INFANCY AND EARLY CHILDHOOD:
THE PRACTICE OF CLINICAL ASSESSMENT AND
INTERVENTION WITH EMOTIONAL AND
DEVELOPMENTAL CHALLENGES

INFANCY AND EARLY CHILDHOOD: THE PRACTICE OF CLINICAL ASSESSMENT AND INTERVENTION WITH EMOTIONAL AND DEVELOPMENTAL CHALLENGES

Stanley I. Greenspan, M.D.

INTERNATIONAL UNIVERSITIES PRESS, INC.
Madison   Connecticut

Library of Congress Cataloging-in-Publication Data

Greenspan, Stanley I.
 Infancy and early childhood : the practice of clinical assessment and intervention with emotional and developmental challenges / Stanley I. Greenspan.
  p. cm.
 Includes bibliographical references and index.
 ISBN 0-8236-2633-4
 1. Developmental therapy for children. I. Title.
 [DNLM: 1. Child Development Disorders—diagnosis. 2. Child Development Disorders—therapy. 3. Community Mental Health Services—organization & administration. 4. Family Therapy--methods. WS 350.6 G815i]
 RJ505.D48G74 1992
 618.92′89—dc20
 DNLM/DLC   91-35367
 for Library of Congress   CIP

Manufactured in the United States of America

This book is dedicated to the families who have allowed me to collaborate with them on behalf of their emotional and developmental progress.

Contents

Acknowledgments

I wish to thank Serena Wieder, Stephen Porges, Georgia De-Gangi, Diane Lewis, and Valerie DeJean for their clinical and research collaboration, Pat Martin and Sarah Sorkin for editorial, and Sue Morrison for word processing assistance.

Introduction

The evaluation and treatment of infants, young children, and their families is challenging and satisfying, at once simple and complex. Infants and young children are very direct; what you see is what there is. An eight-month-old doesn't disguise his true feelings; he is either engaged and related or aloof and withdrawn. But there are many factors influencing behavior and many aspects of development that all relate to one another. For example, an aloof and withdrawn eight-month-old will be influenced by his relationship with his caregiver and family functioning, as well as his own physical tendencies (e.g., over- or undersensitivity to sound or touch). He will also be influenced by the relationships between the different aspects of his development, including his sensory, motor, language, cognitive, affective, and interpersonal capacities.

The evaluation and treatment of infants, young children, and their families is challenging for the same reason that it is complex: one is working with the relationships between many different influences and aspects of development. But more important are the many opportunities for favorably influencing emotional and intellectual growth. One may help the infant and his or her family develop new adaptive capacities and overcome difficulties in a relatively short period of time. The clinical work and its impact can be dramatic. In contrast to work with adults, where the therapist may experience the security of gradually and indirectly helping the patient understand and help himself, the work with infants, young children, and their families provides direct and distinct opportunities to foster favorable development. The therapist will either take advantage of or miss these golden opportunities.

The clinical work with infants, young children, and their families is unusually satisfying because of this unique opportunity to foster dramatic shifts toward adaptive development. The infant or child and his or her family may learn to relate in entirely new ways. Worrisome patterns, such as withdrawal and avoidance of human relationships, aggressive behavior, or fragmented, disorganized thinking may shift to adaptive patterns, such as warm trust, relating, cooperative behavior, and organized, logical thinking.

In the chapters that follow, there will be detailed discussions of the steps in the assessment and treatment process, as well as detailed case studies. Part I will present the "Basic Model" for clinical work in infancy and early childhood. It will demonstrate how constitutional–maturational, family–cultural, and interactive patterns influence the infant or child's feelings, thoughts, and behaviors at each of six developmental levels.

In Part II, over twenty detailed case studies will be presented. The case studies will be organized according to the age of the child at the time the family came in for an evaluation, and will include cases in each of the first four years of life. The case studies will provide the reader with a sense of clinical work in the trenches with a wide range of infants, young children, and their families. These case studies will also convey to the reader the range of clinical situations and types of challenges from which our approach to assessment, diagnosis, and treatment was constructed.

The recommended assessment and treatment approaches (Parts III and IV) emerged from years of work with these types of cases. Each case would help to tease out an element in the assessment or treatment process. For example, the importance of assessing certain constitutional–maturational variables, such as an infant's oversensitivity to touch, sound, or movement, and integrating an approach to these variables (including their effect on caregivers and families) in the treatment process, emerged from working with cases which presented unique and often extreme constitutional–maturational variations. Originally, the assessment and treatment process focused predominantly on caregiver perceptions, caregiver–infant interactions, and family patterns. The infant's individual differences at birth and shortly thereafter eventually was also seen to be important. Only over time did the importance emerge of observing the infant's constitutional and maturational differences at each stage of early development. But these observations made it possible to understand the complex interplay, for example, between a two-year-old's sensitivity to touch or sound, his interactions with his caregivers, his own emerging picture of himself, and his caregiver's perceptions and fantasies. Now it is possible to give equal clinical weight to the caregiver's fantasies, feelings, and behaviors, the infant's and caregiver's interaction patterns, and the infant's or young child's own individual differences.

The case studies in Part II should be read twice; initially, to gain a sense of the clinical phenomena one deals with in infancy and early childhood, as well as to understand the basis for the recommended assessment and treatment approaches. A second reading will enable the clinician to reflect on how the assessment, diagnostic, and treatment process works with different types of challenges and to compare the approaches in the book with his or her own clinical methods.

Part III will present the steps in the clinical assessment process, beginning with parents or caregivers discussing their concerns, and including the developmental history, observation of the infant–child and caregiver and family interactions, assessment of the constitutional–maturational variables, caregiver and family patterns, and construction of the formulation.

Part IV will discuss the process of intervention. An approach called floor time will be used as a framework to discuss the microscopic elements in the treatment process. Floor time, it will be seen, is a way for a parent or clinician to relate to an infant or child. This way of relating is based on the principles of following the infant's or child's lead, supporting his or her intentions, being sensitive to individual constitutional differences, and simultaneously fostering the child's focus or attention–capacity to warmly engage emerging ability for two-way communication and, with children over eighteen months, the child's representational or symbolic capacity in different emotional domains. The discussion of the treatment process will include therapeutic approaches for each developmental stage and each type of problem. It will discuss the types of caregiver/infant–child and therapist–child interaction patterns that facilitate developmental progress and a child's ability to overcome emotional and developmental challenges. Approaches to direct work with caregivers and families, and a special type of caregiver-oriented therapy, will also be discussed.

The appendixes include discussion of special issues, including the administrative challenges involved in setting up a clinical infant development program in a community.

Clinical work with infants, young children, and their families is still in its infancy. It is hoped that the reader will incorporate the pioneering spirit of this field into his or her own work and further develop assessment, diagnostic, treatment, and preventive approaches.

PART I

The Basic Model

Chapter 1

THE BASIC MODEL:
The Influence of Regulatory and Experiential Factors on the Six Organizational Levels of Experience

The diagnosis and treatment of emotional and developmental disorders in infants and young children requires the clinician to take into account all facets of the child's experience. It is necessary, therefore, to have a model with which to look at how constitutional–maturational (i.e., regulatory), family, and interactive factors work together as the child progresses through each developmental phase.

The developmental model formulated in this chapter can be visualized with the infant's constitutional–maturational patterns on one side and the infant's environment, including caregivers, family, community, and culture, on the other side. Both of these sets of factors operate through the infant–caregiver relationship which can be pictured in the middle. These factors and the infant–caregiver relationship, in turn, contribute to the organization of experience at each of six different developmental levels, which may be pictured just beneath the infant–caregiver relationship.

Each developmental level involves different tasks or goals. The relative effect of the constitutional–maturational, environmental, or interactive variables will, therefore, depend on and can only be understood in the context of the developmental level they relate to. The influencing variables, therefore, are best understood, not as they might be traditionally, as general influences on development or behavior, but as distinct and different influences on the six distinct developmental and experiential levels. For example, as a child is negotiating the formation of a relationship (engaging), his mother's tendency to be very intellectual and prefer talking over holding may make it relatively harder for him to become deeply engaged in emotional terms. If constitutionally he has slightly lower than average motor tone and is hyposensitive with regard to touch and sound, his mother's intellectual and slightly aloof style may be doubly difficult for him, as neither she nor the child is able to take the initiative in engaging the other.

Let us assume, however, that he more or less negotiates this early phase of development (grandmother, who lives with him, as well as his father are very "wooing" caregivers). At age three, when the developmental phase and task is different, he may have an easier time, even though his mother hasn't changed. His intellectual mother is highly creative and enjoys pretend play as well as give-and-take logical discussions. No longer anxious about her son's dependency needs, she is more relaxed and quite available for play and chit-chat. The task is no longer simply one of forming a relationship but of learning to represent (or symbolize) experience and form categories and connections between these units of experience. Mother's verbal style is now quite helpful to him, especially given his need for lots of verbal interaction. In other words, the same caregiving pattern can have a very different impact, depending on the tasks of the particular developmental level. Each developmental level of experience is, therefore, a reference point for the factors that influence development.

What is potentially unique about this particular clinical and research model (Greenspan, 1989) is the ability it gives us to look at the back-and-forth influence of highly specific and verifiable, constitutional–maturational factors on interactive and family patterns and vice versa, in relationship to specific developmental processes (and to relate these processes to later developmental and psychopathologic disorders). There have been very useful intervention models that focus on specific influences such as the caregiver's feelings, fantasies or support system or on certain phases of early development (Fraiberg, 1980; Provence, 1983; Provence and Naylor, 1983; Brazelton, 1990). The goal of this model is to look at all the major influences throughout the different stages of development. Each of these factors will be discussed individually, followed by a brief case illustration and discussion of how they work together.

DEVELOPMENTAL LEVELS

In this model, there are six developmental levels. They include the infant–child's ability to accomplish the following:

1. Attend to multisensory affective experience and at the same time organize a calm, regulated state and experience pleasure.
2. Engage with and evidence affective preference and pleasure for a caregiver.
3. Initiate and respond to two-way presymbolic gestural communication.
4. Organize chains of two-way communication (opening and closing many circles of communication in a row), maintain communication across space, integrate affective polarities, and synthesize an emerging prerepresentational organization of self and other.

5. Represent (symbolize) affective experience (e.g., pretend play, functional use of language). It should be noted that this ability calls for higher level auditory and verbal sequencing ability.
6. Create representational (symbolic) categories and gradually build conceptual bridges between these categories. This ability creates the foundation for such basic personality functions as reality testing, impulse control, self–other representational differentiation, affect labeling and discrimination, stable mood, and a sense of time and space that allows for logical planning. It should be noted that this ability rests not only on complex auditory and verbal processing abilities, but visual–spatial abstracting capacities as well. The theoretical, clinical, and empirical rationale for these developmental levels is discussed in appendix 4 and in *The Development of the Ego* (Greenspan, 1989).

At each of these levels, one looks at the range of emotional themes organized (e.g., can the child play out only dependency themes and not aggressive ones; is aggression "behaved" out?). One also looks at the stability of each level. Does a minor stress lead a child to lose his ability to represent, interact, engage, or attend?

In regard to their use in day-to-day clinical work, the six developmental levels can be collapsed into four essential processes that characterize development in infants and young children. These processes have to do with how an infant and his parents or caregivers negotiate the various phases of their early interactions. It is necessary to understand how these four processes serve as a basis for diagnosis and treatment.

1. SHARED ATTENTION AND ENGAGEMENT

Usually in the first four months of life, the baby learns to look, listen, attend, and also to experience pleasure and comfort, dependency and warmth with the caregiver. But it is important to look for this core process in two- and three-year-old children as well. Is the problem the youngster is having, even though it may be a sleep problem or a behavioral problem of hitting another kid, related to difficulties with proper negotiation of this core process of attention and engagement?

2. TWO-WAY COMMUNICATION

Normally, between four and eight months, babies are learning how to go beyond a simple state of connectedness and shared attention into a state of cause-and-effect interaction. At this point, there should be an emotional, social, and intellectual dialogue going on, in addition to a motor dialogue and a sensory dialogue, between the caregiver and the baby. Is this dialogue now "cooking," is there a two-way communication?

One way to think about two-way communication is the process of opening and closing circles of communication. When the mother, father, or therapist takes an interest in the child, the first circle of communication is opened. When the child responds, the child is closing the circle, and when the parent responds in turn, he or she is opening another circle. When the child responds again, he or she has closed a second circle. A circle of communication involves following a child's lead with interest, responding in some way, and the child then responding to the parental initiative. The child's response closes the circle. In very simple communications, such as with a four- to six-month-old, a parent may get just one or two circles. By fifteen or sixteen months, it should be possible to get twenty or thirty closed circles in a row, as the baby takes a parent by the hand, walks to the refrigerator, and points to the door, or tries on a hat and has fun imitating a gesture of the caregiver or therapist.

A difficulty in two-way communication processes in older children may show up as a problem in controlling aggression. The core problem may be that gestural communication was never negotiated. For example, most children learn to comprehend limits from gestures, not from words. By sixteen or seventeen months, the look on Daddy's face or pointing will tell most babies whether they are safe or in danger. A toddler knows whether he is approved of or not based on this, a more complex version than the four- to twelve-month level of two-way communication. Two-way communication establishes very important behavioral parameters.

3. SHARED MEANINGS

The third core process involves the level of shared meanings, when by eighteen to twenty-four months, the baby is learning to use representations (symbols or emotional ideas) to comprehend his or her world. One sees pretend play, phrases like "Me mad," "Me sad," "Give me that." Any time words convey intentionality or play involves representations or symbols that have emotional themes or content, the child is into this third level of shared meanings. A child who does well at the early level of engagement and has two-way gestural communication may have a problem at this higher level. The problem could be a fantasy. A child who is withdrawn and seems to be not attached could be fearful that if he gets close to people they will bite him. A three-and-a-half-year-old who has a fantasy of being bitten will pull away from people. A therapist cannot assume right away that what he sees in front of him is necessarily the essence of the problem. A complete diagnostic workup is needed to discern what is happening at the level of shared meanings and symbols.

4. EMOTIONAL THINKING

The fourth process is representational differentiation, or emotional thinking. From about ages two-and-a-half or three to about four-and-a-half to five years of age, children learn to categorize shared meanings. They categorize units of thought or ideas into different configurations. They see connections between images or representations or symbols. They can categorize in dimensions of time—what's now, what's in the future, what's in the immediate past. This ability is critical for limit-setting and impulse control—"Something I do now is going to impact on you later" or "If I do this, I'll be punished later." They are doing it in terms of space—what's immediately in front of me, what's in the next room, what's around the corner. This capacity is critical, because knowing that the mother is in the next room and not in California makes a child feel much more secure. To be able to conceptualize a sense of space and distance and to define what is me and what is not-me, what is inside me and what is outside me (a child's basic boundary); what is reality and what is fantasy all relates to what is self and what is nonself. Emotional thinking also includes the ability to categorize different emotional themes: What is dependency? What is aggressiveness? What is assertiveness? What is the difference between healthy assertiveness and destructive aggressiveness? Children at this age are learning to make these kinds of distinctions and categorize these sorts of experiences.

In addition, children are learning to integrate feeling and thought. A younger child can talk sad and look happy, and the therapist may not think anything is wrong. The two-year-old can be gleeful while saying, "Die, Die." But if a four-year-old behaves the same way, the therapist should wonder, "Hey, something isn't working here." One would expect the four-year-old to have an integration of the idea and the emotion.

In a number of areas, categorizations of units of intrapsychic life allow a child to begin to make connections and to reason between them. The four-and-a-half-year-old can figure out, "I hit Johnny because yesterday he hit me." That's a reasoning using time and feelings—a piece of anger in one time interval relates to a piece of anger in another time interval. Or, "I didn't get what I wanted," a frustration with love, "therefore, I'm mad." As development continues into latency and adolescence, it is this fourth process, the ability to categorize and make connections and various permutations of these connections, that gets more sophisticated and evolves into the ability to deal with the peer group and form an identity.

It is important to note that each of these new organizational levels puts demands on the infant to organize new types of experience. For example, engaging the animate world or caregivers and becoming emotionally involved and dependent on human relationships demands that the infant adjust to the unpredictable behaviors, mood shifts, and frustrations of a real person. While he can bang a block on the floor and reliably hear a sound, he may not get back a vocalization or receive a hug every time he vocalizes or reaches out invitingly with his arms. When the infant learns to use words and can form an internal picture of his mother, he now relies on his word and his picture to convey certain internal feeling states, such as security. The language and symbolic mechanisms underlying this representational ability may not be initially as reliable as mother's continuing physical (and tactile) presence. Auditory or verbal sequencing difficulties or sensory hyper- or hyporeactivity in any modality can easily compromise such emerging symbolic capacities. Yet, at the same time, the ability to engage, as well as the ability to represent or symbolize experience, provides enormous flexibility and new adaptive range for the growing infant. In this respect, each new level of organization is, indeed, a double-edged sword.

CLINICAL ILLUSTRATION: OBSERVING THE FOUR DEVELOPMENTAL LEVELS IN A THREE-YEAR-OLD

A three-year-old girl would hardly look at and would not talk to the therapist. However, she was clearly warmly engaged with her father and held onto him as if he were a security blanket. She came along readily with him into the playroom, and when he invited her to play, she said, "Play with me," and indicated her desire to get down on the floor and play with him. She was attentive to her toys and held several dolls very tightly. She was also very attentive to her father and made sure he was in view. If anyone else came near her, she would both hug her dolls and want to either touch her father or be near him. As the therapist tried to talk to her or show her toys, she tended to tune in only to what she was most interested in—her daddy and her dolls. With great effort, she could pay attention to another person; she could listen to a voice or exchange gestures. She was attentive and could focus for a few minutes on what she wanted to, but she was unable to move around and take in visually and auditorily the room, all the people in the room, or the toys in the room; nor could she move smoothly and easily from one attentional realm to another.

She engaged her father very warmly and used him as her security whenever something intruded or made her feel scared. However, she hardly spoke a word; if other people in the room talked or moved around, she gave her father mostly looks or smiles, or tentative and frightened glances.

She related warmly to the dolls but had a difficult time engaging new people whom she tended to look at fleetingly; but she would not talk to them. She would place the dolls inside or outside the doll house; she answered questions with "yes" or "no." When her father started to play with her, he had to do all the talking. He also had to carry out all the action for her; she would say only "yes, "no," or nod.

She slowly warmed up but kept herself less than fully engaged with the interviewer. She did smile and giggle, but there was a sense of reserve that constrained her range of warm, pleasurable feelings. In contrast, there was a sense of involvement and connection between the girl and her father, although he too was rather constricted in his range of affect and didn't show a lot of exuberance or pleasure.

In terms of two-way communication, she was initially quite passive: she let her father initiate the dialogue. For example, he would say, "Do you want to play with this doll or that doll?" She would nod or shake her head or occasionally say "yes" or "no." Communication even with him was limited to closing one or two circles. She would respond to his questions with some circle-closing answers, but would not elaborate or show any inclination to continue the dialogue. Even though she tended to be passive and cautious, there was a sense that she was aware of what she wanted to do. Her verbal responses were quite deliberate, and from her passive position she orchestrated the drama that her father played out around her. She behaved similarly with the clinician about fifteen minutes into the session. She was gradually becoming more relaxed.

As the clinician exchanged simple gestures with her, he sought to expand the range of the gestures to include different themes, like exploration, conflict, aggression, as well as warmth. She was able to engage cautiously in each. In her drama that dealt with aggression, for example, she stomped on "the monster" with her foot and had her doll attack the monster, but she closed only two, three, or four circles in a row, instead of ten or twenty, as one would expect at her age. She abruptly switched themes, which suggested that aggression made her anxious. She was able to mobilize a verbal component to her gestural signals, however, by responding to "why" questions with low-level answers, such as the boy who wants to be in the house, because "he wants to eat dinner." When she played out a theme of dependency, she fed the dolls repetitively, but she did not develop the theme further. She evidenced a constriction in her range of affect at the gestural level and was unable to close many circles in a row.

She showed both the ability for representational elaboration and differentiation (i.e., the ability to connect ideas). When asked who gets angry at her, she was able to say "Mommy and Daddy"; when her father asked her "Why?" she said, "Because I wouldn't share my ice cream." She had a few instances of elaborate representational play when, for example, she wanted the doll to go to sleep in the house, and wanted to put various other animals into the house. She seemed to have a plan in mind. But she did not spontaneously elaborate on any related themes. Either her father or the clinician constantly had to engage her, and help her be representational.

Therefore, she was capable of shared attention, very gradual engagement, two-way gestural communication, representational elaboration, and the early stages of representational differentiation. At each stage, however, she evidenced a significant constriction in the range of affect and depth and elaboration of the drama or dialogue. She often depended on the other person to move her from one theme to another. She was more comfortable with themes of dependency than themes of aggression. While she was able to stomp joyfully on the monster, she changed themes quickly afterwards. She continued and developed the dependency themes more easily. Her father seemed similarly tense and constricted. Mother was not present in this session, but she too tended to avoid assertiveness and tended to be anxious and overprotective.

We therefore see how in a relatively short period of time the clinician can observe how a child does or does not evidence the capacities associated with each stage of development. We also see how the clinician can look at the depth and range of theme dealt with at each level, as well as the degree to which they are elaborated (number of circles opened and closed in a row). The child described above was consistent in behavior over a number of sessions. These patterns were also consistent with her history. Not surprisingly, she was having difficulty interacting, talking, and playing with peers in her preschool program. A plan was developed for her parents to help her become more elaborate at each stage and to become more comfortable with aggression and assertiveness.

The four processes described above and illustrated in this clinical vignette are influenced by different factors. These factors determine whether an infant and his family successfully negotiate these levels of development. As indicated earlier, these factors include constitutional–maturational and family patterns.

CONSTITUTIONAL–MATURATIONAL PATTERNS

In order to specify the constitutional–maturational characteristics that should be observed, the following list may prove helpful:

1. Sensory reactivity, including hypo- and hyperreactivity in each sensory modality (tactile, auditory, visual, vestibular, olfactory);
2. Sensory processing in each sensory modality (e.g., the capacity to decode sequences, configurations, or abstract patterns);
3. Sensory affective reactivity and processing in each modality (e.g., the ability to process and react to degrees of affective intensity in a stable manner);
4. Motor tone;
5. Motor planning.

A new instrument to clinically assess aspects of sensory functions in a reliable manner has been developed and is available (DeGangi and Greenspan, 1988, 1989a,b). The following section will further consider the constitutional and maturational patterns.

Sensory reactivity (hypo or hyper) and sensory processing can be observed clinically. Is the child hyper- or hyposensitive to touch or sound? The same question must be asked in terms of vision and movement in space. In each sensory modality, does the four-month-old "process" a complicated pattern of information input or only a simple one? Does the four-and-a-half-year-old have a receptive language problem and is therefore unable to sequence words he hears together or follow complex directions? Is the three-year-old an early comprehender and talker, but slower in visual–spatial processing? If spatial patterns are poorly comprehended, a child may be facile with words, sensitive to every emotional nuance, but have no context, never see the big picture (the "forest"); such children get lost in the "trees." In the clinician's office, they may forget where the door is or have a hard time picturing that mother is only a few feet away in the waiting room.

In addition to straightforward "pictures" of spatial relationship (i.e., how to get to the playground), they may also have difficulty with seeing the emotional big picture. If the mother is angry, the child may think the earth is opening up and he is falling in, because he cannot comprehend that she was nice before, and she will probably be nice again. Such a child may be strong on the auditory processing side, but weak on the visual–spatial processing side.

My impression is that children with a lag in the visual–spatial area can become overwhelmed by the affect of the moment. This is often intensified by precocious auditory–verbal skills. The child, in a sense, overloads himself and does not have the ability to see how it all fits together. Thus, at a minimum, it is necessary to have a sense of how the child reacts in each sensory modality, how he or she processes information in each modality, and particularly, as the child gets older, a sense of the auditory–verbal processing skills in comparison to visual–spatial processing skills.

It is also necessary to look at the motor system, including motor tone, motor planning (fine and gross), and postural control. Observing how a child sits, crawls, or runs; maintains posture; holds a crayon; hops, scribbles, or draws; and makes rapid alternating movements will provide a picture of the child's motor system. His security in regulating and controlling his body plays an important role in how he uses gestures to communicate his ability to regulate dependency (being close or far away); his confidence in regulating aggression ("Can I control my hand that wants to hit?"); and his overall physical sense of self.

Other constitutional and maturational variables have to do with movement in space, attention, and dealing with transitions. Further research with the role of these individual differences in an infant's regulatory capacities will pinpoint the processing, reactivity, and motor style that leads to attentional and behavioral problems (DeGangi and Greenspan, 1989a).

As can be seen, the constitutional and maturational variables are one set of influences on the child's ability to regulate behavior, affect, and later on, thought. These variables may, therefore, also be thought of as "regulatory factors" when they are a prominent feature of a disorder of behavior, affect, or thought. Such a disorder may be considered a "regulatory disorder."

FAMILY CONTRIBUTIONS

In addition to constitutional and maturational factors, it is important to describe the family contribution with regard to each of the four core processes. If a family system is aloof, it may not negotiate engagement well; if a family system is intrusive, it may overwhelm or overstimulate a baby. Obviously, if a baby is already overly sensitive to touch or sound, the caregiver's intrusiveness will be all the more difficult for the child to handle. We see, therefore, the interaction between the maturational pattern and the family pattern.

A family system may throw so many meanings at a child, that he or she is unable to organize a sense of reality. Categories of me/not-me may become confused, because one day a feeling is yours, the next day is the mother's, next day it is the father's, the day after it is little brother's; anger may turn into dependency, and vice versa. If meanings shift too quickly, a child may be unable to reach the fourth level—emotional thinking. A child with difficulties in auditory–verbal sequencing will have an especially difficult time (Greenspan, 1989).

The couple is a unit in itself. How do husband and wife operate, not only with each other, but how do they negotiate on behalf of the children, in terms of the four processes? A couple with marital problems could still successfully negotiate shared attention, engagement, two-way communication, shared meanings, and emotional thinking with their children. But the marital difficulties could disrupt any one or a number of these developmental processes.

Each parent is also an individual. How does each personality operate vis-à-vis these four processes? While it may be desirable to have a general mental health diagnosis for each caregiver, one also needs to functionally observe which of these levels each caregiver can naturally and easily support. Is the parent engaged, warm, and interactive (a good reader of cues). Is he or she oriented toward symbolic meanings (verbalizing meanings), and engaging in pretend play, and can the caregiver organize feelings and thoughts, or does one or the other get lost between reality and fantasy? Are there limitations, in terms of these four levels, and if so, what are they?

Each parent also has specific fantasies that may be projected onto the children and interfere with any of the four levels. Does a mother see her motorically active, distractible, labile baby as a menace and therefore overcontrol, overintrude, or withdraw? Her fantasy may govern her behavior. Does a father, whose son has low motor tone, see his boy as passive and inept, and therefore pull away from him or impatiently "rev" him up.

In working only with the parent–child interaction, and not the parent's fantasy, one may be dealing with only the tip of the iceberg. The father may be worried that he has a homosexual son, or the mother may be worried that she has a monster for a daughter (who reminds her of her retarded sister). All these feelings may be "cooking," and they can drive the parent–child interactions.

In the first session of a diagnostic workup, I let parents talk about the child; I don't interrupt very much. I listen for their associations. When, for example, they finish telling me what the symptoms are, I say, "Tell me more about Billy." Often elements of their fantasies spontaneously emerge in that first session. In the second meeting I have with a family, I go through the developmental history. I try to learn about their wishes for their baby and how they felt about the baby at each stage and age. I take the parents through the four processes: finding out how they negotiated shared attention and engagement, two-way communication, shared meanings, and emotional thinking. For example, was the child a self-starter who initiated activities and pulled them in, or was the child passive so that they initiated the communication? What was going on in their lives, in terms of what they were thinking and feeling? What was going on in their marriage? Often, fantasies will develop further during this second meeting.

Then I have a third meeting with the parents, which is devoted to them as individuals and as a couple and to the family as a system. I want to know their backgrounds, their emotional makeup, and what they were like as children growing up. In the third session, if it hasn't come up before (we now know each other better), they will often talk about their worries; for example, about a brother who was hyperactive and destructive or about a sister who was a show-off or about the way their mothers aggressively criticized them, and how they worry about being too like their mothers. A governing fantasy may emerge that explains why a parent shies away from a baby's aggressiveness (e.g., the parent doesn't want to be too controlling like his or her own mother). Or, perhaps, a parent is trying not to be as aloof as his or her mother was and is instead overly bossy with the eighteen-month-old. In a similar way, I try to discover, as a part of the family's overall fantasy about itself, the couple's and family's collective fantasies about the new baby.

INFANT-CAREGIVER RELATIONSHIP PATTERNS

We have discussed the developmental levels, the constitutional–maturational variables, and the family, couple, and parental characteristics, including the organizing fantasies the parents have about the child, and how this all plays out in the four developmental levels.

Next, we will focus on the caregiver–infant relationship. As indicated earlier, it is this relationship that mediates these other variables, and in addition determines how each of the four developmental processes is successfully or unsuccessfully negotiated.

Often, parents will bring a baby in, and I will watch the parent–infant interaction in the first session, while I am hearing about their concerns. With an older child, a four-year-old, for example, I will have them wait to bring the child in, because I want them to talk freely at the outset.

Usually, I let each parent play with the child for at least fifteen or twenty minutes, and then I will play with the child for about the same amount of time. I look for a pattern of interaction in the context of the four core processes. I also look for the range of emotional themes in each of the four core processes and the stability of these processes. For example, a four-year-old may be playing out wonderful fantasies of fairy princesses going off to a castle and being tied up by an evil witch and then being saved by the hero. While I am interested in the content, I first keep an eye on how the child is relating with his caregiver (and later on with me), as well as the breadth of emotion and the stability of the relatedness.

How are they negotiating shared attention? Is the child attending well until the parent intrudes; then, does the child pull away and become distracted? Or is the child only attentive to his toys, marching to his own drummer and not attending to the parent? Is the parent laid back and slow to make overtures? Depressed caregivers will often talk to their child in a slow rhythm with much longer pauses than expected. Sometimes a child who is potentially a good attender begins to get preoccupied and to march to his own drummer, because the parent's rhythm is not compelling enough to keep him involved. I may be able to confirm his skill when I interact with him myself. A therapist must observe the baby or child with his caregivers and himself and then reach a conclusion about the baby, the parent, and how they negotiate each developmental process together.

After observing the quality of shared attention (actually, one is observing all these developmental processes simultaneously), I observe how the child and the parent are engaging, I look at the depth and warmth and the richness of their sense of connectedness, the chemistry between the two of them. A therapist must train himself to look simultaneously at a multiplicity of issues.

Next, I observe two-way communication focusing initially on gestural issues. What is the quality of child and parent's eye-to-eye contact, smile-to-smile, affect-to-affect, like? What is the frown–smile interaction like? Are their motor gestures interactive? Are they opening and closing gestural circles together, or gesturally are they each marching to different drummers? In looking at gestures, one also observes size and complexity of the pattern. Are basic emotions of acceptance, approval, pride or rejection, hostility, danger or bossiness communicated via this system, or is the communication system so constructed that only one of these is being dealt with? In looking at the two-way communication, I am looking at the baby's side, the mother's or father's side, and the interactive pattern.

Next, I look at shared meanings. For example, with a two-year-old or older, is there pretend play? If so, what is the theme of the play? But, before I get to the content of the theme, I look at how elaborate the drama is. Is it a shallow drama of simple dependency, with the dolls hugging—hugging, hugging, and nothing else happening—or is it a rich drama that is flexible and encompasses a broad range of themes? How deep is the drama, in terms of the complexity of each theme? Is the drama constricted or wide ranging in terms of affects? Then I look at the content. Is the child predominantly concerned with separation, dependency, aggression, neediness, sexual curiosity, or all of the above, and what happens in the drama? Is the scared child helped or left to the tiger or the evil witch?

Lastly, I look at the level of emotional thinking, the categorization of meanings, and how the child connects up different ideas. Is he using "buts" and "becauses"; is he connecting up subplots with a larger plot?

At both levels of "ideas," I look at whether the parent supports symbolic activity or not. Does the parent, when the child is playing out themes of aggression, say, "Oh you must be tired . . . you must be hungry," thereby changing the theme and distracting the child. Or, when the child is playing out dependency, does the mother pick him up and hug him as opposed to letting him play it out with the dolls? In this instance, the mother may be saying to the child, "Go back to an earlier level of concreteness and behaving. Don't stay at the symbolic level because symbols are more scary to me than behavior." For some parents, the symbol is more anxiety provoking than the behavior. They would rather go to a lower level.

Even when a parent stays with the representational or symbolic level, he or she can be more or less reflective. The child says, "Get me my juice now." The unreflective concrete parent says, "yes" or "no," indirectly supporting the child's sense of urgency. Even a "no" supports the urgency because the child's demand is taken literally. The reflective parent says, "Boy, you sure sound like you need it immediately," thereby helping the child reflect or symbolize his sense of urgency. After a brief discussion, and depending upon the circumstances, the parent may get the juice or help the child get it for himself, or let the child accept a delay and wait. The key is the parent's tendency to take the child literally or to help the child symbolize. In areas of their own anxieties, parents tend to be more concrete.

While most parents may respond to a child's demand-ingness with a concrete "no," some parents will be concrete in all areas of a child's affects, including sexual curiosity, dependency wishes, interest in assertiveness, and so forth. For example, a child says to a parent, "I want to see your bottom!" An anxious, concrete parent might say, "No! Don't talk that way!" A reflec-tive parent might be concerned with where such a wish is com-ing from and reflectively ask, "Where does that idea or wish come from?" (The parent will be wondering if a brother or sister or friend said something, etc.) After the wish is reflected on, the parent might explain to the child why his or her goal will not be implemented. Interestingly, in looking at degrees of concreteness or degrees of reflectiveness, one can look at which of the child's themes brings forth a reflective or concrete atti-tude. The average parent would be concrete if her child is too demanding, but would deal with sexual curiosity in a reflective way. A very concrete parent would deal with both in a concrete manner.

I next look at how well parents deal with logic and reality. Does the parent give accurate feedback to the child and encour-age him to elaborate his ideas in a logical way? Or does the parent get avoidant or so mixed up, confused, and lost in the child's world, that emotional thinking is compromised? Does the parent support the use of "but" and "because" to connect up ideas?

PUTTING THE PIECES TOGETHER

Therefore, for each of the four levels, or core processes, it is necessary to look at the child's constitutional and maturational status, the family and parent and couple patterns, and the actual caregiver/parent–infant interaction. For each of the four levels, one must have a sense of the family variables, the constitutional–maturational variables, and the caregiver/parent–infant interactional variables. For each level one must look at what is influencing the successful or compromised negotiation at that level. Therefore, a therapist wants to be able to reach a conclusion about a child three years and older on all four levels, and for the child less than age three years, on the levels they should have attained (e.g., for a 2 1/2-year old, through the first three levels; for a 14-month-old, the first two levels—attention and engagement, and two-way communication).

Looking at all the variables for each developmental level may seem very complex. However, it is not as complex as it may seem because not every system always contributes equally. In some cases, the maturational system may be the major contributor, and the family may be playing a minor role. In other cases, it may be the parent's projections that play the major part, and while there are some unique maturational patterns, they are a minor theme, perhaps setting the stage for some of the parental distortions, but not in itself the controlling variable.

One nevertheless needs to have a conceptual framework that touches on all these points in order to avoid, for example, dealing with the maturational system and ignoring the family and interactions, or vice versa. If the therapist focuses on just one developmental level (e.g., the current one) and fails to look at others (e.g., the earlier levels), he or she may be missing the predominant issues. If the child is "spacey" and not engaged, and the therapist is dealing with meanings, he may be missing the boat. He may play and talk with a child who needs instead to be wooed into a relationship. A distracted, unengaged child's main problem may be conflict at the level of meaning. Using suggestions on how to engage the child may not deal with his fear of aggression, being "eaten up."

Therefore our model looks at the constitutional–maturational, family, and interactive factors, as they influence a series of developmental processes. This model can accommodate and further elaborate many of the currently and historically important research trends in infancy.

For example, there is an important and valuable literature on "temperament" as a way of capturing the infant's innate tendencies. Our focus on specific constitutional and maturational variables attempts to build on what we know about temperament in a new and, we hope, promising manner. Most of temperament research relies on parental reports of the infant's capacities, rather than "hands-on" assessment of the infant. In addition, most temperament constructs tend to assume that there is a general tendency within the infant toward such global behaviors as introversion or extraversion, or shyness and inhibition. In this model, these global behavioral tendencies are hypothesized to be secondary to highly specific "hands-on" verifiable infant tendencies, such as tactile or auditory sensitivity or motor tone and motor planning difficulties. Furthermore, we seek to relate each maturational tendency to specific developmental processes which are also influenced by family variables.

In addition, there is a growing literature on attachment difficulties using an experimental paradigm focusing on the infant's reaction to a "strange situation" (Ainsworth, Bell, and Stayton, 1974). This important body of work not only helps categorize caregiver–infant interaction patterns, it relates problems in later childhood to qualities of the infant–caregiver attachment pattern at one year of age (which can also be related to earlier caregiver patterns). In our model, we attempt to examine interaction patterns at each of the six developmental stages and also relate them not only to caregiver patterns, but to the infant's individual variations in terms of physical and maturational differences (an important component of the infant's adaptive capacities).

The goal of the model presented here is to understand how all the relevant factors influence a child's behavior. Behavior is viewed not simply as what a child does, but how a child organizes experience. As the child's capacity to organize experience changes, there are new relationships between various family, constitutional–maturational, and interactional factors that influence this capacity.

BRIEF CASE ILLUSTRATION

A seven-and-a-half-month-old infant's mother worried that "He cries any time I try to leave him, even for a second. If I'm not standing right next to him when he is sitting on the floor, he cries and I have to pick him up. He's a tyrant. He's waking up four times at night and is a fussy eater. He eats for short bursts [breast-feeding] and then stops eating. I'm feeding him all the time."

The mother was feeling cornered, controlled, manipulated, and bossed around. Her baby was like a *fearful dictator* (therapist's term). She said, "That's the perfect way to describe him." The father was impatient with the mother; he felt that she indulged the baby too much. He was getting "fed up," because she had no time for him.

Mother was frightened of aggression and was very dependent on her own mother. She was very fearful that her baby would show any discomfort; she wanted the baby to be happy (meaning no crying or discomfort). It made her "shake" to think that her baby could be uncomfortable. The father, an angry sort of person, took the opposite approach—a "John Wayne," tough-it-out strategy. In interactions with the baby, each showed his or her characteristic pattern.

The baby was very interactive and sensitive to every emotional nuance. As he came into the room, he immediately caught my eye. We exchanged smiles and motor gestures. He interacted with his parents with smiles, coos, and motor movements. Father intruded somewhat. He would roughhouse until the baby would cry, put the baby down, and then roughhouse again. Mother, in contrast, was ever so gentle, but she had long silences between her vocalizations. During her long silences, the baby would rev up, get more irritable, and start whining. There was whining with the mother and fearful crying with the father. Even before he could finish his motor gestures or vocalizations, his mother moved in and picked him up, or gave him a rattle, or spoke for him. In this way, she undermined his initiative. Even while whining, however, he was interactive and contingent.

Upon physical examination, this baby was sensitive to loud noises, as well as light touch on the arms, legs, abdomen, and back. He had a mild degree of low motor tone and was posturally insecure. He was not yet ready to crawl.

From a regulatory perspective, babies who are constitutionally most worrisome are those who are oversensitive to the environment, to normal sounds and sensations, and at the same time, have poor control over their motor system. Because of their motor immaturity, they are unable to do much to correct their sensitivities themselves. They are passive victims of their own sensory and motor systems.

Mother, terribly frightened of her own and her infant's potential assertiveness, was unable to help her baby learn assertive coping because she was so overprotective. At the same time, however, she was *undernurturing*, evidenced most notably in the empty spaces in the rhythm of her speech. She was not silent consciously. She wanted to do everything possible for her baby, but her own depression and anxiety kept her from having a securing or soothing vocal or gestural rhythm. The spaces in her vocal pattern conveyed a sense of emotional emptiness. At the same time, father was impatient and moved in too quickly. The baby was having challenges from all sides.

Related to the mother's patterns were worrisome fantasies that her baby would be sick and not survive. These were related to anger at her own very ambivalent mother. Behind father's John Wayne approach was his relationship to his own austere, tough-guy father. Father had been taught to "control" his needs and longings very early in life.

In terms of mastering the first developmental challenge of shared attention and engagement, the infant's constitutional and maturational patterns did not compromise development. This was an attentive, engaged baby, but at the second developmental stage, intentional communication and assertiveness, he was a passive reactor. He was not learning to initiate two-way communication, to be assertive and take charge of his interactions. His low motor tone was compromising his ability to control his motor movements. His sensory hyperreactivity was compromising his ability to regulate sensation. He was frequently overloaded by just the basic sensations of touch and sound. At the same time, he wasn't receiving support from his mother through the nurturing and rhythmic caretaking that would foster self-initiative. Father obviously wasn't supporting assertive communication either. Both the maturational and the family patterns played themselves out through the caregiver–infant interactions.

This family required therapeutic work on a number of fronts simultaneously. We went over the infant's special constitutional–maturational patterns. Hands-on practice helped the parents help their baby be attentive and calm. We worked on how to play with the baby; how to get in front of him and help him to take more initiative. We also worked on how to help mother to be more patient and wait for the baby to finish what he started, and how to support his initiative (e.g., putting something in front of the baby while the baby was on his tummy in order to motivate him to crawl and reach). We worked on getting the mother to put more affect into her voice and to increase the rhythm and speed of her vocalizations; we worked on getting the father to be more gentle. We explored the parents' own feelings about the interactions—the father's tough-guy background, the mother's fear of her own assertiveness, of her baby being injured, and their own associated family patterns.

Gradually, the baby began to sleep through the night and became more assertive and less clinging and fearful. He also became happier. He was slow to reach his motor milestones, so an occupational therapist began to work with him and to give the parents advice on motor development and normalizing his sensory overreactivity. In four months, this infant was functioning in an age-appropriate manner with a tendency toward a cautious, but happy and assertive approach to life's developmental challenges.

CHILDREN WITH SEVERE REGULATORY PROBLEMS

There are a number of children who come in with severe communication problems, sensory under- and overreactivity and processing difficulties, motor delays, and "autistic" features, with the diagnosis of pervasive developmental disorder or atypical development. Such children often have problems at all of the developmental levels described earlier: attention, engagement, two-way gestural communication, and the symbolization of emotions.

At each developmental level there are problems on all fronts: familial, maturational, and interactional. The constitutional problems with sensory reactivity and processing (of a severe nature, especially auditory–verbal processing), motor tone and motor planning, family system problems, parent–child interaction problems, as well as problems with the parents' own reactions and fantasies about the child undermine attending, forming relationships, being intentional, and using words or complex symbols and gestures to convey needs or desires. Treatment involves a comprehensive approach. Often, however, with these children, professionals may try to work with splinter skills at the symbolic level and not enough with the regulatory difficulties and the early levels of engagement, shared attention, and gestural interactions. Four times a week play therapy that focuses on all developmental levels, occupational therapy twice a week (for some children), speech therapy twice a week, parent counselling once or twice a week, and a psychoeducational program five half-days a week are elements of a comprehensive program. With such a program, many children we have treated in the last few years have done remarkably well, better than I would have expected at the start. Within six months, for example, withdrawn preschoolers are comfortable with dependency and closeness, seeking out their parents, and learning to be intentional. Within one year, they are beginning to symbolize affect and become comfortable with peers. Over time, specific severe learning disabilities become the focus of treatment as the pervasive emotional difficulties improve. Compared to children where the focus is on controlling behavior and splinter skills, working comprehensively on the underlying regulatory difficulties and their associated emotional patterns leads to children having greater warmth and spontaneity.

For each case, one must pinpoint the family system dynamics, the parents' fantasies, the baby's constitutional–maturational contributions, and the caregiver–child interactions for each developmental level: attention and engagement, two-way communication, shared meanings, and emotional thinking.

CONCLUSION

The infant and child's ability can be viewed in the context of sensory, motor, interactive, and family patterns. Each of these variables can, in turn, be viewed in the context of a number of developmental–emotional levels of functioning. This model provides a construct that is sensitive to an infant's individual differences, family, and environmental patterns on the one hand, and his emerging adaptive and psychopathological patterns on the other hand. It provides a bridging construct between genetic, prenatal, perinatal, or early developmental variables and later developmental outcomes. This type of construct may be particularly useful for understanding the developmental course of conditions where multiple etiological factors interact with one another or where the impact of certain etiological factors is part of a dynamic system. It also has implications for constructing a comprehensive treatment approach that can work with the multiple intervening variables that influence the course of development.

PART II

Clinical Case Studies

Chapter 2

Birth to Twelve Months

CASE NUMBER 1: LUCY

Lucy, a five-month-old girl, was brought in by her mother and father because they were worried by her crying spells of "up to a half hour." Mother was in a parent support group and said, "Lucy will stare for a few minutes at other babies and mothers and then gets bent out of shape, and cries and cries and cries. She needs constant attention." She also reported that at home Lucy required "constant holding" or else she would cry. Whenever mother went into a new environment, such as a friend's house, Lucy would get "wound up. She won't settle down until we get her home," she said.

Nevertheless, Lucy was sleeping through the night from six in the evening to six in the morning; she took one-hour naps during the day, often two to three times. As she grew older, she was becoming irritable, however, and would find it hard to go to sleep.

Her motor milestones seemed to be progressing. At five months of age she could sit by herself, reach for her glass with

31

both hands, and was already confidently rolling over both ways. Mother mentioned that Lucy, at her happiest, would play peek-a-boo, light up and smile, and also vocalize. She felt that her daughter was more attentive to her voice than her facial expressions. She would brighten up and be interested in her mother for at least five or ten seconds before taking time out, and would also deeply and warmly engage with big, broad smiles. She seemed to prefer high-pitched noises to low-pitched ones, startled easily with loud noises, and would cry for fifteen to twenty minutes if something scared her. Mother also reported that Lucy liked to be touched and bathed.

Lucy was breast-fed for the first three months. Then mother weaned her and started bottle-feeding her with a milk-based formula (Enfamil) augmented with rice cereal, peaches, and strained vegetables. She was in the 75th percentile for weight and in the 90th for height on the growth charts.

The parents reported that the question of a seizure disorder in father had recently been causing the family some stress. This seizure disorder was secondary to trauma he had received to his occipital lobe in an automobile accident. Medication had caused some blurry vision. Medical workups had not revealed any progressive difficulties.

Mother reported that she was a "nervous wreck" and worried that being so nervous was affecting the baby. From a physical health point of view, the pregnancy was unremarkable. However, due to being turned in the wrong position, Lucy had been a C-section baby and the cord had been wrapped around her neck. She had been eight pounds, nine ounces at birth, had 9/9 Apgars, and looked alert and healthy.

Within a short time, she had proven her alertness by turning toward mother's voice and being easily engaged with mother's vocalizations or even facial expressions. Mother had been impressed by her firmness. At five months old, she was progressing reasonably well in terms of her motor milestones. "But I've been a nervous wreck," mother said, "worrying whether Lucy would be okay or not, and worrying whether I could be a good mother." Mother confessed that she was a nervous kind of person. She had been in therapy and taken antidepressant medication intermittently due to a tendency to be both anxious and depressed.

Both parents played with Lucy well, mother thought. "Daddy is more gentle than me, though," she added. "I am so stressed, that I didn't want to hold her or look at her sometimes. I'm afraid I didn't bond with her, that I wasn't excited enough with her, too scared that I would do something wrong. I was afraid the medication for my depression was off and that would make me do something wrong."

As mother talked further, she said that sometimes when they had company Lucy became extremely upset. She was easily "startled by strangers." "I can't calm her down," she went on. "Sometimes I feel like hitting her when she is demanding and crying uncontrollably. I worry about this and worry I'll go out of control." (Mother's history suggested a rather careful and cautious person who never had any history of acting impulsively with adults or children.)

Mother's conversation turned to her own mother, who was a very intrusive and aggressive person, and who could easily say, "I hate you," and mean it. Lucy's mother had always been afraid that she would lose her temper much like her mother did. (The maternal grandparents were both survivors of the Holocaust and mother felt that their experience of it was still influencing her, and through her would influence her own children.)

As Lucy interacted with each of her parents, she was very attentive and socially responsive. She smiled, made different vocal sounds, and looked around. She focused equally well on her mother or father. She also took me in, smiling and flirting with me quite easily. As mother interacted with her, she stayed very close to her daughter, an inch or two away, rather than giving her some room—three or four inches, for example. When Lucy made a sound, mother would make three or four sounds so quickly that Lucy hardly had time to take control over the rhythmic interaction. Also, mother kept touching Lucy as she talked to her. She would stroke her and try to hug her, all at the same time. Mother was clearly a very physical person. Whenever Lucy got upset, she would use touch and holding in an effort to calm her, rather than trying to use words or facial expressions. Lucy wasn't given even two seconds to calm down before Mother was with her, rubbing her back, stroking her feet, trying to rock her in different rhythms, all within twenty or thirty seconds. Even when Lucy was sitting with father, mother was attentively engaged with her, distracting herself from me, saying, "Oh my! I think I better go hold her. She looks like she is going to cry."

Father was gentle in his interactions and gave Lucy more room. He looked a little preoccupied and depressed, and his rhythm was a little too slow for a bright, attentive, and socially responsive baby. She would do two or three actions in sequence, such as taking an object in her hand and holding it out for father. Rather than take it, he tended to keep working on trying to get her to repeat a sound he made. When I pointed out that she was now trying to engage him in something new, he seemed to take a split second or two longer than one would normally expect to shift gears. He looked a little puzzled, and then got the idea of it. Later, when I talked to him about this, he admitted he was still very preoccupied with the effects of his accident. He worried about his seizures and was especially concerned that he might have a seizure and hurt Lucy. He said that he had been somewhat depressed and thought that the seizure medication might be dulling his appreciation of his daughter.

When I examined Lucy, I noticed that she had good motor tone in all extremities and was very responsive, in a pleasurable way, to being touched. She enjoyed my facial expressions and vocalizations, brightening, looking, cooing, and vocalizing back, much as she had with mother. While holding her, I talked loudly to mother who was sitting across the room. Lucy soon started crying, showing a sensitivity to loud noises, which mother had reported. I tried moving her in space. She was excruciatingly sensitive to any sudden movement, especially in the vertical direction; she was a little better horizontally. As I watched her play, I noticed that if I took one toy away and hit it, Lucy would get upset and start crying quickly. But if my movements were very slow and gradual, allowing her to be visually in charge of the action, she would enjoy it and be less likely to cry.

I suggested the parents help Lucy use her solid abilities for shared attention and engagement and beginning abilities for two-way communication to take better charge of her world. It would involve her shifting from using proximal modes of communication, as she did with mother, to more distal modes (more vocalization and visual cuing, especially when Lucy was upset, as opposed to just touch and rhythmic rocking). We talked about the current rhythm of interaction and Lucy's need for more time in order to calm herself and take the lead in play. Mother recognized that she would need to slow down her rhythm and try to deal with her anxiety differently. She appreciated the insight she was now gaining. Father, also, seemed to feel a little better about the situation, particularly once he aired his feelings about the accident. He was able to review his medical history more realistically and verbalize some of his anxieties about hurting Lucy, and his fear that he was preoccupied and not as attentive to her as he might be. Both parents were very gratified to know that Lucy was so competent.

I also suggested that mother and father might have special play times with Lucy where they could practice their interactive skills and actually coach one another. I explained that they complemented each other nicely. Father, in some respects, was much more sensitive to Lucy's need for independence, letting her do more things on her own (he had been extremely independent in his own family). Mother was so socially cued into Lucy that she could certainly point out missed opportunities to father. We practiced a little in the office, with each one coaching the other one quite successfully. They seemed to enjoy and relax one another, rather than make each other tense. (One could imagine tense parents making each other more anxious by looking over each other's shoulders. If parents have a solid marriage, as these two had, the involvement with each other's child rearing abilities could actually relax them; because each one was quite nervous and enjoyed the mutual exchange of support and reassurance).

Furthermore, we discussed how mother could try to break down the interactions into circles of communication. Before she responded to Lucy, she would first have to figure out what Lucy was trying to do. It would prevent her from "flying by the seat of the pants" and doing three or four things before Lucy had finished one. Mother would have to practice saying in her mind, "Okay. Now Lucy is trying to get me to look at the ball, or trying to make funny sounds at me." Then she would respond and build up. We practiced doing this as well, and mother discovered how to gain that extra split second that she needed to follow Lucy's lead.

We worked not only on mother following Lucy's lead and letting her be the more assertive one, but also on self-calming; on ways of giving Lucy a little more time to use her considerable strengths to calm down. We also brainstormed on the idea that Lucy was slightly sensitive to loud noises and sudden changes in her environment. The principle was that of gradual exposure to new or changing experiences. For example, we experimented by hiding a ball in one hand and seeing whether Lucy could get curious; or whether she would follow an object when it traveled from high up, down to her level on the floor. This was to be done very slowly and gradually; then slowly speeded up. With these exercises, she would learn to be more flexible, using her vision and even her hearing to find objects and to deal with the changing environment, especially a changing human environment. I suggested that, when Lucy was brought into a new place with new people, mother give her lots of time, and perhaps not put her immediately in a room with six or seven other parents and children. Mother could try spending some time with Lucy and perhaps one other person, in a corner of the room where Lucy wouldn't feel overwhelmed; then gradually introduce her to the group. The principle of not overprotecting Lucy, but also being very gradual with her, was an important one.

In a follow-up meeting, a month later (when she was almost 7 months old), Lucy showed good progress. Through her own assertiveness, she was taking much more of a lead in the interactive play. Lucy would lie on her stomach, instead of just sitting up, and was beginning to slither a little. Mother was much more relaxed and letting her take a lead, and father had a better rhythm of interaction. For example, in her play with father, Lucy began making faces at him, cooing and reaching toward his nose. He smiled and giggled back. He commented on her curiosity about his nose, but with a vocal rhythm in tune with Lucy's. He then offered his hand to her, and she began playing with his fingers—a very nice interaction. Mother, for her part, was still a little tense when Lucy cried; she would grab her too quickly, but was much better at trying, at least for a few seconds, to talk to her and to use facial expressions. Or she would attempt to help Lucy calm down by pointing at things out the window, rather than just using frantic rocking.

Mother reported that Lucy was now less upset at other people's houses; still crying but able to calm down. Taking Lucy into a corner of the room out of the hustle and bustle seemed to be working. At home, Lucy was still having trouble entertaining herself, though; she always wanted to see mother in the same room. She would tolerate playing on the floor for only a minute or two while mother stayed nearby, talking to her; then she'd demand to be picked up. Progress in this area seemed to be slow, but gradual.

As I watched Lucy interact with her parents and myself, I noticed that she was still too passive and her parents were still a little too eager to move in quickly. We talked again about letting Lucy assert herself more. Now that she could be on her tummy and slither around a little, I demonstrated how to get down with her face-to-face and put things in front of her. The parents would let her work toward these objects, encouraging her with a lot of affect cues. Mother had some difficulty with this tactic. "Isn't she going to be in pain when she has to reach for something that she can't quite get?" she asked, worriedly. I stressed the importance of some exercise for Lucy, and assured mother that her daughter's groans, sounds, and even cries were not necessarily signs of discomfort, but more often signs of hard work.

Lucy continued to sleep and grow well. She was now in the 75th percentile in weight and 99th percentile in height. When I saw her again, she was nine months old, and her progress was continuing in a slow but steady manner. She was beginning to search for things that she couldn't see. Crawling confidently now, she would go after her toys and was quite contingent with mother, who showed she was learning to play without moving in too quickly. Father, by this point, had gotten some reassurance from his doctors that he did not need his medication any more. He was much more relaxed, warm, and engaged with Lucy; more with it in terms of the rhythm of his vocalizations and his motor gestures.

Mother talked a great deal about Lucy's anger which was showing itself more now that she was asserting herself. Mother wanted to work around the anger, saying "I don't want Lucy to be angry like my mother was angry or carry the tradition of my family." She, therefore, wanted to calm her daughter down before she got angry. We talked about anger, just like love and warmth and assertiveness, all being legitimate human emotions, and that sometimes Lucy would need to practice her protesting ability, in the same way she needed to reach out sometimes to be picked up. Mother associated Lucy's anger with her own childhood where anger had been quite terrifying, as her mother was such a formidable person. She said, "I'm not going to be intimidated by my daughter, just like I was by my mother." We talked about her fear being a little premature, given how young Lucy was; but it was well understood, in terms of what she was seeing in Lucy, and of the family tradition. This seemed to help mother feel more relaxed about Lucy's assertiveness.

Lucy continued to do well and entered the toddler stage as a competent and assertive little girl. Under stress, she could become passive and needy; and mother, under stress, could become overprotective and anxious. For the most part, however, they had confidently moved from the stage of shared attention and engagement into the stage of two-way communication. They had a flexible pattern of two-way communication with a broad range of behaviors and emotions. Only when frustrated or under stress did they tend to return to passivity and an overprotective interactive pattern.

Now that Lucy was well on target, we agreed that the parents would call me as needed. I alerted mother to Lucy's confident engagement, great attention, and mastery of two-way communication; but I emphasized that the area which the family would need to negotiate over the next few years would be this issue of assertiveness. As Lucy grew more comfortable with her assertiveness, mother would most likely worry about it, because of her own upbringing and her own tendency to be anxious around aggression and assertiveness. Mother recognized the effort it was going to take not to succumb to her own tendencies.

I next heard from them when Lucy was about twenty-seven months old. Mother telephoned, concerned that perhaps she was again falling into a pattern of making her daughter "too passive." When they brought Lucy in for a follow-up visit, she was a highly verbal little girl, capable of nice pretend play with dolls and doing organized themes. She was still able to share attention, as shown by her warm, deep engagement, pleasurable smiles, and two-way gestural communication. She was now building good representational and symbolic capacities into these tendencies. However, when I watched mother and Lucy play, I did notice that mother's worry was, in fact, manifesting itself. Mother tended to try to control the rhythm of symbolic play, much as she had done with Lucy's presymbolic gestural play. For example, mother said, "What do you want to do now?" Lucy answered, "Play some more." Lucy then had the dolls drinking juice. "Drink juice and play," she added. When the question of a little chair arose, Lucy said, "Let's bring a chair." "What for?" mother asked in a friendly manner. Lucy paused for a second. Then mother jumped in, saying, "Oh, I know. The chair will be for this doll. Let's make this doll the mommy, and this doll the baby, and the mommy will give the baby some juice. Here, you be the mommy." As mother took charge in this, Lucy's expression of pleasure seemed to decrease. She looked spacey and sad, and became a little passive. She didn't do exactly as mother had suggested. Instead, she knocked over one of the dolls and turned, as though she was trying to get away from mother, to do something else. Mother said, in a slightly anxious way, "Oh, this doll fell down. She must be hurt. Let's get the doctor." Lucy passively tried to pick the doll up and said, "Fix doll." She was mimicking mother's vocalizations. As mother continued to take charge, Lucy's enthusiasm waned.

I decided to intervene. I told mother I could see how hard it was for her to let Lucy fully take the lead, now that Lucy was using both a wide vocabulary and her marvelous imagination. While Lucy played by herself, I talked with mother. "I want her to perform," she said. "That's my secret wish for her." When asked what the driving force was behind this wish, mother reiterated her earlier fear of "being a bad mother." She said, "I'll prove I'm a good mother by making Lucy do what she should." I commented that she might best prove herself a good mother by helping Lucy be a self-thinker; at this age, performing wasn't carrying out another person's wishes, but it was "thinking for herself." Lucy had to learn to use ideas to guide the play. This would help her control her behavior better. Mother smiled knowingly. She had heard this advice before. I said that I was simply reminding her of some earlier principles, and I acknowledged the feelings that were making it hard for her to follow these principles. She again associated Lucy's competence to her own mother's dominance. She said, "Lucy is so competent now that at times I feel she is smarter than me." Lucy's use of ideas was obviously making mother feel that Lucy had become somewhat dangerous to her. Under the guise of encouraging Lucy's competence, she was inadvertently playing out an unconscious wish to make sure that her daughter would not dominate her.

As I then watched mother and daughter play some more, mother became more relaxed and began to follow Lucy's lead. Lucy took charge again, a smile returning to her face. They looked through some toys; Lucy tentatively started to ask

"What's this?" and "What's that?" Once she saw that mother wasn't going to take over, she took some of the toys and arranged them into a theme; the theme was "who lives in this house?" She said, "Maybe this person lives in a house," or "That person lives in a house." Each time she seemed to look to mother to see if she would interfere; but mother said, "Oh yes, I can see where this one lives in a house. What are they going to do next?" Lucy soon had a whole family living in the house. Each family member was deciding which bedroom to have. The theme focused on order and finding where one was supposed to be, such as who would be in the bedroom and who would sit where around the table. Lucy was obviously starting her play with a safe theme around order. It was nice to see her take the lead.

We talked about sustaining Lucy's opportunities for increased assertiveness as well as following her lead. Mother revealed that Lucy was a little cautious with some of her more assertive friends. I suggested exposing her to more of a variety of friends so that she could learn to share and interact even with her more assertive friends.

We arranged for a follow-up visit in about a month to help monitor Lucy through this new stage of development.

In summary, Lucy was a child who had only mild constitutional contributions to her mild regulatory difficulty. She had a slight sensitivity to loud noises, being moved rapidly in space, to things being moved rapidly away or toward her, and transitions to new situations. A more significant contribution was the environmental side of the equation—an extremely anxious mother who had good reason for her own anxiety, in terms of her own family history as the child of Holocaust survivors. The mother was on antidepressant medication and had a lot of depressive ideation; she worried about being a bad mother, and while trying to be a good mother she was very overprotective. The overprotectiveness was played out with Lucy in the stage of two-way communication. Mother would make communication one-way by overcontrolling her daughter and moving in too quickly. She was interfering with Lucy's ability for self-care and for taking the initiative in their two-way communication. Compounding the family's difficulties was mother's anxiety about father, and father's anxiety about his own seizure disorder. Since he was able to verbalize some of his worries about injuring his child, he was able to move from less available, non-contingent relatedness to greater empathy and availability.

A series of four sessions had helped Lucy and her parents negotiate two-way communication during infancy and early toddlerhood. When the same issue of assertiveness came up again during Lucy's preschool years (when she started using representational capacities, emotional ideas, and the beginning of emotional thinking), they were, fortunately, able to come back again. I plan to follow them for a few visits, and then remain available in a preventively oriented capacity, since, in all likelihood, this issue with assertiveness may pop up again at further developmental junctures.

This case is a clear model of preventive intervention in that it makes use of minimal interventions by maximizing the parents' ability to work through issues on their own. Such intervention remains available, however, at critical junctures in the developmental process when mild constitutional–maturational variables are coupled with environmental patterns that could sow the seeds for some moderate to severe character problems. The early introduction of greater adaptation and flexibility into parent–child interaction patterns can often help infants and young children negotiate their emotional milestones in flexible and wide-ranging ways.

CASE NUMBER 2: JUSTIN

Justin came in as a four-and-a-half-month-old with his parents. They worried that he wanted to "be held all the time." He cried a great deal and the pacifier only helped minimally. "When he gets upset," mother said, "he flails his arms and it's hard to comfort him, even if you hold him. He doesn't like it if he is on his back." Father added, "He likes looking around but not interacting with us as much. He keeps looking away at other things." They also reported that he was getting up four times a night and then took a long time to go back to sleep.

While hearing about these worries, I observed Justin. He was a laid-back child and it took a lot of work for mother, father, or me to get him to smile. He would look at you, but didn't reach out with a smile or any other emotional expression. When you offered him a pen or something shiny, like a spoon, he would give a faint little smile, look at it, but never reached for it. He did increase his attention, however, and clearly could relate to the object or the person handling the object. He also watched as his father left the room to go to the bathroom and, similarly, when his mother moved from one chair to another.

Mother reported that if she put Justin down, he would start crying, and if she left the room, he would really start crying, as though it was a double insult. She felt he wasn't relating to her that much now, and was worried that it would get even worse when she went back to work in three weeks. They had a live-in helper who, she felt, had the same patterns with Justin, but she wasn't present at this first meeting.

Mother also reported that he ate well and was having Similac, rice cereal, and applesauce. He was gaining weight and was physically quite healthy.

The pregnancy and delivery were unremarkable except for a moderately high bilirubin due to an A/O blood incompatibility. He was eight-and-a-half pounds and his Apgars were 9/9. He left the hospital after a few days and had been physically fine since. Mother also noted that he had good muscle tone after he was born, could hold his head up, and could do things like put his fingers or hands in his mouth.

As I observed mother and Justin, mother tried talking to him as she held him in her lap; her voice was quite anxious and she seemed uncomfortable and clumsy at doing this. She didn't seem to know how to get a response. Then she got passive and helpless and stopped talking to him. When she talked, it was in an intermittent fast tone and followed by complete silence, and then another fast tone and complete silence. She tried putting a rattle in his hand. At first, he didn't grab it, but then he was able to take it and look at it. Mother then tried moving him around, up and down, and he got upset and anxious, clearly showing that he was very uncomfortable. When she tried to stroke his arms to relax him, he clearly didn't enjoy the touch, evidencing, perhaps, some tactile sensitivity.

By contrast, father took the baby and just tried to hold him on his shoulder. He comforted him and didn't try to interact very much at all.

In an examination of the baby, I found he had slightly low muscle tone. He evidenced a slight delay in motor development in terms of the security with which he held his head up, but coordinated his arm movements with things he was looking at and might be interested in. Stroking his back and arms and legs, I noted that he was quite sensitive to touch on the back and a little less so on the arms and legs, evidencing some tactile sensitivity. He could respond to a range of vocalizations, both high and low pitch, but tended to require a lot of vocal input before he looked and gave a little smile. He seemed to be slightly underreactive to vocalizations, but didn't become disorganized or distant when the vocal cadence got very complicated. He seemed to respond to steady, persistent vocalizations within a medium range of pitch and loudness. In the area of facial animation, he also required a lot of input, seeming to be less rather than overly reactive; with a lot of animation, he did well and could begin looking and smiling more. He also responded reasonably well to a range of lighting situations, and did not seem to have difficulty with bright lights.

My initial impression was of a baby at some risk: he was a little low in his motor tone, slow in motor development, laidback, and not very reactive (in fact, a little underreactive) to auditory and visual input, and a little overly reactive to touch. He had a worried mother who was very clumsy and uneasy in her interaction patterns, and did not feel confident in her wooing ability; and who was planning to go back to work.

In this first session, I didn't learn a lot about mother's own background, except to wonder about her degree of discomfort with the baby. Father, too, seemed uncomfortable, but he also seemed satisfied by whatever small comfort Justin achieved. Toward the end of the session, mother talked about wanting her baby to cling less, and to know that she was the mother. She wanted him to love her; but she mentioned, too, wanting to go back to work as soon as possible.

We went over his pattern of reactivity in each sensory modality, discussing his need for a lot of persistent, calm, slow input, in terms of his auditory and visual systems; and that he needed to be held with firm pressure and not rubbed lightly on the back or the arms. He tolerated light touch better on the abdomen, though. We reviewed how to hold him firmly, while offering him lots of visual and auditory input, as well as how to apply deep pressure. We discovered he responded slightly better when I let him bounce in my lap and then hugged him. His attention also improved when there was gross motor activity and joint compression, together with the firm pressure. I demonstrated how we could get his smile to deepen with these persistent overtures. I used vocalizations, and interesting facial expressions, along with firm pressure on the back or arms. I did some bouncing in the lap followed by joint compression.

We also reviewed the legitimacy of mother's concern, given that she and Justin were still working out their relationship, and the fact that she was going back to work full time. When we discussed her flexibility she mentioned that her income was essential for the household, to "put food on the table." She admitted she could begin at half-time and then gradually work up to five-eighths time so that she could be home during a large part of the afternoon. I stressed that this was a better idea. Both she and Justin would feel more comfortable if they had more time to get to know each other and work out their patterns together.

I suggested that mother and baby work with a colleague of mine a few times a week on patterns of interaction. She would practice learning to help Justin calm down and be more attentive and engaged using the procedures we had outlined.

Mother worked on these patterns and returned with Justin six weeks later. She felt that he still cried a lot when there wasn't a person around, and got frustrated easily, but she was pleased that he was trying to crawl and was relating to her more. He was looking and smiling and even beginning to interact a little bit. He was still waking up four or five times in the night, and she and her husband were becoming exhausted. Even though Justin was looking and smiling, and beginning to interact more, mother was worried that there were still lots of times when he didn't look at her. "Particularly when I come home from work," she said. "He will ignore me for the first hour or so. He takes a long time to warm up." I empathized with this, pointing out that he was a baby who did take a long time to warm up. I told her that Justin was probably still very sensitive to events like separation, just as he was sensitive to her walking out of the room. His reaction was rather deceptive because he didn't usually show his sensitivity through anger, but more through withdrawal.

In observing their play together, I noticed that Justin was much more engaging and smiling than he had been the first time he came in. He was very responsive to mother's voice, showing a nice organized look and a big smile when she talked to him for a minute or two. He had a pattern of smiling and looking for a few seconds, then looking away for a second or two, and then coming back. He didn't sustain it. He seemed to need to take a break from the intense looking and smiling more often than most babies his age. It appeared that he got overloaded more quickly than other babies, even though he needed a lot of wooing and input. He had a seemingly narrow zone. Many babies who are underreactive can sustain their attentiveness and pleasure for a little while; other babies who are overly sensitive will tune out quickly after just a few seconds of looking and smiling engagement. He had some elements of both. It was as though Justin had a narrow range that took him a long time to get to. Then, he could enjoy it and focus. But when he got slightly overloaded, he needed time out to regroup.

Justin looked and followed his mother as she moved about. He followed toys to the floor; he also made some nice exchanges with his rattle. He handed it to her. She took it, looked at it, and handed it back to him. He also reached for a little toy globe I have that is brightly colored and can be spun around. He and mother smiled as they exchanged it with one another. Mother, however, was still quite uncomfortable in her interactions with him; she vacillated between a nice moment or two and passive silence. She would look confused, and then sometimes overload him with too quick a cadence of words, or hand him too many things in a row. She was able to slow down and maintain a nice reciprocal rhythm for isolated moments, and then she would create other islands of clumsiness. When she went too fast for him or withdrew, he would tune out rather quickly and look blankly around the room, seemingly unfocused and disinterested. It was still impressive, though, to see the gains he and mother had made.

Father did not come this time. Mother thought that he felt too uncomfortable to participate; he had been doing a lot of holding and cuddling, but was still reluctant to try more interacting.

In talking about her history, mother reported that she had been an only child and that her parents had been very formal and aloof. Her mother, she suspected, had been depressed during her childhood, but she wasn't quite sure. She thought there was a family history of depression, but the family was very "secretive and closed." She suspected that her mother's mother had also been depressed and that an aunt had perhaps been treated by a psychiatrist for depression. On her husband's side of the family, she reported that there had been one uncle who had been hospitalized for schizophrenia, she thought. She knew of no other mental illness. She herself remembered being a good student in school, but had never felt very comfortable with intense emotions. She had acquaintances, but not close friendships throughout her childhood. She felt that she and her husband had a friendship, but not a deep or passionate relationship; "We don't fight very much," she added. Having grown up as an only child with very formal parents, she said she felt "ill-prepared for a baby who was changing his mind all the time." I empathized with how hard it must be, given her lack of preparation—not having had brothers and sisters to take care of—to all of a sudden be a mother, particularly the mother of a challenging baby. We talked about how, perhaps, she and her baby could learn about relationships together. She smiled and seemed reassured by this.

When I saw Justin as an eight-month-old, mother was still worried about him. "He doesn't attend to me as long as I would like him to," she said despondently. "He still looks at me, may smile at me, and may even interact, but then he looks away." She felt that he flitted from one thing to another too much. Mother had brought the housekeeper to this session. She was worried that he attended longer and seemed to respond more deeply for this live-in helper, who spent the greater part of the day with him because mother was working.

Mother said that Justin wasn't crying as much and was playing a little more independently. He also was sleeping better; now that he was a little more independent during the day, she was comfortable in letting him cry more on his own at night. She no longer felt compelled to go back into his room if he woke up again since he could now cry himself back to sleep after five or six minutes. She was following an approach where she would look in on him and see if he could settle himself down. She was having to go in to him only two or three times an evening, rather than four or five. He continued to be a good eater.

While watching mother play with him, I noticed that she still had her pattern of intruding and then being passive. She did this with speedy vocalizations or took his fingers and tried to force him to hold something, or handed him too many objects in a row; and she had the same anxious, tense quality as before. Whenever she overwhelmed him, he would tend to turn from her and look around the room, then try to look back to her and smile and engage. Nevertheless, they had some moments of nice warm engagement with an exchange of objects or smiles, or even some sounds. But mother's rhythm continued to be uneven and, perhaps, clumsy, although she vocalized her discomfort.

I then watched the housekeeper interact with Jason. She was a very passive, laid-back woman but one who could persistently woo and engage. They had wonderful, warm, pleasurable, mutually attentive engagements, with nice peek-a-boo games, exchanges of objects, and warm smiles back and forth. He disengaged less from her and only after thirty or forty seconds of engagement. When he looked away, she would, in her own quiet, calm, way, reengage him. She seemed ideally suited for him.

In play with me, Jason was very joyful and vocal and motorically interactive. He smiled deeply and was highly contingent. His motor tone seemed to be improving and he was tolerating touch on his back and arms a little more. I noticed that I could hold his attention for a good sixty seconds. He would give three or four deep, rich smiles, particularly if I let him sit up in my lap, bouncing and holding him firmly on his arms with my fingers on his back. He responded to a wide range of my vocalizations and different facial expressions, and was willing to engage me in peek-a-boo games. We handed the globe back and forth, then his rattle, or other objects. He was generally flirtatious with subtle little smiles.

When I got down on the floor with him, I noticed that he was not quite able to crawl yet. He would reach objects by slithering forward. I could go head-to-head with him and he could assertively move toward me; he seemed to enjoy being on his stomach and interacting from that position. I had mother and the housekeeper do that too. Mother felt uncomfortable, but was willing to practice; the housekeeper felt more at ease with it. We talked about giving him more practice, now that his motor tone seemed better and he was almost ready to crawl.

Mother surprised me by saying that, perhaps, she "needed to stop working entirely," or reduce her time, because she wasn't forming the relationship she wanted to with her baby. She thought that she and her husband could afford it after all, since they had some savings, and this was a time she didn't want to miss. I had originally felt it important not to press her into spending more time with her baby, except to urge her not to work full time. As she was reflecting on his, I empathized with the pleasure and joy that I thought she would have, being as close to her baby as she wanted to be. I supported her consideration of all the options. I also helped her elaborate on her worries about not being a good mother. She hadn't felt prepared; and as she spoke of some of her concerns, she said, "If I do stay home and still can't get into a good relationship with him, then I will really feel terrible." When I asked her in what ways she thought she would feel terrible, she talked about times in her childhood when she felt clumsy and couldn't get other children to like her; she felt that she hadn't had the "natural moves" that other children had. She now blamed this on her parents being so formal and uncomfortable with emotions. Mother, then, got some very nice, warm interactions with her baby. As I drew her attention to them, she smiled and became hopeful that she and her baby could learn how to be close together.

When Justin was ten months old, mother came in and reported that he was continuing to make progress. He was not sleeping through the night, although there had been a few difficult evenings where she let him cry for fifteen or twenty minutes to make the final adjustment. She felt more confident in helping him take the final step at night time, because he was more adept at self-calming and not as dependent on her.

In general, parents often feel more comfortable helping children work through some of their separation challenges when the children demonstrate more self-comforting and self-calming skills during the daytime. It is usually helpful to work on the same theme or issue in the day to master it "in the light of day," before attempting to master the same issue during the evening.

At this time, mother also talked about leaving work entirely. She had actually reduced her work schedule from two-thirds to half-time again. She was contemplating leaving work imminently and getting ready to become pregnant again, so that by the time Justin was two, he might have a brother or sister. She seemed comfortable with this set of plans and hoped that she and he would become even closer once she was home with him full time. She also reflected on her jealousy toward the caregiver, but in a constructive way, saying, "I can't expect him to prefer me if I'm not home with him as much as she is."

In their interactive play, mother spontaneously picked up a baby doll that Justin was beginning to explore. She rocked it close to her. He crawled over and grabbed at it, making overtures as though he wanted it. They started a very interesting dialogue with a certain message and meaning to it. Mother was talking to the baby doll and vocalizing for it, but soon after Justin came over, she got distracted and tuned him out; she was looking for another toy rather than staying with the first one. I commented, "You just had a beautiful moment, but then for some reason you decided to disengage. This time, you did it before Justin did it to you." Mother smiled, and admitted that she hadn't been aware of it; some other toy had caught her eye. On reflection, she wondered whether she was doing to Justin exactly what he did to her. She thought that perhaps she was doing this at home, too, that she had become so sensitive to his rejection, she rejected him first. She realized that she did it only in a microcosm of play, as she was dutifully attentive to him in a general sense. She then remembered how sensitive she was as a teenager to boys not liking her or rejecting her. "I would often try not to like them first," she said.

Shortly thereafter, mother and Justin explored a Snoopy doll together. He crawled over to mother and started touching Snoopy just as mother was. Mother then spontaneously had Snoopy talk to him, making different silly sounds and saying, "Do you want to give me a hug?" Much to my surprise, and mother's surprise too, Justin looked, smiled, and started imitating the sounds that mother was making for Snoopy. He said, "Ga-ga, boo-boo," and even some "da-da" and "ma-ma," although he couldn't repeat and imitate the exact words mother was using. This was, by far, their best interaction ever and a momentous occasion. Mother smiled deeply and warmly, and felt for the first time, as she later explained to me, "fully like a mommy." It wasn't so much that Justin had imitated her words, but that the depth of warmth and connectedness between the two of them was better than it had ever been before. This was reflected in mother's relaxation and in her being quite original and creative in the way she had Snoopy talking. It had drawn Justin in for this wonderful interaction. Here, they had not only cause and effect interaction, but also emotion, vocalization, motor manipulation, and even the beginning of a psychological drama.

After this wonderful interaction, Justin was his usual self. He became disengaged and relaxed for a while, looking at different things. When he rejoined mother with other nice reciprocal behavior, vocalizations, and emotional gestures, she was able to stay with him. They exchanged nice sounds together directly—some "ba-ba's" and "da-da's," and "ma-ma's"—and then played a little game of hiding and saying "bye-bye." Justin tried to find mother when she hid behind the chair, playing out some separation themes, but in the safety of the office.

As they played, this same subtle disengagement issue emerged. Sometimes in the middle of a peek-a-boo, or chasing his mother behind the chair, Justin would disengage and get distracted by something else. Mother would look pained for a second, then she would disengage from him and start talking to me or begin to turn her back on Justin, or even fumble in her pocketbook for something. When he turned and was ready, looking eagerly at her to reengage, she was still turned away or preoccupied. Mother was missing the fact that sometimes Justin would take a time out because he got overexcited and needed to take a break. His disengagement was a form of taking a break, but she still took it as rejection. But this time when I pointed it out to her, she was able to see it much more readily and said, "I guess it's hard to teach old dogs new tricks." She related a few instances at home where she felt she had probably done the same thing. She seemed much more self-observant now and much more ready to regroup quickly.

We talked about working on remaining engaged so that Justin could take his time out and reengage. They were already very successfully sustaining these periods of engagement, as well as adding on periods of shared attention and engagement. They had nice, complex two-way communication patterns in which Justin was opening and closing at least four or five circles in a row and using motor actions, vocalizations, and a range of emotion. Justin was looking more and more age appropriate.

Mother continued her progress, and about a month-and-a-half later stopped working entirely. She felt more relaxed, more assured of herself as a mother, and more comfortable with spontaneous emotions. Although father did not rejoin us, mother reported that he and she were getting along better and that there was more warmth in the relationship; she was more comfortable taking the lead and drawing father in.

At fourteen months old, Justin came in, walking now, and immediately went for some toys. He became fascinated with the whale. Mother jokingly tried to start a game with Justin, saying that she was going to hide the whale and put it behind my chair. Justin made some wonderful facial gestures, looking puzzled and curious, and then started searching. He found the whale behind my chair and brought it to mother. When I asked if he would bring it to me too, he grinned and giggled and brought it to me. When I said, "The whale wants to give you a kiss," and made a little movement, he put his cheek up and let the whale touch him. He then took the whale and wanted to touch it to my face. He was beginning to use a few words like *mom* and *that.* Mother reported that she had counted twenty different words already, and that his language acquisition had grown dramatically since she'd stopped working. He looked happier and more deeply content than I had seen him before; mother felt that, with her home full time, he had gotten "happier and happier." She added that he was only occasionally waking up at night. He might cry for a while, but she was comfortable in letting him cry it out, although if she was concerned about him teething, she would go in and comfort him. "He still demands my attention too much some of the time," and won't let me go out of the room. He pulls my newspaper or magazine if I am trying to read, or pulls on my leg if I am talking on the phone. He cries if I don't give him the attention he wants."

We talked about how it was now time for mother to use Justin's considerable potential for interacting. If he used "the distal communication modes" more, he would learn how to be close to her, even when she wasn't holding him. Eventually, he would become more secure in his ability to comfort himself. We talked about vocalizations, facial gestures, and motor gestures, as ways of communicating with Justin when he was on the other side of the room. If she was reading a magazine, for example, she would look up every few minutes while he was playing and do some distal communication with him. She had been getting into another pattern, common to many parents, of letting him pursue her until she felt she had to flee from him for a few moments of peace and quiet. Justin sensed her desire to get away and it only made him more ardent in pursuing her. We came up with the idea of giving him twenty or thirty minutes of floor time, fully and intensely, focusing on distal communication interactions. Then mother would take an organized time out for herself. She would tell Justin she was going to be on the phone or read the newspaper, but every few minutes she would look up and interact with him, using gestures and words.

In the play part of this session mother and Justin had nice reciprocal interactions. He took a little doll and put it in the truck she was playing with and pushed it around. He took her hand and showed her how to put a man in the car. With a look of enormous satisfaction, he indicated that he wanted her to put a man in another car so that they could make a kind of train. Mother felt pleased at the initiative and leadership he was showing. They were exchanging many affective, vocal, and motor gestures together, closing at least five or six circles in a row.

Near the end of this session, mother needed some further reassurance that it was okay to set limits on Justin, when after twenty or thirty minutes of floor time, and after lots of distal communication, he still persisted in interfering with things that she wanted to do. Limits were now appropriate. She could say "no" or "wait" and Justin could understand what these words meant. The notion of learning to wait would be a very important ingredient in their distal communication system.

This case illustrates preventively oriented intervention with a child who had risks from two sides—his low motor tone and slightly delayed motor development, and his underreactive auditory and visual–spatial sensory processing patterns—which made it hard for him to engage and stay engaged. Also, his tactile sensitivity made it difficult for him to be comforted by his mother. He evidenced a unique style of having a very narrow zone in which he felt comfortable with information; it would take a lot of visual and auditory input to woo him; he would be attentive and engaged for a few brief seconds and, then, become overloaded and need to disengage and look around.

His unique constitutional–maturational pattern aggravated mother's and the family's psychological patterns. Mother, as indicated, was uncomfortable with closeness and emotion, having grown up in a very formal family. She was always sensitive to being rejected, often rejecting first before someone would reject her. Father tended to use massive avoidance when confronted with psychological challenges, and was also not comfortable with emotions. The housekeeper was much more consistent and persistent, but tended toward passive comfort and didn't have a lot of wooing power. Therefore, we had a situation where Justin's own constitutional–maturational pattern made it hard for him to engage the world and led him to disengage quickly after being engaged; and mother's sensitivity to rejection and her difficulty with emotions made it hard for her to achieve a natural rhythm of wooing with her son.

Working with both sides of the equation enabled this family to gradually make progress. By the middle to the end of the first year, Justin was becoming more and more richly engaged, more attentive, and slowly more interactive. He was still rather passive and laid-back, though, still finicky and fussy, and having sleep problems; and mother was still feeling somewhat clumsy and uncomfortable with her mothering abilities. However, by the end of the first year and toward the beginning of the second, gradual progress led to Justin taking over the interactions more, and showing greater initiative. Mother became comfortable enough with her mothering role to give up work not only to prepare for a new child, but also to consolidate her relationship fully with Justin so that he wouldn't be more involved with the housekeeper than with her.

This case shows how slow such progress can be, taking a good part of the first year and the early part of the second. It also shows that slow, gradual progress can be the best progress because mother and Justin fully worked through their differences and difficulties and challenges. By the early part of the second year they are now both experiencing a great deal of competency. Fortunately, Justin has been able to catch up and become fully age appropriate in terms of evidencing healthy toddler patterns that include behavior and emotional complexity and interaction. They are patterns built on a foundation of solid attachment and a solid capacity for shared attention.

Perhaps the lesson for this case is that a seemingly serious and worrisome problem in the first year of life can turn into an opportunity for building a solid foundation. If one takes one's time and works with the psychological patterns in the mother and the family, as well as the constitutional and maturational patterns of the child and the interactive patterns between them, one can build a solid foundation and see optimal development within a reasonable period of time.

CASE NUMBER 3: GAVIN

An economist brought in her three-and-a-half-month-old baby, Gavin, because he had stopped looking at her and was very disinterested; she was worried that he was "autistic or becoming autisticlike." As I watched them interact, I found the mother's worries to be justified. This baby was very aloof, staring at different objects. It was very hard for the mother to engage him. The best she could do in the first session was to get a fleeting look, with no smile nor any sign of pleasure. There was none of the imitative mouthing or motor activity and joyful smiles which one often sees with a baby that age.

The baby was also a bit sensitive to touch, a bit stiff in terms of motor tone, and didn't like to lie on his tummy; he liked to lie on his back better. The baby did focus on inanimate sounds, like a telephone ringing. Also, in terms of auditory processing, there seemed to be low arousal. It took a lot of input to get him to turn toward a sound. He seemed to be more hyporeactive in auditory processing than in some of the visual processing (e.g., he studied interesting shapes and objects).

The mother was trying to interact with him without being overly intrusive. She varied the pitch of her voice, the position of her face, and held him reasonably gently and securely and warmly. She was quite sad that her baby wouldn't look at her. The father was a little more impatient and tended to intrude, and the baby recoiled from the father a little more. But the father was, for the most part, a warm and gentle person. The couple seemed to have a decent marriage, to care for one another, and to be equally concerned about the baby. As we discussed the family further, the mother revealed that she had returned to work full-time, about two weeks before her baby started tuning out, leaving the child with a baby-sitter. The mother was a busy professional who traveled one hour to her job. She was terribly distressed that in the evenings when she came home, and even on the weekends, she couldn't get her baby to reengage. She reported that he was a healthy eight-and-a-half-pounder, and in the first two months was very alert and attentive and calmed easily. The pregnancy and delivery went well and his Apgars were 9/10. He showed some precociousness in terms of social interest, and even some beginning smiling at two months, but "he lost it." This change made her even more upset. She was wondering what to do, feeling guilty about working, and conflicted about whether or not to continue working. Her main worry was whether her child was slipping into an autistic pattern and whether or not her going to work caused this.

Based on the initial session, there were suggestions that events seemed to be contributing to this baby's withdrawal. There was also a mild constitutional vulnerability; namely, tactile sensitivity and slightly low motor tone. Yet other babies, without such a vulnerability, might not have reacted this way to the mother going back to work with a constant baby-sitter (caregiver) in the home.

Preliminary suggestions included giving ideas to the parents on how to help their baby attend through tactile approaches (a great deal of gentle pressure rather than a light touch); a passive range of motion exercises relating to his motor system; and trying different ways of holding with movement and large muscle activity (e.g., sit-ups in the parent's lap), to help him attend more. We also worked on a skill the mother already seemed to possess—how to vary the pitch of her voice and pull him in and how to take a fleeting little look for a second and pull it into a longer look. The father, although less naturally gifted, worked on that technique as well. We also worked on playing to the baby's interest in sights, combined with both parents becoming very animated. They learned the value of engaging the baby's attention for two seconds (instead of one).

I suggested to the mother that she work only half-time for a number of months (to be determined), so that she could be with her baby at least half the day. I had no question that this change was necessary for this child in order to pull him in. This adjustment was quite a compromise for her. She was directing a big research program, and had a lot of work to do at home in the evenings on her computer, and she was still doing full-time work. She agreed to be away for only four to four-and-a-half hours each day. She negotiated with her boss to work half-time, which was going to mean about three hours in the office, because of her travel time.

When the parents came back two months later, the baby was much more connected and involved. On the next visit, the baby was fully engaged—smiling nicely, gurgling and cooing, and evidencing nice motor gestures. Now, the baby, at five-and-a-half months of age, still didn't like to be on his tummy. We worked a little more on playing with the baby from the tummy position and noticed that when he was on his tummy, and motivated for social interaction, he would lift his neck up and get into a good position for looking. The parents had been doing this mechanically for him, because he had a little trouble with motor control and a little bit of sensitivity yet in the trunk area, but he could, with motivation, do the motion himself. He eventually became very interactive, although now he enjoyed his mother more than his father.

The father was politicking for the mother to be able to go back to work, because she was "taking so much time in the evening doing her work that [he feels] she is tense." Her mother was still living in the house to help out, but was about to return to her home, and they had not yet settled on a full-time, permanent caretaker for the baby.

It has been my experience that there are certain babies that are more rejection-sensitive than others. Whether these babies also tend to be somewhat hyporeactive to auditory input, or have some tactile hyperreactivity, I am not sure. But I have noticed that it is very important for babies who are rejection-sensitive to have consistent caregiving. One could argue that every baby needs a consistent caregiver to avoid problems. But to avoid major problems, there is no question that the baby, in this case, would not be ready to tolerate another shock to his system for a while. I suggested that the mother spend perhaps another hour or so at work as the baby got a little older and as the caregiving situation with the new caretaker became more secure.

This was a baby who was difficult to interest in the world around him. There were no disruptions in sleeping and eating. He was fairly sound constitutionally, except for the tactile sensitivity in the trunk, low auditory arousal, and some questionable motor planning and motor tone lags. The baby was a little slow in his crawling, but otherwise his motor development came along nicely. In contrast, when the very finicky, hyperreactive babies experience separation, they become more clinging and vigilant, and develop sleeping and eating disturbances. But the babies who are a little hyporeactive are the ones you can lose, in terms of engagement. They can fall between the cracks if a therapist doesn't see them until they are eighteen months old, and at that point they may have a diagnosis of a communication problem with autistic features. The history of some of these babies begins like the case I have just described.

CASE NUMBER 4: JAMES

James's parents came in to consult me about their son when he was just a month old. He was born a healthy, seven pound, five ounce baby, with good Apgars (9/9) and a healthy adaptation. In the first month he gained an appropriate amount of weight and height and nursed vigorously and satisfactorily, with mother breast-feeding.

Mother was worried, first, because she wanted to make sure he was "okay," and, second, because she felt that he was "too demanding," even though he was just a month old. She felt "Maybe I'm not satisfying him enough and that's why he's especially demanding." Father was perplexed and felt that the problems were more with the mother than with the baby. Then it turned out that father was working until eight or nine o'clock at night and didn't have much of a sense about his baby other than to feel "I love him very much." Mother described James as eating a lot and being up "all day long." He liked to "be held and stimulated," she said. "He looks at things; he'll look at his mobile, but he doesn't give me a special look."

As mother talked, I was observing little James in her lap and he was able to look over in his mother's direction as she was talking. She was holding him on her knees and he looked toward her rather than toward me as she talked. At other times he would look up and around the room. When I asked mother to show me how she liked to interact with him, she was able to change the rhythm of her voice and make interesting facial expressions, all within reasonable bounds. She varied the rhythm of her voice and made gradual and slow facial expressions and seemed gentle, soft, and sensitive. She also stroked his arms and legs gently. For his part, James was able to use each of his senses to take an interest in the world. He seemed to look; he seemed to turn toward her voice and tune in; he had reasonable head control. In the few instances when he became whiny and cried during the time we were talking, he responded to her rubbing his back, holding him on her shoulder, or looking at him and trying to comfort him with sounds and looks.

When I asked if I could also interact with him, I found that his motor tone was on the low side in all four extremities and in his trunk; and his control of his neck wasn't quite as good as I like to see. He was, however, able to look at me and move to my voice and generally sustain an interest without getting too upset. His reaction to touch didn't seem overly sensitive.

As I worked with him, I noticed that in keeping with his low motor tone, there was a subtle tendency toward being a little laid-back. It took a lot of talking and facial expression to have him look or follow me. He wasn't a baby who tuned in easily or quickly; but I didn't place a lot of confidence in this short cross-sectional impression, and he was only, at this point, one month old. In general, he seemed to be able to take an interest in his world through all his senses and use his motor system to help coordinate this interest. He also seemed to have the capacity to regulate himself, because he was able to calm down after being upset. He was healthy, eating and sleeping all right. The only concern that I wanted to monitor was his slight inability to engage. I suspected that a slightly underreactive baby might make a very sensitive mother feel less than successful when she was not having as much impact as she expected. Such a baby might also have less capacity to pull father in, especially since this father was working extra hard and perhaps avoiding getting into a relationship with his son.

As mother talked more about her reactions to her baby, she revealed that her own mother was very rejecting of her; she felt that she had led her own mother to feel that she was too demanding. "I always thought that something was wrong with me," she said. "I was needy and demanding all through my childhood and my mother always seemed to want to hide from me. I always felt she was hiding when, for example, she was in the bathroom for long periods of time."

She went on to say that when her baby had been up for a long period of time, she couldn't always get him to look in her direction; also, he would cry irritably and be hard to calm down. She realized that perhaps he was tired, but since he wouldn't go to sleep, she would begin to feel that she was "not doing things right." Mother also felt that her husband was shutting her out and not providing much support or warmth.

Father felt that he was trying to be relaxed and calm about the whole situation, but then indirectly revealed the extent of his heavy work schedule. He wasn't home very much to share with mother the emotional drama of having a baby or to provide much physical help, although mother did have some help part of each day at home. Mother felt she needed to have couples therapy with the father to work out the reaction to the new baby.

When James was three-and-a-half months old I saw them again. At that point, he was sleeping through the night. He was still a little fussy, but by ordinary standards not very fussy (though mother was still overly sensitive to his fussiness). He liked to be on his back more than his tummy, although he was having a little trouble lifting his head, and he loved to be massaged and talked to. When we moved his hands, he looked and was beginning to smile and even "swipe at things." Mother noted, however, that in a group situation (she was in a mother's support group), he seemed to withdraw and look spacey and be less available; she wondered whether all the noise and commotion was hard for him. Mother also reported that she got embarrassed when he cried at this same parents' support group.

She thought she got tense with him, feeling "you shouldn't be that way," and was worried that "he would be angry" at her.

Father was still working late and mother was very resentful of that, even though they had started some couples therapy. But the therapy only lasted a few weeks because she didn't like the therapist. At this point, father threw up his hands as if to say, "See what I have to live with?" He was clearly using avoidance as a tactic rather than trying to get in there and be supportive and helpful.

During this session, the parents explored their own past a little. Mother amplified the pattern that she had with her own mother, adding that her father "never came to [her] rescue to help [her] out" when her own mother hid from her or passively retaliated by not giving her what she needed; for example, her mother had refused to stay with her in kindergarten for more than a day or two when she was frightened about being alone. We talked about some of her worries; she could intellectually see where she projected some of them onto the situation with her baby.

Father talked about his historical and chronic characterologic pattern of avoiding conflict, giving in to his wife passively, but then trying to avoid her. They were both aware of the pattern. Father was aware that he had started using massive avoidance when he was a teenager, just to try to get by and "circumvent difficult situations." He talked a little about his fear of holding James and dropping him; he was also concerned about his wife criticizing him for doing things wrong. He clearly hadn't yet spent enough hours in the trenches to be confident as a father. We talked about him trying to protect the hours between six and eight-thirty in the evening. James usually went down for the evening around nine, and after that, father could return to his office to do calls at night. Their time together would be central for mother and father to begin to work out some of their differences, and for him to be included in the family. He began making efforts in this direction.

When working with James during this session, I could see that he still had low motor tone, but, with a lot of work on my part, was able to give me a big robust smile and enjoy my funny faces and my different vocalizations. When I talked to his parents in a very animated and loud way, however, he seemed to get a little overwhelmed and began looking distant and spacey; he seemed to be sensitive if my voice got too loud or high pitched. But he was still able to be engaged, although it took a fairly controlled rhythm to sustain a quality of relatedness, his pleasurable warmth, and his engagement. With a lot of work on my part, he would sustain his focus for a while. Otherwise he would look spacey and tuned out, particularly if he had too much auditory input. I had the parents working with me on the floor. We put him on his stomach, seeing if he could hold his head up consistently; he did for the most part, although he tired after a few minutes. I also looked to see if he could reach for things in front of him and show some of his warm, pleasurable affect in that position as well. (As indicated up to that point, the parents had been mostly working with him on his back.) His muscle tone was a little bit low and I thought it useful for him to spend more time on his stomach. We talked about James doing "floor time" on his tummy and letting him work a little harder. We put a finger or something that interested him in front of him and watched to see if he could coordinate some of his visual interest; then mother or father made some unusual sounds, and we monitored his auditory interest, motor movements, and his ability to be slightly more in extension when he was on his back. Both parents practiced this in the session and were able to do it successfully. Mother, however, worried that he was uncomfortable; she kept worrying that something "would happen to him if he was upset." Father was less worried about this, but was also less able at keeping James's interest sustained in terms of his vocal rhythms. Even with her extra worries, mother had a natural gift for keeping James interested and looking at her. Father, on the other hand, tended to have long silences between his vocal utterances and wasn't quite as animated in his facial expressions; this led James to tune out a bit more. The parents agreed to practice some of these exercises. They were made aware that James needed extra practice on his motor system because his tone was a bit low, indicating he might be a little slow in some of his milestones. The infant was slightly laid-back, like his father, and we wanted to get him working and asserting himself as early as possible.

I saw James again at five-and-half months. Mother reported that she was feeling more confident now that he was bigger and stronger and was progressing nicely. She was less worried that she was doing things wrong. She reported that he was less fussy and smiling more and that she could elicit smiles pretty easily. She was even considering going back to work half-time. She felt somewhat conflicted about it but for the most part thought that, now that she had a good, stable live-in helper, it would be all right. She would still be with James for half the day.

Father was not getting home by five-thirty or six in the evening, but was there by seven in order to spend at least an hour or an hour-and-a-half with James. He was also able to spend some early morning time with him, and was a little less avoidant with mother. What emerged, interestingly, as father talked about his impressions of his son, was his disappointment that the infant was running about a month behind in his motor milestones, in terms of the initial rolling over and learning how to sit up. "I don't want James to see my disappointment," he said. Yet, he desired "magic moments" with him. Clearly part of father's avoidance was to prevent people from seeing his own anger, competition, or disappointment in others.

Watching James interact with his parents, now, I noticed how he was able to be warmly engaged, with bright pleasurable smiles; be attentive and persistent; work on their laps, on his back, and also even on his stomach; hold his head up consistently; reach for things, making some vocalizations, and coordinate his arm movements. But he was very unstable when trying to sit on his own, and it looked as if this milestone was going to be delayed. Nevertheless, he was more confidently rolling over in both directions.

When I examined him, his motor tone remained a little on the low side, but did not seem to be interfering in a significant way with motor progression or with his social, emotional, and intellectual adaptation. He still had the quality of being some- what cautious and passive; and it still took a lot of work from both mother and father, as well as myself, to get him to smile, to vocalize back, and to reach for objects. As both parents played with him, it became clear that they were doing about 80 percent of the work. Even in those instances where he had the age-appropriate emotional milestones mastered, the parents would do much of the work for him, and by overdoing it, were in a sense supporting his passive response. For example, mother would put her own face about eight inches in front of him and begin making sounds, seeing if he would make a sound. However, she would make one sound, then another, then another, and then another instead of pausing and waiting with an eager expression on her face. She scarcely gave him a chance to respond to the first one before going on to the next. When she wanted him to reach for a little red ball that he seemed interested in, she put it in front of him and focused on it. Rather than using vocalizations, such as, "Oh, are you going to be able to reach it?" she kept putting the ball closer and closer to him until he hardly had to reach at all. I then demon- strated how James could do more of the work, using vocal and visual support to help him reach out. I knelt down beside mother and put the ball a few inches in front of the infant. I told her she couldn't move the ball, but she could encourage him. Then she used her considerable charm and magnetism with him (he seemed to love her voice) to help him just reach out a little bit more. He grabbed the ball, and smiled with satisfaction. Mother was impressed and pleased that she didn't have to be passive and could be quite active and engaged while helping James become more assertive. Father had the same tendency toward doing the work for James, but his vocalizations had more of a staccato quality. When he, too, became a little passive, much like James was, father and baby had a "stand- off." Both parents practiced interacting with James and focused on how to help him be more assertive and take control over his world a bit more. We worked in general on distal support, using vision and vocalization to help him support his assertiveness and maintain a sense of mastery of his emotional, social, and inanimate world.

Over the next several months, the parents continued to work with James who seemed to be making gradual, but slow, progress. They still had some difficulty in helping him be as assertive as one would like, related, in part, to James's slow motor development. Mother continued to be somewhat over-anxious and overprotective and father not quite as engaged as one would like, but there was clearly slow and steady progress.

When James was sixteen months old, he presented as a handsome, cute, walking toddler who came in and took toys out of the toy box and brought each item to mother or father. He was nicely focused and intentional. He made some minimal sounds, facial expressions, and organized motor gestures as he took a toy. Then he pointed to it and made a sound or two for mother or father to help him explore it. He moved cars along the ground and made some additional sounds. He was clearly warmly connected to his parents, sharing attention and a warm sense of engagement and pleasure with them. He had also established two-way gestural communication, at least of a simple nature. The parents were both reciprocal with him and relaxed, supporting the two-way communication and the shared attention and the warm, pleasurable quality of engagement. (I should mention that James had learned to walk at about 14 months old and the pattern of being about a month to two months delayed in motor milestones had continued.) James put a person in a truck which he rolled along; then he tried to put a larger animal in a small truck. He seemed to enjoy the cars, exploring them, pushing different ones in different directions, and making sounds all the while. He seemed quite content to play on his own, relating to his parents, but not necessarily drawing them in or trying to draw me in.

Most noticeable, however, were his minimal vocalizations and sounds. He did not make a complicated series of sounds with vowel and consonant sounds, but more general global sounds, and then only intermittently. (It reminded me a little of the way father had spoken to James during the earliest sessions.) When mother went down on the floor to play with him, she was verbally supportive, with good reciprocity and good rhythm. But she tended to give a running commentary, allowing James very little chance to make sounds of his own. She was almost too good in her reciprocity, still, leaving him very little work to do. Her verbal communicating was undemanding; she did not stop to see how he would respond to her, either vocally or motorically. For example, when he moved the cars around she would say, "Oh, you are moving the car near me, now near Daddy, now near Dr. Greenspan. Oh, where is you car going next? Uh oh, it's going over here." James would look at her, smile, occasionally make a sound, and continue moving his cars. She was evidently a good commentator and stayed engaged. She would comment on everything James did, showing some sensitivity to his cues. However, she was not really opening and closing circles of communication; she was not setting up a pattern of responses upon which James had to build. When he moved the car, she could have said, cupping her hands, "Oh, gee it's going to come here into my hands." Then she could have waited to see what he would do with it, whether he would respond to either her gesture or her words. Instead, she just kept a vocal commentary following his lead with no implicit demand for him to build on her responses.

James handed father some crayons. Father, working with James, held the boy's interest in the crayons. Father drew a hand and James scribbled on it. James then went to play with the cars; father took one car from him and ran it up and down the boy's arm. He turned away and put a man in a different car, as if wanting to avoid his father. Father then went back to the drawing game with him; James was able to scribble over something father had done, but father seemed a little uncertain about how to engage his son. He wanted to get some interaction going, but half the time seemed to annoy James—James would turn away—nevertheless, the other half of the time James built on some of father's responses. They smiled warmly toward one another, were quite engaged, and did open and close some circles. However, father seemed to feel clumsy. One time when he said, "James, can you put this man in the car again?" James did it. Another time when he asked James if he wanted the crayon, James nodded his head "yes," showing that he had some receptive language that was of an age-appropriate nature. But he was not yet making many sounds or words on his own.

Father revealed that he himself had been very slow to talk, not talking until he was three years old. Mother had been an early talker, putting together three-word sentences by the time she was eighteen months old. Both were concerned about James neither talking nor imitating lots of different sounds. They described him as being very attached both to the baby-sitter and the housekeeper, but avoidant of new people. He would sometimes cry for one to one-and-a-half hours in a new situation. He was also not very adventuresome. He held onto mother in new situations, although at home he was slightly more assertive. They described the baby-sitter as being a very passive and protective person who didn't demand anything from James in terms of vocalization, motor activity, or the like. When he went to the park, James would interact with other children, but if they made too much noise or commotion, he would run over to mother and look a little spacey for a while. Clearly, he did seem to enjoy others. He would jump in with lots of pleasure, but he would interact for only a little while.

They also reported that James was easily frustrated and would cry for half an hour or so when he didn't get what he wanted. So, we talked about how to help him become more assertive and also begin more vocalizations. We reviewed how mother tended to be very undemanding in her interactive style. While her supportiveness was consolidating their warm relationship further, it was not giving James the chance to respond to her and initiate clearer circles of interaction. We discussed how to do this, in terms of using James's receptive language skills. I demonstrated ways of creating alternatives where (depending on the verbal cues) he could choose from among them. For example, if he was building a car, mother might cup one hand and with the other take another toy and say, "Which direction? Where do you want to make the car go, James?" Or she might offer him two things that he wanted; he would have to communicate his choice to her by making some gesture or vocalization. I told the parents not to worry about whether he vocalized or gestured with pointing or looking. The idea, now, was to get him to take the lead in two-way communication, building on their responses. We wanted to see many circles of communication being closed, either with a vocal or a motor gesture. We practiced some more and they went home to work on the task at hand.

At seventeen months of age, although James came in walking, he was still somewhat unstable. But he was able to interact with his parents in an organized manner, with a lot of shared attention, a sense of relatedness, two-way gestural communication, and the beginning use of some words, like "Da-Da," and "cat." There was much inflection in his voice, and he had a hard time with his sounds. He could follow two-step instructions, like, "Give me that . . . " or "Bring the cup that . . . " but some of his language emerged through structured drills. His mother would say, "Who's that?" pointing to father, and he would look and say, "Da-Da." Clearly, some of his use of words had been trained; in spontaneous play, his use of words was minimal. Although James had some increased vocalization, it was still low for a seventeen-month-old.

Mother also reported that James still tended to cling somewhat to her and the baby-sitter, and still didn't seem to enjoy other children as much as she would like. However, in the playground he was playing with other children about half the time. He continued to get upset if there was too much commotion or too much activity, but if the other children were playing more quietly, he would join in and parallel play with them.

James's baby-sitter was present during this session; while father tried to play with James, the child was making nice exchanges of toys, both giving and taking from his nanny. Father worked hard to engage him, finally succeeded and then he said, "Let's take the car to the supermarket." James took the car and put it in the garage of the house. There was good, shared attention and engagement, two-way communication, and even the beginnings of some presymbolic elements to his play. One wondered, though, about how much father had been doing his homework, given the fact that James seemed more comfortable playing with the baby-sitter.

When the baby-sitter played with James, he was very engaged, listened carefully, followed her gestures, and responded with gestures. She said, "Let's put the dolly in the house," but he didn't do it; he listened to her intently and seemed to be trying to understand what she was saying. She took the lead a great deal, not demanding that he take much initiative or assert himself very much. There were two and three and four circles closed in a row, but mostly with him reacting to her. "Here's the car," she would say, rolling it to him. He would then take it and roll it and she would take it and roll it back to him. He might roll it, but not necessarily in her direction. He did explore the house, however, and followed her simple commands; for example, if she held her hand out and said, "Give me that," he would give it to her. He was also able to search for things she hid in her hand, which she did only on my suggestion, to see if he was interested and able to do it. Another exercise involved her taking a doll and saying, "Where is the mouth?" He pointed to the mouth, showing that he knew body parts. She did the same thing for the arms and legs. James became a little more assertive from time to time when he was exploring the toys, and he would hand things to her, with some sense of energy. But for the most part, the baby-sitter overdid, overprotected, and made life a little too easy for him, although it was clear that she had a warm, compassionate quality of relatedness with him.

With mother, James became a little more active and assertive, but she continued as before, giving a running commentary. He barely had time to breathe let alone take initiative on his own. She would say, "Let's put the block on top of the car." When he didn't do it, she quickly jumped in with other suggestions, gesturing to him, showing him, and verbalizing what to do. One time when she was overwhelming him too much he took the car she was using and brought it to father, looking as if he was going to do something funny and interesting. This was his first spontaneous reaching out to father during this session. A moment later, while still playing with father, he took a basket, put it on his head and smiled, pretending it was a hat. This was, perhaps, his most organized and high-level presymbolic kind of component, but he only did this once during the entire session. He took great joy and pride in it, and father smiled warmly. It was interesting that James needed to pull away from the two women a little to do this.

James seemed very good at focused attention, had a good quality of engagement, but he was not progressing to the level of complexity necessary for two-way communication, particularly in terms of his own initiative and his being able to string together five or six circles of communication under his own steam. He seemed to be more passive and reactive. Contributing to this appeared to be two women, his mother and his babysitter, both of whom were very good at engaging, sharing attention, and two-way gestural communication; they tended to take the active role and stifle his initiative. His low motor tone and natural tendencies supported his passive–reactive compliant mode, rather than an assertive leadership one. Father still didn't seemed quite involved enough, although James was clearly ready for him to get more involved. His highest level of symbolic activity, putting on the hat while smiling broadly, was a presymbolic and assertive activity related to father.

I felt that James's lack of assertiveness was contributing to his delay in articulation, although his comprehension, as indicated, seemed all right. The family interactive component, coupled with his low motor tone, was also contributing to his articulation, as well as the tendency for passivity and a passive–reactive orientation. At this session, we talked about working further with him on taking the initiative; both the babysitter and the mother would focus on energizing, and remember to pause to give him time to respond. They would count the number of circles in which he clearly took the initiative, rather than paying attention to the circles in which he reacted to them. We discussed how father might correct his schedule and alleviate his anxiety about, as he put it, "competing" with these two powerful women whom he felt "did it much better than [he]." When his son reached out to him in this session, he became aware that James did in fact like him and that he could have a role in helping the boy become more assertive.

The slow and painstaking way this case progressed is not unusual. It is an example of preventive guidance with a child who was somewhat at risk for the kind of patterns we have described here, and an approach that often works best both for the family and the youngster. Over time, the family makes its own approach more flexible and the youngster makes overall sound progress in terms of the developmental epochs he needs to master: shared attention, engagement, and two-way communication. The constrictions and limitations on the flexibility or the range in this case, in terms of assertiveness and complexity and use of vocalization, will often have a double cause (motor tone on the one hand and the family interaction patterns on the other hand). This flexibility gradually improves over time, so that by the time a youngster gets on in development, he is becoming more and more flexible; rather than other patterns in which overall developmental milestones may be limited or inflexibility may increase. Families often only change gradually and slowly; therefore, slow consistent progress should not be underestimated in terms of its value.

James's progress was more evident in the next session a few months later when he was nineteen-and-a-half months old. This time, father spontaneously played with him first, and there was a warm, nice quality of relatedness between the two of them. James looked at me, but then ignored me and got into really playing with father. They took cars from the toy box and put them in the house, James leading the way with good concentration, good focus, and lots of intentionality. He looked at his father for approval as he put the car on the first floor and then on the second floor. They reciprocated well in terms of visual contact and circle closing, and also in terms of James making sounds and seeking approval while doing his work with the cars. Occasionally father distracted him with, "Look over here" or "Look over there," trying to get him interested in another toy rather than following his son's intentionality. I helped father see that James was taking the lead and that, by distracting him, he was inadvertently undermining the boy's leadership. Father reflected for a moment that in wanting his child to do something even more dramatic, he was perhaps inadvertently competing with his youngster. He said, jokingly, that maybe he was afraid his youngster would become more assertive than he was.

James put the cars in another house and then began arranging a man in one of the cars. He made the man in the car go into the house again, looking to father for approval. Father tried to stay with his lead, taking another car and having it go parallel with James's car. The boy seemed to enjoy this and at one point even had the cars crashing a little bit. When he did this, father had his car turn over and James beamed with pleasure. Father said, "You did it!" Perhaps, this was an acknowledgment of some of the competition father was talking about, now being played out in a more joyful way with father willing to let James be the boss.

Near the end of this play session James took father's little car and put it in his big one. It was perhaps a final statement of his taking over. Father's and James's progress was impressive for its early symbolic inklings as well as the greater warmth between the two of them.

The parents reported that at home there was a lot more relaxed horsing around between father and son and that James was imitating father in the bathtub, blowing water at him, laughing. They would play at switching off the lights. James would try to trick father by making it dark when father was in the room. They were clearly learning to enjoy each other.

The play with mother, during this session, also reflected greater assertiveness. Mother still talked too much and gave a running commentary, but she was more aware of what she was doing. She would stop herself, and at times let James take the lead.

During this time, he made more vocal sounds, but still did not use words very often—a few "Da-Das" and "Ma-Mas," but no stringing words together or working hard to vocalize. Even in his own private language of many sounds, this wasn't occurring.

When James played with the baby-sitter, she had difficulty shifting from her passive, overprotective mode. She didn't like to vocalize a lot and preferred to do things for him. She tended to sit passively and almost paralyzed, although we tried to help her relax and enjoy herself. But she clearly felt uncomfortable being observed by three people.

The parents indicated that James was beginning to play a little longer with other children, but was still cautious if they got too assertive, were too aggressive, or there was too much activity; then he would go either to his baby-sitter or his mother.

We talked about their continuing to work on increasing James's assertiveness and interaction. They would try creating opportunities which demanded his assertiveness and moments when he would feel overjoyed by it, such as in his car play with father. We also discussed ways to get him working harder at vocalizing when he wanted things: when he pointed at something and began to make a few sounds, the parents should play "dumb," rather like the television character Columbo. James would then have to vocalize and articulate more. It was generally felt that because of his low motor tone and difficulty with articulating, it took more effort for him not only to take motor initiative, but also vocal initiative. To help him add more and more sounds so that he would grow accustomed to using this aspect of his motor system along with his gross motor, I suggested that the parents neither move in too quickly to get him what he wanted or even acknowledge that they understood what he wanted. Instead, they would look intensely at him, listen, vocalize back, but more from the point of view of the old Columbo, "What are you trying to tell me?" attitude.

We also began talking about working on his fine motor skills, which seemed a little delayed, as a way of helping him enjoy the fun of scribbling with crayons. At the moment he would fist the crayons—he did not seem to have as much control as one might like. I described how they could make his difficult scribbles more enjoyable. Through making counter scribbles they could easily turn his scribbling into a game.

In the most recent session, James was calm and focused as before. As he played with mother, he examined the doll house and was very connected to her. He used lots of animated gestures, pointing, and sounds as they worked out a drama with the house and its many doors. James found a man and said something like, "Is this?" He examined it and began putting another man into the house. Mother was responsive this time, but did not give a running commentary. She helped him with whatever was happening next, responding to his every gesture with a gesture. Without taking the drama further, she paused patiently to see where he wanted to take it next. She was doing much better. When he put a man next to the trapdoor, mother took her man and asked if he wanted her to put it in the trapdoor, using gestures and words. He pointed and indicated that she should, and she put her man down the trapdoor. James made his man do the same. He then made a sound like, "Dis, dis, dis," as he grabbed the man and put it back in the trapdoor, looking from mother to the door. He tried to put a big man in the door, but it was too big. Then he shook his head and said the word, *no*, acknowledging that he couldn't do it. Mother put her hand out and said, "Me help?" and he gave it to her, nodding, and she tried to put it in but couldn't make it fit. James grabbed it out of her hand, put the man in a car and made him drive instead. Then he pointed to her to take another car. When she did, he crashed his car into hers, with a big smile on his face. He seemed a lot more interactive, more vocal, and more assertive than before, especially with mother. Also, mother was doing much better in terms of being responsive and contingent without taking over.

With his father, in this session, there was also a warm, engaged quality. He, too, was able to be continually involved, as he had been in the prior session. "What are we going to do?" he would say to James. James pointed to the door; he put the dolls through the door, and he took the man out of the house and put him in a car; he took his car, brought it to mother, and showed it to her. She showed that she was impressed. He then grabbed a yellow egg and put it in the car and said, "This," and gave it to her. James ignored father for a few minutes while he was bringing mother other presents. He took two dolls and put them in two cars and rolled both of them to her, smiling broadly again, and saying, "This, this." Mother, suddenly feeling guilty about absorbing all the attention, said, "Do you think Daddy wants the yellow egg and some of these cars?" James smiled, turned around, and wheeled the cars and yellow egg to father, who smiled and said, "Thank you." Father and James continued to play for a short time, racing cars alongside each other, occasionally crashing them. They then got involved in a game of seeing how far a big doll could ride without falling off. James tried a small doll, then a medium-size doll, and then a big doll to see how many could fit without falling down. He tried to put them in the cars, while continuing his this's and that's, his pointing and other vocalizations.

As I watched both parents play with him on the floor in this spontaneous, interactive way, I noticed that James would tune into one and then the other; but he could also march to the beat of his own drummer for a while, ignoring them both. I also noticed father's tendency to control the action too much. He followed the lead some of the time, but at other times he would take over, much as mother had done earlier. It was almost as if he had been watching her. He would begin telling James what to do, by asking questions like, "Do you want to move the car here?" "Do you want to move the car there?" "Do you want to bring me those men?" "Do you want to see if these guys can fit in the car?" We discussed his tendency to slip into a rhythm with James that was trying to get the child to do more. I pointed out that as father tried to get James to do more the boy would do less, because whatever he was doing was not on his own initiative. The ideal interactions had James taking the lead, building on his interests, and followed by his building on the parent's interest.

At one point, James began saying some this's and that's and making some other sounds which were funny and unclear. We worked, at that moment, with the parents making sounds back to him. I had noticed that, while they interacted and gestured with him and tried to talk to him, they didn't necessarily make interesting sounds back at him to get a vocal rhythm going. This time, when James made a sound, they made a sound back, as if to say, "What are you trying to say?" He then made his sound again, they repeated their sound, and they closed about six circles, each making sounds. We focused on trying to match James's vocalizations with more interesting sounds. By increasing the frequency of sound, as well as talk to him, they would help him refine the words he was already using.

Over the next month or two, he began using more single words, like *here, there,* and *that,* along with his pointing. He even used conceptual words like *up* and *down.* Although still a little bit delayed, in terms of his articulation, his receptive abilities have continued to develop and he is now getting into pretend play of a slightly more elaborate nature; the dolls are getting special hats and occasionally a baby doll is being fed. Since mother has recently gotten pregnant, his feeding the doll seems to be related to the family dynamics around the new baby.

In summary, James is now at the early representational phase, uses emotional ideas, is very related, has good attention, and good two-way communication. Although he is still a little cautious when playing with other children, his play is interactive rather than parallel. He is beginning to use single words to convey intentions and wishes; while still having a tendency to be passive, he is making slow and steady progress toward greater assertiveness and flexibility. His parents are also making steady progress in helping him experiment with taking the lead, in spite of his low motor tone and general tendency toward a little bit of cautiousness and passivity.

Overall, this case, which is ongoing, has been an example of developmental monitoring. The clinician helps the parents maintain their child's progress, even when there is slight risk on the motor side and on the family dynamic side. Further-more, he facilitates increasing the child's flexibility and asser-tiveness at each milestone of emotional development.

FOLLOW-UP NOTE ON JAMES

On a follow-up visit, when James was twenty-five months of age, he was very engaging, and looked much older. As he led his parents into the room, he had a very with-it quality about him, relating to me warmly, gesturing quickly, pointing to the toys he was interested in, and sitting down to play with the doll house, action figures, dolls, and trucks. Mother sat down with him to play and father sat on the couch. I noticed quickly that James's assertiveness and intentionality were greatly improved and he had more depth to his relatedness. His smiles, looks, pointing, and vocal gestures revealed a clearer, more organized gestural pattern. He nicely orchestrated mother, father, me, and the toys. He seemed to have come into his own in a few short months. When I had seen him last he had been much more tentative, less gesturally sophisticated, and much more cautious and passive in his approach. In spite of his greater assertiveness, however, James was not yet stringing together two words. He was using "dis," "that," "car," and single word descriptives, mostly to convey intentionality; he would point at something he wanted and say a word that sounded like "this," or "that," or close to the name of the item he wanted. (His parents mentioned that at home he was stringing together two words sometimes like "Da Da go," but had not yet really mas-tered phrases. He was, however, much more vocal and inten-tional in his use of sounds.)

James initially took some sunglasses out of the toy box. He went over to father and, smiling broadly, put them on him. He then took them off father, and smiling broadly, put them on mother. Then he sat down and began exploring the toys, grunt-ing and groaning as he put cars in the house. When mother tried to do something he didn't want, he would say "dis" and "no." Mother was contingent and supportive, but tended to vocalize what James was doing with an ongoing narrative instead of setting up opportunities for real gestural and vocal interaction and engagement. In other words, she would say, "Oh, James is putting the car in the house and James is now taking the car out." She would even say things like, "What are you going to do next?" but she didn't create an opportunity for him to engage her other than to feel her nice warm support.

At one point, with mother's support, James took his horse and put it in the house; he then took the horse out of the house and had a man ride it. When he put the man and the horse back in the house, he looked at mother proudly and pointed. "This," he said with a big smile on his face. There was a nice, warm, with-it quality as he showed off his complicated early symbolic play activity. He then started knocking on the door and, still beaming, said, "Knock, knock," to the house. Mother again smiled warmly and admiringly. I commented to mother about the importance of creating interactional opportunities. She wanted to see how this could be done but deferred to her husband who then took over the play.

Father sat down and they began playing with cars going in and out of the house. Father said, "Look at the truck coming in the back of the house." James said, "What?" and began looking thoughtful. "The trucks are in the back of the house," father continued, lining them up in the back of the house. Finally, looking very thoughtful for a minute or two, James got up and went around to the back of the house to see what father was doing. He then took one of father's trucks and put it on the chimney. "Here," he said, pointing to the chimney. This was a very nice example of an interactive opportunity where father, by building on his son's interest in the trucks and the house, created a new twist on it by having the trucks line up in a certain position.

Needless to say, James on his own wasn't creating many of these interactive opportunities; he was happy to play while supported by mother's and father's admiration. He enjoyed showing off to them, looking at them and gesturing to them, but did not involve them directly in the interactive play.

After James had been playing with father for a few minutes, he tried to involve mother in the play by taking some toys to her. She asked questions like, "What goes in there?" referring to the house, and he was able to respond with words like *car* and *truck*. During this time, James was gesturally and behaviorally organized and extremely well connected. Even when his words hadn't been intelligible, his gestures, facial expressions, and his orchestration of his two parents had been very deliberate.

After interacting with his mother for a while, James went back down on the floor with his father to play with a helicopter. He took a string that had a hook at the end of it from the helicopter and connected it up to a car. He then towed the car along, saying, "This, this," while pointing at the car and smiling proudly. This was James's highest level of interaction with an object; he had figured out how something worked and moved it along, and he had also shown pride in his parents' warm appreciation of his feat.

James, at twenty-five months old, is very warmly engaged, showing good focus and concentration, and is able to focus his attention for a few minutes or more. He has also established excellent two-way communication at the gestural level and progressed to very complex gestural patterns. He indicates wants, desires, and needs and orchestrates interrelationships between both parents. He even plays out beginning pretend dramas involving taking cars inside the house, putting them out of the house, putting them on chimneys, having soldiers or dolls ride in the cars, and so on. By making the car go and, furthermore, by placing the doll inside the car, James is not only beginning early symbolic play, but also showing that complex ideas are guiding this play. He is also beginning to use simple words, such as *this*, *that*, and *car*, and to use two words together to indicate a want or desire: *no daddy*, or *here, dad*. But most importantly, he is showing more initiative and assertiveness, increasing the breadth of his range of both complex gestural patterns and early symbolic patterns.

Thus, we see a two-year-old who is functioning at the very early representational level in both play and use of language. While he is a few months behind optimal levels for his age, he has turned an important corner toward becoming (1) symbolic, and more importantly, (2) broadened in the range and depth of his emotion at the gestural and early symbolic levels. This indicates a healthier adaptation in terms of breadth at the age-appropriate developmental level.

I should add that in a relative sense one does not overfocus on whether a child's level of representational play or complexity of language is plus or minus five or six months. At this age one is more concerned with the breadth of experience incorporated into the complex gestural mode, or the early representational mode at all. In both cases, James's mastery leads one to be optimistic about his further development, even though he experienced some delays early on.

The chief concern for James had been his cautiousness and passivity, and his lack of assertiveness and focused shared attention. With improvements in these, one can be optimistic that even if there are some articulation problems on the language side, James's development will improve with time. Psychologically he is functioning quite ably now. His problem is now more in the mechanics of language than in language as an instrument of intentionality.

Further follow-ups at ages two-and-a-half and three indicate that James is becoming a secure, warm creative, bright, and verbal preschooler. He has learned to create complex pretend dramas, hold logical conversations (with complex sentences), and assert himself in a collaborative manner with his parents and peers. Most importantly, he is a joyful and happy child.

CASE NUMBER 5: ELIZABETH

Mother came alone to the first session when Elizabeth was three-and-a-half months old. Mother was an attorney who immediately gave me a picture of her background and the prestigious places she had gone to school, but then she quickly told me, "I have a feeling that my baby doesn't like me. She doesn't look at me. I feel incompetent and helpless. After my baby was born, I felt that others could do it better, almost like I felt when I was trying my first case—others could do it better than me." Mother added, "I look at her and I feel sad when she isn't looking back at me."

Mother was thirty-nine years old when she had her baby, "Life was fleeting by," she said. "Now I can look at her sometimes and feel how cute she is and it gives my life meaning. But I also worry that she's not looking at me." She described Elizabeth as a "sweet and placid baby," while further reiterating that she had a baby nurse for the first two months. "I was an only child," she explained. "I needed to plunge in, to learn how to be a mommy, but I didn't do it. Now I feel awkward and uncomfortable." Mother reported that she had a housekeeper who was going to come in and help her. The housekeeper was a woman in her late forties, whom mother hoped would help her feel more confident. She told me that her husband was a "driven stockbroker," who worked hard and didn't get home until seven-thirty or eight o'clock at night. She said she hoped to get back to working hard again soon.

As mother was talking, it appeared that she was a woman who was operating with tight control of her face and her vocal tone. She seemed passive and cautious, and said she felt helpless and empty. There was a sense that she needed to be filled up by someone else and was finding it hard to fill anyone else up. This quality was conveyed even in the way she reached out with her words. Her affect was constricted. Her thinking was organized but somewhat concrete, seeking to serve a few details without great elaboration on the different feelings she mentioned. At the same time, she seemed to have a desire to be reflective and to figure things out.

Mother reported that her own history had included two miscarriages in the last two years, and that she had stayed home and only worked half-time during this pregnancy to avoid another miscarriage. There was lots of nausea and general discomfort. She said of her labor and delivery, "I had so much

pain that I didn't feel a rush of love when I saw Elizabeth."
Interspersed with this, mother informed me that she had been
a history major at college, and had always thought of herself as
an emotional and rather romantic person. But she "never realized how scary it could be to have a baby."

She went on to reveal that she had always been scared of
taking care of other people, even as a baby-sitter. As early as
fourth grade, "I was always afraid of death and dying and that
bad things would happen if I took care of people." She described a dream from childhood where she "launched out to
get to infinity, but could never get there." She felt that she was
always striving and would never reach the success she wanted.
Her parents were both academics, and she saw them as "very
emotionally controlled" people. She, herself, always did well
academically, but "I grew up feeling lonely and not knowing
how to relate easily to others," she said. She never felt relaxed
and comfortable with others. On reflection, she said, "In a sense
I am not prepared for having a baby."

Mother further reported that other than not feeling well,
the pregnancy was unremarkable in terms of any complications,
and that the delivery went smoothly. Elizabeth was born a
healthy six pounds, seven ounces with 9/10 Apgars, and with
no complications. Within the first week of life, she seemed to
be able to look around, but mother noticed that she wouldn't
look at you unless you talked a lot at her and then would only
do it some of the time. Mother felt that father was a little better
than she at getting Elizabeth to look more focused. The baby
would calm down easily when crying, but again it seemed more
straightforward for father and the nurse than for mother. Elizabeth's motor tone seemed fine; she could put her hand to her
mouth, felt firm when held, and fed well on a bottle. Mother
said, "I was too nervous to try breast-feeding her."

At the second meeting, mother brought Elizabeth with her.
She appeared to be a small three-and-a-half-month-old baby
who didn't look at either her mother or me very much, except
for a fleeting second here and there. If mother persisted in
talking to her, she did respond with an occasional fleeting look

toward mother's voice, but there were no robust smiles toward either mother or me. Mother was very tentative in the way she interacted with Elizabeth. She whispered in a king of monotone, rather than varying her pitch and pulling the baby in. She held her stiffly and anxiously at a distance. I also noticed that as mother interacted with the baby, she got discouraged easily. In her whispering and monotone, she would pause for a few seconds longer than one would expect, flattening the rhythm, so that even if she had the baby's attention for a second, she couldn't vary her pitch to hold her look. Mother lost her repeatedly; she would go silent for five or six seconds and then start up again in a tense, "dirgelike" whisper. She hardly varied her facial expression at all, nor did she vary the way she held the baby—about eight inches from her and with stiff, rigid hands around her abdomen and back, as if this was how she had seen it done in a textbook. The atmosphere between the two of them was one of an eerie kind of tension and lacked warmth and feeling. Elizabeth either stared off at the wall or fleetingly looked past her mother.

I then worked with Elizabeth. She came comfortably into my lap, without any fuss or change in her facial expression. She had good motor tone, perhaps even higher than expected, but it was consistent throughout. At one point as I was talking with her, she got a little fussy, but she calmed easily when I put her on my shoulder and applied gentle pressure to her back. As I played with her and stroked her arms and legs gently, I didn't notice any smiles of great pleasure or warmth. Nor were there any aversive signs—no turning away of the head or look of discomfort—when I lightly touched her arms, legs, abdomen, and back, or pressed those areas firmly. I worked with her, making interesting facial expressions and moving my head back and forth. I noticed that she responded a little better, in terms of following my face, when I was very animated. When I spoke with her, she did not focus well on my voice. If I was very persistent and varied my pitch only slightly from one second to the next, giving her a slowly changing pattern, she could begin to focus more, for as long as perhaps two-and-a-half seconds before she tuned out. She, therefore, had a rather fleeting pattern of joint attention with me. She would focus from one to two-and-a-half seconds or so, and then tune out and look at a lamp or something around the room. Occasionally she had a faint, beginning grin on her face, but no broad, robust smiles.

Elizabeth was patient with me during the fifteen minutes or so I worked with her. She didn't get upset or fussy as I tried lying her on her back on my lap. I had her do sit-ups with me holding her hands, and then held her in front of me. The fleeting pattern was consistent in all positions. She would do best when I combined very animated facial expressions with a very slowly changing vocal rhythm. If the vocal rhythm became too fast, or monotonous like mother's, I could only hold her attention for about a second. She did not enjoy brisk movement in space, but preferred very slow rhythmic movements, both horizontally and vertically. She seemed to enjoy slow, rhythmic rocking rather than very rapid movements, which tended to startle her.

It appeared from this first session with Elizabeth that she was having difficulty reaching the first milestone of shared attention and a sense of warm, affective engagement. She was finding it hard to tune in to vocalizations, but was doing very slightly better with visual experiences. She, therefore, appeared to be a little hyporeactive in the area of processing vocal experience. She was also mildly sensitive to brisk movement in space. Her response to touch and her motor tone, though, seemed appropriate for her age. Therefore, she seemed to come into the world as a laid-back baby who was a little hyporeactive, requiring lots of wooing and work. Coupled with these individual differences, Elizabeth's mother was a very tense, anxious person who could provide little vocal/verbal experimentation to find the right rhythms to engage her. Based on her background, mother also felt easily rejected and empty, almost requiring, as she put it, "a baby who could fill me up." In some respects, Elizabeth fitted the description mother had given of herself as a child—someone who was waiting for the other person to woo them. We therefore had a situation where Elizabeth's individual differences and mother's individual differences were making the early phase of shared attention and engagement hard to negotiate.

Elizabeth evidenced a lag in negotiating the first critical developmental process of shared attention and engagement, in part due to her own constitutional and maturational pattern and mother's personality structure. This first developmental process is the beginning of attention and concentration, and forming and enjoying relationships, both critical ego functions. Identifying the challenge early led to assisting Elizabeth and her mother and father. They learned to adjust their pattern to Elizabeth's unique maturational pattern and the early stages of ego development were successfully negotiated.

We talked about the baby's individual differences and some of the patterns mother had described about herself and the grave dilemma described above. Mother, as bright as she was, said she was relieved that it wasn't all her fault; Elizabeth's characteristics might make it hard for any mother to pull her in. Fortunately, instead of regarding it now as an "impossible task," mother saw it as challenging. We talked about working with Elizabeth for periods of fifteen to twenty minutes at a time doing a series of exercises. These would involve shifting vocal rhythms and cadences and tone extremely slowly, using lots of facial animation; and trying to increase Elizabeth's focus and engagement simply from one second to two seconds, then two seconds to three seconds. I pointed out that once babies achieve over three seconds of engagement, their ability to take in more information from the world increases accordingly, so that the process becomes more self-sustaining. The most difficult seconds are the first ones. I explained that as she experienced more success in having Elizabeth take an interest in her, she might relax more and her own pleasure would come through. She obviously had gained a great deal of pleasure from having Elizabeth, and Elizabeth was very important for her, but she was worried, understandably so, that Elizabeth wouldn't like her. She felt that she "wasn't doing as good a job as other people could do," that it was hard for Elizabeth to sense the enormous pleasure she was having.

We started to work on mother using a light touch and firm pressure with the baby. I had surmised that Elizabeth enjoyed it by the lack of any negative reaction to it. I suggested that mother also use both a passive range of motion and achieve motor control on Elizabeth to help her attention. We practiced pull-up/sit-up games where Elizabeth would do deep-knee bends on mommy's lap; and we stroked the baby's arms and legs, both lightly and with firmer massagelike rhythms, while talking to her and making funny faces. These activities would help Elizabeth have more sensory experiences with her mother and also enable mother to have a fuller experience of closeness with her daughter. She would begin to experience Elizabeth through all her senses.

Mother was in a state of confusion, for the most part, about how to communicate with her daughter. "How do I keep talking to her when I have nothing to say?" she said perplexedly. She felt compelled to say something interesting and important and was convinced that the actual meanings of her words were important. She said, "Being a lawyer, I've learned to be precise in my language." We talked about how Elizabeth would respond more to the rhythm and cadence of her voice than the content of her speech, and that this was a chance for her to say anything she felt like and not be criticized. Mother giggled at the thought of having so much license. We also talked about how, historically, she had often felt that she had had to choose her words carefully; her lawyer father had been the one who taught her about "the precise meaning of words." His rigid, compulsive, and somewhat critical style had made her fearful as a little girl, and she felt she hadn't received much flexibility from her mother. Having been a legal secretary, her mother often deferred to her father. The house was set up around a controlling and often critical and rejecting theme, so that mother felt that she always had to be careful for fear of annoying her parents. She intellectually surmised that she had often swallowed her own anger, adding, "but I was never even aware that I might be angry."

As mother was talking about her dilemma, she relaxed and reached out to her daughter—such behavior that she could never do at home. Then she revealed that she had been in therapy when in graduate school. At that time, in her early twenties, she had felt quite depressed and was even "suicidal" for a brief period. In spite of having thoughts that "life was not worthwhile," she never "did anything about it." During the period of her deepest depression, she had a hard time finding friends. She was working all the time and felt hopeless about ever finding a man to marry.

Her revealing this fact to me was quite significant, particularly in light of her secretiveness about it during the earlier session when we talked about her difficulty in reaching out to her baby. It suggested the beginning of a process of relaxation and a willingness to open herself up, not only to me but perhaps to her baby. She was, in a way, saying that she was afraid of what might come out if she just babbled and said whatever came to mind; and she had a lot of reason for being emotionally tight. As we talked further, we also discovered a way she could sometimes chit-chat when she had nothing to say. She could just comment on the wonderful things her baby was doing: "Oh, look at how you are looking at me, or not looking at me," "Oh, you'd rather look at the clock" or "You'd rather look at [whatever]." By commenting on what the baby was doing, and what she thought the baby might be feeling, it gave her a way of talking at times when other thoughts didn't come to mind. She enjoyed this prospect.

In the next session, mother talked more about her husband and the family relationships. She described him as "hard-driving and ambitious, yet honest." They had met toward the end of her time in law school. They started dating, but then lost touch with each other. Later, when she moved to Washington DC, to work with a law firm, they ran into each other. Like her, he seemed "ready to get married." Initially, their relationship was more friendly than "passionate," but it had evolved, she

felt, into a "nice relationship." Sometimes father had gone to
childbirth classes with her, but he hated psychiatry and didn't
want to get into "all this emotional stuff"; he was not about to
join her in these sessions. Currently, days could go by where
he would get home late and not see Elizabeth. He did enjoy
playing with her on the weekends, making funny faces at her.
Mother wasn't sure how deeply involved he was, although she
thought he would get more involved as Elizabeth grew older.

During this follow-up session, I noticed that Elizabeth, now
four-and-a-half months old, showed a little more energy in her
face. She was staying engaged with mother for two or three
seconds rather than one to one-and-a-half seconds. She still
drifted off into staring into space, but there was a critical increase, clearly, of a split second or two. Mother got anxious
whenever Elizabeth looked away and we talked about "respecting Elizabeth's need to look around." I reminded her that we
were trying to find the rhythm Elizabeth had, and, perhaps,
the best way to work with her was to keep her looking and
engaging for a second more, but at the same time to respect
her rhythm. Once the baby disengaged, mother was to let her
relax and look at whatever she wanted. Then she would try to
woo her back in. Mother did this, with the two of us working
on it together. She made many associations between her own
empty feelings as a child and how she now felt when Elizabeth
stared off into space. I empathized with her, and, while re-
viewing some of these historical feelings, I coached her as to
how to vary her voice pitch more and change the way she held
Elizabeth. Elizabeth began to look for another half-second and
to give a bigger smile of pleasure. In this session, mother varied
the pitch of her voice a little more and had a smile or two for
me as we talked about her own background. She was also a
little more relaxed with Elizabeth, who was showing her slightly
more engagement and shared attention.

In the next meeting, when Elizabeth was about five months
of age, she was clearly reaching more and grabbing things that
mother would hold. She could also sit up a little on her own.
She was looking at mother for a good three or four seconds

now. Once or twice she even had a real big smile as mother made funny faces. Mother was more relaxed in her own vocal rhythms and no longer paused for long silences when Elizabeth momentarily disengaged; she varied her voice pitch more, and smiled in a more relaxed way. "Oh, sometimes you like to look at the chair or the lamp better than Mommy," she said, talking to Elizabeth. "Don't you know you hurt Mommy's feelings when you do that?" Even though mother was verbalizing her hurt indirectly, she was doing it with a light touch and a smile on her face. Whenever Elizabeth looked at her, she would say, "Oh, how cute you are and what a nice looker you are!" Mother reported that now she was getting more of her baby's attention, she was feeling a sense of warmth with her for the first time; consequently, she felt less empty inside. "I'm more confident that I can finally do it," she said.

Around this time, mother was getting to know a new nanny who had come to live with them for what she hoped would be a long time. There had been a period of no help between the nurse and the new nanny. Mother described the nanny as a naturally warm person who, "unlike me, tends to reach out to people." She thought this would be good for her daughter. The nanny had experience with lots of children (she had three children of her own who were now grown-up) and mother felt she would be of help to both mother and daughter. She wondered whether she could bring the nanny; I thought that would be a great idea.

In my own mind, I was pleased to have this series of sessions alone with mother before the nanny became a critical figure in the family. I'd been able to see mother make progress on her own.

In the next session, when Elizabeth was about five-and-a-half months old, I noticed another step of improvement in her ability to focus and engage. She now looked for a good five to eight seconds at me and mother, depending on who was playing with her. Sometimes she would smile, and sometimes she would just intensely study our faces. When I played with her, she seemed to prefer doing deep-knee bends while simultaneously looking at me; sometimes she could look and smile when I was just holding her on her back or up in front of me. Mother was even more relaxed. She actually laughed when Elizabeth gave her a funny little expression. The baby still looked away, but mother wasn't as nervous about it. She'd catch my eye and say, "No matter how much fun she has with me, she will still want to look at the lamp or out the window at the trees."

Mother was able to coordinate the rubbing of Elizabeth's hands and legs with interesting facial expressions and some nice slow variation in her vocal rhythm. She was also putting Elizabeth down on her stomach from time to time and getting down on the floor, herself, nose to nose. From six to eight inches away, she would try to help Elizabeth sustain looking, and even put things in front of her to see if she would reach—mother being the temptress.

We discussed Elizabeth's ability now for give and take. Mother could perhaps not only encourage her daughter to reach for something, but could also have her hand things to her, and vice versa. Mother enjoyed trying some of this and Elizabeth was successful at reaching for an interesting red ball. When mother took it out of her hand, Elizabeth easily took it back from her.

The nanny came in during this session. She was quite a natural caregiver. She was warm, engaging, had a nice even disposition, but, because she was an outgoing person, at times tended to overload Elizabeth. She would talk to Elizabeth so fast that the baby would start tuning out and staring off into space. The nanny would say, "She's just getting to know me, and when she does, she'll like the fact that I like to talk a lot." We discussed how Elizabeth liked to look at things and was learning to enjoy people's voices and how she did best with nice slow rhythms that were gradually varied. Over time, she would be able to enjoy someone who talked real fast and loudly. Fortunately, the nanny was sensitive to this, and even during the latter part of the session had slowed down her rhythm and was getting Elizabeth to look and smile at her more.

By six-and-a-half months of age, Elizabeth was sitting up solidly, playing on her stomach nicely, smiling happily, taking things from mom, reaching for blocks, squirming on the floor, and vocalizing with delight. Mother was much more relaxed, enthusiastic, and very responsive to her daughter's signals. She took a block from the baby and handed it back, responding to Elizabeth's sounds with sounds of her own. The nanny was doing similarly well with her.

They all seemed to have negotiated the stage of shared attention and attachment, and now were moving easily into the stage of two-way communication. The only concern I had at this stage was around mother tending to move in too quickly when Elizabeth was trying to do something for herself. When the baby would reach for a block, mother would put it next to her rather than let her work for it a little. If Elizabeth was beginning to whimper or get the slightest bit uncomfortable, mother would pick her up and put her on her shoulder and walk her around. Her voice became more anxious whenever the baby got a little bit upset. We talked about how competent Elizabeth had become and about the fact that mother could relax, even when the baby was a little upset.

What we saw here, then, was a mother and infant who had learned mutual shared attention and to be contingent with each other. But the stability of that new learning was affected by how well mother was able to do it under some stress, such as when Elizabeth was upset: mother tended to move in a slightly overcontrolling, overprotective manner. Mother smiled knowingly, and toward the end of the session was relaxing more, even when Elizabeth was a little fussy. She let the baby try to calm herself down before moving in and helping her. I emphasized that we were talking here about split second differences and mother not feeling quite so anxious. Interestingly, mother said, "I was afraid Elizabeth would get mad at me if I didn't hug her quickly." She went on to reveal how she had always been scared of making her parents angry, or any friend angry, and that even to this day she was cautious with her husband, fearful of making him angry. Clearly, she associated crying with anger, and she felt the best way to handle it was to make the other person "not mad at you."

Mother, at this point, was also talking about returning to work, but only half-time, at the most. This was because she was "beginning to get the hang of this being a mommy."

On the next visit, when Elizabeth was seven-and-a-half months old, they continued their nice style of warm interaction and shared attention, engagement, and two-way communication. However, mother still showed a tendency to do a little bit too much. She would say to her, "Do you want this or that?" I encouraged mother to follow Elizabeth's lead. When she did this, Elizabeth began smiling, reaching, and being more assertive. She banged on a metal plate and pushed a ball back and forth, and explored mother's ring. Mother tended to respond too quickly and too controllingly. She took off her ring and gave it to Elizabeth rather than letting Elizabeth continue to explore the ring. When the baby moved her hand in the direction of a ball, mother would take it and give it to her, rather than letting her move in an inch closer. I suggested she make some interesting facial expressions to see if Elizabeth would reach out even further.

The baby was making more sounds at this time and was even more solid in her ability to sit and begin to squirm along the floor. At home, mother reported that she was beginning to say sounds like "Ga" and "Ma." She had always been a good sleeper and had recently shown that she was able to go back to sleep easily on her own if she woke up in the middle of the night. But mother was having difficulty in letting her put herself back to sleep for fear, again, "that the crying would make Elizabeth angry" at her; she didn't want her to be angry. Mother added that Elizabeth was also sometimes waking up in the evening and wanting to play.

The main issue now was how to help mother deal with her own fear of Elizabeth's being angry, so that she could let her daughter be more assertive and do more on her own, rather than be overprotective or too quick with her reactions. The same issue seemed to emerge at nighttime, in terms of Elizabeth's learning and solid self-calming skills.

At a follow-up meeting, when Elizabeth was eight-and-a-half months old, she was already beginning to crawl. She smiled warmly and deeply, but was not vocalizing as much as one would like to see, given her general movement forward in other areas. She was still having difficulty, when she woke up in the evening, with going back to sleep. We talked at great length about mother's fear of aggression and about her now being away from Elizabeth for a few hours each day, while working part-time. We also talked about her own fear of separation and anger. Mother still seemed to want to "sweep it under the carpet," preferring to talk more about her own fears of aggression while growing up.

Elizabeth was now developing in an age-appropriate fashion. She had reached the stage of two-way communication, but a constriction was emerging in this, particularly in the area of assertiveness and self-sufficiency. Mother's anxiety about aggression was interfering with Elizabeth's assertiveness which she needed for more age-appropriate use of sounds, and expressive language development. Interestingly, Elizabeth seemed to be very focused and followed mother's gestures well: she pointed, and even seemed to understand a few simple words like *no* or *there*, suggesting that her receptive language was probably fine.

On a follow-up meeting, Elizabeth was now walking. She came into the office holding mother's hand, and was quite intentional. She reflected extraordinary focus and concentration at twelve months of age: she examined toys, played little facial games with mother, made expressions back at mother for a good minute or two at a time, and could play with a puzzle or a toy for longer. (The early worry about Elizabeth being inattentive and not being able to engage with shared attention no longer seemed to be an issue. It is interesting to speculate here whether the easy to tune out type of children, who might be at risk for attentional difficulties, in terms of becoming self-absorbed or not staying with a focus, could be helped with the kind of work that this mother was able to do with Elizabeth, including increased motor activity.)

As she and mother played, Elizabeth closed four or five circles of communication without any difficulties. Mother was very vocal, animated, and responsive and was less overcontrolling. Elizabeth was still not showing the amount of vocalizations that one would expect at this age, but was making more sounds and more spontaneous use of sound, with an occasional word like *Ma* or *Da*. As she moved near the couch mother moved in quickly and anxiously. She was worried Elizabeth might hurt herself, even though Elizabeth noticed on her own that she needed to duck. Mother was still perhaps quite nervous about her daughter, but was moving, nonetheless, in the right direction.

The progress continued so that by fifteen months old, Elizabeth looked excellent. She was playful, had good attention, a purposeful use of gestures and words like *out, now, up*, and *down*, lots of intentional gestures, and lots of organized interaction. Mother still talked a great deal about anger and themes of separation, but now was able to talk it out rather than act it out with her daughter. Since then she has come in with lots of anxious questions around the area of anger and separation. She seems able to support Elizabeth's development while struggling with these issues on her own, particularly her relationship with her husband, memories of her own past, and worries about colleagues at work.

The little girl continued to do well over a number of months. She arrived at the stage of using emotional ideas, began talking in brief sentences, and got into pretend play. Mother was able to do regular floor time each day with her, helping her use her symbols for elaborating her feelings and wishes. Interesting themes have continued to emerge in Elizabeth's play revealing a nice age-appropriate progression of using ideas or representations. For example, during a session in my office, when Elizabeth was thirty months old, she played out a theme with whales. The whales would start out being nice to each other, then started biting; one whale was very scared of the other whale biting. Around this time, mother told me, Elizabeth was anxious and a little avoidant of other children's aggression, although she stayed in there and kept playing with them. But she tended to move away and not be counterassertive back if someone took a toy of hers. Nevertheless, mother was pleased that she wasn't withdrawing and seemed happy with other children. Also mother reported that, at times when other children in Elizabeth's play group would get aggressive, she would come over and cling to mother. At other times, she could assert her will for a new toy.

Mother was now beginning to think about a new baby and was talking about a baby brother or sister. Elizabeth seemed to "want" her baby brother or sister, although she didn't quite understand what it would involve. However, after mother talked about it, she would set up her own doll and feed it, showing some comprehension of what mother was talking about. There seemed to be a very minor constriction in the range of Elizabeth's ability to deal with assertiveness and aggression. She was a little more fearful than other children in this age, but at the same time she was fully representational, showing nice patterns of elaboration with her representations; and mother was able to support most of these. Mother, too, felt nervous around aggression and separation, so we had a mild constriction which would be about average for most children of this age. Very few show equal flexibility in all thematic areas once they get to be representational. So Elizabeth was evidencing age-appropriate personality functions, with a slight constriction in the area of aggression and assertiveness. It was particularly nice to see that she was enjoying friends and had one little girl that she liked to play with frequently.

It is also important to note that father was, as mother had predicted, getting more and more involved with his daughter. He was now treating her like a little princess and taking her out on weekends. He was still coming home late, though, during the week. Elizabeth seemed ready for her father's involvement, and did not show any annoyance at or resentment or avoidance of him. She thoroughly enjoyed the time that he did give her.

We worked, at this time, not just on Elizabeth's greater comfort with themes of assertiveness or aggression in play, but also on how to help her be even more elaborative in her thematic development and pretend play, with mother and nanny, as well as her own playmates. The goal here was that as Elizabeth grew more elaborative and more representational, she would gain access to the ideational representational world. This would, in itself, be an assertive act.

In a subsequent meeting, when Elizabeth was playing with the toy wild animals, it was interesting to hear her say to mother, "You talk for the animals," particularly when the animal needed to be angry or aggressive. Mother skillfully replied to Elizabeth, "What do you want me to say?" Elizabeth whispered into mother's ear. Then mother would say things like, "I'm gonna eat you up, I'm so mad." So, gradually, but surely, the little girl was learning to become more comfortable with the assertive and even the angry side of life, although first through mother's mouth rather than her own.

As she became more comfortable with assertiveness, she also became defiant. This made mother quite anxious for a number of months. She wondered about what to do when Elizabeth said, "No, I won't!" and marched around the house throwing temper tantrums; or yelled when she didn't get her favorite food or couldn't watch her cartoon as long as she wanted to. This direct confrontation of anger to anger reverberated with mother's earlier fears around aggression and again brought up many of her worries from her own childhood. We reviewed these and talked about Elizabeth's need for balance between having limits set for her and being allowed to enjoy flexing muscles. She needed to be allowed to verbalize being the "king of her domain." We worked on how mother could empathize with Elizabeth's desire to watch more television, have more cartoons, and be the "boss of the house"; and how this could enter into some of the pretend play themes. We also talked about how Elizabeth could sometimes have her way, but for the most part she would still need to go to bed on time and have her meals on time, and so forth. It was hard for mother to find the right balance, and to some degree continues to be difficult for her, but she is making steady progress. Elizabeth, too, is negotiating this phase as she is becoming more and more assertive and at the same time learning to internalize her limits. Mother is now pregnant again, and Elizabeth is showing mixed feelings about a little sister. Sometimes she feeds her dolls and talks about how she is going to have a baby, too; at other times she tells mother that no one is going to "play with my toys."

The current goals include mother and Elizabeth working on expanding Elizabeth's play time with other children so that she gets more, rather than less, practice with this; and dealing further with the balance between them of warm nurturing activity and the power struggles that inevitably come up in the preschool years. Elizabeth is now a very attentive, very happy and engaged little girl. She is capable of elaborative pretend play, both hugs and kisses and asserts herself (with some anxiety around the assertive dimensions still). She is moving into a nice balance of being able to deal with reality and shift back and forth to fantasy. She seems to have growing positive self-esteem and assertiveness, as she negotiates relationships with new friends and does well in her preschool program. She has good fine and gross motor coordination and mother is enjoying her more and more. As mentioned earlier, the only issue between the two of them involves how to deal with assertiveness and aggression, although, occasionally, issues concerning separation do emerge. Elizabeth is a little over three years old now and has certainly made good progress. It is interesting to see how the early difficulty with attention and engagement was almost entirely corrected. The legacy of the early challenges is more in the area of her flexibility for dealing with assertiveness and aggression.

In summary, this case illustrates work with a little girl who was at risk for negotiating the early stages of development. Constitutional factors (the little girl's difficulty with responding to vocal–verbal experiences fully, being a little underreactive) were aggravated by mother's difficulty with wooing and engaging, due to her own early childhood (feeling empty and fearful that what she had to offer was "not good"). These early challenges were overcome through preventively oriented counseling. I should add here that mother and daughter were only seen, at the most, once every other week. When the treatment began working, they were seen once a month to once every two to three months. Often in a case like this, the mother will require individual therapy, either with the same therapist or with another therapist, to go along with the parent–infant work.

This case, therefore, shows nice progression where the ability to work with the family over a long period of time not only helps them over the initial hurdle, but also over some of the derivatives of this initial hurdle as it plays out in the later stages of development. Thus, mother's difficulty with negotiating Elizabeth's assertiveness and separation at eight months, in terms of the full flexibility and range of two-way communication, plays out again at the symbolic level. Preventively oriented therapy is vital for helping the family in an area of conflict that mother is not about to resolve fully, short of, perhaps, more intensive treatment of her own. It prevents the conflict from getting acted out in the relationship between Elizabeth and mother.

By the time we were working on the representational or ideational level, we were only meeting every few months. Even these infrequent meetings can play a critical role in helping a mother and/or father help their child negotiate areas of development that they themselves may have found difficult, and may still be working on. This ability for ongoing contact tends to make the equilibrium shift in a more favorable and flexible direction. It would obviously have been nice to involve father in the work, and one of the limitations of the work was father's lack of involvement; although it was nice to hear, through mother, how his relationship with Elizabeth improved as she got older and more verbal. In this case, father, whose rigidities may have been too severe for him to get involved, nonetheless was able to become flexible. It was, perhaps, secondary to his wife's and daughter's increased flexibility; Elizabeth was eventually able to woo him in. The father, with this low tolerance for looking at emotions and dealing with emotional issues, may have had a very hard time if his daughter had stayed less engaged and less attentive.

In summary, then, this case illustrates the importance of working with both the constitutional and the parent–infant interaction, as well as the mother's own feelings. One works the best one can with the whole family while being flexible in one's expectations, realizing that there are "many roads to Rome."

CASE NUMBER 6: JAMIE

This case presented initially with mother coming in and talking about her history of chronic depression. She had been treated with antidepressants, as well as electroconvulsive therapy (ECT). Nevertheless, she was still chronically depressed and was currently in psychotherapy and on antidepressant medication. She was worried about how to relate to her four-month-old baby Jamie saying, "He doesn't look at me, he cries whenever I touch him or hold him," and that either there's "something wrong with him or something wrong with me." She described in great detail that he never looked at her, smiled at her, and always cried when she came close to him or looked at him. In contrast, she said that her husband related a little better. The baby would relax and not cry with him, although mother felt there was still no pleasure, no enthusiasm, no smiles, and no positive emotion in the baby's relationship to father either. In addition to mother and father, there was a nanny at home, a young twenty-one-year-old from the Midwest with whom, mother felt, the baby related even better; the baby had given her occasional faint pleasurable looks and perhaps even a "smile or two."

Before obtaining a history, I was able to watch mother and baby interact. What struck me immediately was how mother held him—very stiffly, almost like one would hold a doll. Mother looked anxious and worried, and she had almost no facial expression. Her vocalizations were in a depressive-like monotone with a few utterances like, "Baby, baby look," followed by a long silence of about three or four seconds. Then she would make another monotone-type utterance, "Baby, baby look." I saw no facial expression, no movement, in terms of rocking, and very little orienting of her own body posture to that of the baby. Also, when mother did try to look and talk to her baby, her voice, in addition to being a monotone, was very low in volume, a whisper. The baby looked past mother with an expressionless vague quality. After about ten minutes he became irritable and began crying and twisting. There were no looks, smiles, frowns, or motor gestures, only an indifferent, flat, vague stare.

When father held the little baby, he was more relaxed. He picked the baby up and did some walking around, first holding him on his shoulder and then trying to use more roughhousing kinds of play, like moving the baby up and down quickly. But he, too, talked in a relative monotone, with little facial expression, except for this swift moving of the baby up and down and to the sides. The baby looked a little more at father, but as they had indicated in the history, there were very few smiles or warm looks. The baby vacillated between looking at father and looking around the room.

During this first visit, I had an opportunity to hold and play with the baby. I found that he started off by looking around me, not at me, glancing to the left, right, up, and down; his look was fairly vacant. As I used vocalizations, mentioning his name and how cute he was, and at the same time trying to use lots of facial animation with very slow variations in pitch and rhythm, I was able to elicit a little smile and then another one and then another one. It took about five minutes of work to get these three little smiles and five seconds of focused interest. When I became too animated in my facial expression or when my voice pitch went up and got really enthusiastic or my rhythm became very fast in order to keep his attention, he cried, as though what he was experiencing was unpleasant. I also found it interesting that when I left his field of vision and put my head to the left or right seeing if he would turn, he began to cry as though the change was uncomfortable for him. I tried talking in a slightly louder tone to his parents while I held him, and noticed he began again whimpering and crying. Nevertheless, he did seem to enjoy brisk movement up and down and doing little sit-ups in my lap.

The history revealed an unremarkable pregnancy and delivery. The baby was a large eight pounds, two ounce healthy little boy with 9/9 Apgars. He seemed to have good motor control and was able to be both alert and calm, responding to sights and sounds as well as touch and movement in the first few days and weeks after birth. By the second month, however, mother had noticed that he was not as responsive to her looks or father's looks, or their vocalizations. As she thought back, she couldn't be sure whether this was true at birth. She thought she had been able to get his attention as a newborn more effectively than she could now. She said, "He's learned to hate me."

Mother's own background, as indicated earlier, included chronic depression beginning in late adolescence. She was now in her late thirties, and had, in spite of this chronic depression, been able to finish college and graduate school. She was now an accountant who worked eight to twelve hours per day.

Father was also a busy accountant, working a similar schedule. He presented himself as a rigid, controlled person who liked things done in an orderly fashion, on time, and on his schedule. He showed little interest in emotions and feelings, and was "frustrated" that his son was "hard to warm up." He was especially angry with his wife whom he viewed as "deficient in her mothering abilities." But he was willing to talk about how to improve his wife's mothering abilities, viewing his role as one of supporting the family. While recognizing that she worked, father also wanted her to be a "better mother." He was quite angry for all the ways he felt she was "not being a good mother" and, by implication, also not a good wife. He wouldn't go into detail about how she disappointed him, but alluded to many instances. Furthermore, he was rather closed about his own background and upbringing, claiming it was "not terribly important."

By the end of the first session, it was clear that this little baby and his family would need some intensive work: already at four months of age he was showing patterns of not fully engaging or attending to the human world, although he could be drawn in with some work and some skill. But even more worrisome than his pattern was the parents' interactive pattern. Mother seemed completely unable to work flexibly at engaging him and helping him attend more effectively; and father seemed somewhat disinterested, except for his one way of rough-and-tumble type playing which worked to a limited degree. I suggested that they come back a few days later with their nanny for a follow-up meeting. I would be able to observe her skills with the baby and then determine how to involve her in a program that would help both the baby and the family.

At the next session, I watched the nanny interact with the baby. She had more warmth and a greater sense of relatedness than either parent, and clearly had taken an emotional interest in this little baby. She held him gently as she tried to interact with him, positioning him about six to eight inches away from her face and making little facial gestures and sounds at him. She had a conventional approach, trying to talk and make sounds. (She reported she was the oldest of five and had used this approach when baby-sitting for her younger siblings.) She was able to catch the baby's attention fleetingly, as I had. He gave her a faint look and a quick smile, but only for a second or two. There were no robust, warm smiles or focused looks lasting any period of time. But at least there was a sense of relatedness and connection. She confirmed that it was hard to get him to look and show pleasure in her. More often than not, she just let him "do his own thing," as she went about cleaning the house. At other times, when she tried to play with him and he seemed less responsive than she expected, she would wind up getting discouraged after a minute or two. She might try getting him to look at pictures in a book, but he only showed a fleeting interest.

The nanny was the oldest of five in a Midwestern family. She described her father as being rather bossy and her mother as being warm, but nervous and controlling. She, herself, hoped to be a parent someday and was using this work as a way to get from the Midwest to the East where she hoped, in a year or two, to find another kind of job.

During this second session, I had a chance to work with the little boy again and found the same kind of interaction as I had before. I was able to further document my impression that he was sensitive to high-pitched noises, loud noises, and overly animated facial expressions; he tended to focus in and out a fleeting second or two, then look at other things, and then tune in again for a fleeting second or two. There were only the faintest of smiles. At the same time, his muscle tone seemed fine, as did his beginning motor planning capacities. It was hard to assess his auditory or visual–spatial processing because his looks were so fleeting; and it was impossible to tell whether he would respond better to simple or complex rhythms. He still enjoyed robust movement in space, up and down and side to side, as much he had in the first meeting.

Toward the end of this session, a plan was formulated: the parents would work with a colleague, a nurse with a lot of experience in counseling parents on infant–parent interaction patterns. I explained that this was necessary to help their little baby learn to attend and enjoy interactions with people more. We reviewed the many factors contributing to his difficulty in negotiating this early process of shared attention and engagement, including his sensitivity to loud sounds and high-pitched sounds. He was also sensitive to visual input that was very complex, such as extremely animated facial expressions. In addition to these individual constitutional and maturational differences, we reviewed the family patterns, such as mother's depression and her feeling hopeless and helpless with him. She, herself, acknowledged that she felt so tense it was hard to relax and try the different things that she knew she should be trying. Father acknowledged not his own patterns, but mother's limitations. He recognized that, at the very least, a parent–family component and an interactive component were contributing factors. On mother's side there was a history of depressive illness, but no history of thought disorders or other severe pathology. Father indicated no history on his side.

Mother, baby, and, quite often, nanny began regular twice-a-week visits to an infant specialist. The specialist helped them work around this baby's constitutional and maturational patterns, and to pull him into a greater sense of relatedness and shared attention. After five or six visits, they went to once-a-week visits. The sessions focused on helping mother relax and experiment with variations in voice pitch, emotional signaling, and in tuning into the split second or two when she could get her baby's attention. She was able to become more animated and more varying in her voice and facial gestures, and over time, began eliciting a faint smile. She recognized the need to be very gentle and slow in her approach, which was natural for her style, but she found it was "hard work" to get the energy level up high enough to offset her natural slow and depressive rhythm; she still tended to whisper and pause for a long time between her words.

The nanny adjusted more quickly, realizing, with the help of the infant specialist, that this baby needed more, not less, interactive practice. She understood that looking at pictures in a book was not going to be as useful to him as his having a chance to look at her wonderful bright eyes, smiling face, and changing vocal patterns. She began working with him at twenty-to thirty-minute intervals during the day, three or four times a day. She encouraged him to look at her and show pleasure in her for more than one or two seconds, then three or four, five or six, and eventually seven or eight seconds. Mother did the same in the evenings when she was home from the office.

Within two months, the parents, nanny, and baby returned for a follow-up visit with me, and mother announced a "big improvement." She said, "I can sit down with him now without his crying, but I can't really calm him well yet. But at least he doesn't cry when I hold him." She described "magic moments," adding, "I now feel that I'm making it sometimes." When I saw him on this visit, he was a big six-month-old and showed a broad smile. At the same time, he actually made some vocalizations, moving his arms and legs in rhythm with his vocalizations and his smile. He was able to do this with mother, even though she was still a little slow in her rhythm and didn't vary her voice and facial gestures as much as would be optimum. But she did it a great deal more than she had at the first visit. The baby smiled, vocalized, and moved very well with his nanny. Father seemed to have learned something from mother and nanny and was doing less roughhousing and more looking at his baby, even making funny sounds and faces. But he seemed less able than nanny to elicit smiles. All in all, the interactions were characterized by less tentativeness and more affect, pleasure, and a greater sense of connectedness.

During this session, we were able to get baby and mother down on the floor, nose-to-nose. She put her face about six inches away from him and held out her finger. He was able to reach for it while looking and smiling a little. At the end of the session, mother exclaimed, "When he cries, I will still have to give him to someone else, but I feel I'm making progress."

When I played with him, I noted that he had nice motor tone and was able to smile and attend and reach out for my fingers. However, the degree of depth to his pleasure, the number of vocal sounds he made, and the amount of work I had to do to hold his attention for four or five seconds still led me to the conclusion that a great deal of work needed to be done.

The work continued with the infant specialist, and on the next follow-up a month-and-a-half later, mother reported that the baby no longer cried when she was with him. He was almost crawling and she felt that he was showing more pleasure and was more attentive to her, as well as to father and the nanny. This time, during the play with mother, he was reaching for her watch as well as her hair. He was very persistent in his grabbing and intentionality, looking at her and occasionally smiling when she made nice sounds back. She still showed her cautious rhythm, which had improved over the first visit, but not dramatically so over the second visit. But she let him take her bracelet. He was able to play with it and then give it back to her. She found it hard, though, to get the idea of cause-and-effect interaction, which he seemed capable of; she preferred just to smile and coo and get him attentive and smiling, as if she was unable to transfer into his stage of two-way communication.

The play with the nanny had more of an interactive quality to it. She took off her earrings and let him grab them. She would hide them in her fist and when he pointed in that direction, she would open it up; the little boy had a big smile on his face. Father, however, seemed very preoccupied. He returned to his rough-and-tumble style of the first session, although with some coaching he did some simple interactive games.

Over the next eight months, progress was gradual but continual. In the most recent session, at fifteen months of age, this little baby walked in, gave me a nice, but quick, smile, and evidenced good, focused, and organized behavior. He took toys out of the toy box, handed them to mother or to me. He jammed them, took them back from me, examined them and then handed them back to me. He responded to my gestures with his gestures and mother's gestures with her gestures. She was still whispering and talking low, with long pauses, and interestingly, baby had a very calm, passive, slow-moving style. But he was clearly engaged and related, organized, focused, and capable of complex behavioral and emotional interactions. What seemed to be missing at the fifteen-month-old level was a degree of enthusiasm and robustness to his emotions and energy level. He treated mother a little like an acquaintance, rather than someone he felt deeply and strongly about. He was able to warm up to me, but again only slowly. With his nanny, however, the little boy showed more intense pleasurable emotion; he giggled and was able to do similar kinds of complex behaviors and interactions. The main challenge now seemed to be determining how long nanny would stay with them and what would happen if she needed to move on. There was the possibility that in three or four months she might be leaving for a new job, although the parents were hoping to keep her for another year.

Father was more involved now. He said, "I think he likes me." He prided himself on the fact that his little baby would run up to him as soon as he arrived home and sometimes hand him a toy. Sometimes he would take something that father had brought home from the office and enjoy it. Father felt that there was some "acceptance now." Mother was also taking more pride in her child, feeling that he liked her better now and that they had a "real relationship."

It was clear, however, that while this youngster was now on schedule, in terms of his major emotional milestones—he could attend, be warmly related and engaged, had mastered two-way communication, and was moving into the more complex forms of two-way communication—he still lacked emotional range and depth, particularly with his parents. He was a very calm youngster who could recover from cries or upsets, but he would still get upset with loud or high-pitched noises. He seemed to be bright in the way he approached understanding the world—examining toys, searching behind things and under rugs for toys that I had hidden, and so forth. His calm, methodical style seemed well suited to help him handle some of his sensitivity to auditory pitch and intensity. He seemed to have good visual–spatial skills, judging by his interest in figuring out how the different toys worked, and his comfort in moving in and out of my playroom and my office and finding his way back and forth each time. It looked as though he had made a major recovery from the challenges in his early months of life, and that his parents were also getting more involved with him and feeling more confident in their parenting roles. Many challenges remain in this family and work with them will continue.

CASE NUMBER 7: JILL

Jill, a ten-and-a-half-month-old baby girl, was brought to see me by her mother because of a "sleep problem." "She wakes up every few hours," mother said, "and cries until I nurse her—and she's already ten-and-a-half months old." Mother went on to say that she liked to hold her and "not let her cry." As a newborn, she had slept for three or four hours, and at three months old was sleeping through the night. At four-and-a-half months old, however, when she was moved from the bassinet to the port-a-crib, mother began nursing her to sleep and she would wake up twice in the night. At six months of age, the family moved to a new house and Jill began waking up more frequently. Additional factors were the fresh paint and a DPT shot, after which she had had a fever and was irritable; mother had noticed some edema around the shot. Her sleep patterns had become more erratic during the past month—she had had roseola, with a 102 degree fever and vomiting. At its worst, mother reported, she was waking each hour. "She was screaming different cries and wouldn't stop, only wanting to nurse." Before this most recent illness, Jill had begun to wean herself off the breast, but during the last month she had become more "anxiously desirous of only having breast milk."

My initial observation of this ten-and-a-half-month-old indicated an adorable, but somewhat overweight child, with slightly low muscle tone, who was having difficulty maintaining her posture while sitting. She was not quite crawling, but managed to slide along, dragging one leg behind the other. She smiled briefly at me in a flirtatious way, clearly engaging me and feeling warm toward me. She was focused and attentive while doing this and was able to take toys in her hands and hand them to me once I started becoming playful with her. As I hid a toy, she searched under my hand for it, in an attentive, quite organized, and purposeful manner. She looked at me, smiled, and was clearly reciprocally interacting with me. With her mother, she showed similar interaction patterns, but mother had a very anxious, overprotective style; she usually did not let Jill initiate the interactive behavior she was capable of. In spite of this, Jill maintained a warm, engaged, and pleasurable affect, but tended to become more passive with mother, letting mother do for her, while looking around with nice, bright smiles.

The developmental history revealed that mother had a normal pregnancy and uneventful delivery. Jill had been a large eight pound, six ounce healthy baby, who was very alert and, according to mother, very responsive—looking and listening and even showing faint smiles by two months of age. Mother felt that she was more responsive to sights than sounds, but liked both. She tolerated a wide range of sounds, including loud and high-pitched noises. She did, however, evidence some sensitivity to light touch when having her arms and legs stroked, and was initially uncomfortable about having a bath, even with nice warm water. But, she would adjust to this after "a few minutes."

Mother indicated that Jill was slow to develop motorically, being last to sit among the children in her parent group, and slow to hold her head up. (As I noted, she was still not completely stable when sitting.) She began sitting at around seven months and scooting along at about nine-and-a-half months. (Mother never crawled, but went right to a walk and father hadn't walked until 15 months of age.) Mother also reported that her daughter started vocalizing even by four months of age, and already, she felt, had good comprehension: she could respond to "Give me the spoon," by giving the spoon to mother and said, "back, back" and "Ba Ba" for grandmother.

Jill's early months were characterized by "lots of colicky behavior," where she was irritable and hard to calm down, but she would calm with nursing. Mother reported feeling very anxious and worried, whenever the baby was upset. "I feel like I'm doing something wrong," she said, "and I try to anticipate what she needs to help calm her down." She went on to describe her own difficulty with tolerating frustration or anger in anybody—her baby, her husband, best friends—and her general tendency to "make everything nice-nice." She described a conflict between her husband and herself: the husband wanted to let their little daughter cry a little more and learn to calm herself; mother wanted to move in quickly for fear that her daughter would be uncomfortable.

While watching mother hold Jill and play with her later in the hour, I realized that mother, in addition to being anxious and moving in quickly, tried to control the interaction a great deal. She led her daughter into searching for the ball under her hand, rather than following her bright little baby's lead. They did interact and there was reciprocity, but baby tended to be passive and mother tended to be very subdued with long pauses between her vocalizations.

The pattern that emerged between the two of them was one of a passive baby who permitted herself to be controlled by mother. She responded to mother's overtures and gestures, and mother, looking anxious and frozen at times, would then become controlling and overprotective. The rhythm between them was slow, with some silences, lots of mutual passivity, and overcontrol on mother's part.

At the end of this first session, I suggested that we continue with a more complete evaluation next time, including family functioning and a detailed history. For the time being, I suggested mother could help her baby be more assertive by letting Jill take more of a leadership role in the interactions. Mother said, "I don't know if I can do assertive play. It's so unnatural to me." We discussed this for a while and agreed to continue our discussion at the next session, particularly in view of mother's deep feelings of discomfort about perceiving annoyance or anger in other people. We also talked about letting the baby lie on her tummy more. She tended to sit up or be on her back a great deal and didn't like the tummy position. I showed mother how to play with Jill on the floor from a tummy-to-tummy position; mother would get down on her stomach, nose-to-nose, face-to-face with her baby, letting the baby take the lead, reach for things, and crawl toward her.

We also talked about trying an elimination diet with certain foods; it might help us understand some of the colickiness and fussiness Jill had had when younger, and that persisted now as part of her sleep problem. We decided to remove dairy products, salicylate-containing fruit, chemicals (additives, preservatives, food coloring, dyes, etc.), and sugars.[1]

---

[1] In a follow-up session when Jill was eleven-and-a-half months old, mother reported that her sleep had begun improving after dairy products were eliminated from the diet

Father accompanied mother and Jill to the second session, and so this time I could observe the three of them. The little girl was still not crawling; she scooted along the floor, but had slightly increased her steadiness; and mother showed some tendency to follow Jill's lead more, although she was still inclined to be quiet, passive, controlling, and overprotective. Jill remained much more passive than her general level of comprehension and brightness would indicate that she needed to be. She did use more sounds, saying "Ba Ba" and "wolf" and "Hi," during the interactive play, but she kept the play to simple interactive sequences. She handed mother dolls, took something mother handed her, searched for something under mother's hand, and so on.

Jill's play with father was a little more active and interactive. Father had more of a talent for engaging her in her play and making implicit demands on her to respond to him. For example, when she looked at me to hand me a doll that she and father were playing with, he pointed to me and asked if she was going to go over to me. She looked at him and then got up and tried to crawl in my direction. Mother, in a similar situation, would have most likely not thought to create this opportunity or would have taken the doll from her and handed it to me directly.

During this session, it also became clear that Jill not only did not respond well to bathing, but the parents had questions about the degree to which she cuddled and the degree of her tactile sensitivity. They found that when they stroked her abdomen or her back lightly, she tended to get stiff and that she didn't cooperate much in the cuddling process. When they tried to embrace her she seemed passive and limp in their arms, and occasionally squirmed a little as though uncomfortable.

---

and got worse when they were reintroduced into the diet. At a later meeting, it also became clear, from continuing the elimination diet, that chemicals, preservatives, and sugars were associated with poor sleep. At a still later session, there was also a questionable response to fruit containing natural salicylates. Jill's sleep pattern seemed to be worse when on them and improved when off, but the results were not as clear as with the chemicals, sugars, and dairy products.

As the parents and I worked through Jill's motor history there were indications of her being somewhat "loose"; this looseness seemed to play a role in her not cuddling well (as well as a tactile sensitivity). It also seemed related to her slowness in holding up her head, sitting up, and now in crawling; all of which I had observed during the interactive play sessions. We decided at this time to obtain an occupational therapy (OT) consultation and continue to work on the "floor time" exercises. The parents would play with her for twenty- to thirty-minute intervals each day, working on increasing her assertiveness through interactive play, where she would be permitted to take the lead. Jill's assertiveness would become critical to carrying on the drama. For example, when she seemed interested in something, her parents would engage her in that object. She would be encouraged to crawl over to it and reach for it, or make sounds and point to it. At the same time, talk to her about what a nice doll it was, or what a nice pan or plate or dish it was, depending on what she was interested in. If she became frustrated and began to cry a little, they would offer support and security through words, facial gestures, and emotional gestures. But they would not move in to pick her up quite as quickly as usual. Of course, whenever she clearly needed to be cuddled and hugged, they would be nurturing and tender.

In the third session, after the occupational therapy consultation, it became clear from the OT evaluation that there was, indeed, tactile sensitivity of a moderate nature and low motor tone (motor age of about 7 to 8 months in comparison to her chronological age of 12½ months).

Also, at this time mother talked more about her own history of being a "frightened child" and very dependent on her own mother. She had tended to have long relationships with boyfriends because she was "afraid of separating," even when the relationship was no longer any good. She talked about how security-oriented she was and how frightened of aggression she had been for most of her life. In the marriage, she viewed herself as providing the dependency and security, and her husband as being more ambivalent. He agreed to this, but thought he represented the more assertive side of their marriage, seeking out new experiences. He also viewed himself as being more interested in the baby learning to be more independent. In their marital relationship, it became clear that they had trouble empathizing with each other's strong points—the very strengths they had married each other for. Mother now had difficulty with father's desire to help Jill be more assertive and also with the independence he enjoyed in his relationship with the child; father had difficulty with some of mother's security and dependency needs. As they became aware of this, they began to realize that their baby needed both the security and empathy, and the experience of assertiveness, too; at an intellectual level, they became aware that they needed to join forces more (father had been deferring to mother) in planning the best approach for their child.

We decided that they would see the occupational therapist twice a week for a while to work on sensory normalizing exercises, and other exercises to improve motor tone, postural control, and some motor planning skills.

During this session, their interactive styles with the baby showed continued improvement, although mother was still somewhat cautious and controlling and unenthusiastic in her chit-chat and banter with the baby. Father was more active, and at the same time seemed to be sensitive to the baby's needs. In spite of Jill's simple interactions and games being more at the eight-to-ten-month-old level, she showed a great deal of warmth, pleasure, and comfort, and high-level abilities in terms of receptive and expressive language; but she still could not pull together three or four consecutive circles. She played simple peek-a-boo games, handing games, but not the complicated ones normally seen in a youngster of this level of brightness and receptive language ability.

When talking about the family in a subsequent session, mother revealed another important aspect of her own family dynamics—a sister who had medical illnesses and with whom it was "quite difficult to be angry." "I tended to inhibit it," she said. "As an adult, I was aware that I was quite jealous of her and copied her a lot. But we all had a very protective attitude toward her. We thought we had to take care of her." Mother also had an older sister who she said picked on her a lot.

A month later, at the next session the parents reported that they "were all doing much better." Their little daughter was now sleeping through the night, crawling more confidently, and was able to throw a ball to father from a sitting position. They demonstrated this for me in their free play session. Jill and father threw a ball back and forth; she reached out for him and he threw the ball to her. As he caught the ball she clapped her hands, imitating his having clapped for her. When father asked her to get him a book that was lying on the floor, she did, bringing it back to him with a big smile on her face.

The play with mother showed increasing complexity in both interactions and the number of circles they could close together. Jill became interested in mother's keys and got hold of them. Mother hid them behind a chair and the little girl crawled to them and brought them back to mother. She smiled broadly, comprehending that mother was playing a game. Mother was able to show joy and pleasure, although she still became anxious after a few minutes. She worried that she was frustrating her daughter too much. She talked about how hard it was for her to know where to draw the line on what was frustration or what was good assertive play. We played out this theme, varying the amount of the frustration with the keys and then with other objects that her daughter enjoyed. Mother would create opportunities for her daughter to be assertive by trying to find things that were hard for a small child to do, such as opening the doors in a playhouse.

She began to realize that her daughter could tolerate a little more frustration, although clearly mother was still quite anxious about it. Gradually, we saw two- and three-circle interactions, and a slightly increased range of affect on the baby's part—not just the joy and pleasure that she had always shown, but some real assertiveness, curiosity, and pleasure in her own sense of mastery. We hadn't seen any real signs of anger, but that perhaps was yet to come.

In a recent session, the parents reported that Jill's sleeping pattern had continued to improve. Both baby and mother, who was still breast-feeding, were now off salicylate-containing fruit, sugar, chemical additives, and dairy products. (During a holiday, mother had eaten foods containing sugar and preservatives, and Jill's sleep had deteriorated. Now that mother was off these foods again, the baby's sleep had improved.) The parents had noticed improvements in both gross and fine motor skills, which they attributed to the work with the occupational therapist. She was now using seventy words, with lots of jabbering, and plenty of imitation; for example, as mother would go through the mail, Jill would take the letters and pretend to look through them. Mother reported that Jill remained fearful of other children, and added that she was confused about what to do when her daughter took a masturbatory interest in her own body; she had begun playing with her genitals a great deal.

Later, when mother and daughter were in the pretend play sequence, they exchanged necklaces. Mother wondered if Jill could put the necklace on the doll. Jill took the doll, and tried to put the necklace around it, but got frustrated because the necklace was too large. She gave up easily, and mother was reluctant to inspire Jill's interest in continuing to try for fear that she would become too frustrated. I suggested that she could do it, if I put the doll near her again and caught her attention with it. She tried again and again, finally got angry, and threw the doll down. I wondered out loud if mother wanted to help her with it. Mother reluctantly brought the doll back again, and together they succeeded in getting the necklace around the doll. There was highly intentional, collaborative behavior, but mother was clearly finding it difficult to work on her daughter's pleasure in mastery and assertiveness.

Even while respecting her daughter's lead more than before, mother still tended to be controlling and to try to set the agenda, rather than follow her lead. With father, the play had a different tone. He spontaneously began by hiding napkins and the little girl searched for them. Father controlled the rhythm a little, but not nearly as much as mother. Jill showed greater range of affect and greater enthusiasm as father made demands on her; he folded one napkin into intriguing little shapes and she tried to put it over her head and make shapes with it on her own.

We talked further about following her lead, creating opportunities for assertiveness, increasing the number of circles closed, and helping her increase the range of her affective expression. I urged father to make more time for her, to interest her in him, so that when they were at home together, she'd want to play more with him. Even though Jill had played nicely with father during this session, she seemed a little more dependent on mother.

In the most recent session, Jill came in and played for a long time with mother. When I said, "Would you like to play," she immediately got down from mother's lap, an interested look on her face, and took out toys from the toy box. She took the lead and examined each one, while smiling eagerly at mother. Mother held out her hand, asking if she could see the toy. Jill would hand it to her once she had looked at it herself. Mom described both the action of the toys and what Jill was doing, but was involved only in terms of being a describer. Jill looked and smiled at her, but mother, as gentle and reciprocal as she was, wasn't interacting with her as much as she could. She indicated to me, almost parenthetically, that she was afraid of being too controlling; she was, perhaps, erring now toward not being interactive enough. I agreed with her and shared her concern.

Soon Jill looked over at father and there was clearly more warmth and chemistry; apparently father had done his homework. All of a sudden, Jill wanted to give one of the dolls to him. "Here," she said, crawling over and handing it to him. Father said, "Thank you." She crawled over to him again with another toy and another nice smile, and he said "Thank you" again. She finally handed him a third toy saying a word that wasn't entirely clear but was obviously intentional. Mother, then, picked up the doll from father and said, "Hello." She gave it back to Jill who looked amused. Jill picked up the doll and handed it back to father, and they handed things back and forth to each other a few times. It was interesting to watch mother being supportive without very much interaction; she took the more passive position for "fear of being too controlling." When father took the lead in their play, he made nice sounds while handing Jill some dolls. But when he suggested that they play hide-and-go-seek with one of the dolls and he tried to take one of them, she shook her head no. She refused to look any place for the doll even when he persisted. Father suggested that she give one of the dolls to me and she said, "No," shaking her head; but she made hand gestures in my direction and then ambivalently moved a nearby doll further away from me. The more demanding father was, the more the robust the interaction. The fact that both parents followed Jill's lead, as well as mother's increased passivity, may have had an influence on this interesting moment.

Jill still appeared to have a low level of energy for a fifteen-month-old and was a little bit on the passive side. Her attention, though, was excellent and her language skills were good (both her vocalizations and her receptive skills); she was crawling confidently and even walking when father held her hands. There was a warm sense of pleasure and confidence about her. What still seemed to require improvement, however, was the range for affect, and also the complexity of interactive play. She needed to learn to take the lead and string together multiple circles.

At this point, her presenting problem (the sleep problem) was now taken care of and the family was now trying to facilitate her general development. Their main concern during this recent session was how to help her be a better "coper." Mother still wanted to do for her and protect her, and father wanted to let her cry a little more (when, for example, they were talking on the telephone and she wanted attention). We discussed ways she might learn to calm herself when upset—mother didn't have to calm her all the time. They could use talking and vocalization and facial gestures as distal communication skills to help her relax and calm down. This would utilize her visual and auditory abilities as tools for calming. We also focused on situations when she might feel upset, for example, if she fell while trying to walk. Before distracting her, it would be important to empathize with her, because of her great comprehensive skills. They could say that they knew she was feeling "like she had a boo-boo." They could point to the spot and nod their heads to indicate their understanding. After empathizing with her discomfort, they would move on, to say that perhaps playing with a little doll or doing something else might make her feel better. We talked about the difference between the overprotective style, which moves in and picks her up, robbing her of the opportunity to realize that she can calm herself with verbal and visual support, and the alternative style, which anxiously distracts her so that she feels that she can't focus on the hurt or the upset feelings at all. There is even a third style of denial which totally ignores her discomfort, pretending that it doesn't exist at all.

The parents reviewed their own stresses in the marriage—father would get angry at mother for being too protective, and mother for father's insensitivity. There was further discussion of each of their backgrounds and the need to find a middle ground between the two of them. In fact, the perfect posture for their daughter was one that probably harnessed both their instinctive and intuitive responses.

The work continues with the occupational therapist, and there is good reason to believe that Jill will continue to make progress in her skills for assertive and affectively broad ranges of interaction characteristic of the two-year level. At the moment, she is lagging a little behind and her parents are working on their own difficulties concerning the kind of practice she needs. Nevertheless, they are providing more of that practice, and, through occupational therapy as well as with her sensory overreactivity, she is getting help motorically so that she can engage in more robust interaction patterns.

In summary, this case is a good illustration of a child who came in with a sleep problem, but was having a more general developmental difficulty. Jill had progressed nicely through the early stage of attentiveness. There was some increased reactivity to touch and she had difficulty in calming down, but overall, she was progressing into a nice warm attachment with her mother and father (closer to mother, but getting closer to father now). She had simple reciprocal intentional interaction patterns characteristic of the third phase of development. At this third phase, however, we began seeing a lack of progress into the complex three- and four-circle sequences, characteristic of the toddler stage, and no increase in the range of affect, assertiveness, or curiosity, or a deep sense of pleasure. Other factors were Jill's mild motor delays, low motor tone, and tactile sensitivity, as well as mother's profound overprotectiveness and father's deference to mother.

The intervention approach included a number of elements: the elimination diet to help reduce some of the irritability leading to frequent awakenings at night; strengthening motor capacities and sensory normalizing capacities; working with the parents to modify their own emotional proclivities, especially mother's overreactivity to a child who tended to be passive and overly sensitive and father's exiting from the interactive play; and, perhaps most significantly, hands-on floor time practice during the sessions, and lots of floor time at home, to increase the interactive abilities of Jill and her parents. The floor time would encourage more complex prerepresentational interactions: the parents would follow Jill's lead, and most importantly, help her to take the initiative and become more assertive. Her sensory reactivity, together with the mother's overreactiveness and overprotectiveness, would no longer be a basis for a more chronic pattern of passivity, and interfere with her acquisition of self-coping and self-comforting skills.

This is a good example of an early regulatory problem that had both motor elements and family interactive elements to it. The overall approach only took about six sessions and addressed general development in an effort to help the child sleep better.

CASE NUMBER 8: ROSIE

Rosie came in as a two-month-old with her parents. Mother was quite depressed and worried and father seemed stoic and aloof. Rosie had been born prematurely at thirty-two weeks gestation and weighed three pounds, two ounces at birth. She was in the hospital for four weeks with a series of complications including mild hyaline membrane disease. The parents had stayed with her in the hospital every day—mother all the time and father whenever he was not working.

When Rosie was discharged from the hospital, she was gaining weight satisfactorily. She was on Theophylline for her breathing for about three weeks and than was weaned off it.

At two months, Rosie was looking inward rather than robustly taking in her world. Occasionally, one could get some looks or some faint attentiveness to the human voice, but only with a great deal of patient effort; and this response was fleeting. For the most part, she was listless, with low motor tone in both extremities and in the trunk and neck area. Mother was, herself, looking listless and inward. She seemed quite depressed. Mother held Rosie as she talked about her, but made no effort to engage her daughter, work with her, or increase her interest in the world. She talked a great deal about how worried she was that Rosie would have "brain damage." She thought some terrible prophecy would come true for her baby.

Father tended to have more energy to try to interact with Rosie, but did it on a very mechanical basis. He used a lot of tactile input, poking at her cheeks and her tummy to see if he could get her to be alert. She responded by slightly turning away from this sort of rough handling. At the same time, she was feeding adequately from a bottle on a soy-based formula, and was gaining weight satisfactorily. She had a reasonably strong cry when she was hungry or upset, and was also sleeping through most of the night.

As I examined Rosie closer, I further confirmed a mildly low tone in each part of her body. I also noted that she had a slight tactile sensitivity in the trunk area, but not in the arms or legs. She would turn her face away a little when I stroked her tummy, showing slight discomfort; but when I stroked her arms and legs, she tended to open her eyes more and begin to look more alert. In appealing to her with vocalizations, I noticed that if I persisted with high-pitched, but slow rhythmic sounds, she gradually opened her eyes more often and even began following movement from left to right. It was unclear whether she responded to different facial expressions at this age, but in response to my high-pitched, but slow rhythmic vocalizations, she was equally good at turning to the left and the right. As I worked with her, I began using a gentle touch to the arms and legs. She seemed to enjoy it, and as she brightened up more I got glimmers or shared attention and, perhaps, even faint engagement.

During this first meeting, I worked with mother and father to try to achieve this same degree of involvement. They were able to do this a little, but mother had a hard time noticing that her baby was a little more bright and alert. She remained preoccupied with her preconceived notions and worries about Rosie being "brain damaged." However, father was able to see the change in his daughter, although he often overstimulated her tactilely and lost the little bit of involvement (a look here and there) that he had begun to get.

I suggested to the parents that they have an occupational therapy consultation for Rosie's low motor tone and her limited degree of tactile sensitivity. I told them that they could learn ways of handling her to help her take a greater interest in her sensory and affective world, and at the same time help her learn to normalize her motor tone. I also suggested that they see a nurse colleague of mine to work on their emotional inter-actions with their baby. They would go for a number of sessions in a row, returning to see me in a month. They were already in an effective program for regular pediatric well-baby care.

Mother had been in therapy on and off. We talked about the value of her getting back into some counseling to work through some of her depressive feelings. She understood well that she was "overwhelmed" and that she was not as available to her baby as she would like to be; but she said, "I can't shake this ominous feeling I have about the dire outcome."

When I saw them a month later, Rosie was able to sustain looking and listening for a good four to five seconds. Her motor tone (she was now seeing an occupational therapist with the parents once a week) was clearly improved, but was still on the low side. The tactile sensitivity around her abdomen remained, although it seemed to have decreased as she was more alert and interested in her world. At three months old, she was still not engaging or smiling a great deal, but she did seem slightly more attentive. Mother, too, was showing more interest. She was using rhythmical sounds to draw her baby out and held her in a firm way. But she had long silences in her vocalizations and still complained about being preoccupied with "terrible thoughts." She reported persistent images of awful things happening to the baby, around the themes of brain damage, and retardation. Father was angry at mother. He was getting "fed up with her not being able to shake off the depression." He was also working late hours in the evening, rather than helping support the development of his new baby.

Upon further exploration with father, it turned out that he had quite a bit of mental illness in his family—severe depression in his mother and in his maternal grandmothers. He had handled his mother's mood swings, particularly depressive mood swings, by being a rather stoic and indifferent child, trying to spend a lot of time outside the family. As he talked about this, tears welled up in his eyes and, for the first time, some affect shone through.

The parents continued their work. Father was not accessible for individual work with anyone, but mother was working with her counselor on her depression. She continued to work with the occupational therapist, although she stopped seeing the individual infant specialist for her interactions with the baby. She felt that she could "carry on on her own," as she was "getting the knack of it." She was, however, agreeable to returning to see me on a monthly basis.

Over the next series of months, these same themes continued to play themselves out. Mother kept worrying about Rosie being retarded because she was a little behind motorically and in her vocalizations and her social cuing. But Rosie continued to get more interested in the world of sight and sound; was more responsive to touch; and began smiling at about six months of age. Mother was convinced that the baby would be "retarded" because she was smiling two to three months late. I persuaded mother not only to make adjustments for Rosie's prematurity, but also to take the attitude that getting there slower is not necessarily worse. I explained that with a baby who has been through so many difficult shocks and challenges, it was important to look at the learning curve and not at any particular timetable for milestones. I urged her to interact with Rosie as though she were a four-month-old and not try to do six-, seven-, or eight-month-old types of interactions. Mother was, for example, trying to get the baby to imitate different sounds, which she was not ready to do, and to perform motor acts beyond her present abilities. She and Rosie were beginning to feel frustrated with each other. For example, Rosie would start smiling and engaging with mother's nice rhythmic, high-pitched sounds. Mother would then try to make a complicated sound and get frustrated when Rosie wouldn't mimic her. Or mother would hand her something and she wouldn't take it or would ignore mother's motor gesture. Mother would, again, get frustrated and say, "Rosie is obviously behind, brain damaged, retarded," and so on. Father would take these opportunities to criticize mother for being unrealistic in her expectations of their daughter. He later explained that his wife was very critical of him, too. "She is always criticizing me and finding fault with me," he complained.

Nevertheless, having gained some insight about his own pattern of withdrawal from his own family, father was staying attentive to his daughter's needs. He was neither as stoic or aloof as he had been and was beginning to come home earlier in the evening. While he was fighting with his wife, he was at least also involved in helping with some of the practical aspects of baby care. He was also trying to interact more with Rosie, and his patterns were getting less intrusive and more appropriate. He was more gentle. He stroked her without being tactilely intrusive, and was learning to vary his pitch and rhythm of voice. Rosie responded with smiles for both of her parents. At this point, she could sustain a longer smile with father, because he didn't overchallenge her as much as mother.

This pattern gradually improved over the next few months. By nine-and-a-half months, Rosie was actually closing the gap between her chronological age and her developmental age. She was, for example, picking up little food bits by herself, changing them from one hand to the other, and using her thumb and forefinger well with things like Cheerios. Even with her low motor tone, she was beginning some early crawling motions by slithering across the floor. Most surprisingly, she was beginning to vocalize sounds like "Ba-ba" and "La-da," words that had a number of different sounds to them. Also, there was something very similar to "Ga" sounds coming out, and she waved "bye-bye" and "hello" when her parents left or came into the room. She was clearly reciprocal by this time. As I watched mother and daughter play, they reciprocated not only vocalizations. When mother handed her a toy, Rosie took the toy and handed it back to mother, showing delight and a nice smile. She even searched in mother's hand for things when mother closed her fist. She did the same thing with me and with father. According to mother, she was very vocal and made lots of different sounds when she ate, although I didn't actually observe this.

Interestingly, Rosie had stopped sleeping well. She was waking up two or three times a night as if, through her alertness to the world, she had decided to enjoy more of it. (Mother wondered whether she might be cutting her teeth.) At home, Rosie was reaching out to be picked up, making different sounds of frustration if her diaper was wet or she felt hungry. She seemed to be quite curious.

Mother was tempted to focus only on Rosie's inability to crawl and ignore all the dramatic gains she was making. Rosie was rolling over quite well and, as mentioned earlier, was beginning to slither across the floor, sometimes backwards when she wanted to go forward. Whenever she was upset, she seemed able to recover well. Mother reported that she had had Rosie with some other babies on a visit to some friends, and she did "seem as good as the other babies."

With some help, mother saw that she was still projecting a lot of her negative feelings onto her daughter. She recognized that Rosie needed her patience and for her to engage the baby at her current level to help her catch up and become age appropriate in most areas. Mother began showing greater affect variation and less listlessness and sadness but, nonetheless, wasn't able to relinquish her preconceived notions easily. She did talk a little bit more about her own family and some of the roots of her negative imagery. She mentioned that her own mother was a person who never could tolerate optimism, joy, or pleasure, and tended to withdraw from her children whenever they got "too competitive" with her.

Rosie continued to develop well, making solid progress over the next year. Each visit seemed to result in a greater sense of competency. She showed a deeper sense of pleasure, more confidence in her assertiveness, and a consolidation of age-appropriate abilities. Mother was also doing better, but remained anxious about Rosie's ultimate prognosis. With each succeeding visit her anxiety seemed to ease a little. When Rosie was twenty-one months old, for example, mother worried, "Am I filling her up enough? Do I give her enough?" She was convinced that she was somehow short-changing Rosie since her daughter was so competent, and wondered whether Rosie needed more from her than she could give her to keep her competence going.

Father, in contrast, seemed to want to avoid Rosie having any pain or discomfort. Far from his earlier stoic and avoidant attitude, he now showed some extra sensitivity to Rosie's cries, wanting to pick her up and comfort her right away. He didn't question his ability to help her, but in a sense wanted to "make up for lost time."

Rosie, for her part, was a cute, nice sized twenty-one-month-old, who looked a little scared about being in new surroundings; but she warmed up over time and flirted with me with smiles, using two-word sentences, such as naming a toy with "that doll" or "that girl." She also asked for things, using two words joined together with verbs and nouns. She was very warm and close to both parents, holding onto them and then venturing out to play with toys and sometimes coming over to me. When I got on the floor with her, she even got into some pretend fragments. She labeled one small pretend play animal a kitty-cat and another one a man and then had the man touching the kitty-cat. There was excellent attention and focus as she played. She then made a toy dog walk and gave the dog to me to see if I would continue to walk it. She similarly involved her parents in this kind of play. Her fine motor seemed appropriate as she held a crayon and scribbled with it, showing good control. She was walking at this point, but looked a little clumsy and still obviously had slightly low motor tone.

The main question the parents had at this time was that she sometimes got timid with other children when there was a lot of commotion. She was a little shy of them, they said, and could be fearful, but would usually warm up after a period of time.

For the most part, though, she was warm and engaging, in the early representational stages of development, and quite happy. Interestingly, when mother would be upset and cry (when she talked about her own family), Rosie would pat her and say, "Okay?" Both mother and father seemed to support her early representational play and had clearly made a lot of progress. At this point, we talked about how to give her more rather than less opportunity to play with peers and to learn how to deal with the confusion and extra challenges of interacting with children her own age. To do this, mother or father should be available as a buffer and they should build from one child to a second and then perhaps even a third, in terms of group settings. We talked about how nice it was that Rosie's only challenge now was something that we normally see at this age with many children, particularly those who are a little tactilely sensitive—they tend to be a little shy and cautious and need to warm up gradually to the complexity of peer relationships. Rosie seemed to have all the equipment ready to do that.

At age three, when Rosie returned to see me with her parents, it was interesting to observe that she was now a very sturdy, strong-looking little girl who came in on her own, but looked initially scared and angry. She was slow to explore and warm up with the toys. At times, she seemed frozen with anxiety. But on her own, with minimal help from me, she worked herself out of it, got used to the toys, and got used to me. She then developed some nice representational play; for example, with the ballet girl going into the house and climbing up the chimney. She developed a little drama about the girl coming down from chimney into the house and exploring the different parts of the house. At one point when I made a comment, she said, "Why did you say that?" in a very sophisticated way. She then played with some dolls that had some monster components to them, and I became one of the monsters. She became scared and took it literally, rather than enjoying it. At one point, she told me she had "dreams," but wouldn't elaborate on them. Each time she got scared, she recovered quickly and got back into nice pretend play, with warm engagement, and was reciprocally interactive with me. She was rather stoic. I was impressed that she had intact basic personality functions; she was anxious, serious, and scared at times, but had a warm engaging smile and a good capacity for representational elaboration. She clearly had some conflicts around anger and fear, but was able to deal with these.

We were observing the continuation of certain personality characteristics that appeared first as tactile sensitivities, when Rosie was a baby, and later as cautiousness when she was two years old. They were partially related to mother's difficulties with anger and her overall depressive attitude toward the world. Recently, Rosie had told mother about a dream she'd had in which "mom was a witch throwing away a doll" of hers.

When mother played with Rosie, they were nice and reciprocal with one another, although mother was clearly cautious,
anxious, and depressive around monster or aggressive play.
Father was warm, enthusiastic, and representational with her,
and there was a good fit. It appeared that they had worked out
much of their conflict.

Mother reported that Rosie was now physically more competent; she had learned to swim. When she drew, she was still
fisting a pencil, but was showing better control over making
squares and circles. She had begun to challenge mother more,
rather than be fearful. One time, mother told me, when they
were engaged in pretend play, Rosie had enthusiastically taken
the part of a witch, even using a witchlike voice. Other aggressive themes were beginning to appear in her pretend play. She
was even defiant at times. However, for the most part, Rosie
was cooperative.

We talked about continuing the floor time regularly, as a
means of allowing her to develop her excellent representational
abilities. The parents were encouraged to add more floor time
and more problem-solving chit-chats whenever Rosie seemed
to be challenging limits. Since she was already emerging from
her tendencies toward fearfulness, floor time would also help
her use her great recovery power to try gradually to reexperi-
ence situations that were a little scary for her. Furthermore, I
suggested that the parents arrange for more children to play
with Rosie at home; mother had not exposed her to much
group play. Even though Rosie had one or two little girl friends
whom she liked, she was still a little shy in group situations.

Rosie was making good, consistent progress over time. It
appeared that she would continue to do well while mother and
father continued to work with her and became more flexible
themselves.

In summary, Rosie was a child who started off with lots of
constitutional vulnerabilities, which were related to low motor
tone, and a complicated premature birth with many attendant
risk factors. Her early cognitive and emotional delays, coupled
with her low motor tone, brought out in mother a depressive

core: she had seen in her daughter negative images of herself. Mother had ominous fantasies about her little girl being brain damaged and began relating to her in a depressive, unengaged way that could have easily made her prophecy come true. Father's avoidant style was also maladaptive. He would become aloof from family situations that distressed him, as he had done with his own family. Given Rosie's need for consistent and sustaining environmental experiences that would help draw her out, interest her in the world, and engage her, she needed parents who were neither aloof and avoidant nor depressed. The parents' emotional patterns, coupled with her constitutional and maturational pattern of low motor tone and hypoarousability, made this a doubly vulnerable situation. She needed a comprehensive pattern of care: occupational therapy, parent–infant counseling, and some counseling for mother. The family gradually got back on track, learning to engage Rosie at her own level. As she mastered each emotional milestone, she began showing patterns of constriction around dealing with aggression and assertiveness, and also increasing fearfulness. Rosie is resolving them slowly.

With a course of therapeutic work implemented on both sides of the equation—Rosie's constitutional and maturational vulnerabilities and mother's and father's difficult environmental patterns—she is working through her difficulties, recovering, and entering into a normative, developmental progression.

CASE NUMBER 9: MEGAN

Mother and father came in with their four-month-old baby, a pretty little girl called Megan. They complained that she cried all day long if not held and was getting up every four hours at night. "I feel tired and exhausted," said mother, a biochemist who was on maternity leave and working two days a week. Other than the baby wanting to be held all day long, Megan's development was fine, mother thought, in terms of motor, language, and intellectual development.

Megan was delivered normally and full term, at the end of a planned, unremarkable pregnancy. She was six pounds, twelve ounces, with 9/9 Apgars and physically quite healthy. However, from day one, mother reported, "she always was kind of fussy and needed to be held more. Only that's gotten dramatically worse in the last month or so. She loved to look at me and focus on my voice, even within the first week of life." She also liked it when her four-year-old brother looked at her, for she enjoyed being "entertained."

Mother said Megan was now able to hold her head up, but could fuss and cry for hours and hours. She could put her hands up to her mouth and seemed to feel "nice and secure" in mother's arms. From the first week, Megan examined and looked at people, and by two-and-a-half months had developed nice smiles; she was now taking delight in people entertaining her. She had been free of any physical illnesses and, mother added, "likes her daddy." Father, sitting in the room, nodded and said that Megan enjoyed both of them. She liked either one to hold her, but preferred mother if they were both there. "My only problem," mother concluded, "is that she cries so much."

She said she was breast-feeding Megan, augmenting the diet with a soy formula. She stressed more than once that the infant's desire to be held was unrelated to her being hungry; once she had nursed, she was clearly not interested in having anything more to eat. Her older child suffered from eczema and hayfever and she herself had a history of hayfever. She reported that her own diet consisted of cereal, milk, decaffeinated coffee, muffins, whole cereal, tuna, cheese, noodles, cottage cheese, vegetables, chicken, beef or turkey, and lots of juices—apple, cranberry, or strawberry.

I watched mother and daughter play together. They engaged with beautiful reciprocal gestures, little Megan smiling broadly and deeply at mother and giggling as mother talked to her and with a nice engaged rhythm. There was also nice rhythmic movement of arms and legs in synchrony with mother's voice. Mother looked to me like a "natural." She helped Megan maintain her focus and her pleasure for thirty or forty seconds at a clip before they both took a time out and then reengaged in another wonderful moment of mutual rapport and engagement. Megan moved her mouth in synchrony with mother's words, vocalizing with guttural sounds back at her mother. She was struggling to comprehend everything her mother was saying.

Dad and Megan played similarly well, although he was a little less gifted than mother. Megan still focused, looked, smiled, and cooed as father talked to her and let her play with his little finger. He got her smiling and laughing with funny little sounds and faces.

With me, Megan gave a few smiles, but was more cautious. She, nonetheless, was comfortable in my arms and quite trusting. Her motor tone was fine in both arms and legs and trunk, and she enjoyed light touch and heavy pressure to her arms and legs. She could follow me equally as well as she had her parents when I made funny faces and vocalized, revealing that she responded to both visual and auditory input. She also liked movement up and down and to the sides, in terms of movement in space.

As I watched mother play with Megan more, I noticed that, in spite of Megan's being a terrific interacter, she didn't have to do much of the work. Mother was so natural and talented that she did almost 80 percent of the wooing.

Megan was very responsive and reactive, and she was also obviously quite sophisticated: she followed both complex and simple vocal rhythms and seemed to be quite alert to noticing little things around the room. For example, if I talked to mother, Megan quickly looked at me and when father talked, quickly looked at him; she was easily interested in sounds that came in from the outside, such as a car honking or a cat meowing or the birds chirping outside my window. She, therefore, seemed a focused, attentive, and very alert child who could be interested in most things.

In talking with the family about their history, mother iterated that she herself was a product of rather cold parents and felt she "never got enough as a child from them." She had always wanted to have a family of her own so that she could give her child more love and attention. She felt her parents cared for her and loved her and were there for security, but she had always wished they were warmer, like some of her friends' parents. She recalled that she could never "get any satisfaction" from becoming mad at her mother because she could never make her mother upset. Her mother always had an even temper and refused to get involved in "power struggles." Her father, she felt, was a little warmer than her mother, but he worked a great deal, had been a successful engineer, and wasn't as available as she would have liked him to have been. She had two older brothers who were seven and ten years older than she, who, she said, were "doing their own thing." Although she was the baby of the family, she felt that she had never been sure whether her mother really wanted her. She had grown up with the feeling that perhaps she was "an accident." But she had never been able to get her mother to tell straightforwardly why she'd waited so many years to have her.

Father came from a much warmer family. He was clearly a very warm and tender individual, as was mother for that matter. He felt his mother was much too intrusive with him and was too, in a sense, "warm and into my skin." He felt he needed some distance and space, but that he and his wife got along as well as they did because she could be warm and secure with him, without overdoing it as his mother did.

At the end of this first session, it wasn't entirely clear why Megan demanded so much holding from her mother. Certainly, during the session here, we saw her being quite comfortable and confident without being held all the time. She tolerated my playing with her and holding her, albeit a little more cautiously than with mother and father, revealing a good capacity for relating to the world and for warmly engaging.

We decided, in a preliminary way, to look at two elements that might help Megan be less demanding of mother and calm down a bit. First, it was reasoned that constitutionally Megan had sound equipment for the most part. She was not tactilely sensitive, had good motor tone, was cognitively quite sophisticated, and able to use visual as well as auditory processing for both shared attention and to engage her world. The only constitutional–maturational component that might be contributing, we reasoned, was her superalertness. It made her all too aware of the different things going on around her, and, therefore, caused her to feel a little overwhelmed at times. This could certainly move her in the direction of wanting to be held by mother for extra security. But it didn't seem to be a major constitutional–maturational contribution in her case. Second, on the family side, mother was certainly trying to make up for the lack of warmth and mothering in her own childhood; she was giving to Megan and wooing her so naturally and terrifically that perhaps she didn't give the infant enough chance to woo back and to practice her initiative.

But it was reasoned that these two factors were probably minor contributors and not the only causes for the pattern we were observing. The third factor explored was mother's diet, often a contributing cause of problems of self-calming and self-regulation. Aspects of mother's diet (she was breast-feeding) or Megan's formula could have been making her a little more fussy or irritable at certain times during the day.

We, therefore, decided to do an elimination diet, along with working on Megan's next developmental emotional milestone, which involved her learning to become more competent in two-way communication and more assertive. We took two simultaneous approaches. In the elimination diet, I suggested that mother remove three food groups at once and then challenge Megan to see if her fussiness and demand for excessive holding would get worse after being off these food groups for ten days. We combined the milk and dairy category with the honey and sugars category, and also with chemicals, including additives, preservatives, and dyes, since mother was taking all three of these in her diet. A second stage dietary category was salicylate-containing fruit, which includes many fruits other than grapefruit, bananas, pears, melons, and exotic fruits; these fruits include apples, apple juice, citrus fruits (other than grapefruits, which are OK), and grapes. The herbal teas that mother drank would be in this second group. If we found a positive for any group, we would then go and separate the group and look at individual foods in it. Mother was going to go for ten days without these foods and then eat a lot of them to see if there was a difference in Megan's pattern.

I also suggested we start floor time, with Megan lying on her tummy, to help her take initiative and begin to reach for things. Mother would work on inviting Megan to woo her a little more. She would be conscious of who was taking the lead in the interaction and try to divide it up fifty–fifty. She practiced wooing, then she'd let the baby do the wooing a bit more. Megan seemed quite capable of wooing mother with her warm smiles and coos; she had needed the chance to respond more to this exceptionally gifted mother.

I saw the parents again about three weeks later. It turned out that Megan was quite sensitive to the first group, the mild–dairy–sugar–honey–chemical combination. When that group was divided up we discovered in subsequent testing that she was quite sensitive to dairy and, to a lesser degree, sensitive to the sugar–honey–chemical group. The dairy, however, seemed to be the biggest culprit of those three. When mother took dairy completely out of her diet we saw a rather marked improvement in Megan's ability for self-calming, particularly during the late afternoon when she tended to get more tired, finicky, and fussy; with the dairy out of the diet, she seemed to be able to hold together and play a lot better. In fact, when mother occasionally went back on dairy, Megan would have a fussy day or two, confirming that the baby had this sensitivity.

While experimenting with Megan's diet, mother also worked with Megan's assertiveness. As the baby became more assertive in the wooing she enjoyed taking greater charge of her environment. Being a very bright, unusually sensitive, and unusually aware baby, she needed to take more control over her world, including at least fifty–fifty control over the relationship with mother, rather than being more on the reactive side. As she got closer to eight months, she emerged as calm, confident, and wonderfully bright, in many respects a remarkable baby with two very gifted parents. She was now taking more initiative in the interaction, wooing mother as much as mother was wooing her. At the same time, she was much better at self-comforting, calming herself down, and playing independently, as well as warmly with mother.

This case of a baby with a mild regulatory difficulty, evidenced by her excessive need to be held and calmed down, illustrates that it is often worth doing an elimination diet along with assessing the baby's constitutional–maturational pattern, the family pattern, and the parent–child interaction. A diet sensitivity will often express itself by accentuating the baby's regulatory challenges, particularly at certain times of the day. This, then, will alter the interaction pattern during those times and can stress some of the family interactions. Here, we saw subtle and minor contributions from the parent–infant interaction and the family patterns, as well as the nondiet related maturational pattern. The more significant contribution came from the dietary pattern. The changes in diet, coupled with helping this baby become more self-confident through taking more initiative in her relationships, seemed to do the trick.

Chapter 3

Twelve to Thirty Months

CASE NUMBER 10: STEVEN

When Steven's parents brought him to us, he was seventeen months old. He had been a preterm, low birthweight infant, and had a history of moderate cerebral palsy with severe involvement of the lower extremities and lesser involvement of the upper extremities (increased muscle tone). During his first year, to his parents he had seemed primarily despondent and aimless. His gentle, gifted mother was able to get him to respond a bit to touch, but there was very little two-way communication through interactive vocalizations, eye contact, or facial expressions.

When I first saw Steven, his language and cognitive development were at about the six- to eight-month level and he was aimless and random in his movements as he crawled around the room. His aimlessness had been increasing, causing his parents and professionals who had seen him to be concerned about autistic features. An evaluation a few months earlier concluded that in addition to his motor impairment, he had and would

139

continue to have a severe cognitive and social impairment with cognitive functioning no better than the 50th or 60th percentile and an overall diagnosis of severe pervasive developmental disorder.[1]

Initially, the mother was extremely caring and understandably worried about Steven, and therefore very protective toward him. She used a great deal of gentle touch to interact with him, but was less involved in working with his interactive gesturing. The father, a very successful, "take-charge" person, communicated his deep love for Steven with demands and, at times, an impatient and intrusive approach. He would hold the toddler by the arm, demanding, "Look at me, say something to me." Father was worried about the possibility that Steven would be retarded or autistic.

Our first goal was to help Steven's parents learn how to achieve a state of shared attention and engagement with Steven. Mother worked trying to get his attention through visual contact and gestures. Approximately a month-and-a-half into our work, after initially feeling frustrated about Steven's lack of engaging and intentional gesturing, father learned to see that whenever he spoke too loudly or moved in intrusively, Steven would turn away and try to crawl in the other direction. Once father recognized this, he began to modulate his voice. Interestingly, because Steven was sensitive to high-pitched sounds, he liked his father's low voice, and they gradually became more comfortable with each other. Mother became increasingly skilled at adding a variety of gestures to her already sensitive style of approach which helped to provide more for Steven to attend to.

---

[1]Our work with children like Steven and their families often involves two to five weekly sessions with the speech pathologist; one to five weekly occupational and/or physical therapy sessions; two to five sessions weekly with a skilled clinician/play therapist to work with the child, and with the child and parents together on interactive skills; and counseling with parents to help them facilitate the processes of shared attention and engagement, two-way communication, shared meanings, and categorization of experience. Sessions with a special educator and, for preschoolers, an integrated educational program that addresses their cognitive, physical, and socioemotional needs are often indicated.

Some two-and-a-half to three months into the work, we had our first two-way communication, and closed a circle (see p. 7). This experience introduces the child to the notion that he can have an impact on the world, that the world makes sense. The first circle may be the hardest to close, but it is worth trying for.

During one therapeutic session, Steven, while seemingly involved in aimless behavior, began to turn a wheel on an office chair. Father was trying to tune in to Steven and to avoid intrusion. I suggested to him that he turn the wheel in the other direction. Father did this; Steven turned the wheel back again, thus closing his first circle of communication. That first circle led to many additional ones.

By about six months into the work, we were up to closing two circles in a sequence, and were also addressing the issue of perseveration. Steven would often roll a toy car back and forth over and over again, or open and close a door repeatedly. Understandably, adults often respond to perseveration by trying to distract a child or order him to stop his behavior. I feel that such a response is just a one-way communication, the kind of behavior we are trying to discourage in child or adult. We tried instead to create circumstances in which the perseveration itself would become the basis for interaction. So if Steven was rolling the toy car in a perseverative way, father's hand became a bump in the road, and Steven had to get over the hand. As he was struggling to push the hand away, and even getting annoyed at the obstacle, Steven was closing some circles. If he was pushing a door back and forth, mother would get on the other side of the door and offer resistance, or start a gestural dialogue around the door. By making every perseveration the occasion for interaction, we capitalized on Steven's motivation to engage in repetitive activity, but made it more fun for him, a little more interesting, and, most important, interactive. We did this gradually, and reached "three-circle" sequences of interaction.

Around this time, a language spurt occurred. Suddenly Steven began imitating everything this parents said. This stage is typical in normally developing children, and we are wondering whether getting children with disabilities "hooked" into communication at the preverbal, gestural level may provide a necessary foundation for an imitative language spurt. At this point, Steven told his first joke. A cream-filled candy bear had splattered against the wall. Steven said, "Poor bear!" and giggled.

As we now began to see elements of shared meanings emerge, and the use of more symbols in an organized, purposeful way, we tried to build on this process. If Steven said, "Juice," his mother would ask, "How much?" and he would say "More." Mother would ask, "How much more?" and he would have to indicate with his hands a little more or a lot more. We always encouraged closing more circles, expanding his communication, sometimes pretending not to understand in order to entice Steven to point and use a word.

When Steven was about three years old, he jumped to putting two ideas together. When his infant brother bumped himself one day, Steven, highly motivated to express his concern, said "Jay hurt his head. Help him."

At this time, eighteen months into the work, we saw that Steven needed to learn to shift gears between the fantasy play of dolls and cars and "reality chit-chat," like describing what he wanted to eat. We worked on both fronts at once. Although Steven was expanding his communication with his parents, he couldn't do this with peers. His behavior would become aimless when children his age were around.

We began a very intensive program of bringing peers into Steven's home. I suggested that mother and father begin gradually, but work up to having children visit three or four times a week. The parents were reluctant: It is hard to find children who want to play with a child with a motor delay; it is easier to play with the child oneself, now that one has become skilled at this. But once a child like Steven has gained the ability to sequence ideas together and to communicate, he needs to work things out in the "real world."

Steven's course was slow, but he was able to start relating to other children and took a great interest in them. Now, in a mainstreamed preschool setting, he is able to do complicated "fourth level" categorizing of information and comparing ideas. Of his brother he now says, "Put the baby in the closet. He cries too much!"

Steven is also beginning to handle what, when, and who questions. For example, in pretend play father asked, "What happened to the car?" Steven replied, "The car is broken." "What's broken?" father asked. "The brakes," he stated. "What should we do about it?" father inquired, and Steven replied, "Let's take it to be fixed."

During a recent visit to Steven's school I observed that Steven turned as his father walked in and said, "Hi, Dad." He turned to the little girl sitting next to him at a table and said, "I'm going to Jane's house today." Father asked, "What are you going to do there?" With a big smile, Steven answered, "We're going to eat." I watched Steven navigate purposefully around the room, joining various groups of children.

Our current challenge involves helping Steven move from what is sometimes a passive, concrete approach to problem solving to a greater ability to think on his feet and direct his own communications. To do this, it is necessary to avoid overdirecting him, because when we do, we are using one-way gestural communication rather than creating opportunities for two-way communication. In playing with puzzles, for example, when Steven looks confused, it is important to avoid the temptation to say, "You can turn the piece this way or that way." Saying, "Gee, I'm not sure how this shape goes," puts the onus back on Steven.

This approach seems to be working. With the support and assistance of his parents and therapists Steven has learned not only to take the initiative but even to challenge them. (His parents have mixed feelings about his coming home from school and saying, "I want to have Joshua over to play, not Sam.") Occasionally, in his regular classroom, Steven gets into a verbal tussle with another child, arguing over who is going to be the boss of the pretend play of the moment. At the same time, Steven retains his warmth and gentleness and is developing a nice sense of humor. Most important, Steven has and conveys a sense of inner joy, purpose, and spontaneity, rather than the mechanical, rigid quality one sometimes sees in children with uneven development.

As we work with children like Steven, we must remember that parents as well as clinicians will be tempted to concentrate on teaching "splinter skills"—using personal pronouns properly, saying the alphabet, identifying colors. One must remember that a child who doesn't yet know how to relate or to interact gesturally needs first to achieve these more fundamental skills. In our experience, what keeps children with severe communication problems looking mechanical, perseverative, and unnatural is their failure to master presymbolic aspects of communication and social and emotional development. Once a child has the relationship capacity and the gestural competence of a typically developing eighteen-month-old, symbolic elements will often follow naturally. Also, once the relationship capacity and gestural system are in place, the child will be able to interact and negotiate effectively as he masters symbolic processes.

Sometimes, with the best of intentions, parents copy what they observe early interventionists doing, for example, by working on a particular skill. Therefore, it is critical for professionals to spend the time and effort to incorporate their specific techniques into spontaneous interactive sequences. Professionals need also to help parents understand and learn how to read and respond to the child's spontaneous cues. Specific techniques and approaches can then be incorporated into natural, pleasurable interactions.

Specific skills are useful to a child only when he realizes that they are, indeed, tools at his disposal, to use in mastering the environment as he sees fit. When a child is treated as the passive recipient of information, he is learning primarily to be passive and reactive, whatever specific skills he may be gaining. But when a child is inwardly motivated to explore and act upon the environment, when he learns through the reactions of other people and his interactions with them, then he is truly learning how to organize his world.

FOLLOW-UP

In Steven's most recent sessions he took another big leap. He had been pretend playing with lots of representational elaboration and differentiation and was getting into themes of triangles between him and his parents, saying, "I want Mommy for me." He playfully pushed father away and said, "Mommy is mine, not yours." When I asked why he wanted mother all for himself and didn't want father to have mother, he said, "Some questions can't be answered."

In his most recent session, he came in and took another step forward in assertiveness. He was, for the first time, directing the entire drama with both his parents and me. He was telling each of us what to say and demonstrated he had also taken another major step toward talking about feelings, such as angry feelings. At the same time, I noticed that he still liked to beat to his own drummer and preferred to tell someone what to say rather than to build on the questions one asked him, particularly questions in difficult areas like feelings. About half the time he was closing complex symbolic circles, but the other half he tended to drift off into his own world.

A good illustration of what Steven was able to do, and also of some areas where he needed further work, was when he began a drama with a "baby going in the car to the hospital." As he zoomed the baby along, he described its journey to the hospital in a very detailed way. He announced the baby would sit in the back seat and then said, "Daddy? Do you think it should be in the back seat or the front seat?" as if trying to get father to make a decision for him. When the baby arrived at the hospital he went to find the doctor. Steven played the role of father with the baby and he had the doctor "fix up the baby." Then the baby wanted to "go back home." As soon as the baby got home, it climbed into the crib and said, "I want to get out of the crib." Steven then played the part of the car driver, who had driven the baby home. He said to the baby, "You have to stay in the crib." The baby said, "No, I don't want to go in the crib." The baby would crawl out of the crib, and Steven, as the car driver, would say, "You have to go back in the crib," and eagerly put the baby back in the crib. When I inquired, "How do you feel about the baby getting out of the crib all the time?" he said, with a gleam on his face, "I am very, very angry." I asked him, "How angry?" "Just a little bit," he said, and then he switched it back to being very angry. "He has to stay in the crib," he said decisively.

As he was orchestrating this drama, he began to involve father and mother. "Dad," he said, "you say to the baby,'You have to stay in the crib.'" Father, following the boy's lead, said, "Baby, you have to stay in the crib." Then Steven told mother what to say. On her own initiative, mother asked, "Do you get mad sometimes, Steven, when I make you stay in your bed?" and Steven quietly answered, "Yes, I do." "How much?" I inquired. "Just a little," he said.

In an effort to ignore the discussion of his anger, he decided to take the baby on a trip. Again, there was an issue of whether the baby should be in the front or the back of the car. During this time, he told his parents what to say as he planned the trip. I brought him back to the theme of being angry at mother and asked him what it felt like when she made him stay in his bed. He said, "Make her (mother) stay in her crib. That's what I want to do."

Although he wasn't entirely answering my question, he was getting the gist of it. (Sometimes, he would tend to ignore these questions and I would have to ask them two or three times. Other times he would go off on a tangent if he didn't fully understand all the words.) When we tried to get into the question of whether it was scary to get mad at mother, he didn't seem to follow. "Put mommy in a crib," he reiterated, as a way of getting even with her. He then went back to telling his parents how to talk to the baby. "You stay in the crib." "Don't get out." "Say, 'I will put you in your room.' " "Say, 'You must sleep in your bed,' " and so forth.

At home, the parents reported, Steven has also been showing more assertiveness and orchestrating pretend play dramas. However, mother reported he will get upset if father doesn't follow his instructions exactly to the letter. We talked about how father might sometimes not follow Steven's exact instructions and if Steven seemed to get petulant and annoyed at father, now he might be able to verbalize his angry feelings since he had made the step of being able to do so during his session.

In summary, Steven was now more assertive, beginning to get into the world of identifying feelings, and clearly taking charge, at least in fantasy, of his family. In terms of reality-based chit-chats, however, he often tried to avoid them and turn them into a fantasy. If mother asks him what he did at school, he will say, "Pretend you went to school." Then he will tell mother what to say about what he did at school in terms of who he played with. The logic and infrastructure of such discussions are well developed. But Steven needs some practice in describing his own day in a logical fashion. While he seems to prefer to escape into fantasy, as his assertiveness increases, he should become more comfortable with being assertive in reality discussions also.

His progress has been most impressive. He is now solidly in the realm of representational differentiation and emotional thinking, and has greater emotional range in terms of assertiveness as well as gentleness and warmth.

CASE NUMBER 11: ANITA

Anita came in as a nineteen-month-old with parents who were worrying that she was "not sleeping," was "colicky, finicky, and fussy." She was "constipated and very fearful." For the last four or five months, she had had "blinking episodes" when she seemed to blink uncontrollably for a few minutes at a time, most intensely when the windshield wipers were on in the car. A neurological workup had been unrevealing and a pediatric evaluation also deemed her physically and neurologically intact.

The parents described other times when Anita would become "panicky" and seemed to be acting as though she was seeing something scary, or having something very scary happen to her. Her face would get frozen, and then she would cry uncontrollably for fifteen to thirty minutes. They also reported that she was very scared of vacuum cleaners and other loud noises. Although she was less scared of things she saw, bright lights could also upset her. When she was a little older and verbal, she described visual images of things she was looking at becoming disorganized.

She could, however, be warm and delightful, they said. As I watched the parents play with her, Anita struck me as a very intense, eager, friendly, organized, and focused nineteen-month-old. She attended both to people and things such as toys. She was very intimate with her mother and slowly began relating to the clinician. She was very demonstrative with her gestures and responded to almost every cue of her mother or father. She was already using two- or three-word sentences and beginning some pretend play. She also evidenced considerable overreactivity to sounds (alerting and looking scared when an automobile went by outside the office), to touch (pulling away from mother's or father's attempts to stroke her arms or head) and to movement in space (avoiding any rough and tumble play).

Anita was the product of a normal pregnancy and delivery and evidenced one expected physical, cognitive, and motor milestone. By three or four months she showed evidence of warm relatedness; she would smile, coo, move her arms and legs in rhythm with her mother's smiles and sounds, evidencing a deep level of warmth and affection for mother. She had been slow to warm up to father and initially seemed to be scared of him, but gradually, between four and eight months, she showed some ease in relating to him as well. Anita also found it easy to relate to her nanny, who had been with her since she was a baby; mother had returned to work part time during the baby's first six months, and was working two-thirds to full time by the time Anita was eight months old. Anita's sleep patterns at night, however, had never been established and she was continuing to wake up many times during the evening.

Between four and eight months, Anita began evidencing interactions where she could reach and point, coo, and react to mother. But if the interaction got too robust, or, for example, she was offered two things rather than one, Anita would seem to get upset, and become disorganized, crying or screaming or simply flailing her arms in all different directions. Her fine motor skills seemed advanced. She was able to pick up things with her thumb and finger a few months earlier than expected and this pattern continued into the second year of life.

Recommendations from the earlier evaluations focused on providing mother with skills to help her calm the baby, including swaddling and more regular rituals around bedtime.

During her toddler phase, Anita evidenced complex interactive behavior patterns: she could take mother on a search for toys and she used gestures and words to communicate complex needs. However, this pattern of easily being overwhelmed, remaining sensitive to loud noises and touch, as well as to bright lights and events in her environment, like the windshield wipers in the car, continued.

The various medical, allergy, and neurological workups had been essentially negative, although food elimination diets had revealed Anita's sensitivities to milk, chocolate, and sugar; these substances increased irritability and her tendency toward being overwhelmed.

It was suggested that the parents begin a pattern of care which would have a number of elements to it: (1) They would "institutionalize" the floor time to at least one half-hour session each evening, and one or two sessions on the weekends. When Anita became upset or fearful and started crying during play or interaction, they would hold her and try to use comforting techniques like holding her tightly, applying pressure on the back, arms, or legs. They had learned from an earlier occupational therapy (OT) assessment that, given her tactile sensitivity, trying to stroke her arms and legs only further irritated her. These techniques had only had limited benefit, although, from the earlier OT assessment and general principles, gross motor activity (jumping, as well as moving rapidly) had been found to help calm her. It was now felt that Anita needed to learn to calm herself down. (2) It was further suggested that her ability to represent or symbolize her discomfort through words and play rather than tears or crying would help as a self-calming device. When using a word to describe feeling fearful, Anita would say "scared, scared," and mother would reply "scared, scared." Together the rhythmic use of this sound and the word helped Anita calm down.

Sometimes Anita would rock her doll. Mother would show her that by walking around briskly and putting the dolly on her shoulder, the dolly could feel calmer (much as mother had done with Anita when she was younger). This gave Anita some gross motor activity, some active physical sense of mastery, as well as symbols for the emotions that she and the dolly were feeling together. (3) The parents would use structure and limit-setting as ways of helping Anita feel more secure. Her parents could then help her contain her affect when it became too intense or got out of control. In the past, they had more or less allowed Anita to cry loudly, and occasionally even to bite and pinch mother when she was out of control. Now, while giving extra floor time and extra support for her assertiveness, they set firm limits when Anita crossed a certain line. As we began this process, mother felt more relaxed because it didn't involve leaving Anita to cry uncontrollably on her own. During the increased floor time, the parents were working on Anita's assertiveness, as well as their emotional reactions to her "up-setness": mother's tendency to be frightened at Anita's "up-setness" and feel depressed, and father's tendency to be avoidant. All in all, they seemed to be helping Anita make progress.

Father became more involved with his little girl, and this gave her another person with whom she felt secure. Mother worked on feeling more relaxed, less intimidated, and less depressed. She tried not to see her daughter as a version of herself, but rather as a child who needed her competence and who, in spite of her tendency to cry and feel panicked, in fact had many competencies. She had ignored these considerable competencies while focusing only on Anita's vulnerabilities.

On a follow-up meeting a month later, we found that, for the first time, Anita had slept four hours straight and only woke up once during the night. Mother said,"I now feel convinced that she can make it." Mother also described the few times when she had felt comfortable in saying, "No" to Anita when she had wanted something; mother had begun to set limits. She went on to reveal that there were times she just felt she "had to get away from Anita"—a pattern she had denied earlier. She acknowledged some of her own anger at her daughter, expressing it in the form of ideas, and talked about her desire to get away and, sometimes, to never come home, especially when she was on a trip. As a result of this admission, she could relax more with Anita and actually had less of a desire to run away from her. She was also less overprotective as she had felt so guilty of her angry feelings toward Anita that she had tried to compensate by being overly attentive.

In her play, Anita began evidencing signs of greater assertiveness. She had the little dolly become the doctor who had seen the little dolly getting hurt; then this little dolly started taking care of other children. But, at times, the dolly she identified with most would also get angry and push other dolls.

In spite of her progress, Anita was still showing a great deal of difficulty around separation. When mother would leave the house in the morning, Anita still had a forty-five-minute crying spell; when mother was away for the day, Anita showed coldness and then clinginess and a lot of crying on mother's return. As we wondered together about this, the parents revealed, much to my surprise, that they almost never called Anita when they were away; in fact, mother prepared Anita for her going away by surprising her. Mother felt that by telling her daughter a few hours before her departure, Anita would only become intimidated. Mother would then have to suffer hours of crying and whining. Therefore, she employed "the surprise attack." For a child like Anita, a lack of warning is quite upsetting. It is not surprising that she reacted as she did.

We set about instituting a new pattern: not only would mother warn her a day or two ahead of an overnight trip, but she would also use dolls to dramatize where she was going. For example, a doll would fly to the place mother was going to and Anita would actually construct a scene of the room in which mother would be staying, with one doll representing mother. During her absence, there would not only be pictures of mother, but telephone calls that Anita could look forward to. While she got angry during some of the play and said, "Can't go, can't go, Mommy," this kind of preparation allowed her to feel more relaxed with separations. There would often be short bursts of anger, but then Anita would get over them and could relax with the security of her nanny. Even more importantly, without using her "surprise attacks," mother would feel less guilty about her hidden aggression. Moreover, she would be better able to nurture and woo when she returned from a trip, as well as be more soft and tender in her pattern of saying good-bye to Anita.

At twenty-seven months old, during a session at my office, Anita began showing themes of dolls being "sad." She had already mastered the dolls being assertive and angry and now, somewhat precociously, was able to show dolls feeling sad, rather than just crying uncontrollably or being disorganized. Mother was able to empathize with this. Anita also played out themes of the dolls not wanting to be touched because their skin hurt. At other times, the dolls became overwhelmed, playing out many of the scenes she herself had experienced. As her symbolic capacity became more elaborate, she was using it more and more to deal with some of her own inner tensions and anxieties.

Around this time, Anita had begun in a preschool program, and it was noted that she had become easily frightened of the other children. The teachers tended to want to leave her alone to parallel play with the other children. Mother was thinking about taking her out of the school because she seemed overwhelmed when other children would get the least bit aggressive. We consulted with her preschool teacher about developing a pattern: the teacher would engage Anita, which Anita would be only too delighted to do, and then serve as a buffer between Anita and one other child, so that Anita could get used to the somewhat unpredictable interactions of another child, but first buffered through the teacher. Simple interactions, like rolling a ball back and forth, with the teacher as the mediator, exchanging dolls, having the doll talk to the teacher, and the teacher talk to the other girl with her doll, eventually led to Anita and this one child playing together under the teacher's careful eye. Over the course of a few months, Anita began reaching out to a few other children.

This pattern of neither allowing a child to withdraw or throwing the child "into the water" too quickly often works well in a preschool program when the teacher and aides serve as a buffer. It allows the child to put a toe at a time into the world with other children, particularly a child as sensitive and bright as Anita. Anita was gradually able to do joint pretend play in interactions with other children, and began finding one child whom she could not only rely on as a "close person" but also relate to as she had to her mother.

Later in this session, Anita played out themes of the dolls saying "bye-bye." A baby doll was saying "bye-bye" to a mother doll. Interestingly, mother got anxious when this happened and tried to shift from pretend into reality; she had to be coached to let Anita play it out a bit more. Anita then turned on the windshield wiper of a toy car she was pretending to drive. In spite of her wariness, she could talk about not wanting the windshield wiper to go on.

Mother said Anita was also beginning to sleep through the night for the first time but she had also begun evidencing intermittent nightmares with monsters doing "mean things" to her. However, Anita could talk about these nightmares and, with just a little back rub from mother, often returned to sleep. In a subsequent visit, she began having the monsters scaring mother rather than her; and she then became a monster trying to scare mother. As she played out this drama, the nightmares began subsiding.

By the time Anita was three years old, she was showing unusually precocious cognitive development; she was operating at a three-and-a-half- to four-year-old level. Her pretend play and her ability for representational elaboration and even differentiation, which she had begun to evidence just before she was three years old, were similarly precocious. She had a sound understanding of how different ideas would go together or could explain what or why something happened in her play. There were scenes of animals coming into the house and going outdoors, scaring mother. Anita was the animal indirectly scaring mother, or else she was saving other children who were scared. Sometimes she would then reverse it where the doll she identified with was being scared. But she could relate to the notion that sometimes she could be in charge of the scary feelings and sometimes she felt the scary feelings were in charge of her. She could look up and organize around such discussions.

With friends at school she was becoming more assertive, less cautious, and reaching out into the group at circle time; she was no longer just holding onto the one child with whom she had become comfortable. Meanwhile, mother and father continued to do their floor time exercises with her, even though they sometimes fell into their old patterns. They discussed this between themselves and in their sessions with me, and were hopeful about making the necessary changes.

As Anita reached the age of three-and-a-half, mother got pregnant again. Anita was beginning to deal with the idea of a new baby coming along, and, fortunately, by this time, was sleeping through most nights. She was still uncomfortable in the car, but had, for the most part, become comfortable enough to go on trips even when it rained; she would turn away and look at father when the windshield wiper went on. The blinking symptom had subsided, as well as her general tendency for temper tantrums, panic, and being overly fearful. She was still highly sensitive, yet unusually bright and warm, and still more dependent than not. However, she was also capable of assertiveness and independence, with a precocious capacity for cognitive and intellectual exercises, as well as a precocious capacity for playing out things in make-believe play.

She was now becoming capable of having reality-based conversations about her friends at school, what she wanted for dinner, or whether she was "angry" because her mother had gone on a trip. For example, in one reality conversation she could say, "I want Mommy. I don't like Mommy to go away." She also could say, "I get mad" and "I'm going to throw a tantrum." When she grew frustrated, she would sometimes flail and hit herself. But at other times, she would say, "My dolly wants to hit you." She was still a little bit uncomfortable with her anger and the flailing: she was not sure whether she wanted to hit herself or someone else. She was also in the process of becoming toilet trained. She seemed to evidence a desire to "be a big girl" and learn how to use a toilet, although the sound of the toilet scared her, as did the water swirling around. However, her being able to talk about her challenges indicated she was making progress. For example, during one session, while holding an apple and looking at her mother's big tummy, she said, "I don't want my baby brother to have that apple."

Interestingly, during this time Anita could tolerate a wider range of TV programs than before including chase scenes and scenes with cartoon-level violence in them; previously, even in cartoons, there had been too much violence, and she had grown scared and wanted to turn them off.

Anita has continued to make gradual progress, becoming more comfortable with friends and more assertive in her pretend play. She is better able to label feelings, including angry feelings, and to take the active role in dealing with separation and worry. She is now awaiting, with mixed feelings, the birth of her baby brother or sister and, I hope, will continue to make progress, even with this new challenge. She is identifying herself as someone who is going to have to protect her "apples," but also as one who can feed and diaper the new baby, practicing doing both with her dolls.

This case is a good example of a child with an extreme regulatory difficulty that had constitutional–maturational components, in terms of tactile sensitivities, auditory sensitivities, and vestibular movement. There were also problems on the parents' side in terms of a depressed mother, who was overanxious and identified with Anita's vulnerability, and who acted out a lot of hidden anger at her daughter by abrupt separations or by overcontrolling interactions in the play. There were stresses on the father's side, too; he was a self-absorbed father who used lots of avoidance, even though he professed his love. He didn't provide another object of security which Anita could relate to, and he gave her the impression that he was there, but not there, when she needed him. With these constitutional–maturational vulnerabilities, on the one hand, and parental difficulties in interactional patterns, on the other hand, Anita still managed to negotiate some degree of shared attention with her parents. She experienced a deep, but overly dependent and passive sense of attachment, and had some degree of two-way communication. But toward the latter stages of two-way communication and the beginning of her representational capacities, she was evidencing lots of constrictions in her ability to deal with the more assertive side of life, the angry side of life, and themes, such as separation in the evening and during the day time. She had shown a vulnerability, in terms of the earliest self-calming and self-regulatory skills.

Anita was a little girl who wasn't moving into fuller representational elaboration or differentiation; she had some vulnerabilities in the earliest level of physiologic regulation, as well as in the more assertive and aggressive side of the two-way behavioral communication. This had resulted in a number of symptoms, including sleep disturbance, eye blinking, panic attacks, long temper tantrums, and the emergence of multiple fears, even at a young age.

The approach which best served Anita focused on strengthening her constitutional–maturational capacities and helped her to use her considerable cognitive abilities to promote coping at the representational level through pretend play. It enhanced her assertiveness, stabilizing her moods, and provided structure and limits. The parents were helped to understand their preconscious and unconscious conflicts around Anita so that they could play an active role in helping her develop new coping capacities.

CASE NUMBER 12: DANNY

Danny was a nineteen-month-old boy whom mother and father brought in because he was "hitting and biting mother and being defiant." Apparently he did this less with father and the baby-sitter. Mother came in worrying that Danny was "mad" at her. At night, he was waking once or twice and sleeping for only seven or eight hours. The aggressive hitting and biting were mother's main concerns, although Danny's waking up and general defiance were related concerns.

The developmental history included mother "not wanting a child." At forty years old, "I was given an 'ultimatum' by my husband," she said. As soon as Danny was born, however, she "fell in love with him." Mother reported that the "love affair" had persisted to such a degree that she was "always worried about undermining his confidence or denying him anything emotionally." She described the pregnancy and delivery as unremarkable. Danny was a healthy eight pound, six ounce infant, alert and able to look and listen and calm down easily; his motor developmental milestones were on schedule, sitting up by five months, crawling by seven months, walking by eleven months. He had always been gifted with fine motor skills. He was able to pick up Cheerios by eight months and hold a pencil and make scribbles by fifteen months. His language development was also on schedule, with lots of vocalizations toward the end of the first year. At the beginning of the second year, he was able to say a few words.

Mother described him as being emotionally warm and happy. He smiled by four months and was able to interact with her intentionally by seven or eight months, with gestures, as well as little peek-a-boo and other similar games. In the toddler phase, she felt, he had started to do some more complex interactions, but in this area it was obvious that he hadn't developed as fully as he might.

She went on to describe her marriage as one in which she and her husband stayed together out of "inertia." "There are lots of problems," she added, candidly.

In the first session, I observed mother and child interacting together. During their play, this nineteen-month-old presented as a very explorative child. He was all over the place, in every corner of the room, including closets. While he was exploring everything, such as picking up the telephone, he had good attention and focus and examined each item. But, there wasn't a lot of follow-through. He spent ten or fifteen seconds with one object, and then went on to the next. He was, however, very engaged with his mother, and there was the opening and closing of circles with gestures and even with vocalizations and sounds. For example, he said the word *phone* when he was exploring the telephone, and he gestured to his mother as if he wanted to dial it. His mother looked over to me and said, "He wants a real phone, to make a real call." She shook her head no-no, and he nodded his head yes-yes at her, pointing again that he wanted to dial; meanwhile he was vocalizing, babbling nicely. This reflected that they were not only engaged and could stay focused with each other, but they could exchange information two ways, with each one building on the other one. What followed was a slight battle over the phone: mother gestured for him to stop playing with the buttons and he refused. Her tentativeness was obvious here. Her voice didn't go up, on a one to ten scale, with greater degrees of assertiveness, nor did her facial gestures or motor gestures accentuate a strong desire for Danny to stop. She tended to get whiny and helpless, and then physically restrain him with a very anxious, tentative voice. He persisted and only stopped when she physically restrained him, still feeling like he had the right to do what he wanted to do. He clearly wasn't getting the range of gestural feedback he needed, given his explorative nature.

While he seemed to have shared attention, a quality of engagement, and an exchange of simple gestures, as part of two-way communication, he did not sustain really complex gestures with his mother; he closed a few circles in a row, but not ten or twenty or thirty circles in sequence as part of a complex, preverbal drama. In spite of his affective range being pleasant and warm, he did not show the range that his general level of brightness would indicate he might be capable of. He looked serious, sometimes pleased, sometimes annoyed, but didn't show great depth of joy or even anger.

When playing with me, he roamed around the room, as he had done initially with his mother, but closed fewer gestural circles. He moved away while making eye contact with me and babbled at me when I asked him what he was doing and what he was looking for or enjoying. He tended to prefer to play by himself than with me, but he made use of me to help him with something or get something. For example, he pointed at me one time when he couldn't reach inside the doll house for a car, so I got my finger in there and was able to get it out for him. He nodded and seemed to enjoy it. But he didn't get more involved with me after that.

When he played with mother again, I focused on seeing if he could elaborate a more complex dialogue with his opening and closing of circles. Unfortunately, she got impatient and overcontrolling with him instead of waiting for him to build on her responses. When she would gesture or say the equivalent of "what next?" and he didn't respond immediately, she would move in with two or three additional issues. She did not wait and give him some time to build on what she had initially tried to do.

In the second meeting, mother and Danny were gesturally very engaged and connected, just as they had been the first time. Their facial and motor gestures and vocal gestures indicated they were sharing attention and had a sense of relatedness between them. There seemed to be an increased depth to their sense of pleasure, engagement, and joyfulness, with a greater range of affect. They entered into some dialogue over whether he wanted to draw and have a pencil. Through head nods and vocalizations and pointing, they negotiated which pencil he would use and how he would hold it. He demonstrated a nice grasp of the pencil, and there were many circles closed in a row during this dialogue. He also took the initiative and related to me more this time, exchanging a ball with me and throwing it. Then he said, "Mom"—he wanted to throw the ball to her—followed by the word, "Ball." Gesturing pleasurably, he threw it to her and she threw it back to him. He smiled and said, "Ball," again, pointing to mother and throwing it to her. When I waved to him to throw it to me, he looked at me and made a "no" gesture. "Mom," he said again as he threw it to her. I asked if he would hand me the pencil. He looked at me, said, "No," again and handed it to mother. The evident progress was partly related to a suggestion between the first and second sessions that mother practice during floor time with Danny (I will go into more detail later as to the suggestion that I made).

When they returned to playing, after a brief rest, I encouraged them to try some pretend play. Mother took a puppet and began using it to bite Danny's leg. He responded by turning away. Mother did not look amused and said, "See, he doesn't like me to play with him in this way." She seemed unaware that the main theme emerging from her was somewhat intrusive and aggressive.

Later on in the play, after they had done some drawing together, Danny threw her the ball. He smiled nicely and used the word *ball* again. Mother looked up at me and said, "He just threw me the ball to get me out of his hair." I commented to her, "Maybe that's the game he wants to play—'Get out of my hair.'" She said, "Great. 'Get out my hair.' So I'll leave him alone." I said, "Why take him so literally? Sometimes, even 'Get out of my hair' and rejection can be part of a playful interaction, not to be taken literally." She said, "When should I or shouldn't I take him literally?" I empathized that this was a key question for her, that was, perhaps, hard to figure out. She then related that she found it difficult to know the difference between when he was doing something as a part of his play and when he felt strongly that way; and consequently, whether she should obey him or take his behavior with a grain of salt. So here we had a mother taking her twenty-month-old son literally and having hurt feelings. Often the "literalness" was around rejection or separation or her not being worthwhile. This was an important dynamic to discover and will be returned to momentarily. At the beginning of the session mother had said, "I almost didn't come back this session. I felt very self-conscious about your watching my play. What could you tell? I felt so unnatural. I am a good play partner." Her fear that I would think otherwise seemed to be related to the issue of "literalness."

In the third session, father came in for the first time and said, "I want Danny to be assertive and experiment with taking risks. I'm afraid if we curb his aggression too much we will inhibit him too much." Nevertheless, father was concerned that his son had bitten and gouged people in the face. "He's our first and I think what he does is abnormal," he said. "He even bashes his own head on the floor sometimes." But he insisted that he didn't want "to inhibit him and make him into a 'wimp.' " Mother than said, "And I don't want to hit him or give him mixed signals by modeling my hitting." "We disagree on strategies on how to handle him," father said. He went on to describe himself as a fairly compulsive, sloppy, disorganized, slow, methodical person, who after many years in the federal government now worked as a real estate broker, selling commercial property.

As mother described herself, she came across as a person who was chronically depressed, and felt overwhelmed and fragmented; a person who responded to the emotions of the moment—very different from father's more compulsive style which tended to shut out any emotions.

Mother felt they had lost their sense of communication and connection and confessed she was thinking of "leaving the marriage." Father felt the need for a "renewal," and added that he knew what she wanted. He had complaints about the marriage lacking sexual intimacy while she complained that he did not communicate with her; there was none of the old feeling of talking together and being together. She also had no interest in his "methodical way thinking"; and he found it hard to empathize with her emotionality.

As we talked in this session, each one dug into their own background. It became clear that early in their marriage they had empathized with each other a little more than at present. After Danny's birth, however, they had lost some of their ability to take an interest in each other's style and mode of thinking. They didn't know how to regain it. They had almost no time with each other; they never went out on Saturday evenings; and once they got Danny to bed in the evening, each almost always went his or her own way. So there was little time spent together to rekindle some of their early feelings.

With further discussion, it became clear that their difficulty in understanding each other was parallel to the difficulties with Danny. Mother couldn't understand Danny's motivation and returned to the question of how to interpret his gestures or speech. When he said, "Get away," should she interpret it literally or see it as an interactive experience? Father also realized that he had trouble understanding Danny's emotions, but not his basic messages. He wanted to know how to empathize with Danny's desire to be angry sometimes and also his desire for limits. This was confusing to a parent who liked things laid out logically and methodically. Mother's and father's problems with each other were, therefore, mirrored in their problems with interpreting Danny's behavior.

Of special interest was a comment that mother made when she said, "Why can't Danny learn to stop behaving so aggressively? Why does he feel that just because he's mad he needs to hit or bite?" I wondered aloud whether or not his being concrete in displaying feeling, his notion that a feeling leads immediately to an action, was paralleled by her sometimes feeling concrete and literal. She wondered what I meant by this. I pointed out that she was saying, both in the session with Danny and today, that sometimes when he gestured for her to leave the room she felt compelled to do it; in other words, to take his intention and immediately add a behavior to it. This was exactly the same thing that Danny was doing. He took an intention and immediately put it into behavior. If she felt the need to respond physically every time he had an intention or a wish, she was only confirming a literal and concrete way of relating to the world. I further elaborated over many sessions at appropriate moments that at this time in his life he was learning how to go from this literal or concrete behavior orientation to the world of emotional ideas, where he could now begin to contemplate wishes and intentions without feeling inclined to put them into behavior. If eventually his intention could exist as a thought or a wish, he could begin to delay and reason about it, thinking of many different behaviors from make-believe elaboration of the wish, to inhibiting the wish; to finding some substitute way of satisfying or even relinquishing the wish. All of these were options once he could elevate the wish to the level of ideas. However, if she remained concrete, she wouldn't give him this experience and help him move to this transition. I went back to the example of when they were playing together and he gestured to her to "bug off." If she could empathize with gestures and even a few simple words like "Mommy away," and have a dialogue about him wanting mommy away, he would begin to separate the wish from the deed; she would be acknowledging his want and desire, and, at the same time, empathetically stay with him by continuing to engage him. If he upped the stakes and kept pointing at her to leave, she could empathize with how much he wanted her to leave. And she could even become a little quiet for a second or two, showing some respect for his wish, but at the same time remain in the room with him, engaged. She could then try to play the drama out with dolls or to gesture around it and see how it would develop further; in other words, Danny's pointing that she should leave might only be the first step in his drama.

During this session, we also talked about the parents' need to work with each other in empathizing with each other's way of communicating. We agreed that they had to begin spending some time together, a minimum of a half-hour each night plus one evening on a weekend, so that they could have their own version of "floor time." They couldn't even begin working out the kind of difficulties they had, perhaps involving deep-seated emotional feelings and conflicts, unless there was some sense of shared attention and engagement. As they tried to comprehend one another, we could begin to see how many hurdles they ran into and the nature of those hurdles.

During the middle stages of this evaluation, we had also talked about a pattern with Danny that might prove helpful. We talked about doing half-hour floor time sessions each evening, focusing on opening and closing circles and having his gestural and preideational patterns be as elaborate as possible. He tended, at least in the first session, to be a little bit fragmented and could use help in stringing together many of these circles into a more elaborate drama; whether it be just a gestural drama around drawing or a kind of presymbolic drama with cars and trucks moving, or perhaps even moving into some early representational or symbolic play. I especially emphasized the need for floor time with father, because it was clear that Danny and mother were involved in a very intimate relationship, but one that was being acted out with power struggles and anger.

We also talked about defining—creating limits which would consist of two components. The first was lots of gestural interchanges around limits, with mother working on varying her voice pitch and her facial gestures as a prelude to using physical restraint, and even using varying degrees of physical restraint. I suggested that father do the same thing. Due to mother's anxiety and father's rather isolated affect, Danny wasn't getting a lot of emotional or gestural preverbal feedback for his challenging behaviors. This was also due to his parents' mixed feelings about his aggressive behavior—father secretly not wanting him to be a wimp and mother fearful of somehow depriving him (in part related to her original wish not to have him). They were both being more ambivalent about setting limits with him than they might be. The second component was a sort of "gentle giant" approach to limit-setting: they wouldn't let Danny's behavior get to the point where they needed to blow him out of the water with their frustration, but they would move in gradually and extremely firmly. It was clear to me that with mother Danny felt in charge and also felt her tentativenss. The tentative mother would have to become the "gentle giant" over time, and father would have to be a collaborating "gentle giant," and much more involved.

Another suggestion was to explore elimination diets to see if these would facilitate better behavioral control and also a better sleeping pattern. Different groups for the elimination diet were suggested, including dairy products, such additives as preservatives and dyes, sugars, caffeine and chocolate, peanuts and nuts, salicylate-containing fruit, and wheat products. Danny would go without each food for ten days and then be challenged with each for two or three days, or until his behavior worsened or the symptoms got worse.

We also discussed a bedtime ritual during which Danny would have the chance to spend a lot of warm cuddling time with mother and father as well as an opportunity to play quietly in bed. During these rituals they could facilitate closing circles, gestural interaction, and, if possible, some early symbolic play. Once this whole pattern was in place, they would gradually work on Danny putting himself back to sleep in the evenings: letting him cry for increasing periods of time, looking in to make sure he was safe, and weaning him from their coming to him in the middle of the night.

Both parents were made aware of their different reasons for concreteness in relating to each other and with Danny. Mother took Danny literally, not realizing that a little boy doesn't wish to be taken literally, but needs to be understood in terms of his wishes, without the wishes necessarily being granted; the wish does not have to be translated into behavior. Danny was being given the idea that wishes and behavior are the same, inhibiting his moving from the behavioral and gestural level to the ideational and representational level. In addition, father needed to work on his sense of confusion with Danny and realize that the child had two needs—to be assertive, but also to have limits. Father needed to stop using so much avoidance or isolation of affect when he felt confused.

Over the next three sessions, these same themes were expanded, in terms of the family patterns. More complex gestures and early symbolic play gradually emerged in Danny's floor time, both in the office, and at home with his parents. Father became more involved, and Danny played out aggressive themes with him, such as cars crashing. With mother, Danny, interestingly, chose themes of "leave me alone"; often when trying to draw he turned his back to her, but then flirted with her, brought her in, and then mildly rejected her. Mother, finally, recognized his feeling of wanting to be left alone. "He doesn't want me," she said. She also saw that when she stayed in there, empathizing with words like "Mommy away," and then looked sad for a second, Danny giggled. He would then pull her back in, often using a physical gesture, like touching her nose or handing her a crayon to draw with him. They experimented with a gradual approach to limits, being firmer in the "gentle giant" way but also giving lots of gestural interaction when Danny was about to throw one of his tantrums or bite or kick someone. They could see the look on his face that preceded this. If they didn't let it get to the point where he actually did kick, they could usually stop him. Whenever Danny had the glint of mischief in his eye—the beginning of a pattern in which he would usually touch another child first on the head before starting with his pinch—they would raise their voices, point their finger at him, and say "no-no." Then they would motion for him to come to them (he was reluctant to do it at first, but after being physically restrained the first couple of times, he responded to their gestures), and they would say to him, "Danny," and look at him, "Hit yes or hit no?" Danny would giggle and then say, "No hit." With this pattern, he gradually hit and bit and poked less and less frequently.

It was discovered that Danny had a slight sensitivity to salicylate-containing fruits and products with caffeine in them. He tolerated some sugar, but not chocolate. He also was mildly sensitive to a lot of dairy products eaten in the course of one day, but he could tolerate a small amount of cheese. With these dietary refinements, plus the play patterns and patterns of understanding that had been initiated, he began sleeping through the night. He also showed slightly improved capacities for concentration, although this was fairly good in the first place.

The work with Danny and his family continues in short-term treatment where the parents are seen once every four to eight weeks (for about eight sessions) to consolidate the gains they have already begun to make. While Danny's behavior continues to improve, the parents' own marital relationship is moving much more slowly. Mother is still not sure whether she can recapture the chemistry with father, and father still feels he would like to try. They are spending a little more time with each other, and mother shows some more pleasant affect in father's presence—a little more smiling and more flirtatious glances. How well they can work things out remains to be seen. Their progress will need to be monitored over the next few months. They may still need to be referred for some couples work directly. Most importantly, however, Danny is making nice progress. He is emerging as a confident, outgoing, warm, and, most of the time, respectful child.

CASE NUMBER 13: TOM

Tom was a very verbal, two-and-three-quarter-year-old boy who had begun potty training a few months earlier. Originally, he had been having a bowel movement once a day in his diaper, but ever since beginning potty training he had started withholding his bowel movements. He was able to say, "Diaper," and then "No." He was withholding for two to three days at a time. The parents came in quite concerned about this pattern. They were giving him a chocolate-flavored mineral oil (Neocotail) to help him with his bowel movements, but it wasn't working.

Pregnancy and delivery were uneventful and had progressed normally. He was a healthy eight pound, eight ounce baby, who was alert and responsive in the weeks following his birth. He was a little overly sensitive to commotion and could get irritable, but was comfortable in being touched and being moved up and down in space. As a baby, his motor tone had been good as had his motor planning in terms of getting his hand to his mouth. He had enjoyed looking at his parents and responded by turning toward their voices. As mentioned, he seemed a little sensitive to commotion and tended to wake up three or four times a night, but responded very well to being left to cry for five or ten minutes. By six months of age, Tom was sleeping through the night. He had been breast-fed until he was eight months old, supplemented with soy-based formula. His motor milestones were all on schedule, as were his emotional milestones, although he tended toward being a little passive and negative rather than fully assertive. For example, at four months, he would wait for his parents to woo him, rather than being outgoing in his wooing. At eight months, in the two-way communication stage, he tended to be more reactive and even negative, rather than initiating assertively. If he wanted to be picked up he was more likely to cry than to reach out. But he entered into two-way communication with peek-a-boo games and the like.

Tom had always been a fussy eater. He was selective about his foods and, as a toddler, liked only peanut butter and jelly and certain kinds of fruits. He wouldn't try new foods, although there was no evidence of sensitivity to touch around or in the mouth, or other evidence of tactile sensitivity. At about eighteen months, he frequently woke up with either nightmares or night terrors, but could calm down with his parents' support. They reported that the negativism of his early toddler months gave way to anger if he didn't get his own way. Temper tantrums between eighteen and twenty-four months were not uncharacteristic, but he could be calmed down rather easily. He had an older brother who tended to regard him as a "pest," but he was able to be generally supportive with Tom.

The parents said that Tom also liked to play independently, and at times could be daring, jumping off a chair. He also had a blanket that he had liked to hold since his toddler years. Mother felt he tended to cling to her and be whiny at times. But he also liked going places with father, such as to work. On a typical day, he would play Legos with father, and do pretend play, such as being a waiter taking orders from his mother or father. Then he would bring them over cars or trucks that he wanted to play with. Sometimes he would make these cars or trucks crash.

His parents thought that Tom was very verbal and understood complex directions, but that he was tense and high strung. They also felt that he was creative. Although Tom was quite verbal for his age, it was clear that he was not adept at finding his bearings in a new setting or understanding exactly where he was. Interestingly, he got frightened when seeing clowns or people who looked strange, and he didn't like cartoon monsters. The parents found him to be an interesting blend of daredevilry, where he would jump off a chair, and being frightened of new experiences. Although he seemed verbally gifted, at times he seemed quite cautious in this respect.

In terms of family patterns, the parents related that they had lots of "pressure and tension." Mother saw herself as a tense person. She looked tense, too. Father was gone much of the time and she felt overloaded and overworked. She felt that she was probably getting overly tense about Tom's bowel movements. Her overall style with him, she admitted, was nagging and perhaps anxious. She was always making sure he was "doing the right thing."

They played with Legos, building tracks and a tunnel; then they took luggage onto a train and put people on the track and the train. There was some concern about the train running over the people and crashing. It ended up with the child crashing the train and laughing. They built towers and knocked them down. Then a fire truck crashed into a tower and people on top of the tower fell off. Father enjoyed the play as much as Tom.

The play with mother had similar themes. Trucks crashed and towers came tumbling down. But mother was more intrusive and interfering, trying to get him to switch to something nicer. She would say, "Why do the trains want to crash?" She was worried about the people being hurt. He seemed to ignore her concern for the hurt, and gleefully had people crash. She was less in tune with him than father was, in terms of encouraging the themes to go in the direction Tom wanted them to go.

The little boy talked about school and playing cars and trains with a friend of his named Teddy. He mentioned playing Ghostbusters with another friend, and was interested in good guys and bad guys. His teacher reported that he got along fine with his friends. He was not an instigator and could defend himself well when other children tried to take things that were his.

At the end of this first session, we talked about both parents spending a half-hour each day doing floor time. Mother would especially work on trying to follow Tom's lead and become more comfortable with his assertiveness and sense of mastery. She would try to support his assertive and aggressive instincts rather than interfere with them. I suggested that, since he was very verbal, they could have some problem-solving chit-chats; he could describe what happened at school, as well as talk about how he felt about the potty and going to the potty. Another possibility was to encourage prolonged times on the toilet. They could help him relax on the toilet by letting him talk about activities that he had done with the parents, such as the good guys and bad guys, or the trucks crashing; even his fantasies. Reading him a book might also help relax him while on the toilet. We also spoke about setting firm but broad limits, and not trying to overcontrol or overprotect him; letting him take the lead and be more assertive and aggressive, but setting firm limits when he crossed a line, which he didn't seem to do very often.

Father, who seemed natural with Tom, was quite busy. We talked about him making sure he had more time with his boy each day; he seemed to find supporting Tom's assertive and representational side easier than mother, who would have to work at it a little harder.

Tom's diet was of some concern, and I suggested supplementing the mineral oil with lots of fluid and also lots of fiber. Vegetable and fruit fiber and, perhaps, some grain fiber would provide good internal sensations and stimulation. The resultant bulky, moist feces would help stimulate his desire to go to the bathroom. This, coupled with his greater comfort with assertiveness and his relaxation in the bathroom, would help him be more relaxed in his potty training.

The program was put in effet and when the parents came in a month later, they reported Tom had seen another child put a diaper on and asked for one. He decided to make "poo-poo's" in the diaper after hopping around for five minutes. He was able to say, "Poop," and mother would put the diaper on, then he would make a "poop." He had also begun talking about a big rocketship. If he went to the potty, which he would do on occasion, he'd talk about the rocketship coming out from inside him.

Mother felt that he was sometimes able to relax on the toilet. She was growing more confident at reading him a story, or letting him use his considerable language skills to verbalize and fantasize while on the potty. When he did go, he was able to say to her, "Are you happy I went? Is Daddy happy?" He was also able to say, "Tummy ache got better when I go to the potty," or "I go in my diaper." He had always comfortably urinated in the potty, and this continued.

We talked about mother allowing him flexibility to use the diaper. At times she would encourage Tom to wear the diaper and go on the potty simultaneously. If he felt like using the diaper rather than the potty, he could; but he might sit in the bathroom on the potty with the diaper beside him. He readily agreed to this compromise and from his look thought it was a neat idea. Now he had a choice: he sometimes went in the diaper on the potty and sometimes he decided to "have the rocketship come out" and go in the potty itself.

On a follow-up session, the parents reported that he was beginning to take an interest in a "girl friend" at school and he actually tried to kiss her. When mother asked, "Did you try to hold Emily's hand?" he said, "I kissed her. But then she got away." He was also becoming more assertive, not just defending his turf at school, but taking more of a lead role in his play with other children. The teachers had reported a greater sense of confidence, too: in nursery school, where he had been particularly afraid to either use a diaper or go to the potty, he began asking for a diaper and sitting on the potty when he had to go. He was also sharing better with other children at school, being less negative and needing to get his own way less; his eating habits got broader; he was even able to say he was sorry, rather than being stubborn; and he started responding better to limits with his parents without arguing as much. Mother reported that he was even getting more tender and loving with her.

When I observed Tom on his next visit, he seemed much more relaxed in terms of his play with his parents, looking happier, with a deeper sense of pleasure. His pretend was more elaborate: he put a family of men and women in a house, and played out a drama with them, they fed each other, went to sleep, and had some "fights with each other." He also related to me more comfortably and clearly, and when we talked about potty training and about going to the bathroom, he was able to tell me, "Afraid bottom dropping out." He repeated this phrase a number of times when we talked about what made him not like going to the toilet.

We continued Tom's program of floor time with mother and father, and chit-chat time with a problem-solving focus. They encouraged him to talk in both the problem-solving time, as well as floor time dramas, about some of his fears of losing things in the potty and losing things in general. We talked about continuing his high fiber, high fluid diet and some of the mineral oil.

Over the next month-and-a-half, he gradually shifted from using a diaper three-quarters of the time, to using it half the time, and then only a third of the time. Finally, he began going in the potty regularly all the time and having nice solid bowel movements once a day. As he was sitting on the potty during one of these more recent times, he stopped talking about the rocketship coming out and began talking, instead, about how nice and big his "doody" was; he looked at the "doody" with some pride after he finished. When I saw him in a follow-up visit he pointed to his bottom, he said, "Bottom here." He then started building some towers with obvious pride and pleasure.

His relationships with other children continued to get even better, with more cooperation. Both parents were sharing in the pleasure of Tom's growing assertiveness. They continued floor time and problem-solving time, helping him use his representational capacity for more elaborate access to his many feelings.

As he continued to develop, his maturation and psychological growth progressed nicely. He was gaining good gross and fine motor skills, good language and cognitive development, and fine interpersonal and emotional relationships.

In formulating this case, it appeared that Tom was basically a constitutionally and maturationally sound child who had progressed through the normal expected intellectual, motor, and cognitive milestones. But he was running into some difficulty, during the phase of representational elaboration, with comfortably learning the self-care involved in potty training. His withholding seemed to be related, in part, to the fear of losing something. It could be speculated that he was afraid of losing a part of his body, which could be valued and treasured for its power (e.g., his rocketship); a fear that seemed partially related to mother's very anxious and undermining attitude toward his growing assertiveness. It may also have been related to his own maturational pattern and cognitive style: he was more gifted verbally than he was in visual–spatial terms (he could not negotiate his way around an unfamiliar house, while at the same time his ability with words was excellent). In addition, his tendency to become anxious over clown faces and visual configurations that were not familiar to him can often be seen in children who may be lagging in their visual–spatial integration abilities in comparison to their considerable verbal abilities. Children who lag in visual–spatial integration seem to have a harder time putting all the pieces together. They are better at seeing the details, the trees, than the whole, the forest. Their ability to organize an integrated representation of their bodies may therefore be more difficult, especially in relationship to parts of their bodies invested with conflicted feelings (in this case assertiveness and aggression).

Another contributing factor was father's persistent absence. While he was naturally supportive of his son's ability to represent his assertiveness, he was not as available as he could be. At this critical age, the child's close relationship with mother often needs a balance from father, particularly if mother is uncomfortable with growing assertiveness.

Had this case continued for longer, we might have learned about mother's fantasies particular to Tom's bowel training and whether there were unique anxieties relating to this. Nonetheless, the family shift in focus toward supporting his assertiveness helped him begin working through some of the issues we have discussed. We saw him progress from consternation at losing things from his body, to taking pride in what he produced from his body. As this was happening, we observed him becoming more comfortable with representing the assertive side of his life. He seemed to grow, generally, in terms of being less negative and less withholding with his friends, teachers, and parents. Also, on the physiologic side, a high fiber diet with lots of fluid seemed to support his developmental thrust by giving him good internal signals for learning this aspect of self-care.

In summary, Tom's initial symptom, relating to withholding his bowels, served as an opportunity for supporting general growth and helping him learn to represent the assertive side of life.

CASE NUMBER 14: LEAH

When Leah first came to see me, she was twenty-five months old. Mother had been thinking of an evaluation for some time because of a history of Leah being negative and "overly sensitive," and in the last few months, since her little brother's birth, this behavior had increased. She was waking three and four times during the night and didn't seem "happy" during the day. She would walk around with a solemn look on her face and was often "testing," mother said, as if she was "trying to get me to yell at her. I always feel like I am doing something wrong and can never get her to be happy," she added. For example, on a recent trip to the beach, Leah was happy for ten minutes, but then in tears over something. Either the sand castle wasn't quite right, or the food didn't taste right, or mother took too long to get to her, and so on. She was described as strong willed, wanting it "now" or even "a few minutes before she even asked for it."

Mother worked part time (third to half time) and had been in therapy, and father was a busy lawyer who had also been in therapy.

Mother also noted that Leah was very cold to her and wasn't at all "warm" to the new baby; she said that Leah could be happy and outgoing sometimes, but would often ignore her when she returned home from her part-time work.

At other times, she felt Leah evidenced gifted intelligence, was verbal for a two-year-old, and could be happy when playing with a little friend. She loved to be read to and could really enjoy herself in the sandbox. Occasionally, mother and daughter had nice walks together.

The developmental history included a normal pregnancy and delivery and Leah was a seven pound, four ounce healthy infant. Mother stopped working entirely for the first five months. When she described the family pattern during that first year, however, mother revealed that father had a drinking problem, along with a temper, and there had been fighting between them. Leah, as a baby, was described as physically healthy but easily irritable and colicky, sensitive to loud noises. To be comfortable, she had needed to be held "in just the right way." Mother put great efforts into trying to comfort her, but often felt unrewarded for her efforts, as if she wasn't doing things right. Nevertheless, Leah started sleeping for longer periods of time, and by the time she was three months old was only waking up twice during the night. She was able to be attentive to sights and sounds, but tended to get easily overstimulated. Then it could take as long as a half-hour, involving lots of rocking and holding, to settle her down. By three to four months old, Leah was evidencing a warm, engaging smile, but was easily distracted by noises. She was also described, at four to ten months, as assertive, with lots of fussy times. She could be demanding, but quite intentional in her demandingness, pointing at the toy she wanted or making loud noises, until mother gave her the thing that appeared to be on her mind.

Her development between twelve and twenty-four months was as follows: she learned to walk at fourteen months, and had a two-month period of great joy and pleasure as she walked around controlling her own mobility and discovering the house. Mother felt her daughter often walked away from her, rather than toward her. But they did have "moments" when they could be happy together; she might show Leah pictures from a book or comfort her by sitting her on her lap as they looked at pictures. However, by sixteen months, they had entered what mother described as "the beginning of our negative phase." She was pregnant and tired. Her husband, she felt, fought with her more when she got tired and was less available to him. His drinking got worse as she attended to Leah; and as she grew more tired from being pregnant, he became even more tempestuous. His drinking did not worsen during the later stages of her pregnancy, however.

The family relationships were described by each parent in the following manner. Father saw himself as a person who controlled himself. He tended to be passive and avoid confrontation or conflict, but would drink when he got anxious. He felt he was "happy" to see his daughter, and she was often happy to see him, but if she was demanding, he would withdraw and get annoyed. "I don't have much tolerance for strong emotion," he confessed. Mother described her daughter's demandingness as making her feel "empty inside," as if she were "not doing something right." She said that she vacillated between "frenetically trying to do something to make her happy, and becoming controlling and annoyed with her. "I get short tempered," she said. "As I do this, I tend to feel emotionally cold inside and then feel guilty for not feeling a lot of love."

I had a chance to observe mother and Leah playing together. Mother was somewhat tense and there was very little sense of emotion coming from her during the play; her gestures and affect expressions seemed empty. She went through the motions, but it gave the clinician the feeling of being in a room with people who had a very mechanical quality to them. Leah looked at the clinician as much as she looked at mother, but with no real flirtation or joy. The little girl, for her part, was involved in pretend play and was obviously a bright and verbal youngster. She could talk in three- or four-word sentences. She was, nonetheless, very solemn looking and marching more to her own drummer than interacting with mother. At first, she made a little doll go down the slide. Mother, somewhat blandly, asked her "What happens next?" Leah looked back at mother, obviously gesturing her understanding of mother's comment. But she didn't follow up with any verbal comment of her own; she looked back to her doll and the slide and then got hold of a big house and said, "I want to put the people in there."

Leah continued to "tune out" her mother. Meanwhile, mother would let long periods of silence go by, and looked puzzled and somewhat paralyzed with anxiety. Only after a long pause did she try to comment constructively on what her daughter wanted to do with the people in the house. By that time, Leah was already beginning to look around the room for additional toys to bring into her emerging drama. She continued her methodical, vaguely organized play. She occasionally used elaborate descriptions, such as, "Now I am going to have the dolls try to find a horsey for them to ride," while she looked around for an animal. Mother looked on passively in silence, neither jumping to help her find a horsey nor showing interest in what the dolls were going to do on the horsey. After a pregnant pause of about ten seconds, she tried to follow Leah's lead by saying, "Gee, do they want other animals, too?" In this, too, Leah ignored mother, looking at her with a solemn angry look, as though to say, "Too little, too late." This more or less characterized their play during the initial playroom session.

When father got down on the floor and started playing with Leah, his style was more intrusive, rather than avoidant or laid-back. As father started manipulating Leah's dolls and the horses and other animals she had gathered together for the dolls to ride, he said, "Oh, I think they are going to go here and I think they are going to go there." He had an enthusiastic, but somewhat aggressive look on his face, and his play had a somewhat anxious, clumsy, intrusive quality. With clear annoyance in her voice, Leah said, "They are my toys!" She pulled his fingers off the toys with her little hands. The possessiveness was quite clear. Father, then, jumped back in, and the next ten minutes were characterized by Leah turning her back to him. As she tried to push him away, father tried to push himself into her play. They actually had quite a lot of interactions around this theme of him intruding and her trying to turn him off. As father got discouraged, interestingly he became more active, and then attempted to engage her in some "horsing around." He tried to pick her up, throw her in the air, and have her jump on his tummy. Screeching angrily, she squirmed away from him, and got back to her toys. He was not able to get into a comfortable rhythm with her and vacillated between attempting physical play, being overintrusive, and occasionally having a few minutes when he just observed and seemed to regroup. For the most part, though, he was involved and Leah was involved with him, although in a negative and avoidant way. They communicated with each other in the sense that she responded to him clearly and logically, and he responded to her cues by trying to take over.

When I got down on the floor and played with Leah, I noted that she was quite capable of engaging in contingent and reciprocal interactions. I joined her theme of trying to get the different dolls on the horses, and she seemed to take charge of the drama, but accepted my assistance. As I handed her dolls, she looked at me, and occasionally nodded her head. When I asked, "What next?" she would explain that the horses were going to go over here, or that this doll was going to go on the horse next, or this doll was going on the horse after that. Her verbal, elaborative productions were responsive to my simple comments or questions; her gestures were elaborating on mine and the interactions were clearly related to one another. She was able to operate on a simple pretend level without any "buts" or "becauses" or elaborate themes; and the themes revolved mostly around getting the dolls on the horses and seeing where the horses would go. At the same time as this representational interaction between the two of us, there was also a quality of mutual engagement and a sense of relatedness. Her ability to control and limit impulses was quite good; even when she got frustrated with the doll not being able to do what she wanted it to do, she didn't bang or throw the horse, but simply tried persistently again. Her mood was even during these efforts. She was able to organize a number of units of representation or make-believe into a reasonably long sequence, such as staying with the theme of the dolls and horses. At the same time, however, her emotional range was limited to looking serious and sad. She occasionally showed some annoyance when the horse or the doll wouldn't do what she wanted it to do, but there were no signs of pleasure or joy, or of her broadening her themes out of simply trying to get the dolls to ride the horses where they wanted to go. Her play never broadened into themes of curiosity, or themes of exploration, or even themes of anger. There were certainly no emerging themes of warmth and closeness, other than her general sense of warm relatedness.

In short, she was an organized, intentional youngster with complex behavior. She could use short, intentional sentences. She was engaged with me and her parents, and capable of beginning representational play and interactions. But she was very serious and sad looking, and lacked pleasure, joy, and spontaneity.

Leah's parents had obvious difficulty engaging her in a broad range of representational and prerepresentational involvements. Mother's quality of emptiness and the lack of joyful affect between herself and her daughter, as well as mother's tendency for long pauses, were most striking. They were consistent with my observations of many depressed mothers—the rhythm of their affect, cues, and gestures literally leaves the youngster feeling empty. In contrast, the interactions with father were characterized by his intrusive style; the child was constantly fending him off. Both parents could be logical and organized, but one seemed to be leaving Leah empty while the other seemed to be trying to control and overload her.

She could focus, relate, interact intentionally and use representational modes to organize experience. But her mood was sober, her affect range limited (little joy or spontaneity). Her thematic overtures were around issues of controlling the action, making sure the dolls and people were doing things her way.

Also relevant to this case was the dietary history. There was a history of a sensitivity to the peanut and nut family, resulting in rashes and irritability. We did elimination diets to look at certain food groups, including dairy, sugar, chemical additives and preservatives, salicylate-containing fruit, wheat, and yeast products and eggs. Leah became somewhat irritable when challenged with sugar and chemicals, grape and apple juice (two of the salicylate-containing fruit juices), as well as with the nut family. There was also a slight sensitivity to dairy products, but in a questionable area.

Leah's basic personality and ego functions were at an age-appropriate level in terms of her ability to relate and engage, use gestures intentionally, and use early representational modes consistent with her age to communicate. She was able to control her impulses and to concentrate and maintain a relatively even mood, at least under unchallenging situations. At the same time, there were indications of a rather marked constriction in the range of affect she had available to her: she evidenced no pleasure, showed no spontaneity, and even very little creativity in her play. Her history indicated moodiness and lability of affect, and poor frustration tolerance in many situations from early infancy. None of these were observed in the sessions, but they did seem to relate historically to her overreactivity to sounds and to aspects of touch. I should also mention that during the playroom evaluation, it was evident that her gross motor coordination was age appropriate, but she was about two months behind on fine motor coordination.

It appeared, therefore, that she showed constrictions in the flexibility of her age-appropriate personality functions with a narrowing of the range, particularly in the areas of pleasure, joy, and spontaneity. In addition, she had difficulty handling frustration and a tendency toward greater lability in her moods. This would fit into the diagnostic category of a regulatory disorder and also the category of constriction in the range of age-appropriate functions.

The treatment approach developed for this family was to first see if working with Leah and her family in a relatively infrequent way, to help them develop interaction patterns at home (which could facilitate more age-appropriate flexibility), would do the trick. It was decided that we would meet once a month for a series of eight to twelve sessions to help the family institute at home the elements of the following program:

1. Each parent would do a minimum of a half-hour a day of floor time, following Leah's lead.

2. During the floor time, mother would work on "filling up Leah more," in terms of the rhythm and pace of her gestures and the relaxed, joyful affect she would try to mobilize. This was explored during the interpretive early sessions with mother. She became aware, for example, that her tending to feel anxious led her to feel "like a bad person inside"; and when she felt "like a bad person," she withdrew and became quiet for fear that only more "badness" would come out. With just this awareness she was able to enter a more relaxed, chatty rhythm

with Leah and say things like, "Oh, what are we going to do next?" and "Oh, look what you have done here." Her voice took on a slightly more enthusiastic and supportive quality. This was not easy for her to do. But over a series of three sessions, the pace and rhythm of her voice improved, as did the support of her husband; and gradually her quality of relatedness with Leah improved, too.

3. Father, helped by his floor time exercises done during the session, would work on becoming more respectful of Leah. He learned to wait for her to take the lead. He no longer jumped in too fast or too hard as if trying to take over, which would result in his getting irritable and even more aggressive. Although his style remained a little bit on the aggressive side, Leah didn't have to turn her back on him or push him away; he learned to take her first cue, then pull back and be silent for a few seconds while he watched what she wanted to do.

4. During floor time, both parents had an initial goal—to see if they could march to Leah's drum for a half-hour during each day. A secondary goal was to focus on two issues: help her increase the complexity of her play so that there would be many subthemes and subplots, rather than just one drama; and help her expand (expound) with more joy, creativity and assertiveness, as opposed to negativism, soberness, and seriousness. It was expected that as she experimented with assertiveness and joy, she would learn a better coping style when she was frustrated in other situations.

In general, I have noticed that children who are frustrated easily are often also frightened of more constructive assertiveness. They fear that it may lead to separation or character attack. By engaging in floor time where they practice their assertiveness under supportive circumstances, they become more comfortable with an assertive attitude toward the world; it helps them try to change the situations which frustrate them, rather than crying inconsolably or becoming disorganized in their behavior or affect.

One goal, therefore, was for Leah to engage with her parents in daily floor time. Here the range of personality functions could be explored and experienced, with a special eye toward joy, pleasure, creativity, and increased assertiveness. Mother and father were both aware of their own characterologic tendencies in their interactions with Leah. Leah's solemn, controlling style tended to instill in each of them their characteristic patterns—mother felt empty and cautious (like "a bad person") and father felt like he had to "push his way in." Both of them could relate their reactions back to their own childhood patterns, which won't be explored here.

During the sessions in my office, I would work with Leah's parents at trying to help Leah experience an emotional theme that she was perhaps avoiding. An early example was when Leah, in spite of a more supportive attitude on the part of her parents, would cautiously repeat the same kind of representational theme. One day, when she was only willing to line all the dolls up repeatedly in the house to get them ready for bed, I helped Leah experience some greater broadness in her range. I made her wonder about the importance of ensuring that every little doll was in exactly the right position next to the other ones. She chided me by saying, "Don't touch that." I said, "You mean touching them wouldn't be what you want." She nodded her head yes. I empathized that she had good reason for not wanting people to touch each other. Then she showed one doll biting another doll, and I empathized that it could hurt sometimes when people touch too much. The touching was obviously her way of representing the more general issues of joy and pleasure. As she went back and forth between touching and hurting, she showed her first smile and giggled. When she had one of the dolls touch the other one, I said, "Oops! Look what happened!" She giggled as though she hadn't meant to make that mistake. I then made the dolls almost touch each other and then finally touch each other a tiny little bit. Leah gave another little giggle.

The parents were watching this play and got a sense of the equilibrium that Leah was operating under. On the one hand, she wanted everything orderly and controlled, and on the other hand she really wanted to experiment with pleasure; but she was scared that pleasure and touching could hurt or lead to aggression. (Part of this was related to her own tactile sensitivity.) Touch, for her, had been physiologically difficult. She had been sensitive to touch since birth, and would still become difficult about being bathed, having her hair brushed, and changing her clothes. At the same time, the touching had taken on some family meanings. Father was clearly quite intrusive and aggressive and she may have been, for good reason, frightened of too much closeness with him. Mother, with her tendency to become removed and somewhat depressed and feel bad and hollow, may have (and this is speculative) responded to some intimacy by pulling back. Although she couldn't recall this second pattern having happened with Leah, mother did recall it happening with her husband. At times when his intimacy would frighten her, she would pull away.

In any event, we could speculate not only about Leah's tactile sensitivity, but also about how this would make her physically sensitive to touch. This extra physical sensitivity could then take on family meanings, based on some of the family characteristics. Although it wasn't critical to explore these patterns with Leah, for she could not have understood them, the parents found it valuable to at least speculate about a few of them. What was significant to Leah, however, was the association between touching and pain, which she could comprehend. It was valuable for her to play that out a number of times. Then, for the first time, she began to show some real pleasure during her sessions with me. The parents were relieved to see that Leah could be helped to become more flexible. As she became more joyful, they relaxed considerably and a new equilibrium began to emerge. Initially, she showed little islands of joy and pleasure just once or twice, both in the office sessions and at home. The parents came to value them. They appreciated how much more relaxed they felt, particularly as they gained insight into their own patterns.

As Leah approached two-and-a-half years old, the parents were encouraged to begin doing problem-solving time as well as floor time. Given their daughter's unusual verbal abilities, the problem-solving time involved short logical dialogues around issues of the day—whom she played with, what she liked or didn't like. In their explorations, they would try to draw out of her what made her upset or mad. Leah surprised them in being able to say, "No like baby brother Paul," or "No like this food," or "No like hair brushed." The parents tried to respect her wishes. Certainly, they wouldn't always leave Paul whenever Leah said, "No like Paul." But they would try to let her learn to brush her own hair, change her own clothes, and respect her need to take a long, long time to do these things.

In addition to the floor time and problem-solving time occurring each day, the parents also improved their ability to deal with limits. They used problem-solving discussions to help Leah anticipate the times in which she got overly negative or refused to do things; then they would outline with her the possible punishments for being negative (she was rarely overtly aggressive). For example, she would sometimes refuse to go to bed or even go upstairs, forcing her parents to carry her; or she would refuse to come to the table, or clean up her toys. During the problem-solving discussions, Leah was encouraged to explain why she behaved in certain ways; but her parents also reviewed with her what would then happen, such as no cartoons, no special dessert, and so on. Because Leah was precociously verbal and had good comprehension, she could understand some of these connections. The parents were fairly firm with her limits, always remembering the basic principle of increasing floor time while increasing limits. We also focused on the parents' own tendencies, and explored their childhood roots to some degree. We looked at how these tendencies expressed themselves in the marriage.

Mother decided to follow a diet pattern in which she eliminated the same foods that Leah was sensitive to. She became quite compulsive. For example, she avoided all chemicals, additives, and preservatives, including some of the salicylate-containing fruit that she noticed Leah as sensitive to; tended to keep questionable dairy products to a moderate level, rather than using a lot of dairy products; eliminated peanuts entirely from her diet; and allowed sugar only on special occasions. She noticed that both she and Leah became more irritable on these special occasions, but by anticipating them she and Leah could both cope.

Over a period of six months, through this pattern involvement, Leah became increasingly relaxed and pleasurable, and mother came to enjoy Leah more. Leah's sleep patterns improved so that she was sleeping through the night. She was more assertive and comfortable with peers; and her play and general relationships took on more broad-based themes of joy, laughter, as well as serious, orderly play. In a recent session Leah came in and developed a drama with a series of ponies. She lined them up in an orderly way, but then they went on an adventure where they tried to find a special magical pony who could do special tricks. This magical pony could jump upside down and be thrown in the air. As Leah was developing the drama, mother was supporting her with a "more filling up" kind of rhythm and pace. Leah threw the little pony in the air and giggled and laughed. She made it do many tricks. She, too, moved around the room in a more flexible way, evidencing many tricks, just like her "magical pony."

In this case, the treatment was carried out with a limited number of sessions. I saw the parents and Leah only once a month, because the parents were able to carry out the program at home. In other cases, if the parents' ability is more limited, either because of lack of flexibility of their personalities or other circumstances, more sessions in the office are needed. Leah's father has become much more flexible with her. Nevertheless, he still gets irritable with mother and there continue to be some marital tensions. Overall, while Leah is doing better with each of her parents than they are doing with each other, their greater ability for self-observation is making it possible for them to support Leah's continuing emotional growth.

CASE NUMBER 15: RYAN

When Ryan's parents first brought him to see me, he was twenty-two months old. "He refuses to eat, he's hyperactive, and he won't sleep for more than an hour or two at a time," mother, a busy journalist, complained. "I am depressed and father is frustrated and fed up." Added to her concerns was her fear that Ryan was very small for his age and not gaining adequate weight.

In her overview of the situation, mother quickly reported that Ryan had had lots of difficulties as a very young baby. He was the product of a planned, full-term, unremarkable pregnancy. He was vaginal delivery and weighed eight pounds, six ounces at birth. In the hospital, he threw up most of the food that he was fed and was fussy and irritable all the time. He showed no ability for looking at his parents, listening to their voices, or calming down with holding or stroking. When they noticed that the vomiting was clearly projectile, a diagnosis of malrotation of the intestines was made and Ryan had emergency surgery. Fortunately, the bowel was not infarcted, but the baby spent the next eight weeks at the hospital. As soon as he went home, he became reobstructed and was back in the hospital for two more weeks.

When Ryan came home for the second time, he only slept for an hour at a time and he refused to feed, keeping his mouth closed. The parents saw the G.I. person at the local children's hospital who determined that Ryan was allergic to milk and soy. He was put on Nutramagin, but took only twenty ounces a day, with a little cereal added. He never slept through the night, and as he got closer to four or five months old, he slept for two or three hours, stayed up for a half-hour, and then went back to sleep. All through his infancy, he remained highly distractible and irritable.

When Ryan was fifteen months old, mother took him to an infant clinic at the local hospital, where a clinician suggested trying a small dose of Ritalin, about 1½ milligrams (¼ of a 5 milligram pill); he developed erythema multiformae in reaction to the Ritalin. Furthermore, at that point he was also found to be sensitive to milk, having developed asthmatic type coughing, and also to soy; with eggs he developed severe diarrhea; with dairy products, hives.

At fifteen months, Ryan weighed only eighteen pounds. Not only was his weight gain inadequate, but he also had difficulties with his attention span and activity level. It was also noted that he did not enjoy eating. He would try to get out of his chair and scream, reaching for whatever his mother was eating and not what he was eating; he would finger his food, but not put it in his mouth.

Because of Ryan's problems in sleeping, eating, distractibility, irritability, and the parents' overall level of distress, the infant clinic suggested that the baby be admitted for six to eight weeks on the inpatient psychiatric unit. Mother was horrified by this suggestion. Intuitively, it didn't make sense to her to be separated from her baby at the time when he was in such dire straits. She felt that if there were problems between the two of them, they should learn to work it out; she doubted that she could be the sole culprit behind all his difficulties. She, therefore, decided not to work with that clinic any further and sought additional consultation elsewhere.

Her main concerns at that time were Ryan's sleeping and eating patterns. "He won't sit down," she said. "But when he does, he will take three or four bites of something and then gets up and two minutes later may sit down again." His general activity level and irritability level were also concerns. She felt that she was busy all the time just trying to feed him. At the same time, she seemed very tentative toward her child and would spend much of the day running back and forth between her high-pressure job and her child. In spite of working with the different help she had for Ryan, she kept wondering whether she should "just quit [her] job or just work part time."

Mother was close to tears and feeling understandably overwhelmed. Nonetheless, she showed considerable dedication and the capacity for "staying in there" under dire circumstances.

Father looked calmer, but a little more impersonal. He was less involved with Ryan, but he was organized. He seemed concerned, but a little aloof from the day-to-day realities of his son and wife.

When I saw Ryan he was a small, twenty-two-month-old with an unenthusiastic sense of relatedness. He appeared organized and connected to mother and to me, the clinician, but without any sense of emotional intensity or warmth. He was intentional in his gestures and simple use of words; about half the time, however, he could tune out mother, father, and me, going in and out of states of attention and relatedness. He would look bland and unenthusiastic, but could be purposeful in his play with toys and purposeful in his gestures and use of words with people.

Mother reported that her live-in helper had been with the family for about nine months. She was somewhat outgoing and organized, but more on the passive and sedate side; and she was patient. She could take an hour-and-a-half in giving him lunch, providing lots of distraction to help him eat.

As she revealed her situation, mother would occasionally focus on herself and say things like, "I don't care about my job"; "It's a no-win situation"; "I can't control him"; "I don't know what to do." At times, she would throw up her hands in defeat.

When elaborating on her difficulties with Ryan, she said that she was usually more successful in getting him to eat when she focused his attention on other things. Distracting him was the key; without distraction she said, "Forget it." She said he took one-and-a-half to two hours to fall asleep, and she would often have to be with him for the first forty-five minutes. After he woke up at about 6:30 in the morning he could be hyper the rest of the day and sometimes did not even take a nap.

As I observed mother and son play together, I noticed that mother was quite laid-back, but she would intermittently push her face right up to his. She vacillated between being overly passive and overly intrusive. Her depression and the long silences between vocalizations did not give him a rhythm that he could easily grab on to: two or three words, long silence, and then two or three more words; her gestures also carried the same pattern. Their verbal interaction seemed somewhat fragmented: "What's this?" mother said. "Crayon," Ryan answered.

"Why don't you write on this?" she said, directing him. Ryan picked up a doll, instead, and said "Anna baby," giving it a name. Then he handed a transformer to mother and said, "Go car." When he turned to color something with the crayon, mother said, "Make a picture for me." He was slow, methodical, very passive and unexpressive, but careful and attending. He responded to mother with his gestures and his looks and had an overall sense of relatedness. For example, mother said, "Put the lady doll in there," and the child took the lady doll and put it into a carriage. After he had picked up a number of dolls, mother said, "How many do you have?" and he said, "One, two, three, four," and counted.

I was impressed with the fact that he was gesturally organized, with two-way communication; but he showed little affect or enthusiasm or change of facial expression. When mother asked him, out of the blue, "What did you tell Santa you wanted?" (it was near Christmas time), he said, "Bike, car." Then she said, "Where does Santa come from in the house?" and he said, "Fireplace." He showed that cognitively he was quite sophisticated and able to answer her questions. Shortly after this, he took the whale puppet out; mother took it from him, saying, "He will bite you." He took the whale back and then, in a pretend way, started to bite her. Mother reacted with "Ouch!" (This was their best sequence of pretend play, with him taking the whale and her pretending to be bitten by the whale.) This showed, I thought, what the dyad was capable of, in terms of using fantasy and pretend play and elaboration.

For the most part, however, they didn't operate at this level of representational interaction. Between them, there was a subdued quality, with each one being inclined to march to their own drummer. They had some vocal and gestural interaction, but without much enthusiasm or vocal intensity of affect. Ryan tended not to close mother's circles when she verbalized something; he would continue what he was doing, either taking out different toys and manipulating them, or putting them into the house, or manipulating dolls and putting them into cars or carriages. Their style with each other was rather passive and uninvolved. It lacked enthusiasm, emotional depth, or intensity. Their capacity for opening and closing symbolic circles was, for the most part, latent, as evidenced by the sequence of the whale biting mother after she was going to bite Ryan. Perhaps, this sequence also showed what they were both a little scared of, and why they avoided each other.

I suggested that mother try engaging Ryan more energetically. I wondered if it would be too tiresome or draining, given how demanding he was with the eating. Mother said quickly, "He rejected me as a baby by tuning me out and turning away, so I became passive." I thought this direct statement rather dramatic and insightful. Unfortunately, mother was not stating it as an insight at the representational level where she could understand her feelings, but was saying it as a statement of fact. She was, in other words, recounting behavior, saying, "He rejected me and I, therefore, reject him. He does to me and I do to him." I commented on her saying that this was a matter of fact and not something to reflect on. She smiled a little. "I guess you're right," she said. "I'm not just feeling that way—that's what I do to him and he does to me. Maybe I'd better rethink it."

After this exchange, mother and son went back to playing. Ryan put a baby doll in a truck, and mother asked him whether the baby wanted to go into the house. As he put the baby in the house, she said, "Very good." He then identified another toy as a "camera." Mother said, "Give it to me. I'll take a picture of the baby." He complied and she took a picture of the baby. I commented on the fact that, perhaps, they were ready to develop some pride in one another, rather than continuing with their mutual rejection.

In observing Ryan's play with father, I noticed that they engaged well and were also organized in terms of gestures and behaviors. Ryan used sentences and phrases, sometimes without clear understanding. For example, the boy would say to father, "Get toy for me." Father would identify different objects, such as a car and Ryan would nod yes, get it, or no, don't get it. He was very direct in this instructions to father. Father was gentle and warm, very patient, and contingent. When his son was already looking at the house, he would say, "Let's look at this house," and they'd examine it together. As Ryan took objects out of the toy chest, father helped him identify them, how they worked, and whether or not they fit in the house. Overall, father was more even than mother, and more laid-back. Although he did not show a wide range of emotion, much less enthusiasm, during the play with Ryan, he was somewhat contingent and responsive. When I asked father if he was enjoying the play, he said that sometimes he finds it repetitive and boring, and didn't usually play with Ryan. We, therefore, talked about the value of playing at home as well.

While the evaluation continued, we talked about using floor time for working on the intensity of Ryan's engagement and affect. I mentioned that they already seemed quite related; they had good two-way gestural communication with him. Even so, mother and father did not generate much enthusiasm or energy when helping Ryan use emotional ideas in his play. I showed them how available he was to more elaborate drama, as illustrated by the theme of the whales, and suggested that they play more energetically. By joining in the drama with him, they would create interactive opportunities. Ryan might, then, be eager to play out some of the issues on his mind; he seemed quite able to play out his feelings. Mother, in a dutiful way, agreed to try, and father, reluctantly, said he would try to spend more time on the floor. He did recognize that he had left a lot of the child-rearing to mother, who he knew was overwhelmed.

We also talked about implementing an elimination diet to see if there were other foods contributing to Ryan's difficulties with sleeping, his irritability at home (which I didn't see at the office), and his difficulty with eating. We listed the different food groups to withhold for ten days, and then reintroduce as a challenge: sugars, additives, preservatives, and dyes; salicylate-containing fruit; peanuts and nuts; dairy products; eggs; soy; wheat and yeast. Also, I suggested that the parents be alert to other groups to which he might be sensitive.

The general feeling was that we postpone and direct treatment for Ryan's sleep disturbance. However, I suggested that we get an occupational therapy (OT) evaluation to look specifically for sensory reactivity difficulties, particularly in the oral area, and any other subtle differences or difficulties in the area of motor tone and motor planning.

Within a few weeks, after eliminating milk, eggs, and soy from Ryan's diet, the parents discovered that the removal of all three reduced his diarrhea and gas, his hyperactivity, and his wakefulness at night. They had yet to eliminate sugar, wheat, and fruit.

The OT evaluation revealed that Ryan had a rather severe hypersensitivity to touch around the mouth, and there was some indication of postural insecurity and insecurity regarding movements in space, particularly those that involved swinging, orbital and circular spinning, and movement into an inverted body position. Ryan preferred self-generated movement rather than movement on playground equipment or by a person.

The occupational therapist recommended eliminating peripheral distractions at feeding time—only a few toys would be available on the food tray; expanding the number of meals to three complete meals and two snacks; cutting back on Ryan's evening bottle, so that if he vomited at night, it would be less worrisome; exploring wheat allergies; placing Ryan in his high chair and providing social interaction during feeding time; and limiting the feeding time. If he stood up in his chair and protested, they were to remove him from the chair and not feed him outside. They would then remove the food until the next snack or mealtime. It was also suggested that a sense of possession be instilled—"my cup, my plate"—to eliminate his wanting to eat his parents' food.

In talking with the parents more about their own family background, I discovered a history of depression on mother's side of the family, but no history of mental illness on father's side. Mother went into the subject of her depression quite deeply. She expressed "feelings of giving up." "I don't care," she said, "I can't make decisions." Later she added, "I'm over-whelmed emotionally." Father felt he escaped from the house to work; family life was too hectic. His wife was always worried and complaining; and his son was always coming between the couple having any time alone because of his neediness and demand for constant feeding and attention. Mother and father reported having had a nice, but not very intense, emotional relationship with each other before the birth of their son; they felt ill-equipped to cope with such a challenging child. They were committed to one another and not thinking about separa-tion or divorce, but felt they were simply living "day-to-day," with no pleasure or relaxation in their lives.

Father kept wanting mother to be firmer with Ryan and to enforce limits; mother felt that she "was the cause of his difficulties" and didn't want to make them worse. She realized that "he was a very sensitive baby."

By the time of this follow-up session, the remainder of the elimination diet had been completed and it was determined that not only milk, eggs, and soy, but also salicylate-containing fruit and chemicals, and sugar were problems for Ryan. They intensified his irritability, his wakefulness at night, and his dif-ficulty in staying settled during feeding time. Now that they were removed, he was sleeping a little bit better, was less active at home, and was more focused. Mother wondered about going all the way and getting organic foods for him in order to remove all the chemicals.

Mother also reported that she was finding it helpful to have sessions with the occupational therapist. She had learned different exercises to reduce tactile hypersensitivity in the mouth, such as putting in a finger and rubbing the soft and hard palate, and other little games that would normalize sensa-tion in the oral area. In addition, she was getting advice on varying the textures of food so that Ryan would experiment with them. Some textures would be normalizing as they would put different types of pressure on the hard and soft palate and the lips. She felt she was having some success with this, in terms of his taking over a little more of the feeding. However, father seemed to feel that she was going to too many therapists.

When talking further about Ryan's developmental history, mother reported that he had been very socially alert from the time he was about four or five months old, after getting over the original surgery; but he was also very clingy, especially to her. He even wanted to follow her into the bathroom. He insisted on being held day and night by either mother or the woman who was helping take care of him. Mother said she "felt always guilty because he almost died." She had breast-fed him until he was about six weeks and then weaned him onto the bottle. Even though he was so clingy during that first year, mother remembered him as being willing to vocalize when she vocalized. He would reach out in a controlling way, rather than in a truly interactive way, but there was no question in her mind that he was "quite intentional." In the second year, Ryan experienced asthma, eczema, and diarrhea, as a result, she thought, of sensitivity to the foods he was eating. He was up every two hours, a pattern which had continued until this time.

As I watched him play with mother and father over the next few sessions, a certain pattern became clear. Mother would vacillate between being silent, while Ryan moved trucks and cars in and out of houses or identified toys on his own, and getting involved in an intrusive way; in this latter case, she would anxiously open and close her own circles. For example, she would say, "What's this?" If Ryan didn't answer immediately, which he often didn't do, she would say, "That's the boy doll. What does he want to do with the little girl?" Then she would say, "That's the girl doll." Before he could respond, she would be off telling him something else. As she spoke, she often had her hands on his body. When he occasionally put his fingers in his mouth, she would quickly grab them and take them out of his mouth, worried that he would get "some germs" in him.

At times, Ryan would respond to her gesturally in his play, but his response resembled a counterpunching rhythm; he would turn his body away avoidantly, or exhibit other negative gestural comments. For example, on one occasion, mother put a puppet on her hand and tried to talk to him. "What are you going to say to the puppet?" she asked. When he didn't reply, she said, "Say hi to the puppet. Say hi." Ryan turned away and said, "No." Then he took a block, put it on another block and toppled them over. Occasionally, he would acquiesce and respond as mother wanted him to; but throughout their play, there was very little assertiveness on his part, and very little enthusiasm or depth of emotion, either pleasurable or angry. Even though Ryan could speak in short phrases, his representational or symbolic play was minimal. I noticed that while he was very gesturally sophisticated and intentional, in terms of his relationship to mother, father, and me, he rarely closed gestural or verbal circles. He sometimes avoided mother by turning away, sometimes acquiesced, and did close a circle. More often than not, though, he shifted themes by turning his body away and changing the subject, usually in reaction to mother's intrusiveness.

With father, the pattern was somewhat similar. Although he was less intrusive and anxious and fragmented, he tended to control the rhythm of the interaction and do things for Ryan. There was less of a sense of intense relatedness with father; even though Ryan's affect had been negative with mother, there had been a greater quality of relatedness.

Ryan tended to be shy with me. He would hand me things and make gestures and occasionally say a word or two to me in play, but he let me know clearly that it would take a long time for him to warm up to me. According to mother, Ryan was also shy and cautious with other children, playing in parallel play in a somewhat avoidant posture.

At the end of this preliminary phase of the evaluation, it appeared that this bright, cognitively age-appropriate youngster was functioning slightly below age levels, in terms of his level of emotional organization. He was functioning at the early representational level, between eighteen and twenty months, rather than twenty-two to twenty-four months. But he was enormously constricted, in terms of the range and depth of affect in his representational elaborations, so that the quality of his relatedness was globally constricted. In addition, he was locked into a passive, avoidant, counterpunching, negative pattern of interaction with his intermittently intrusive and intermittently depressed mother; and the pattern was similar with his somewhat uninvolved, only partially related father.

So here was a child who was engaged and capable of two-way communication and early representational capacity. However, he was experiencing massive constriction in terms of each level of development that he had achieved. As a result, he had little ability to negotiate the emotional aspects of life. Even though Ryan had had access to age-appropriate developmental levels for such negotiation, his severe constrictions were not allowing him any range to negotiate. Since he lacked an ability to elaborate, either in the assertive, aggressive domain or in the pleasurable domain, he was left to negative, avoidant postures, such as reacting to being fed and negatively negotiating self-regulation with sleep. It wouldn't have been surprising if other somatic patterns or disturbances in somatic regulation would emerge, given the lack of representational or prerepresentational depth and range.

In addition to the family patterns described above, which contributed to this pattern, was Ryan's constitutional–maturational individual differences. Ryan's constitutional vulnerability was, fortunately, not as overwhelming as I had originally suspected when hearing the profound nature of his symptoms and his history. Given the avoidant and negative posture Ryan had taken throughout his early life, I expected to find much more tactile sensitivity and motor tone and motor planning problems. We did find, as indicated, hypersensitivity to touch in the oral and mouth area, accounting for this being a target organ for his negativism and avoidance; and problems with postural insecurity contributed to his being unsure of his body in space. This insecurity was also contributing to his comfort with passivity and negativism, and his not taking risks in terms of motor assertiveness. These constitutional variables intensified the interactional aspects of his limitations. Furthermore, Ryan's early history of surgery and other medical procedures, such as nasal–gastric tubes following the surgery, had undoubtedly contributed to his developmental difficulties and accentuated the constitutional and interactional patterns.

The treatment approach involved a number of elements. There was the ongoing OT consultation, more particularly around feeding and better postural control. Mother was learning new ways of feeding Ryan that would help normalize sensation in his mouth, such as letting him take more control of his oral experiences; by trying different textures of food; and by mother doing some deep touch in his mouth. This would be briefly intrusive but would help normalize sensation. I also suggested some motor exercises that would gradually help Ryan feel more comfortable in space and with posture. Mother would be able to practice them in Ryan's weekly OT sessions.

Ryan's treatment also involved working on the mother–child and father–child interaction patterns. The parents would each do floor time with Ryan for a minimum of a half-hour each day and in regular consulting sessions. They would use the floor-time experience to understand better the relationship they had with Ryan and how they were undermining or supporting development. In these sessions, the parent–child interactive patterns were explored: mother's intermittent depression and intrusiveness and her son's concomitant negative and avoidant patterns, and father's lack of involvement. The parents' own emotional reactions to these patterns were also explored.

Over time, mother was able to establish a consistent rhythm; she gave Ryan a little more space and time to respond and generate leadership rather than just react against her. We focused on his opening and closing of gestural circles and then symbolic circles. Mother would first have to figure out what Ryan was trying to do before she could move in and give him three or four new options, or answer the questions that she herself had raised, as she was prone to do. After a few sessions of working on this, mother smiled, recalling how, as a child, she had always been "the boss and the queen bee" among the other children and directed the dramas. She had had a very "aloof, yet controlling mother" who, she said, "gave me nothing of warmth, but made me very tough in terms of being a controlling person myself. I would never let her control or exploit me."

Mother was able to relax and begin smiling and even giggling during her play with Ryan. Her relationship with me and her husband was also easier. Ryan could take the lead. In one session, for example, he put the whale puppet on his hand and held his mouth open. Instead of trying to act out a feeding scene, which she had been prone to do in earlier sessions, this time she said, "What does the whale want?" Ryan said that the whale was hungry. She asked him, "What food would he like?" The boy determined which of the pretend food things he wanted to eat. As simple as this little interaction sounds, it was a major improvement for her to wait for him to direct the feeding drama. In a subsequent session, when the whale was eating food, mother wondered aloud how the whale felt when it was spitting out some of the food. Ryan, now close to thirty months old, said, "Well, mad." Mother asked what the whale wanted to do. Ryan then started making the whale bite everything in the room, knock down toys, and even throw some toys. Both mother and I empathized with how mad the whale could get. His affect broadened and brightened after this; it was the first time he had used representational modes to deal with anger. He was also much more gesturally animated, using his complex gestural system to deal with angry feelings. After this, he was more relaxed about assertiveness in a general sense. Overall, mother's rhythm had fewer silences and intrusion, and she was showing more respect for her son's growing initiative.

With father, the task was somewhat different. He had less trouble being unintrusive, and intellectually knew how to relate to his son, but it was very difficult for him to get deeply involved. Initially, he was reluctant to do the floor time and actually wanted to interfere with mother receiving occupational therapy support or her own counseling. "She should be able to handle it on her own," he said. He had almost no awareness of the degree of her depth of depression. On one occasion, when father wasn't in the room, mother confided that "the marriage was just like two roommates, with little love or intimacy or warmth." She was only staying in it because of the degree of depression and hopelessness she felt in general.

The work with father included raising the whole issue of what he got out of the family, and what pleasures he felt with his son and his wife, particularly as he was reluctant to do the floor time and be more involved with his wife. This led to some exploration of his early family upbringing, including the fact that he had had a somewhat self-centered, but anxious and needy mother, and that his father had passed away at an early age, when he was nine years old. He felt fortunate that his older sister had been there to help take care of his mother. He admitted that he had pretty much buried himself in books and work and had always avoided intimacy which had depth of feeling. Nevertheless, he had always managed to have some friends and dated in high school and college; but he avoided intense relationships, he felt, partly because intensity reminded him of his mother and her helplessness. That he had married a fairly depressed and fragmented woman confused him; he said that he felt he had married someone who could be competent because she was a journalist. He had either not looked at the fact, or had ignored the fact, that his wife had some characteristics in common with his mother; although his wife was, in some respects, a very strong woman in spite of her depression.

As these patterns in father's life were raised, he relaxed a little and started enjoying his floor time experiences with his son. Ryan began experimenting a little more with motor assertiveness, the kind of roughhousing that children of this age ordinarily do; father even went to one OT session where he got some ideas about how to help his son do some of this roughhousing as a way of improving postural control.

Slowly and gradually, Ryan increased his intimacy in the play with father. Initially, it was just with more looks and smiles and greater intensity of affect; then his overall quality of relatedness grew more animated, and symbolic play evolved. For example, in a recent session with father the little boy was being somwhat cautious and whiny. He noticed a flashlight and asked what it was. Father, in his own quiet but now warmer style, neither took over nor avoided the question. "Let's see if we can figure it out," he said, and he began pressing the different switches. He then showed it to Ryan who started pressing the switches himself. Suddenly, his son pressed the button that made the light go on. He enjoyed shining it at father, and every time he shined it at father, father made a funny face and he started giggling. Then he gave father the flashlight and when father shined it at him, Ryan made funny faces. He started ordering father around, saying, "Do it more," or "Put it over there." Then he imitated a TV character and told father to hide behind the chair and shine the light at him so that he could pretend that he was on stage. He began to get some of the puppets and was starting to do a puppet show when the time for the session ran out. It was impressive to see Ryan take charge. I admired how, with father's warm support and the theme of light shining on him, Ryan had given the light over to father in order to perform.

In a recent session with mother, Ryan (now $2\frac{2}{3}$ years old) came in eager, alert, warm, and verbal. He got all the toys out and told me to put the doll in the chair. Talking in complex sentences now, he took charge of the drama, involving me and mother. He began identifying one of the toys as a boat and another one as a truck. He announced that one part of the room was going to be where the boat was going (water), and that the truck was going near the water. The dolls on the chair were to go on the water first, and then go into the truck. He decided to have me manipulate the car, while mother manipulated the boat; he handed each of us toys and dolls from the "shoreline" (in the chair) to take into our different vehicles.

Again, what was impressive here was his control of the drama. He looked animated, smiling with pleasure and mastery. Meanwhile, mother was able to obediently follow and take some pride in his initiative.

At present, Ryan is eating much better and gaining weight more readily, sleeping through some nights, and only waking up once during other nights. He is still somewhat cautious and shy with other children; the current goal is to have other children, whom he seems to enjoy, come over three or four times a week. This will enable him to get more practice in one-on-one situations where he can learn to relax in interactive play, just as he now does with mother and father.

Ryan is still not completely comfortable with the full range of assertiveness in all situations. He is gradually becoming more comfortable, however, showing pleasure and joy, a sense of mastery, and some assertiveness in situations that he is comfortable and trusting in, such as my office. I have talked with the parents about having the teacher draw him more into peer-to-peer activities in his class, where he tends to avoid the assertiveness and unpredictability of the group.

This is a youngster, then, who has shown gradual and steady progress over a period of about ten to twelve months. He has been able with his parents' help to overcome many of his original symptoms and to both gesturally and representationally expand the range and depth of both pleasure and assertiveness, and begin experimenting more with aggression. He is confidently approaching age-appropriate patterns in terms of both developmental level and the range and depth of experience he can organize and communicate.

Chapter 4

Thirty to Fifty-Four Months

CASE NUMBER 16: ROBBIE

Robbie was four years old when he first came in with his parents. His mother described him as "a mysterious little boy" who was unhappy with himself. He was the middle child of three children. She felt that his older brother had done very well after having some therapy when he was younger, and she saw some similarities between the older child and Robbie. She also felt that there were differences. The older one had a lot of separation anxiety, but Robbie was more like a ray of sunshine one minute and then "fell apart" the next minute. Mother thought he was imaginative, except that he would often come out with extraordinary statements like, "I am an egg." He also tended to "tune out." When he did this, she would make a joke of it by saying, "Earth to Robbie. Earth to Robbie." "When he tunes out," she explained, "he is just marching to the beat of his own drummer and you can't get his attention, let alone get him to talk to you." Yet, mother also described him as a "scientist/clinician." He could tell how insects digest food, and, while looking at a picture had recently said, "My cat looks like a dying star."

Sometimes Robbie would make up facts and say to her, "No, that's not so. You are not the boss." He could be warm and affectionate at times and say, "I like you," but at other times would tune her out. He tended to be friendly with other children, but had no special friends; in nursery school children liked him, but he tended to be a loner and would do things like make funny noises when other children were around which would sometimes frighten or annoy them. He was rarely interested in inviting a friend over to play. Occasionally, when he did, he would withdraw and pretend to be an "egg" or a "science book," and refuse to talk to his friend.

Mother revealed that, historically, he had severe respiratory allergies (to dust, cats, molds, and pollens) and was also allergic to orange juice and chocolate, and to some degree to dairy products. As part of his allergic symptoms, he would get pale, listless, and irritable. Sometimes he seemed to "cave in" from tiredness. He could also burst out crying when he seemed overloaded or overwhelmed by too much activity. In either case, he could scream in total rage for fifteen to twenty minutes.

His irritability was perhaps the most difficult symptom for mother. "It drives me crazy," she said. "He will sit on my lap clinging to me, but then everything that you do for him is wrong and nothing will make it right." His parents reported that Robbie had a hard time learning how to talk and had been in speech therapy for six months to help him articulate certain sounds. Also, mother questioned his comprehension, particularly when he tuned out. The speech therapist had been working with that, too.

Mother described herself as a volatile and emotional person who got lost in her own emotions. Father described himself as warm and understanding, and was described by mother as "a wonderful bear of a person." In response to mother's self-description, father said, "I don't like her volatility. It irritates me. I yell at her. She's childish and illogical."

Robbie's developmental history included the following facts. He was not a planned baby, but was a healthy seven pounds at birth; the pregnancy had been healthy and delivery uneventful. He was colicky for the first month but responsive and alert. Although he was overly sensitive to sounds, touch, and bright lights and was hard to calm down, at the same time, he was reasonably cuddly, and by two to four months old was smiling and engaged. Mother felt he related to her warmly, but had this tendency to be easily irritable and overstimulated all through the first year. She felt that her own anxiety and tendency to be very volatile and emotional made it harder for him to settle down. Nonetheless, he learned to engage her and be warm, and by eight months old was interacting with peek-a-boo games, exchanging balls, and clearly had established two-way gestural communication. But he could easily get fragmented in his play. He would start banging his hand on the floor or doing things in a random fashion.

In the toddler phase, mother felt that Robbie had not progressed to complex gestural interaction patterns; he had stayed at simple interactive patterns, easily falling apart and getting upset, as well as throwing temper tantrums when he became overloaded. She would frequently feel irritable with him; father was working hard during this time and was often not available. As a toddler, Robbie was also frequently ill with allergic bronchitis, which mother associated with a dairy sensitivity, and a proclivity for upper respiratory tract infections. Mother's health was also poor then; she got migraines, was often irritable and upset herself, and, to add to her difficulties, she underwent surgery to remove a thyroid nodule. She was now on thyroid supplements.

When Robbie was almost two years old, mother became pregnant with the next child. By the time his sister was born, mother was feeling better, she was less physically ill, exhausted, and irritable. She reported that Robbie began talking early, but continued his pattern of irritability and temper tantrums and "falling apart." He began nursery school between two-and-a-half and three years old and hated it. He refused to go and started getting lethargic and tired very easily, which was when much of the allergy workup was done. His allergies to molds, dust, and other substances were partially handled with allergy shots. At three years, nine months, he got involved in therapy because he was so negative and irritable. The therapist described him as running around a lot, being hard to engage, distractible, generally tense, and fragmented in his behavior. The therapist also thought Robbie needed speech therapy, and he was evaluated by two other people who concurred with the therapist. He began having speech therapy both for difficulty with articulation and with comprehension; the speech therapy was ongoing. Mother felt that the original therapy was not helping Robbie very much and was therefore seeking another evaluation.

In the first playroom session with Robbie, he appeared to be a motorically clumsy youngster. He came in alone, confidently holding my hand, and went immediately to the toys. He was friendly and engaged, but avoided eye contact. He made a few facial gestures and some disorganized motor gestures of a highly irregular nature: he moved his arms in different places, pointing without any seeming intentionality. He looked very much like a child who had both some involuntary motor movements and a lack of synchrony in his motor system. There was lots of babbling, vocalizing, and quick chit-chat. It was clear that he could use language, but it was directed under his breath at himself. He could answer some of my structured questions and talk clearly at times, and at a later point in the session, he counted five numbers forward, but refused to cooperate in counting backward. There were some complex sentences. For example, he told me that the "crystal ball is for magic," indicating some good conceptual understanding. However, when we talked about his family, he was confused about the date of his birthday and the age of his brother and what they liked to do together.

Robbie played with the toy house, opening and closing doors, and putting things inside the doors. He seemed to prefer the self-oriented chit-chat, as he played, but, most important, he never appeared aloof or unengaged. He would always look at me, smile, and make some gestures; if I asked him a specific question, he seemed to make an attempt to answer it. He was able to engage me in his play with the house and the little wooden people. He put them down the slide and smiled, seeming to enjoy a logical gestural interaction pattern with me; but there was no real story and he didn't add any symbolic content, which he seemed capable of given his verbal ability.

Initially, therefore, he seemed engaged, tense, but avoidant and marching to his own beat. His mood was even, his attention was focused on what he was doing, but he had a lot of discoordinated motor movements. His obvious difficulty with articulating clearly what he wanted to say made it hard to understand him.

After fifteen minutes into this session, Robbie insisted on having mother come in and join him, but wouldn't say why; he seemed pressured to want her to come in. When she joined us, she was very relaxed and supportive, and responsive to his signals. She tried to join him in pretend play and after ten or fifteen minutes of chit-chat, the clarity of Robbie's language improved. They played out some pretend themes with a whale and a crystal ball and an octopus going into a house. As they played out the drama, what emerged were fragments of a story rather than a whole story. For example, Robbie said that he was scared of the whale and that the whale was hiding in the house. But the outcome of being scared and what happened after the whale was hiding never became clear; there was no cohesive plot developing between these subplots. (These story fragments were more at the 3- to 3½-year-old level than the 4- to 4½-year-old level; in fact, he struck me as a bright 3- to 3½-year-old rather than a 4 to 4½-year-old.)

As Robbie continued playing, he would get distracted by something physical in the room, such as a new object to explore, and mother would try to bring him back to the story. I was impressed with her ability to be very patient and engaged with him, although at times she could also become fragmented, flitting from one subplot to another, and not keeping in mind the larger theme. She did have an unusual ability to be relaxed, tune into him, and create a sense of warm acceptance.

By the end of this first meeting my impression was that Robbie could relate well. He had an even mood and reasonable concentration; a moderate comprehension of sound, but unusual discoordinated motor patterns and decreased articulation. He often seemed to tune out and retire to his inner world, depending on the type of content or information he was dealing with; it was a partial disengagement. By himself, he was tense, and with mother, very pleasurable, but he seemed passive and compliant rather than assertive or muscle-flexing in the themes he developed. There were no aggressive themes to the pretend play, although he was, as pointed out, warm. My feeling was that he had established some sense of shared attention and relatedness, but his relatedness was partially vulnerable, not to the extent that he dissociated entirely, but insofar as he dissociated from the sense of relatedness and sharing information. He had established some degree of two-way communication, but was unstable when under stress. He would pull away and march to his own beat both gesturally as well as symbolically. Although he seemed to have progressed to more complex gestures, and even to representational elaboration in terms of sharing meanings and ideas, he was operating in a fragmented way and tended to regress toward one-way rather than two-way communication. He had not yet shown evidence of progressing to a stage of representational differentiation, except in isolated fragments. Here, out of other people's symbolic communication, he could consistently build a cohesive interrelated theme or story line, either around a real piece of logical conversation or around a make-believe conversation.

So, we had a four- to four-and-a-half-year-old child who was functioning somewhat vulnerably and partially in the two-and-a-half- to three-and-a-half-year-old range. He had tendencies toward partial regressions in two-way preverbal communication, quality of relatedness (not becoming unrelated but withdrawing from two-component relatedness); and had his sense of shared attention more directed toward inanimate objects than people, although he always maintained some sense of connection to the human world.

In a second session, Robbie walked in, again rather clumsily and with a funny expression on his face, but he was related, attentive, had an even mood and good control of impulses. He was still hard to understand but seemed to use more complex sentences, some of which were seemingly out of left field: "That's a piece of clay surrounded by fire," he said, referring to a picture he was looking at. While examining some of the doll-like toys, he said, "The arm is off the He-Man doll. He is from the He-Man said, but I don't know his name." This was an example of a more logical, organized sentence. It would often take two or three sentences to pull him back in so that he could answer another question. He remembered the crystal ball from his first visit and developed a partial story around it, saying, "That's from a long time ago." He conceptualized that the crystal ball could tell things that would "happen in the future." There were islands indicating a conceptually bright youngster who did not have the ability to organize. He engaged me more this time, but his engagement ebbed and flowed, never withdrawing and never consistently remaining engaged. Again, he responded to questions only if they were very structured.

When I attempted a more reality-based conversation with him, he was able to engage in some logical types of conversation. For example, he told me, "I like your pen. It's funny looking" (it was a crooked pen). When mother came in, he got out a gun and said, "Let's play." He then seemed to want to joke around and said, "Candy corn made me funny." Except for small comments, he was, for the most part, fragmented in regular conversation. He couldn't stay with it and would withdraw to some private amusement, like "Candy corn made me funny," or drift off into play in the midst of a conversation.

At the end of this session, mother reported that she and Robbie didn't "talk in reality conversations. We talk in metaphors," she said. She felt that she had a bright little genius who could talk highly indirectly and symbolically, so she tried to find meaning in his fragmented pieces of logic. Mother seemed anxious when talking about this, and it was clear that she was, in part, denying some of her worries about him and the reason why she had brought him in.

While the evaluation continued, the parents reported that Robbie was still operating in a way that worried them; using noises and funny sounds instead of words; hitting and flailing when upset; covering himself up with quilts and doing seemingly silly things; being avoidant and antisocial with other kids, and at times being loud and miserable with long episodes of temper tantrums.

A speech evaluation revealed that Robbie's main difficulty in the articulation area was in mispronouncing the vowel sounds. In addition, he had a word retrieval problem. His comprehension seemed good, and in many respects was age appropriate or higher, but it was uneven in ways that didn't necessarily make logical sense. At times, he was scored way above age level and at times, particularly in relationship to some social conventions, he could misperceive the intentions of others. Most troublesome was his difficulty in using speech for social interaction and purposeful communication. His pragmatic speech remained uneven.

The therapy focused on his articulation, word retrieval problems, and on teaching him better social use of speech.

An occupational therapy (OT) evaluation revealed that Robbie was a delightful four- to four-and-a-half-year-old who was displaying difficulties in fine and gross motor skill development and in sensory integration. He had difficulties in postural control, processing of movement in space, balance, muscle tone, motor planning of sequence movements, and bilateral motor coordination. He displayed some tactile sensitivity to environmental stimuli, a lot of fidgetiness, and some visual distractibility. He had fine motor difficulties with delays in developing his bilateral assistive skills, such as scissor use and buttoning.

The visual–motor skills—block construction, puzzles, design copying—were age appropriate with the exception of drawing, which appeared immature. Both fine and gross motor skill fell approximately six to twelve months behind, which represented a significant delay.

Both speech and language therapy was continued and OT for the motor and sensory reactivity and processing problems was begun once a week.

It appeared that Robbie had had difficulties at a number of developmental levels. These difficulties had not entirely derailed him, but had created instability and delay. Thus, in his early regulatory abilities he was irritable, distractible, and easily overwhelmed. He had progressed to be engaged with others and drifted into two-way communication. Although Robbie had some representational capacity, there was no depth or range, and he hadn't arrived at the stage of representational differentiational or emotional thinking (the fourth core process or sixth stage).

Contributing to these developmental difficulties were both constitutional–maturational factors and environmental factors. Robbie had a constitutionally based difficulty with both gross and fine motor control, including low motor tone, motor planning, posture, and coordination, as well as many aspects of fine motor and perceptual motor development, and sensory reactivity and processing. In addition, the motor system seemed to have affected speech articulation. There was no clear evidence for a receptive language problem, except functionally, perhaps secondarily due to attentional problems.

Factors in Robbie's environment also contributed to his difficulty in negotiating these developmental stages. Mother was a fragmented, labile, intense person who was undergoing a great deal of stress herself in Robbie's early years, including thyroid surgery and migraines. Father, a calmer person who tended to overwork, was intimidated by mother's labile emotional style and stayed out of the picture too much. The parents were not providing the necessary environmental experiences that could help Robbie develop compensatory capacities for his own maturational unevenness; at times, they intensified some of his difficulties, which contributed to his unstable pattern of emotional progression.

Robbie's capacity for representational differentiation would be necessary in order for him to develop age-appropriate reality testing, self-esteem, focus, and concentration, as well as a capacity to relate to peers. As indicated, mother tended to become fragmented and irritable. She tried to rationalize his lack of reality orientation by entering into his metaphors and idiosyncratic way of using ideas. She wasn't helping him differentiate by doing this. Father, on the other hand, was not involved enough with Robbie to provide a corrective influence and was still using patterns of avoidance with mother's overemotionality.

A treatment plan was developed that involved the following elements: Robbie would undergo speech therapy and OT, once a week. The parents would begin to engage Robbie in a number of new and different ways; each parent would be involved in at least a half-hour a day of floor time where the focus would be not only to follow Robbie's lead, but, once following his lead, to maintain a two-person communication system. In this way, Robbie would be prevented from withdrawing into his own world and from maintaining a sense of relatedness between himself and another person which excluded the other from the dialogue Robbie was creating between his toys. Instead, the dialogue would be two-way, with the other person becoming either a fantasy figure or a collaborator in the drama under construction.

Mother and father worked during this session at ways of gently reentering Robbie's world every time he tuned them out. For example, he might play with the house and begin to slide the doll down the chute and, perhaps, come up with some idiosyncratic phrase like, "The doll is jumping out of the moon." The parents would say, "Okay, where's the moon going to be?" and Robbie would look at them as though they were a little peculiar for jumping into his illogical fragment of a thought. But by entering his world, however silly the content, they were helping him become reality based by helping him take into account another person and his or her intentions. For example, they might say, "How can I help this man jump out of the moon? Is the slide going to be the moon?" Gradually, but surely, he tended to assign them a role. "Put your finger here," he might say, indicating that they should hold the slide. Sometimes he would smile and say, "This is a slide," and let go of his idea of the moon; or he might intermittently grab something and say, "This be moon. You hold it."

Another example might involve mother and father talking to him about a puppet game. He had had the whale bite one of their legs, then bite a car. One of them might say, "I wonder how the whale is feeling?" and put a puppet on their own hand, asking, "Is the whale mad at me?" Then Robbie might start interactive dialogue with their puppet. Up until now, they had pretty much let him follow his own route and had not tried to pull him into the interpersonal world. Generally, by opening and closing circles of communication at symbolic and gestural levels with them, they pulled Robbie more and more into the interpersonal world.

In addition to doing that a half-hour a day, the parents were instructed to practice reality-based, logical conversations for at least twenty minutes at a time, as many times a day as they could. For example, they would ask Robbie about what he did at his preschool program. If he looked at them blankly or said something silly like, "The chimney has water in it," which he did say from time to time, they would use this as a transition into something realistic. Did something at school happen with a chimney or with water, they might ask, or was he just saying something to say something. He would usually give them a silly grin. At times, they would discover that he had played with water; other times he would smile and say, "Did nothing today," at which point, because of his word retrieval problems, they would help cue him up a little. "Well," they might say, "in the nothing you did, did you do it next to little Sally or little Johnny? Who was in the group near you?" He would then give concrete details about who was near him and, with some cuing up, could say who he played with and with which toys. Slowly but surely, he could piece together more and more fragments of logical conversation.

Robbie's teachers were similarly encouraged not to let him wander in his own mental world. They would serve as a transition between him and other children, drawing him and another child into interactive, symbolic, and pretend play in a corner of the room; particularly when he was overwhelmed by excessive stimulation in the group.

Along with these elements, Robbie began individual play therapy three times a week. This involved a therapist who was sensitive to his cues and signals, as well as his interesting and somewhat creative way of looking at the world. The therapist entered his world, opening and closing many circles of communication. In addition to following his lead, she also spent about ten or fifteen minutes in each session on more logical conversation about what he was going to do the next day or when he went home. Piece by piece, the therapist tried to help him organize his thinking more.

The parents were also helped to set limits when Robbie had temper tantrums or would flail around wildly. In the past, they had let him flail around, or tried to figure out what to do to give him what he wanted; now they would use a lot of gestural contact, trying to engage him in gestures, followed by conversation. Then they would use a lot of physical holding, especially firm pressure to his back to help him reorganize. The occupational therapist reviewed with them some tactics that had worked well for Robbie in the OT sessions. These tactics included large muscle movements, where he would jump or get joint compression, as well as firm pressure to the arms, legs, and back. The occupational therapist had also discovered that certain textures of sound and rhythmical use of sound, including music, would help Robbie reorganize. It was suggested that his parents and teachers, as well as his speech pathologist, use some of these tactics to help him focus.

Over time, Robbie reflected slow but steady progress. A few months after this program began, he came in for a follow-up session with me and already looked better. He smiled and engaged me with a greater sense of relatedness. He gestured more continually with me, with better concentration. His mood was positive and a little more optimistic. He was still hard to understand, but used difficult words in a more organized way. When he opened a book about prehistoric animals, he said, "Pterodactyls and dinosaurs," informing me that he was interested in them. Then he got out some play materials—castles and figures—and said, "This is Grayskull and this is Snake Mountain. These are going to be the good guys and these are the bad guys. They are going to fight." I asked him why. He said, "Because one is good and one is bad," looking at me as if to ask why I was asking such a silly question. He couldn't elaborate on what the bad guys had done and what the good guys had done, but just wanted to bang the bad guys into the good guys. Finally, when I pressed him, he said, "Don't know what made them that way."

At the same time, Robbie couldn't tell me about school or recall his teacher's name, or tell me which individual children were "pains or nice." He did, however, say that his mother and father were nice, and that some children were either "not nice" or "nice." If I didn't make myself very available, he would drift into his own play. He didn't attempt to pull me in, but when I got down on the floor and reached into his play, he readily accepted me with much less resistance than before and without my having to move into his world. Here, he showed that after only a few months he had arrived at an early stage of representational differentiation and emotional thinking. He was actually making connections between his representations. He seemed closer, now, to a four-year-old level, with some constrictions still in the depth and range of his abilities; he was engaging better, was more attentive, and showed more two-way gestural communication. Interestingly, there had also been a general improvement at home, with less irritability, fewer tantrums, less "peculiar behavior," and fewer "left field" verbalizations. He still retained his scientific bent and his unusual curiosity, which delighted mother. (She had been afraid that he might lose some of this with his therapy.)

In subsequent sessions, the theme of good and bad guys fighting for dominance continued. On one occasion, when I couldn't follow his lead, I said, "I'm slow to get our message," and he said, smiling, "I should say so." He would set up elaborate dramas, while mumbling to himself. There was enormous preparation as the bad guys were preparing to attack the good guys and the good guys were defending against the bad guys. Again, he preferred to play alone but would readily accept me into the play. In one of these sessions, I helped him make a transition from the make-believe world to the real world. I commented that he seemed very interested in the good and bad guys and took great care in understanding how they were going to attack each other. I bet him that this wasn't only in play, but there must be some good and bad guys at home, too. He then spontaneously elaborated that he was quite "mad" at his sister. "She wrecks my things. I can get very mad. It depends on what she wrecks." He let me know that he was always "mad at some people," and that he hated it when people wrecked his things. A theme emerged in which people who overwhelmed him were viewed as wrecking things. It was his main complaint and could happen at school or at home; in particular with his younger sister and less so with his older brother. There was the first inkling of a personal approach to people at school, as he mentioned two or three children by name—one who was nice and two or three who were mean.

My impression at this time was that there was much better elaboration and logic in his play, and he was beginning to build some bridges between his make-believe world and his reality world. Some of the motivations for his living in his own private world—to handle his enormously aggressive and angry feelings—were beginning to become clear. I empathized with him that sometimes it was easier to deal with mean people when one could be the boss of the whole world, as in his world of make-believe (he smiled knowingly), but in school or at home it was a little harder to deal with the bad guys (he nodded).

Robbie was working on these same themes in his individual therapy. His parents had been alerted to his need to verbalize and play out themes having to do with anger and fear and to create his own feelings of being overwhelmed through themes of being destroyed and wanting to counterattack. However, his parents vacillated between following out their assignments for doing floor time, problem-solving time, dealing with limits, and falling back into their old patterns. Nevertheless, they generally made steady progress with this program of therapy. Their ability varied according to father's job demands and the stresses in mother's life. She had a great deal going on in her own family of origin. More often than not, they were able to return to the baseline of being more available to Robbie. Here they helped him organize his reality, empathizing and helping him stay engaged while in his fantasy world. Robbie's progress has been very gradual. For example, in a subsequent session, he again talked about good and evil. When I inquired why they were that way, he said, "They are born that way." But these small increments have added up to considerable progress over about a year-and-a-half of treatment. In his most recent session, he came in and was immediately warm and friendly. He engaged me with a nice sense of relatedness, giving core gestures, and evidencing an even mood, good impulse control, and a continuing sense of relatedness without tuning me out. He paced around the room in his typical uncoordinated motor pattern fashion, with a gleam in his eye, touching everything; he was seemingly happy to be there, keeping me in his vision. For the first time, he remained very logical throughout the whole session, organizing more of the conversation, and keeping me involved with him. He was in an extremely infectious and happy mood, opening and closing circles of communication easily, and evidencing organized thinking. At times, though, he was evasive, and had difficulty holding a complete reality conversation. When I asked him how things were going, he said, "Can't recall." I replied, "It's so hard to know whether it's been a good day or a bad day?" "It's been a good day," he answered. I said, "For example?" and he said, "I can't recall examples." He gave me a sophisticated look. I remembered his word retrieval problem and asked him if it was sometimes hard for him to recall specifics. He nodded and said, "Yes." I said, "You mean like what you did at school today?" "Yes," he said. "I can't remember the specifics, but I have a feeling that it was okay." I empathized how hard it was, sometimes, to recall specifics and asked if he could remember, for example, what he had had for breakfast? He shook his head and said, "No." I said, "What if I help? For example, did you have fruit?" and he said, "Oh, yes. I had some bananas." I said, "How did they taste?" and he said, "Good. I liked it." I asked him if it was frustrating not being able to remember the specifics. He said that sometimes it was and sometimes it wasn't.

I was impressed with the interactive nature of his logic and speech and his own sense of awareness of the difficulty he had in retrieving the specifics of his day. I said that I imagined it was hard, sometimes, to recall how he felt, not just what he ate, and he nodded in agreement. I asked him what kind of feelings he could sense he had most of the time these days. He said, "Unhappy a lot of the time; occasionally I get mad." We talked about these feelings and later I asked him if he got scared sometimes, and he said, "Yes." I asked, "Of what?" and he said, "The types of things that it's reasonable for a child to be scared of." I was somewhat amused and also intrigued by this answer. It appears by this answer and many others that he had become extraordinary in abstracting general categories. He was quite sophisticated in this ability and was usually on target; he was no longer pulling in things from left field, but responding in the area relevant to the issue being discussed. Where he had trouble was putting meat on the bones, or seeing the trees for the forest. He was superb at constructing the forest, but his word retrieval problem, coupled with his good abstracting abilities, led him to rely heavily on his abstracting abilities. Recalling the specifics secondary to his short-term memory word retrieval difficulties was much harder work. I empathized here, too, with how difficult this was for him and he nodded knowingly.

Then we talked about his angry feelings and he said, "Of course I get mad sometimes." When I asked for an example, he became pensive and, for the first time, came up with a specific. (Maybe it had helped that I empathized with his difficulties with specifics earlier.) He said, "When Mom interferes with my fun." "What would be something fun for you that Mom would interfere with?" I asked. "When I want to climb in the car window and she doesn't want to let me," he replied. "You mean she doesn't let you climb in the window all the time?" "Right," he said. Throughout this session Robbie was very good at answering all my "why" questions and excellent at coming up with his unusual abstractions, revealing that he could sometimes fill in the trees that went along with the forestlike abstractions.

At another point in this session, we were talking more specifically about his interests in school, what and with whom he liked to play. (He had recently shown indications of forming more intimate friendship patterns with a few select children whom he liked a great deal. He still was easily overwhelmed in a large group and preferred to move off into a corner at school with one or two children, but he was inviting children to his house and was enjoying their company.) He called one of the children he played with his "best friend." He mentioned that he liked to play with "tiny snakelike animals and real animals, too." When I asked him why, he said, "Because I'm a scientist and I'm going to be a scientist and scientists like to figure out how things work."

Throughout this whole session, there was an amazing quality of warm, appropriate, light-hearted kibitzing along with some serious discussions of feelings. His mood was enormously positive, but most impressive was a kind of chemistry of relatedness and a sort of pleasure and involvement that had not been in evidence before. Earlier, he had always shown an unusual capacity to remain related, even when off in his own world; but never with this degree of consistency or spark.

Robbie told me more about his friends, particularly Michael, who liked to be a "scientist," too. Then he was willing, even, to draw a picture of his friends for me. When mother came in at the end of his session, she asked him how he was doing and told me that he was finding school more relaxing. For the first time he was having consistent, warm, intimate friendship patterns. He was more alert and engaged at school, and getting rave reviews from all his teachers (in a regular school program); at home he was chatty and cooperative—there were almost no tantrums to speak of. He could remain in logical conversations with mother, as well as enjoy escapades into creative fantasies and figuring things out. She was excited because she thought he had retained his creative thrust and now was fully related to her and his father, as well as to other children at school. While Robbie and his mother were in the room together, I asked him how his parents were doing. I said that I had heard that he was doing terrifically well. "In my opinion," he said, "Dad is away too much." His formal use of language was made light of by the little gleam in his eye and the smile on his face. He said, "Mother is doing terrific. She's the best!" He also indicated that he liked playing with father, but he wanted him home even more.

At this time, I was impressed with how good he looked overall. His basic ego functioning was now fully intact and his reality testing clearly established. He was stable in mood; had good focus, good concentration, and good ability to represent many different feelings and differentiate them, and even see relationships between some of them. There was increased flexibility and warmth in the way he related, and certainly greater development of the themes he would talk about. He also closed his circles easily and took the lead in doing this. He even evidenced some assertiveness, moving the session from theme to theme, rather than responding only to me, or withdrawing and only engaging when I would pull him out. He still evidenced his word retrieval problem, but was complementing it with a great capacity for abstracting and coming back in from the general to the specific. He supplied general categories first and then back-tracked to the specifics, rather than constructing the category from the specifics, as his mother naturally did. His father had a cognitive style similar to Robbie's, although it was not as fully developed.

With his mother I discussed continuing to work with the "trees" and the specific feelings, and helping him become more natural in describing the details of life and then abstracting from them. I was, needless to say, impressed by the amazing progress that Robbie had made in only a year-and-a-half.

He had begun as a youngster who had only marginally established his reality testing and relating capacity. Now Robbie was not only functioning fully in an age-appropriate way, but had integrated his creative potential with age-appropriate ego functions.

This case illustrates how a child who is not moving toward age-appropriate reality testing and instead is living in a fragmented world of fantasy can be assisted to move forward in his development.

CASE NUMBER 17: DAVID

David presented as a four-and-a-half-year-old with delayed speech development that was compounded by a series of emotional and behavioral problems. These included hitting both mother and father, being moody, not responding to questions or comments, and often seeming to "space out." He was not yet toilet trained, and had tantrums that could last a half-hour or longer when he didn't get his way. The parents were worried that his tantrums interfered with his playing with other children. He would not interact with other children and, at best, did parallel play. It was very unclear how much he comprehended about what anyone was saying, given the fact that he could only say a few words clearly. Most of his utterances were garbled sounds. Earlier evaluations had revealed that, in addition to his severe articulation difficulty and delayed speech, he had decreased motor tone, although he was able to walk and jump by age four-and-a-half. (The motor milestones were delayed but occurring in an expectable sequence with about a 4- to 6-month delay, secondary in part to low motor tone.)

The medical workup was negative in terms of metabolic studies, chromosome studies, and regular pediatric well-baby evaluations. Furthermore, David showed indications of unusual cognitive abilities. He knew his alphabet, seemed to remember stories, and occasionally would spontaneously say things like, "played wagon" or "in there." But he was not able to hold an interactive conversation. He enjoyed wrestling, tickling, and other forms of roughhousing if it didn't get too much, but he didn't like having his hair brushed. He could hold a pencil and draw a circle, but could not draw a square or a triangle.

The family had a history of learning disabilities. Father had a learning disability, and there was a "retarded cousin" on his side. On mother's side, there was a history of depression—her aunt was hospitalized. In addition, mother had a history of petit mal epilepsy with an unknown etiology.

The pregnancy and delivery were unremarkable, and early development was characterized, according to mother, by the fact that "he didn't cry much. He seemed happy, he smiled, slept through the night, and was very observant." He liked to touch things—"he would study first and then engage," she said. She felt he was attentive and somewhat related during the first year, although quite passive in terms of the two-way communication expected in the second half of the first year. But she felt he would respond: when she handed him a rattle, he would look at her and take it. Rarely, though, did he initiate an activity.

In the second year, the parents began to recognize David's problems. Although he did make sounds, he was not using any words, and there was a question about the clarity with which he indicated his needs and desires. He would occasionally point at what he wanted; or cry in a diffuse way. But more often, he seemed "spacey" or following his own beat.

According to mother, David wanted her to be with him all the time. During his second year and into the third, he would cling to mother and was fearful of being with other people. Only in the last six months had he begun to stay alone with father.

Father felt that he, himself, was "removed" from the family in the second and third year of his son's life. He was preoccupied with work and also did not feel terribly involved with David.

At about age two, David began banging his head, but would respond to the parents' physically restraining him. When he spent time with other children, he would occasionally hug and stroke them, but he did not have symbolic play interactions or verbal interactions with them. They had found that since age three he would occasionally do some imitative play. For example, if mother were to put a puppet on her hand, he might copy her by putting a puppet on his hand and making some sounds.

I observed the parents playing with David during this first visit. Mother took a puppet and bit David on the nose with it; he copied her, biting her back. When she asked some questions, he seemed to ignore her and tune out, although occasionally he made some eye contact. It seemed that in spite of the imitative gesturing, there wasn't a spontaneous give-and-take of gestures or words or emotional expression.

When father tried to get a pretend game going he gave David something that looked like a gun and said, "You shoot me, shoot me dead." He then attempted to tickle him, engaging in a flurry of activity. David smiled a little as he was being tickled, but then became passive. He turned his back to his father and started exploring toys; he seemed interested in how the toys worked. Between father and son, there was very little reciprocity on either a symbolic or a gestural level.

Both parents seemed to want to be close to David. He was intermittently engaged with each of them, but only on a simple gestural level with smiles and looks and an occasional word. There was no indication of complex gestures and no interactive use of symbols or representations.

The impression of David at the end of this first session was that he was functioning as a one-and-a-half- to two-year-old at his highest levels, and had some splinter skills. His lowest level of functioning was represented by tuning out: he would be indifferent to his parents' questions or gestures, or avoidant in favor of exploring how toys worked. Even in his exploration of toys, he seemed to be at the level of a one-and-a-half- to two-year-old. But, at the same, it should be noted that he showed some capacity to concentrate well, particularly when he turned his back on his father and explored toys. He also showed a glimmer of warmth and emotion whenever he gave a faint little smile or look of recognition.

At the follow-up meeting, the parents revealed further medical history. David had had an atretic right ear canal and tympanotomy tubes had been put in his left ear. It was thought he had a 40 percent hearing loss on the right side but on the left side his hearing was normal. It did seem adequate for speech development, although since the age of about two he had been receiving speech therapy. He had had a single febrile seizure at age two-and-a-half, but the ensuing computerized axial tomography (CAT) scan and an electroencephalograph (EEG) had been normal.

David was a C-section baby. Mother reported that he moved vigorously in utero. The pregnancy and delivery were otherwise unremarkable. His birth weight was eight pounds. He breathed and cried immediately and had 9/9 Apgars. He took a bottle well, and went home with mother. During infancy, he had had two dislocations of his right elbow, the first one being the result of a fall and the second one being related to a pull injury. His thyroid, while in the normal range, was on the low side of normal, and a neurological evaluation when David was three years old revealed that he was physically functioning well, but in the borderline range in terms of cognition and language. The examiner also wondered about underlying cerebral palsy because of the low motor tone and some "extensor thrusting." Chromosomal and metabolic studies were also normal.

The psychological evaluation of David as a three-year-old showed "delay in his development, with uneven skills." At that time, he was generally functioning at a two-year-old level, with scattering up to two-and-a-half in terms of some of the nonverbal forms of board tasks. However, the impression was that he functioned at the eighteen-month-old level in terms of his social development. Precocious interest was noted in letters, numbers, and colors. There was note also of his irritability, difficulty with transitions, and his inappropriate or lack of relatedness to other people. The psychologist noticed that David seemed clingy and dependent at times, and aloof, distant, and overindependent at other times. She was reluctant to give a diagnosis, in terms of a psychological assessment, other than that he had slow and uneven development.

A number of professionals had verbally given David's parents the impression that they thought he was "borderline retarded, or educably retarded." Their conclusion was that he had considerable behavioral and emotional difficulties, and that his social and emotional behavior lagged even further behind his cognitive and language performance.

At the next meeting, I observed more of the parent–child interaction patterns. Father moved in much too quickly. He didn't let David develop his own gestures or initiatives, either symbolically or gesturally. When David was functioning in the higher range of his abilities, such as beginning some potential pretend play with a car, his father would move in and take control of the car. He would try to take charge of the play.

Mother didn't demonstrate as much energy as father in her play with David. She often seemed preoccupied with herself, and quite depressed. At other times, she would become fragmented and overload him. He vacillated between being "spacey," when she was not generating enough energy to pull him in, and whiny, when she got too active and animated in a fragmented way. Besides whining and crying, he would become a little disorganized and still not generate much gestural and symbolic interaction. It was clear that mother felt overwhelmed and guilty. She recognized that in many areas of her life she vacillated between a kind of frenzied helplessness and a depressive preoccupation. Some of this was consistent with her earlier history of relationships.

Father, a busy economist, recognized that he was frustrated and angry that David was having the problems he was having. Father had been a slow developer, but "unlike David, I got it together." Father revealed a lot of warmth and empathy for his son, but at the same time didn't know what to do with all the impatience and anger, and the feeling that David had, as he put it, "let [him] down." As father talked, there was a not-so-secret aspiration that his son could be much better coordinated and the athlete father had never been.

As both parents became aware of some of the underlying feelings contributing to their styles of interaction, they were eager to read David's signals a little more clearly and begin playing in a more constructive and supportive way.

A program was developed that would further elaborate and tease out some of the evaluative and diagnostic issues, and, we hoped, prove helpful to David. The parents were instructed to try to engage David at the four levels described earlier: first and foremost, to get his attention and maintain some pleasurable sense of connectedness by following David's lead in an activity that he was already enjoying. Then they would try to open and close some circles of communication—simple gestural ones and then more complex gestural ones. They were not to worry about his advanced number and letter interest or even any symbolic interactions, but rather, they would let the symbolic part of the play emerge spontaneously. They were asked to empathize verbally with what David was doing, and were encouraged to follow his lead and respect his initiative while at the same time closing circles. Whenever he ignored them, they would pull him back in and try to help him build on their responses. (The tactics for doing this are described in the treatment section.) Each of the parents were asked to do this for at least half an hour each evening at home; and mother, if she had time, two or three times a day.

In addition to this home program, the speech pathologist who was working with David three times a week was consulted. She was working on his pronunciation, aspects of his receptive language, and his ability to carry out instructions. The consultation included helping her make more use of spontaneous play and interaction in the speech work, so that David would get a sense of his own efficacy and intentionality in that work. The speech pathologist revealed that David's speech capacity had an uneven quality to it and ranged from the middle of the second year of life, in terms of intermittent reciprocity, to scattered verbal skills in the two- to three-year-old range. David was occasionally able to put together two or three words or follow simple commands. On rare occasions, he could even follow a two-sequence command, such as, "Please get that block and put it here."

David also began to see a play therapist twice a week. The therapist would follow his lead and help him learn to symbolize his emotions, as well as to interact in a more organized gestural way. The play therapy was organized along the four levels suggested earlier, and David's parents were to become involved to some degree to help them improve their interactions at home.

Not only did the parents have considerable anxiety in their interactions with David, but also in their marital relationship. The tension between them was often tangible when they would voice differing opinions on how to work with their son. It was clearly connected to the amount of anger they felt toward each other; each felt let down by the other. I suggested that they begin weekly psychiatric sessions. There they could discuss their problems and also receive further guidance on how to deal with some of David's more worrisome behavior, such as his withdrawal and his perseveration. (Although David did not perseverate in the playroom with me, the parents reported perseverative behavior. We discussed trying to tease this behavior into interactions to make the perseverations interactive.)

In summary, then, a comprehensive approach was developed for David: daily work with the parents; regular sessions with a child psychiatrist; speech work three times a week; and play therapy twice a week. Furthermore, David received an occupational therapy evaluation for his low motor tone, motor planning problems that were suggested by his developmental history, fine motor lags, and suggestions of some sensory reactivity difficulties. Once-a-week occupational therapy was added to his complete program.

Since the beginning of this program, David has shown consistent improvement. Within the first four months, a rather large improvement was noted, primarily in the quality of connectedness. When David came to see me, four months after this program was instituted, he had a gleam in his eye and was clearly much more affectively involved with his parents. Even though he hadn't seen me for four months, he gave me a knowing look, instead of ignoring me as he had done earlier. He could interact with mother using four to five gestural sequences in a row, and he was able to add on symbolic make-believe to these gestural sequences. For example, he might take out a car, with which he was enamored, and have a doll sit in the car. The doll would then get out and be given a bath. As he gestured to give the dirty doll a bath, he might look at mother, give her a faint grin, and say, "Dirty." "Yes, dirty," mother would reply. "Now we have to clean him up." After four or five of these elements, David might switch to another activity. As he played this out with mother, he might smile at me, too, and make other postural and facial gestures.

The play with father took on a similar tone. Father chose to play out more aggressive scenes with soldiers and shooting. David concentrated on what father was doing and could interrelate a series of gestures and ideas with father also. Father was warmer, more supportive, and more contingent on this follow-up visit. He had practiced at home and previewed this play with the therapist who was working with David on a weekly basis. In the sequence with father, father began it somewhat impatiently, as he had in the earlier visit, but this time David smiled back. Father relaxed and took the lead. He let the boy take the gun from him; and David smiled faintly and said, "Boom, boom. Boom, boom." Father then returned the "boom, boom" and they exchanged three or four gestures and words, making "booming" noises back and forth.

David had made considerable progress. He was related almost the entire time with both the parents and with me. He could organize a series of five or six gestures in row, closing circles and giving them the flavor of a normal social interaction, and he used a series of symbols or ideas in his play that were natural and coordinated with the gestures. He had a warm, likeable quality to him and he showed excellent concentration.

Over the next six months, David's progress seemed to level off. He did not seem to increase his symbolic comprehension. When mother or father asked him simple questions in their play with him, he could follow their gestures but was only able to close simple symbolic circles. For example, they might ask, "Does the car want to go left or right? Does the car want to go here or here?" He would move the car in one or the other direction. The more they structured it, the easier it was for him to close a circle. If they asked him, "What does the car do next?" he would look puzzled and then become random in his behavior or tune out a little. It was also hard for him to shift gears from pretend to a reality-based conversation, even when asked, "What do you want for lunch?" He found it even more difficult to close circles in a reality-based conversation, although, when he was familiar with the routine, he could respond to certain structured tasks with his speech pathologist and his occupational therapist. After a while, the parents became demoralized over David's lack of progress. They wondered whether or not he was, in fact, "retarded," and whether he was capable of making significant gains.

Upon close examination of the parent–child interactions, it appeared that David's parents were not giving him a lot of practice in taking the lead. Even though they were working with him and engaging him and closing gestural circles, they were still, in subtle ways, structuring the experiences for him. In their eagerness to have him close multiple circles, they were giving him practice in answering only yes or no questions. We focused on their anxieties and worries and how they wanted to make him "perform well." But I pointed out how this engendered a certain type of overcontrol, where he wasn't able to get a sense of what he could do. We worked on following his lead more effectively. For example, when he seemed puzzled about the car, rather than saying, "Do you want to move it here or there?" they would gesture back with another car and say, in simple words, "Where car go?" They would learn to be patient. With this kind of play, David eventually said, "Car go there." He pointed to a chair and then made the car go up the chair.

When the chair became a garage, he was beginning to show signs of greater sophistication in his play.

Over the next four months, there was great improvement in David's abilities. He not only was closing gestural circles and symbolic circles, but also was closing quite complex circles with a continuing sense of "being connected and with-it." On his next visit, he looked at me, smiled, and interacted with appropriate gestures and words. He spontaneously told me about school and a teacher named "Teed." When he didn't understand a question that I asked him (a follow-up to his telling me about school), he would answer randomly. But even with his random verbal response, he looked and gestured with intention. We talked about the kind of toys he liked to play with and he selected some new toys. He told me he liked "soldiers and trucks." As he was trying to get a soldier into the truck, he said, "The soldier's too big for the truck."

This kind of play was now characteristic of the parent-child interaction. They let him take more of the lead and were solidly supporting him. He was making good progress at the preschool level, and was solidly at the prekindergarten level.

At home, the parents reported that David was much easier to engage and maintain in engagement: they were having little conversations and exchanging lots of gestures with him. But he still had temper tantrums when he was frustrated and would bite and kick. However, they were not feeling so intimidated by his temper tantrums; they had been working on setting more effective limits, using gestures, words, and physical restraint as needed.

His progress continued and in a further follow-up session he showed greater elaboration in his play. He was using representational modes in his play that were intimately connected with his gestures. For example, in one such session he asked his mother to "get monster house." Mother got it and held it up. He said, "Okay." Mother asked, "What's happening?" "They are climbing up," he said. Then mother said, "What next?" "Look for hotel," he replied. He then played out the monsters trying to scare people in the hotel. This was the first time he had shown elaborate make-believe dramas. But the parents admitted that while he was doing more creative play and using symbols and words, they were still feeling frustrated. They wished he could hold conversations about school or solve simple problems such as what he wanted for dinner. They felt they were having to structure their interactions with him much too much.

We talked about how to spend twenty minutes a day on problem-solving or reality-based conversations. Just as they did with pretend play, they would help him with cues, but only the minimal amount he needed in order to have a give-and-take conversation. This way, they would become more demanding in terms of setting at least half of the agenda, when talking about school or a TV program, and so on.

Over the next three or four months, David improved in this capacity as well, and the parents began using these problem-solving discussions to talk about his "temper tantrums." Now, for the first time, he began using words and pretend play to deal with feelings. Around this time, he first talked about feeling mad and "wanting to be boss."

The parents were both delighted, but also a little frightened by this development. Now that David was armed with words, they were afraid he would be "mad at them" most of the time. Once they realized that this advance would actually make him less frustrated and mad, they relaxed a little; even if he were mad, their empathizing and engagement with him would persuade him of how much they cared for him. The parents dug into their own pasts to remember how they had dealt with anger as children and growing up. Both had their own conflicts which we won't explore here.

It is important to know, however, that many children with developmental delays have an especially difficult time dealing with angry feelings. The ability to represent anger and deal with it constructively is a critical milestone in moving to more logical modes of relating to the world. In a sense, if children are comfortable with anger they don't need to use regressive modes of fragmentation—withdrawal and avoidance—as much.

But they cannot deal with the anger until they have developed the representational capacities and the circle-closing gestural interactions that will allow them to deal with the feeling constructively. Therefore, at a certain point in the treatment, helping the child to verbalize angry feelings, through pretend play, becomes very important. It builds on the respect for the child's assertiveness and helps him develop in terms of gestures and representations as a precondition for this.

As David's progress continued, his speech pathologist and play therapist wondered whether they should cut down the frequency of the work. I urged them to continue at the present rate until David was functioning completely at age level in all ways, a goal that they had not even anticipated when the work began. There is a tendency in cases such as this to work less aggressively when a child is making progress. Parents and therapists will want to "give him more time to play with friends, peers, etc." This desire to relax the pace often represents an unconscious wish to be satisfied with a lesser goal for the child. If the parents are motivated, there is usually enough time to play with peers on weekends and after special programs. Also, if the work is done skillfully, with empathy and warmth, and the child's lead is truly followed, as opposed to his being coerced, he will usually find the sessions sufficiently rewarding and a boost to his self-esteem, so that he won't feel tired or overworked.

Later, as his progress continued, David began interacting and using his new skills with other children. In school, the teacher noticed spontaneous use of verbal interaction and pretend play with other children in typical and expected ways—tea parties, cars crashing, soldiers fighting. David became shy when the action became too aggressive. He would withdraw a little and return to more parallel play where he could observe from a safe distance. But he clearly showed a capacity to recover and again be involved with children.

Over time, he developed a special relationship with one little boy who became a "friend." He talked about this boy at home and invited him over. They had nice play sessions together where they would giggle and laugh, run around and jump, and also do pretend play with trucks, cars, and soldiers. This was a major psychological hurdle for David who had never had a "close friend" nor shown a capacity to evidence pleasure with a child his own age. His friend also had had some uneven development with learning delays, but was a little more socially advanced than David. David used the relationship to improve his own social interactive skills. With this child he learned how to share, how to experience joy and pleasure, and even how to protect himself when his friend wanted a toy that he wanted to play with first. He learned to say, "Me first."

His progress is perhaps most evident in his more recent sessions, at age six-and-one-third, about two years after beginning this comprehensive program. I should mention that while David was making this solid progress, his parents began letting up on their floor time at home. They did not realize that the source of his progress was their own toil and sweat on the floor. With encouragement, the parents regrouped and resumed their support. In a recent session, he played with mother and she tried to give him "the mean dolls." He said, "I don't want meany. I don't want those." Dad joined in by saying, "Maybe the policeman should come over and do something with the bad guys." The parents seemed very relaxed as if enjoying their play. As mother tried to take the lead, David for the first time evidenced an ability to compete with her and take over the rhythm. Mother said, "What's happening here?" and when she tried to distract him from what he was doing, he looked at her and said, "Come here." He directed her to the drama that he was developing with trucks that were taking some rocks from one place to another. Then father got intrusive and began taking the truck over from his son and putting it in his face (as parents relax, they sometimes go back into old patterns). David, showing his greater assertiveness, now grabbed the truck from his father and said, "Look, the truck is going bang-bang." He turned the truck into a gun and started shooting at father. He then made father into the bad guy and ordered him to the other side of the room. This served two purposes: getting father out of his face and also letting David take charge of the drama.

David then built a fortlike structure out of the pillows, and he and father shot at each other from across the room. He smiled and giggled and seemed pleased, not only at the elaboration of his drama, but at the ability to keep father under control. Later on in that play, he made two girl dolls slide down a slide. He said that the little one was a girl and the big one was a "lady" and that they were sliding down the slide. He made the slide a part of the house and talked about which doll was bigger than the other. Finally, one of them got injured and had to be fixed up by the doctor.

In his play with me during this session, David was very relaxed. He had good intentional gestures, a with-it quality, and seemed able to relate to me almost like a child of his own age. There emerged a theme of "putting on masks"—one for me, that he gave me, and one for himself. He showed me how to put the mask on. (It was a mask from a popular robot-type toy.) Then he said, "Let's fight the monsters together." He kept coming back, giving me my mask, and asking me to join him in the fight, as one group of robots was fighting another. He was very interested in figuring out how the robots worked. "Can this robot do this or that?" he asked. During all of this, he was also able to engage in seemingly idle chit-chat. I asked a question about a friend at school. He would try to answer for a minute or two, but then floated into the pretend play. With my help he could refocus to the talk about the friend at school. He vacillated greatly between struggling to tell me and avoiding the issue by drifting back into pretend.

My impression of him was that he was warm, relaxed, related, and focused, but did not yet have full differentiation of his representational capacities. Nonetheless, he was quite elaborate and creative in his representational capacities and had many islands of differentiation for emotional and logical thinking. But his tendency to drift back into pretend thinking when the questions got too hard or it was too difficult to find the words to describe his thoughts indicated that the solid ability to shift between reality and fantasy was not yet established. In this sense, he was more characteristic of a four-and-a-half-year-old, but in some of the elaborations of his play he was clearly in the five to five-and-a-half-year-old range. I tried to empathize with him about how he felt when he couldn't find a word or couldn't answer a question. I asked him how he felt. He was able to tell me, with great difficulty, that sometimes he gets "mad," and he kicked the doll.

The parents and I talked about the challenges lying ahead. We discussed stringing together numerous logical ideas into cohesive themes so that David could hold a more normal conversation, a skill that we usually see developing between ages three-and-a-half and seven. We also wanted to maintain the elaborateness of his pretend dramas and help him articulate his feelings more and more; particularly his feelings of frustration and anger secondary to some of the articulation problems which had a mechanical and motor component to them. Furthermore, I emphasized how important it was for the parents to empathize with David's frustration at this time.

In a recent session, at age six-and-a-half, David demonstrated that he had made another huge shift and gain. When he walked in the door he had a look of complete normalcy and a terrifically eager, friendly, warm sense about him. He smiled and said, "Hello, Dr. Greenspan," with a very warm, open posture. He was clearly happy to be visiting an old friend whom he obviously remembered. As he walked in, the parents began talking about some of the battles with him at home. David was wanting to play with a certain popular toy that father didn't like because, he felt, it was too aggressive and "weird." I spontaneously turned to David (rather than organizing the pretend play sequences with mother, father, and then me as we usually do) and made it the center of a family discussion. I said to him, "I gather from your daddy that you like this toy." He said, "Yes." I asked, "Why?" He said, "I like to play with it because it is fun." I inquired, "Can you?" He said, "No, daddy doesn't let me." "How come," I asked. He said, "He thinks it's too scary." I said, "Is daddy a scaredy-cat?" David began giggling. "No," he said, smiling broadly and giggling. There was a real knowing look to his smile—it was clearly fun to make fun of his father, but a little bit scary. He wasn't quite ready to do it, although he was bursting with pleasure about the idea that his father was a scaredy-cat.

This conversation, which we would have been unable to have a few months earlier, suggested to me that he now had excellent abilities to hold a logical conversation. He could build on my ideas and I could build on his ideas in a more normal, ordinary conversation without having to cue him too much. He was now able to deal with what was actually a conflictual situation at home in a logical, problem-solving discussion. This was a major milestone; and the amount of pleasure and joy he showed in making fun at his father, together with his logical ability, suggested that he had made major gains in his ability to be pleasurable and emotionally assertive, as well as to be logical intellectually. His articulation had dramatically improved, as had the depth of his warmth.

Interestingly, both of his parents were still a little patronizing and overstructured in their chit-chat with him, as well as in their pretend play. I had to remind them that David didn't need them to cue him up any more, nor did he need a patronizing approach. (They would say, "Now, David. Tell Dr. Greenspan A, B, or C.") I reminded them that he could think for himself now and that it was very important for his parents to respect this ability. By being patronizing and overstructured, they would hold him back from the considerable progress he was making.

As compared to the previous session, David did not drift off into fantasy. He played out elaborate fantasy dramas as he had in prior sessions. However, now he could hold a conversation about school, friends, or the special toy he liked, for five or ten minutes, or as long as I was willing. Only when we had finished the conversation would he begin doing his pretend play.

At school, he was progressing well. He enjoyed playing with other children and continued to have a "best friend," as mentioned earlier. He was showing more of the characteristics of a four- to seven-year-old child. He was becoming increasingly comfortable in using words for feelings, such as being mad or sometimes being sad; his tantrums were only occurring when he was tired or in a real power struggle with his parents.

In summary, then, this is the case of a child who, when he came in for his original diagnostic impression, appeared to be operating only intermittently: in terms of shared attention and engagement and of having achieved two-way gestural communication with some irregular and splinter representational skills. Some maturational unevenness was contributing to these developmental patterns, which put him anywhere from (at that time) one-and-a-half to three years behind his actual age; these problems included low motor tone and motor planning deficits; articulation deficits in terms of language, and receptive language deficits. The family's unfavorable interaction patterns added to the complexity of the case. The father was overly intrusive, impatient, and angry at the child and the mother vacillated between being fragmented on the one hand, and anxious, withdrawn, preoccupied, and depressed on the other hand.

Thus, we had a youngster who had both maturational and family interactive contributions to his difficulties. He was evidencing difficulties in a number of areas of development—emotional, social, language, and, to a lesser degree, motor. A comprehensive program focused on his current level of development and on each of the etiological factors contributing to it—the maturational side, through occupational and speech therapy, the family side, through family counseling, and the interactive side, through parent–child interactional help and play therapy. The program helped him move ahead developmentally in such a way that the foundations were improved as he was making progress.

This case is a good illustration of a youngster with multiple difficulties who made progress because of the very comprehensive nature of the program. It emphasized parent–child work at home, as well as with various professionals working collaboratively to help David build the foundations that he needed.

CASE NUMBER 18: KYLE

Kyle, a four-year-old boy, came in with his parents who were worried that he had a "BM problem." He was described as a "tyrant, a king-type" of child, who would, for example, come downstairs and order his parents to come and hold his hand to take him wherever he wanted to go in the house. They reported that he was very stubborn, very negative, and very insistent on his own way. "We are afraid to escalate battles with him because he is so stubborn," they said.

Kyle was older than usual, about age three-and-a-half, when he learned to control going to the bathroom for his bowel movements. At first he would often wipe himself with his hands, upsetting mother greatly; and sometimes he would smear on the walls, which "very much" upset mother. After many power struggles with her over his smearing, he did learn to go in the potty. But it lasted for only two months. When Kyle was visiting a museum with his grandparents during the summer, he had begun making it in his pants and going to the bathroom every few mintues. This had become his pattern. Now he was going to the bathroom ten times a day, each time making a little.

Corresponding to this pattern of multiple bowel movements, and making a little bit each time, was the birth of a younger brother who was now one year old. In the summer, when this had started, his brother was just beginning to crawl. Needless to say, mother, who was upset with bowel training to begin with and very upset that he was smearing and using his hands to wipe himself, was now completely frustrated and perplexed with Kyle's pattern.

Both at school and in a summer day camp program, teachers had described Kyle as a nice, "pleasant, polite" child who related well to other children. The parents said that he had some friends he liked to play with, particularly one friend from his preschool program whom he idealized a great deal. The children seemed to enjoy doing pretend play together. The parents also reported that this friend had recently been away on several trips with his own parents, and that Kyle had missed him. Mother said, "I guess he loves to play with him so much."

The parents revealed that there was little or no pretend play with them, although apparently Kyle loved rough-and-tumble play with father. Mother thought that Kyle did not show a lot of affection or cuddling with her, although she felt that they had a warm, loving relationship.

According to the parents, Kyle's language development was better than his number skills, but he still used baby talk at times. He was left handed and still held a pencil with a fist, but he could make a square and circles, even though he was fisting the pencil. He was a late walker, who didn't walk fully until eighteen months, and even now he was not very well coordinated or a good athlete.

When discussing Kyle's history, the parents remembered that at four months of age he didn't have a bowel movement for two weeks, and they needed to use suppositories.

From the presenting picture, Kyle seemed like a child with slightly delayed fine motor skills who was stubborn and finicky, and having his own unique pattern of bowel movements.

After this first session, I talked to the parents about the elements of a complete evaluation. I would see them for additional sessions to find out more about Kyle's and their own history and to observe, play with, and talk with their child. In the meantime, I suggested that they begin using floor time as a way of establishing more pretend play with him. Furthermore, I suggested they institute problem-solving time and pay attention to opportunities for setting limits, and also examine his diet. They would try to identify differences in his mood or negativism on certain days, and see if there was any correlation between them and his diet. We discussed, in addition, the possibility of getting an occupational therapy workup for the fine motor problem, but decided that we would hold off until I had a chance to see Kyle.

By the time I met with the parents for a second time, Kyle's bowel movements had decreased from between ten and fifteen to between three and five times a day. Mother said that he would "stand in a corner, either pushing or holding back." Then he would go to the bathroom "and a little piece would come out." She reported that she was feeling less angry at him and that they had started doing some floor time. Father had winced at the thought of floor time when I had first mentioned it, but now he told me that the emerging theme in his play with Kyle was bad guys and protecting the good guys from the bad guys. Kyle had been showing lots of anger through burning and fighting and knocking down houses in his pretend play. He had apparently verbalized some feelings to mother—"You don't love me because I'm bad," he'd said. When he played with mother, he liked "being a baby," where he would cuddle up in her lap, clearly trying to get some of the cuddling that was not yet part of their relationship. He had elaborated on this theme of being a baby by saying he was "baby Kyle" and he liked his mushy underpants. Also, he liked to "help people who are sad." He developed a song, "Don't Leave Me, Mommy." With father, he liked to roughhouse. Along with this, dad reported that he was also less defiant and that things were continuing to go reasonably well with school and friends. Mother, however, worried about whether he was getting enough sleep. He was going to bed at eight-thirty and getting up at six-thirty in the morning, but he sometimes seemed tired and cranky.

In this session, the parents also talked about issues with limit-setting. Mother said that when Kyle was upset or angry, he would hit her on the arm or leg; for example, if she made him stop playing with some toys before he felt he was ready. He liked to whine a lot and sometimes became very critical of her. "Don't like your hair," he might say. We discussed setting limits any time he crossed the boundary of expressing his dislike or anger in words and used any kind of physical force that could potentially hurt someone else. The general principle was to use floor time as a way of increasing intimacy and availability, creatively using fantasy, and, at the same time, increasing limits, firmness, and structure. I encouraged them to allow him greater responsibility for self-care; when he was in the bathroom he could practice wiping himself and taking care of his own BMs.

When we reviewed Kyle's developmental history in more detail, what emerged was a normal pregnancy and delivery. Kyle had been a little "finicky" for the first few months, crying and having trouble calming down, but generally he had slept for three or four hours at a time; and he had fed reasonably well (breast-feeding for the first 4 months and then bottle-feeding on a soy formula). His motor control had, perhaps, been a little slow—he'd had a hard time finding his mouth with his hands. Mother remembered that he had initially "not felt as firm in my arms as his younger brother," but he had progressed reasonably well with the motor milestones, although he had been slightly slow in learning to walk at eighteen months. By three or four months, he smiled and enjoyed being talked to and made funny faces. By eight months, he had established two-way communication, albeit passively: he would play peek-a-boo and take things and hand them back, but it took a great deal of work to get him to respond this way. During his toddler years, he again tended to be rather unassertive and negative; but he was able to engage in complex interactions, such as taking mother's hand and looking for a game he wanted to play, or gesturing to her with sound and pointing when he wanted a certain food.

The pattern described was of a slightly motor-delayed, passive, compliant, and negative infant and toddler. He had, nonetheless, negotiated his early emotional milestones of shared attention, developing intimacy, and two-way communication. When he reached between eighteen and twenty-four months, he had not elaborated on pretend play with his parents, but began speaking in two- or three-word phrases. He had established vocalizations much earlier, and could make his needs known, in terms of "give me that"; or a combination of pointing and naming games for objects that he wanted. He still used negativism and avoidance to deal with conflict: when his mother wanted him not to spill juice on the table, Kyle would usually wait until she wasn't looking and do it anyway. If she got mad at him, he would cry. He rarely confronted her directly, but would usually use more passive modes to get even with her.

As mentioned before, Kyle enjoyed playing with his peers. He sometimes had trouble asserting himself and would sometimes cry to mother if other children took his toys away. Nonetheless, by twenty-seven to twenty-eight months, mother mentioned he was involved in interactive play, doing some pretend play; although mother also said she never looked closely at what Kyle was doing.

In terms of family patterns, father felt that he was always close to his son, and that they liked to rough and tumble together. He said that he let mother handle the "day-to-day stuff" like BM training and other "details." Father was a warm person, who seemed tense and anxious nonetheless, but very committed to Kyle. Mother came across as a sweet and warm person, who seemed to have a warm relationship with her son, even though she rarely cuddled with him. (Kyle did show some hints of mild tactile sensitivity; for example, he did not like his hair brushed nor did he like brushing his teeth. But there was no clear indication that he didn't enjoy light touch or being bathed. Mother even said that Kyle had never seemed to enjoy being cuddled by her.) She seemed to be very tense, particularly in the area of cleanliness and neatness. She reported that, in her own childhood, she'd had many compulsive rituals, and she felt she had a "hang-up" about cleanliness. She then talked about how much the smell of feces disgusted her; yet, in her own childhood, there had been some indication of her playing with feces as well. "It completely threw me when he began playing with his feces," she said. "It's the one Achilles heel that I have." Both parents seemed to realize that their own tensions and anxieties around this issue might be contributing to the difficulty.

At the following session, when Kyle came in he was a nice looking, very calm, yet tentative four-year-old. He moved slowly, talking in a rather passive way, but he was clearly engaged and warm and trusting. His mood was even; he had good impulse control; he concentrated well to an extraordinary degree, focusing on either me or the toys. However, he had a narrow range of affect, with not much intensity or enthusiasm to his pleasure or his anger. It was as if he was going through the motions. He smiled a little and showed obvious pleasure, and there was excellent language, both receptive and expressive.

Several themes emerged in Kyle's play. The first involved Kyle getting toys out of the toy box. He wanted to explore all the toys: he set up dolls with good guys who were hugging; he set up bad guy dolls who were "fighting." He then transformed one bad guy into a monster that ate up "all the other persons." Out of this aggression there emerged a mother trying to find the baby doll. She searched all over for this baby doll. Kyle then found a whale doll. The whale was asleep on the roof of a house while some kids played inside the house.

As Kyle was playing out these different themes, I noted that, for the most part, they were little fragments of themes—two minutes here and two minutes there—rather than having real thematic development in one area. For example, the last theme involved the whale on top of the house. It was never clear what the whale was doing and what would happen to the children, except that there was some apparent danger from the whale.

When Kyle seemed to have finished playing, we began talking about his daily life. First we talked about friends. He said, "My best friend is moving, but will live close so that my mom can drive me to him." He reported that his friend only had Nintendo to play with because his other toys were packed up. (He was very logical and thoughtful in his description, although somewhat avoidant of the emotional aspect of his friend moving.) He told me, "We take turns and play his games and then he plays my games."

Kyle said that his parents were "nice," but "I can get angry at them if they don't let me play enough." It was the only thing he "got angry at." When he told me about his brother, who was one year old, he said, "He has an ear infection. He is nice, but also can be a pain." He did some drawings for me, fisting the pencil. Although he didn't have very good control, he seemed to have a good concept of what he wanted to make on the page. He used the whole page, making different designs on different parts of it. "I will draw a bird," he said, but he couldn't quite execute it.

My impression after this first session was that Kyle's basic personality and ego functions were intact, in terms of relatedness, attention, reality–fantasy differentiation, impulse control, and even mood; however, he was somewhat constricted. On the one hand, he was methodical and concerned with details, but on the other hand, he was passive, showed little emotional elaboration, and seemed somewhat fragmented in his thematic development. He lacked emotional intensity. His fine motor skills were also slightly delayed, and I wondered whether his motor planning might need an occupational therapy (OT) workup. Kyle struck me as being more like a bright three-and-a-half-year-old, rather than a four-year-old, although that distinction, admittedly, may not be critical.

When Kyle came in for a second session, he showed great expressive and receptive language ability, as he had earlier, by answering and responding to why, how, and what questions. He used contrasting elements and qualifiers in his speech. He was as warmly related as before, and had good concentration and focus, good impulse control, and an even mood. As he started taking out a castle and some other toys, he referred spontaneously to a friend, Paul, whom he said had "got a bigger castle than me." "But," he added, "we share pieces." In this session, he seemed more likeable and available. There was a slight increase in the intensity of affect. He was very easy-going. As the session progressed, his thematic development showed a small improvement, with less fragmentation and a little more depth. For example, he played out a scene with a cow who got onto the farm truck with other animals that were going to drive it. "See, this one is fixing the motor," he informed me, "and this one is driving; and this one is pressing down this and that." There was great attention to detail and plenty of independence to the play. He informed me of what he was doing, but didn't necessarily engage me or involve me in the play.

He then moved to a theme where one of the dolls was "missing arms and legs." He said, "They want to jump on one leg." He stayed focused on the missing arms and legs for longer than he had with any of the themes in the first session. He talked back and forth between the missing arms and legs, suggesting what they could do with the one leg they had (revealing his interest in finding a way around limitations). He then shifted to a rocketship going to the moon and the themes of power and accomplishment, staying with these themes for a while. He appeared to vacillate between things being missing or defective, and making the best of what you have and themes of power and assertiveness.

Toward the end of this session, I asked him about specific feelings that still hadn't been touched on. We talked first about scary feelings. He told me that he was "scared of the dark," especially when it became dark at night. He did not relate particular fantasies about the dark; he just said that "it was kind of scary." I turned to the subject of anger. He said, "I get angry at mom if she takes away TV for my hitting my brother. I don't stop. I get as mad as she is at me. I get mad back at her and I feel like punching her that hard." When I asked him about dad, he said, "Same with dad, only more." (Interestingly, in both instances, he was describing his retaliation for their anger at him.) When we talked about two situations that might get his parents angry, he spontaneously denied that he needed things "right away." He said, "I can wait for things." He also said that he wasn't "jealous of his brother." On the subject of happy feelings, he revealed he was happy "eating dinner and dessert." He mentioned a few foods that he particularly liked.

At the end of this session, I was impressed that Kyle seemed more mature than he had been in the first session. He looked more like a four-year-old. I felt that he had progressed in the course of a few weeks from an immature three-and-a-half-year-old to a more mature four-year-old. His thoughts seemed more complicated; he focused on detail and elaborated more in the themes of his play. He didn't quite have the capacity to create grand epics that some four- to five-year-olds have, but then very few children can do this. He showed increased pleasure, and he was more likeable because of the greater depth and intensity of affect. As in the first session, I was impressed that his basic ego functions, reality testing, relatedness, concentration, impulse control, and even mood were approximately age appropriate. But here, too, he still showed some constrictions. He tended to deny anger and jealousy toward his brother, indicating low-key acceptance; and he still showed a passive orientation since he would only respond to his parents' anger with his own anger. However, he did seem more flexible with his assertiveness in this session and acknowledged many more feelings than he had the first time. I wondered to myself whether or not some of the constrictions we were seeing were already undergoing change; the parents were doing more floor time with him, and they had also become focused on their own personality traits, making life less tense at home. Overall, I was impressed with Kyle's coping capacities and his ability to flexibly grow and change.

In the next session, I met with his parents again for an update and to give them a picture of what I had learned from earlier meetings with them and Kyle. They reported that he was now going to the bathroom on a regular basis. His bowel movements were less of an all-consuming issue now that they had established the patterns that we had discussed: increasing floor time; talking and problem solving with him about his pattern of going to the bathroom, trying to understand it from his perspective; and setting limits when he was truly out of control, such as hitting his mother. Together with these patterns, mother was more attentive to being warm, cuddly, and available and less preoccupied with fecal odors, and father was trying to be a little less tense. Kyle was having bowel movements one to three times a day, with some small "pebblelike feces and some big ones." When tired or upset with something at school he would tend to go more often. He still wasn't wiping himself, mother reported, but she was working on changing this, and sometimes he would still get feces stuck in his underpants.

"I still get into too many power struggles with him," mother complained. She further reflected that her own family had been so intrusive with her bowel movemens that she was overinterested and overcompulsive with her son. She reviewed her own time at high school and college, where she had regularly gone for two weeks without having a bowel movement. Interestingly, she reported that she hadn't had normal, daily bowel movements until she got pregnant.

In light of these insights, she felt that there were far fewer power struggles between Kyle and herself, although still too many. While he remained stubborn, he was more delightful at times, and he was showing less chronic negativism. She said that if he hit, she punished him by forbidding his TV viewing. It had been working since he was now better able to set up internal limits. She was less "crazy with him," she said. "I won't, for example, come downstairs when he calls, yelling and screaming. I deal more with the bigger limits."

Kyle's parents thought that he seemed happier with his friends. He was playing more often after school, even though friends had always been a strong asset for him. The relationship with his best friend seemed to be deepening, in terms of pleasure, and, in general, he was playing with a deeper sense of happiness. Mother and father were still concerned that he wasn't as expressive with his feelings as they would like him to be. For example, when he didn't like something, he wouldn't tell them why. Or when he got angry with his brother, he wouldn't talk about his feelings. He tended to avoid, deny, or just say "don't know," or "Okay."

They did feel that in their chit-chats with him, he tended to be more concrete. He would talk about TV shows or the Redskins, but not much about feelings. Even when they tried to help him name his feelings, he stayed with the concrete details of life. He did occasionally talk about being scared of the dark or missing a friend who couldn't come over to play, which they felt was nice progress. They gave, as another example, Kyle's reaction to going up the Washington Monument. He wouldn't say he was scared of being high up, but only that he liked the "floor which was lower down."

They had noticed that Kyle was less interested in using pencils, crayons, and pens to make different shapes, although he was very good at building with blocks and Legos. Nevertheless, they were encouraged by the "50 to 75 percent" improvement they had seen in Kyle between the beginning of this evaluation and this current stage; they were eager to further understand the nature of his problems. Therefore, they planned to continue their floor time, the problem-solving discussions, and working on limits. They also wanted to add on some fine motor exercises for him, coloring, drawing, and the like. We agreed to observe his progress for a while before deciding whether he needed an OT fine-motor workup. We also discussed how to begin talking with him about his feelings in a more personal way. I suggested that they continue the floor time in a very nonintrusive way for the next few weeks and then introduce the subject of his BMs and his pleasure in smelling or smearing.

My understanding of Kyle's situation was as follows. He had contributions from the constitutional and maturational side that were affected by fine and gross motor delays. Much of the fine motor delays and some motor planning delays were related to him feeling insecure in his control of his body; but these delays were also associated with his difficulty in learning certain automatic functions, a difficulty that had become a source of greater anxiety. In addition, he had a possible mild tactile sensitivity and a tendency to deal with frustration through passivity and avoidance, rather than assertiveness or confronting the problem. This often happens when a child doesn't have as much confidence in assertion through his motor system. On the parental–environmental side, both parents seem quite engaged and involved. They seemed capable of helping him share attention, engage warmly in the world (although mother had a hard time negotiating the tactile and physical side of intimacy), and of establishing two-way communication. However, in a general sense, the parents had trouble fostering assertiveness and self-sufficiency. They easily fell into a pattern in which they inadvertently supported his passivity by taking charge for him.

In Kyle's early development, neither the environmental contributions or the constitutional–maturational delays were severe enough to derail his progression through the emotional milestones. There was greater constriction and more passivity, negativism, and avoidance than one would like to see, but the basic milestones of engagement, shared attention, and two-way communication were well established. However, when it came to establishing representational capacities, the parents had had little involvement in his fantasy and make-believe world, and in terms of emotional ideas, had given little help for elaborating feelings and behaviors. They had provided minimal access for his playing out and symbolizing the aggressive and assertive side of life. While Kyle's language was normal, he evidenced very little use of language for emotion or fantasy and pretend. Compounding this, on the environmental side, mother was acutely anxious around bowel training and both anxious and intrusive with regard to her son's interest in fecal odors. Father did not get involved in this, but also seemed anxious and unable to help Kyle negotiate these phases either.

In terms of representational life, then, there were two limitations in the environment. One was restricting his use of representational life for elaborating a range of emotions intensively, especially the aggressive and assertive side of life; and the second involved a lot of focal anxiety around his mastering the self-care necessary for bowel control. It would appear that the symptoms of repetitive small bowel movements, with interest in smearing and smelling, was representative of and related to both his passive and avoidant response to his mother's overintrusiveness. It was also typical of his more general passive approach to conflict and his difficulty with representing or even acting out his assertiveness.

His parents were readily in tune with this picture of their son and shared my goals for his learning to be more assertive and more representational in general, and for diminishing the anxiety around the BMs in particular. Mother had gained a lot of insight by just talking about her own background, and father had become more relaxed, to the point where he was now engaging his son in assertive pretend play during floor time. The parents agreed to a series of three to six consultations spread out at monthly to six-weekly intervals. They would continue their floor time, problem-solving time, and limit-setting goals at home. We decided to watch Kyle's fine motor progress together to decide whether anything further would need to be done here.

On a follow-up visit a few months later, the parents came in and reported, "He is doing great in all ways." Kyle's bowel movements had become completely normalized. He was going once or at the most twice a day, with cooperation and with some pleasure. There was no smearing and no secret soiling of his pants. Mother, needless to say, was thrilled by this. They also reported that he was generally more cooperative and less negative and was verbalizing much more of his wishes, needs, and feelings. Mother said that he would occasionally still touch her with kind of a light gestural tap, but he no longer hit her. She was encouraging him to put his feelings into words and, for the most part, he was much better about verbalizing his anger.

In terms of his fine motor ability, there were some improvements. Just from the extra practice, he was beginning to hold the pencil appropriately, using his thumb and forefinger, although he was still having trouble making some of the shapes. Since he was showing sufficient progress, we decided to postpone the consultation for fine motor. He was already making many letters of the alphabet; and his auditory memory for following directions and for making sound–letter connections, in terms of prereading skills, seemed to be quite good.

The parents felt that he was growing by "leaps and bounds," in terms of his floor time and fantasy life. He had action figures involved in long conversations with one another, and playing out themes of protection and fighting. As he played out both sides of the drama, the parents were impressed with both the detail and the elaboration of these themes. Sometimes he even made a little doll into his brother and pretended to shoot or hit him or blow him up. He was able to talk about having mxied feelings toward his brother, being mad at him some of the time and liking to play out some of his anger in make-believe. At other times, he admitted he enjoyed his brother and found him "cute."

In normal conversation, Kyle showed an increased range of emotions. He talked about being disappointed and sad sometimes, and at other times he could say, "I am angry," if, for example, a friend disappointed him or wouldn't play what he wanted to play. With his best friend, who had moved away, he talked about the situation being okay. "I get to see him sometimes," he said. But he also talked about feeling "sad and too bad and missing him a lot." He was able to play with other friends, and be more flexible in terms of reaching out to other children about whom he had previously said, "I don't want to play with them." Now, he was able to say, "They are not my favorite, but there is no one else." He had also become more flexible in planning activities with his parents. If he had to wait to do something special, even a whole week, he would remember and anticipate it, saying "Next weekend will be my chance to go to X or Y."

Both parents were now in a quite different relationship with Kyle. Father was more relaxed about the assertive and aggressive themes in his play, and less competitive and dominating with him than he had been earlier. Father had gained insight into his own pattern of subtle domination during floor time with his son. Whenever Kyle had tried to get the "upper hand" or be the dominant one, father had switched the theme until he, himself, was in control. In an earlier session, father had become aware that this subtle form of competition was undermining his son's ability to feel competent and assertive and to experiment more with assertiveness. Mother recognized that, while she loved her son very much, she tended to both infantilize him (treat him like a baby), yet also be controlling and anxious about his bowel movements. She was frightened of his ability to "defeat" her. The floor time, problem-solving approach had helped the family equilibrium shift. The parents showed greater respect for their son, who was now able to use fantasy and emotional ideas to elaborate his behaviors and his feelings, and to get into more of the assertive domain of life. He was learning that he didn't need to use only passive and negative modes to deal with conflict or anxiety. Most importantly, he was learning to use representational modes for all types of feelings—feelings about loss, about love, and about assertiveness. With his parents' decreased anxiety around the bowel movements, and the growing maturation of his own nervous system, he was now able to have good self-care and good self-regulation in the area where the initial symptoms had presented themselves. Interestingly, there were also nice signs that even his fine motor skills were generally improving.

We observed, in this case, a child who had mild constitutional–maturational and environmental contributions. They had limited his progression once he reached the representational area of development, resulting in constrictions around assertiveness, and constrictions in terms of representational depth and richness around all feelings. An intervention which focused on reestablishing this developmental progression and reducing the parents' focal anxiety around his bowel movements not only corrected the presenting symptoms, but also returned him to expected patterns of personality growth. In a relatively short intervention of less than eight sessions, over a period of three or four months, this youngster was back on track.

CASE NUMBER 19: TONY

As soon as Tony, a thirty-six-month-old boy, came in with his parents, he gave me a quick, warm smile. His manner was somewhat trusting and assertive as he walked in a little clumsily. He looked at my desk and around the room and then began wandering around aimlessly, taking no notice of me or any of the toys or items on my desk. His activity level was slightly high, but not extremely so. While he wandered around aimlessly, there was a sense of emotional connectedness to his parents, but an indirect one. He didn't look at them and make eye contact and he didn't exchange gestures with them. He stopped for a moment and let his father hug him and seemed to relax and enjoy it. After that, he did look occasionally at his parents, but he did not give them big smiles.

After a few minutes of watching Tony wander, I noticed that some islands of purposeful activity were emerging. For example, he took out a toy and, with father's help, was able to press a button that made it go "pop." He began opening and closing one of the doors leading out of the office, examining how it worked. When his parents said to him, "No, don't touch that," he was responsive and turned away. But he did not come to them, did not vocalize back to them, and did not even look at them; he just wandered to something else. He was clearly responsive to the parents' verbalizations that were setting limits.

As he walked around the room, Tony made lots of high-pitched sounds and squeals, like "Eek, Eek," and some other noises that were either gruff or high-pitched. There were no distinct syllables or babbles, indicating a private language; and no suggestion of his trying to say something either to the toys or me or his parents. I also noticed, as the family was getting organized, that mother looked depressed and tired as she tried to engage him. She said at one point, "Look, here. Here is a fire truck." He would notice it, take it from her, examine it, and then wander off.

At one point, perhaps indicating his highest level of inter-active organization, he got curious about the door leading from my office into my living room (not the door he came in by). He tried to open it. He went back and got mother by the hand, took her there, pointed to the latch, and made some motions indicating that she should try to open it. Mother said, "No, you can't go there." She was about to take him back to the middle of the room, using physical restraint, when I suggested that she might want to use his interest in the door to negotiate with him gesturally. Perhaps, Tony could indicate to her the level of his curiosity or interest, or, perhaps, they could negotiate a little about doing or undoing the latch, and so on. He was able to keep coming to the door, as she permitted this, and to maintain this more purposeful activity. He pointed at the latch, taking her hand to it; she lifted him up a few times and he tried to jiggle the latch. While he was doing this, he made sounds and was focused, and mother was gentle and supportive, and contingently responsive to his signals.

Since the family had told me over the phone some of their concerns about Tony's loss of language abilities and tendency to withdraw (and we were already involved in watching Tony), I suggested that father play with him first and help him get adapted to this new environment; we would talk later. Mother tended to follow Tony's lead and be responsive and contingent. For example, she would build on his interest in a fire truck by saying things like, "Here's another truck. Where's the fire truck going to go?" Even though he ignored her, she was making attempts to be responsive and contingent. She also responded to his gestures, moving a truck in one direction but then trying to move it in another direction to see if she could get some interest going. While mother was doing this, I should mention that she had some affect available: her facial animation was reasonable, as were her motor gestures and so forth.

In contrast, father tended to be less depressed looking, but more tense. He tended to structure things more and take over more, but in a somewhat anxious and fragmented way. For example, as soon as I suggested that he might want to play, he said to his son, "Let's play ring-around-a-rosie." He grabbed Tony's hands and tried to get him to dance around with him. His son cooperated to a degree, but wouldn't fall down when father said, "All fall down." Then father quickly said, "Let's play catch," and he threw the ball, rolling it at his son. Tony vaguely kicked it back in his direction. Then father said, "Do you want to read?" and quickly grabbed a book. Interestingly, Tony was able to open the book and turn some pages with him. Father, nonetheless, continued to introduce each new subject at a fairly rapid pace, making it difficult for Tony to take the lead himself. It was impossible for father to follow Tony's lead because he was too busy introducing new subjects. After watching this for a few more minutes, I sensed father's desire to relate to Tony and get some interaction going with him. I suggested that he might want to try building on what Tony was doing, to follow Tony's lead, and then try to build some interaction. As father relaxed and saw what Tony wanted to do, Tony took father by the hand and led him back to the same door he had been playing at with mother. He tried to get father to do something with the lock. I suggested that it was okay for Tony to play with the lock as much as he wanted. Father tried to show him several times how to open the latch, but Tony wouldn't copy him. Tony would look, but then turned away and wandered to another part of the room. Even though father was able to stay with the task rather than distract his son, Tony still couldn't follow father's desire to have him open the latch on his own.

Tony became frustrated with the door; he whined and cried at it. He was perhaps at his most organized when showing interest in the door. He kept at it for at least three to four minutes, returning to it many times. He even closed three or four circles of interaction around the door, in spite of not being able to imitate father's latch-opening behavior.

Following this, Tony wandered around the room, playing with some cars and examining other objects. Father fell back into his old patterns of play—he would quickly grab some other toy near Tony and try to distract him from the one with which the boy was already playing. Tony usually responded by tuning his father out and trying to continue whatever he was doing.

Throughout all this observation, Tony used no words or intentional-type sounds, other than sounds of frustration in terms of a babble. His behavior varied between aimlessness and purposeful interactions in which he could close three or four circles in a row, such as with the door play. Later, during the session, he was hungry and pointed to mother's pocketbook. She nodded that he could get some food out. He went and took out some cookies, and looked at mother again. She nodded approval, and he took out a cookie and ate it. This and the door play were his highest levels of organization.

Later, when Tony discovered a chair that turned, he spun it around a little and laughed. Father asked him if he wanted to spin in it; Tony came to his father, smiling, and then wandered away. Father switched gears, asking him if he wanted to look at a book. Father asked him if he would turn the page. Tony turned a page and then wandered away again. At one point, when Tony was eating his cookies, father asked him if he would give him a cookie, which he did. As Tony ate, he showed nice organized eye contact with his father. He slowed down and relaxed, making a number of focused gestures at his father and some warm smiles.

In general, Tony's style was to engage a little and then disengage, aimlessly wander around and then reengage. If his parents didn't draw him in, he would often brush by them or make some other contact. If they drew him in with suggestions like, "Look at the book" or "Look at the picture," he would go over to them for a moment before he wandered away again. In his highly motivated states involving the food and door, he stayed engaged for a good few minutes. I should also mention that when I made overtures to him, he was friendly, occasionally coming close to me, occasionally looking at me, and once or twice he gave me a faint smile. He was also responsive when I gestured with my arm that he was getting too close to my books or my papers; but he did not try to involve me in play any differently than he involved his parents. He obviously did not feel as comfortable with me, but was not aversive to me either.

The pregnancy and delivery were uneventful. He was a seven pound, six ounce baby who was physically healthy with 9/9 Apgars, and was very alert in the first weeks of life. By two months, mother said, "He was awake ten to twelve hours a day. Perhaps we were playing with him and keeping him awake too much." She said he was an easy baby, sleeping through the night by three to four months of age. He loved to look around and enjoyed sounds, particularly music. "He still likes music, especially classical," mother said. In infancy, Tony didn't show any negative reactions to sounds, and only later, between eight and ten months of age, did he show a slight aversion to a vacuum cleaner. Even so, he was able to adjust to that sound after hearing it once or twice. He had always loved rough, brisk movement, being picked up and moved around; he still enjoyed rough and tumble in his play. He also liked all kinds of touch—smooth gentle touch; being bathed; firm touch. Mother felt that he had been, in many respects, more alert and eager to look around and relate to them than most babies. Tony nursed for the first six months, and was weaned onto a milk-based formula. He was still getting milk, but he also now had a lot of juice and ate a wide range of foods. He had always been a "good eater." Mother felt that in the first few months of life he followed her face, looked at her, and responded to her voice, as well as to her facial expressions. She was home full time during this period, and enjoying him. When he was about eight months of age, mother returned to work part time. She stopped work entirely when he was about fourteen months of age because she wanted to get pregnant with her second baby. During this time Tony had a steady baby-sitter whom he responded to well. Also, mother's mother lived nearby and helped out with the caregiving. Tony had gotten to know his grandmother very well.

By three to four months old, Tony was smiling warmly and was very engaging and vocal, making lots of different sounds. Mother recalled a photograph of Tony at four to five months: he was reaching out with his arms to be picked up. He was already gesturing quite a lot and could let them know what he wanted by pointing and other gestures. Mother also mentioned that Tony was extremely aware of strangers. By four months he was showing caution and even anxiety when a stranger came to pick him up or take him from mother. He seemed to recognize his own boundaries of feeling secure and insecure. He would turn away and stiffen his body if a stranger approached him too rapidly, even if the stranger was a friend of mother's or a relative. He took a while to get warmed up to new people.

If they flirted with him for a while from a distance, he would eventually allow them to pick him up and play with him.

Between four and eight months of age, in addition to reaching out to be picked up, he liked to play peek-a-boo and other interactive games. Father vividly recalled that by the time Tony was nine months old and was crawling quite solidly, they would each get on opposite sides of the room and crawl toward each other as though they were playing a football game, charging at one another and then falling into each other's arms to wrestle. Tony loved to play this repetitive roughhousing game. He was also using lots of vocalizations and making intentional and distinct "ma" and "da" sounds by ten months of age, and pointing to objects as he looked at his parents.

Both parents agreed that toward the end of the first year Tony's personality was crystallizing. He was a very alert, superaware baby who was highly cautious of new experiences and new people, but, with patience and familiarity, he could slowly warm up to them. They felt he had been developing into a verbally gifted child who would be very aware and bright, but a little bit on the cautious side. Tony's temperament had seemed much like their own, especially father's. Father revealed a history of anxiety and patterns of avoidance, which had reached a crescendo in college; he had gotten quite depressed and was paralyzed with anxiety for periods of time in terms of studying and work, but was able to overcome it with treatment. Mother did not have a psychiatric history; in fact, with the exception of father's depression, neither parent reported clear psychiatric histories in either family.

As a toddler, Tony had pointed at everything, but he especially loved books. He would say, "Book," and "Read." He was very determined and focused and when he wanted a book read to him, he would go and grab it and bring it to his mother or father. He would look them in the eye and say, "Read, read." He also enjoyed pushing his trucks and pulling things. Mother recalled enjoying singing "The Wheels on the Bus" to him. During this period, he would explore different parts of the room and the house, and would come to his parents for reading. He wanted to have them read to him "all the time." He also loved shape-sorting toys and took great delight in putting them in the right hole, and he smiled enthusiastically when his parents were admiring of his ability. He also loved a particular video and would ask for it by name and point to it. They were impressed with how focused and deliberate he was, how much he enjoyed being read to, and how he orchestrated this with them.

During the latter part of Tony's toddler stage, when he was about sixteen or seventeen months old, mother exposed him more to other children, in a play group or at a playground. She immediately noticed that he was a "shy, observer type." He would seem to be a little overwhelmed at first, but then he would go and join the other children for a little while. Then he'd come back and hold onto mother for a while and then go back, playing near the other children or interacting with them a little. When in a house where he had a chance to be with other children for long time, Tony could slowly warm up and would play near them, and, occasionally, he had some gestural-type interactions with them.

By the time he was twenty-one months old, Tony had become quite verbal and had a vocabulary of somewhere between 150 and 200 words. He could also recite the entire alphabet and count to ten; identify a variety of shapes, animals, and other things; and knew a number of verbs and was beginning to do some phrasing. There was no evidence of any echolalia and, according to his parents, he had initiated speech and used vocabulary in a spontaneous and meaningful way. They gave numerous examples of Tony describing a toy or telling his parents what he wanted. He also liked to play interactive games, such as "Wheels on the Bus," but seemed to favor more structured kinds of games. I should also mention, as indicated earlier, that his motor milestones were in the normal to early range—sitting by five-and-a-half months, walking at ten months, and using words by nine to ten months.

This rather positive pattern of a somewhat verbally precocious, perhaps overly alert (stranger anxiety at 4 months), somewhat cautious child began changing around eighteen months
of age. Until then, he had been coping rather well with his
balance of verbal precocity, awareness, and mild to moderate
cautiousness.

Around that time Tony began having a series of middle
ear infections, with discomfort, fluid, multiple antibiotic treatments, including prophylactic antibiotic use, and eventually had
tubes put in to help drain the fluid. Hearing was not impaired,
however. But during this time, Tony gradually became more
anxious and frightened, with repetitious nightmares and daytime fears of strangers, new children, and even clowns and
certain types of costumes.

When Tony was twenty-eight months old his sister was
born. He cried jealously whenever mother held her. Once when
his grandmother tried to approach him after the strain of sister
being born, he gave her an angry grimace. Shortly thereafter,
he began to "weep silently for no apparent reason, showed
little interest in toys, cried bitterly upon seeing his sister every
morning, and spent much more time by himself." He also
would hit his little sister or push her. His parents had to keep
an eye on him.

He gradually began losing his speech and became more
withdrawn. Tony's parents took him to a number of doctors
soon after he began losing his speech. At first, they saw a social
worker who tried some limited play therapy once a week. The
therapist felt that his speech loss was a traumatic reaction to
the birth of his sister and his ear infections, but the therapy
had little benefit.

In the fall, his "autisticlike" behavior became much more
pronounced, and the parents aggressively tried to get a diagnostic workup of Tony's problems. They felt he was more disengaged, had lost interest in books and toys, and had begun to
spend more of his time in a hyperkinetic remote stare. Occasionally, he would seek the simple sensory stimulation of touch.

(Only recently, they felt, had he shown some marginal improvement from his most "acute phase." He was now showing some renewed interest in books and toys and was a little less remote. He had stopped seeking simple sensory stimulation.)

While continuing this play therapy, the parents sought a consultation with a psychiatrist oriented to the kind of problem Tony was experiencing. They were referred to another therapist to whom the parents felt they could not relate. "She didn't know what she was doing," they said. They were then referred to yet another psychiatrist who did a diagnostic workup. It was suggested that Tony have a physical workup to rule out any organic pathology. Over the next few months, he had laboratory procedures, including EEGs, brain scans, X-rays, neurologic workups, chromosome studies, metabolic studies, and electromagnetic resonance studies, all of which were negative.

The parents came to see me at the suggestion of their current therapist. They were anxious to see if any further light could be shed on their son's condition and to get a more definitive recommendation about an optimal treatment pattern. Their most prominent concern was his complete "lack of speech." He made a lot of noise, but not to communicate. Occasionally, they could "hear some consonants and vowels," perhaps even the word *doggie*, but much of it was diffuse. They were also quite worried about both his aimlessness and his hyperkinetic and unfocused behavior which varied, they reported, from day to day. "He can run back and forth and jump up and down, examine, flap, or wring his hands, shout or babble without any obvious purpose," they said. "At other times," they added, "he can be relatively calm and focused, will sit and listen to music or sometimes look at pictures or watch TV." I had observed his ability to gesture with nonverbal signals, such as when he felt hungry; to continue to understand some aspects of speech. If, for example, the parents said he was not to do something or mentioned a favorite food or TV program, he would respond to that; just as he would to daily directives, like "Go to the bathroom" or "Brush your teeth."

During this whole time, the parents reported that Tony continued to be cuddly and warm with them. He would hug them and sometimes sit in their laps, enjoying their closeness. They also reported that none of his puzzling behavior seemed to have affected his gross motor skills. He was "strong and agile," and his physical health was good. The routine pediatric visits were showing solid growth and weight gain, although the parents felt that Tony was less sure of himself with fine than with gross motor tasks. Nevertheless, he could pick up little bits of food and occasionally fist a crayon and scribble in circlelike motions.

When I talked to the parents about their reaction to Tony's difficulties and their own past history, mother reported that she had been eager for a child. It had not been hard for her to leave work to raise a family. Father expressed more anxiety and worry about having children and talked about his own history, particularly his depression in his college years. He was very interested in interacting with his son, but tended to be a little anxious, intrusive, and overstructured. It seemed that with some help and support, he would be able to accommodate his son. Mother appeared to be a warm, empathetic woman, somewhat stressed, depressed, and worried about her son, but still able to be supportive, contingent, and responsive in interacting with him. They both reported being worried about Tony and exhausted by their concern. But their collective anxiety had not precipitated power struggles or difficulties between the two of them; they felt they were supportive to one another.

The preliminary impression was that Tony had reasonable constitutional and early maturational patterns. His early individual differences were, most likely, only making him partially vulnerable. He had the type of constitutional vulnerability that, under ordinary circumstances, could have conceivably been an asset for this little boy. It might have given him some difficulty when he got into preschool peer groups or began nursery school involving lots of activity—he might have been slow to warm up and slow to join circle time—and he might have had some separation difficulty. But he would not have had the kind of constrictions we were seeing here. The usual picture for children who develop a pervasive developmental disorder around this age is of much more severe constitutional–maturational risk on the side of receptive language skills and expressive language skills, and a tendency to tune out or avoid rather than a tendency for precocious fears and the like. When considering the psychological stress Tony suffered, one has to wonder about his parents' availability to him to help negotiate this stress during a time that must have been very stressful for them as well. The history is not entirely clear, although they state that they were available to him and supportive of him all the time.

There is another element in this case that is worthy of consideration. Did the ear infections and continuous use of antibiotics create some general systemic and physiologic stress that made him more vulnerable to the psychological stresses? A physiologic disruption of some kind, secondary to the use of antibiotics, may need to be considered, as well as allergic reactions and other types of sensitivities to the antibiotics.

Even though the etiology of Tony's deterioration is elusive, one can postulate three general factors:

1. A mild to moderate constitutional–maturational vulnerability;
2. Psychological stress and trauma;
3. Some intervening physiologic stress associated with the middle ear infections, as well as the continuous use of antibiotics.

The nature of Tony's symptoms, given the age-appropriate earlier development, make this case one which raises more questions than it answers. It is presented in part to illustrate a pattern that one sees not infrequently. The pattern is one of seemingly pervasive loss of functioning in a child who has had age-appropriate earlier patterns of development.

When talking with the parents about Tony's treatment, I stressed that they should not try to make him skip over where he is in their effort to arrive at where they would like him to be. I suggested that we work backwards from his top level of functioning, now about the fourteen- to sixteen-month-old level, taking into account that he functions at a much earlier level of development when he is disengaged and completely aimless. (When he was engaged around the door or taking father's hand to help him get food, he operates at his highest level—that of a 14- to 16-month-old. But when he disengages or is aimless or is only closing one circle, he is operating more like an 8-month-old or even a 4-month-old.) The treatment must, therefore, include the goals of reestablishing his relatedness and interest in the world; his capacity for two-way communication; increase the complexity of his gestures while maintaining engagement; and begin presymbolic and symbolic activities, while maintaining affective ties and using symbolic activities to deal with affective and interpersonal issues. To achieve these goals, I made six recommendations:

1. He would be seen four times per week in individual play therapy, involving the parents, and once a week with parent counseling.
2. He would be evaluated by a speech pathologist and have a minimum of twice-a-week speech therapy.
3. He would be assessed by an occupational therapist, looking for differences in sensory reactivity and motor planning and fine motor control. The number of weekly sessions (1 or 2) would depend on the findings.
4. The parents would do floor time with him, for twenty- to thirty-minute intervals each; mother during the day and the evening, and father in the evening. They would focus on shared attention and engagement, two-way communication, and increasing gestures, working up to early presymbolic play. I reviewed with the parents how to do this, and the therapist would also work with them.
5. I also suggested that they do an elimination diet regarding milk and dairy products, chemicals, and sugar, and later on different types of fruit, as well as peanuts, to see if he is sensitive. Food allergies may be interfering

with his capacity for attention and focus and follow-through.

6. Finally, I recommended to his therapist that we follow up the possibility of a reaction to the use of antibiotics and explore this diagnostically.

This case will be closely followed. There are some positive factors: he has retained his affection and cuddling with his parents (when I saw him, he was quite trusting, warm, and engaged with parents, even though aimless). He has retained his ability to organize things when highly motivated and operates as high as the fourteen- to sixteen-month-old level—all without any organized treatment. He should learn to relate and be more organized in his interactions. He should also be able to get to the symbolic level of functioning. Once the behavioral and emotional problems improve, it may be possible to see more clearly his unique pattern of individual differences. This, however, will be a long and intensive course of treatment occurring over a period of many years.

CASE NUMBER 20: SAM

Sam's parents brought their three-year-old to see me because they were worried that his language and speech were not what they expected them to be. They described Sam as physically "doing okay." Now, at age three, he had about "sixty words." They felt that until recently he had said more complicated things, such as "I saw nanny." Lately he was saying, "I saw bye-bye." He could say single words, however, like *waffle, toast, juice,* and things that he wanted. He could also say certain action words like *walk,* but their biggest concern was his limited use of language.

The pregnancy and delivery were described as unremarkable. Sam had been a good-sized eight-pound baby who had been fussy, colicky, and "not easy." He had, however, enjoyed being touched, and enjoyed being moved up and down. In fact, he'd seemed to crave movement. He had not startled to loud sounds, and had slept through most loud music. If he did get upset, the parents described themselves as having done "everything for him," in order to help him calm down. Sam gradually became slightly more comfortable by the time he was four months old, and his parents, though weak historians, remembered him as having smiled and been happy at this age. But by eight months of age, they remembered him as being "very active." At nine months, he was already walking and "cried a lot." When he was fussy "we tried to guess what he wanted and give it to him" they said. By ten to twelve months, he would take one of their hands and try to walk them to go get something. They described Sam's general development as progressing as expected for the first ten to twelve months of live. He seemed a little more fussy and finicky than other babies and they had tried to cater to this by rocking him and getting him things he wanted. Both these patterns had seemed to calm him down.

The parents felt that after twelve to sixteen months or so he had never developed more complex gestures. For example, he would take mother's hand, walk her to the refrigerator, open the door, and point to the food he wanted; or he would take father on a search around the house to find the toy he wanted; or he would take father's hat off, imitate him, and smile, and then show he wanted to play "throw me up in the air," by gesturing to father to do it. (Only in the last few months had Sam gotten into more complex behavior, where he would imitate father or seemingly fool around.) In addition, they described the fourteen-month to about twenty-eight month period as having had a similar quality throughout it. Sam had engaged in some complex gestures and began making more and more sounds, eventually saying a few words, but hadn't gotten very elaborate in terms of either his gestural or verbal communication.

There was no indication of any particular family stress, although upon further examination it appeared that father was going through a difficult time at work. Mother felt that she was home most of the time, although she had consistent help. She spoke about being worried about her husband being worried, and her husband being somewhat of a workaholic, coming home late. But according to her, there were no other particular stresses in the family.

Mother felt that Sam's fine motor skills were not developing, just as his language was not developing. He was still scribbling, holding a crayon in his fist. At age three he wasn't making any particular shapes. He did, however, mother reported, love approval from people he liked. He'd look at them and say, "Bye-bye." He could repeat his alphabet, which he seemed to have learned by memory; and more recently, in his play, he had taken to lining up things, such as trucks. On further reflection, mother indicated that, although Sam loved to be touched and hugged, he didn't like baths. But he did like his skin rubbed with all kinds of different textures. Mother also felt he loved roughhousing and rough and tumble—he almost craved it—and that he liked loud noises.

Mother was worried that Sam now had a shorter attention span than when he was a baby. If confronted by a lot of toys, he would play with each one for a few seconds. Or if she was trying to engage him, he would be easily distracted by a noise.

In terms of his diet, he loved carbohydrates and dairy but he didn't like sweets. He had been on medication for a chronic middle ear infection for quite a time. He had been prescribed Keflex, which had a strawberrylike flavoring. His hearing had been tested and appeared to be in the normal range.

Among the family patterns was the fact that mother had had a miscarriage a few months earlier. She had been feeling somewhat sad, but not terribly depressed. She thought the family relationships were basically warm and emotional, although her son would kiss only her. She said, "He becomes extra warm to me when I'm upset. He is very sensitive to my moods." She described his play with father as consisting of more hide-and-go-seek and rough-and-tumble and roughhousing, chase-type games (father was not able to make this first session due to his work schedule). Father usually didn't get home until between

seven and nine o'clock at night and she thought that this contributed to Sam's poor sleep patterns. Sometimes he went to
sleep at nine o'clock, sometimes ten-thirty P.M., and often had
a hard time falling asleep. When Sam had tantrums they could
last ten or twenty minutes; and it took him another ten minutes
to recover. He didn't interact a lot with new children, but was
willing to do parallel play with them in a play group. On occasion he played chase games and other interactive games with
children.

Mother characterized the family pattern as "always doing
for Sam." She mentioned that this was particularly difficult
when father was under stress at work and she was trying to
make everyone feel good, especially father.

Sam presented as a good-sized, shy three-year-old who hid
behind his mother as he walked somewhat clumsily into the
playroom. I suggested they might play together. He was clearly
being coy with me, glancing occasionally at me, but then hiding
behind his mother. As soon as he came in the playroom, he
tried to get mother to leave the playroom with him and pulled
at the door. He looked at me. Meanwhile, mother was a little
tense and intrusive, putting a puppet in his face and talking
quickly; as she made the puppet kiss him he tried to push it
away. Then he grabbed onto her leg and held on. Later, as she
sat down, he clumsily crawled along while hugging and grabbing her. I noticed he seemed to enjoy crawling over her, and
hugged her above and beyond just trying to hide behind her
to avoid looking at me. He got up and tried to open a drawer
where toys were kept, and figure out how it worked. He was
trying the different things in the drawer and seemed to have
an interest in mechanical things. He looked at me quickly again,
with a coy look, and then quickly looked away.

Mother then handed him a ball. When she mentioned that
he could throw the ball, he smiled and threw it down. As he
threw it a second time, really hard, he had kind of a look of
sadistic glee on his face. Mother said, "Oh," and he replied,
"Oh, oh." They had an exchange of "Oh" and "Oh, oh" around
his throwing the ball. She called his name when he was throwing

the ball. He ignored her. Sometimes he seemed to "close the circle" and respond to her gestures or vocalizations with gestures or sounds (no words) back, and at other times he would seem to tune her out and ignore her. Mother tended to intrude on him and change his play. If, for example, he was throwing a ball, she would try to pick up a doll or something else to get a new activity going, instead of moving in and throwing the ball back and trying to get some vocalization going or some complexity to the ball throwing. She zoomed cars up and down his body, presumably to get him to respond. There was always lots of physical contact in her play. Sam would usually look at her, sometimes seemed to push her away, and at other times began crawling all over her as she moved the cars up and down his body. They exchanged grunts and "Ohs" and high-pitched noises; they gesturally recognized one another, and showed a lot of warmth and connectedness, but rarely did they exchange complex gestures. There were no words.

He persisted in hiding from me, but intermittently peeked out with a coy look. Then, looking away, he hid behind mother again.

When Sam tried to leave the room, he and his mother played with the door. He opened it and she would close it. He would look at her and angrily push it open; and then she would smile and push it closed. Sam would make some sounds and again push it open. This seemed to be a fairly organized interaction, but at a simple gestural level. Suddenly, with an abrupt change of pace, mother said, "Let's play ring-around-a-rosie." She grabbed his hand, and started dancing with him. She said, "Ring-around-a-rosie," and he would say, "fall," and they would fall down together. This was their best and only verbal and gestural intraction. At one point, though, mother tried to help him draw. He fisted the crayon and scribbled chaotically.

As the session progressed, mother became more playful. She showed warmth and support in her interactions and less intrusiveness and anxiety. As she played with him, she told me that he sometimes said, "Come now" when he wanted to go somewhere.

I suggested that she might try to "close as many circles as she could." I explained that a circle was when Sam would do A, and she would then do a B related to his A. She would then see if she could encourage him to do a C, so that he would build on her response and "close the circle of communication." They began playing with a toy house that had lots of doors and compartments to open, and many slides within the house to slide a little doll down. At first mother just tried sitting. She appeared perplexed as to how to join the play, now that Sam was opening and exploring the doors with good focused concentration. He opened the house door, mother handed him a truck, and he put the truck in the house. There were sounds accompanying this, but no distinct words. This was their best circle. He then continued to examine the house with great focus and concentration, opening up each door and putting dolls in one or the other. He clearly understood how the different slides within the house worked—if he put a doll in one hole, it would come out another hole. As he was showing this good focus in examining the house, mother and Sam closed some nice gestural circles together; she handed him objects that he put in the various compartments and caught some of them as they came out of the compartments; he held his hand out and she would give him something. They made nice eye contact and their play had a rhythmic quality. There was some exchange of sounds.

Sam, as evidenced in the way he examined the different aspects of the house, could intermittently focus his attention and concentration. He was warmly engaged with mother, and the quality of warm engagement seemed quite pleasurable on both sides, with lots of physical hugging and handling. When it came to interacting, however, his repertoire was more limited. He was capable of simple gestural interactions, such as taking a toy from mother and putting it into a compartment in the toy house, or indicating the office door and pointing at it. He even tried to open it, while making vocal and facial gestures, revealing that he wanted out of the office. He could do this similarly around some of the toys in play. But he didn't evidence any complex gestures by stringing together three or four gestures in a row, or doing complex imitations, even though, in an isolated sense, he had done some of that by following the rules for "Ring-around-a-rosie, all fall down." He evidenced minimal use of words in a gestural sense, using words not to convey complex symbolic meanings, but more to convey simple intentions.

His mood varied from excited to sober. He responded to limits in a variable fashion but for the most part was never out of control. There was no evidence of representational (symbolic) play or true representational (verbal) communication in terms of any emotional theme, even dependency.

In terms of developmental patterns, he evidenced scatter in the twelve- to twenty-four-month-old range, with most of his gestural and behavioral patterns suggestive of the twelve- to sixteen-month-old range. Sam was able to organize himself around simple focused tasks, such as examining the house and its various compartments. He also could organize himself around being shy or being negative, as shown by the way he avoided me and hid behind mother and in the way he wanted to get out of the office. But even at the gestural level, he didn't show a lot of range in terms of affects or behaviors. There was evidence of some curiosity about the house and how it worked; some assertive and explorative play, and intentionality in getting mother to hand him the dolls and things; and there was some warmth and closeness with mother. But there wasn't the infectious range of charm that would tend to bring others into his play. Even at the gestural level he seemed to be constricted, although not severely so.

While lacking representational capacities, there were hints, however, that this level of awareness and his comprehension of his world might be higher than his expressive capacities. This was suggested by the way he took in a new situation, and also by the way he organized his pattern of shyness and mechanically examined how things worked. In his ability to comprehend spatial relations and mechanical relationships there were suggestions for circumscribed areas of higher level functioning.

The clinical impression of Sam was of a child who was delayed in organizing some of his basic ego functions. At age three, he was not yet at a representational level, although he had variable intentional gestural capacities. At the same time, he seemed emotionally comfortable with closeness and dependency, but didn't have flexibility to negotiate new situations comfortably or negotiate around other emotions. His ability to concentrate and modulate behavior was variable. Contributing to his deficit in basic ego functions was a marked receptive and expressive language delay, fine and gross motor delays, and indications of sensory overreactivity and sensory processing difficulties. He was between one and two years behind in terms of his functional capacities. Normally, we would see representational capacities emerging between eighteen and twenty-four months.

After further observation, the program for him required additional evaluation including:

1. A language evaluation (including hearing) by a speech pathologist, with the possibility of two or more sessions a week of language work.
2. A sensory and motor evaluation by an occupational therapist, to look for sensory reactivity and sensory processing difficulties, with the possibility of one to two sessions a week.
3. A neurologic and pediatric evaluation to assess possible organic contributions.
4. Parent and family evaluation with the possibility of following through with counseling for the parents to help them set up a home program and deal with their own emotional reactions and patterns.
5. An evaluation for interactive play therapy with the possibility of three to five sessions a week.
6. A psychoeducational preschool program would also need to be considered.

A comprehensive treatment program was initiated and within a four-month period of time there were initial indications of significant progress. In a follow-up visit, he was much more engaged on a continuous basis and evidenced greater focus and capacity to attend. In fact, he appeared to be entering a phase where he was extremely sensitive to interpersonal dynamics, easily becoming overstimulated, irritable, and overly active. During this phase, there was also a rapid increase in the acquisition and use of language. He would intermittently respond to three- or four-word sentences and would use three-word sentences when motivated, such as wanting to go outside.

At this time, the main challenge appeared to be the driven and fragmented quality to his functional communication. Gestures and symbols were now used, but not always in a logical, organized manner. When his gestures and words were the most fragmented, he could also appear as aimless and random as he had originally. Yet even during these episodes of seemingly aimless activity there was still a sense of his awareness of and concern with those around him. At his most intense level, his therapist felt that he was engaged, but in a more need-fulfilling way than a way that would suggest mutual regard and empathy.

It was noticed during this time that his mother followed his lead nicely and was always tuned in to him, but she had a tendency to respond to his gestures or words too quickly. In responding so quickly, she often compromised his potential attempt at explaining more fully either through his behavior or words what he wished or what his goals were. Mother, therefore, was contributing to the frenetic fragmented quality of the interaction and communication patterns. Father tended to be slower and give him more time, but was less gifted at following his lead.

During states of transition where the child wanted something badly, we observed some very organized communications and interactions. For example, he wanted to go outside and hit a tennis ball. Father: "Hit ball in here." Child: "No—Go outside." Father: "Right now?" Child: "Now." Father: "Can't we wait?" Child: "Want to go outside." Finally, when they did go outside, the child was able to hit a tennis ball with excellent coordination and with an extreme look of pleasure and satisfaction.

The next challenge was to help this child slow down his thinking and behavior and learn to become more organized and differentiated in his feelings, thoughts, and behavior. This next step would require his parents to work patiently with him on opening and closing symbolic circles of communication. He is making excellent progress toward more differentiated modes of communicating.

His comprehensive program continues with a focus on taking advantage of his enthusiasm and pleasure in having his needs met in relationships and harnessing this enthusiasm and pleasure through lots of patient negotiations involving sequences of gestures and words. After almost a year of therapeutic work, his fragmented and formerly aimless patterns have given way to more organized styles of relating and thinking. There is still a way to go, but important developmental stages have been successfully negotiated.

CASE NUMBER 21: ALAN

Alan was a three-and-a-half-year-old boy brought in by his parents because of problems in his thinking and conversation, and with his helping himself. They said he tended to "march to the beat of his own drummer," and that a neurologist who had seen him diagnosed his problem as one of "abstracting." The parents said Alan knew numerous songs and even had perfect pitch (music was a big part of his life), but if they asked him a question he'd just repeat it and didn't seem to understand how to give an answer. They characterized him as "jittery"—he would "hop around a lot"—and his voice tended to be anxious and tense. He enjoyed being around children but didn't interact with them very much; he might even toss objects and occasionally hurt another child instead of engaging in pretend or interactive play. His parents said he seemed somewhat impervious to them. His play was intrusive and tended to scare other children; for example, he would take away another child's car without showing any sense of another person's feelings about possessions.

With his mother, Alan played a little more. She explained he would try to keep an object and not return it to her, such as in a sharing game of throwing the ball back and forth. She felt he was trying to get her "irritated." But he also didn't seem able to distinguish between her being angry at him, excited with him, or accepting of him. He would ignore her angry looks or glances, sometimes giggling excitedly.

Mother also felt that Alan did not have much of a relationship with his father. She said that they were kept apart; to which father chimed in that his wife kept his son and him apart because she wanted to control everything. "She thinks she knows best," he said.

Alan's parents reported they had noticed his poor fine motor development and coordination when he was about three years old. An evaluation led to an occupational therapy evaluation. He was now receiving occupational treatment once a week to improve his fine motor skills. (Apparently the examination revealed that there was some decrease of motor tone in the upper extremities and some problems with motor planning.)

While his parents were giving me the history, I watched him playing. Although he looked serious, his play engaged me: he was looking at me, pointing at toys, looking again for permission to go the closet. I nodded to him that he could go. There were occasional comments of "What's this" or "What's that," and he seemed interested in trucks. When I commented to him that we had some big trucks, he looked expectantly and was able to say, "Where?"

Mother revealed that he had trouble answering "why" or "how" questions. He did have some conversational abilities, but they seemed less mature than a three-year-old's, not an almost three-and-a-half-year-old's. She added that he ate and slept well and could be close to both her and father; he would cuddle them both at times, although he seemed to prefer her. Father chimed in again, "That's because she keeps us apart."

In discussing family patterns, father felt that mother was controlling and overprotective, needing to do this her way. Mother presented herself as a somewhat anxious, protective person who worried a lot. She was working half-time and had babysitters, who changed with some regularity about every six months. Father said, "I'm angry at her, but I tend to give in." He felt there was a lot of "guerilla warfare" in the family.

Mother felt that father tended to be too passive and avoidant and would withdraw from conflict. He had had some illnesses and deaths in his family, she said, including his own mother's death. She felt he had been unavailable to both herself and the child. "I took over by necessity," she said. Father disagreed. He felt that she overreacted to his getting depressed once in a while. Yet he agreed that he would pull away when he felt his overtures were not welcomed by her. There was clearly a lot of marital tension and disagreement over whether mother was anxious, controlling, and rejecting, or whether father was passive and avoidant. Both agreed that they each had some of those tendencies; it was a question of who threw the first stone.

Alan's developmental history included being adopted when he was three months old, at which time he was not very reactive or responsive. While sleeping and eating patterns were good, he seemed unavailable to sights, sounds, and the parents' emotional gestures. He was slow in his motor development, being late in crawling and sitting up. He did, however, seem to catch up when it came to walking and walked between thirteen and fourteen months. "Now he runs like a whirlwind," mother reported, and he had learned to skip and hop six months earlier. His motor planning, which had led the parents to the neurologic and occupational therapy evaluations, was slow, however, in terms of complex, planned movements. His fine motor ability was also low in regard to such activities as holding a pencil, writing, drawing, and tying shoelaces.

They felt that during Alan's first year he gradually came out of his nonreactive, unresponsive state, and was by six or seven months engaged with them; he could smile warmly, but was very passive and never took the initiative. Only recently did they feel that he initiated hugs with them, for example, although he had been receptive to their hugs earlier.

While we were going over the history, I was interested in watching him play: he was putting the whale puppet on his hand. When I interrupted him for a second and asked, "Does the whale talk?" he almost had the whale talk back at me. He toyed with it and then put it down. He seemed to be struggling to comprehend what this pretend whale could do.

Mother reported that in his second year, after Alan had learned to walk, he seemed to be in "perpetual motion." His behavior became intentional. When she initiated play with him, such as handing him a ball, he would take it but he wouldn't necessarily hand it back. He would play intently with cars and trucks and was warm if you approached him; while at other times, he would wander around the room, fidgeting, looking at things, and exploring many different objects. As he got toward the middle of the second year, he began pulling the hair of other children and also pulling mother's and father's hair. On occasion, when he got frustrated, he would lie on the floor and bang his head.

His speech was delayed, but toward the end of the second year, he did start vocalizing using lots of different sounds. He didn't use words until about age two-and-a-half, and had only recently put words together into sentences (at age $3\frac{1}{3}$, about 2 months before this evaluation began).

There were no significant medical illnesses; mother reported that she did not know what his genetic history was; he had been adopted from Asia. As mother talked further and completed Alan's developmental history, she also revealed, somewhat reluctantly, that she was very frightened because one of his teachers, and one of the evaluators, suggested he might have some "autistic features." She was worried that, because of his ability to sometimes march to his own drummer, move aimlessly around, and seemingly be unrelated, he could become or was autistic.

In play with mother, Alan was able to relate and engage, share attention, and begin two-way communication, both at a gestural and a verbal level. As they were playing, mother asked him, "What do you think the doctor is doing?" I was taking notes; and he was able to say, "He writing." Mother was quite responsive, not only supportive and attentive, but also contingent. She responded to his overtures gesturally and symbolically. As they played with cars and trucks, mother empathized with his pleasure in motor activity; they also played with the doll house, making some of the soldiers go to the top of the house and some to the bottom of the house, and some jump off the roof. He used selective words like *jumping*, *falling*, and looked serious, exhibiting a narrow range of emotion. Mother was tense and, at times, overcontrolled him, but at other times was supportive and gentle.

When father played with Alan, he said, "Look here, I found a globe," as a way of getting his son's attention. His son went to mother though, ignoring him. Father seemed shy and in need of encouragement. Instead of taking over, he became passive and silent as his son went back to mother. He admitted confusion when his son brought things out of left field or ignored him. I watched as he kept trying to bring out a toy that would interest his son. But he had a passive, serious, unelaborative emotional expression and not much wooing power. The child looked at the toy for a second, and then went back to playing with mother, often jumping in her lap and at other times making the truck he was holding go into her knee.

At the end of this first session, it appeared that there was a history of uneven motor development and motor planning problems. Alan had a history of being passive and not taking much initiative, but seemed to progress through some of the levels, or core, developmental processes (e.g., sharing attention and engaging, learning two-way gestural communication). But he was having trouble with very complex gestures and fully engaging at the level of symbolic differentiation in the stage he was at; and he had only partially engaged in full representational elaboration, in terms of developing themes and make-believe. He was knocking at the representational door, so to speak, but not yet fully in it. Even though he had mastered the early stages of two-way communication, engagement, and shared attention, he had not yet mastered the use of emotional ideas and emotional thinking, although elements of them were in place. In terms of handling aggression and frustration, he tended to withdraw to pre-two-way communication stages and become aimless or very avoidant. During most of the time in my office, though, Alan was related and showed solid gestural communication, reasonable focus, and some capacity for warmth, especially with mother.

It seemed clear, at the end of this first session, that this child did not evidence any serious or worrisome autistic features. But he was showing a pattern of uneven development and was lagging in social and emotional, as well as aspects of cognitive and language functioning. I talked with the parents about obtaining a speech evaluation, in addition to the occupational therapy (OT) evaluation that he had already completed; doing elimination diets to see if he was sensitive to any foods that were undermining his capacity for controlling his aggression and maintaining his attention better than was now the case; about the parents doing floor time with him to expand the gestural level to very complex modes, in the hope that this would enable him to begin entering more into the symbolic level of emotional ideas and begin pretend play. We also talked about increasing his access to peers while the mother or another adult served as an intermediary to increase peer-to-peer interactions without aggressive acting out.

At three-and-a-half, Alan was already in a special education developmental disabilities program for preschoolers because of his uneven motor development and his lack of age-appropriate language development, as well as his emotional and social and behavior difficulties. We consulted with his school to mobilize the same kinds of floor time perspective we were developing with the parents.

I also talked to the parents about their relationship with each other. I stressed the importance of father doing daily floor time and not allowing his feelings about mother to cause him to be passive or avoidant. I referred them to a couples' therapist to work on their relationship in terms of each of them having the perception that the other was culpable. Perhaps if each could deal with his own patterns—father, his avoidant pattern, and mother, her overcontrolling, anxious, and fragmented style—they could work better as a team. They did seem committed to each other and wanted to work together to help their child.

A few months later, the parents returned, reporting having worked very hard at carrying out the instructions. They had done floor time every day and tried to help Alan use his existing language for some problem-solving discussions; such as making choices about what he wanted to eat or which game he wanted to play, or describing what he might have done at school.

The speech evaluation revealed that Alan was at least in the average range in intelligence, seemed selectively to attend, and had age-appropriate comprehension, although it was somewhat uneven. He could do some things above age level and some things below age level. He did not show major articulation problems, but there were some minor difficulties, such as with word retrieval, an area for which the speech pathologist had recommended some exercises.

Later, in a follow-up meeting, the parents said that they had been carrying out the recommendations of the occupational therapist and speech therapist. They had been doing lots of floor time and were working on reality-based problem-solving type discussions where they helped him close a logical circle of communication using words. Father had become very involved with Alan, and mother was trying to have him increase the complexity of his play gesturally. She felt that he was showing some spontaneous emergence of symbolic play, an area that he hadn't been fully involved in. This may have, in part, accounted for his tendency toward more primitive modes of interacting, particularly aggressive interactions, and some of his inability to deal with peers.

When I saw Alan three months later, he gave me a nice greeting and engaged me much more warmly than the first time. There was a smile on his face as he said, "Hello." He immediately asked, "Where's the Halloween toy?" I got it out of the closet and he looked at me and started playing with it. I asked him if he liked it and he said, "Yes." But then he tuned me out and played with his toy. I felt that I had to work to keep him engaged; if I did, he opened and closed circles, stayed related, and talked to me in sentences. When I asked him if there was anything he wanted to tell me about things he had done, he said, "I went to an amusement park." I asked him what was there, and he said, "A ferris wheel." His mother then chimed in, "He's making that up." I indicated that I thought it was a pretty good answer, whether he was making it up or not. As he was playing with certain toys selectively, I wondered out loud why he liked certain toys, and he said, "Because *I like them!*" While the answer was a low-level response to a "why" question ("I like it because I like it"), the intonation suggested a comprehension of the "why" kind of question.

In his play he tended to be somewhat fragmented and to use the toys he saw in front of him rather than trying to find others. But he did begin some pretend play; he had an animal on a truck and talked about the wolf biting the little girl doll.

In the play with his parents, this time with father first, Alan told him he was "going to turn the truck into an airplane." When he made it fly, father tried to follow his lead, but slipped into passivity and silence rather than continually building on the themes. I encouraged father to be more relaxed and more active with him, without worrying so much about taking over. As the session went on, he relaxed more and they could do better pretend play together. There was a long sense of relatedness, and it was clear that Alan was closer to his father this time than the first time—he didn't run away from him to mother. They were beginning to make progress together. Toward the end of their play session, they had a nice sequence where the truck turned into an airplane. Alan flew it around and onto mother's lap but then flew it back into a sort of hanger-type thing that father had constructed with his hands. When father wondered out loud if the airplane needed a place to rest, Alan smiled broadly. He demonstrated here that he could be close to father, incorporate mother into the play, but still keep a focus on father.

In his play with mother, Alan wanted to know if a machine-looking toy was a machine. He tried to plug it in and wanted to know what happened. When he discovered it was a tape recorder, he wanted to sing "Happy Birthday" onto the tape. Mother asked him if that was his favorite song, and he said, "Yes, Happy Birthday." Then she talked about the kind of presents he wanted for his birthday, and he was able to tell her. He seemed to thoroughly enjoy mother and she seemed more relaxed.

Their current concerns were that when he was around a lot of noise he became "hyper." One of the children in his preschool program was very noisy and he had told them, "It hurts my ears." His mother reported that he was also having trouble dealing with other people's anger; he would cover his face if either parent got angry with him. If mother raised her voice too much, he would cry. She also felt that he tended to perseverate somewhat in his games repeating the game movements or using prepackaged sequences rather than being innovative like other children his age. We talked about the play partner creating the innovative twist in the play (e.g., putting a doll in front of the forward and back moving car) and helping him talk about his feelings concerning noise. They could create play sequences where one animal or one doll would be noisy; then he could put into words some of the ways noise made him feel. Also, we discussed similar ways of talking about people's anger through pretend play and some reality chit-chats, since he now seemed verbal enough to get involved in this.

The parents had been anxious about becoming innovative in the pretend play for fear of overwhelming him. I suggested they do it gently, one step at a time, but for them to go out of a particular pattern so that he could become more innovative. His lack of innovative play was more likely due to his own anxiety about being assertive than directly due to organicity. I also mentioned that some of his uneven motor development and word retrieval problems made him seek the security of repetition more readily.

I suggested that father not spoon-feed Alan as much in their play. He could attempt being less passive and more challenging in terms of what he brought into the play. Father tried to make it too easy. With mother, we would work on consolidating her great rhythm and warmth, and also try to diminish some of her controlling style by encouraging Alan to challenge her for the lead a bit more.

With mother, it was noted at this time, Alan was becoming more involved in make-believe play and fantasy. But because he sometimes preferred to play with the girl dolls and sometimes shied away from aggressive play (it should be mentioned that he was quite assertive and masculine in his style and orientation), mother was worried about his "gender identity." When mother talked about her own conflicts with assertive, aggressive men (her husband was very passive), it became clear that she was projecting many of her own conflicts onto her son. As much as she wanted him to be an assertive, confident male, she was also very frightened of what was beginning to emerge in the themes of his play—his interest in power and assertiveness. She exaggerated some of the more curious interests he had in the body and in girls and girl dolls. While empathizing with mother's underlying concerns and their historical connection with her feelings toward her own very aggressive brother, I talked about the importance of empathizing and accurately reading the child's communications during this phase. It would help him move fully into the stage of representational differentiation and emotional thinking. At this stage, the parents' ability to accurately read his communication, as well as their ability to empathize and help him elaborate his communications in terms of emotional ideas, were of equal importance. The parents needed to know themselves, their own inclinations, and some of their own fears. Mother was a very emotional and open person who, in a relatively short period of time, could see how she might be anxious about the very things she wished for; that is, for him to be a competent and assertive male.

Now that Alan was beginning to differentiate some of his emotional ideas, we also talked about him beginning to label and discuss his feelings more, both in rational dialogue as well as in the floor time and pretend play modes.

In subsequent sessions, both parents were clearly doing their homework as well as reflecting on their own feelings about their son and their style of interaction. They helped him get together with other children while continuing to do their inter-actions with him. As he became more cooperative with them, the themes that emerged during sessions here were related to his vacillating between trying new, more assertive, and powerful themes in his play, such as being king of the jungle or some-times being a powerful gorilla who would knock down houses, and his fear of things being broken, such as arms being broken off of dolls. His parents were helped to go both ways with him, support the more power-oriented play, but also empathize with the scary feelings associated with things being broken. He be-came more verbal and more elaborative in his make-believe as these scenes were played out. For example, as he played with father in one session, he said, "Let's get more toys." He became assertive as he searched around like a big, tough guy. But as soon as he came upon a broken doll, he said with concern, "This one is broken." Then he immediately switched; "I want lots of toys." When he came across another broken one he said, "I don't want this one. Let's put it away and hide it." "Why do you want to hide it?" his father asked. "That's for a baby to play with," he answered. "I don't want to play with things that are for babies." Father wondered why the broken things would only be for babies and asked if Alan could perhaps fix them. The boy said, "I'm not into fixing things." He then started playing with the Potato Head doll and father started talking for the Potato Head, wanting to know how they should play. Alan started taking out other animals and said, "This is a duck. Look how funny it is." He made the doll act silly and then experi-mented, for the first time, with another duck by breaking the leg off it. 'Oh, look! It's broken," he said, including this com-ment in a dialogue with Potato Head. He then became a little nervous and went back to a more powerful posture by saying, "Let's forget the Potato Head and go on to the wolves."

Throughout this play, he was connecting up his islands of emotional ideas, one to the other, and playing out an important emotional drama. Interestingly, in keeping with mother's concerns about his feminine identification, he played with Barbie dolls during this session, but he picked out a Barbie doll which had one leg missing. "She has one leg off and one leg on," he said. He eagerly searched for the lost leg, and mother, rather than get anxious, was able to join him in the search. He eventually found the lost leg and fixed the doll; then he picked out some cars and tried to hook them up. Mother said, "They are not going to hook up." He said, "Where's the Scotch tape? Maybe we can hook them using that." Mother said, "They're still not going to hook up." He found some tape and figured out a way to hook up the cars. Having made a nice long train out of the cars, he was smiling broadly. Mother was surprised and intuitively understood that his ability to hook up the cars spoke to his competence and his assertive orientation in life.

At about this time, the parents revealed that father was very frightened of violence and worried that his son would hurt himself—this was part of his passive orientation. Mother continued to struggle with her projection of issues about Alan's masculinity, but she was becoming more and more aware of her own conflicts. She was able to help him at home, and during subsequent meetings, with his curiosity about a baby-sitter who was pregnant. He wondered about where children come from, and whether "he could have a baby some day." Mother empathized with his feelings about that and at the same time helped him ask the questions he wanted to ask about the baby-sitter.

In a more recent session, at age four-and-a-half (approximately one year after beginning treatment), Alan came in with his parents and immediately began looking for toys. He had a serious expression on his face, but engaged me easily in a clear, organized conversation. He asked "how" and "why" questions, and made circle-closing conversation, both about day-to-day concerns of a rational nature and make-believe play. For example, as he was examining one of the toys I asked which one he was interested in. He said, "This one," and then he said, "Mom, how does it work?" I said, "Why did you ask mom rather than figuring it out for yourself?" and he said, "Because she has a big brain." I said, "How about dad?" "Mom is smarter," he said. "Are you saying dad is a dummy?" I said. Then he giggled and laughed and started to chant, "Dumb daddy, dumb daddy," although he immediately became anxious and serious looking. He wasn't yet comfortable with poking fun at father or entering into a more open competitiveness with him; and some of his favoritism toward mother was still evident. Yet, this sequence illustrates his growing ability to construct logical connections between complex thoughts and to communicate logically.

Although he seemed to favor mother over father, he related much more warmly to father than he had originally. Their relationship was continuing to develop in obvious ways. With mother, Alan entered into a pretend play sequence where she was a doctor who would take care of him. He said, "But you ran out of medicine." He had had a boo-boo on his knee, "Call CBS," he demanded, the place where they get medicine, the pharmacy. Mother said, "Well, the medicine doesn't work." "Get some more," he said. Mother said, "Still doesn't work." He said, "Well, get me some more juice or maybe give me some lemonade. That's my favorite." After mother pretended to do that, he said, "Now I'm better." Mother said, "How did you get better? Was it just giving you the medicine or the juice?" He said, "Well, I also have a special machine and it has lemonade in it and it gives me lemonade whenever I want it." He then took a toy and made it into the machine. Mother wondered how the machine worked, and he said, "Like magic. The machine and the lemonade helped me." This was an interesting drama in terms of his expectations of mother and the development of the magic machine as an extension of his expectations of mother.

With father, he played in a more inconsistent way, and said after a few minutes, "I'm getting too bored." He was able, however, to bring father over to the lemonade machine and together they tried to build an even better machine. This was the theme of their play, although intermittently he went back to mother and expressed that he was bored with play and wanted to go outside. It appeared that in a thematic sense his issues with mother revolved around how she could take care of him; he had not yet fully decided whether he was capable of building his own machine or whether he would form a collaboration with father to build a machine.

At age four-and-a-half, he seemed appropriately in the early phases of some triangular issues. He was deciding how to work out his needs for nurturance and care and also how to work out his competition and rivalry, as well as his self-sufficiency. From a structural point of view, he had lots of "how" and "why" questions, easily elaborated fantasy in his play, also rational dialogue. At times his play had more of a quality of proximity. He would add on elements to it that were available close by rather than planned, but at other times his play seemed planned. So Alan was showing a more elaborate capacity for fantasy, as well as a more differentiated capacity for connecting up his emotional ideas. He was working on emotional issues which were age appropriate. He was also beginning to have best friends and talked a little about them. He said that sometimes he got upset if kids were mean to him; mother reported that he never felt angry, only sad or upset. (It appeared that some more work in helping him elaborate specific feelings in a representationally differentiated way would be important for him, particularly the angry side of life, but also the competitive side of life with which he was struggling with father.)

In other areas of development, his teacher said that he still had unusual body movements, which became more intense when he was anxious. He mostly liked to draw circles, she said, though she felt his fine motor skills were improving; he could now write his name. He played with both boys and girls at school and especially enjoyed playing with active boys; but he had a favorite girl he liked to play with, too, whom he liked to invite to his house. His best friend at day care was a boy, while his best friend around the block was a girl. He proudly said she had hugged him one time. The teacher's only worry was that he seemed obsessed with "drawing circles." Mother was still concerned that at times, after a lot of activity or work with drawing or coloring, he became tired and put his head on the floor, looking as if he was carrying around the burdens of the world. Both mother and teacher were impressed with the fact that now when he got angry, he would say, "I'm mad" or "I hate you" but didn't hit. However, mother said that he couldn't always find the word he wanted to use and sometimes was a little slow constructing his sentences. But she reported that he was giggling more and his senses of humor and joy were improving.

It appeared that overall from a structural sense he had progressed into age-appropriate levels of functioning. He was now able not only to share attention, engage, and have two-way gestural communication, but was also using emotional ideas to elaborate what was on his mind and categorize his ideas into patterns of emotional thinking. He could now see the connection between different themes in his pretend play and he was organizing rational dialogue. He evidenced some mild constrictions around competition, rivalry, and aggression, feeling hurt and sad rather than angry at times; he was struggling dynamically with his dependency on mother's nurturance and negotiating how to "build his own machine"; not only did he want it to give him the medicine, but he also was discovering how to form a collaboration with the machine around father. These are nice, age-appropriate challenges for a four-and-a-half-year-old.

In summary, then, this was a youngster who had constitutional contributions, in terms of motor delay and motor planning problems, a history of some early deprivation, in terms of being adopted from an orphanage at three months, and some ongoing environmental struggles with his parents, mother being anxious and somewhat fragmented and father being avoidant and passive. This youngster was experiencing a number of problem behaviors, representing his inability to negotiate the stages of representational elaboration and differentiation on his own. Over a period of a year, he progressed to being able to stabilize the earlier stages and become fully involved in the more age-appropriate stages that we wished he could get involved in.

Therapeutic work continues to help him learn more about his feeling and conflicts, only now he clearly possesses the structural capacity to understand and work through specific feelings, fears, and conflicts. He still receives his occupational therapy to help him with his motor coordination and some mild aspects of sensory overreactivity (e.g., to sound). Finally, the parents are still working on their marriage.

CASE NUMBER 22: RICK

Rick was born three months premature, at twenty-eight weeks gestation, and was three pounds at birth. He had severe cerebral palsy that affected both lower extremities in particular.

Rick was three-and-a-half years old when mother brought him to see me. She complained that he was "a discipline problem at school, banging spoons and not stopping. His teacher wanted to put him in a cardboard box for time-out," she said. She felt that Rick's behavior was best when they were together. When they were separated, "He falls apart," she said. Mother felt that Rick and his brother, Paul, eighteen months older, who does not have any motor difficulties and has grown up physically healthy, play nicely together. They liked to roll cars and bang them into one another and occasionally even give each other pretend food. Sometimes Rick would pretend to be washing dishes and say, "I am Cinderella," or "I am a gorilla," when playing with other children on a playground. She went on to describe Rick as occasionally quite creative and inspired, even when playing with his brother or other children; he might get the idea for a pretend sequence, such as "dinner party." Rick tended to get fragmented, once he'd had the initial inspiration.

As mother talked further, another concern with Rick became apparent, not just his not listening, but also his "attention." She wondered if he "had attention deficit disorder," because he floated in and out of states of attention—paying attention one second but then not the next—and he could easily get distracted. She also worried about Rick's receptive understanding of the world: Was he inattentive because he didn't comprehend what was going on or was his receptive language okay and his only real problem in the motor area? Or did he have both motor and attention problems, but none with receptive language? She wondered how "bright" he would be. She was especially worried that he would not be as bright as his brother.

In terms of early development, the pregnancy was uneventful, other than the prematurity. As noted, Rick was born at 28 weeks of gestation. Mother recalled being disappointed that Rick wasn't a girl. Rick was critically ill with pulmonary difficulties immediately following birth. Rick then had had a grade 4 intraventricular hemorrhage, which had caused the cerebral palsy. The doctors had even discussed discontinuing medical treatment, and later they feared that Rick would not have as much function as he does in fact have. He needed a shunt put in to prevent hydrocephalus, and there were worries, because of Rick's optic nerve, about blindness, as well as obvious worries about severe neurologic and cognitive difficulties.

As both parents were talking, father came across as a warm, involved, organized and assertive man. He was, nonetheless, a workaholic, and not home quite enough to give mother the support she needed. Mother emerged as a sensitive, very warm and engaged person, but she was also a little fragmented and anxious, even ephemeral at times. The parents seemed to have a warm relationship with one another, and were cautious not to be critical or angry with one another.

Rick came home on a monitor when he was two-and-a-half months old. (He had been taken off the respirators when he was one month old.) After he was home, mother reported it was hard to feed Rick, and he vomited each evening. He was very thin and "emaciated" as a baby. Mother also reported that he was very tactilely defensive around the mouth, turning his head away from any kind of touch in the oral or facial area. The early months mostly involved getting food into Rick and keeping him as physically healthy and comfortable as possible. At eleven months of age, Rick had functioned at about the five-month-old level, in terms of motor development. There was some question of a seizure disorder at that time. The doctors were uncertain whether it was a mild clonic jerk, based on just a spinal reflex, or a true seizure; he was on Deprocain for six months. Rick was also on a milk formula and toward the end of his second year of life was frequently noted to vomit when angry.

When Rick had started two-way communication in the toddler phase, he'd had a hard time following, tracking, and staying on a task; Rick was consistently poorly focused and had poor follow-through.

In terms of his motor milestones, by the time Rick was two years old, he could hoist himself up on his stomach and play with one arm, and could roll over well. Somewhere between fifteen and twenty-two months, he was beginning to manipulate toys as part of his growing two-way communication. At around twenty-four months, he learned some signing and used it to indicate wants and needs. Mother reported that Rick, at around age two, had started going to a special program at a child center where he could get therapy and early schooling. He had loved going to school and had a big smile on his face.

Throughout his development, Rick had been affectionate and loved to be held. He would reach out to mother and father. Rick let his emotions fly and would vocalize his upsetness.

Intermittently, the parents talked about themselves and their own families of origin. The emerging pattern involved a father who was constantly describing himself as a workaholic. His main concern in life was that of losing power in his job. He was very detail-oriented, yet warm and nice and supportive to the children. He kept talking about inequality in the children and about his not getting enough support from his wife. Mother came across more as emotionally intense and as a very sweet and warm person who wanted to treat Rick as an individual. It was clear that she felt overwhelmed a good deal of the time and needed more support from her husband.

The first time I saw Rick, he came in crawling and smiling. He seemed to be a related child with a good basic personality function. As he came in the door, he called to his mother. "Mom," he said, looking scared about coming alone. Once he had crawled inside my room, using one hand more than the other, he looked around eagerly at all the toys. He grabbed some puppets and began putting them on his hand as he sat up. He made them mumble some words and "go to sleep." He was quite intentional in the way he manipulated the puppets and the way he looked at me and his mother. His language was functional, even though not always understandable. He did seem to talk in sentences. He received information, but seemed to tune out, so it was hard to know what he understood or whether he chose to tune out what he didn't understand. Rick tended to operate with islands of pretend sequences. For example, he had the puppet trying to throw the ball. He said to the other puppet, "catch," but then he shifted gears quickly, making the puppet mumble something to mother. He looked over at me to make sure I was paying attention, and then he handed me the puppet; but when I put the puppet on and tried to have it say something back to him, he had already turned away and was playing with the doors of a little house. He was trying to see how some little puppets could fit inside. If I spoke his name and said, "Rick? What do you want me to do with the puppet?" he'd look at me and then point toward the play box, indicating I should put it back. One time he did say, "Put it here." He could clearly speak in short sentences. He also had a very good quality of warmth in his engagement and, at the gestural level, was very communicative with two-way communication. Only very infrequently, though, did he build on my symbolic communications with symbolic communications of his own. When I called his name, he responded with a gesture, but rarely did he respond with words to my words or with additional pretend play to my pretend sequence.

His pattern was very similar with mother. In her style of interaction, mother tended to be very good at following his lead. She was extremely warm and able to mirror and monitor what he was doing; but she put next to no demand on him for interaction. In other words, when he had the puppet on his hand and was trying to talk, she said, "Oh, the puppet is talking." When he switched to a little horse and had the horse go toward the doors of the doll house, she said, "Oh, now there is a horse and it is going to the house with the openings." He was pleased at her commentary. Mother didn't realize that inadvertently she was supporting Rick's fragmented, interactive style. She was not putting on him any demands for interaction. For example, she didn't take another horse and say, "Oh, my horse is now in front of your horse. What are they going to say to one another?"

At the end of this first session, I was impressed that Rick had mastered a sense of engagement. He had some capacity for limited shared attention (2 to 4 seconds at a clip), and, also, had well-established two-gestural communication of a fairly complex nature. He was using emotional ideas, that is, early representations, but fragmentedly, rather than in an elaborative or cohesive manner. It wasn't clear yet whether he had some islands of organized emotional thinking or representational differentiation. Given the insults to his nervous system so early on, I was pleased and impressed at the amount of solid development that he had accomplished. I thought he had strong potential for making further progress. Even though he was three-and-a-half, and only functioning at about the two-and-a-half-year-old level in terms of his functional capacities (emotionally, socially, and cognitively), I was still quite struck by his having progressed solidly into the symbolic range. It was now a question of elaborating this in a more cohesive way; improving his attention, and having him then develop more abilities to categorize experience and differentiate it. I was also impressed with his mother's ability to empathize and be warm. I felt she had the potential to help him stay with his focus more, elaborate more, and eventually categorize and differentiate.

In a subsequent session mother's concerns were further amplified when Rick said in a subsequent session, "I'm a dog. I want dog food." Mother worried, could he really think of himself as a dog. When she asked, "Where do you go for lunch?" he said, "To the dog food store." She also had concerns about how Rick would sometimes stutter, and how, sometimes, in his play he wouldn't hold up his part of the action because he couldn't understand.

At this time, Rick was in a special county program where he was receiving speech and occupational therapy and, in a small group of eight to ten children, was also receiving early education services. The other children in the group had mixed handicaps, as he did, but many of them were not at his cognitive or interactive level. There was some question about whether this program was providing as much social and interactive experience as Rick needed.

At the end of these preliminary sessions, I pointed out to the parents that their concerns with Rick were very much on target; he did need to improve his concentration and focus, his receptive language skills, as well as his comfort with organizing and asserting himself socially and emotionally. However, I also pointed out that from their initial description of Rick, I had been surprised by his competence, his warmth, and his engaging, special charm. I told the parents I was particularly impressed with his creative bursts, both reported and observed.

We talked further about how Rick's motor delays and suspected attentional difficulties (perhaps secondary to some of the neurologic challenges he had around birth), as well as receptive language unevenness and articulation difficulties, were all conspiring to make him less attentive than he otherwise might be. I also pointed out how some of the family interaction patterns might not be giving him as much practice as he needed to learn better ways of attending, following through, and elaborating. Different interactive patterns might help improve his receptive language and his articulation, too. Mother's extremely empathetic style was excellent for establishing engagement and warmth—Rick was terrifically charming—but, at times, mother made communication so easy that there was no basis for real interaction. She followed the pretend play but didn't create opportunities for interaction. She could make her horse confront his horse, for example, or put her hand in front of the house and wonder aloud how the doll was going to deal with the hand in front of the house. Just by thickening the plot in such a way that Rick would have to develop a new subplot, mother would help him create solid interactions.

Mother talked about how her anxiety tended to make her passive and cautious. She was always afraid of hurting Rick or doing something to make him "feel bad about himself." We discussed her ambivalence and how she was sometimes annoyed with Rick. She associated him with her brother who was less competent than her. She admitted that she sometimes compensated for her anger at Rick by being overly passive and compliant with him, not giving him enough interactive opportunity.

With father, we focused on his workaholic tendencies and his attention to detail. He was usually more concerned with bathing Rick and making sure he ate the right food. Father said he was so concerned with working hard and maintaining "power" at work, that he was afraid to come home where he would feel more vulnerable. I suggested that floor time was a perfect place for him to deal with his own vulnerabilities. There, his attention to detail and concern with power might take a secondary position to "flying by the seat of his pants." He laughed and giggled at this possibility; over time he had already become somewhat better on the floor with Rick and was prepared to try to do more.

We decided to work at monthly intervals, with the parents practicing a number of exercises at home. They would do "floor time" with Rick. The focus during floor time would be on increasing his attention span from three or four seconds to ten or twelve seconds before he switched to another theme. For example, if he put a puppet on his hand, father would put on a puppet and try to get a dialogue going. If he switched to a car, father would say "Hey, wait a second. I want to switch to the car with you, but what did this puppet say about the car?" If Rick was able to say, "Well, the puppet changed his mind and he now wants to drive the car," that would be great and they would make the transition. But if there was no bridge, father would pressure Rick to create a bridge, or stay with the puppet a little longer until he could figure out how to make the bridge. In this way, Rick's focus and attention would increase. The parents would also be closing circles by keeping Rick focused on the puppet until he made the transition to the car. He would only be able to switch through building on the parents' communication. For example, when he said, "My puppet says hello," and mother put a puppet on her hand and replied, "Hello," he would have to say, "Goodbye, I'm going into the car." He would be brought back to the puppet until he did. Therefore, not only would he be building bridges, but he would also be learning to open and close circles.

I suggested that the parents use floor time for monitoring Rick's growing assertiveness and his method for dealing with themes of anger and aggression in his play. Given the fact that children with motor delays often have trouble confronting their anger, they may use sweet seductiveness or warmth and charm to get their way; but they are often afraid to make the toy soldiers fight or the stuffed animals get mad at each other. As Rick's parents learned to increase his focus and attention and helped open and close his circles, they would also work with him on Rick's manifestations of assertiveness. Since Rick seemed quite comfortable with having dolls hug, I felt that he would not have much difficulty with longing or nurturing or closeness.

We discussed how the parents might confide more in each other to better articulate their own inner dynamics relating to Rick. Mother was both mad at Rick and worried about him. Father perceived in Rick the "loss of power" he feared might occur at work; he stayed away from him by being a workaholic, to keep his power. I hoped these insights would help them relax with each other, so that they could each talk about their feelings.

We have subsequently met at monthly intervals for a number of years. In spite of Rick going through a bout of seizures, he has made continued and steady progress. He can now hold quite a normal conversation with complex sentences, including coordinate and subordinate conjunctions (e.g., "but" and "because"), and answering why questions. Rick has definitely maintained his creative and engaging flair.

Rick, as indicated, has shown gradual improvement in his ability to differentiate. In a recent session, he came in and held what I would consider a normal conversation, with good focus for thirty to sixty seconds on each theme; he was answering lots of why and how questions, and making "because" links between themes. He was asking intelligent questions, too. He took charge of the play and wanted to know where the castle was. He played out themes of anger and assertiveness with the hero dolls and then negotiated with his father about whether they were going to go to McDonald's for hamburgers. He articulated his case carefully saying, "You promised me a hamburger after the session, and I want an ice cream, too." His father said he didn't have time because he had to get back to his office. Rick replied, "You work too much and that's why mommy gets mad at you sometimes." His father giggled and promised him that he would go to McDonald's. Rick asked me about some toys that were missing from my office. He wanted to know, "Why don't you have them here?" Looking at me with a little gleam in his eye, he asked, "Are your children taking my toys?" He had maintained his charm and insight, and now was fully differentiated in his representational abilities. In the course of our conversation, it was heartening to hear him make many references to enjoying not only friends, but also more of family life.

PART III

The Process of Clinical Assessment

INTRODUCTION

The biggest single challenge in clinically assessing a child's development and his relationship to his caregivers is how to be comprehensive without getting lost in the details. There is no choice but to try to elicit all the relevant information and make sense of it. Limiting the number of sessions for reasons of expediency or because the time or financial constraints may lead the therapist to jump to premature conclusions and mislead rather than help the child and the family.

In some cases, the therapist can conduct an evaluation more quickly, because the problems are relatively straightforward. Even so, in order to identify or rule out certain types of problems or abilities, he or she has to investigate multiple aspects of the baby's development, as well as interactions with the caregiver, and patterns of family functioning.

Chapter 5

Comments on the Process of Clinical Assessment

Each clinician may develop his own way of doing an evaluation. However, any assessment should (1) encompass certain baseline data; (2) organize data by indicating how each factor contributes to the baby's ability to develop; and (3) suggest methods of treatment. A comprehensive assessment usually involves the following elements: presenting "complaints," developmental history, family patterns, child and parent sessions, additional consultations, and formulation.

PRESENTING "COMPLAINTS" (OVERALL PICTURE)

I frequently spend a whole session on the presenting "complaints" or picture, which includes the development of the "problems," the infant's and family's current functioning, and preliminary observation of the infant or child both with the caregiver(s), or, in the case of a child over three, without them as well.

I will usually suggest that the parents bring the baby with them to the first session. Even though I spend most of the time talking to the parents, I have my eye on the baby and I watch what is going on spontaneously between parents and baby. If an older child (3 or 4 years of age) is involved, I will have the parents leave the child at home the first time, if possible, so the parents can talk more freely.

I begin by asking the parents, "How can I help?" and I try to listen to their responses. I encourage the parents to elaborate about the child's problem, whether it has to do with sleeping, eating, or being too aggressive or too withdrawn. If I ask a question, it is usually to clarify something they have said, such as, "Can you give me some examples of that?" "How is this different now from what it was six months ago, and when wasn't it a problem?" I try to find out when the problem started, how it evolved, and its nature and scope. For example, if a two-and-a-half-year-old is aggressive with peers, I want to know whether it is with all peers or only certain children. I am interested in what precipitated the problem and what may be contributing to it. Was there a change within the family, such as the father getting a new job? Was there marital tension? Were new developmental abilities emerging which paradoxically were stressful to the child?

When the parents say, "Well, I think we have told you everything about the problem," then I will ask, "Is there more to tell about Johnny or Susie that would help fill out the picture?" It is much more helpful to ask open-ended questions than to ask specific questions about cognitive, language, or motor development at this point. One gathers together more relevant information when the parents elaborate spontaneously. Parents also reveal their own feelings and private family matters if the therapist is empathetic as he helps them describe their child. Therefore, a clinician should strive to be unstructured; ask facilitating, elaborative questions rather than yes or no or defining questions; and never be in a hurry to fill out a checklist.

The initial session also should establish rapport with the family and child in order to begin a collaborative process. The developmental process discussed earlier in relation to the child—mutual attention, engagement, gestural communication, shared meanings, and the categorizing and connecting of meanings—may occur between an empathetic clinician and the parents. How the clinician relates to the parents reflects how they will be encouraged to relate to their baby. If the therapist asks hurried questions, with yes or no answers, he or she sets up an untherapeutic model. It usually takes parents a long time to decide to come for help. They should be able to tell their story without being hurried or criticized.

As part of this presenting picture it is important to learn about all the areas of the child's current functioning. If the primary focus is initially on aggression and distractibility, one wants to know the child's other age-expected capacities. One considers if the child is at the age-appropriate developmental level and if so, the full range of emotional inclinations. Is the eight-month-old capable of reciprocal cause-and-effect interchanges? Is a four-month-old wooing and engaging? Is a two-and-a-half-year-old exhibiting symbolic or representational capacities? Does he do pretend play? Does he use language functionally? How does he negotiate his needs? At each of these levels, how is he dealing with dependency, pleasure, assertiveness, anger, and so forth?

Toward the end of the first session, I may fill in more gaps by asking questions about sensory, language, cognitive, and fine and gross motor functioning. Usually, I have a sense of these capacities and patterns from anecdotes and more general descriptions of behavior. I listen for indications of the child's ability to retain information; how he does or does not follow commands; word retrieval skills; word association skills; and fine and gross motor and motor planning skills.

Some clinicians write down what parents say right after the session; others write during the session. Taking notes need not be an interference if one stops throughout to make good contact. I take detailed notes during the first fifteen or twenty minutes because I want as much information as I can get in the parents words.

By the end of the first session, one has a sense of where the child is, developmentally. One has a sense of the range of emotional themes the child can deal with at his developmental level. One has an awareness of the support, or lack of support, the child gets from his fine and gross motor, speech and language, and cognitive abilities. One also forms an impression of the support the child gets from his parents. One observes how the parents communicate and organize their thinking, the quality of their engagement, their emotional availability, their interest in their child. One has a good sense of their relative comfort or discomfort with each emotional theme. In general, the therapist observes how the parents attend, engage, intentionally communicate, construct and organize ideas, and are able or not able to incorporate a range of emotional themes into their ideas as they relate to the therapist.

DEVELOPMENTAL HISTORY

In the second session, I construct a developmental history for the child. (However, sometimes marital or other family problems burst out during the first session. The parents may be at each other's throats; the mother and/or the father may be extremely depressed. In such cases, in the second session I will focus on the individual parent problems, as well as family functioning.)

I will usually start the session in an unstructured manner. I want to hear how development unfolded and what the parents thought was important. I encourage them to alternate between what the baby was like at different stages and what they felt was going on as a family and as individuals in each of those stages. I try to start with the planning for the baby and progress through the pregnancy and delivery. Next, I cover the six developmental stages, outlined earlier, in order to organize the developmental history. (A guide for the areas to be covered in the developmental history, and direct observation of the infant and caregiver, is presented in chapter 6.)

FAMILY PATTERNS

The next session focuses in greater depth on the functioning of the caregiver and family at each developmental phase. For example, the mother may say that she was a little depressed or angry, or that there were marital problems at different stages in the child's development.

Sometimes clinicians who are only beginning to work with infants and families feel reluctant to talk to the parents about any difficulties in the marriage. However, an open and supportive approach can elicit relevant information. One might ask, "What can you tell me about yourselves as people, as a married couple, as a family?" I am also interested in concrete details of a history of mental illness, learning disabilities, or special developmental patterns in either of the parents' families.

Some families will not hesitate to discuss marital difficulties or other problems. Sometimes there will be discussion of how the "problem child" relates to the father and mother in terms of "power struggles." If they describe a pattern, for example, between mother and child or father and child, I am likely to ask, "Does that same pattern operate in other family relationships—between mother and father, for example?" Is the pattern a carryover from a parent's own family? By following the couple's lead, I try to develop a picture of the marriage, careers of one or both parents, relationship with other children and between all the children, the parents' relationship with their own families of origin, as well as friendships and community ties.

Sometimes the family as a whole functions in a very fragmented, presymbolic way. They gesture, "behave at" each other, overwhelm each other, withdraw from one another, but they don't share any meanings with one another. Nothing is negotiated at a symbolic level. Even though each individual may be capable of functioning on a symbolic level, something about the family dynamics cancels out that ability. In this context, I want to know how the family handles dependency, excitement, and sexuality, as well as anger, assertiveness, empathy, and love.

For each unit of the family—the parents, each parent–child relationship, as well as the family as a whole—I want to find out how the different emotional themes were dealt with at different developmental levels. (Family and couples assessment and therapy will be more fully discussed in chapters 17 and 18.)

CHILD (OR INFANT) AND PARENT SESSIONS

I spend the next two sessions with a focus on the child or infant. I conduct the session differently with an older child (a 3- or 4-year-old, for example) than with an infant. With an infant, I may ask the parent to play with the baby to "show me how you like to be with or play with your baby or child." The parents may ask, "What do you want me to do?" "Anything you like," is my response. I offer the use of the toys in my office or tell them they may bring a special toy from home.

I watch each parent with the child, playing in an unstructured way, for about fifteen or twenty minutes. I am looking for the developmental level, the range of emotional themes at each level, and the use of and support that the child is able to derive from motor, language, sensory, and cognitive skills. I am also watching for the parents' ability to support or undermine the developmental level, range in that level, and use of sensory, language, and motor systems. After I watch the mother and father separately, I watch the three of them together to see how they interact as a group, because sometimes the group situation is more challenging. Later, I will join them and start to play with the child (briefly in the first session and for a longer period in the second session).

During this time, I want to see how the child relates to a new person whom he knows only slightly. In addition, I want to determine how to bring out the highest developmental level at which the child can function. For example, if the parents do not support symbolic functioning in their three-year-old, I will try to get pretend play going. If an eight-month-old is being overstimulated, I will try to get cause-and-effect interactions going. If a four-month-old looks withdrawn, I'll try to flirt to pull him in. I will try to calm down a fussy five-month-old with visual or vocal support, gentle tactile pressure, and a change of positions. I will work hands-on with an infant to explore his tactile sensitivity, motor tone, motor planning, and preference for patterns of movement in space.

One can learn a great deal through observation, as outlined in chapters 11 to 15 on floor time. By way of example, one could say to a child who is moving a train, "Oh boy, I can see that you know how to make this train go." The child may put a doll on the train, make the doll a conductor, and add a passenger. The passenger may have a baby while the train is going through a tunnel, and at the same time a doctor makes sure the baby is all right. A three-year-old who generates such a "drama" is sophisticated cognitively and evidences a rich fantasy life.

With children two-and-a-half to three years and older, depending on the child's comfort in being separated from his caregiver, I may reverse the sequence. I may have the first session with the child alone to explore how he or she engages with me, attends, initiates intentional two-way communication, and shares and categorizes meanings.

During this time alone, a three-and-a-half-year-old may stand in the middle of the room and look me over, while I look at him. If I don't try to control the situation too quickly and can tolerate ten or fifteen seconds of ambiguity the child may start to play, ask me a question about the toys, or talk about his family. What the child has to say, without me saying, "Tell me what your mother told you about why you are here" or "Do you want to play with the toys?" can be very valuable. A child may look around and say, "I heard there were toys here. Where are they?" Such a statement indicates an organized, intentional child who has figured out why he is there and acts on his understanding. Another child may look puzzled and, after a silence, ask in a formal manner, "Can I sit down?"

Some four-year-olds will talk to me throughout the session. We can have an almost adult-to-adult kind of dialogue about school or home, nightmares or worries, or just a chat about anything, as one might have with a neighbor. Other children will behave aggressively and want to jump on me or wrestle. They become too familiar too quickly.

During interaction with a child, I note what the child is like physically, his speech and language, gross and fine motor skills, and general state of health and mood. I observe the way he relates to me, that is, the quality of engagement—overly familiar, overly cautious, or warm. I look for how intentional he is in the use of gestures and how well he sizes up the situation and me (without words). I try to determine his emotional range and his way of dealing with anxiety (e.g., does he become aggressive or withdrawn?).

The next step is to learn what is on the child's mind. One looks at the content of the play and dialogue, as well as the sequence of themes that emerge from them. The therapist's job is to be reasonably warm, supportive, and skillful in engaging the child and helping him elaborate. If the therapist makes the interaction too easy by being overly seductive, he does not learn about the child's problems in relating. On the other hand, because the experience is new and scary to the child, the therapist should not make the interaction too hard.

With older children, I will have the parent come in, either toward the end of the first session or in the second session, in order to watch the mother and father play with the child. If the parents come in first, the child may not want to play with the therapist alone because he is used to his parents being in the room. If the child comes in alone, because he is curious about the room and toys, he often establishes a primary relationship with the therapist. If the child is at all cautious, however, one may say, "Would you rather have mommy or daddy come in, too?" If the child elects to have his parents come in, have the parents and child play and talk first, then join them later.

ADDITIONAL CONSULTATIONS

As part of a complete evaluation, a child should have a pediatric evaluation to rule out physical illness. Suspected metabolic or genetic disorders should be investigated as well. If there is a question about a neurologic disorder, one should consider having a pediatric neurologist look at the child. If there are problems with receptive language, including word retrieval, word association, sequencing, or expressive language, a speech pathologist should be consulted. For questions about motor or sensory functioning (reactivity and processing) an occupational therapist should be consulted. If motor and language testing and clinical observation leave questions about cognitive or psychological capacities, a cognitive and/or psychological assessment may be considered.

FORMULATION

After learning about the child's current functioning and history and observing the child and the family first hand, there should be a convergence of impressions. If a picture is not emerging, one may need to spend another session or two developing the history or observing further.

One then asks oneself a number of questions. How high up in the developmental progression has the child gone, in terms of (1) attending and regulating? (2) establishing two-way intentional communication; (3) sharing meanings; and (4) emotional thinking? How well are the earlier phases mastered and, if not fully mastered, what are the unresolved issues? For example, does a child still have challenges in terms of his attentional capacities, the quality of engagement, his intentional abilities?

Determining the developmental level tells you how the child organizes experience. To use a metaphor, it provides a picture of the "stage" upon which a child plays out his "drama." The presenting symptoms—nightmares, waking up at night, refusal to eat, as well as other concerns and inclinations—make up the "drama." The "stage" may be age appropriate. For example, a four-year-old, who can categorize representational experience, has a drama of being aggressive to other children, but this drama is being played out on a stage that is age appropriate. This child has the capacity to comprehend the nature of his aggression and use "ideas" to figure out his behavior. On the other hand, there may be major deficits in the stage (i.e., attending, being intentional, representing experience, or differentiating experience). If there are flaws in the stage, one wants to pinpoint the nature of those flaws.

For example, if a child is not engaged with other people, he may be aggressive because he basically has no regard for other people's feelings. He may not even see people as human. Alternatively, another child may be aggressive because he cannot represent feelings and therefore acts them out. Still another child may represent and differentiate his feelings, but have conflicts about his dependency needs.

One also looks at the range of experience organized at a particular developmental level. If a child is at an age-appropriate developmental level, does he accommodate such things as dependency, assertiveness, curiosity, sexuality, and aggression at that level. On the other hand, even if a child is at the right developmental level, the stage may be narrow. In other words, he might be only at that developmental stage when it comes to assertiveness, but when it comes to dependency, he is not quite there, and when it comes to excitement, he functions at a much lower level. In other words, if he dances the wrong step, he could fall off the stage. One also looks at the stability of the developmental organization. Does even a little stress lead to a loss of function or are the functions stable?

Therefore, if the stage has cracks or holes in it because there are major problems from earlier developmental issues, I will say there are defects in the stage. If the stage is solid (no defects), it is either very flexible and wide or very narrow and constricted (e.g., it will tolerate a drama of assertiveness but it will not tolerate a drama of intimacy or excitement). In addition, it is stable or unstable.

Next, one wants to know about the contributing factors. One set of factors relates to observations about family functioning; the other set of factors relates to the assessment of the child's individual differences. The parent–child interactions are the mediating factors. These factors are discussed in chapter 1, "The Basic Model."

In chapter 1, which may be usefully reread at this point, the different constitutional–maturational factors and family factors, as well as other relationships to the developmental level, are discussed. In addition, the framework suggested in this section is illustrated in each of the case studies in chapters 2, 3, and 4.

Chapter 6

A Guide for the Developmental History and Direct Observation of the Infant/Child and His or Her Parents or Caregivers

The developmental history includes: the planning for the baby that precedes the pregnancy; conception, pregnancy, and delivery; followed by the different phases of the child's development up to the present. In each phase, the therapist needs to know about the child's physical development; he always asks about physical health, such as infections, general well-being, weight and growth patterns, and acute or chronic illnesses. The therapist monitors intellectual development; sensory, motor, and language development; emotional and social development; the interactive patterns between the caregiver and the child; and the interactive patterns between the parents and the family as a whole as well as their relationship to their community. These different factors can be systematized in the following manner.

1. *Prenatal and Perinatal Variables.* These variables all have some impact on the infant's constitutional status and developmental tendencies, although the extent of the impact is unknown. The prenatal variables include: familial genetic patterns; mother's status during pregnancy, including nutrition, physical health and illness, personality functioning, mental health, and degree of stress; characteristics of familial and social support systems; characteristics of the pregnancy; and the delivery process, including complications, time in various stages, and the infant's status after birth. The perinatal variables include maternal perceptions of her infant, maternal reports of the emerging daily routine, and observations of the infant and maternal–infant interaction.

2. *Parent, Family, and Environmental Variables.* These variables include evaluations of parents, other family members, and individuals who relate closely to the family along a number of dimensions. These assessments include each member's personality organization and developmental needs, child-rearing capacity, and family interaction patterns. Evaluations of the support system (extended family, friends, and community agencies) used or available to the family, and of the total home environment (both animate and inanimate components) are also included. Of special importance is the capacity of the parents and family to calm and regulate the infant; reach out and foster attachment; perceive the basic status of pleasure and discomfort; respond with balanced empathy, that is, without either overidentification or isolation of feeling; perceive and respond flexibly and appropriately to the infant's cues; foster organized complex interactions; and support representational elaboration and differentiation.

3. *Primary Caregiver and Caregiver/Infant–Child Relationship Variables.* Evaluations in this area focus on the interaction between the infant and his or her important nurturing figures. Included are the equality of shared attention, comfort, and regulation, and the capacity for joint pleasure and intimacy, as well as flexibility in tolerating tension and being able to return

to a state of intimacy. Later, the capacities for reciprocal interaction to form complex emotional and behavioral patterns, and to construct and differentiate mental representations, are important.

4. *Infant Variables: Physical, Neurologic, Physiologic, and Cognitive.* These variables include the infant's genetic background and status immediately after birth, including the infant's general physical integrity (size, weight, general health), neurologic integrity, physiologic tendencies, rhythmic patterns, and levels of alertness and activity. Special attention should be paid to the infant's individual differences, including sensory hypo- or hyperreactivity, motor tone, motor planning and sensory processing, and cognitive level and style. At the same time, it is important to determine how these factors could foster or hinder the child's capacities to experience stimulation and regulate or organize experience; develop human relationships; interact in cause-and-effect reciprocal patterns; form complex behavioral and emotional and cognitive patterns; and construct representations to guide behavior, feelings, and thinking (DeGangi and Greenspan, 1988, 1989a,b; Porges and Greenspan, 1990).

5. *Infant Variables: Formation and Elaboration of Emotional Patterns and Human Relationships.* The following variables involve the relationships between infant and caregivers which help the infant develop the capacity for a range of emotions (dependency to assertiveness) and relationship patterns, in the context of a sequence of organizational stages. These stages include the capacity for purposeful interactions; complex, organized social and emotional patterns; constructing representations; and differentiating internal representations along self versus nonself time and space dimensions (Greenspan, 1981, 1989b).

HISTORY AND OBSERVATION

In taking a history, it is preferable to ask the parent to describe the child's development and the complementary development of the family, parental, and couple patterns, from the time when the child was only an idea in their minds to the present, as best they can recall and in the way in which they are comfortable. Often the parents will skip around somewhat at first. They may talk about a phase in the child's development that worries them, such as a time when language functions weren't occurring as rapidly as they would have liked, or when the child started getting too aggressive, or when a grandparent died, and everyone in the family became upset. After talking about these times that have particular emotional weight or value, the parents may return to a more systematic account. Sometimes, the parents will not present highlights first, but systematically walk through development from the beginning to the current time. Other times, parents who seem to be fragmented in their behavior might say, "Ask me questions. I need to be guided.

The best approach is to let the parents speak first on their own. If they ask for guidance, the therapist should reassure them that they should recall their own associations, because they know what is important. With a little encouragement, parents will usually recount the things they think are most important. After this phase, if they do need some guidance, one can walk them through each of the relevant phases of development with an open-ended question like, "Can you tell me about how you decided to have the baby?" or "Can you tell me about the pregnancy?" "Can you tell me what the delivery was like?" Asking such questions is the best way to find out new and important information. When the parent seems to have exhausted spontaneous narrative concerning a particular developmental phase, it may then be appropriate to move in with specific questions, such as, "At four months of age, how did your baby show you he wanted to be close? Did he reach out or wait for you to read his signals?

At each stage of development, a therapist wants to look at how the baby and the parents negotiate the phase and what the reactions of the parents are emotionally to the phase as a couple and as a family unit. The therapist should pay attention at a particular phase, to whether, for example, the father begins to withdraw, or marital problems start, or the mother becomes depressed. The therapist seeks to identify whether the reaction is related to the challenges of the baby's developmental phase—a very important motivator in family relationships.

To begin, it is helpful to know what the relationship is between the parents, what their family circumstances are like, and whether the child was planned, wanted, or unwanted. It is also helpful to know what feelings, fantasies, and hopes the parents had for the wanted child, or what concerns they had that kept them from wanting to have a child. Such information gives a therapist a picture of the emotional context that the parents' relationship and their expectations provide for the child.

A therapist needs to know about the mother's and father's health at the time of conception and about the circumstances of conception and a history of prior pregnancies or attempts at pregnancy (e.g., miscarriages). The therapist needs to follow the mother's health during the pregnancy and to check for illnesses, such as viruses, changes in blood pressure, blood glucose levels or habits such as alcohol, tobacco, and drug use, which have potential impact on the developing fetus. He or she needs to know about issues of mood, anxiety, and tension. A picture of the prenatal patterns should be developed such as reactions to the baby's heartbeat and first kicks; or whether the baby seemed responsive to temperature or sound. How was the couple's relationship proceeding? What were the mother's reactions, the father's reactions?

The therapist wants to know about the parents' anticipation of the challenges of taking care of the baby as the pregnancy concluded. Some parents look forward to the baby becoming a reality outside the mother. Other parents go through a beginning separation process. If having the baby in utero was warm, reassuring, and pleasurable, it may be upsetting to anticipate a first step in what will be a long series of separations as the baby develops. Other families worry about the challenges of caring for a demanding, yet very fragile baby, on the one hand and on the other hand the separation from the extreme closeness of pregnancy, particularly on the mother's part.

The therapist seeks full term or early information about the circumstances of the delivery, whether it was vaginal or Caesarian; aided with forceps, natural or with medication; any perinatal complications and the state of the baby's health including weight, size, and signs of anoxia at birth. Were there complications? Also important is the way the baby behaved immediately after birth, mother's and father's immediate reaction to the birth, and their ability to be with the baby or not be with the baby. Initially, it is very important to know the process by which the parents and the baby began to know one another, how the parents began "falling in love" or not falling in love with the baby. The process by which parents and baby began to know one another can occur moments after birth, with looks or touching, or gradually over a period of days and weeks. For a baby with complications, who requires special medical procedures, the ordinary process of getting to know one another may be challenged by having to make contact through an incubator. The therapist wants to explore how communication occurred, given the particular circumstances.

THE FIRST DEVELOPMENTAL PHASE—REGULATION AND INTEREST IN THE WORLD (EARLY MONTHS OF LIFE)

The therapist proceeds to develop a systematic history by determining how the baby does in relation to adaptive goals for each stage of life. In the first stage, during the early months of life, it is necessary to determine how the baby negotiated the first adaptive goal of calming down, regulating, and taking an interest in all facets of the world, through his sensory system. The therapist has the parents talk about these broad adaptive goals. How did the parents and baby negotiate this first stage? A baby calms down and takes an interest in the world through vision, hearing, touch, smell, and movement in space. The therapist checks on the baby's ability to react to sensation to see if the baby is overreactive in any modality. It is necessary for the therapist to profile whether the baby is hyper-or hyposensitive to touch, sound, visual input, such as bright lights, colors, visual complexity, or being moved up and down. What is the baby's motor tone and motor planning ability?

The therapist wants to get a sense of the baby's early sensory processing ability. Does the baby seem more visual (looking and comprehending what he is seeing) or is he more responsive to sound (turning to the left or right when the mother speaks softly)? Does the baby decode complex rhythms or just simple two-cadence rhythms?

For example, a baby who is hypersensitive to touch will look unhappy or pull away from a soft, gentle touch. What type of touch does the baby prefer, a light touch or firm pressure? Whether the baby enjoys cuddling, being stroked, having his hair combed, or being bathed all give clues about the baby's pleasure in touching and his comfort with using his motor system to achieve closeness, warmth, and relaxation, and to begin exploring the world.

In summary, one asks two basic questions about the early months of life: Is the baby gradually learning how to calm down, that is, does being talked to, held, touched, looked at, and interacted with through vision calm him down? Second, is the baby gradually showing more interest in the world? Does he tune in better to sounds and sights, or is he becoming more irritable and less able to calm down, and is he disinterested in the world of sight, sound, and touch? If the latter is true, one wants to discover some of the reasons through the history-taking process: Is the baby extra sensitive to touch or sound, to being moved in space? Is he beginning to show some early signs of motor tone or motor planning difficulties or difficulties with processing information?

History-Taking Procedure (Stage 1). A parent may report that a child was colicky and irritable and couldn't quiet down. He was very interested in his surroundings, almost hypervigilant. He looked around a lot, studied his mother's face, responded to her voice, but couldn't go to sleep readily. He seemed constantly uncomfortable and cried for the first three months. This description gives the therapist a sense of how far along that baby was in terms of the adaptive goals for the first couple of months of life. He was very interested in sensations, perhaps too interested in the outer world, but he had a hard time controlling that interest in order to calm down and be regulated; therefore, he was irritable and crying.

Then the therapist needs to ask specifically: How was the baby's attention? Was he interested in so many things that he was distractible very early on? Did any experiences help the baby calm down? What did the parents try to do? Did they know intuitively what occupational therapists would recommend for a tactilely sensitive baby? Did they apply firm pressure on the back or the arms? Did they talk to and look at the baby, or did they only rock the baby frantically? Did they try elimination of items from the baby's or, if breast-feeding, the mother's diet? In other words, how did the parents negotiate the first stage of development in terms of the broad adaptive goals?

When the therapist has a sense of the first set of parameters, he should systematically review the known symptoms. Does he have a general sense that the baby was colicky, unable to quiet down, slept only two hours at a time, was very vigilant and interested? Is the baby very reactive to sight and sound, or overly reactive to touch and dislikes being bathed or having his body stroked?

Next the therapist considers each sensory system systematically to pick up symptoms he may have missed. (He may get about 60% of the picture from the parents' unstructured discussion of that stage.) The therapist should ask again about sensory reactivity—tactile sensitivity, auditory hypersensitivity, visual sensitivity in terms of light or color intensity, and movement in space (up and down and around).

Once he has reviewed sensory reactivity, he goes on to discuss sensory processing. Did the baby seem to respond to and focus on complex vocal patterns? Next the therapist pursues motor tone. Does the baby move in a loose and floppy manner or do his motions seem tight or confined? What is the baby's motor planning ability? Could the baby get his hands up to his mouth? Could the baby move his arms in relationship to the parent's movements or vocalizations?

Lastly, one examines more closely any emotional and social goals that weren't already taken into account in the broader view of adaptive goals, in order to complete a general picture of the baby's capacities.

The therapist then tries to determine how well the parents, as well as the family as a whole, were able to facilitate the adaptive goals. He or she needs to have a model in mind of supportive behaviors that promote development. In this first stage, the ideal family pattern is to be both calm and regulating and interesting in multisensory ways.

As one explores the family's reactions and its ability to negotiate this early stage with the baby, one wants to observe how the family is promoting development. Is the mother enjoying helping her baby discover the world? Is the father enjoying this process? Is the family organizing around this first challenge of discovery and learning to be calm, regulated, and comfortable? Or, alternatively, is the family overintruding on the baby or treating the baby impersonally, like a rag doll? Does either parent vacillate between withdrawing and overintrusiveness, because of maternal depression or preoccupation with family difficulties? Whether the baby does well or not at this time will be a product of both his individual constitutional and maturational characteristics and the way the parents, as individuals, and the family as a unit, negotiate the first developmental phase.

The therapist may ask, "What did you feel about your baby during these first couple of months of life? How did you like to play with your baby? What did you like to do during this stage? What did you enjoy and not enjoy? What did you find hard and what did you find easy?" As the therapist listens, he asks himself: Did the parents enjoy offering interesting sights,

sounds, and touch? Did they enjoy calming kinds of experiences? He may hear such statements as these: "We have just
moved across the country"; "My grandmother had just passed
away, and I was very depressed"; "The baby's father had just
lost his job, and we were fighting a lot"; "The baby's brother is
hyperactive and having learning problems at school"; or "I can't
even remember what we did with the baby. I'm just glad we
survived the time." The therapist can get a sense that the family
may have been under great stress, irritable, hyperactive, and
unable to calm a sensitive baby. This baby's sensory regulation
was not negotiated well.

On the other hand, a mother may say she didn't enjoy
much of anything: "I was very down. After the baby was born,
I was feeling very low. I was fearful a lot. I could barely get up
in the morning. My mother came to visit and that only made
me feel worse. Thank God she left after two weeks. My husband
was his typically workaholic self, and I was home alone. I was
happy to feed the baby." The therapist may get a sense of
a mother with postpartum depression who was apathetic and
withdrawn. If this mother comes in with a baby who has low
motor tone, almost overly calm and laid-back, and also a little
"spacey," it would appear that the baby's multisensory interest
in the world wasn't negotiated well.

Thus, the therapist begins to get a sense of the family
pattern by finding out how the parents provided regulation
and interesting experiences to involve the baby. Once he develops the family's general patterns of behavior, he can look for
them to repeat themselves through each of the developmental
stages. Such patterns hold for individuals, the couple, as well
as for the family as a whole. They may include depression,
apathy, physical unavailability, unavailability due to aloofness
and lack of interest, or intrusiveness and overstimulation. The
latter may be due to anxiety or not knowing what to do, or a
kind of undermining, overcontrolling, perfectionist attitude
that precludes the flexibility to adjust to the baby's needs. The
pattern may reveal disorganization and chaos, even though the
family or parent may be sweet and well intentioned. A very

passive, anxious, and tentative parent may not be able to talk much to the baby or to reach out to offer support. As a therapist works with a certain population, he develops these and other characteristic caregiver or family patterns.

A therapist always needs to ask, "Were you worried about anything special during this stage?" He wants to be alert (throughout the history-taking process) to hints of emotional difficulties in the parents' history or mental illness in the family. He also needs to pay attention to what is going on with older children. Parents often compare the younger child to an older child, and the therapist may get a sense that a sibling has a problem. The parents may bring up marital problems. A mother may talk about her husband being supportive or not supportive. The therapist should go off at a tangent for a few minutes with such emotional or marital problems, "roll" with them, and then say, in order to stay with the developmental history, "We'll go back into this later on in this session," or "Next time we meet, I want to hear more about what was going on with you and your husband at that particular time that made the baby's development so difficult for you." Perhaps the baby stirred up something in the marriage. If the baby was very demanding, and the mother was too tired to make love with her husband, he may have become angry and upset enough to start having an affair. The mother may want to talk about the marital problems, because the therapist is interested in her child, and the problems stem from the child. It is preferable to have both parents there, because each has a lot of information, and their interactions as they give their history enrich the therapist's picture. Sometimes the father's work schedule does not allow the parents to be there simultaneously, but I try for joint meetings whenever possible, particularly for the early sessions.

Thus, the basic model calls for the therapist to look at the first stage of adaptive goals and to examine each specific system, including the family pattern and the parent–infant interaction.

The parents' ability to communicate this information to a therapist will perhaps take less time than it takes to read this description of history taking. Parents who negotiated this stage easily may be able to tell quickly how the baby loved to look and listen and how overjoyed they were with the baby's attention to them. A therapist may quickly get a sense that everything came together well during this period.

SECOND DEVELOPMENTAL PHASE—ENGAGING AND FORMING RELATIONSHIPS (2–4 MONTHS)

The second stage of development involves the baby's ability to form an attachment or "fall in love" (i.e., when the 2–4 month-old baby begins to show a preference for the human world). What does the baby enjoy with the mother? How does the baby show his enjoyment? How does the mother feel about the baby's pleasure or lack of pleasure? The baby who responds to parents with robust, warm smiles that convey a sense of deep pleasure and with a cooing voice and synchronous arm and leg movements, contrasts with a baby who strikes the parents as indifferent, aloof, withdrawn, or avoidant of their looks. The therapist wants to look at how the mother and father each negotiates this stage of intimacy and engagement and their reactions to it. Either parent may have fears about closeness or being overwhelmed, controlled, or exploited by the demanding baby. Family patterns, such as jealousy of the father toward the mother, jealousy of older siblings toward the new baby, and how the family copes with those feelings will be of interest to the therapist.

History Taking Procedure (Stage 2). The therapist can ask such simple questions as, "How did your baby let you know how he was feeling that he was falling in love or taking a special interest in you or not showing pleasure in the relationship? What happened during that time?" A parent might respond, "Oh, my baby would smile beatifically and he would make sounds at me or he would move his arms. Whenever there were strangers around, he would always hug me tighter." Or one may get a different answer: "I can't remember very well about that time of life. There was so much going on." Then one might say, "Can you remember if and when she showed any special interest in you? Was there a special smile or a special sense of joy?" The parent's recall is a tip-off as to what went on at that particular stage. The therapist is looking at the sequence of the baby's adaptive goals. He is building a picture of why this baby is having trouble at his current age. The first set of questions had to do with: Did this baby ever learn to calm down, to attend, to respond to stimuli? The second set is: Did this baby use his ability to take an interest in people, to form relationships? He wants to know if the baby was aloof, indifferent, distractible, spacey, or shallow. "Well, he was different from the older sibling. When his sister smiled and reached out, I could tell that she loved us. But he was kind of laid-back and would just as soon suck on his fist or look at a light. He never took a special interest in us." Such a picture indicates when a problem with relationships might have started. The therapist tries to determine the full extent of the child's relatedness capacity—the eagerness with which the child related, how he responded to maternal or paternal overtures, and also, how well he recovered from stress. For example, if the mother was away for part of a day or a whole day, did the baby become aloof and indifferent and take two hours to woo back? Or was baby aloof only for a few minutes and then could be wooed into a relationship?

One must proceed systematically through each of the systems. "Well, did your baby show you that he loved you mostly by looking at you or mostly by talking to you?" is a question to determine how the baby used his sensory equipment. "Did the baby show you his love mostly through movement patterns or mostly by lying there and letting you pick him up and hug him?" The response to this question provides a picture of how the baby used his senses, such as vision and hearing. How did he respond to touch, as a part of loving? How the baby used his motor system and motor planning is indicated by whether he hugged and cuddled nicely or was limp or not able to get comfortable. One gets a sense of the sensory and motor systems, not in isolation, but as they foster the adaptive goal. Some children with delays and motor tone problems still manage to find a way to foster the adaptive goal; other children with less severe problems are not necessarily fostering the adaptive goal. To look at language development, when the baby can make some sounds, one needs to ask, "How did the baby use sounds to pull you in or to react to your sounds?" One begins to get a sense of how all the systems contribute to falling in love.

Questions about the family are again relevant: "Well, how did you feel during this time?" If the mother or father weren't delighted with the baby's first smiles and signs of pleasure, it becomes clear that the parents were not falling in love with their baby. What went wrong here? If one is observing a three-year-old, one may have to go back to the beginning to reconnect such issues, because the parents and child may not have been relating very well to each other for two or more years. "How were you feeling? What was going on with you? How would you compare that to your older child or the middle child?" One looks at how all the different possible family patterns relate to falling in love.

THIRD DEVELOPMENTAL PHASE—TWO-WAY COMMUNICATION (4–8 MONTHS)

Between four and eight months, the baby should learn about purposeful, two-way communication (somatopsychological differentiation). He usually begins to be highly intentional, not only in motor exploration, but also in each area of emotion, in order to negotiate dependency, pleasure, security, and even anger. Reciprocity and opening and closing circles of communication become important at this point.

Therefore, the therapist wants to ask how the baby began letting the parents know what he did and did not want. How did the baby become or not become intentional? Is the baby a clear signaler and initiator or does he seem to lie back and expect someone to read his signals? Or is he a child who seems active and interested in everything?

As the therapist talks to the parents, he or she will observe whether they are good reciprocal interactors by how they respond and how they describe their baby's development. Parents who say, "Well, I can't remember. I think he occasionally used to bang his fist on the table," are quite different from the parents who recall how the baby gleefully squeezed his father's nose when the father would say "toot toot," and the baby would squeeze his nose again.

One or two examples of the baby's behavior can provide a sense of the pattern of the baby's intentionality or lack of it. A lack of intentionality is linked to fragmented, chaotic, or more withdrawn patterns. Whether or not the baby uses intentionality to achieve closeness, such as reaching out to be held, is indicative. Does the baby satisfy his curiosity by exploring toys or parts of his mother's and father's faces or hair? Does he assert himself by pointing, as opposed to crying and having temper tantrums? The passive, fearful baby, the withdrawn baby, the chaotic, distractible baby, or the passive baby will emerge during this period.

It is interesting to note that with handicapped children, during this four- to eight-month period, there is frequently very little support for initiative and very little response to the baby's cues. It is not unusual to hear that parents working with an occupational or physical therapist were moving the baby's arms and legs to help with motor tone and posture, but doing almost nothing to harness the baby's communicative ability or his initiative. This could be one reason why children with handicaps are often, unnecessarily, quite passive. Thus, if there is any special problem, such as a handicap, it is especially important to find out about the parent's reaction—how they felt about the problem, what was going on in their marriage, what this did to their relationship, and what effect it had on older siblings.

When one inquires about family functioning at this particular stage (or any other), one should keep in mind that at different stages, different adaptive tasks place different stresses on the family. A family that may have done well with regulation and interest in the world and forming attachments may start having trouble in stage 3, when purposeful, organized communication is the adaptive goal. A very controlling, structured family may function well in the first two stages, particularly if they are very loving, but falter when the baby starts to take the initiative. The baby says, "I want 50% of the leadership here," and many parents say, "No way!" The parents may become more controlling, and power struggles ensue. A maladaptive response occurs because the family isn't equipped to deal with this new developmental challenge.

Sometimes the child's positive mental health can actually be the first step in a negative cycle, and a therapist needs to look for and understand that possibility. A three-year-old may appear negative, belligerent, and oppositional. But if the therapist does a careful history, he may find that the child was doing well up to about eight months. He was a high-intensity, very organized, and very purposeful six- and seven-month-old, and only when he came up against a very controlling father or mother did his negativism and oppositional behavior start. That child is very different from one who is oppositional because he has no attention span or has a severe problem with aggression. You might approach it differently, even though it may look the same at age three-and-a-half. Thus, the history becomes a very revealing and important determinant of the therapist's approach.

History Taking Procedure (Stage 3). To elicit information about the stage of purposeful communication, one can start with an open-ended question: "How did your baby let you know what he wanted? Did your baby get to a stage where he could be purposeful or intentional? Could you tell when he wanted to be picked up and when he wanted to play with something, when he was hungry or angry? How did he let you know those things?" The parents may say, "Well, it was hard to know. He would cry, and I would know that he might be hungry sometimes." "Well, what if he wanted to be picked up?" "Oh, I would just have to guess." "You mean there was never any time when he would kind of reach out and look you in the eye?" "No, my older one did that, but he didn't do that. Sometimes he would look kind of glassy-eyed, and I would pick him up, because I figured I hadn't picked him up in a while." This account does not give a sense of a very intentional child. On the other hand, a parent might say, "Oh, from the time he was six months on, he would point and make different sounds. I knew exactly when he was hungry from one sound and exactly when he wanted me to cuddle him." "Well, how did you know he wanted to be cuddled?" "He would make a low-pitched sound, he would reach out with his arms, or he would bang on my leg." Here is a highly intentional child. "Well, how did you know when he wanted to play with a toy at eight months?" "Oh, he would be taking that toy and banging it on my leg, and I would know that he wanted me to play with him." One child who couldn't crawl at ten months, because he was motor-delayed, was highly intentional and would roll from across the room over to his mother and look up at her; she knew that he wanted to be picked up or played with.

Once the therapist has a sense of how the baby is negotiating the stage of intentionality, he goes through the review of systems again. How much of a contribution is made by fine motor, gross motor, sensory reactivity, sensory processing, or language functions? The questions are geared to determine how the baby is using his abilities to foster intentional communication, that is, to let one know what he wants or to react to what one wants.

To go into greater depth in the emotional area at eight months, one breaks up the emotional and social areas beyond just the adaptive goals into how does this child deal with dependency, pleasure and excitement, assertiveness, and anger. The questions are: "How did your baby let you know that he wanted something?" (to determine assertiveness). "How did he let you know when he was mad? How did he let you know when he wanted you to be close?"

To explore family functioning, in terms of the goal of intentional communication, one asks, "How did you feel during this stage? What did you do? What kind of games did you like to play with your baby?" The therapist has in mind the ideal parental response to harnessing intentional communication. The most supportive adaptive family pattern is to follow the baby's lead, to respond to his cues in an empathetic and temporally effective way. The parents should not overcontrol the baby, poke the baby, or do everything to the baby, but should allow the baby to initiate and then react to that initiative. Relevant questions are: "What did you like to do and what did you like to play?" The parent may describe games, such as picking at the baby, poking the baby, tickling the baby, which illustrate a one-way street. If they are not reacting to the baby, the therapist may get a sense of a somewhat intrusive, overcontrolling parent. One may get different reactions from one or the other parent. The mother may be very sensitive and respond to the baby's cues: "Oh, I used to watch for the baby's look on his face, and when the baby would say something to me, I would try to talk back, and then he and I would talk to each other and kind of gurgle." This is an ideal kind of description. Or, "I could tell that he was ready to play, because he would stop banging his toy, and I would go to him, and I would roll the ball back and forth with him." Again, this is an ideal interaction, as opposed to, "At this age, he was able to laugh every time I tickled him, whereas before that he wasn't very responsive." This is more of a one-way street, stir-the-baby up kind of notion. Or, "We had great fun together. He would laugh and giggle." "What did you do to laugh and giggle?" "Oh, I would throw him up in the air and I would tickle him." Just roughhousing is fine up to a point, but in isolation, it just revs the baby up and doesn't give him a chance to develop intentional communication. The therapist gets a sense of whether the parents are harnessing the baby's natural ability.

FOURTH DEVELOPMENTAL PHASE—COMPLEX SENSE OF SELF (9–18 MONTHS)

At around nine to eighteen months of age, one moves into the stage of behavioral organization and the emergence of a complex sense of self. One now looks at the adaptive goal of the baby's being able to categorize or abstract the social patterns of interaction.

The next stage the therapist focuses on is the period between nine and eighteen months or when the baby learns more complex styles of communication and to categorize or abstract the social patterns of interaction. For example, when the baby is hungry, he can take his mother's hand, walk her to the refrigerator, bang on the door, and point to the food. The baby can take off his father's hat and imitate his father's mannerisms. The baby learns to decipher his parents' facial expressions and gestures in order to figure out such important emotional messages as whether or not he is safe or in danger and whether or not he is accepted or rejected. He learns whether or not his personal features are a source of pride to his parents, or whether his parents are trying to change him. This two-way communication is a most important component of development, because the baby is learning to form a complex, abstract, prerepresentational image of himself. He is becoming a partner in a relationship that allows him to abstract the larger social meanings around emotions such as closeness, approval, and dependency. The child is also learning to communicate across space with gestural patterns; to employ auditory and visual–spatial processing; and to develop much better motor control. He uses fine motor skills to manipulate objects; in addition to walking he coordinates his gross motor system, so that local motion can be used to control himself and to communicate. The child begins to control and negotiate such basic concepts or themes as security and independence, focused as opposed to uncontrolled aggression, as well as assertiveness and exploration.

The baby goes beyond simple give and take, and now orchestrates complex behaviors with goals, and begins to abstract presymbolically the features of his environment. He begins to know during this stage that the angry mother and the nice mother are not different people but the same person. He can be across the room, look at mommy's expression, and feel as if he is in her arms, even if he is spatially independent from her, because he can abstract her gestures and figure out that she's making approving and supportive remarks.

History-Taking Procedure (Stage 4). During the history-taking process, it is important to probe the following: the child's ability to communicate across space, to abstract the basic emotional and social patterns of life; his ability in negotiating with his sensory and motor equipment the emotional polarities of life, such as independence–dependence, passivity–assertiveness, as well as a sense of mastery. If the parents' description of the child's patterns of behavior does provide a sufficient sense of the child's negotiation of this developmental stage, the therapist should enquire about complex behavior the child exhibits. "What are the most complicated things your child does—socially, emotionally, language-wise, and cognitively?" If one hears about the child taking the parent by the hand to look for toys or to get the refrigerator opened or imitating the father, one knows the child is generally at an acceptable level. On the other hand, if one hears that the child is playing only simple peek-a-boo games or is negative or withdrawn, the child is not acquiring greater social and emotional complexity. The key is whether or not the child is stringing together many cause-and-effect units of interaction.

It is helpful at each of these stages to ask about the child's ability to open and close circles of communication. As indicated earlier, a circle is opened when the child shows an interest in something. If the parent responds to that expression of interest with a gesture or comment—pointing at something the child is pointing to, or verbalizing the child's interest in a particular food; and if the child then builds on the parent's signal by pulling closer the object he is pointing at or picking up the food, the child is closing a circle of communication. If, however, the child gets distracted and goes from pointing at the objects to looking at television, or moves to yet another object, the child is not closing a circle of communication. In other words, a circle of communication has three components: the child shows an interest, A; the parent builds on that interest, B; and the child builds further on the parent's communication, C. If A, B, and C are related, a circle is opened and closed. If they are not related, a circle has not been opened and closed. At fifteen to sixteen months, the child should be able to open and close ten circles in a row, whereas the eight-month-old may do only two or three circles in a row.

Therefore one wants to know whether complex patterns of interaction are developing through these circles being opened and closed. One wants to know further if the child is equally good at developing complex patterns of communication in all areas of emotion. How does the child negotiate getting picked up or getting dependency and closeness needs met? How does the child negotiate assertiveness and curiosity, such as by taking the father by the hand and searching? How does the child deal with aggression? Pleasure? Excitement?

One wants to know about the stability of the behavioral patterns. How much does stress, such as separation from a parent, physical illness, hunger, or fatigue, lead to a loss of the ability for organized behavior (opening and closing many circles in a row)? In other words, how stable is the pattern over time and what kinds of stress tends to destabilize it?

One wants to know about the parents' ability to support the child's development with expressions of admiration. The ability to be one step, but not three steps, ahead of the child and to help the child develop even more complicated patterns, should be contrasted with critical, jealous, intruding, overcontrolling or withdrawing patterns on the part of the parents. A parent can either overprotect and treat the child as younger than he is or move far ahead of the child, as though to burden him with goals he cannot reach. Marital troubles can stem from the child becoming more assertive and getting into power struggles with his parents. The mother and father may differ about how to handle the assertiveness. The father may prefer a tough guy approach, and the mother may take a more indulgent approach. The mother may react to the child's greater independence by becoming upset and taking it out on the father, who in turn gets upset. If the father feels ignored by his toddler who still prefers the mother, the father may undermine the mother at every opportunity. The therapist needs to explore the ability of the parent to admire, support, and encourage the child; to set limits on the child; and to use gestural modes of communication. At the same time, the therapist has to contrast the parents' tendencies to undermine the child's development.

Another aspect of family patterns is worth discussing at this point. With this systematic overview in mind, we can look at some practical aspects of taking a history and observing. Certain family patterns and relationships will be consistent over time, patterns do not always differ in each developmental phase. At times, however, the child's unique behavior during a particular developmental phase may affect the parent, and the family patterns. For example, a seeming marital conflict, which could emerge from a father's work schedule or a mother's relationship with her own family, may in fact be stimulated by a certain developmental shift in the child. As the child becomes more independent, the mother may decide to become more involved with her own mother and nuclear family. This involvement may bring her into conflict with her mother, which then makes her more irritable with her husband who, in turn, becomes upset with her and his in-laws. In such a scenario, it is easy to lose sight of the fact that what set the drama in motion was the child becoming more independent and the mother feeling anxious about it.

A review of systems takes into consideration that the baby should be walking (by at least 14 or 15 months). He should be using his greater navigational ability to play hide-and-seek games or to explore new parts of the room and come back to his mother. Fine motor coordination should be supporting greater organization; more sophisticated language development should lead to preverbal sentences or at least a few words used functionally, not just randomly. One looks at how all these systems are contributing to or undermining the adaptive goals. The tactilely sensitive baby may not be getting into assertive kinds of play. The child who has an auditory processing problem may not be able to receive information from afar. For example, he may look at his mother from across the room while playing. His mother may say, "Hey, that's terrific," whereupon the child begins to cling to her leg. He doesn't seem to get the idea that she's approving from across the room because he is unable to abstract her gestures and sounds in order to figure out her approval. He is unable to sequence the sounds together and abstract the pattern.

Next, one probes the family pattern. The goal is for the family to admire the baby's new abilities, not to feel jealous or envious of them. Many families become surprisingly competitive with their children during the toddler stage. The parents may overcontrol the toddler who is learning so many new things. One looks for the parent to admire and encourage the child and to try to introduce complexity a small step beyond (not 2 steps beyond or 20 behind) where the baby can reach alone to make life interesting for him. With many handicapped children, one sees patterns of infantilization and overprotection, without enough admiration and respect for the baby's abilities. One asks how the parents felt, what games they played, what they liked to play, to get a sense of whether they were able to support the more adaptive goals. If not, one tries to find out what was happening in the family at that time.

In summary, one asks about the child's ability to enter into more complex patterns of communication, the parents' ability to support this behavior, and how this plays out in different emotional realms. Do they enhance the ability of the child to abstract social relationships and social patterns, to use more distal modes of communication through vision and hearing across space, and to integrate the various polarities of life, such as dependence–independence and passivity–assertiveness? The ability of the child to integrate different polarities is reflected in the child's ability to play independently while feeling connected to the parent only through gestures across space. Does the child have the ability to be angry, recover, and be close within the same play session? Can he be assertive and seek mastery, and at the same time seek warmth and intimacy?

FIFTH DEVELOPMENTAL PHASE—CONSTRUCTING EMOTIONAL IDEAS (2 TO 3 YEARS)

Between eigthteen and twenty-four months to about thirty months, the toddler gains the capacity to use ideas to symbolize or represent emotions. One wants to know about the child's functional use of language and complex gestures and make-believe play. How did the baby negotiate his or her needs, such as physical hunger, dependency, pleasure and excitement, or assertiveness? When did the baby begin using symbols as a way of organizing his world? How well did the family support this goal? Were the parents functionally oriented in terms of language? When they wanted to discipline or when they wanted to explore new things, did they use words and concepts? (even gestural interchanges can support concepts); or were they very concrete (e.g., "Do it this way. Do it that way.")? Did they order the child around and give him no chance to develop his own ideas?

The next stage to explore historically is the point at which the child gains the ability to construct emotional ideas. How well can he use internal representations to deal with emotional, social, and intellectual issues?

The best indicators of this ability come through pretend play, when the child causes dolls to hug or fight, or have a tea party, or take a rocketship to the moon. The child's use of intentional, as opposed to descriptive language (e.g., only able to label or describe things) also indicates he is organizing emotional ideas. The child who uses language intentionally will tell the parents, "Me hungry," "Me mad," "Give me that. I want it."

The use of language to negotiate interests and eventually to communicate feelings indicates that the child has entered into the stage of organizing emotional ideas or representations.

The child who can say, "Me angry," or "Me love Mommy," can use that ability to verbalize an abstract idea or play it out with dolls to reduce his sense of urgency. The child who can say, "I love you," doesn't have to cling to his mother. The child who can say, "Me angry," doesn't have to hit his friend. If the use of the word reduces the sense of urgency and the need to act out the feeling, then the child has truly learned to represent his feeling. On the other hand, if the word accompanies the action, he hasn't.

History-Taking Procedure (Stage 5). To inquire about this ability to express emotional ideas, one simply needs to ask the parents if the child engages in pretend play and to give examples of how the child uses words. If the parents report elaborate pretend play sequences and language that conveys intentionality or desire and helps reduce urgency, then the therapist knows that the child is using emotional ideas or representations. If, on the other hand, the child shies away from pretend play and uses words only descriptively, then the child lacks representational capacities.

Once the therapist decides that the child has reached the level of abstraction, he should ask the parents how the child uses his ability in emotional areas such as dependency and closeness, aggression and assertiveness. If the child can make the dolls hug and can say, "I love you," as well as, "Me angry," when the dolls fight, then the therapist knows the child can use his new ability to express both the angry side and the warm, intimate, dependent aspect of his life. He should be able to apply the same ability to mastery, exploration, sexuality, and excitement. One also wants to inquire about the ability to use language and ideas for limit-setting. Can the child say, "No. Me no do that"? Can he comprehend the parent's verbal limits and follow them?

At this stage one wants to inquire, not only about the child, but also about the parents' ability to express feelings. Is this a parent who is comfortable with using ideas and labeling feelings or is this a parent who prefers that feelings should be left under the carpet and not expressed? Is anger taboo? Is the notion of a child's saying, "I'm mad," frightening to a parent? Are words used to describe excitement and sexuality taboo? Are words used to describe closeness and intimacy misperceived as a sign that the child is too clinging or too needy? If so, the parent is uncomfortable with the symbolic mode. What kind of play does a parent enjoy with the child? The response will indicate the parent's level of comfort with different emotional demands. If the parent does not enjoy pretend play but finds it too childish or silly, the therapist will presume some anxiety about the world of make-believe. A parent who likes only bland themes of play may be contrasted with a parent who is comfortable with all themes. Parents are typically more comfortable with themes of dependency (dolls hugging) than with aggressive themes (dolls fighting), although some may be more comfortable when the dolls show assertiveness.

As the child goes from age two to three, the therapist also wants to look at the complexity of the dramas he is developing, and how far the parents are prepared to go to help him. Do the parents follow the child's lead in the play, or do the parents interfere? The therapist asks them to describe how they play with the child. Does the parent become bossy or withdraw when he or she doesn't like what the child is doing? Is the parent able to engage in a certain level of symbolism, for example, to talk about the angry doll? But does that same parent become anxious and pull away when the complexity gets too great, as when the child begins to explain why the doll is angry? A parent who is quite literal and concrete may feel that the child's make-believe play and creative use of ideas is worrisome, because it betrays the child's deeply held feelings. That the child can reveal his ideas in the form of play suggests that the child is coping with his emotions. The concrete parent, however, will feel instead that the child is overwhelmed by his emotions, and won't be able to facilitate the child's discussion of his feelings.

At this stage, one wants also to look at how the child's ability to use ideas influences relationships within the family. Does a child's interest in the human body, his undressing and dressing of dolls, or his interest in body parts, stir up conflicts about sexuality between the mother and the father? Or does a child's greater verbalization of aggression or greater independence from the other stimulate conflicts in the mother or the father that get played out by the couple or within the family?

In terms of family, as well as parental patterns, one wants to look particularly at the tendency to withdraw from the child at this time, to overcontrol the child's use of ideas, or to stereotype the child's use of ideas along very conventional, hackneyed, or contrived lines; all such tendencies suggest anxiety on the parents' part. At this stage especially, one needs to look at the tendency of parents to project their own ideas onto the child. As a child becomes verbal and more involved in pretend play, it is easy for parents to disturb the child's productions, because of their own feelings about people and ideas. The child who is trying to play out a scene of aggression when the dolls hit each other, may lead the parent to say, "Oh, let the dolls hold hands. Aren't they loving each other?" Or, the child who is trying to show dolls loving may stimulate the parent to say, "Oh, why are they so mad at each other?" Because of the greater symbolism and complexity of the child's play, in terms of its make-believe quality, it becomes easier for the parent to distort the play and to bring the parent's own hidden agenda and inner feelings to bear on every drama. Often the parents' conflicts emerge superimposed on the child's play.

One may see such behavior less clearly at earlier stages of development. The child may, for example, be simply playing a peek-a-boo game with his parents. The parent may describe that game without much distortion or characterize the child's looking as aggressive, rather than curious. One should ask the parents how they interpret or understand the child's play. If the parent describes what the child was doing, how he or she interacted with the child, and how he or she interpreted what the play meant to the child, one will begin to see emerging certain characteristic emotions (such as hostility, dependency, jealousy, competitiveness) that makes up the parent's world.

SIXTH PHASE OF DEVELOPMENT—EMOTIONAL THINKING (2½–5 YEARS OLD)

This next stage of a child's development has to do with emotional thinking or representational differentiation. At this point, one looks at children as young as two-and-a-half to three years and as old as four-and-a-half to five years to gauge their ability to organize behavior and feelings by making connections between the ideas.

By way of example, a child begins to organize ideas that have to do with make-believe as opposed to those that have to do with reality. The child can then distinguish between fantasy and reality. He organizes ideas that have to do with "me" and "not-me," which helps to separate the subjective from the objective. Children also start to organize ideas in terms of time, such as ideas that have to do with now, compared to tomorrow or yesterday. Children at this age do not think in terms of long stretches of time, but they can understand short intervals of past, present, and future time periods. They can understand concepts of space—their house, someone else's house, grandmother's place in California. Besides separating out the dimensions of self or nonself, time, and space, the child also begins to distinguish dimensions of the thematic–affective realms. He begins to categorize emotional proclivities, such as dependency, aggression, and assertiveness at the level of ideas.

The ability to categorize experience helps the child formulate his basic ego functions: reality testing, impulse control, even mood, and the ability to concentrate and anticipate (these adaptive goals represent the essential functions needed for school). The therapist needs to determine how the child distinguishes fantasy from reality. Regarding impulse control, it is important to determine how much sense the child has of a "me" operating on a "you." A sense of the sequence of time allows the child to know, "If I do something now, it will have this effect in the future." He can control his impulses through his reason, not only because his rote memory tells him he has been slapped on the hand for doing something. He can reason that, "I'd better not do this, because I'll be punished," or "I should do this, because I'll get rewarded for it."

A more stable mood comes from the ability to categorize experience. A two-year-old is likely to change moods every few minutes, but a three- or four-year-old has a more even mood, because he pulls fragmented emotions into categories that allow him to be angry or happy for a more extended period of time.

Again, the therapist wants to know if the child is moving in the direction of the adaptive goals and how his sensory, motor, and language systems are contributing to or detracting from his progress.

History-Taking Procedure (Stage 6). It is necessary to ask simple questions about how the child communicated with the parents as a three- and four-year-old and later, if the child is as old as five. One needs to listen to whether the child uses "buts" and "becauses" and whether he juxtaposes two ideas in his sentences. Does he say, "I shouldn't have to go to sleep, because it's early?" One gets a picture of the child's ability to connect ideas by observing how he or she understands complex directions. The child's ability to carry out an instruction like, "First put your plate away, then go sit down in the other room" means that he can hold in mind two interrelated, sequential ideas, and suggests that he has reached the stage of connecting ideas.

During pretend play, the therapist now expects the child to play out more complex dramas involving two interrelated themes (e.g., the good guys attack the bad guys, because the bad guys attacked them first). The therapist therefore asks the parents for examples of the child's ability to convey this kind of complexity in pretend play and in communication with the parents. If the child shows an ability to form and connect up different categories of feelings, one then looks for the ability to handle more complicated versions of the same feelings. For example, is the child able to separate reality from fantasy and to tell a parent that a dream is make-believe, although it feels real? Is the child able to shift gears from make-believe play to reality? Or does the child think the dreams are real? Does he refuse to or become unable to stop being Batman or Superman? It is necessary to make distinctions here: there is the child who likes to fool around and pretend to be Batman, and when his friend comes over, takes off the Batman outfit and plays his friend's favorite game. And there is the child who seems to keep the Batman outfit on in inappropriate situations and gets very upset when someone insists that he is not Batman. One looks at the child's ability to shift between fantasy and reality as a sign that he or she can organize emotional ideas into larger categories, such as make-believe and real.

One should also look at the child's ability to control his impulses, not only through fear, but also by comprehending that there are do's and don't's, punishments and sanctions. One wants to hear evidence that the child has mastered this ability to form categories of experience. The child who says, "Well, I won't do that, because I know you will punish me," shows that he has that ability. Also, the child should demonstrate that he is able to distinguish among the different emotions of dependency, aggression, assertiveness, excitement, by being able to play out different themes and to make connections between these themes. If during pretend play, the dolls are lovey-dovey and hugging until the monster comes, and the dolls then become angry in order to fight off the monster, the child demonstrates that he understands categories of emotions and experience.

At the same time that the child shows he can categorize emotions and experience, one also wants to know if he is categorizing dimensions of time and space. Does he know the difference between yesterday, today, and tomorrow, or between right here, next door, and far away? One should ask the parents for examples of what the child does when he visits a friend, say. Does he ever talk about whether the friend is near or far? Or when it comes to wanting something, can he comprehend that he has to wait ten minutes, two hours, or two weeks?

One needs to look at the parents' comfort with differentiating and connecting ideas: some parents are very intuitive and don't like analyzing how ideas relate to one another. For example, one parent said, "I like my child to march to his own drummer, and I like to speak to him in riddles." Her child might express a series of disconnected ideas such as, "The children are crying," followed by, "The children are happy," but never connect how the children changed from crying to happy. This child has difficulties in distinguishing reality from fantasy and logically bridging his communications.

The notion of opening and closing symbolic circles, as at the gestural level, becomes important at this point. Do the child and the mother or father engage in communication that encompasses the logical opening and closing of circles with symbols? For example, if the child says, "Look at the soldier doll," and the parent says, "I see him. What's he going to do?" the child might say, "The soldier is going to jump on the motorcycle and go to his fort." The child just closed the circle that he opened when he mentioned the soldier; the parent creates the opportunity for further elaboration of the circle by showing an interest and asking what was going to happen next; the child closes the circle by telling the parent what happens next. This microscopic interaction creates a basis for the logical use of symbols, because the child's symbol is connected to the parent's symbol which is, in turn, connected to the child's symbol. The symbols are connected in a logical way; there is a bridge between each element in a series of communications. On the other hand, if the child says, "Here's the soldier doll," and the parent says, "Oh, I see him. What's he going to do next?" and the child then says, "Look at the moon," the child is not closing a symbolic circle but is using symbols in a more fragmented and random way. This child needs help in establishing a logical structure from a parent who says, "I like the moon. But what about the soldier?" to see if the child can close the circle around the soldier, before the child speaks about the moon. Perhaps the soldier eventually will go to the moon in his rocketship. Even phantasmagoric play about going to the moon can involve a certain logic, if the spaceship has a rocket engine, and if the pilot communicates with a copilot about navigation. The parent who is uncomfortable closing circles and creating a logical superstructure may not help the child categorize his experience. Similarly, the parent who gets lost in the trees and can't see the forest, or gets lost in the emotion of the moment, may become fragmented by the child's rich imagination and not be able to help the child open and close his circles of symbolic communication.

Exploring how the parent relates to the child in make-believe play and during day-to-day conversations about school and friends can give the therapist a sense of how the parent deals with the child in different areas. For example, how do the parents negotiate dependency when the child wants to be picked up or cuddled or says "I love you?" How do they deal with the child when he says "I'm angry," or "The dolls are angry"? Is the parent logical in dealing with dependency, closeness, or sexuality, but illogical and not able to differentiate or close circles with the child, when it comes to anger? Because of their own anxiety, parents are sometimes more random or fail to be logical with regard to certain emotions and not others. Therefore, one looks at the ability of the parent to support the categorization of experience in all the different modalities and emotional areas.

While some parental anxiety with logic stems from conflicts about aggression, or sexuality, or separation, other parents are, by nature, more fragmented and illogical in the way they use ideas. Sometimes each parent reports that he or she can be logical when talking to the child; in pretend play each can help the child open and close circles. However, when siblings are around, and the family is all together, everybody tends to become chaotic, fragmented, and more illogical in the use of ideas. Sometimes the family's difficulty in negotiating dependency or aggression plays a part in this fragmentation; other times the problem may have to do with the way the individuals organize experience as a group. Therefore, the therapist wants to look both at the child's ability to master this stage of emotional thinking in terms of the parents' reports, but also to identify the roles of the parents in supporting or discouraging that ability.

If the child is older than four years, one wants to look at how well the child is moving from comparing and connecting ideas to elaborating on them. The child's ability to create elaborate new fantasies or complex dramas with subplots will be characteristic of this next stage of emotional thinking and even more so in the stages that follow.

Finally, one wants to derive from the child's history a sense of how the child is negotiating aggression and limit-setting, relations with peers, sharing, assertiveness, and curiosity about family life. Such curiosity may be about body parts, sexuality, where brothers and sisters come from, and the parents' privacy behind bedroom doors. Issues such as nudity, sexual overstimulation or understimulation, as well as aggression, should be further explored at this age. This age is particularly important for the child's development of his sense of self. Through his greater ability to use logic, he is forming a more integrated image of himself in relationship to others. He is also forming opinions about concepts such as dependency, sexuality, and aggression in a logical, conscious way.

At each stage, in addition to looking at the child's developmental progress, the parents' reaction to the child, and their ability to support and harness the child's progress, as well as the roles of the couple and the family, one wants to ask specifically about what else of importance is going on in the family. Is there a death of a grandparent, an illness, a financial setback, or a family problem seemingly unrelated to the child? For example, at the birth of a sibling, what were the child's reactions, the parents' reactions? Love? Jealousy and anger? Less time for everyone? How do the parent and the child, the couple and the family negotiate a new challenge? Do they become concrete and rigid and make a lot of rules? Do they become disorganized and fragmented? Do they withdraw? Is there a lot of fragmentation and aggression, or can they integrate the new element into family life and keep a balance? Can the family elevate both warmth and love for the new baby and healthy sibling competitiveness to the level of emotional thinking, so that the emotions can be worked with, for the benefit of the child, the parent–child relationship, and the family as a whole?

In addition to the birth of a sibling, one wants to be aware of physical illnesses at any stage, as well as illnesses of other family members, marital difficulties, financial setbacks, or problems with grandparents or other relatives. The parents' involvement in the larger community needs to be addressed, since their concerns will affect their relationship with the child, particularly in stressful communities where there is drug abuse, violence, crime, or when the parents' income level has changed.

In summary then, a history and observations should work together to give a picture of how the child functions and where the child's development has gone awry; they should elaborate the child's unique and exceptional competencies. The history should provide a useful working hypothesis of what the therapist expects to find when he or she observes and interviews (plays) with the parent(s) and child together, or the child alone, depending on the age of the child. And often the direct observations will lead to new questions that need to be raised in terms of history. For example, a child's intense sexual curiosity may lead the clinician to ask more about this aspect of the child's development than he did originally.

The therapist wants to be able to ascertain from the history and observations which stages of early development the child seems to have negotiated successfully and the extent of each negotiation (i.e., broad or narrow). In other words, has the child negotiated regulating and attending to his world; learning to engage or fall in love with the world; learning two-way communication; learning to use emotional ideas or representations; and learning to categorize and connect representations? How far has the child come along based on his age? If the child has made it through each of these stages, has he made it through with limitations? Can he negotiate aggression and assertiveness, but not dependency and closeness? Can he use two-way communication and emotional ideas to handle dependency and closeness, but not aggression and assertiveness? Has he negotiated each stage with some limitations in the range of experience he can incorporate at that stage, or does he have the stage negotiated and the range negotiated, but not in a stable manner? Does the slightest stress, physical illness, a transient separation from parents, or angry feelings tend to lead to a loss of the child's ability to organize a particular stage? Is the ability regained, or does stress lead to a more chronic loss of that ability? If one looks at the stage achieved, the range of experience organized, and the stability of the achievement at that stage, one should have a good profile of the child's development.

OVERVIEW OF COMPETENT AND POTENTIALLY DISORDERED INFANT FUNCTIONING; A GUIDE FOR CLINICAL OBSERVATION AND HISTORY TAKING

DEVELOPMENTAL DIAGNOSIS—HOMEOSTASIS (0–3 MONTHS)

Competent functioning is suggested if the infant is relaxed and sleeps at regular times; recovers from crying with comforting; is able to be very alert; looks at one when talked to; and brightens up progressively more when provided with appropriate visual, auditory, and/or tactile stimulation as he goes from birth to three months of age.

Severely disordered functioning is suggested by the following:

1. The baby sleeps almost all the time; shows no interest in anyone; does not respond to interesting stimuli, such as lights, colors, sounds, touch, or movements, or
2. The baby is always upset or crying; stiff and rigid. Becomes completely distracted by any sights, noises, touch, movement, gets too excited and cries; or

3. The baby shows a mixture of the above patterns with neither predominating.

Moderately disordered functioning is suggested by the following:

1. The baby seems apathetic or sad, uninterested in anything. Responds a little to touch or movement, but is not very interested in seeing or hearing objects nearby; or
2. The baby is upset and crying most of the time, is too alert; looks at too many things; gets somewhat distracted by things he can see, hear, or feel.

DEVELOPMENTAL DIAGNOSIS—ATTACHMENT (2–4 MONTHS)

Competent functioning is suggested if the infant is very interested in people, especially mother or father, and other key caregivers; looks, smiles and responds to their voices or their touch with signs of pleasure and interest such as smiling, relaxing, "cooing" or other vocalizations indicating pleasure. The infant seems to respond with deep feeling and multiple sensory modalities (e.g., with vision, audition, tactile senses, movement, olfactory senses, etc.).

Severely disordered functioning is suggested by the following:

1. The baby is disinterested in people, especially mother, father, and/or other primary caregivers (e.g., always looks away rather than at people); looks withdrawn (as though eyes were turned inward); human approaches (i.e., holding) lead to rigidity and turning away or further withdrawal; chronic flat affect; or
2. The baby insists on being held all the time; will not sleep without being held; or

3. The baby is a mixed type, showing a mixture of the above with neither pattern predominating.

Moderately disordered functioning is suggested by the following:

1. The baby only occasionally looks at people or responds to their voices with a show of interest, either a smile or putting a hand out or kicking; afterwards, however, the baby shows no special interest in the human world. The baby experiences no comfort in being held. Flat affect a good deal of the time; or
2. The baby seems almost too interested in people, clinging to mother, father, or other primary caregiver; cries easily if not held; goes to strangers and holds on as if they were parents. The baby is not very interested in playing alone (e.g., exploring a new toy).

DEVELOPMENTAL DIAGNOSIS— SOMATOPSYCHOLOGICAL DIFFERENTIATION (3–10 MONTHS)

Competent functioning is suggested if the infant is able to interact in a purposeful (i.e., intentional, reciprocal, cause-and-effect) manner; smiles in response to a voice; is able to initiate signals and respond purposefully using multiple sensory modalities and the motor system; purposefully employs a range of emotions (e.g., pleasure or protest, assertion, etc.); and at the same time is able to get involved with toys and other inanimate objects.

Severely disordered functioning is suggested by the following:

1. The baby may interact but not purposefully; seems oblivious to caregiver's signals; does not respond to his

or her smile, voice, reaching out; "marches to the beat of a different drummer"; or

2. The baby demands constant interaction, cannot tolerate being alone at all; has temper tantrums or withdraws if caregiver does not respond to his signals or initiate interactive signals all the time; or

3. The baby shows a mixture of the above with neither pattern predominating.

Moderately disordered functioning is suggested by the following:

1. The baby responds occasionally to caregiver's signals, such as smiles or sounds, but it is hard to predict when he or she will do so; the response is very intermittent, often random rather than a purposeful social response, or it is limited only to one type of signal, such as caregiver's voice, but not smile; or

2. The baby is able to interact, but seems overly sensitive to any emotional communication from the caregiver; looks sad and forlorn at the slightest sign that the caregiver is preoccupied; gets very easily frustrated if his signal (e.g., smile and hand reaching out) is not responded to; is disorganized; or

3. The baby shows a mixture of the above problems with neither pattern predominating.

DEVELOPMENTAL DIAGNOSIS—BEHAVIORAL ORGANIZATION, INITIATIVE, AND ORIGINALITY (10–17 MONTHS)

Behavioral Organization. Competent functioning is suggested if in an organized manner the infant manifests a wide range of such socially meaningful behaviors and feelings as warmth, pleasure, assertion, exploration, protest, and anger. For example, the child can play or interact with parents stringing together a number of reciprocal interactions into a complex social interchange. Such an interchange might consist of a game where parents and child take turns chasing each other around the house, or where looking at pictures together contains interest and curiosity in the context of a warm interchange with parents and child taking turns viewing, pointing, or vocalizing. The child is able to go from interacting to separation and reunion with organized affects, including pleasure, apprehension, and protest.

Severely disordered functioning is suggested by the following:

1. The child rarely initiates behaviors and/or emotions; is mostly passive and withdrawn or seemingly uninvolved or excessively negativistic; flat affect may predominate; or

2. The child's behavior and affect are completely random, chaotic. The toddler will almost always appear "out of control" with aggressive affects predominating in a context of highly disorganized behaviors. The child has no sense of purpose; or

3. The child shows a mixture of the above with neither pattern predominating.

Moderately disordered functioning is suggested by the following:

1. The child can manifest a few socially meaningful behaviors in a narrow range (e.g., can only protest, or only compliantly "go along"); the child is involved only with social interactions around an inanimate world (exploring a new object); he or she has no capacity for integrating pleasure, warmth, assertiveness, and anger in a social context; or

2. Lots of behaviors and feelings are manifested, but in a poorly organized, unmodulated manner; there are rapid behavior and mood shifts; the child is occasionally

involved in socially meaningful interactions, and has no focused curiosity; or

3. The child shows a mixture of the above with neither pattern predominating.

Behavioral Initiative and Originality. Competent functioning is suggested if the child initiates complex, organized, emotionally and socially relevant interactions, yet also accepts limits; continually surprises parents in a "delightful way" with new behaviors, capacities, social skills, complex emotions (e.g., can initiate cuddling with parents; can bring a favorite game or puzzle and convey a desire to play); can explore new objects, and after a "warmup," new people, especially when parents are available.

Severely disordered functioning is suggested by:

1. Passivity, compliance, withdrawal, or
2. Usually being out of control, with aggressive behavior, disregarding limits and others' feelings; or
3. Mixed type, showing a mixture of the above with neither pattern predominating.

Moderately disordered functioning is suggested by the following:

1. The child occasionally takes the initiative, but usually only responds to others' initiatives and may also be negativistic; little or no originality (i.e., no surprises or new emotions or behaviors); instead tends to be repetitive; no focused curiosity; or
2. The child takes initiative but is demanding and stubborn; tends to repeat rather than develop new behaviors or interactions; or
3. The child shows a mixture of the above with neither pattern predominating.

DEVELOPMENTAL DIAGNOSIS—USE OF THOUGHT AND IDEAS: REPRESENTATIONAL ELABORATION/ SYMBOLIC CAPACITIES (17–30 MONTHS)

Competent functioning is suggested if the child uses representational elaboration in descriptive and social–emotional interactive contexts. For example, the child either uses words or wordlike sounds to indicate wishes and intentions. The child can use dolls or other objects to play out a drama (e.g., feeding scene or shooting scene, etc.). Symbolic elaboration appears to cover a range of emotions including love, closeness, dependency, assertion, curiosity, anger, and protest.

Severely disordered functioning is suggested by the following:

1. The child shows no symbolic behavior such as words, symbolic play (e.g., one doll feeding another), or complex actions implying planning and anticipation; the child's behavior is fragmented or stereotyped; or
2. There is symbolic activity, but it is totally disorganized and fragmented, totally used in the service of discharge-type hyperactivity; words or play activities *never* develop into an organized drama.
3. The child shows a mixture of the above with neither pattern predominating.

Moderately disordered functioning is suggested by the following:

1. There is some symbolic behavior such as the use of a few words or doll play, but it is mostly limited to the descriptive use of a symbolic mode (e.g., naming objects or pictures); there is little or no capacity for social, emotional, or interactive use of thoughts and ideas. (The child can name objects or even describe cars crashing, but is unable to use ideas in an emotional sense. He is unable to say, "No, I like this or want that"); or

2. Symbols are used (e.g., words or play) but often in chaotic, disorganized fashion; dramas have only fragments of discernible meaning; or
3. The child shows a mixture of the above with neither pattern predominating.

DEVELOPMENTAL DIAGNOSIS—PURPOSEFUL, REALISTIC USE OF THOUGHTS AND IDEAS: REPRESENTATIONAL DIFFERENTIATION AND CONSOLIDATION (26–30 MONTHS)

Competent functioning is suggested if the child relates in a balanced manner using the representational mode to people and things across a range of emotions (e.g., warmth, assertiveness); is able to be purposeful, know what is real from unreal; accepts limits; can be self-limiting and also feel good about self; switches from fantasy to reality with little difficulty.

Severely disordered functioning is suggested by the following:

1. The child is withdrawn, unrelated to people; he or she uses words or symbolic play only with "things." If words or symbolic play are used with people, then the difference between the real and the unreal is unclear. There is no sense of purpose or intention in the social use of the symbolic mode; or
2. The child relates to people and things symbolically in a totally chaotic, unrealistic manner; there is no reality testing or impulse control. The child's self-esteem and mood is labile; or
3. The child shows a mixture of the above with neither pattern predominating.

Moderately disordered functioning is suggested by the following:

1. The child relates slightly to people with words, play, or other symbols, but in a narrow range of emotions; some purposefulness and reality orientation is present, but the toddler is vulnerable to the slightest stress; or

2. The child relates to people and things using words or play across a range of emotions and themes, but in a chaotic, unreality-oriented manner. He or she can only relate to reality orientation with structure (e.g., needs lots of limits and repeated help with what is pretend and what is real); or

3. The child shows a mixture of the above with neither pattern predominating.

OVERVIEW OF COMPETENCE AND POTENTIALLY DISORDERED CAREGIVERS

FUNCTIONAL APPROACH TO CAREGIVERS—HOMEOSTASIS (0–3 MONTHS)

Competent functioning is suggested if the caregiver is excellent at helping infant to become fully regulated and comforted; can use multiple sensory and motor modes, voice, vision, movement (rocking), as well as a variety of affect states and empathetic skills in ways that tune into the infants' individual differences in a regulating manner. The caregiver interests the infant in a variety of animate and inanimate stimuli. He or she gains the infant's attention in a relaxed, focused manner and helps the infant use multiple sensory and motor modalities, such as vision, sound, touch, and movement, as a way to explore the human and inanimate world. Caregiver stress generally does not interfere, except temporarily, with this capacity.

Severely disordered functioning is suggested if:

1. The caregiver is completely unavailable to comfort the infant (e.g., aloof, self-absorbed, very depressed, etc.);

caregiver presents no interesting stimuli, animate or inanimate; or

2. The caregiver is grossly hyperstimulating and chaotic; undermines the infant's own regulatory capacities; or
3. The caregiver shows a mixture of the above with neither pattern predominating.

Moderately disordered functioning is suggested if:

1. The caregiver is intermittently available (e.g., can comfort for brief periods or when infant is not too upset); but at other times is withdrawn, aloof, or otherwise unavailable. The caregiver is intermittently interesting to the infant and gains his attention on occasion; or
2. The caregiver tries to comfort, but is out of synchrony with infant or with lack of mutuality; is overly intrusive and occasionally hyperstimulating. The caregiver gains the infant's interest, but is intermittently chaotic and distracting (e.g., too much stimuli or too intense); or
3. The caregiver shows a mixture of the above with neither pattern predominating.

FUNCTIONAL APPROACH TO CAREGIVERS—ATTACHMENT (2–4 MONTHS)

Competent functioning is suggested if the caregiver provides optimal attachment with deep rich emotional investment expressed through smiles, looks, touch, and talk. Loving interest can accommodate occasional anger and disappointment, and survive caregiver stress (e.g., illness, tiredness, etc.).

Severely disordered functioning is suggested if:

1. The caregiver is totally unavailable; lacks emotional warmth (e.g., is mechanical or disinterested; does not look at, smile, talk to, or touch the infant); or

2. The caregiver has a slightly chaotic emotional investment; is overwhelming, has an intrusive, hypomanic quality; seems impervious to the infant's moods or states; or
3. The caregiver shows a mixture of the above with neither pattern predominating.

Moderately disordered functioning is suggested if:

1. The caregiver shows intermittent emotional interest as reflected in some looking, cuddling, talking to, and/or stroking; may be limited to one modality (e.g., looking only, or holding and touching only); whatever emotional contact that does exist is very vulnerable to caregiver stress; or
2. The caregiver appears very interested in the infant, but seems overly anxious and overprotective (e.g., always smiling, stroking) and worried that the infant be "happy"; or
3. The caregiver shows a mixture of the above with neither pattern predominating.

FUNCTIONAL APPROACH TO CAREGIVERS—PURPOSEFUL COMMUNICATION (SOMATOPSYCHOLOGICAL DIFFERENTIATION) (3–10 MONTHS)

Competent functioning is suggested if the caregiver reads and responds causally and with empathy to the entire range of the infant's communications across all sensorimotor modalities and affect states. For example, he or she reads and responds causally or reciprocally to smiles, vocalizations, glances, facial expressions, and motoric behaviors in the context of pleasurable dependency, as well as of protest and assertiveness. This capacity is resilient to stress.

Severely disordered functioning is suggested if:

1. The caregiver is impervious to the infant's communications; fails totally to recognize or respond purposefully (causally) to the infant's signals in any modality (e.g., no responsive smile, looks, vocalizations, or appropriate reaching out in response to infant's inviting gesture); or
2. The caregiver misreads and overresponds to all signals. There is a chaotic intrusive quality; or
3. The caregiver shows a mixture of the above with neither predominating.

Moderately disordered functioning is suggested if:

1. The caregiver responds causally and purposefully only intermittently or in one modality but not another (e.g., only sometimes responds to a smile; may totally misread or misinterpret [i.e., doesn't respond to] entire areas of affect such as assertiveness or tenderness); or
2. The caregiver overresponds and/or misreads some signals and, when anxious, tends to confuse his or her own feelings with the infant's feelings. This is either limited to certain affects or sensorimotor modalities or states of stress. For example, the caregiver responds contingently to smiles but overresponds to the infant's protests by overfeeding the child (i.e., sees protest as hunger); or
3. The caregiver shows a mixture of the above with neither pattern predominating.

FUNCTIONAL APPROACH TO CAREGIVERS—BEHAVIORAL ORGANIZATION AND INITIATIVE (10–17 MONTHS)

Behavioral Organization. Competent functioning is suggested if the caregiver can interact in a complex organized manner and help the child organize one step further; and is able to do this across a wide range of themes (e.g., love, dependency, separation, anger, etc.). The caregiver can incorporate many themes into one interactional sequence, including polarities of love–hate and passivity–activity. The caregiver recovers well from stress, tolerates frustration and the child's negativism, and is able to pursue and be available without being overly controlling.

Severely disordered functioning is suggested if:

1. The caregiver is unavailable to the child when the child is organizing complex behavior (e.g., withdraws, feels "the child doesn't need me anymore"); or
2. The caregiver always becomes intrusively confused and mildly disorganized when the child's behavior affect becomes complex, such as the child introducing a number of themes or signals. For example, the caregiver cannot switch with the child from one game to another or tends to switch and introduce new ideas too quickly, confusing and disorganizing the child. The caregiver cannot tolerate the toddler's intensity of feeling or becomes too easily ashamed of themes such as sex or aggression and becomes intrusive or disorganized; or
3. The caregiver shows a mixture of the above with neither pattern predominating.

Moderately disordered functioning is suggested if:

1. The caregiver can interact in an organized manner around a few limited themes or when not under any stress. For example, he or she will play organized, interactive games around love, but withdraws as soon as aggression or assertion comes to center stage; or
2. The caregiver intermittently tends to become intrusively confused and mildly disorganized when the child's behavior becomes complex or introduces a theme (aggression, for example) that the caregiver finds frightening. Intermittently, he or she cannot switch

with the child from one game to another or tends to switch and introduce new ideas too quickly, confusing and disorganizing the child.

3. The caretaker shows a mixture of the above with neither pattern predominating.

Initiative. Competent functioning is suggested if the caregiver admires the child's initiative (with a gleam in the eye); can follow the child's lead; encourages the child to go one step further (e.g., is a great noncontrolling coach), and can do this across thematic areas, which include dependency, assertion, curiosity, aggression, pleasure, and so on; at the same time, the caregiver can set limits effectively to help the child take the initiative in self-control. He or she permits separation; remains available and knows when to pursue the child lovingly.

Severely disordered functioning is suggested if:

1. The caregiver is withdrawn and unavailable to any initiative by the child, however appropriate; or
2. The caregiver overwhelms the child; provides no opportunity for the child's initiative; becomes chaotic and physical; undermines and overcontrols; does the initiating in all areas; or
3. The caregiver shows a mixture of the above with neither pattern predominating.

Moderately disordered functioning is suggested if:

1. The caregiver is intermittently unavailable to the child's initiative, depending on the thematic area (e.g., he or she will encourage initiative around play with puzzles; may "pull away from" the child's initiative around pleasure, including interest in the human body, sexual parts, sucking, etc.); easily disorganized by stress; or
2. The caregiver intermittently tends to overcontrol and undermine initiative; tends to be anxious and intrusive; or

3. The caregiver shows a mixture of the above with neither pattern predominating.

FUNCTIONAL APPROACH TO CAREGIVERS—REPRESENTATIONAL CAPACITY AND ELABORATION (17–30 MONTHS)

Competent functioning is suggested if the caregiver interacts in a representational (symbolic) mode across a variety of age-appropriate themes using multiple sensorimotor capacities (e.g., he or she can interact using language and/or symbolic play in all thematic areas such as love, pleasure, dependency, aggression, competition, envy, hate, curiosity, etc.). The caregiver can supportively pursue thematic areas which may be mildly frightening to a child. He or she can gradually develop richer and deeper symbolic communication (e.g., the caregiver can further child's play sequence without assuming the initiative). Caregiver can maintain representational (symbolic) mode in face of stress.

Severely disordered functioning is suggested if:

1. The caregiver lacks all capacity to engage the child symbolically; engages the child in a concrete fashion only (e.g., can deal with feeding and cleanliness), but cannot interact imaginatively, as with words, to describe feelings, or through play with dolls to represent people or activities; or
2. The child's symbolic capacity is supported in a chaotic, fleeting, hypomanic manner (e.g., mother keeps switching topics, etc.); the caregiver often totally misreads the child's communication; or
3. The caregiver shows a mixture of the above with neither pattern predominating.

Moderately disordered functioning is suggested if:

1. The caregiver has some symbolic interactive capacity but limited only to some themes, dependency but *not* curiosity or assertiveness, and/or to one or two sensori-motor modalities (e.g., can play symbolically, whereas language use is concrete only). Withdraws if child tries to engage in "avoided area"; or

2. The caregiver interacts symbolically but only according to his or her own agenda, thereby undermining the child's capacity for elaboration; may do this in only some thematic areas (e.g., when the child develops play where two dolls feed each other, the caregiver becomes anxious and switches to a shooting game); controls by activity and intrusiveness; easily undermined by stress; or

3. The caregiver shows a mixture of the above with neither pattern predominating.

A FUNCTIONAL APPROACH TO CAREGIVERS—REPRESENTATIONAL DIFFERENTIATION AND CONSOLIDATION (26–36 MONTHS)

Competent functioning is suggested if the caregiver is able to interact symbolically in a purposeful (causal, reciprocal) manner to a wide range of themes, including love, dependency, pleasure, assertion, aggression, impulsivity, curiosity, and so on; and he or she can respond in a flexible manner, including support, encouragement, empathy, and firm limit-setting. Stress does not interfere except briefly.

Severely disordered functioning is suggested if:

1. The caregiver is unable to use a symbolic mode in a logical or causal manner (e.g., depressed mother only interacts occasionally and never completes interaction in a logical sequence). For example, when the child shows a doll being "naughty," mother cannot finish the

sequence, even with the child's encouragement, to show how the child is either punished or learns a lesson. Mother cannot use language to set limits and thereby help the child see the consequences of his or her actions; similarly she is unable to convey through language a sense of pleasure or pride in the child's accomplishments; or

2. The caregiver has totally disorganized symbolic interactions (e.g., mother with severe thought disorder or very manic); or

3. The caregiver shows a mixture of the above with neither pattern predominating.

Moderately disordered functioning is suggested if:

1. The caregiver intermittently compromises in purposeful symbolic communications due either to stress, inability to deal with certain thematic areas, or for other reasons (e.g., no limit-setting in response to anger or explosiveness; but is able occasionally to interact meaningfully to child's symbolic expressions of dependency); or

2. The caregiver interacts symbolically, but frequently not purposefully or causally (caregiver "marches to the beat of his own drummer"); intermittently tends to be disorganized in communication patterns; or

3. The caregiver shows a mixture of the above with neither predominating.

Chapter 7

Examination of the Infant

During a hands-on examination, a baby will go through various stages of alertness and attention, which will include crying. The baby may begin in a state of sleepiness and move to gradual alertness and then to full alertness—looking and listening. The next stage may be emotional engagement, when the baby responds pleasurably, but then may begin to feel irritable and overloaded before crying, and then may begin crying vigorously. The clinician may help calm the baby and the cycle may repeat or with support the child may remain calm and alert. Whether the baby comes in calm and relaxed or crying, the clinician must realize that during the course of any day, babies go through these different states, and he needs to observe how the baby negotiates them. How does the baby recover, for example, from an irritable state and get back to a calm state? Especially important is how the clinician or the parents assist the baby with the transition.

Neither the clinician nor the mother or father should feel incompetent and inadequate when the baby is in the more irritable or crying part of the cycle. The clinician should find in the baby's behavior a basis for understanding the baby and how to help the baby calm down and relax, which may be helpful to the parents. Babies will vary in the amount of time they spend in one or another state, the ways in which they recover, and the ways in which one can assist them to recover.

OBSERVATION OF THE MOTHER AND BABY PLAYING TOGETHER

Perhaps the best way to begin is to have the mother play with the baby for about ten minutes, while the clinician observes her doing the things she does routinely at home. (By way of example, the baby is presumed to be 3 or 4 months old.) The clinician observes how the mother interacts with the baby; for example if, in rhythm with the mother's smiles and vocalizations, the baby smiles or coos, accompanied by some coordinated arm and leg movements. He or she should also notice how the baby attends to rattles or other interesting objects.

INTERACTION OF THE CLINICIAN WITH THE BABY

The clinician should begin to interact with the baby in the same way the mother did, while the mother is still holding the baby or the baby is on the floor. He should make interesting sounds, facial gestures, and try to generate warm affect to see if he can woo the baby into a state of warm relatedness. It is necessary to experiment with different pitches and volume of voice and emotional and facial expressions. One can also experiment with different distances from the baby by moving closer and then farther away. The clinician should try to get the baby's attention for more than just a second or two. If the clinician can elicit some sense of engagement with smiles and other affect gestures, he will want to observe as well whether the baby can synchronize some motor patterns by moving arms and legs in rhythm with his facial expressions.

The clinician should then try to gently take the baby into his own lap to attempt to continue the state of relatedness and to observe how the baby engages and disengages with him. He should see how long he can hold the baby's attention with vocal rhythm. How long does the baby stay in a focused, attentive, pleasurable state? Does the baby disengage after several seconds and look around and then reengage with you? Every baby will have his own pattern of pleasurable engagement and shared attention. Is the baby a "long" sustainer or a "brief" sustainer? Does one have to work very hard to maintain engagement with vocal rhythms? The clinician should vary the pitch, volume, firmness, and rhythm of his voice, as well as the animation of his facial expression and the way he is holding the baby, in order to determine what facilitates the best state of shared attention and engagement or what tends to hinder that state.

SENSORY REACTIVITY, SENSORY PROCESSING, AND MOTOR TONE

After giving the baby a break, the clinician should check the baby's motor system. It is effective to start by holding the baby's hands firmly and, with a lot of vocal support, let him pull up in your lap to a standing position, in essence doing deep-knee bends. The clinician can get a sense of the baby's motor tone and strength, for example, by seeing how the baby holds his head up. How well the baby can push up with his feet gives a sense of his tone throughout his body—his trunk strength and tone. The three- to four-month-old with good tone will be able to help an adult pull him up by holding onto the adult's hands, doing deep-knee bends in a rhythmic pattern of exercise.

When the baby relaxes in his lap, the clinician should move each of the baby's legs and arms around to see if the tone feels tight or loose, or if there is any asymmetry.

The clinician might play with the baby, while varying his posture, to see how he responds in different positions to facial expressions and different vocalizations. He could be perhaps lying flat on his back in the clinician's lap, as opposed to the initial 90 degree angle position when the clinician supported his back with the baby facing him. When the baby begins to enjoy the interaction, the clinician can remove the baby's clothes to observe how he likes touch. The clinician might start off by stroking the baby lightly on his extremities, first one leg and then the other, then his hands and arms, with a light, ticklish kind of motion. The clinician should note if the baby smiles and coos and pays attention or if the baby gets irritable and tries to turn or pull away, as though the touching is uncomfortable for him. It is important to notice which limb or area, including the abdomen and back, seems to be a source of comfort or discomfort when touched. One might use a gentle, light touch to see if he smiles and looks, or whether he begins to look uncomfortable and turns to avoid the touching.

Next, one might check to see if he enjoys firm pressure. One might gently squeeze each leg (in the calf, in the thigh, and then around the soles of the feet), and then do the same with his hands, forearms, and upper arms. Does he enjoy firm pressure on the extremities, and, if so, which ones? One must look for his look, smiles, state of shared attention, or his irritability, pushing or turning away, or looking uncomfortable. One should apply gentle pressure on his stomach and back, as well as his neck, lips, face, and the top of his head, to see where he might enjoy being touched, either with a light touch or gentle pressure.

One might also take something rough and put it on his stomach under his shirt to see if he will enjoy it and leave it there or whether he will try to get rid of it. One may also put the rough item on his arms and legs and watch his response.

One should also note during the entire exam how the baby responds to different sounds—soft and loud, high and low pitched—and to different intensities of light and color. One should also note the response to simple and complex vocal rhythms and to items with complex visual detail or with simple designs.

MOVEMENT IN SPACE

The clinician also needs to look at the baby's movement in space. After talking and making faces to try and woo him into a state of relatedness, the clinician might hold the baby out in front of himself with his hands around the baby's trunk. He should move the baby up and down, and then from side to side, at first very slowly and gently, gradually increasing the pace until either greater joy or some beginning discomfort becomes evident. At the point in the movement that one notices discomfort, this is the point at which the baby finds the movement too brisk; for some babies, it is the "quicker the better"; other babies will find moving beyond a very gentle rhythm uncomfortable.

The clinician should notice whether the baby likes looking and listening better when he is held out at a 90 degree angle in one's lap, or whether he prefers to be on his back. One may also have him lie on his stomach across one's knees or on the floor. If he can lift his head up a little bit, can he interact in that position? Which position does he enjoy best? One can try different kinds of rocking motions to see which tends to lead to an ideal state of alertness and engagement. Does he enjoy brisk rocking? Does he enjoy slow, rhythmic rocking? Which rocking does he enjoy when he is calm, as a general support for his state of attentiveness, and which does he enjoy most when he is upset and wants to calm down?

AN EXAMPLE

To give an example, let's say we have a three-month-old who engages wonderfully with his mother. He has a warm, deep smile, a nice state of shared attention, and is somewhat extraordinary in terms of the degree to which he can listen and look, particularly when someone is vocalizing at him. He shows an unusual interest in sound across a wide range, including high and low pitch and complex and simple rhythms. He seems to favor a slightly firm, louder voice and talking in fairly complex rhythms, which suggests a good auditory processing system. He enjoys facial expressions, although not to the same degree (he is more of an auditory baby), although he clearly enjoys looking as well.

He has good motor planning, as demonstrated by his ability to put his hands in his mouth and move his arms and legs in rhythm with another person's voice. He is able to assist in being pulled up and has nice motor tone in his arms and legs, which facilitates his ability to get his hands to his mouth and to carry out the kinds of maneuvers that he wants to do.

In checking his sensory system, the clinician found that he enjoys sensation on most parts of his body, but shows some differences. For example, he loves light touch all over, although a little less so on his abdomen. He especially enjoys light touch on his arms and legs, and especially his legs. He seems to enjoy gentle pressure all over, but again, not so much to his abdomen, which may explain, in part, why he doesn't like to be on his stomach quite as much as he likes to be on his back.

He enjoys calm, slow movement in space, but not moving up and down too briskly in the vertical direction. When he is upset, he seems to enjoy most a calm, very rhythmic rocking. As he gets older, it would be useful to watch his exposure to rough-and-tumble versus more relaxed play.

Based on a more systematic evaluation of his sensory modalities, he seems to enjoy the vocalizations and what he sees as well, but the latter wasn't as much an organizing or calming influence for him. Most prominent is his deep sense of pleasure and relatedness and his rather precocious ability to sustain his attention for long periods of time, particularly with vocal exchanges.

In summary, he is a baby who is functioning at or well beyond his age level in a general adaptive sense, with a lot of strength in his auditory and vocal systems and his warm, engaging affect. There are some individual differences, in terms of the way he enjoys touch, with a little less so to his abdomen (both light and firm pressure), and the way he enjoys movement in space, a little less so in the vertical direction than in the horizontal direction. Overall, he is a competent three-month-old who is, in most areas, ahead of his age level.

INFANTS AT DIFFERENT AGES

In this section, we discussed a part of the "hands-on" aspect of the examination, with a focus on a three-month-old. However, the clinician will be assessing babies of different ages. The goal is to observe initially how the infant relates to the parent(s) and the clinician in terms of age-expected developmental organization (e.g., attention in a two-month-old; attention and engagement in a four-month-old; attention, engagement, and two-way gestural communication in an eight-month-old; attention, engagement, two-way gestural communication, and representational [symbolic] play and dialogue in a two-and-a-half-year-old).

Following the initial observation, the clinician should assess the affective, interactive, sensory, motor, language, cognitive and movement-in-space inclinations of the child, as described earlier, but with flexibility in relationship to the child's age and abilities. For example, with an eight-month-old it is helpful to let him lie on his stomach or be on all fours as you interact with him to see if two-way communication is possible; in a two-year-old, in addition to engaging with the child in pretend play, observing how the child walks and holds a crayon will reveal aspects of motor tone. One might touch arms and legs as part of age-appropriate play to determine tactile sensitivities.

Chapter 8

Sensitivities to Foods and Aspects of the Physical Environment

As a part of a routine evaluation of an infant or young child, it is worthwhile to consider (along with family stresses, and individual differences, such as tactile and auditory sensitivities) sensitivity to aspects of the physical environment, including certain foods, and exposure to substances such as petrochemicals, formaldehyde, or paint fumes.

The research literature on physical sensitivities is not conclusive. The area of food sensitivities, whether to dairy products, sugar, additives, preservatives, wheat, or other products is quite controversial, in part related to the claims of the well-known Feingold approach. Both the believers and those scientists who believe food sensitivities are mostly in peoples' imaginations report their findings with great emotion. Interestingly, the research literature is more balanced than one would anticipate.

There are studies that support food influences on behavior (Prinz, Roberts, and Huntaranj, 1980; Virkkunen and Huttunen, 1982; Virkkunen, 1983, 1984; Bolton, 1984; Kruesi, Linnoila, and Rapoport, 1985), and that eliminating certain food

375

groups can be helpful in reducing symptoms such as migraines and overactivity (Egger, Carter, Wilson, Turner, and Soothill, 1983; Egger, Carter, Graham, Gumby, and Soothill, 1985). But there are also studies suggesting either no influence of food on behavior, clinically insignificant influence, or only selective influence on very sensitive individuals (Gross, 1984; Behar, Rapoport, and Adams, 1984; Wolraich, Milich, and Stumbo, 1985; Milich and Pelham, 1986; Ferguson, Stoddart, and Simeon, 1986; Connors, Caldwell, and Caldwell, in press).

The different research findings in part may be related to methodological challenges. For example, very few studies eliminate sugar or chemicals from the diet for two weeks before a challenge phase (chronic exposure may obscure a response). Also, studies vary on how much of a substance or food they expose a child to and what constitutes a clinically significant response. Obviously, the research design used can reflect a bias, especially because the area is so controversial and emotional (e.g., no elimination phase prior to exposure, low level of food or substance, insensitive measurement tools, or high degree of disturbance required for result to be clinically significant or vice versa).

There is very little research on elements in the environment, such as paint fumes, formaldehyde, petrochemical-based solvents and cleaning fluids, and their effect on behavior. For example a lot of people report headaches, sinus problems, irritability, distractibility, and hazy thinking when they are in the presence of paint fumes for a period of time. Indoor pollution has received a lot of attention in the media recently, but it is an area where more systematic studies are needed.

Because the research is not conclusive and because even the most skeptical investigators report extreme reaction in rare sensitive individuals, and trends below a level of clinical significance in others, the clinician needs to pay attention to the possibility that his patient may be that rare individual or may have a variety of handicap that makes even a subclinical level of impact significant (e.g., a child with sensory reactivity-regulatory differences). Furthermore, because the research is not conclusive and sensitivities to foods and chemicals could be greater than now known, and because some clinical populations, such as children with severe handicaps, have not been adequately studied, the clinician must keep an open mind and at the same time take a conservative posture.

The clinician can take an open conservative position by checking out each patient for the presence or absence of food or chemical sensitivities. In this way, the clinician makes no global assumptions about how widespread food or chemical sensitivities are. He only seeks to determine his patient's response patterns.

One way to determine if there is a food or chemical sensitivity in an infant or young child is to set up an elimination diet, as one would do for a rash. The child completely avoids the suspected food group for ten days to two weeks. The child is then challenged with that food group for one to three days or until negative symptoms appear. Negative symptoms include a change in attention, activity level, irritability, impulse control, frustration tolerance, sleep habits, eating patterns, elimination patterns, mood, or any other behavior or feelings or thoughts that deviates from the baseline of this child's expected behavior. One doesn't necessarily look for improvement when the child is off the suspected food group. Instead, one looks for worsening when the child is challenged with a lot of the food. Some foods or chemicals, when introduced, lead to negative behaviors even at low levels. Others require high levels for a day or two.

The clinician first determines if a sensitivity is present and then, depending on the degree of sensitivity, how much of the food can be eaten and how often it can be eaten. For example, some children do fine on certain foods once every three or four days. Other foods have to be avoided entirely.

One doesn't look for immediate improvement in the elimination phase because there may be many things affecting the negative behavior, such as other foods, chemicals, and interpersonal and family dynamics, which could inhibit improvement. But worsening after challenges with the suspected food group leads one to suspect the food that was reintroduced into the diet. If one is not sure, one can repeat the process. As a clinical rather than research procedure, no one is "blind" and there is the possibility of a false positive result. One should, therefore, look for robust changes in the challenge phase and if in doubt one should repeat the procedure.

There are many ways to divide foods into groups in order to do the elimination diet. And there are many different foods and chemicals one can check out. One way to go about this process will be described below.

One may first want to test for pure sugars, chocolate, other foods containing caffeine, and chemicals (additives, preservatives, food colorings, dyes) as a single group. If the child shows a sensitivity, one can separate out the chemicals from the sugars, to see which has more impact. In the case of a breast-feeding mother, the child is tested by means of a mother's diet, because the elements in question will reach the child through the breast milk.

A second group to test for is foods that have natural salicylates in them; these include most fruits and tomatoes. The only fruits that do not have salicylates in them are bananas, melons, exotic fruit like papaya and mangos, grapefruit, and canned pineapples. Most other fruits, such as apples, oranges, tangerines, and berries, do have some natural salicylates. Some children are sensitive to natural salicylates. Also, according to the clinical experience of a few pediatricians, there may be some benefit to taking children off salicylates when they have chronic middle ear infections.

Another food group to test for is dairy products—cheeses and milk. Some dairy-product sensitive people can tolerate yogurt. It is helpful to test for nuts, especially cashews (and including peanut butter), and less often grains, especially wheat and yeast, if there is reason to be suspicious. Other food groups may also be tested for, depending on the child's family history and observations of the child's natural response to different foods.

It is useful to begin the evaluation by asking the family to take on the role of food and environmental detective, to notice good days and bad days, and to keep track of what the child ate or what fumes may have been in his environment. Sometimes parents will say, "After a birthday party, he goes haywire," or "I noticed on days when I clean house, he doesn't do as well." Such anecdotal evidence calls for more systematic study.

In regard to chemicals in the environment, like cleaning solvents, pesticides, paint fumes, natural gas (look for leaks), volatile organic compounds (as in new carpets), polyurethane (to finish wood floors), and other petrochemical-based products, one cannot do a controlled off/on study, as with food. The parent has to notice patterns in the household routine and not assume that bad days are just bad days. For example, the child is behaving badly every Monday, and Monday is the regular housecleaning day when a lot of ammonia-based solvents are used. One might try some other cleaning material or only water for a few cleaning days to see if the child does better. If the child suddenly exhibits poor behavior when the house is being painted, a clinician or parent should be suspicious. Notice if a pattern is present, and make sure his room is well ventilated. There are many substances, such as *lead*, that parents need to be alert to in terms of its long-term negative impact on development. A further overview of household chemicals is available (Greenspan, 1991).

Children who exhibit sleeping problems or irritability that continues beyond the first few months of life, as well as children with difficulties with modulating attention, activity, thinking, mood, or behavior, may benefit from exploration of dietary and environmental factors. Systematic research needs to be done especially on children who have language and motor problems. Children with behavioral problems, and children with overreactivity to touch and sensation or uneven maturation should be investigated for environmental or food sensitivities.

Even if sensitivities to foods, chemicals, and other facets of the environment are identified, they should not be assumed to be an allergy, although allergies may be present. Factors that can influence behavior may be "sensitivities" in the same way that adults may respond differently to coffee or to a newly painted house. The "detective approach" to observing (i.e., looking for good and bad days) and conducting elimination diets is, therefore, a useful way to identify if such sensitivities are present.

Chapter 9

The Functional Emotional Assessment Scale for Infancy and Early Childhood

The clinical approach to assessment emphasizes understanding the infant and young child's emotional and social functioning in the context of relationships with his or her caregivers and family. The emotional capacities of the infant and young child relate to the infant's ability to deal with his or her real world. This approach to the infant and young child's functioning can be contrasted to a formal structured test approach. The formal test approach looks at what an infant can and cannot do in relationship to a defined set of stimuli or test procedures. In terms of assessing adults, the functional approach would attempt to look at how an adult functioned in the real world, whereas the formal structured test approach would attempt to predict how the adult will function in the real world based on a narrow set of procedurally derived behaviors. Formal tests are often used when more direct functional assessments are not possible. In this sense, regardless of how quantitatively they are scored, the data produced by formal tests tend to be approximations.

In assessing infants and young children, especially those with atypical or challenging developmental patterns, the formal structured test approach covers only a small part of the infant's real capacities, and often provides incorrect and misleading information at that. The formal tests themselves were, for the most part, developed and standardized with infants and young children who were not evidencing unusual challenges or special needs. Formal tests are not geared toward bringing out a challenging child's unique ability and potential. Yet it is the special needs child who requires early assessment and intervention. In addition, many infants and young children have difficulty in attending, relating, and conforming to the tests' most basic expectations. Skilled examiners aware of these factors may use only the challenging infant's general behavior around the test situation as an indicator of his or her abilities. The less experienced examiner often mistakenly attempts to derive and draw conclusions from a numerical score. In either case, the test situation is not the best context within which to observe the infant's functional capacities.

Incorrect and misleading formal test data often lead to incorrect recommendations for services and educational placements and programs. Most importantly, a delayed or atypical child may deteriorate with the wrong placement; hardly a desirable outcome for such a laudable goal as early identification and appropriate early intervention. Unfortunately, as states and communities have been attempting to assess and offer services to more and more infants and young children in need of appropriate special services, the problem of incorrect service recommendations may be becoming greater. Recently, I have been seeing more and more toddlers and preschoolers who have been misdiagnosed and offered incorrect services and educational placements based on misleading standardized test scores. The test results have often been six to seven months off in comparison to more complete clinical evaluation. Since many of these children have been under the age of two, the error is quite significant.

All evaluations of infants, young children, and their families must begin with a clinical assessment of the infant and/or young child's functional capacities as described earlier. Specific structured tests, however reliable, valid, and easy to administer, must only be used to build on the overall clinical functional assessment. Often time can be saved and resources conserved by only using formal structured assessments very selectively, for example, when there are critical questions that have not been answered by the clinical functional assessment. More importantly, however, errors in educational placement and service recommendations will be minimized with an approach that has as its foundation a clinical functional assessment of the infant, young child, and his or her caregivers and family.

This chapter presents a method of systematizing the clinical functional assessment of the infant and young child. It focuses on the infant's core emotional and social capacities at each stage in his or her development. It also outlines the related motor, sensory, language, and cognitive capacities that go along with each of the core emotional and social capacities. The data from which the clinician will make judgments are derived from a free, unstructured interaction between the infant or child and his or her caregiver, as well as the clinician. These unstructured interactions are started by simply asking the caregiver to interact or play with the infant or child as they might at home. If further suggestions are needed, phrases such as, "Just the way you like to interact with each other"; "The way you like to enjoy each other"; "The way you like to be together"; and so on, may be useful. If necessary, a series of semistructured interactive opportunities are offered to the infant or child to help elicit their core competencies. (These interactive opportunities, which can be suggested to caregivers or carried out by the clinician or both, will be described later in this chapter.) These free, unstructured, and, if necessary, semistructured interactions are close to the infant's natural way of interacting with his world. They can be done both in the office and at home and can be repeated as many times as necessary in order to gain a true picture of the infant/young child and caregiver's capacities. It is often very helpful to see the infant/young child and his caregiver(s) interacting on at least two or more separate occasions. In reaching an overall clinical judgment, one must also include historical data and caregiver reports of current functioning. While this scale was developed to systematize the observable clinical data part of the evaluation, the clinician may also use it to systematize historical and/or current functioning data and integrated judgments using all sources of data.

The scale that follows can be used in two ways. It can be used descriptively to profile the infant and young child's emotional, social, and related developmental capacities. It can also be used in a quantitative manner by rating each capacity on a 0 to 4 scale:

0 = Capacity not present
1 = Capacity fleetingly present
2 = Capacity intermittently present
3 = Capacity present most of the time
4 = Capacity present all the time in all circumstances
N/A = Not Applicable, because there was no opportunity to observe the presence or absence of this capacity

For each item the child may receive an N/A, 0, 1, 2, 3, or 4 rating. These ratings can then be added together. A *potential* score can be derived by adding together each item observed at the 4 level. This is the child's potential age-expected capacity. The score attained can be put over the possible score and a percentage derived.

While this procedure can be carried out for each area of functioning, only the Primary Functional Emotional and Emotional Range categories may be described quantitatively. The other categories should only be used in a qualitative descriptive manner. The areas of functioning that will comprise the scale are the following:

1. *Primary Emotional Capacities.* The attainment of primary emotional capacities at each developmental level determines if a child has progressed to his age-expected functional emotional developmental capacity. When a primary functional emotional capacity is not present it suggests the infant has not achieved his age-expected developmental level.

2. *Emotional Range—Sensorimotor (including speech).* This area focuses on the range of sensory and motor equipment, including speech, the infant or child is able to employ in mastering his primary functional emotional capacities (e.g., using motor gestures, touch, words, etc.). At later ages these capacities will involve the use of sensory, motor, and speech capacities to support higher level functional and conceptual abilities.

3. *Emotional Range—Affective.* This area focuses on the different affective themes (e.g., dependency, aggression) that the child can organize at his age-expected developmental level (e.g., one child can use words and pretend play in relationship to the theme of dependency—the dolls hugging—while another child can only use play and words for aggression).

4. *Related Motor, Sensory, Language, and Cognitive Capacities.* This area comprises selected developmental items not already covered in the primary emotional capacities. Many capacities that would ordinarily fall in one of the cognitive categories will be seen to be covered as part of a functional emotional capacity.

5. *General Infant Tendencies.* These are constitutionally and maturationally based capacities.

6. *Overall Caregiver Tendencies.* These are facilitating and undermining caregiver patterns.

At present, the quantitative use of the scale should only be for descriptive purposes. While based on the developmental model described in this work, this particular scale has not yet been used with a large number of normal, delayed, and dysfunctional infants and young children and their caregivers. The categories that are used in this scale, however, have been rated reliably, discriminate between clinical and nonclinical groups, evidence age related stability, and expected shifts with developmental progression (Dougherty, 1991; Hofheimer et al., 1981,

1983; Poisson, unpublished) and are related to the (G.L.O.S.) scales (Greenspan and Lieberman, 1989a,b).

In using the functional emotional assessment scale, the clinician should first assess the age-expected primary emotional capacities of the infant or young child. He should then assess all the prior primary emotional capacities which, one hopes, were mastered at earlier ages but continue as part of the child's basic capacities. He should then assess emotional range (sensorimotor) and emotional range (affective). If the infant or young child evidences an optimal emotional range in both emotional range categories for his age level, the clinician need not assess developmentally earlier categories of emotional range. On the other hand, if the infant and young child evidences constrictions in his emotional range, the clinician should keep assessing the developmentally earlier category of emotional range (one or both) to see if the infant or young child was ever able to establish a broad and flexible emotional range in the sensorimotor or affective areas. The clinician should next observe how the child functions in terms of motor, sensory, language, and cognitive capacities to see if these are consistent with, behind, or advanced for the child's functional emotional capacities. These should only be used qualitatively. Next, the clinician should assess the infant's constitutional tendencies and the caregiver's capacities.

The clinician arrives at a number of judgments regarding the infant's capacities, which includes the developmental level in terms of primary functional emotional capacities; the sensory motor range; and affective range. He also gains an understanding of contributions from the infant's constitutional and maturational tendencies and the caregiving patterns.

The clinician will see if a child is at or below the age-expected functional emotional development, as well as how well earlier functional emotional capacities have been mastered. Also, the clinician will gain an impression about the infant's emotional range. A child who is, for example, at a developmental level lower than expected with regard to functional emotional capacities, but has an optimal emotional range at that level, is not necessarily at greater risk than a child who is at his or her age-expected functional emotional developmental level, but with a constricted sensorimotor and affective range. The clinical interpretation of the child's profile must be a clinical judgment based on the child's overall adaptation. A child who, because of a medical illness, is a little delayed but is now developing at an appropriate rate in all areas may be at less risk than a child who is already chronically constricted in his emotional range (e.g., a 2½-year-old who talks and does some pretend play, but avoids pleasure and only deals with dependency through physical touch and impulsive behavior may be more at risk than another 2½-year-old who operates in all ways fully like a two-year-old).

In general, one first determines the child's developmental level in terms of primary functional emotional capacities. This provides a sense of where the child is developmentally.

Then one determines how flexible or wide-ranging his adaptive and coping capacities are at that level (i.e., his sensorimotor and affective emotional range). If one wants to see how stable his capacities are, one looks at the ratings themselves. Lots of ones and twos ("fleeting" or "intermittent") suggest unstable capacities. Threes and fours ("most" or "all of the time") suggest stable capacities. A stability score can be derived if needed by dividing the sum of the rating numbers by the highest possible score (i.e., all 4s for ratable capacities).

One then may look at the associated sensory, motor, language, and cognitive items to see which areas are ahead, at, or behind the functional emotional capacities. For example, fine motor and motor planning capacities may be behind while receptive language and cognition are advanced. If this child is also constricted in his emotional range, especially in dealing with aggression, one may wonder if the lag in fine motor and motor planning is contributing (i.e., a lack of security in the fine control of his motor system). Another child may evidence lags in his primary functional emotional capacities and his affective emotional range and be advanced in his motor, sensory, language, and cognitive areas. Here, one may wonder about his interactive opportunities with his caregivers and his family functioning.

After one gains a sense of the child's developmental levels in different areas, one should look at the infant's constitutional and maturational patterns (e.g., over- or undersensitive to touch or sound) and his caregiver's capacities. One now wonders about how each of these may contribute to the developmental profile. For example, an intrusive caregiver coupled with a tactilely and auditorily hypersensitive child may contribute to a certain developmental profile (e.g., a fearful, cautious child who avoids assertive behavior).

While it is always tempting to use rating scales to simplify complex clinical judgments, it should be clear that the goal of the Functional Emotional Assessment Scale is to assist the clinician in systematizing and fine-tuning clinical judgments, and in incorporating judgments about functional emotional capacities into research protocols. In working up a case, the scale is of assistance in pointing out critical areas for further clinical inquiry.

For example, an infant's profile evidences the following: a delay in achieving intentional communication (i.e., opening and closing circles of communication); a narrow emotional range (not using vocalization or evidencing assertive exploratory behaviors); auditory underreactivity, and a withdrawn depressed caregiver. Such a profile would alert the clinician to explore the infant's constitutional and maturational pattern of underreactivity and look for related constitutional and maturational patterns, including motor capacities dealing with vocalizing and sensory processing capacities dealing with auditory processing. It would also alert the clinician to explore the caregiving capacities, learning more about the depressed caregiver, other caregivers, and the family. Most importantly, it would alert the clinician that he or she should explore in great depth the interactive patterns that were not supporting intentional, purposeful communication. It would also create an immediate concrete goal for the potential intervention once the diagnostic workup was complete, namely to foster intentional interactions and initiative.

Therefore, the goal of this scale is to operationalize complex clinical judgments about what is often considered to be the vague and difficult to describe world of emotional capacities. Functional emotional capacities can be described just as can motor, sensory, language, and cognitive capacities. The goal is now for each clinician to routinely do it!

In the next section, the Functional Emotional Assessment Scale will be presented. Table 9.1 is an example of how a rating sheet might be formulated for use during the session. This is just a sample—each clinician may want to devise his or her own sheet to suit the particular situation. For example, abbreviated descriptions may be used, as in Table 9.1, or just the headings and numbers. Following the presentation of the scale, there will be a description of how to conduct the session with the infant or child and his caregiver in such a way as to elicit the infant's emotional and social capacities.

THE FUNCTIONAL EMOTIONAL ASSESSMENT SCALE

REGULATION AND INTEREST IN THE WORLD

By three months, the infant can be calm; recovers from crying with comforting; is able to be alert; looks at one when talked to; and brightens up when provided with appropriate visual, auditory, and/or tactile experiences.

Primary Emotional
1. Shows an interest in the world by looking (brightening) at sights or listening to (turning toward) sounds. Can attend to a visual or auditory stimulus for three or more seconds.
2. Can remain calm and focused for two or more minutes at a time, as evidenced by looking around, sucking, cooperating in cuddling (e.g., melding with caregiver), or other age-appropriate activities.

TABLE 9.1
Functional Emotional Assessment Scale:
RATING SHEET

Rating Scale: 0 = Capacity not present
1 = Capacity fleetingly present
2 = Capacity intermittently present
3 = Capacity present most of the time
4 = Capacity present all the time in all circumstances
N/A = Not Applicable, because there was no opportunity to observe the presence or absence of this capacity

Rating

REGULATION AND INTEREST IN THE WORLD (3 MONTHS)
Primary Emotional:
1. Shows interest in different sensations for 3 + seconds _____
2. Remains calm and focused for 2 + minutes _____

Emotional Range—Sensorimotor:
1. Looks at sights for 3 + seconds _____
2. Listens to sounds for 3 + seconds _____
3. Relaxes, smiles, vocalizes, or looks in response to light or firm touch _____
4. Relaxes, smiles, vocalizes, or looks in response to moving of limbs _____
5. Tolerates/shows pleasure in gentle movement in space _____
6. Tolerates/shows pleasure in smells _____
7. Relaxes/shows pleasure when held firmly _____
8. Relaxes/shows pleasure when rocked rhythmically _____
9. Recovers from distress within 20 minutes, with help from caregiver _____

Emotional Range—Affective:
1. Shows interest in caregiver _____
2. Shows interest in happy caregiver _____

TABLE 9.1 (*continued*)

3. Shows interest in assertive caregiver _____

Selected Capacities:
1. *Motor:*
   a. Holds head upright on own _____
   b. Lifts head by leaning on elbows _____
   c. Hands open 75% of the time _____
   d. Rolls side to back/stomach to back _____
   e. Reaches for toy _____
   f. Manipulates toy _____

2. *Sensory:*
   a. Follows objects in horizontal plane _____
   b. Follows objects in vertical plane _____
   c. Responds to a variety of sounds _____
   d. Tolerates deep pressure-type touch _____

3. *Language:*
   a. Vocalizes with at least one sound
      type _____

4. *Cognitive:* (Same as Sensory and Language)

Emotional Range: Sensorimotor
1. Looks at interesting sights for three or more seconds (brightens or turns to sights).
2. Listens to interesting sounds for three or more seconds (brightens or turns to interesting sounds).
3. In response to touch (light or firm), relaxes, smiles, vocalizes, or looks.
4. In response to moving infant's arms and/or legs, relaxes, smiles, vocalizes, or looks at caregiver or own limbs.
5. Tolerates and/or shows pleasure (e.g., smiles) in gentle horizontal and vertical movement in space (e.g., caregiver moving infant up and down and side to side).

6. Tolerates or evidences pleasure in routine smells (e.g., a fruit odor like lemon, an after-shave lotion, or perfume).
7. When held firmly, relaxes or evidences pleasure.
8. When rhythmically rocked, relaxes or evidences pleasure.
9. Recovers from distress, with help from caregiver (e.g., holding, rocking) within twenty minutes.

Emotional Range: Affective
1. Shows an interest in the caregiver by looking, listening, or evidencing curiosity and pleasure (as compared to only being interested in inanimate objects or nothing).
2. Shows interest, through looking, listening, or signs of pleasure, when the caregiver makes happy, joyful facial expressions and vocal tones (e.g., caregiver smiling and laughing with great joy).
3. Shows interest when caregiver is assertive and reaches out by means of his or her facial expressions and vocal tones (caregiver talking in a regular tone of voice about, for example, "What a wonderful nose and mouth and little chin you have"; "Will you hold this rattle? You can do it! You can do it!").

Selected Associated Motor, Sensory, Language, and Cognitive Capacities Not Already Included Above
1. *Motor:*
   a. Holds head upright on own;
   b. Lifts head by leaning on elbows while on stomach;
   c. Hands open 75 percent of the time;
   d. Rolls from side to back or stomach to back;
   e. Reaches for rattle or other toy;
   f. Manipulates rattle or other toy.
2. *Sensory:*
   a. Follows objects in horizontal plane (e.g., light);
   b. Follows objects in vertical plane;
   c. Responds to a variety of sounds;

    d. Tolerates deep pressure-type touch.
3. *Language:*
    a. Watches lips and mouth of speaker;
    b. Vocalizes with at least one type of sound.
4. *Cognitive:* (same as sensory and language)

FORMING RELATIONSHIPS (ATTACHMENTS)

By five months, infant evidences positive loving affect toward primary caregiver and other key caregivers; looks and/or smiles spontaneously and responds to their facial expressions, voices, or touch with signs of pleasure such as smiling, relaxing, "cooing."

Primary Emotional
1. Responds to social overtures with an emotional response of any kind which may include pleasure (a smile), but also may include a frown, other facial expressions, vocalizations, arm or leg movements, or postural shifts.
2. Responds to social overtures with an emotional response of pleasure (e.g., smile, joyful vocalizations, etc.).

Emotional Range: Sensorimotor
Shows emotional interest or pleasure in caregivers'
1. Vocalizations (indicate which type works best—high or low pitch; loud, medium, or soft tone);
2. Facial expressions;
3. Touch (indicate part of body—back, abdomen, face, arms or legs—and type of touch—light or firm, that works best);
4. Gently moving the infant's arms or legs;
5. Moving infant horizontally or vertically in space (indicate rhythm that works best—fast, slow, etc.).

Emotional Range: Affective
1. Evidences a relaxed sense of security and/or comfort when held or rocked.

2. Evidences signs of pleasure (e.g., smiles, happy sounds) when either talked to, held, looked at, moved around, touched, or all of the above.

3. Evidences a curious, assertive interest in the caregiver (e.g., looks and studies caregiver's face).

4. Anticipates with curiosity or excitement the re-presentation of an interesting object that has been presented a moment earlier (e.g., a smiling, vocalizing caregiver making interesting sounds leads to anticipatory looks and facial expressions).

5. Evidences signs of discomfort or lack of pleasure or sadness when during interactive play caregiver is unresponsive for thirty to sixty seconds (e.g., while playing, caregiver stops interacting and is silent and still-faced).

6. Evidences anger or protest when frustrated (e.g., angry cry or facial expression).

7. Can recover from distress with caregiver's social overtures, such as vocalizing and making interesting facial expressions, within fifteen minutes.

Selected Associated Motor, Sensory, Language, and Cognitive Capacities Not Already Included Above
   1. *Motor:*
      a.   Pushes up on extended arms;
      b.   Shifts weight on hands and knees;
      c.   Readies body for lifting while being picked up;
      d.   Can reach for a toy;
      e.   Can roll from back to front;
      f.   Sits with support;
      g.   Can cooperate in being pulled to a sitting position;
      h.   Can bring hands together;
      i.   Can grasp objects voluntarily;
      j.   Can hold rattle.
   2. *Sensory:*
      a.   Reacts to paper on face;
      b.   Looks toward sound;
      c.   Tolerates roughhouse type play.

3. *Language:*
   a. Regularly localizes source of voice with accuracy;
   b. Vocalizes two different sounds;
   c. Vocalizes to caregiver's facial expressions and sounds.
4. *Cognitive:*
   a. Can focus or attend for thirty or more seconds;
   b. Looks and scans for objects and faces;
   c. Smiles at face in mirror;
   d. Looks toward object that goes out of visual range;
   e. Looks at own hand;
   f. Manipulates and plays with toys, such as a rattle or ring.

INTENTIONAL TWO-WAY COMMUNICATION

By nine months the infant is able to interact in a purposeful (i.e., intentional, reciprocal, cause-and-effect) manner; is able to initiate signals and respond purposefully to another person's signals. Uses multiple sensory modalities, the motor system, and a range of emotions in these intentional interactions.

Primary Emotional
1. Responds to caregiver's gestures with intentional gestures of his or her own (when caregiver reaches out to pick up infant, infant may reach up with his own arms; a flirtatious caregiver vocalization may beget a playful look and a series of vocalizations).
2. Initiates intentional interactions (e.g., spontaneously reaches for caregiver's nose, hair, or mouth; uses hand movements to indicate wish for a certain toy or to be picked up).

Emotional Range; Sensorimotor
Responses intentionally to caregiver's:

1. Vocalizations;
2. Facial expressions;
3. Touch (e.g., holds caregiver's hand when being touched or tickled);
4. Moving infant around in space.

Emotional Range: Affective
Uses gestures to initiate:

1. Closeness. The infant reaches out to be picked up or hugs back when hugged.
2. Pleasure and excitement. Can be playful and smile and vocalize joyfully while putting finger in caregiver's mouth or taking a rattle out of caregiver's mouth and putting it in own mouth.
3. Assertive exploratory behavior. Infant touches and explores caregiver's hair.
4. Protest or anger. Infant pushes undesired food off table with an angry look; screams intentionally when desired toy is not brought to him, etc.
5. Fearful behavior. Infant turns away and looks scared or cries when a stranger approaches too quickly.
6. Infant can recover from distress within ten minutes by being involved in social interactions.

Selected Associated Motor, Sensory, Language, and Cognitive Capacities Not Already Included in Above
    1. *Motor:*
        a. Can sit with good balance;
        b. Can hold toy while sitting;
        c. While sitting, can reach up in air for objects;
        d. Can go from lying on back to sitting;
        e. Can go from sitting to stomach position;
        f. Creeps or crawls on stomach or hands;
        g. Holds block or toy using thumb and finger;
        h. Can scoop a Cheerio or small object into palm;
        i. Bangs hands or toy while playing;

    j. Transfers objects from hand to hand.
2. *Sensory:*
    a. Will feel textures and explore them.
    b. Notices when toy or object is put on different parts of body (stomach or foot) (e.g., looks at or touches textured toy).
    c. Not sensitive to loud noises like that of vacuum cleaner, toilet flushing, or dog barking.
    d. Not sensitive to bright lights.
    e. Enjoys movement in space.
3. *Language:*
    a. Responds to name and/or some simple requests (e.g., "No").
    b. Vocalizes different sounds from front of mouth (e.g., "Ba" or "Ma" or "Da") and can use sounds to convey intentions or emotions, such as pleasure or satisfaction.
    c. Responds to different sounds with different vocalizations of own or with selective behaviors.
    d. Can imitate a few sounds (e.g., a "raspberry" or tongue click).
4. *Cognitive:*
    a. Can focus on toy or person for one or more minutes.
    b. Explores and examines a new toy.
    c. Makes sounds or creates visual or tactile sensations with a toy (e.g., cause-and-effect playing).
    d. Can discriminate between different people as evidenced by different responses.
    e. Looks for a toy that has fallen to floor.
    f. Can pull on a part of an object (e.g., a piece of cloth) to get the object closer.

COMPLEX SENSE OF SELF I: BEHAVIORAL ORGANIZATION

By thirteen months, the infant begins to develop a complex sense of self by organizing behavior and emotion. The toddler sequences a number of gestures together and responds consistently to caregiver's gestures, thereby forming chains of interaction (i.e., opens and closes a number of sequential circles of communication). The toddler also manifests a wide range of organized, socially meaningful behaviors and feelings dealing with warmth, pleasure, assertion, exploration, protest, and anger.

Primary Emotional

The infant strings together three or more circles of communication (interaction) as part of a complex pattern of communication. Each unit or circle of communication begins with an infant behavior and ends with the infant building on and responding to the caregiver response. For example, an infant looks and reaches for a toy (opening a circle of communication), caregiver points to the toy, gestures and vocalizes, "This one?" The infant then nods, makes a purposeful sound, and reaches further for toy (closing a circle of communication). As the infant explores the toy and exchanges vocalizations, motor gestures, or facial expressions with the caregiver, additional circles of communication are opened and closed.

Emotional Range: Sensorimotor

The infant can organize three or more circles of communication (with a responsive caregiver):

1. Using vocalization;
2. Using facial expressions;
3. Involving reciprocal touching;
4. Involving movement in space (e.g., rough and tumble play);
5. Using motor patterns (e.g., chase games, searching for objects; handing objects back and forth).

Emotional Range: Affective

Can organize, with caregiver support (i.e., responsive empathetic reading and responding to infant's communications), three or more circles of communication around:

1. Negotiating closeness. Gives caregiver a hug and as caregiver responds with a hug back, nuzzles and relaxes.
2. Pleasure and excitement. Infant and caregiver play together with an exciting toy or with caregiver's hair or toes or infant's toes.
3. Assertive explorations. Infant and caregiver examine new toys, explore the house.
4. Cautious or fearful behavior. Infant hides behind caregiver when in a new setting; negotiates with caregiver degrees of protection needed.
5. Angry behavior. Infant can gesture angrily back and forth.
6. Infant can recover from distress and remain organized while distressed by entering into complex gestural negotiation for what he or she wants (e.g., banging on a door to go outside and play).

Selected Associated Motor, Sensory, Language, and Cognitive Capacities Not Already Included in Above

1. *Motor:*
   a. Walks on own or by holding onto furniture;
   b. Can squat while playing;
   c. Can throw a ball forward;
   d. Can feed self finger foods;
   e. Can stack two cubes;
   f. Can organize one-step motor planning sequence such as pushing or catching or throwing a ball.
2. *Sensory:*
   a. Infant explores and tolerates different textures with hands and mouth (e.g., willing to explore different foods).
   b. Infant is comfortable climbing and exploring off of the floor (e.g., on couch, table top).
   c. Not sensitive to bright lights.
   d. Not sensitive to loud noises (e.g., vacuum cleaner).

   3. *Language:*
     a. Understands simple words like "shoe" or "kiss!";
     b. Uses sounds or a few words for specific objects;
     c. Jabbers.
   4. *Cognitive:*
     a. Can focus and attend while playing on own for five or more minutes;
     b. Copies simple gestures like "bye-bye" or "No";
     c. Can find toy under caregiver's hand;
     d. Will try to imitate a scribble;
     e. Explores how toy works and figures out simple relationships like pulling a string to make a sound.

COMPLEX SENSE OF SELF II: BEHAVIORAL ELABORATION

By eighteen months the infant elaborates sequences of interreaction which convey basic emotional themes.

Primary Emotional

1. Comprehends and communicates, via gestures, basic emotional themes as evidenced by the ability, with a responsive caregiver, to open and close ten or more consecutive circles of communication (e.g., taking caregiver's hand and walking toward refrigerator, vocalizing, pointing, responding to caregiver's questioning gestures with more vocalizing and pointing; finally getting caregiver to refrigerator, getting caregiver to open door, and pointing to the desired food).

2. Imitates or copies another person's behavior, and then uses this newly learned behavior intentionally to convey an emotional theme (e.g., putting on daddy's hat and walking around the house with a big smile clearly waiting for an admiring laugh).

Emotional Range: Sensory and Motor

Elaborates complex interactions (i.e., 10 or more consecutive circles of communication) using:

1. Vocalizations and/or words;
2. Facial expressions;
3. Reciprocal touching and/or holding;
4. Movement in space (rough-and-tumble play);
5. Large motor activity (e.g., chase games, climbing games);
6. Communication across space (e.g., while playing with pots infant vocalizes to caregiver from across room. Caregiver vocalizes back. Infant continues playing and vocalizing without needing to come over and touch caregiver).

Emotional Range: Affective

1. Elaborates complex interactions (10 consecutive circles of communication) dealing with the emotional themes of:

a. Closeness and dependency. Uses facial expressions, motor gestures, and vocalization to reach out for a hug, kiss, or cuddle. Can be coy and charming or even provocative, if necessary, in order to be close. Can also use imitation to feel close (e.g., talks on play telephone while mom talks on telephone with a friend).

b. Pleasure and excitement. Can share a joke with another toddler, or with an adult. For example when the toddler drops some food accidentally and it makes a funny sound ("Splat!") or a mark on the floor, the toddler may giggle and look toward the other person to share in the pleasure. Funny faces, funny sounds, or imitating the behavior of adults or other toddlers may be a basis for giggles and pleasure.

c. Assertiveness and exploration, including relative independence. Can now explore more independently and balance dependence with independence. Uses ability to communicate across space to feel close to caregiver while playing on own (e.g., may go into another room, or to a far corner of the same room, to look for a toy while periodically looking at or vocalizing to the caregiver). May also come over to touch base with caregiver and venture out again.

d. Cautious or fearful behavior. Can now, via vocalizations, motor gestures, or a few words, tell caregiver exactly how to be protective in a new situation (e.g., hides behind caregiver but pushes caregiver toward the toy or toward new people as though to run interference), or says, "No" and hides behind caregiver.

e. Anger. Can hit, pinch, yell, bang, scream, lie on floor as part of an organized pattern well under toddler's control. Can also give the angry cold shoulder to a wayward caregiver. Sometimes, can use the angry gesture, look, or vocalization instead of hitting, screaming, or pinching.

f. Limit setting. Can, for example, respond to caregiver limits communicated through gradually louder vocal gestures, serious-looking facial expressions, and body postures, as well as to simple phrases like, "No, stop that!" "Leave it alone!" "Come here!" For example, with the above type limit setting, the toddler puts telephone down and returns to caregiver.

2. Can use imitation to deal with and recover from distress (i.e., toddler may bang hands on floor and yell after being yelled at).

Selected Associated Motor, Sensory, Language, and Cognitive Capacities Not Already Included in Above

    1. *Motor:*

        a. Can plan motor pattern involving two or more steps (e.g., can bounce a balloon and try to catch it).

        b. Will try to imitate scribble or scribble on own.

        c. Holds crayon or pencil adaptively.

        d. Will put items in cup or toys in a box.

        e. Builds a tower with two or three blocks.

        f. Can put pegs in a pegboard.

        g. Can put round block in the round opening on a board.

    h. Can remove socks.
2. *Sensory:*
    a. Enjoys or tolerates various types of touch (e.g., cuddling, roughhousing, different types of clothing, brushing teeth or hair).
    b. Is comfortable with loud sounds.
    c. Is comfortable with bright lights.
    d. Is comfortable with movement in space.
3. *Language:*
    a. Comprehends some simple questions, carries out simple directions (e.g., with a ball).
    b. Imitates simple words.
    c. Uses words to make needs known.
4. *Cognitive:*
    a. Uses objects functionally (e.g., vocalize on the toy telephone, combs hair with toy comb).
    b. Searches for a desired toy or hidden object in more than one place.
    c. Can play on own in focused manner for fifteen or more minutes.
    d. Imitates behaviors just seen or seen a few minutes earlier.
    e. Recognizes family pictures.
    f. Can use a stick or other object to get another object.

EMOTIONAL IDEAS: I—REPRESENTATIONAL CAPACITY

By twenty-four months the child creates mental representations of feelings and ideas which can be expressed symbolically (e.g., pretend play and words).

Primary Emotional
1. Can construct, in collaboration with caregiver, simple pretend play patterns of at least one "idea" (e.g., dolls hugging or feeding the doll).

2. Can use words or other symbolic means (e.g., selecting or drawing a series of pictures, creating a sequence of motor gestures) to communicate a need, wish, intention, or feeling (e.g., "want that"; "me toy"; "hungry!"; "mad!").

Emotional Range: Sensorimotor
Can communicate symbolically about intentions, wishes, needs, or feelings with:

1. Words;
2. Complex gestures and facial expressions (e.g., making angry facial expressions in an exaggerated manner);
3. Touching (e.g., lots of hugging or roughhousing as part of pretend drama where child is the "daddy");
4. Motor movement (e.g., showing caregiver what to do).

Emotional Range: Affective
Can use pretend play or words employing at least one idea to communicate themes dealing with:

1. Closeness or dependency (e.g., dolls feeding each other, child says, "Want mommy").
2. Pleasure and excitement (e.g., makes funny faces like clown on T.V. and laughs).
3. Assertiveness and exploration (e.g., cars racing, looking at a real car in wonderment and asking "car?").
4. Cautious or fearful behavior (e.g., says, "Scared").
5. Anger (e.g., dolls fighting or hitting, "Me mad").
6. Limit setting (e.g., child says to self, "No hit").
7. Can use pretend play and/or words to recover from and deal with tantrum or distress (e.g., after a few minutes, tantruming child uses words and sounds to argue with caregiver).

Selected Associated Motor, Sensory, Language, and Cognitive Capacities Not Already Included in Above

1. *Motor:*
   a. Catches a large ball from a few feet away using arms and hands.
   b. Jumps with both feet off ground.
   c. Balances momentarily on one foot.
   d. Walks up stairs, two feet on each step at a time.
   e. Can run.
   f. Can stack more than four blocks.
   g. Can both scribble and make a single stroke with a crayon or pencil.
2. *Sensory:*
   a. Enjoys or tolerates various types of touch (e.g., cuddling, roughhousing, different types of clothing, brushing teeth or hair).
   b. Is comfortable with loud sounds.
   c. Is comfortable with bright lights.
   d. Is comfortable with movement in space.
3. *Language:*
   a. Understands simple questions: "Is mommy home?"
   b. Uses simple two-word sentences ("More milk"; "Go Bye-Bye").
   c. Can name some objects in a picture.
   d. Begins to use some pronouns.
4. *Cognitive:*
   a. Can attend or focus for thirty or more minutes.
   b. Can do pretend play on own.
   c. Can search for favorite toy where it was day before.
   d. Can do simple shape puzzles (two to three shapes).
   e. Can line up objects in design (e.g., a train of blocks).
   f. Points to parts of a doll.

    g. Puts round and square blocks in correct places on a board.

EMOTIONAL IDEAS: II—REPRESENTATIONAL ELABORATION

By thirty months, the child, in both make-believe play and symbolic communication, can elaborate a number of ideas that go beyond basic needs (e.g., "want juice") and deal with more complex intentions, wishes, or feelings (e.g., themes of closeness or dependency, separation, exploration, assertiveness, anger, self pride or showing off).

Primary Emotional
1. Creates pretend drama with two or more ideas (trucks are crashing and then they pick up rocks; or dolls are hugging and then have a tea party). Ideas need not be related or logically connected to one another.
2. Uses symbolic communication (e.g., words, pictures, motor patterns) to convey two or more ideas at a time in terms of complex intentions, wishes, or feelings (e.g., "Daddy play with car"; "No sleep, play"). Ideas need not be logically connected to one another.

Emotional Range: Sensory and Motor
Can communicate symbolically about intentions, wishes, or feelings with:

1. Words.
2. Complex gestures and facial expressions (e.g., acting tired and needy).
3. Touch (e.g., lots of hugging or roughhousing like they do on T.V.).
4. Can participate in simple spatial and motor games with rules (e.g., taking turns in throwing a ball).

Emotional Range: Affective

Can use pretend play or other symbolic communication (e.g., words) to communicate themes containing two or more ideas dealing with:

1. Closeness or dependency (e.g., dolls say "hug me," child says, "Give you kiss").
2. Pleasure and excitement (e.g., making funny words and laughing).
3. Assertiveness and exploration (e.g., pretend airplane zooms around the room).
4. Cautious or fearful behavior (e.g., pretend drama where baby doll is scared of loud noise).
5. Anger (e.g., soldiers shoot pretend guns at one another).
6. Limit setting (e.g., dolls follow rules at tea party, "Must sit").
7. Uses pretend play to recover from and deal with distress (e.g., plays out eating the cookie he could not get in reality).

Selected Associated Motor, Sensory, Language, and Cognitive Capacities Not Already Included in Above

1. *Motor:*
   a. Walks up and down stairs.
   b. Throws ball.
   c. Stands on one foot.
   d. Can walk on tip toes.
   e. Draws a line with crayon or pencil.
   f. Can turn a knob.
   g. Can remove a cap.
   h. Can fold paper.
   i. Can make a tower of eight or more blocks.
2. *Sensory:*
   a. Enjoys or tolerates various types of touch (e.g., cuddling, roughhousing, different types of clothing, brushing teeth or hair).

      b. Is comfortable with loud sounds.

      c. Is comfortable with bright lights.

      d. Is comfortable with movement in space.

  3. *Language:*

      a. Understands sentences with two or more ideas (e.g., "You can have a cookie when we get home").

      b. Understands directions with two or more ideas.

      c. Organizes sentences with two or more ideas (e.g., "Want apple and banana").

      d. Refers to self using a pronoun.

  4. *Cognitive:*

      a. Can point to some pictures from a verbal description.

      b. Can name objects in a picture.

      c. Can make a train of blocks after seeing it in a picture.

      d. Can repeat two or more numbers.

EMOTIONAL THINKING

By thirty-six months, ideas dealing with complex intentions, wishes, and feelings in pretend play or other types of symbolic communication are logically tied to one another. The child knows what is real from unreal and switches back and forth between fantasy and reality with little difficulty.

Primary Emotional

1. Pretend play, however unrealistic, involves two or more ideas that are logically tied to one another (e.g., "the car is visiting the moon" [and gets there] "by flying fast"). In addition, child can build on adult's pretend play idea (i.e., close a circle of communication). For example, child is cooking a soup and adult asks what is in it and child says, "rocks and dirt" or "ants and spiders."

2. Symbolic communication involves two or more ideas that are logically connected and grounded in reality: "No go to sleep"; "Want to watch television." "Why?" asks the adult. "Because not tired." Child can close symbolic circles of communication (e.g., child says "Want to go outside." Adult asks, "What will you do?" Child replies, "Play").

Emotional Range: Sensorimotor
Can communicate symbolically, logically connecting together two or more ideas, about intentions, wishes, needs, or feelings with:

1. Words.
2. Complex gestures and facial expressions (e.g., pretending to be an angry dog or cat).
3. Touch (e.g., lots of hugging or roughhousing as part of pretend drama where child is the "daddy").
4. Can organize spatial and motor games with rules (e.g., takes turn in going up small incline or holds hands with others and goes around in a circle).

Emotional Range: Affective
Can use pretend play or words to communicate themes containing two or more logically connected ideas dealing with the following:

1. Closeness or dependency (e.g., doll gets hurt and mommy doll fixes it).
2. Pleasure and excitement (e.g., says bathroom words like *doody* and laughs).
3. Assertiveness and exploration (e.g., good soldiers search for missing princess).
4. Cautious or fearful behavior (e.g., scary monster scares baby doll).
5. Anger (e.g., good soldiers fight bad ones).
6. Limit setting (e.g., the soldiers can only hit bad guys because of the "rules").

7. Uses pretend play to recover from anger (e.g., plays out eating the cookie he could not get in reality).

Selected Associated Motor, Sensory, Language, and Cognitive Capacities Not Already Included in Above

1. *Motor:*
   a. Walks upstairs alternating feet.
   b. Catches big ball.
   c. Kicks big ball.
   d. Jumps forward.
   e. Hops.
   f. Copies circle.
   g. Cuts paper.
   h. Can unbutton buttons.
2. *Sensory:*
   a. Enjoys or tolerates various types of touch (e.g., cuddling, roughhousing, different types of clothing, brushing teeth or hair).
   b. Is comfortable with loud sounds.
   c. Is comfortable with bright lights.
   d. Is comfortable with movement in space.
3. *Language*
   a. Understands and constructs logical bridges between ideas with full sentences.
   b. Uses "but" and "because."
   c. Answers "what," "who," "where," and "doing" type questions.
   d. Comprehends actions/verbs.
   e. Uses plurals.
   f. Uses two prepositions.
4. *Cognitive*
   a. Pretend play has logical structure to it (i.e., pretend ideas are connected).
   b. Spatial designs are complex and interrelated (i.e., a house made of blocks has connected rooms).
   c. Identifies big and little as part of developing a quantitative perspective.

    d. Can identify objects by their function as part of developing abstract groupings.

42–48 MONTHS

By forty-two to forty-eight months, the child is capable of elaborate complex pretend play and symbolic communication dealing with complex intentions, wishes, or feelings. The play or direct communication is characterized by three or more ideas that are logically connected and informed by concepts involving causality, time, and space.

Primary Emotional

1. Elaborates complex, partially planned pretend play with three or more logically connected ideas dealing with intentions, wishes, or feelings. The planned quality (e.g., a special car is used) and "How," "Why," or "When" elaborations give depth to the drama (e.g., child sets up castle with an evil queen who captured the princess. Why did she capture the princess? "Because the princess was more beautiful." When did she capture her? "Yesterday." How will the princess get out? "You ask too many questions.").

2. Participates in reality-based circle closing symbolic conversation using three or more ideas dealing with intentions, wishes, or feelings. In a reality-based dialogue, the child can deal with causality. ("Why did you hit your brother?" "Because he took my toy." "Any other reason?" "He took my cookie.")

3. Distinguishes reality and fantasy (e.g., "That's only pretend"; "That's a dream. It's not real.").

4. Uses concepts of time and space to deal with intentions, wishes, and/or feelings. Caregiver: "Where should we look for the toy you can't find?" Child: "Let's look in my room. I was playing with it there." Caregiver: "When do you want the cookies?" Child: "Now." Caregiver: "Not now; maybe in five minutes." Child: "No. Want it now!" Caregiver: "You can have

the cookie in one, two, or five minutes." Child: "Okay. One minute."

Emotional Range: Sensorimotor
The child is able to use elaborate, complex, logically connected ideas (three or more) and communicate using:
1. Words;
2. Complex gestures and facial expressions (e.g., giving someone a dirty look, observing to see if they react, and giving them an even angrier look if they haven't apologized, and soon!);
3. Touch (e.g., giving caregiver a backrub, looking longingly in her eyes and smiling, and then asking for a new toy);
4. Can organize spatial and motor games with rules (e.g., can partially play baseball or basketball).

Emotional Range: Affective
The child is able to use elaborate, complex, logically connected ideas (three or more) when dealing with:
1. Closeness or dependency (e.g., doll gets hurt and mommy doll fixes it, and doll goes to party and meets the prince).
2. Pleasure and excitement (e.g., says bathroom words like *doody* and laughs, and then goes and says it to caregiver looking for her to laugh or get mad).
3. Assertiveness and exploration (e.g., good soldiers search for missing princess, and find her, but have to battle with evil soldiers to save her).
4. Cautious or fearful behavior (e.g., scary monster scares baby doll, who hides under covers and then gets up and hits the monster).
5. Anger (e.g., good soldiers fight bad ones, and use secret bombs and rockets to defeat the enemy).
6. Limit setting: Child can now set limits for him- or herself by reasoning about consequence (e.g., using ideas causally and in time framework. "If I am bad now, I will be punished later."). Even though he doesn't always follow them, child now is able

to understand rules in terms of limits. He also can form abstract principles. "You shouldn't be mean to them."

7. Separation and loss. Child can now picture mom in home while he is at school or in waiting room while he is in office, and relate some feelings of sadness and loss (e.g., "She is in waiting room. I miss her a little, but I am having fun.").

Selected Associated Motor, Sensory, Language, and Cognitive Capacities Not Already Included in Above

1. *Motor:*
   a. Skips
   b. Hops
   c. Rides tricycle
   d. Catches ball
   e. Bounces ball
   f. Shows hand preference
   g. Copies cross
   h. Strings beads
   i. Cuts across a line
2. *Sensory:*
   a. Enjoys or tolerates various types of touch (e.g., cuddling, roughhousing, different types of clothing, brushing teeth or hair).
   b. Is comfortable with loud sounds.
   c. Is comfortable with bright lights.
   d. Is comfortable with movement in space.
3. *Language:*
   a. Comprehends complex "why" questions such as, "Why do we need a house?"
   b. Can express ideas reflecting an understanding of relative degrees of feelings of wish or intention, "I am only a little mad."
   c. Can repeat a five to ten word sentence.
   d. Can repeat four to seven numbers.
4. *Cognitive:*
   a. Can point to pictures that show an object with attributes that are first described verbally (e.g.,

"What do you eat with?" "What makes food hot?").
b. Can deal with concepts of quantity (e.g., which is biggest, which box has more marbles in it, etc.).
c. Can identify similarities and differences with shapes and verbal concepts (e.g., triangle and rectangle or people and animals).
d. Can recall and comprehend experiences from recent past.

GENERAL INFANT TENDENCIES (REGULATORY PATTERNS): ALL AGES

1. The infant is able to be calm and/or calm down and not be excessively irritable, clinging, active, or panicked.

2. The infant is able to calm down and take an interest in sights, sounds, and people and is not excessively withdrawn, apathetic, or unresponsive.

3. The infant is able to focus his or her attention and not be excessively distractible.

4. The infant enjoys a range of sounds including high and low pitch, loud and soft, and different rhythms, and is not upset or confused by sounds.

5. The infant enjoys various sights, including reasonably bright lights, visual designs, facial gestures, moving objects, and is not upset or confused by various sights.

6. The infant enjoys being touched (on face, arms, legs, stomach, trunk, and back), bathed and clothed, and is not bothered by things touching his or her skin.

7. The infant enjoys movement in space (being held and moved up and down, side to side, etc.), does not get upset with movement, and does not crave excessive movement.

8. The infant is able to maintain motor tone and carry out age-appropriate motor planning sequences (e.g., put fist in mouth, reach for object).

9. The infant enjoys a range of age-appropriate foods and is not bothered (e.g., with abdominal pains, skin rashes, irritability, or other symptoms) by any age-appropriate, healthy food as part of a balanced diet.

10. The infant is comfortable and asymptomatic around household odors and materials and is not bothered by any routine levels of household odors such as cleaning materials, paint, oil or gas fumes, pesticides, plastics, composite woods (e.g., plywood), or synthetic fabrics (e.g., polyester).

If the rating is less than four for any of the above, also rate the items below.

1. Infant tends to be hyper- or overly sensitive to:
    a. Touch (light or heavy);
    b. Sound (high pitch, low pitch, or loud);
    c. Sights (bright lights);
    d. His own movement in space (e.g., being moved horizontally or vertically); or
    e. Smells (e.g., routine household odors, perfumes).

2. Infant tends to be hypo- or undersensitive (i.e., doesn't respond to sensations and may crave them) to:
    a. Touch
    b. Sound
    c. Sights
    d. Movement in space
    e. Smells

(Note that an infant may have a mixture of hyper- and hyposensitivities.)

3. Infant tends to have difficulty processing, organizing (making sense of), or sequencing:
    a. Sounds (e.g., three-year-old following two simple directions such as "take the glass and put it in the sink");
    b. Sights (e.g., three-year-old identifying or copying a design like a circle);
    c. His or her own motor pattern (e.g., tying shoes);

d. Spatial concepts (e.g., figuring out the geography of a new house).

GENERAL CAREGIVER PATTERNS (BY HISTORY AND/OR DIRECT OBSERVATIONS)

In many families there are a number of caregivers. As one becomes aware of which parent or nanny or day care caregiver tends to do what, indicate the person and the amount of time he or she spends with the infant or child each day next to the rating (i.e., Father/3 hrs). You may need to draw additional lines. (Attach additional sheets as necessary.)

1. *Caregiver tends to comfort the infant,* especially when he or she is upset (by relaxed, gentle, firm holding; rhythmic vocal or visual contact; etc.), rather than tending to make the infant more tense (by being overly worried, tense, or anxious; or mechanical or anxiously over- or understimulating).

2. *Caregiver tends to find appropriate levels of stimulation to interest the infant* in the world (by being interesting, alert, and responsive, including offering appropriate levels of sound, sights, and touch—including the caregiver's face—and appropriate games and toys, etc.), rather than being hyperstimulating and intrusive (e.g., picking at and poking or shaking the infant excessively to gain his attention).

3. *Caregiver tends to pleasurably engage the infant* in a relationship (by looking, vocalizing, gentle touching, etc.), rather than tending to ignore the infant (by being depressed, aloof, preoccupied, withdrawn, indifferent, etc.).

4. *Caregiver tends to read and respond to the infant's emotional signals and needs in most emotional areas* (e.g., responds to desire for closeness as well as need to be assertive, explorative, and independent), rather than either misreading signals or only responding to one emotional need. For example, caregiver can hug when baby reaches out, but hovers over baby and cannot encourage assertive exploration or vice versa.

5. *Caregiver tends to encourage their infant* to move forward in development, rather than to misread infant's developmental needs and overprotect, "hold on," infantilize, be overpressured and/or punitive, be fragmented and/or disorganized, or overly concrete. For example:

a. The caregiver helps the baby to crawl, vocalize, and gesture by actively responding to the infant's initiative and encouragement (rather than overanticipating the infant's needs and doing everything for him or her).

b. The caregiver helps the toddler make the shift from proximal, physical dependency (e.g., being held) to feeling more secure while being independent (e.g., keeps in verbal and visual contact with toddler as he or she builds a tower on the other side of the room).

c. The caregiver helps the two- to three-year-old child shift from motor discharge and gestural ways of relating to the use of "ideas" through encouraging pretend play (imagination) and language around emotional themes (e.g., gets down on the floor and plays out dolls hugging each other, separating from each other, or soldiers fighting with each other).

d. The caregiver helps the three- to four-year-old take responsibility for behavior and deal with reality, rather than "giving in all the time," infantilizing or being overly punitive.

The caregiver characteristics described above cover a number of developmentally based adaptive patterns. If in considering these patterns there is an impression that the caregiver patterns are less than optimal (i.e., ratings less than 4), it may be useful to consider the characteristics described below.

Caregiver tends to be:

1. Overly stimulating.

2. Withdrawn or unavailable.

3. Lacking pleasure, enthusiasm or zest.

4. Random or chaotic in reading or responding to signals (e.g., vocalizes and interacts but without regard for infant's signals as in a pinching, poking, "rev-the-infant-up" type caregiver).

5. Fragmented and/or insensitive to context (e.g., responds to one part of an infant's communication but misses the "bigger pattern" as when a caregiver gets excessively upset and hugs her active toddler who accidently banged his leg while trying to run and obviously wants to keep exploring the room).

6. Overly rigid and controlling. Trying to get the infant to conform to rigid agenda (e.g., making the toddler only play with a toy one way).

7. Concrete in reading or responding to communication (e.g., unable to tune into symbolic level in pretend play or in dialogue and instead keeps communication at behavioral and gestural levels. For example, a child is pretending with a toy telephone that he won't talk to his mother. Mother perceives this as a literal sign of rejection and refuses to "play anymore.").

8. Illogical in reading or responding to infant's communication (e.g., the caregiver is so flooded with emotion that he or she misreads what is communicated. A 3½-year-old says, "I am scared of the monster, but I know it is just make believe." The caregiver explains "monsters will never get in the room because the door has a big lock on it and monsters can be nice, too, you know. You shouldn't play with these toys anyhow and how did you get that scratch on your hand?").

9. Avoidant of selected emotional area(s) (e.g., in pretend play parent ignores the child's interest in aggression and always ignores separation themes).

Consider the following emotional areas:
a. Security and safety
b. Dependency
c. Pleasure and excitement
d. Assertiveness and exploration
e. Aggression
f. Love
g. Empathy
h. Limit setting

10. Unstable in the face of intense emotion (e.g., caregiver can support development only if emotions are not too intense;

if emotions are strong, tends to become chaotic, unpredictable, withdrawn, or overly rigid).

SUGGESTIONS FOR ELICITING THE INFANT'S EMOTIONAL AND DEVELOPMENTAL CAPACITIES

To observe the infant's emotional and developmental capacities, observe fifteen to twenty minutes or more of free interaction between infant and caregiver, followed, as needed, by free interaction between the infant and clinician. If the infant or child does not evidence age-expected patterns, the clinician or caregiver may attempt to elicit age-appropriate developmental capacities using some of the suggestions described below. These suggestions are intended only to help get things going. Follow the child's lead, as described in the "Floor Time" chapters, to keep the interactions "cooking."

The capacities to be elicited are listed in terms of the six stages of emotional development. Each set of capacities, while usually first in evidence at a certain period in infancy or early childhood, continues as the child grows. The level a child is at, as well as those he or she may have mastered, should be observed. When the suggestions only refer to the age at which a child first masters a particular capacity, the clinician should improvise a way to support that capacity in an older child (e.g., wooing an older child into a relationship with play and smiles rather than only smiles and sounds).

Regulation and Interest in the World

1. To attend.
2. To be calm.
3. To experience sensation through each sensory modality without being hyper- or hyposensitive.
4. To organize motor movements.

To elicit, hold baby or put baby in infant seat with mother or father near. Offer baby opportunity to look at caregiver or clinician as one offers different types of sensations.

1. *Sights.* Beginning with a six- to eight-foot distance, make funny faces and gradually move closer (no closer than 2 to 3 feet). Hold for thirty or more seconds at what appears to be optimal distance, moving slowly a little to the left, and then a little to the right. Then gradually move away. If baby does not clearly look at you for five or more seconds, repeat exercise while shining a light (use a flashlight) on your face; if still no response, try again putting a colorful toy in your mouth (e.g., a rattle).

2. *Sounds.* Experiment with different sounds, beginning with a soft, medium pitch and going higher and lower in pitch (while still soft). Increase loudness two times. Vary pitch at each higher sound level and note if and when baby looks at you for five or more seconds. To be sure she is looking at you, move a little to the left or right and see if she follows your voice with her eyes.

3. *Touch.* Stroke the baby's arms, legs, feet, hands, back, top of head, and if possible face and lips with (1) light touch (like a feathery tickle); (2) medium gentle touch; and (3) gentle firm pressure (a little squeeze or gentle rhythmic massage). Note reactions: no reaction; positive reaction (e.g., pleasure or attentiveness is increased); or negative reaction (e.g., pulling hand away, crying or making sounds suggesting discomfort).

4. *Smell.* If mother wears a cologne or perfume, you can put a little on your finger and put it under baby's nose. Alternatively, use a little lemon juice. Observe calm, pleasurable, focused, or indifferent response versus crying or pulling away.

5. *Movement in Space.* While firmly holding baby, gently and slowly move him up and down and side to side and then slowly spin around with him. Gradually increase speed and vigor of each type of movement, but stop and slow down as soon as infant gives any sign of lack of pleasure. Note what types of movement are pleasurable or aversive. Observe if he craves vigorous movement.

6. *Motor Patterns.* As caregiver or clinician holds infant, observe if muscle tone is loose (low) (e.g., infant doesn't cooperate in the cuddle) or tight (high) so that infant feels overly stiff. See if age-expected motor milestones are being mastered. Make up games such as holding head up, turning to voice, reaching for toy, and later on, crawling for a favorite rattle, to elicit age-appropriate movements. See if baby can plan sequences of movements, such as putting hand in own mouth or systematically examining a new toy. Mom's, Dad's, or the clinician's hair, nose, or hand can be the toy as well.

Note that many of the above capacities can be observed in the free play of the older infant, toddler, or young child.

Ability to Relate to Others

1. Taking an interest in another person through looking, listening, or moving toward them.

2. Evidencing pleasure in relating to another person through smiles, a joyful look, or just a sense of warm comfort.

3. Seeking out warmth and pleasure with another person through communicating a wish for closeness (e.g., reaching up for a cuddle or jumping into parent's lap, or snuggling warmly).

To elicit, position yourself near baby (who may be in parent's lap, in infant seat, or on floor). Begin to flirt with and woo baby with interesting facial expressions; warm, inviting sounds; and inviting motor gestures, such as moving face from side to side or back and forth. Be patient and start from eight to ten feet away and move in slowly. If the baby seems cautious or concerned, stop moving in and move back and forth, keeping your warm, cooing, funny face, vocalizations, and head movements going. Experiment with the different vocal tones. Also, feel free to put funny toys in your mouth or on your head. Observe if the infant is evidencing signs of relating (e.g., a smile, or vocalizations, rhythmic arm and leg movements, reaching out to you and flirting, or just being coy).

For an older child, any type of play may serve as a vehicle for wooing the child with your voice, smiles, touch, or gestural exchanges. Always move in very slowly, warmly, and sensitively.

Ability for Intentional Communication and Interaction
1. Initiating gestures (smiles, vocalizations, deliberate motor movements, such as pointing, reaching out to be picked up, covering face).

2. Responding to caregiver's gesture with gestures (closing or completing a circle of communication by, for example, exchanging one toy for another, or searching for the desired toy or squeezing Dad's nose after it goes "toot toot").

To elicit, place yourself in front of baby on the floor with the baby up on all fours, lying on stomach, or sitting. Make sure you are three to six feet away at ground level. Create opportunities for interaction. Put a brightly colored squeezable ball in your hand and offer it to baby. If he takes it and examines it, hold your hand out and see if he will give it back. Support your action with words, "Can I have it back?" Use lots of facial gestures (nodding, etc.) and animated hand gestures which say, "Give it to me." If he holds on to it, offer another toy in exchange. If he won't give it up, gently take it out of his hand, and slowly hide it under your hand and see if he takes it back. If he won't take the toy, try putting the toy in your mouth and move close enough for him to take it. If necessary, try over and over with different toys. While interacting, respond to baby's sounds, facial expressions, or motor gestures with sounds and gestures of your own.

You may substitute other activities for the above as long as it creates interactive opportunities (e.g., peek-a-boo game, etc.).

Ability for Complex Interaction and Communication
Initiating and responding in a chain of purposeful interactions. Many circles are opened and closed in a row. Circles of communication using gestures are employed to negotiate basic emotional themes such as closeness, anger, curiosity, exploration, and independence.

To elicit, begin playing with a real or toy telephone and pretend to talk to someone else. See if toddler or child comes over and copies what you are doing or tries to babble on the telephone in his own way. If he takes phone, ask for it back, saying, "I want to talk" and see if he lets you talk for a while, and so on. If he won't give it back to you, flirt with him, offer an exchange, and, if necessary, gently take it and see if he vocalizes or gestures to get it back or just grabs it back. Pick up another phone and see if he will "talk" with you phone-to-phone.

If the phone won't get his attention, put on a silly hat and see if he will take it off your head and use it. Try to get it back like above.

If neither of the above work, walk around on all fours, pretending to be a horsey, and see if he rides you. If you make noises, does he?

If none of these ideas work, follow what was described under "Ability for Intentional Communication." Feel free to improvise and support complex interactions in other ways as well.

The goal is to see if the toddler can close a number of circles in a row.

Ability to Represent or Symbolize (i.e., Create Ideas) Experience
1. Initiating pretend play (e.g., dolls hugging or fighting).
2. Initiating symbolic communication to convey intentions, wishes, or feelings (as compared to just labeling a picture or object).

To elicit, have toys, including dolls, action figures, cars, trucks, a house, furniture, kitchen and cooking utensils, a comb, toothbrush, two telephones, and an airplane or rocket. See what the child starts doing (e.g., pushing a car). Add a little doll to the car, saying, "He wants a ride," and see if the child builds on your gestures and words and begins a pretend drama such as the doll riding to the store. If the child opens the door to the toy house, say, "He [doll] wants to go in," and see if she incorporates your doll into a pretend drama.

If the child just sits still without initiating any play, try to establish some shared attention and a few simple gestural interchanges such as offering to hand him a doll or animal.

He may nod or turn away and in this way begin a gestural interchange. You may put the doll in his lap and say, "Dolly hungry; wants to eat," and see what he does. Or you may begin feeding the doll, put it in the child's lap and say, "Wants more."

You may substitute other initiatives for these if they create an opportunity for the child to initiate a pretend sequence. Do not tell child what to do. Create an opportunity. To evidence this capacity, the child need not do what you expect; he only needs to initiate pretend play (e.g., you say, "Dolly is hungry" and child takes doll and has him hit another doll while saying, "Bad boy").

Capacity for Emotional Thinking
1. Connect pretend sequences together logically (dolls hug and get mad and fight);
2. Connecting symbolic communications together logically ("I don't like broccoli because it tastes bad");
3. Connect visual/spatial concepts together (e.g., figuring out geography of a new house, as evidenced in going upstairs and coming down and finding Mom in the dining room or in knowing directions, finding things that are hidden, or building houses or farms with many interconnected parts).

To elicit, begin pretend play as described above. Only in addition to saying "Dolly is hungry," mention other feelings ("Dolly wants a hug"; "Dolly is mad and wants to fight"). See if and how the dolly you give a voice to is incorporated (or not) into the child's play.

If Dolly is incorporated into the child's play or the child on his own initiates a pretend sequence, ask questions that create opportunities for logical reasoning (connecting ideas). They include, "Why are they hugging or fighting or exploring?" "How did that happen?" "What is this or that?" See if child connects pretend sequences or ideas. He need not respond as you want him to: "Why is the dolly hitting the dog?" Child: "Because they are from outer space and space animals like to fight"; or "I don't know and stop asking questions!" Look for logical bridges between ideas, but not necessarily logical ideas.

Also discuss daily events with the child: "What do you like to play?" "Why/What do you like to eat?" etc.

To elicit the child's ability for spatial reasoning (how the child thinks nonverbally, which includes such abilities as a sense of direction, and constructing drawings of houses or farms), and reasoning about the physical properties of the world (these abilities are hard to elicit in the office), the following activities may prove useful. Hide an object the child takes an interest in, such as a little doll or car or rabbit's foot. First, hide it under a piece of paper with the child seeing you do it and see if she gets it. Next, hide the object in a box. Next hide it in a box and in turn put that box into a bigger box and see if she can find it (now that it is displaced twice). Any variation on this theme may be useful. The goal is to see how well the child figures out ever more complex spatial relations.

Another game that may get at this ability is a variation on the old shell game or three card monte. Through speed of hand, you hide an object which the child likes, such as a key, under one of three boxes or shells. You make it look like it is in the middle one, but it is under one of the corner ones. See how many trials it takes for the child to figure it out. This can be done with cards also (i.e., find the ace or queen). If the child can look for the object in other than the middle by the third trial, he evidences a differentiated level of spatial reasoning.

Other types of activities to elicit spatial abilities might include creating a mazelike structure out of furniture, cardboard, or pillows (like the mirror room of an amusement park), and see how long it takes the child to solve the maze in order to find the new toy or keys.

This section has described only a few semistructured ways of helping a child demonstrate his emotional and developmental capacities. These suggestions should only be used if free play is unsuccessful in eliciting the child's capacities. They only start the process going. The clinician or caregiver needs to follow the child's lead and keep the action moving as described in the "Floor Time" chapters. A judgment can then be made about the child's various emotional and developmental capacities. The above play activities may also be useful in helping the infant or young child practice his or her emerging functional capacities. Clinicians, educators, and caregivers should consider these as examples of the types of activities that help an infant or young child explore his or her relationship with them in a way that supports developmental progress.

PART IV

The Therapeutic Process: Developmental Psychotherapy with Infants, Young Children, and Their Families

INTRODUCTION

The cornerstone of the therapeutic process for infants and young children rests on an understanding of the types of experiences an infant and his or her caregivers require: (1) at each stage in his or her emotional development in order to foster further growth; (2) to work with his or her unique individual differences (i.e., constitutional and maturational patterns;) (3) to enable parents or caregivers to understand their own characteristics and interaction patterns with their children; and (4) to deal with and overcome emotional lags, constrictions, and deficits, as well as associated symptoms.[1]

The types of therapeutic experiences an infant requires may be organized in many different ways, depending on the specific situation at hand. In certain circumstances, the focus may alternate between the parents and family and the caregiver–infant interaction patterns, the caregivers' own fantasies and feelings, and the infant's innate and maturational tendencies and interactive capacities. Often, combinations of all of these elements together will be the focus of a therapeutic effort. A key point to remember, however, is that all the approaches mentioned above must be based on, and provide specific types of, developmental experiences. In other words, to be truly helpful, the interactive, family or caregiver, or infant therapy must not only provide general support, but highly specific types of experiences which can only be determined from understanding the infant's and family's developmental needs.

The specific developmental requirements that are at the foundation of the therapeutic process for infants, young children, and their families are embedded in the developmental approach to therapy which for shorthand purposes may be called "floor time." The following chapters will examine the various dimensions of floor time and apply it to different developmental stages and types of infants and caregivers. Special

---

[1] Appreciation to Serena Wieder for her helpful discussions of the therapeutic process.

approaches, such as parent-oriented therapy, will also be considered. In addition, in the section on diagnostic categories, chapters 20–23, there will be discussions of the therapeutic process in relationship to specific diagnostic groupings.

Chapter 10

The Traditional and Developmental Approaches to Therapy with Infants, Young Children, and Their Families: An Introduction to Floor Time

In order to understand the special features of the developmental approach to therapy with infants, young children, and families, it may be useful to review some of the concepts used in traditional approaches to therapy with children, discuss how a developmental approach would differ, and outline the principles of the developmental approach.

THE TRADITIONAL APPROACH TO THERAPY

Therapy with children traditionally involves a number of types of activities. A therapist may help a child put feelings into words through both play and talk. For example, if three-year-old Susie makes one puppet bite another puppet, the therapist might wonder out loud if the first puppet is mad at the second puppet.

431

If the child elaborates on how the first puppet wants to bite and hit the other, the therapist might feel the child has successfully verbalized his or her feelings. Similarly, if the child nods, as the therapist says, "Boy, the puppet looks mad," the therapist might feel that he or she has successfully helped the child deal with the feeling.

In addition to putting feelings into words, another typical goal of work with children is to help them resolve conflicts. If, for example, a child makes one doll bite another doll, and the first doll seems to become disorganized in her behavior or very fearful or if the scene changes to include monsters, the therapist might feel that the child is playing out a conflict between aggression and fear. Disorganization or withdrawal might be the child's solution to the conflict. The therapist then might be tempted to help the child understand that there are two feelings involved, "mad feelings and scary feelings," and in so doing help the child resolve the conflict.

In addition, the therapist will also have as a goal to help parents refrain from undermining their children's development. If the clinician senses that the parents are unwittingly overly permissive, punitive, abusive, or that they are neglectful or subtly bringing pressure on the child by bringing him or her too much into their conflicts, the therapist might assist the parents in changing these patterns of behavior.

All these traditional approaches may be helpful for certain children at certain ages; however, they cannot reach children as old as three or four who cannot talk or engage in pretend play. Such children have developmental delays or emotional challenges that interfere with their age-appropriate ability to use language. How does the therapist help children who are not yet at the developmental stage where they can represent feelings or conflicts? Furthermore, how do therapists assist parents to not just *not* abuse, neglect, or overstimulate their infants and young children, but to promote healthy emotional and intellectual development? How can therapists assist parents to create experiences that harness a child's developing capacities so that the child can develop emotional and intellectual competencies?

In addition to these questions that relate to dynamic approaches to child therapy, there are also questions regarding behavioral approaches to therapy with children. Behavioral approaches typically seek to reinforce certain target behaviors that are deemed appropriate and desirable and to extinguish or discourage less desirable or negative behaviors. This process occurs through "discriminative learning," which associates certain behaviors with positive reinforcements and other behaviors with either no reinforcement or negative (aversive) conditions. In addition, behavior is broken down into its component parts, so that a complex task can be mastered through the process of "shaping." Shaping involves taking small steps to help a child master a new, complex challenge. Each step must receive positive reinforcement; over time the small steps add up to big steps.

While behavioral approaches offer a means of understanding why certain behaviors persist (e.g., there may be less than obvious positive reinforcement going on), or how to shift the contingencies of reinforcement in the family, as well as how complex behaviors can grow from simple behaviors, there are also a number of issues that behavioral approaches tend to ignore. What is one to do when the main challenge for a child is not so much a specific set of behaviors, but a failure to master an entire developmental capacity? For example, let us say a child behaves aggressively—pinching, poking, and hitting other children. It might help to reinforce cooperative behavior (such as providing praise, M&M's, or stars), when he shares a toy with another child or to use a time-out, or other negative conditions to further discourage the aggressive behavior. A skillful behavioral approach might help the child shift to more positive behavior by using even the simplest piece of cooperative behavior—a kind look, an ability to sit briefly next to someone without poking—as a basis for positive reinforcement. The behavioral approach, however, might lead to too much isolation (time-outs), superficial verbal praise, such as, "You're a good boy," or concrete rewards.

But if the child's aggressive behavior is part of a larger developmental failure, he may never have learned to relate or engage warmly to other people, and others have not related warmly to him. He may see people as things to be hit, poked, or picked on if they don't do what he wants. There may be no difference in his mind between a human being and a chair; both can be kicked when he feels aggressive. (This pattern occurs in many sociopathic individuals who have had a great deal of emotional deprivation early in their lives.) The child has not learned how to empathize with another person's perspective, because he basically has little positive feeling for other people, and he probably has not learned how to regulate or control his aggressive impulses, because he lacks a basic capacity to see that his own behavior can have consequences for others. It is not that he doesn't care whether he is aggressive or not; he doesn't understand the concept of social consequences.

An approach that focuses on behavior alone will miss a larger opportunity to help a child master critical developmental milestones. Trying to get the behavior under control sometimes undermines a more important goal. For example, with a child who hasn't learned that relationships can be warm and supportive, the first step is to help him master a sense of engagement. For such a child, all subsequent learning will depend on his being part of an intimate, trusting relationship. If this first goal is sacrificed, more is lost than is gained. Here an approach that uses isolation as a negative consequence or uses very concrete rewards, such as candy as positive reinforcers, may actually undermine the important first goal of creating a sense of relationship and engagement. Here, focusing on isolated units of behavior can be misleading and can obscure a larger developmental challenge.

Similarly, for this child who doesn't understand that his actions have consequences, a second goal would be simply to foster two-way communication, with a sense of logical cause-and-effect interaction. The child who sees the world and himself as aimless needs first of all to learn that communication is causal and two-way, before he can appreciate the consequences of his interactions. Once the child has mastered these two developmental steps, he might well be able to benefit from systematic feedback that would not rely on specific behaviors but on a great deal of warmth and empathy, with firm limits. Such an approach would be consistent with the behavioral principles, but would not be so mechanical or systematic as to undermine the more basic developmental challenges this child has.

Another example might be the child who won't take turns. It would be easy to try to foster turn taking by using a behavioral approach that focused on systematic reinforcement of turn taking. However, if the more basic problem is a failure on the child's part to understand two-way communication and the nature of his or her impact on the world, the narrow behavioral approach might miss the boat. A mechanical or overly rigid approach to turn taking would undermine the child's learning to experiment with his own initiative and to assess and monitor the feedback he gets from others.

Another limitation of the behavioral approach is that a child may become dependent on certain types of concrete reinforcers; he may want stars and candies but not seem to care about people. The child's focus on "primitive" reinforcers (Greenspan, 1975) might constitute more of the problem than the particular behaviors the child evidences. Similarly, a child who focuses not just on primitive but also very generalized reinforcers, or who doesn't discriminate among reinforcers, will have a special challenge. Such a child might behave the way he does, because he feels rewarded by circumstances that other children would not find rewarding. The child who feels rewarded by other people's discomfort, by things rather than relationships, by any form of attention rather than a sense of pride or respect, may have a significant difficulty, because he hasn't developed certain basic capacities that enable him to feel pleasure from age-appropriate types of rewards. In such circumstances, a broad developmental approach is indicated, rather than one that focuses on isolated behaviors.

DEVELOPMENTAL APPROACH TO THERAPY

Following this review of some of the challenges of traditional dynamic and behavioral approaches, it is important to outline how a developmental approach to therapy with infants, young children, and their families would answer some of the questions that have been raised. The developmental approach does not negate or contradict dynamic and behavioral approaches; in fact, it would use specific components of these, but as a part of a larger developmental framework.

The principles of the developmental approach include the following:

1. The creation of opportunities that assist the child in learning basic developmental capacities. The capacities that learning opportunities must foster include: (a) the ability to attend and focus; (b) the ability to engage warmly and trustingly with others; (c) the ability to communicate intentionally with both simple and more complex gestures. The gestural level must progress to the point where it can be used to negotiate the basic themes of life such as dependency, aggression, approval/disapproval, and rejection; (d) the ability to represent or symbolize intentions and feelings, as seen in pretend play or the functional use of language; and (e) the ability to organize and differentiate represented experience in order to distinguish reality from fantasy, the self from nonself, one feeling from another feeling, as well as the temporal and spatial characteristics of representations. Creating learning opportunities to support these core developmental capacities is perhaps the single most important goal of a developmental approach to therapy.

2. Furthermore, the capacities must be supported in a *stable and broad-ranging manner*. At each developmental level and for each capacity, the child may or may not master age-appropriate emotions and themes at that level (such as warmth, dependency, pleasure, excitement, assertiveness, anger, curiosity, self limit setting, and for older children, empathy and more stable forms of love). For example, the child may have mastered two-way communication in terms of dependency but not asser-

tiveness, curiosity, or aggression. Similarly, the child may master a developmental capacity in a stable way, so that it tends to survive even under stress, such as a mild physical ailment, a brief separation from a parent, or a strong emotional feeling. Alternatively, even a brief stress may undermine a capacity, so that the child loses it. The goal is to create opportunities to learn the key developmental capacities in a stable and wide-ranging manner that encompasses age-appropriate themes and emotions.

3. Developmental capacities depend on relationships caregivers (including therapists and educators) have with their infants and young children. The specific characteristics of floor time that are associated with each developmental capacity and enable the adult to harness and foster that capacity, are described below. Floor-time approaches, to foster attention and engagement, two-way communication, and the formation of representational or symbolic capacities, are described in relationship to different types of children and families.

4. In order to create learning opportunities that foster key developmental capacities, it is important to take into account two contributing factors—the constitutional and maturational aspects of the child's development and the interactive and family aspects of the child's experience. Included are: (a) the infant- or child–caregiver interaction patterns; (b) the family dynamics; (c) the infant or child's own constitutional and maturational patterns, including hypo- and hypersensitivity, sensory processing, affective patterns, motor tone, and motor planning; and (d) the infant or child's own way of organizing experiences. The latter includes his physiological, behavioral, or gestural level and, after age eighteen months, his representational level, as well as the emergence of conflicts between different tendencies, such as conflicts between the child's assertive and aggressive side and the child's interest in safety, security, and dependency.

According to the developmental approach, the main goal, as indicated, is to facilitate the learning of core developmental capacities and to work with the various contributing factors and to prevent and treat developmental defects and constrictions. In order to facilitate these capacities, one needs to understand how each infant and child is unique—the individual differences in the child's maturational and constitutional capacities, the family dynamics, and the interaction patterns between the child and his caregivers. Of course, each family member has his or her own personal dynamics that relate to family experiences while growing up. Therefore, as one works with the core developmental capacities, one is also working with the unique physical and interactive characteristics of the infant or child and his or her family.

Therefore, a key difference between the developmental approach and more traditional approaches to therapy with children is the degree to which one actively promotes the attainment of core developmental capacities and attempts to overcome various delays or disorders in these capacities.

AN INTRODUCTION TO FLOOR TIME

Developmental psychotherapy or *floor time* is an approach that harnesses the infant's and young child's core developmental competencies including capacities for attention and engagement, two-way communication, for representing experience (if he's 18 months and older), and for differentiating experience (if he's over 2½ or 3 years). This is accomplished by literally getting down on the floor with the youngster and engaging him in such a way as to mobilize these four processes.

Parents, educators, or therapists can engage the child in this way; a comprehensive therapeutic program may in fact involve all three in floor time. The parents' involvement in floor time is perhaps the first therapeutic goal. The parents should take twenty to thirty minutes each day for the more unstructured playful side of floor time—interactive or pretend play. For three-year-olds and older, an additional fifteen or twenty minutes each day should be devoted to the more reality-based, logical, or problem-solving aspects of floor time (to be discussed later).

Often the diagnostic workup may indicate that, in addition to the parents' time with the child, direct one-on-one therapy is needed. Direct therapy may be indicated because the child requires certain approaches or the diagnostician observes certain limitations with the way a parent engages (or fails to engage) in floor time. The level of family difficulties or confusion, the lack of capacity of one or another of the parents, or because the youngster is sufficiently challenging in his individual differences and/or his developmental progression, may demand the incorporation of the principles of floor time into the direct therapeutic work. These floor time principles will provide the therapist with developmental approaches to his psychotherapy.

The therapist, in his psychotherapeutic efforts, will also assist the child via traditional psychotherapeutic interactions in ways the parents do not. For example, with a verbal child he may help the child see the connections between one feeling and another and/or between underlying wishes and feelings and behavior. Nevertheless, the therapist should build his "specific" and traditional psychotherapeutic efforts on the foundations discussed below under the heading of floor time. The therapist and parent will share the floor time goals, with the therapist serving as a consultant in helping the parents establish the floor time process, as well as engaging directly in floor time activities as needed.

Because these basic floor time processes are the same for the therapist, parent, educator, or caregiving adult, they will be described in general terms with occasional references to the therapist's special challenges in being a consultant to the parents. While *floor time* is a nontechnical term for a number of growth-supporting processes, the therapist should realize that he may be mastering a number of new techniques and a new way of thinking about his work with young children. At the same time, he is attempting to help parents master these same ideas and to implement them in their relationship with their child.

The professional helps the parents to figure out how to engage the child at each of the four developmental levels (engagement, two-way communication, representational elaboration, and representational differentiation) and to deal with the child's individual differences in mobilizing these processes. Furthermore, the therapist helps the parents assist the child to apply each of these developmental processes to a broad range of human emotions—pleasure, dependency, excitement, assertiveness, aggression, self-limit-setting, empathy, and more mature types of love.

The therapist will find that his consulting work with the parents can be divided into two broad categories. The first involves a more active coaching role; he may suggest that the parents try A, B, or C approach, or actually go through the motions of floor time with the parents, or may model for the parents. The best approach is getting down on the floor with the parents, sometimes whispering into their ears, sometimes wondering aloud why they are trying something one way rather than another, and sometimes providing a few ideas that the parents can use to discover how it feels to engage their child in a new way.

In working with parents, the key is to respect the floor time principles: do not lecture or only model; capture the parents' attention; engage them, interact, and help them use "ideas" to comprehend the floor time process.

A second facet of consulting involves working with the parents' or caregiver's own difficulties in engaging the child in floor time. One might assume that most parents would have an intuitive ability to engage the child in the four processes described earlier; when this ability is not naturally occurring, there is usually a good reason. Perhaps the parents were unengaged in this way as children and so did not have a chance to learn these techniques; the parents may have conflicts with one or another of the developmental processes or about applying them to the different emotional realms. Such conflicts or inhibitions may also be related to the way the parents themselves were raised or to on-going relationships within the family—between husband and wife or with other children. The therapist and diagnostician will discover over time which, if any, of these factors are operating.

Therefore, in addition to his educative, coaching role, which needs to be handled with respect for the parents' need for active mastery and discovery, the therapist needs to be aware of the parents' emotions and tendencies and to clarify for the parents how these tendencies affect their interaction with the child. Such clarification may be achieved on the floor and in sessions alone with the parents, when they can feel freer to discuss their reactions to the child's floor time. For example, the therapist needs to bring out the feelings of the mother who is unable to deal with her child's aggression because it frightens her, or the father who is frightened of intimacy and therefore wants only to roughhouse but not engage in more slow-moving and dependency-oriented kind of play. Sometimes there can be revealing chit-chat off to the side of the play, when the parent may talk about his own background while he plays with the child. At other times, in separate sessions, the therapist can help the parents explore some of the difficulties they may have in engaging the child. Global difficulties will inhibit the parent from engaging in a whole developmental realm with the child (e.g., fear of relating or of interacting), whereas more focal difficulties will enable the parent to engage in some emotional realms, but not necessarily others. For example, there may be focal difficulties in areas such as sexuality, excitement, aggression, or a certain aspect of dependency (separation anxiety). Such focal difficulties may lead a parent who is interacting to become overcontrolling when the true theme of pleasure or excitement emerges.

It should be expected that the parents' conflicts and anxieties have to play themselves out with the child. A parent who is anxious about aggression is less likely to be able to help a child with aggression than a parent who is comfortable with it. Similarly, a parent who is anxious about separation anxiety presumably won't be as able to help the child play out this theme as a parent who is comfortable with it.

However, parents who are motivated by warmth and concern and have the potential for growth can be mobilized by their desire to assist their children. In this way, parents can grow alongside their children. In a sense, the child's developmental challenges help the parents to make developmental progress as well.

In the therapist's direct work with a child, he is attempting to mobilize the four processes that characterize floor time. The therapist may decide that his special skills as a "floor timer" are necessary for the child who is very avoidant, overly reactive, has difficulty remaining focused, or becomes easily agitated. This may also be true in the case of the child who tends to withdraw, becomes paralyzed with anxiety, or has overwhelming fears. The child who becomes fragmented and lost in fantasy, evidences difficulties in processing information, or has conflicts that need to be gently teased to the surface may also be a candidate. The therapist will want to coach himself in much the same way he coaches the parents, paying attention to his own tactics. For example, "How am I trying to simplify my gestures or words for this child with an auditory processing difficulty?" He will also want to pay attention to his own emotional reactions: "Why do I get so bored and avoidant when Johnny tunes me out or becomes repetitive in his play?" The therapist may conduct his direct work either with the parent(s) present, alone with the child, or in both ways, depending on the clinical needs of the case.

An educator's floor time will be similar to that of parents (including the therapist's consultation), except for the fact that an educator will often be working simultaneously with additional educational goals and be using small-group settings. Examples of educational applications will be included in the discussions to follow.

While floor time will be discussed as a therapeutic strategy, it is also an assessment approach. The clinician who initially observes the parents and his own interactions with the infant or child to formulate his initial diagnostic impression should continually revise these (as well as his goals) through his floor time experiences. For example, as the clinician learns about how the child uses his different senses and his motor capacities, his affect expressions, and his evolving ability to organize experience, he will be refining and deepening his original impressions.

Floor time, while a technique, is also a general philosophy about relating to children. The floor time principle of fostering attention and engagement, two-way communication, the elaboration and sharing of meanings, and the categorizing and connecting of meanings can be supported or undermined in all caregiver–child relationships and interactions, as the following discussions will demonstrate.

Chapters 11 through 15 will discuss each aspect of floor time in terms of our developmental model. In addition, special challenges in terms of types of children and situations will also be addressed.

Chapter 11

Floor Time: Engaging and Interacting

ATTENDING AND ENGAGING

The first step is to help the child learn how to attend and to become engaged or connected, and to be calm and regulated at the same time. A parent, therapist, or educator who is working with a child one on one needs to focus on how to pull the child in. "How do I get this child to look at me, to listen to me, to be calm in my presence, and to feel connected to me? How do I get him or her to feel a sense of warmth, intimacy, and pleasure, a sense of good chemistry?" In most relationships, this first step is taken for granted. Yet, many challenging children have a hard time with it.

In order for the floor time approach to be successful, the adult must, first of all, be down on the floor with the child in order to follow the child's lead.

Second, it is necessary to be patient and relaxed (a nervous adult cannot help a child tune in and feel calm and relaxed). Children, whether four or eight months old, or five years old, are sensitive to whether an adult has time and patience. Even adults in a hurry can be calm and relaxed for the few minutes they do have available.

Third, when working with children, especially very young children, the adult must try to capture the emotional tone of the child. It is necessary to resist the natural tendency to try to get another person's emotional tone to be similar to one's own, or similar to the idea that one has of what the emotional tone ought to be. That tendency only makes the child feel controlled or manipulated, or even worse, exploited, even though the child's welfare is the objective. An adult should try to identify with the child to let the child know he is understood. Words are not always necessary; the way of looking at the child or the tone and rhythm of speaking may resonate. Or one might say to a more verbal child, "Gee, I can tell you are feeling kind of tired today," using a tone of voice that does not challenge the child intellectually, but conveys a sense of emotional warmth.

The adult needs to be aware of his own feelings of pleasure and warmth as well as anger, irritability, and being over-whelmed, because these and other feelings will determine how well the adult can tune into the child's emotional tone. A de-pressed caregiver will often evidence an empty emotional tone and talks or gestures slowly with long pauses. Children often find it hard to engage and attend under such circumstances. In addition to the well-known emotional aspects of attending and engaging, there are also important sensory and motor contribu-tions.

In fostering the process of engagement, one must also pay attention to the expectations that are communicated through the caregiver's tone of voice. Some parents have an anxious, "I know you won't look at me" quality. Other parents have a clear, warm, compelling, expectant tone which suggests to the child that he will engage. Particularly with children who are hard to engage, the anxious, unexpectant tone, in comparison to the more expectant tone, can be an important parameter for the therapist to be aware of.

SENSORY MODALITIES AND MOTOR PATTERNS

To capture the child's emotional tone, support a sense of connectedness, and also help the child attend, the adult has to be aware that the child takes in information through all sensory modalities. As described in the assessment section, looking and listening, smell, touch, and the movement of his own body affect how the child attends. Now, however, the challenge is to discover how the child deals with information in each sensory modality in order to know how to actively facilitate his development. What is learned from the assessment is put to good use. We observe, learn, and try different ways of engaging. Therefore, as part of our ongoing therapeutic relationship, we continually ask many of the assessment questions in order to fine tune our approach.

From experience with the child in the classroom or in a therapeutic setting, as a parent in the home, or when helping parents to be sensitive to how the child functions, one must ask what is known about the child in terms of each sensory modality. For example, does the child like loud noise, or is he a child who prefers soft and very gentle sounds? Some children are frightened by loud sounds; some tune out if spoken to too softly. Does the child like bright lights or soft lights? Does the child like to look at "busy" objects, with a lot going on? Does he like a person to be animated, to use hand gestures? Does he like bright colors and all kinds of detail? Or does color and detail overwhelm him by overloading his visual system? Does he like simple, slow, or complex, rapid movement?

What is the child's response to touch? Is this a child who, when gently touched on the hand or the shoulder, relaxes? Or is this a child who stiffens up when approached too quickly and doesn't like to be surprised by a casual, light touch? The child who dislikes light touch may like firm pressure, like a bear hug. Such a child may not like his hair or teeth brushed. Or does the child crave touch, want to be tickled and rough-housed—the more the better. Is he always rubbing up against someone or does he always have something in his mouth in an attempt to keep himself stimulated?

Preconceptions about behavior can interfere with observation and analysis; for example, one might say about a child who likes to chew and to mouth, "Oh, that's bad. Don't do that." In this instance it would be more helpful to say: "This child is telling me something about how he likes to experience touch around or in the mouth." Is the child craving touch or avoiding it? Frequently, parents and educators will say, "Johnny has to learn that he can't fidget or he can't put things in his mouth all the time." A child who fidgets or touches everything drives teachers and parents wild. But the fidgeting child is often one who craves touch. It may be necessary to give that child worry beads to play with or things to touch that are not breakable, so that he doesn't touch the things that a caregiver doesn't want him to touch.

Children have patterns of movement. Some like "horsing around" or wrestling; some like to be thrown up in the air and tossed upside down or to go down slides; others like to run around and jump from the furniture to the floor. One child may crave such movement, while another who becomes startled easily may be cautious about jumping, going down a slide, or horsing around.

A fidgety child who is seeking a lot of touching plays with *everything*. Such a child may fidget not just due to tactile hunger or a desire to play with things, but also because he or she may have a tendency toward motor discharge—a need to move around a lot. In other words, it may not be just a craving for touch, but may also be a craving for movement.

Consider a classroom setting where the teacher wants to convey the meaning of warmth and respect to a child. The best way, of course, is for the child to learn it through his experience of the teacher as a person. However, if the teacher asks the child to look at a picture that depicts warmth and respect, it is necessary for the teacher to respect the fact that the fidgety child may want to look at the picture while walking around and playing with a chair. If the teacher gives the child a few other things to fidget with, such as beads, there is a good chance that the child will walk around, fidget with this and that, and look at the picture. On the other hand, if the teacher gets into a power struggle with the child and says, "You have to sit in that chair, and you have to put your hands in your lap," then the child is likely to put so much energy into trying to sit in that chair and keep his hands still, that there is not a chance in the world that he will look at the picture. Or if the adult tries to scare the child: "Unless you sit in that chair and look, you're going to . . ." he will spend so much energy trying to contain himself, that he won't look at the picture. However, if the adult finds a compromise with the child (obviously, he can't be allowed to run around and hit other kids), to give him a little more space and movement, perhaps to let him stand up, then there's a good chance that the child will actually look at the picture. The request should also take into consideration the sound and lighting level that he needs. Therefore, the teacher will be better able to get the child to concentrate and to teach him about warmth and respect in two ways: through the picture and also through the child's sense that the teacher respects him as unique and special, as opposed to asking him to do something that he may not be able to do. Over time, these methods will enable children to settle themselves down and engage with adults.

In each of the sensory areas, a child can be hyperreactive (very sensitive) or hyporeactive (not sensitive at all) to a sensation. If he or she is hyporeactive, the child may actually crave more of a particular sensation. In other words the child who doesn't respond to touch may need a lot of touching. The craving does not always go along with the hyporeactivity. It is necessary to observe whether the child is hypersensitive or hyposensitive to a particular kind of input—visual, sound, touch, his own movement patterns, smell—and how he tries to cope with his sensory system. Does he seek out loud noises or does he avoid them? Docs he seek out touch or does he avoid it? Does he seek out extra movement or avoid it? How is the child coping? The child's sensory responses indicate the role that the child's physical makeup is going to play in how he can be engaged and helped to concentrate and attend. For example, the child who overreacts to loud noises and to light touch may become distracted, retreat to the far side of a room, "shut down" or become very "spacey," if confronted by an abrupt greeting. An energetic adult can unintentionally overload a child. The child may look "peculiar" or "disturbed" or become rigid in an attempt to tune out the adult. The child may launch into a perseverative kind of behavior, like opening and closing a door, because his sensory system is overwhelmed. Alternatively, a child who is underreactive to sensory experiences may not respond to a gentle, soft person (who interacts well with a hyperreactive child). To say quietly, "Hey, Johnny. Would you like to play with this tape recorder over here?" may not get the child's attention, let alone help him take in the information. An underreactive child may need someone to be energetic and active and to sound excited, in order to "rev" him up and "pull him in."

When an adult's intuition fails to help him to engage a child, it is necessary to take a look at each sensory channel in turn, to develop a profile of the child. One must ask, "How am I going to use each channel to engage and to foster relaxation and calm attentiveness?" Some children are inconsistent and therefore confusing; others are either hyposensitive or hypersensitive across the board, and it is relatively easy to get an intuitive feel for them. Some children may be very sensitive to visual input, like bright lights, and yet underreactive to sound; these children want a loud voice in a calm, dimly lit, not too complicated room. The child who likes visual complexity can respond to someone who is very animated and uses a lot of complex designs to interest and pull in that child (who otherwise would appear to be very distractible and spacey).

Even the child who is easy to work with, who concentrates and engages well, responds better to someone who knows that child's preferences. Even the optimally developing child can be a better concentrator or more warmly engaged, by taking into consideration individual differences, even though they might not be as extreme as those of the child who is having a tough time with the process of engagement. To try to connect with the child through all the child's modalities is to enhance a sense of emotional security by bringing a sense of pleasure and intimacy to the child.

In each sensory modality, it is necessary to try to connect with the child without overwhelming or underwhelming him to the point that he experiences negative emotions. In such a circumstance, he can become frightened and think the adult doesn't like him. ("How come? What's wrong with me? What's wrong with them?" "Where's the lion going to come from next?")

In addition to paying attention to the child's senses, it is also very important for a teacher, parent, and certainly a therapist to respect the child's pace. Some children, even if they crave a lot of input, may be slow to form relationships; other children are quick to form relationships. Pace may relate to the way the children have learned to relate to their parents. A baby or a young child may be slow to warm up when a parent comes home at the end of a day, or may be eager and jump on the parent right away.

The child's style of activity and pace is determined by, in part, the child's way of using her motor system to carry out complex actions. A child who has a motor planning problem cannot sequence many complex or alternating motor movements as part of a more complicated act. The first sign of a motor planning problem is often seen in the baby who can't cuddle, can't figure out how to get his neck into the crook of his mother's neck, or to get hand to mouth to pacify himself. Some children walk at nine months, others don't walk until sixteen months. Some children are very clumsy and are unable to perform a complex physical task.

Related to motor planning are a number of differences in the way a child uses his muscles; one needs to pay attention to this as a part of relating to the child. For example, what is the tone of the child's muscles? Is he a child with low tone or a child whose muscles are tight, with high tone? A parent might recall that a child had trouble holding his head up or learning to crawl, because the child's motor was too low. Or a child may seem strong but can't balance or coordinate his body well, because his tone is too tight (like a musclebound person). If muscle tone is too loose or tight, it affects the way the child responds to his world, because he can't get his motor system to do what he wants it to do. He may feel as if he can't control his body.

Initially, a child needs to use his muscles to get close to his mother, to cuddle, to relax, and to communicate. For example, a child may keep looking and point past something that is being pointed out to him. If the adult is not patient and doesn't recognize the problem, the adult is likely to think that the child is not interested. He's not being distractible; he looked past the mark because he can't readily control his head movement. If the adult says, "Would you get this piece of fruit that I am holding up here next to my nose?" the child may touch the adult's nose instead of grasping the fruit nicely. In give-and-take games between parents and children, the parents may misperceive the child's intent as aggressive. Parents and therapists need to be aware that a child who is in fact engaged, is very loving, and wants to be attentive, may miscommunicate because his motor system doesn't work.

Such a child will take longer to find an adult's eyes. A four-month-old baby may take twenty or thirty seconds, rather than five seconds, to find one's eyes and tune in. Parents who give up at fifteen seconds never discover that the child will find their eyes at twenty seconds. Similarly, one may say to a three- or four-year-old child, "Hey, come on and play here." Although the child hears, his motor system takes him first here and then there, and by the time he gets to the speaker, he or she is on the other side of the room. Rather than getting impatient or annoyed, one might say with words or gestures, "Oh, I can see you are coming closer." If a child has a history of low or high tone, or of being clumsy, it is necessary to allow that child a lot more practice and ways of approximating, before deciding he is not interested in people or objects. Remember, a child engages and attends in part through the use of his motor system.

As one focuses on the emotional tone and rhythm and sensory and motor systems of the child to understand better how to help the child attend and engage, it is also important to take a hard look at one's own empathetic depth and range which will be related to one's feelings and fantasies. Sometimes, the therapist's or parents' limitations in engaging will be due to a set of rigid expectations about a particular child. The therapist's and parents' own fantasies and expectations will be discussed in chapter 17.

TWO-WAY INTENTIONAL COMMUNICATION

If the first goal of the floor time approach is to successfully engage the child, then the next goal is to help that child learn two-way communication. Two-way communication is very simple: the child does A, the adult does B, and the child does C, which is somehow connected to B. For example, if the child shows the adult the pen (A), and the adult offers his hand and looks at the pen and says, "Very nice," and hands it back to the child (B), and the child takes the pen (C), and the adult takes the pen back again, there is two-way communication at the level of gestures. As noted in earlier chapters, we will call such an interaction opening and closing a circle of communication. Any logical conversation between two people is going to have an A, B, and C. Even when two people smile at each other, they have opened and closed a circle of communication (i.e., one person looks at another, and the first person looks back, and the second person smiles back). Most children and adults do this many times in any encounter.

But there are children who don't open and close circles of communication. For example, when such a child shows someone a pen, and the person says, "Oh, that's great," and offers the pen back to the child, that child might say, "Hey! What's that number on the floor? Is it a two or a three?" and the adult says, "Oh, I think that's a two." Rather than saying, "Oh, yes it's a two," or "Thank you," the child may say, "Oh, what are those beads you are wearing around your neck?" Such children are always interrupting the circle before it gets closed. In other words, there is an A and B, or perhaps just an A, and a break in the sequence.

Consider another example. A child points to a toy. The adult follows the child's lead and points to the same toy with a gesture suggesting, "Do you want me to get it for you?" The child, instead of nodding or smiling or simply repeating his pointing, looks blank or starts fidgeting with another toy.

Other children are capable of two-way communication only up to a point. They can open and close two or three circles, but normal conversation consists of opening twenty or thirty in a row. Some children will close two or three circles and then are lost. It is hard to get them back in. By about eight months, children should be able to close two or three circles in a row; by fifteen months, twenty or thirty circles in a row; by two to three years, they should be able to open and close circles as long as the dialogue requires. Certainly, a four-year-old should be able to open and close circles consecutively, for fifteen or twenty minutes, or as long as his interest sustains him.

Two-way communication takes many forms. Frequently, problems are with gestures, not just with words; for example, there is the child who doesn't look back when an adult looks at him, or doesn't look at something the adult points to; and the adult loses him. When an adult is down on the floor playing with a child, the two-way communication could involve just crashing trucks together. The child and then the adult crashes the truck one way, the child crashes the truck another way, and back and forth. But if the child moves the truck and then the adult moves it, the child turns away and plays with a ball, a circle is not closed. Or the child may put a doll in the playhouse, and the adult says, "That's interesting," whereupon the child puts the doll in a different way or takes another doll or asks the adult to hand over the dolls, all the while opening and closing circles. Or a four-year-old may report, "Mommy is going off to the dentist." The adult responds, "I wonder what's going to happen there?" "Oh, he going to look in her mouth." "What do you think is going to happen next?" "I think he is going to fix her teeth, because they were hurting." But some children, instead of responding directly to the subject of the conversation, may say, "Oh, look over there at the piano."

As indicated earlier two-way communication is essential for all learning; it is the basis by which children learn how the world is organized. It is also the basis by which children learn who they are (self-definition), impulse control, and how to determine the intentions of other people. They learn to tell if a situation is safe or dangerous or if their behavior is approved or not. Two-way communication is the only process by which a child gains feedback for his own behavior, thoughts, and feelings. Without such feedback, the child's inner world remains random and fragmented.

It is easy to miss opportunities for two-way communication. If, for example, the adult is not paying close attention, even though ostensibly watching the child, he is not fostering two-way communication. If the adult is talking to the child as the child is acting, and the child is not responding to what the adult is saying but is just going about his play (although the child may look at the adult occasionally), then two-way communication is not taking place. Most devastating to the child's development is when the two-way communication involving smiles, flirtatious glances, looks of annoyance, curiosity, surprise, or disinterest are not present.

It can be hard work to maintain two-way communication. People can begin to lose each other through exhaustion or boredom (e.g., endless repetition). Adults need to try to replenish their energies to keep two-way communication going. Children don't need to have two-way communication all of the time, but they need to have it a reasonable amount of the time. To get down on the floor with the children is to participate with them. If they are crashing trucks and one responds to their gestures, one is interacting with them. Standing aloof and being critical is not interacting.

An adult can interact with children without using words, but through emotions. If a child frowns, the adult can make a smiley face or frown back. Emotional gesturing is intuitive for most people, but some parents, educators, or therapists lack this basic building block. Skilled teachers and day care educators are excellent at emotional gestures; one gifted person can perform like a great orchestra leader, interacting and keeping everyone gesturally connected. Some adults display a lot of animated interaction, but at other times an overburdened person might just sit in the midst of aimless and often somewhat destructive children. When an aimless, self-absorbed, or depressed person does not pull a child into two-way communication, the child loses the ability to organize himself in a logical way. An aimless three- or four-year-old doesn't come from nowhere. There is a lack of two-way communication going on somewhere in that child's life.

Emotional gesturing involves facial expressions, movements of hands and arms (such as pointing), and body posture. The voice, slow or excited, also conveys emotion. The eyes as well are part of facial expression. Awareness of these subtle aspects of the communication system enhances the adult's ability to engage the child in two-way communication.

To foster two-way communication, as part of floor time, it is critical to meet the child on his or her turf. The child is the boss of the floor time drama. There are only two rules: the child can't hurt anyone, including himself, and can't break anything. The adult should, therefore, spend a fair amount of time following the child's lead. If the child wants to crash the cars, let him show the adult how to crash them better. If one worries about educating a child given his overfocus on cars, remember it is possible even to teach a child physics by showing him impact and rebound of his car crashing experiments.

At times, the adult has to intrude himself into the interaction sequence with a child who is not opening and closing circles or who is tuning out. A child who is aloof or indifferent, or who wants to play with a toy by himself, can ignore an adult who says, "Hey, what's that?" If the adult takes a car and moves it alongside the child's car, the child may turn away and keep moving his car and ignore the adult. How should an adult handle a child who doesn't naturally interact, who tunes out? How should an adult get two-way communication going? It is advisable to try the most modest intervention first, such as elaborating on what he is doing, building a garage with one's hands for his car, for example, and trying to elicit his help. If he ignores the garage, the adult can begin to intrude very gently into the child's world. The rule of following his lead is adhered to because the adult is not taking the child to another activity, but is still working with something related to the cars. If the child doesn't voluntarily pay attention to the garage, the adult might block the car's path by moving his hands (a moving garage). The child now has to contend with the adult. As the child pushes away the adult's hand and makes a few sounds, the child has begun to communicate and open and close circles. We now have motor and vocal gestures that are building on the adult's gestures.

With some children who are very withdrawn and aimless, that mild intrusion is what begins to get their attention. Intruding into their world forces them to interact, initially by "Get out of here" actions. The adult then tries to make the interaction playful in a nonfrightening way, by respecting the child's comfort level, in terms of sounds, sights, and movement patterns. By intruding into the area the child is already interested in, whether it's cars or opening and closing doors, over time the adult helps the child get used to interacting. The more repetitive and self-directed the child's behavior, the more important it is not to distract the child, but to join him, and if necessary get in his way so he has to deal with you. You take advantage of his motivation to repeat a pattern and use it to fuel interactions. As the child senses the novelty, pleasure, assertiveness, and mastery of the interaction, he usually begins to initiate more activities on his own. This process works for both very withdrawn children and for very shy, cautious children.

When working with a child who is not using two-way communication, and seems quite reluctant to do so, it is also important initially to demand very little of him. For example, if the child is a verbal child, the adult can put the garage in front of him and ask, "Do you want me to take it away?" All the child has to do is give a "yes" or "no" answer. He can even use gestures—nodding or pointing. Children who don't like to close circles will often be willing to make a little pinky gesture or give a slight nod of the head. However slight the gesture, the child is still communicating in a two-way system. It is important to make communication very easy for the child who doesn't seem to want to communicate and get very involved. The key is to help him get started. Then the process may carry itself.

In a therapeutic or educational setting, it could take a couple of hours or a even a couple of days to sound out a child. But it is necessary to help the child get involved, even if the child responds by pushing the adult away because if the gesture or word is intentional, two-way communication is occurring.

In the psychotherapeutic situation, when a child is withdrawn or unavailable, or just likes to do his own thing and ignore the therapist, the therapist often makes the mistake of just commenting to the child on what the child is doing. If the child is drinking water by himself, the therapist might say, "Oh, you like to drink water," or if the child is smashing cars together, "Oh, you like to crash cars." Meanwhile, however, there is no two-way communication; the therapist is just entertaining himself by his monologue. Such parallel verbalization is akin to parallel play. It is useful at the beginning of therapy to get the child used to the therapist and his voice and to convey interest and support. Later on, with a verbal child, it may even help the child be aware of some of his patterns. But it does not provide an interactive experience. It does not foster differentiation.

After two years, if the child finally looks at the therapist and is willing to relate, the therapist may feel his patience worked. But it doesn't need to take so long to get some interaction going. With the child who is withdrawn, it is necessary to move in gently, but quickly. Occasionally the therapist has to intrude himself, and a parallel commentary is only a beginning step. Parents of children who are not interacting also often comment to the child to try to get some communication going.

They are frightened to intrude, but sometimes it is necessary in a very gentle way to pull the child in. With one very withdrawn child, this therapist found that if one gently put a doll on his leg, he pushed it off. A gentle game evolved ever so slowly of putting the doll on his leg. After a few interactions, he began anticipating the gestures and would move his leg away. Sometimes the therapist would move the doll on his own leg, and the child would nod, indicating approval. The key to such intrusions is to be very gentle and very gradual.

A key principle in two-way communication is to encourage the child's initiative and assertiveness. One of the biggest mistakes is to try to overcontrol the action. If the adult says the word, he wants the child to mimic it. The adult shows the book and wants the child to look at it. The adult wants to be the boss. An adult who is too successful at being the boss might foster a verbal and even bright child, but he might also promote a compliant and passive child.

To encourage the child's initiative, it is necessary to look for opportunities for the child to make discoveries, to take the lead. One can put toys in front of the child and even make oneself into a "toy" to get an interaction going, but then one has to let the child discover how he wants to act, as opposed to acting for the child. By way of example, a therapist described a child who was having trouble learning to take turns in a group setting. The therapist's goal was to get the children to pass the ball around. This particular child would have the ball, and wouldn't pass it along. The speech pathologist would say, in an attempt to get communication going, "Would you give it to me?" and hold her hands out. I asked, "What happens when or if the child won't do it or 'makes a no'?" She said, "I keep trying." I said, "What happens if, after three days, the child is still keeping the ball?" She said, "Well, I probably would finally grab the ball from the child and give it to the other child. He has to learn to take turns!"

What kind of experience is that child getting in this example? In terms of two-way communication, he is learning what can be done to him, but he is certainly not learning about initiative. The goal is to teach taking turns and social communication. When one says, "Give me the ball," and the child says, "No," and one says, "Oh, please?" and the child says, "No," and one says, "Give it to me!" and the child says, "No," three circles of communication have been open and closed. Every time the child says, "No," a circle is closed, and two-way communication is being taught. The child is in charge.

The child's only way of being assertive may be to be negative, to say "No." If the therapist intrudes and takes the ball away in order to get the child to pass it on to another child, the child's initiative is being undermined. There are better ways to assist this child to increase his flexibility. It is the process of two-way communication that is critical. The goal of passing the ball is only a vehicle for interacting. It is always possible to get another ball. Keep up the interaction with him while a second ball is being passed around the circle. One can exchange many gestures trying to encourage him to voluntarily give up the ball. If he tries to get the other ball from another child, the therapist could say, "No," and block his pathway. As the child gets frustrated, and keeps trying to get the second ball, he may close about forty or fifty circles. Some of your best two-way communication occurs when a child is highly motivated. For a child who is not interacting, the ball and passing it along are irrelevant. What is important is exchanging gestures. And when he is being stubborn, you can use his own intensity to open and close many circles. You have to take your eye off your initial goal of getting the ball passed and put it on the more important "process" goal of opening and closing circles.

Thus, two-day communication involves getting down on the floor, following the child's lead, respecting the child, and opening and closing circles of communication with gestures and eventually words. One does not allow the child to tune out by supporting parallel kinds of play. Respecting the child's initiative is critical.

Two-way communication with a child may take place on many different levels. The very simplest kind of two-way communication involves physical touch. When a child feels a touch, he often touches back (the first level of communication). Even when very young babies hug and nuzzle, there is often two-way communication as the baby positions himself as the parent positions herself in response to the baby's movement, and the baby, in turn, moves.

In addition to touch, other senses may be involved in simple gestural communication. A look begets a look. A sound begets a state of attention and a sound in return. One person's shift in body posture leads to a body posture change in another person, which leads to a further shift in the first person's body posture. A clinician often mistakenly assumes that a child is interacting only when the child looks at him. But a vocal or postural or tactile interaction may be occurring even while a child seems to be indifferent, aloof, or aimless. Often these subtle types of interactions may foreshadow more direct looking and obvious signs of pleasure.

Simple patterns of two-way communication lead to more complex patterns. This takes place in two ways: one way is through increasing the number of circles opened and closed in a row as part of a chain. The infant points to a toy; the parent points; the infant moves toward it; and the parent smiles in approval; the infant looks at the parent's face, grins, and speeds up his crawl to reach for the toy. The second way is for the gestures themselves to convey more complicated intentions. The toddler who points to his father's hat and then to his own head may be asking if he can put the hat on. This sequence is more complex than simply vocalizing while pointing to the hat.

Distal communication or communication across distance, which occurs from about eight to twenty months on, means using gestures in a new dimension. Listening and looking become the vehicle for distal communication. A child plays with a tower of blocks and looks up at an adult, who then claps his hands and says, "Hey, that is terrific!" When the child smiles and puts another block on the tower, the adult and child are communicating with each other across space. They may feel as if they are in each other's arms, though they are separated.

Every developing child responds to gestures before words. An eighteen-month-old child understands his mother's motor gestures and the tone of her voice before he understands her words. Even a four-year-old is more sensitive to tone of voice and facial expression than to words. An adult who meets a stranger in an alley who says "I'm a nice person. Tell me what time it is," but who has a menacing look on his face, will pay more attention to the threatening gestures than to the non-threatening words. A four-year-old who intrudes into other people's space by getting up too close and not respecting their privacy is likely to have begun developing the problem between ages one and two, when the rules of social interaction are learned through two-way gestural communication. It is gestures that communicate emotions such as approval or disapproval, and safety or danger.

Chapter 12

Floor Time: Sharing Meanings

After two-way gestural communication, the next goal is to encourage the use of ideas or symbols. The most important way to encourage a child to move from communication through behavior alone to communication with ideas, that is, sharing meanings, is for the educator, therapist, or parent to be available to interact with the child in increasingly complex ways and especially in pretend play. The obvious way a child shares meanings is with words, but even more important to the child is the ability to share meanings through pretend or fantasy play. Five, six, and seven-year-olds, as well as two- and three-year-olds, will use dolls, cars or trucks, or houses to construct dramas. Whether they create simple dramas with cars crashing; more complex dramas with the dolls hugging, fighting, and then reuniting; or grand epics with cars crashing, people arguing, then making up and going to school together, children can share meanings through this kind of make-believe play. In the discussion to follow, the phrases "sharing meanings," "using symbols," "using ideas," and "using representations" are all synonymous.

As indicated, for the educator, therapist, or parent, engaging the child in play where the adult follows the child's lead is a critical way of supporting the use of ideas. After all, it is the idea that is played out in the child's drama that gives the child practice in flexing his "ideational muscles."

In addition to pretend play, the child's use of words, not only descriptively to say, "That's a table or that's a chair," but interactively to convey desires and wishes, is the way in which ideas are exercised in an emotional sense. "Me angry," "Me hungry," "Me want that," "Give me that," "I don't like that," or "I love that," are all ways in which the child conveys feeling using ideas. The word is evidence for the existence of the idea behind the word. Pictures, however can also convey symbolic information as can a complex series of gestures.

Many therapists, parents, or educators feel they are engaging the child in the world of ideas when they are actually engaging the child only in a type of parallel verbalization. For example, the child plays out a scene with dolls having a tea party, holding hands, and being affectionate with one another. Then one of the dolls tips over a tea glass, another one gets angry, and so on. If the therapist only observes this drama, little happens to help the child amplify or use ideas as part of a relationship. If the therapist comments on what the child is doing, but the child ignores the therapist, the therapist is still engaging only in parallel verbalization, without facilitating the child's elaboration of ideas. However, the therapist can engage the child in a discussion that amplifies his ideas. For example, the therapist might encourage the child to elaborate on why one doll got so mad at the other doll when the teacup was tipped. The therapist may enter the teacup drama to speak for one of the dolls by saying, "I'm sorry," whereupon the child might say, "Well, you are still being bad and you have to get spanked 6,000 times." "Oh, please don't spank me." "Well, sorry, that's the way it is." A typical error is to simply describe back to the child what he is doing: "You are feeding your doll so nicely." If the child were able to, he might say, "I already know what I am doing—why don't you contribute some ideas to this drama." Enter the child's world as a play partner, get the interaction cooking. In other words, the goal of the educator, therapist, or parent is to follow the child's lead, enter the child's world of ideas to help the child elaborate and expand those ideas.

As a general rule the adult should try first to get interactive gestures going and build the words and pretend out of the interactive action. In other words, first enter the child's world gesturally and build on interactive action. Do not tell the child what to do or simply ask him questions: interact and pretend.

This sounds easy enough. Most adults are able to do this with eyes closed while day dreaming about something else. Yet, all too often, adults not only engage in parallel verbal commentary, but they may also in some respects interfere with or undermine, rather than help the child's use of ideas. For example, the child who sets up a tea party where one doll becomes frustrated with another doll may feel undermined when the parent says, "Don't you dare bang that tea cup. It's making too much noise," or, "I don't want you to hit the dolls against one another. You may break something." The parent intervenes to treat the pretend as though it is real. He or she gets concerned with the child's play, as if the child were actually out to break one of his dolls to make a commotion, when he was only trying to dramatize a particular relationship pattern through his or her make-believe. When the parent (or educator or therapist) isn't able to enter into the make-believe mode, the child may actually be derailed from his own ability to pretend. In other words, the child who is just learning how to make-believe can easily be diverted into a more "concrete" way of relating where everything is what it appears to be, not what it can be. In the pretend mode, the dolls are playing out a drama. When the parents react to the drama as though it were reality, the child is not allowed to operate in a more advanced way of using ideas or actually to experiment with his picture of the world. Being too literal or too concrete often interferes with the child's progress.

There is another way in which parents, educators, and therapists are too concrete and literal that interferes with the child's attitude about using ideas. For example, the child says, "I want to go out in the rain . . . Now!" The educator, therapist, or parent says, "You can't go out. You must stay in the class-room (house)," and a power struggle ensues. The next day, the child says, "I want to go out," and the adult again treats the child's desire to go out *now* as requiring a literal response of "yes" or "no." On the other hand, the adult may say to the child, "Why do you have to do everything just when you want to?" or, "You seem to think it has to be now." The adult focuses on the child's sense of urgency. The parent and the child in this sense are dealing with a more relevant aspect of the com-munication.

Whenever the parent gets pulled into the child's drama in an immediate and urgent way, the parent may treat the child's reality as the only reality that exists. The child sets up the reality of "I go out now or my world will come to an end." The parent who says, "No you can't go out now," or, "Yes, you can go out now," is reinforcing the child's reality. The parent or therapist who says, "Why so urgent?" or "Now? It has to be just now?" is not accepting the child's reality but pointing out a new reality to the child, and one that is actually more relevant—the child's sense of urgency. Once the child focuses on his own sense of urgency, he is able to take a step back from and reflect on the need, wish, or urgency of the moment. This ability to reflect on one's urges and desires is an important basis for the true use of emotional ideas, symbols, or representations. Time to reason about the urge helps one picture the urge. The child says, "I must go out now," and immediately bangs on the door, without reflecting on the immediacy of his need, even though he is using words. He is not using words or symbols as a means of coping with his sense of urgency. He is still tied to a concrete kind of attitude. Additionally, the more the child and parent discuss or even argue, the more likely gestural and symbolic circles of communication are being opened and closed, giving the child an important learning experience while he is in a state of high motivation. As long as the child's dialogue remains interactive and logical in form, he is "learning."

Consider the following example. A mother came into this therapist's office with her two-and-a-half-year-old who was hit-ting and biting other children. The child said, "I got to go out of the room. I don't want to be in the office." (He is a very verbal, bright child.) The mother said, "You have to wait until we have finished," and he says, "Now!" She got into a power struggle with him about whether he was going to leave then or later. That fairly typical interaction displays a concrete or fixed attitude on the part of an adult whenever a child becomes upsetting. What would be a nonconcrete, more flexible way of dealing with the situation to help the child elevate the interaction to the world of ideas? When the child says, "I got to get out of this office now," instead of taking him literally, by saying that it is either going to be now or not now, the adult should, as indicated above, shift the focus to the urgency of the situation for the child. If the adult says, "No it won't be now," or "Yes, it will be now," he or she is not only getting into a power struggle with the child, but accepts the child's fixed view of the world—"Look there are only two things in this world that count. Either I'm going to be out that door in a second or I'm going to be in here." The adult does not need to join the power struggle to agree that only two options exist. The adult can say, "How come you gotta be the boss? How come you get to decide when you go out the door? How come it has to be now?" To focus on the urgency (i.e., the affect) brings in a new perspective. The child may say, "What? I never thought of it that way." Not taking the child literally opens up negotiation. Why is this so important to the child? This enables the adult to take a step back from a bad feeling. The child is saying, "Either I gotta have exactly what I want or I'm going to be angry," and the adult is telling the child, "Let's take a step away from the urgency of the feeling of the moment and take a look at the situation." Most children who are involved in aggression or other kinds of concrete behavior have parents who are too concrete in the related areas of the child's life. If the parent can become less concrete, develop more of a "Why now?" kind of attitude, the child starts doing better. To find a compromise encourages the child to keep on being a problem solver. To keep dialogue going, within limits, even with an older child, is a key element in promoting a nonconcrete attitude.

The adult has to be able not to be intimidated or scared by the child's feelings. A therapist, educator, or parent who is scared by a child's temper, anger, or jealously tends to become concrete and gets lost. Such an adult needs assistance from someone else—a colleague, a friend, another therapist—in order to gain perspective.

The child who is not able to abstract emotions, label feelings, deal with emotions through make-believe or language, should, if the child is verbal, be helped to label his behaviors. An adult can, in addition to setting limits, say to a four-year-old who is hitting and poking other children, "How do you feel when you do that?" The child may say, "I just like to kick them and poke them when they frustrate me," but he never says he's feeling angry. Without trying to force him by saying, "Aha! You must feel angry," the adult may say to that child, "What are the things you do when you feel like kicking?" and help the child to label all the behavior, such as kicking, poking, hitting, yelling, running around. The next question to ask is, "What do these behaviors have in common?" The child still may not feel the anger inside, but that's the way to help the child describe what he feels inside before or as he is kicking or poking. He may say he feels his muscles tense, he feels like exploding, or he feels like eating. It is important to encourage him to describe his feeling in great detail. These descriptions will initially often be of physical sensations, such as "muscle tense," "feel like jumping," or "feel like exploding." Do not force-feed him by putting such words as *anger* or *excitement* into his mouth.

If the adult lets the child describe the feeling and the behaviors, eventually he will find a label that is appropriate. Obviously, such a dialogue must take place over a long period of time and be very interactive. This dialogue will give the child time to figure out how to use ideas rather than behaviors.

One might divide the use of ideas into two stages: the immediate or concrete use of ideas, which is transitional from behavior to ideas (sort of a behavioral use of ideas), and the abstraction of emotions or affects (using an idea to represent a feeling). It is the abstraction that buys a child time to reason and be able to talk about an urge. It is as if the child says, "I feel mad at you, but I don't have to hit you," or "I feel excited, but I don't have to undress or jump around."

Therefore, there are three ways in which the parent, therapist, or educator facilitates the use of emotional ideas or the sharing of meanings: (1) by joining in the child's world of make-believe; (2) by using words to describe feelings, wishes, and desires; and (3) by questioning the reality of and not giving into the child's sense of urgency in order to help him reflect in a slightly more abstract way than the child would do on his own.

A child who is not using pretend play or words to convey wants and desires never says "I'm mad," or "I'm sad," "I'm angry," or "I feel excited," but only acts out the feelings. One needs to help the child make the transition from acting out the experience, "behaving" it, to instead representing the experience. The behaving child will punch, bite, or kick when angry or will just crash cars when excited. The child who uses ideas can say, "I'm mad" or "I'm angry" and can develop a drama about cars racing with crashes as part of the race, and with good and bad guys competing with one another.

How does one help the child go from one stage to the other when the child seems to be locked into a behavior? It is not helpful to superimpose a pretend drama onto the child's acting out of his experiences. Rather, it is necessary to help the child make the transition naturally (as children do in normal development, between about 16 months and 24 months). As indicated, the first step is to help the child describe the behavior he is acting out and to amplify that behavior. If the child bites, kicks, and pokes when angry, an adult can describe the situation the child is in, such as being yelled at by someone, and what the child tends to do. The child may collaborate in the description. He may be able to describe aggressive behavior he uses but never label any of them as anger or aggression. By describing the behavior the child is likely to evidence in a certain situation, the adult helps the child create categories of behaviors. Categorization is one step closer to the abstraction of a feeling.

In addition to describing behavior, it is necessary to help the child describe what occurs "inside the body" just before and during the behavior. Many children, or even adults, who can't abstract a feeling or talk about feeling angry, sad, glad, or excited, can describe physical sensations in their bodies. In other words, they do not speak about a feeling such as anger, which is a combination of an idea and a sensation in the body; rather they describe only the sensation. They may say that their "muscles feel like they are about to explode," their "body feels tense," or their arms and legs feel "like they have to move." Or, as one older teenager told his therapist, his arm "just felt this sense of pressure, and all of a sudden it was hitting people." One has to help the child describe the sensation in his muscles or stomach or eyes. As the child uses more detail, the metaphors usually become more vivid and more closely related to feelings. "My muscles feel tense, like I have to move them," may change to "they feel explosive," to "they feel like a volcano about to erupt." As one empathetically helps the child describe physical states and categorize behaviors acted out in similar situations, the child can connect the particular sensation with a general category of behavior. He can start to describe a "volcanolike feeling" in his body as associated with his angry behavior. He will gradually begin to label that feeling as "anger." This associative process is similar to how children normally learn when they begin to identify a feeling such as love or anger. They connect different sensations in their bodies with an ability to abstract a category of behaviors, which then is experienced as an "abstracted feeling state."

This process requires great patience. The therapist as indicated should not label the feeling for the child by saying, "You must be angry," "You must be sad," "You must be excited," "You must be feeling loving," "You must be worried about separation or loss." Labeling only intellectualizes and, ironically, lengthens the process. Instead, one may say, "How did you feel when your mother wasn't there?" The child may say, "I don't know what you mean" (if he speaks that directly). The therapist could say, "What was going on when you broke all your toys, or when you were crying and banging your head on the floor? What was happening?" As the therapist proceeds, the child will start to describe his behavior and the accompanying physical sensations.

Once the therapist has helped the child to use shared meanings, that is, abstracted feeling states or emotional ideas, the next step is to assist the child in two ways: to expand the depth of these feelings and expand their range. Expanding the depth of the feeling involves helping the child increase the complexity of his pretend drama. The dolls get mad at one another, and then what happens? One hits the other, one calls the other one a name, they have a big fight, they run away from each other, they come back, and then have another fight. The goal is to move from a simple repetitive theme to deeper, more complex drama that involves a broader range of issues—not just anger, but empathy, love, excitement, assertiveness, fear. The broader the emotional themes that the child can play out or use words to describe, the more he is applying his ability for shared meanings and the broader his emotional world. Some children, for example, will play out only themes of compliant niceness, with hugging and sweet talk. The question is how to facilitate the inclusion in the drama of anger and assertiveness as well. Conversely, when the child plays out only anger and never love or warmth, as well as when the child plays out love and warmth, but never scenes of separation, the goal is to broaden the drama and to make each element in it more complex.

One way to broaden the drama is first to engage the child in interaction by becoming a "discussant" of the pretend play, who helps the child explain what he is doing. Or one can become a partner in the pretend play by taking on the role of one of the characters and helping the child play out the drama. It is also possible in discussions with the child, to interact with him around his ability to use words. If he says, "I'm hungry and want to eat," the therapist should not just say "Yes" or "No," but should have the child amplify and practice using ideas. What does he want? When does he want it? How does it taste, since he likes it so much? When he is angry at his sister, it is not enough to say, "You have to learn to like her." Rather, the therapist should ask him what she did and how he is feeling about it, what the feeling feels like, how intense it is. It is not helpful to be artificial or to interrogate the child as a lawyer would. It is preferable to be empathetic and interested in what the child has to say, either as a player in his pretend play, or as an amplifier and discussant. Cutting off the dialogue doesn't enhance this process. The principle is to support what the child is trying to say in the pretend play or in the verbalization and to help him expand his ideas.

Part of empathizing with the child is to be able to follow his lead. Controlling the drama by inserting one's own ideas about what the child ought to be playing or saying doesn't work. To follow the child's lead, it is necessary to pick up on what the child is trying to say. If he is mad at his parent, therapist, or teacher, he or she needs to find out about all of his feelings by letting him use as many words as possible to describe his anger. If the doll in the pretend drama is mad, it is necessary to find out all about its feelings. Following the child's lead is not always easy, because the adult has to sense where the child is trying to go. He should not lead the child, but be there, perhaps a half-step ahead, to help him move further along. Open-ended questions, such as "What's going to happen next?" are helpful.

Another useful technique is to make summarizing comments about the child's drama, such as, "Let's see, the horse has done A, B, C, D. I wonder what's going to happen next?" Such commentary helps the child feel understood and thus able to take the drama one step further. Similarly, if the child is complaining, for example, about a sibling, about the mother to the father, or about one teacher to another, summarizing one's understanding of what the child has said helps the child then tell the adult more. He knows he doesn't have to repeat what he has already said, because the adult has effectively summarized his feelings. To take the drama one step further, one can ask open-ended questions, either verbally or with a facial gesture, such as, "What next?" "What more do you want to tell me?" One should not structure comments too much. For example, "Gee, that horse has nice curls in his hair. I wonder if you want to curl it?" leads the child to focus on the horse's hair and curling the hair. Such specific comments do not help the child expand the drama in his own way. If, on the other hand, one says, "Gee, there are ten ways in which the pink horse is prettier than the yellow horse. I wonder if there are other things about the horse that are interesting or important," then the dialogue stays open. Or, even if one says to the child, "Gee, you seem to be particularly interested in the horse's hair and tail," that, too, can be an open-ended inquiry or just an empathetic comment even without a question. Open-ended questions, empathetic comments, and summary comments all help the child continue the drama, feel understood, and expand his ideas further.

As part of expanding the drama, it is necessary to keep an eye on both the forest and the trees. The trees are the details of the drama—each way one horse is prettier than another horse, or the ten ways that one car is angry at another car. The forest, however, represents the prevailing theme—that the cars are mad at each other, or the horses are both pretty and each one wants to be the prettiest, or that the baby and the mother really love each other. The summary comment often articulates the theme by encompassing the different elements of the drama for the child. One wants to move back and forth between the specific elements or trees that the child is interested in and help the child amplify those, and comments that summarize and help the child see the forest and expand further.

Another way of helping the child expand the drama is to move back and forth between content and feelings. As the child gets involved in many details of content (the horse has blue ears, a yellow tail, big feet, small teeth), it may become clear that all these particular features of the horse are ways of showing that this horse is better than another horse. After working with the content of the ways this horse is special, one can empathize with the emotion, that is, that the two horses are competing, and one horse wants to be better than the other horse. One gets involved in the content solely to look for an opportunity to bring in the affect or the emotion—competition, anger, loss.

On the other hand, sometimes the child will talk only about the emotions and, for example, say that this horse is mad at the other horse, or this horse loves the other horse, moving from one emotional theme to another. In this case, one may want to amplify the content by asking, "What happened between the two horses that they are so mad at each other? What is the horse mad about?" Ordinarily the adult will intuitively travel back and forth between feelings and content. One needs to consider whether one is hearing mostly content and no emotion, or mostly emotion and no content, in order to help the child amplify both sides of this equation.

One of the hardest parts of the process of helping amplify the child's use of ideas is for the adult to stay with the child's make-believe or dialogue when the content is painful to the adult. For example, when the child says to a parent, "I hate you and I am mad at you," or to a therapist, "I don't want to be here with you. You are bad and you smell," or when the child criticizes a teacher for being unfair, the adult's tendency is to cut off the discussion. The adult is apt to say, "Don't talk to me that way," or to change the subject, or to become bossy and controlling, or to point out the child's failings. It is more important to remember that the child is taking a chance by using words, rather than putting his feelings into behavior. At this point of intense emotion, it is critical to go with the flow and allow the child to elaborate the ways in which he hates the adult and those in which he feels the adult has been unfair to him. After the child fully amplifies his emotions, the adult can, particularly if the child is older than three-and-a-half, raise questions about whether there isn't more to the story than what the child is saying, and to see if the child can understand where his feelings of the moment belong in some overall context. If not immediately, then perhaps later in the day or the next day, he may be able to come back to the moment and understand that his anger is only part of his total feelings toward the adult. It is very important to tolerate the child's feelings and to recognize that the expression of feeling in itself is positive, so long as the child isn't hitting, breaking things, or using language inappropriate to the situation. Although in therapy, using vivid language may be quite appropriate, using four-letter words in public is generally not acceptable. It is often extremely difficult for an adult to deal with a child in a state of intense emotion without undermining the child's use of emotional ideas, when the adult doesn't like the direction of the ideas (e.g., the child is being angry or being disrespectful toward the adult).

It is important not just to tolerate the child's negative feelings toward the adult, but to help the child continue to represent his wishes and feelings, even when upset, frightened, or angry. For example, during feelings of separation, even in a telephone conversation, caregivers can help children put their feelings into words or picture what mommy or daddy is doing, rather than just let the child feel overwhelmed or scared. When the child is angry, one can obviously help the child represent rather than act out his feelings. To the degree parents and therapists can help children represent intense affects, the stability of the representational system, as well as its depth, is facilitated.

It is especially important for the adult, whether therapist, educator, or parent, to beware of feeling bored, aloof or indifferent, or intrusive or angry, and as a consequence, withdraw from the child, change the subject, or try to control the agenda of the child's discussion or play. Even boredom or disinterest is often a sign of some anxiety about the child's ideas, which is unrecognized by the adult. Some parents, teachers, and therapists are uncomfortable with aggressive or sexual themes or those having to do with separation or disapproval. Every adult will have his own Achilles heel, and the more subtle it is, the less aware of it the adult will be. Experienced therapists will usually be aware of their own Achilles heels; that's what makes them experienced. Less experienced therapists or educators or parents will feel bored, antsy, irritable, intrusive, or controlling in regard to what the child is trying to convey. Therefore, the adult should pay attention to negative feelings and regard them as a clue that something is going on that's making the adult feel uncomfortable. Asking rhetorical questions helps adults become more aware of their own problem and helps the child amplify what he is saying, rather than withdraw or intrude. Boredom and apathy usually do not come about because the child has nothing interesting to say. The adult can rationalize his discomfort by saying, "I don't enjoy children" or "I don't find children interesting," but often such an adult finds emotions in general "boring" because they produce anxiety.

One of the most important ways in which the therapist can assist the parent or be an effective consultant to the educator, is by helping adults pay attention to their own reactions to the child's attempt to express feelings or inclinations as ideas. The therapist should remind the parents that they are trying to help the child not only develop a complex drama, but also actually apply his ideas to the different emotional domains of separation, anger, love, intimacy, jealousy, and the like. As the therapist coaches the parent, the therapist should be aware that each parent, depending on his or her own relationship with family and other current relationships, will have blind spots and be sometimes more, sometimes less, able to listen to the child in certain areas. It should be assumed that no parent will be able to listen equally well to all of the child's ideas. Even parents who think they can do such listening are fooling themselves, because some ways they have of listening will be clearly more mechanical and intellectualized and others will be more truly empathetic and emotional. Even the very emotional parent may get overly emotional and overly identify with the child, therefore overwhelming the child with his or her own feelings. The parent who can't stand the child to have feelings of worry and separation may get so concerned that the child begins to reassure the parent instead of elaborating feelings and ideas to the parent. Thus, an adult has many ways of derailing a child from his ability to convey what he has on his mind. The therapist needs to point out to the parents any general difficulty with engaging the child in terms of emotional ideas and specific difficulties in engaging in one or another area.

In summary, the adult should beware of the tendency to overwhelm the child by becoming overly reactive to his feelings, aloof or withdrawn, intrusive or controlling, or to display any other reaction that distracts the child from fully conveying what he has on his mind through play or verbal interaction.

Chapter 13

Floor Time: Categorizing and Connecting Meanings

In addition to engaging, interacting, and fostering the use of shared meanings, floor time helps the child create categories, and connections between categories, for the ideas and meanings that are part of his communications. Helping a child make connections between different ideas, however, can be quite challenging.

Perhaps the most important part of fostering representational differentiation is to help the child open and close his symbolic circles as discussed in earlier chapters. For example, the adult follows the child's lead and amplifies through play or words what the child is doing or saying. Does the child in turn build on the adult's communications? When the child builds on the adult communication (i.e., closes a symbolic circle), he is further differentiating his representational system. He is building a logical bridge between his symbols and someone else's. When the child does not close his symbolic circles, it is important to help him close his circles at the gestural level and simultaneously, or shortly thereafter, close his circles at the

479

symbolic level. In both formal floor time and the numerous spontaneous interactions that occur during the course of a normal day, there are an enormous number of opportunities for helping a child open and close his symbolic circles.

The child may already be verbalizing or playing out particular themes or dramas. For example, the good guys may be fighting the bad guys, with the hero dolls building their defenses against a surprise attack from the evil ones. Simply helping the child elaborate all the elements of his drama, particularly both sides of any potential conflict, is one way to begin the child's journey into categorizing. For example, one might say, "Gee, what makes them good guys?" This question encourages the child to elaborate on how the good guys fight for good, stand up for law and order, never sneak or cheat; or perhaps, how they are just bigger and handsomer or prettier than the other side. One would find out about the child's perception of goodness and badness and the evil characteristics of the bad guys. One might ask, "Gee, what makes them so bad?" The child might respond, "Because they hurt and kill, are greedy and selfish, sneaky and tricky, and they kidnapped the children of the good guys years ago."

There is no substitute for the amplification of all the elements of the drama. In other words, one takes the beginning characterization the child can express, helps the child amplify that characterization, and in so doing, helps the child build categories.

Another way to help the child build and elaborate categories is to encourage him or her to see the whole forest as well as the individual trees. As the child elaborates his categories of goodness or badness, one also helps him see a pattern, with comments such as, "Oh, I can see that these people are all strong, because they are honest and they stand up for the forces of good, and they are fair and don't cheat." In other words, by taking what the child says, repeating it back to him, and summarizing it helps him describe the whole forest and at the same time see how each of his elements fits into the broader category.

It may be especially challenging to help a child elaborate a drama involving "evil" or "bad." A child may create a chaotic drama with people attacking one another, followed by the appearance of a collaboration, then people being overwhelmed or dying, and then people helping one another out. In this confusion, one may have to look very closely to find common themes or labels that can help the child organize the diffuse content. One can encourage the child to tell more about the particular elements in the drama by asking what A is going to do next, or how B is feeling. One can, at the same time, say, for example, "Okay, let's see how we can describe this team or that team," or "Let's see if we can slow down for a second and figure out what's really going on here. I'm getting confused." In this way, the adult helps the child to put elements into a frame of reference. One may say, "Well, I'm not sure who's fighting whom, and what's going on, and who's going to win and why." The child may say, "Okay, here are the good guys, here are the bad guys." This adult commentary can help the child subsume his particular ideas or the particular content of his drama under general categories.

For the child who becomes fragmented and overwhelmed with the emotionality and detail of the moment, the best approach is NOT to further focus on details but to help him be aware of the fragmentation. The most relevant categorization for this type of child may be the theme of chaos: "everything is so confused" or "so wild."

Some children are great at abstraction; they see the forest but not the trees. Such a child may say, "Well, the good guys have had a long history of being upset with the bad guys, and so they are now having a war." The outline of the drama may be clear, but the child never fills in the details. One never knows who is fighting whom, or what the battle is like, or what kind of weapons they are using, or whether the bad guy said something nasty to the good guy. To help this child identify the specifics, one might say, "Well, let's see how this battle plays out." "Who is doing that," and so on. The child's ability to construct categories should be such that he can see both the overall design and the individual parts that make it up.

In addition to the amplification of the elements and themes of the child's dilemmas or conflicts, one may wish to encourage connections between categories by going back and forth between the child's emotion and the content of his drama. The emotions, such as feeling happy or excited, can play the role of the forest, as an organizer of the particular content. "They are doing A, B, C, and D because they are mad." At other times, however, the specific emotions can be the trees, the elements in the drama—who's mad, who's happy, who's excited. Going back and forth between the emotion and the content not only helps the child abstract his meanings, affects, and feelings, but also helps the child begin categorizing.

Elaborating and categorizing emotions leads to building connections. How, what, and why questions, such as, "Why is A doing that to B?" or "Why is the bad guy mad, and how did he get mad?" or "How are the good guys going to get the bad guys and why did they want to trap them that way?" often help the child begin making connections or building bridges. On occasion, an interrogatory manner may interrupt the flow of the child's make-believe play. One can simply wonder out loud, as part of the drama, for example, "Gee, how are they going to do that?" "I wonder what that is? I wonder why?" Such comments or questions often spur the child on to reflect and help build the bridges.

At times, the tendency to use how, what, or why kinds of questions can be misused to force an interpretation of the child's drama beyond the child's own capacity or inclination. To the child who is playing out a drama with wolves attacking bears who are sitting around a fire reading to one another, the parent or educator or even the clinician may be tempted to ask, "Why do the wolves want to attack the nice bears? Is it that every time people are warm and close, something dangerous happens?" This kind of comment suggests to the child how the two themes are linked. While such an interpretation may be useful at an advanced stage of the treatment, it would not be appropriate at the beginning stages of floor time. The how, what, and why questions should be used to amplify, not to interpret. They should be used to enable the child to construct his own bridges, not to establish a connection that the adult may have in mind. Therefore, one might wonder about the wolves' desire to attack the bears just when they seemed so happy with one another, in order to help the child make a connection between the calm warmth and shared intimacy of the bears and the chaos and the aggression of the attack of the wolves.

To assist in the eventual categorization and connection of meanings, the therapist may have to help the child elaborate on meanings that are only hinted at and not put fully into the form of ideas. For example, on the one hand, the bears may be reading books, hugging and cuddling each other, and while there also may be an occasional thunderstorm or an occasional wolf lurking, the child never develops a connection. Comments such as, "Gee, the bears seem so happy and, while there's an occasional thunderstorm or a wolf, they seem so safe and happy it's as if nothing bad ever happens to them," may encourage the child to eventually say something about the lurking danger.

At times, there will be a superficial quality to the drama; it may lack intensity. Perhaps tea parties with smiling faces and the routine of filling and emptying cups is played out over and over again without much depth or feeling. One can again belabor the obvious to wonder aloud, "Gee, it's so nice that they fill those nice tea cups over and over again." Such a comment, if spoken in a positive and respectful way, builds a bridge and opens the door to exploration of feelings. The child might say, "Yes, that's all they like to do, because they don't want to do anything else." "Oh, why don't they like to do anything else?" you might ask. Or the child may say, "Oh, you think that's all they do? Well, at night when the light goes out, you should see what they really do." The child may go on to create monsters and witches and ghosts to populate the evening. When one draws the child's attention to the possibility that he has a vested interest in shaping the drama in a certain way, one is creating a bridge to other possibilities—additional dreams, dramas, and feelings.

Related to the depth of the drama, it is important to be aware that in trying to foster the opening and closing of symbolic circles of communication, one can easily become lost in the details of the child's pretend play or verbalizations. For example, the adult may say, "What's this?" "What happens next?" "What's the color of the car?" In focusing on details of content the adult may lose sight of the fact that it is the child's affective or emotional tone that organizes and gives direction to his thoughts. Sometimes, for example, adults and children get involved in a sing-song or contrived rhythm, where the affect is bland and the ideation a bit fragmented. Adults may talk in an overly formal slow, mechanical manner; for example, the child says, "Look at my car." The adult: "Nice car. What color is it?" The child: "Blue. It goes zoom!" The adult: "Yes, and where is it going?" The child: "Blue car outside." Adult: "Yes, that's our car. Where are we going with it next?" Child: "Going home." Adult: "That's right. Good."

In this example, the child gets a bit fragmented. He goes from the make-believe car to the blue car outside without any bridge or connector. Also, the adult is carrying the dialogue in a fragmented way that continues to stretch out details. The child gets practice using words. But after the child already has command of many words, focusing on details doesn't necessarily help the child organize or give intention to his words. The adult needs to empathize with and relate to the child's affect and help the child use his emotions to give direction to the drama. For example, the child says, "Look at my car!" The adult: "I see it." The child: "It goes fast, zoom!" The adult: "I can see that. It looks exciting that it's going so fast." The child (with a big smile): "Watch, I can make it go like a rocket ship." The adult: "Wow, that's a powerful rocket." The child (beaming with pride): "Here it comes." In this example, the child develops the theme of power, with the adult empathizing with the child's affects rather than just the details. By focusing on the affect and letting the tone of his voice convey natural affect, the adult supports the child's naturally developing capacity for representational differentiation.

It is important to "go with the flow" or take what the child gives. It is not helpful to bring up out of the blue a particular theme or idea, even though there may be good reason to believe that it is in the back of the child's mind—something the child worries about or is interested in. The child will always provide clues to the particular drama he is not elaborating on. The cautious child who is just filling up the teacups suggests by his tension and avoidance of anything else that there is indeed something else out there. One can comment on the process, the way the child relates to you, in a respectful way, to draw the child's attention to his own constriction, his own lack of range or depth. "Gee, I can tell you like to choose your words carefully."

It is also important to be aware that the avoidance of certain themes is an aspect of the child's process or way of relating. The child communicates by what he says, but also by what he doesn't say. For example, the child who always has the frustrated bears "make nice-nice" and never elaborates themes of anger may be avoiding this area of feeling and thought. The omission of this theme is a communication. Helping the child categorize and connect these meanings to others is often helpful. "The bears seem to wish only to be nice. The meaner the wolves are to the bears, the nicer they become. How come?" The child may over time, in bits and pieces, play out themes dealing with fear of aggression to make clear why the bears only like "nice-nice." The same approach is important for the child who only plays out competition and never plays out love or collaboration.

Over time, it will become clear that the child varies in his capacity for elaborating and differentiating his inner world. Certain emotions such as anger, separation, or neediness may be associated with less differentiated interactions. Cohesive and organized elaborations will ebb and flow with fragmented ones. As one helps the child stay with intense affects, and represent and connect them to one another and build on the adults representations as well, one will observe the child's ego develop the capacitites for an organized sense of self, a stable representation of others, reality testing, impulse control, a stable mood, and learning.

Floor time involves helping a child communicate at a number of levels at once. Floor time involves helping a child focus and engage, enter into two-way gestural communication, construct and communicate meanings, and categorize and connect meanings. The clinician may work directly with the child as well as with the parents to facilitate these processes which are at the foundation of healthy emotional and intellectual development.

Chapter 14

Floor Time: Problem-Solving

For children over three years of age, in addition to following the child's lead in floor time, it is helpful to engage the child in a fifteen- to twenty-minute problem-solving discussion—a reality-based exercise that allows the parents and the child or therapist and the child to share the agenda and attempt to problem solve together.

For example, the parents can bring up for discussion the fact that the child hit another child at school or his reluctance to go to sleep; they can explore whom the child played with or what they did. The child may be reluctant to enter into an orderly dialogue that is reality-based; he may prefer to escape into fantasy or pretend play. Some children will resort to, "I don't know," "I can't remember," will attempt to turn on the television, or to deflect the conversation to something more immediate such as, "Let's play a game."

Children who are reluctant to engage in this highly differentiated mode of thinking that supports the fourth process of categorizing and organizing affects show that they need more practice. One must start at whatever stage the child has reached

487

and help him, step by step, exercise this capacity to develop the problem-solving aspect of his personality. The avoidant child who says, "I don't remember," can be helped by cuing the child to recall the events of the day. The child who escapes into fantasy can be brought back to reality by a parent who supports him and empathizes with him about his wish to do pretend play and how hard it is to talk about school or friends. The goal is to empathize with the escape route that the child develops for himself; it is an indicator of the way the child sees the world. A problem-solving philosophy is also helpful for the younger child as well. Even the preverbal child can be helped to collaborate in problem solving by the parents; for example, gestures can be used to convey to a toddler that together they can put away the toys or carry the coat upstairs or get the hair brushed. The patient collaborative spirit rather than doing it for the child or ignoring the child is the key.

The problem-solving discussion should not be a lecture; it should be interactive. The child should be opening and closing circles of communication by building on the parent's comments with comments of his own. Every time the child closes a symbolic circle, it is a miniature practice session in connecting two ideas—the parent's idea with the child's own idea. This process is, in fact, the way representational differentiation occurs in normal development.

It is important to engage in problem-solving discussions in relationship to all the age-appropriate emotional themes. For example, with a child who is having trouble representing aggression, a parent should discuss how he feels just prior to hitting another child or how he feels just before withdrawing or avoiding a problem at school or home.

As a part of problem-solving time, the caregiver should help the child observe how his specific behavior is part of a bigger pattern. For example, the child is whining for the parent to do something for him, such as put food on his fork. In problem-solving discussions around this event, the parent can say "No, I won't," or "You do it for yourself," or "Stop whining."

Alternatively, however, the parent can focus on the larger pattern; the child enjoys being passive and having the parent do his thinking for him. (This will often be based on an assumption, such as, "You are supposed to do everything for me and I have an inalienable right to whine until I get you to.") By focusing on the larger issues rather than just food on the fork, the parent creates an awareness in the child of a certain pattern that they disagree about. By identifying this larger pattern, the parents are fostering self-observation, perspective taking, and ultimately, a more collaborative spirit in the child. Even though the child may whine and cry, and refuse to give in, it is far better for the battle to be over the big issue than over the specific details.

The sequence of feelings that precede a problem behavior is helpful for both the child and the parents to understand. Months of work may be required for the child and therapist or parent to reconstruct this set of feelings. Initially, it may be just a blur to the child, expressed by "I don't know" or vague hems and haws. He may escape into fantasy, avoidance, or concrete games. To patiently empathize with the child's difficulty in knowing how he felt may facilitate, slowly but surely, some capacity for the child to represent his feelings. A child may progress from saying, "I don't know," to "My hand just wanted to do it," to "My muscles felt tense," to "I just wanted to hit him," to "He frustrated me," to "The frustration felt like a volcano welling up inside me," to "I felt like I was about to explode," to "I felt so mad, I just wanted to bite his head off." The more the child can abstract his own feelings with metaphors that convey true affect, the less he will need to discharge the underlying impulse directly into behavior. In essence, the ability to represent is the antidote for the tendency to discharge or inhibit. To represent means that one can expose a feeling to reason and integrate that feeling with other feelings. The more profound and advanced this ability, the better one is able to reason. In a sense, the ability to construct and differentiate representations is a first step in sublimating impulses. When the child is cognitively able, it is also helpful to have the child anticipate challenging situations, likely feelings, and the automatic or reflexive behaviors that follow the feelings, as well as explore other options. "Will Johnny try to take your toys again tomorrow? How will you feel? What will you do? What else could you do given how you feel and how the other person feels?"

In addition, it is important to realize that problem-solving discussions and representational differentiation will not occur without firm limits. The child who can give in to his impulses won't feel the need to represent his feelings; acting them out is too satisfying. Firm limits need to be set in a broad and nonintrusive way. The choice of what to limit should give the child the maximum opportunity to negotiate issues that are not of critical importance. One mother, who was trying to involve her child in a discussion, told him to sit still, not move the ball on his lap, and take his finger out of his mouth; she attempted to control every aspect of his behavior. It was not surprising that neither she nor he had any energy left for more important limit-setting, such as not hitting other children. Parents should allow children maximum freedom in areas that are not all that important, such as whether they jiggle their arms when they talk or walk around during a discussion. It is not necessarily disrespectful for a child to move around when he is thinking and talking if he is more comfortable that way, and especially if it helps him organize his thinking.

Therefore, there are two approaches that foster development: floor time and problem-solving time. Floor time techniques foster a sense of shared attention and engagement, two-way communication, and the elaboration of emotional themes in symbolic or representational forms. To some degree, floor time also enhances the ability to differentiate or categorize representations. To a lesser degree, problem-solving also fosters engagement, shared attention, and opening and closing gestural circles of communication (two-way communication). However, logical problem-solving dialogue mainly fosters, for children three years old and older, the reality aspects of the fourth process of emotional thinking or representational differentiation. Problem-solving approaches are especially challenging for children with developmental delays. The following examples will illustrate these challenges which in reality exist on a continuum.

INCREASING COMMUNICATION DURING PROBLEM-SOLVING TIME WITH A DEVELOPMENTALLY DELAYED CHILD

Johnny, age three, occasionally says a few words. Over half the time, he ignores his mother, but sometimes, he points to the refrigerator to indicate that he is hungry. His mother's natural tendency is to say, for example, "Do you want some ice cream?" He'll say, "Yes," and she will give him what he wants, thereby closing a circle of communication as part of a logical discussion.

However, the mother could close six or seven circles with another kind of dialogue. Instead of, "Do you want some ice cream?" she could say, "Oh, what do you want?" If the child looks as if he does not understand, she can mimic his expression by saying, "I don't know?" The child is likely to make an "I don't know" gesture with his hands. Then the mother can offer a gradual approximation of what the child wants, accompanied by multiple cuing of choices. (The mother should not make it easy for the child; he should have to work for it.) She should ask, "Do you want something to eat?" and point to her mouth. He might nod his head and say, "Yes," and she could ask, "What?" If he looks blank again, she could mimic him to give him a few seconds to see if he can name the food he wants. If he can't, she should then list four or five choices—popsicles, milk, bread, and so forth. If he looks blank again, she could again say something like, "Well, let me help," and then narrow the choices down to three and show him pictures or the real things so that the child could indicate what he really wants. The mother could say further, "Do you want to open the refrigerator yourself?" pointing to him and gesturing toward the refrigerator door, or ask if he wants her to open it. The child might decide to do it himself. A ten-second interaction about food can become a two- or three-minute interaction with six or seven circles closed in sequence. These interactive sequences are best done when the child is motivated to communicate. There is nothing like a child who wants his favorite dessert or feels he needs to go outside now, or has to have a certain toy, to encourage the closing of many circles. The rule is, never close just one circle when you can close six or seven.

The general principle illustrated here is to take advantage of a naturally motivated state in order to try to teach children to close as many circles as possible. One must always begin very gradually. Without supplying the answer or making it easy for the child, one must always ask the why, how, or what question first. If the child can't answer, one cues the child by beginning with the maximum range of choices and then narrowing the choices. The more circles one closes as one narrows the choices the better. Combining gestures with one's words is the most effective way to facilitate the opening and closing of circles.

PROBLEM-SOLVING AND REALITY-BASED DIALOGUES WITH CHILDREN WITH PERVASIVE DEVELOPMENTAL DELAYS OR DYSFUNCTIONS AND SEVERE RECEPTIVE LANGUAGE DIFFICULTIES

Children who are nonverbal and only irregularly capable of intentional gestural communication often have difficulty interacting with clinicians or parents. Clinicians mistakenly tend to make complicated statements to these youngsters about their emotions and to keep up a running commentary on the child's affect and the child's behavior. A therapist might say, "Johnny is angry at the teacher," if Johnny looks angry or is biting, kicking, or throwing a ball at the teacher. Or when Johnny is obviously wanting to do something, he might comment, "Johnny wants to go to the refrigerator." Or, if Johnny is interested in a toy, say, "Johnny likes opening and closing the gate on that house."

It is perhaps not surprising that such children develop idiosyncratic speech patterns, given this kind of highly idiosyncratic dialogue. For example, let's assume that two-and-a-half-year-old Johnny, who has severe developmental delays, has receptive and expressive language abilities equivalent to those of a seven-month-old. If one observed a dialogue such as the one outlined above, with a normal seven-month-old, one would say that the clinician or parent was interacting in a stilted, mechanical, unnatural way. If one analyzed the interaction on videotape, one would find that such a parallel commentary on the child's behavior offers little opportunity for reciprocal interaction. The communication is one way; the parent comments on the child, the child often does not acknowledge or respond with gesture, words, or expression to the adult's comment.

This type of commenting is part of a long tradition in work with children, because one tends to speak this way with older children who have good receptive language skills and are quite verbal, but who choose not to talk at the moment. One comments on their affect in the hope that they hear, even if they may not always acknowledge one's remarks.

However, one must consider whether such a tactic has any role other than to keep the adult busy and feeling useful. In fact, one could argue that the exercise distracts the adult from the more important work of "creating interactive opportunities"—helping the youngster open and close circles of communication by creating a pattern of gestures that one would normally see in a six- to seven-month-old.

Although these severely delayed children often have the language ability of a normal six- to seven-month-old, they may differ from a child that age in many ways, due to the unevenness of their motor, language, and affective development. Nonetheless, the child's opportunity to make progress depends on getting him into interactive patterns that encourage him to take the initiative, the adult to respond, and the child to build on the response. This unit of interaction, the simple opening and closing of the circle, is the building block for natural, spontaneous, and, more importantly, purposeful and meaningful communication on the child's part. Any other type of communication will be mechanical and less helpful to the child. The problem-solving discussion with a delayed child must begin with helping him be intentional rather than focusing on words or symbols.

Therefore, when the child is wandering aimlessly or banging his fists angrily on the floor, therapists, parents, or educators should create an interactive opportunity by positioning themselves in such a way that the child must engage and interact with them. For example, if a child is opening and closing a door perseveratively, instead of saying, "Johnny likes to close the door," or trying to distract Johnny, one might insert a finger in the door. If the child indicates (not necessarily with words, but with gestures or by grabbing the finger and pulling it out of the way), "Get your finger out of the door," the adult should point to the finger and look helpless. Such simple, direct, and interactive communication comes closer to the way one would normally interact with a seven- to eighteen-month-old.

It is unfortunate that sometimes the therapist interferes with what the child wants to do, but the therapist is actually drawing the child into interactive opportunities, as opposed to letting the child perseverate or engage in parallel behavior.

To give another example, if a child is having a tantrum, the parent, rather than saying, "Johnny mad" or "Johnny upset," which Johnny won't understand, should try to comfort the child. The parent should move in very gradually using deep pressure on the back, some rhythmical movements, and rhythmical vocal tone, saying, "Let's calm down, be calm, relax." The parent should not expect the child to understand the words but the tone. The child may turn away, but such a gesture is a response to the parent's behavior. The parent can attempt to comfort the child again; the child may again turn away. In this sequence, they are opening and closing circles of communication.

It is preferable that these circles be positive rather than negative. If the child is perseverating by moving a car, for example, the parent may very slowly move a car in the direction of the child's car, and the child may begin an interaction pattern car-to-car. Or if the child is trying with difficulty to reach something, the parent can look at the child and point to himself, and slowly begin to assist the child. If the child accepts the parent's assistance, with an eye or hand gesture, that gesture, too, closes a circle of communication.

Part of creating interactive opportunities relates to the vocal gestures of the adult. Not infrequently, therapists and parents fall into a rhythmical pattern of sing-song baby talk with a language-delayed child. However, overly soft sounds are more appropriate to lull a child to sleep than to encourage the child to interact. The sing-song tones do not have the normal conversational rhythm with its expectations, crescendos, and variations. Therefore, it is often useful to help parents talk to their children in a normal tone and rhythm using simple words and phrases, while supporting the words with lots of gestures. For children with delays, problem-solving and reality-based dialogues begin with intentional gestures. On the other hand, when therapists or parents carry on endless parallel commentary, or forms of one-way or stereotyped communication, the ability of the child to initiate and participate in self-motivated intentional interaction can remain severely limited.

Chapter 15

The Six-Step Process to Meeting Emotional and Behavioral Challenges

Another dimension of floor time and problem-solving time is its use as a foundation for a six-part process that helps children cope with many challenges, from handling aggression to building self-esteem. This process is most appropriate for older, verbal children, but elements of it can also be applicable to younger, less verbal children.

Step 1 is to make sure there is a good baseline of floor time that incorporates a sense of shared attention, engagement, and two-way communication involving gestures and ideas. Such a baseline leads to the establishment of rapport, warmth, and intimacy, necessary to a sense of initiative and mastery for collaborative problem solving.

Next, one uses the problem-solving approach, that is, the logic of exploring the world of ideas, to help the child identify the nature of his challenge. Whether this challenge is curbing his aggression, dealing more effectively with peers, or mastering a difficult subject at school, one wants to help him articulate the goal from his perspective. One wants also to help him articulate why he might be involved in a self-defeating pattern in trying to reach his goal. Perhaps the child behaves aggressively because he is mad at his parents, or because he is frustrated. Perhaps he wants to be "the boss" all the time. By a series of problem-solving discussions, one tries to tease out the child's perspective on what he is doing and why he is doing it. One also helps the child anticipate challenging situations, associated feelings, reflective behaviors, and other options. As the child becomes aware of his own feelings, if cognitively sophisticated enough, he can relate potential options to his feelings. He should also be helped to consider the other person's feelings. An adaptive option deals with both. The goal of problem-solving discussions is not a particular answer but a process of reasoning that anticipates situations, for self and others and related options.

At the same time, one implements step 3, which is to help the child find a more effective way, not only to accomplish his goal, such as curbing aggression or feeling better about himself, but to do so in a framework that meets his own objectives. In this way the child is enabled to be close to certain friends, to get more attention from his parents, to deal with his frustration, to feel like a boss. How can he have his cake and eat it too? In step 3 it is important to empathize with the child's perspective and help him think about meeting his own needs more flexibly. Being aware of his own needs is of enormous help to a chlid in finding a better solution for himself.

In step 4, one breaks the goal down into as many parts as possible, so that the child can have a sense of success as he masters one step at a time. In curbing aggression, for example, he may try to control himself initially only at school. He may only gradually move to trying to be nice and supportive to other people as well. Sleeping problems, toilet training, various "habits" can also be approached in "tiny" steps. A typical example is a child who is perhaps trying to master a particularly difficult subject at school. It is important for the parent and the educator to break down the challenge into as many steps as possible, so that there can be a sense of mastery along the way. The child who is having trouble with his math facts, for example, often has trouble picturing quantity. He doesn't have a way of intuitively knowing that ten is twice as big as five, and twenty is twice as big as ten. If one asks such a child to show quantity with his hands, he may make ten look as if it is twenty times bigger than five or only a tiny bit bigger than five. Developing a sense of picturing numbers in terms of quantity is often a first step in learning math facts and numbers. So if one just tries to make a child memorize better, he will feel like a failure. On the other hand, one can play with the child's favorite blocks and have him stack them up, ten and then five, and look at them. As a second step, without the blocks, one can have him show with his hands (and his imagination) what the ten and the five look like. Then, as a third step, one can begin with very easy numbers, like $1 + 1 = 2$ and $2 + 2 = 4$, and make sure that he can always come back to this ability to picture without concrete props. By breaking down the task into a series of steps, one may help him gradually learn his math facts. The challenge is to break down a goal into many small steps that meet the child's need for satisfaction, and avoid self-defeat.

Step 5 is the establishment of firm limits on misbehavior or patterns of avoidance. Often children won't want to practice, even when a task is broken down into small, doable steps. Children may prefer to watch television. Children may not want to curb their aggression, because it feels good. Here's where firm limits become important. The principle of firm limits includes: (1) definition of the limits through negotiation with the child, so that he understands what the limits are and can have some input into defining what seems to him to be fair sanctions for his misbehavior; (2) being firm in the implementation of the limits agreed upon (or if not agreed upon, reasonably set). An important caveat is to set limits only on one or two problem areas at a time and to set limits on categories of behavior rather than individual behaviors (e.g., on hurting others rather than just on hitting Sally). Furthermore, incentives should be created and constructed so that the child feels successful most of the time.

Step 6 requires application of the principle that whenever limits are increased, floor time needs to be increased as well. There is a tendency to get into power struggles with children as limit-setting increases. Sustaining a framework of good will may be hard with a child who is already angry at the adult about the limits. "Hanging out" with the child becomes imperative in order to be in his presence, so that he can work out some of his angry feelings and feel the adult's closeness and interest in him. Therefore, one should always increase floor time as one increases limits.

The multistep process just described serves as a basis for addressing many common problems: sleeping and eating problems, aggression, separation anxiety, self-esteem problems, and even learning problems at school. These six steps can be viewed as an extension of the basic floor time problem-solving technique, applied in particular ways to particular problem areas. The process can be used by the therapist directly with the child, by parents on their own or with the therapist's assistance, and by educators with the assistance of the therapist and/or the parents.

Chapter 16

Floor Time: Different Types of Children (Shy, Withdrawn, Angry, Distractible, Negative, Concrete, Clinging)

While every child is special and unique, some fall into familiar patterns: a child may be a bit shy, more outgoing, quick to anger, or get disorganized easily. Although it is helpful to recognize such differences, it is also necessary to describe what the child is like in order to figure out what one knows that may help one understand why the child is the way he is. The goal is to help him use his special qualities rather than to allow them to become liabilities that make life more difficult for him.

THE EXCESSIVELY SHY CHILD AND THE WITHDRAWN CHILD

Some shy children are very sensitive. They might be sensitive to the way someone looks at them, to the loudness or pitch of

501

a voice, or to the way one touches them. Some children display physical differences in the way they react to touch, sound, bright lights, or being moved around in space.

One kind of shy child (a four-year-old for example) is cautious in part because experiences involving sound, sight, or movement can be overwhelming. These children warm up to new situations very gradually; they "go into the pool one toe at a time." All educators are familiar with children who come into the classroom in the fall and are very slow to warm up to new children, to the teacher, and to the physical surroundings. In a couple of months, such a child may be moving more into the group, approaching more corners of the room, playing with more of the toys, and asking the teacher for help, rather than keeping to himself. Such a cautious, sensitive child may be saying, "I'm interested in you. I want to be a part of the world, but I need to do it at my own pace," which is a very gradual one. For this child, circle time, group time, and recess may be a little more scary than one-on-one play, sitting at his desk drawing, or talking to the teacher.

Another kind of shy child is not necessarily overly sensitive to experiences, but may enjoy marching to his own drummer; that child has a harder time tuning in to others. He may, in fact, be just the opposite of the overly sensitive, shy child and may be, in some respect, undersensitive to words or sounds or touch or things he sees. In order to begin tuning in, that child needs someone to talk to him for a minute or two. He seems to be tuned in to his inner voice, so that when someone starts talking to him, he only seems to be listening, and only after a while does he recognize that someone is talking to him. Then when he says, "Would you repeat that?" one can easily become irritated and say, "But, I've already told you." But in fact you haven't really told him; one has been talking to his face but not to his mind. These children can appear withdrawn or unavailable; they differ in the way they react to touch, sound, lights, or to being moved around in space. They may require not a lot of time to warm up but a lot of wooing and pulling in by the teacher and the other children. They may love relationships and love to be involved, but it's not natural for them to seek out experiences.

These two types of shy children need different kinds of help. To respect the first child's need for caution, for example in a classroom situation, an educator may want to empathize with how new things are and how scary they can be. It is helpful to encourage the child to talk about how he experiences new situations—playing with other children, doing a new kind of drawing, or listening to a new kind of music. As he shares his feelings, it is possible to gradually increase the number of experiences available to him. An educator must try to break down into small steps the way the child is wooed into the group, into relationships, or into different kinds of academic exercises. He must know that someone appreciates that he likes to take things slowly and is on the same wavelength with him. He should feel that it doesn't make any difference how long it takes him to get where he is going; that it is only important that he achieves a goal and makes progress. If a particular challenge looks too hard, such as sitting around in circle time, the educator shouldn't give up on it, but neither should he or she force this type of child to "jump into the water." One breaks down the task into smaller steps: he might be in a little circle in a corner of the room with just one other child, and then a second child, and then a third child, and then a fourth child, until he becomes comfortable enough to take his small group and bring it into the larger group. So the key for the shy, oversensitive child is to be very supportive and empathetic, as one helps him take very gradual steps.

Whether doing floor time or working in a group with the oversensitive child, the same pattern holds. One wants to be aware of all the processes or levels of floor time: attending and engaging; two-way communication (beginning with gestures); interacting with ideas or words, both in pretend play and in discussions; and connecting up these ideas or words, that is, emotional thinking. It is necessary to realize that the child is only gradually being exposed to a greater and greater state of shared attention, engagement, and more complex two-way communication. The child may start off able to communicate very, very tenuously when one is kind and nurturing—giving him juice, for example. Or if he is shy about taking a toy elephant and putting the soldier on the elephant, one can help him by picking up the soldier and putting it next to the elephant, so that he has only to pick the soldier up and move it over another inch. By the second or third month, one can encourage him to move beyond dependency. If he asks the adult, by pointing his finger, to bring the elephant over, the adult might point back to the elephant and to him, to indicate that the adult fully expects that he can crawl over and get the toy himself. One hopes that he can get to the point where he can assert himself and flex his muscles to have the elephant and the soldier fighting other elephants. As he asserts himself physically, he should become more assertive in his play as well. One is constantly trying to broaden the range of the child's interactions in different emotional areas—from nurturing to assertiveness, and also coping with anger.

At the third stage of using ideas in make-believe play and language, one might observe not just whether the child picks up the elephant or one gives him the elephant, but the kind of drama he actually plays out with the elephant. Initially it may be the elephant just drinking water, but eventually it may be the elephant fighting off all the other elephants who want to get to the water first. He is gradually expanding his horizons, not only at the level of behavior, but also as he uses make-believe play at the level of ideas.

Similarly, at the fourth level of using reason, logic, and thinking, the child may progress from being barely able to ask for something, such as chalk to draw on the blackboard, to arguing about why his drawing is better than another child's drawing.

It is necessary to break down these processes into many small steps to achieve progress in the way the child engages and establishes two-way communication; the kinds of dramas or pretend themes he develops; and how he applies his reasoning to interactions with a therapist or educator. Floor time is a wonderful opportunity to bring him along very gradually. By following his lead and yet always trying to add another dimension to his interactions and play, it is possible to help him experiment with becoming more assertive and self-confident.

The key for the oversensitive child is to respect his uniqueness and to use his caution and methodical approach—his focus on detail and his concern with doing things gradually—to his own advantage, to establish a good internal sense of competence. It is a mistake, on the one hand, to throw him into the water. He may be overwhelmed and scared. He may do something because he is forced to, but he will not necessarily develop confidence as a result. On the other hand, if one leaves him alone on the assumption that he will do whatever it is when he is ready, he may never get ready. He may decide that the ostrich approach of keeping his head in the sand will allow him not to have to do anything differently. One wants to find a comfortable middle ground.

The other type of shy child, who tends to march to his own drummer and has a hard time tuning in to words or other experiences, often tends to withdraw. He is not scared, but it may be that during group activities at school, for example, he requires a lot of extra effort, energy, and activity to pull him into the group and to keep him involved with others. An educator would approach this child somewhat differently than the overly cautious type of shy child, considering the four developmental levels in floor time. In order to sustain his attention, it is not necessary to introduce new experiences so gradually, but one has to use great energy and enthusiasm in wooing him. One may have to do 75 percent of the work initially to woo him in. One will need to be very animated in facial expressions, talk in a loud voice, and then vary the pitch quite a bit. A signal that one is succeeding is that his eyes may brighten up as one works to keep him attentive and engaged and to elicit positive emotions and pleasure on his face. One may work on interactions between the child and other children in the group, when the other children are energizing him and pulling him in. They may have to play very exciting and interesting games to keep him mobilized. For example, a game that requires him and the other children to imitate each other may particularly intrigue him, whereas a game of drawing a picture side-by-side with another child may lead him to tune out, because he won't naturally look at the other child's drawing.

At the stage of two-way communication, one may see that this child tends not to close his circles of communication. A therapist may say to him, "Look at what my horse is doing." He may look at the therapist for a second, but then go back to his duck, ignoring the horse. The therapist may have to pull him in again by saying, "You didn't say anything about my horse"; he may give the therapist a look, mutter, and go back to his duck. Perhaps the third or fourth time, he will say, "Your horse better stay away from my duck." When he says that, he's closed his circle. It may take several more tries for him to build on the therapist's responses and get real two-way communication going—a look in his eye or a smile or a hand gesture or an actual verbal comment. The therapist may have to do a lot of work to help this child close three or four circles in a row.

Although the therapist establishes two-way communication, each time the child may pull away and go back into his world, as though he enjoys his own thoughts and ideas better than those of others. The appearance may not be entirely accurate. The child is comfortable with his own ideas and finds that figuring out what other people are saying is more work. He finds that keeping to himself is easier, not necessarily more interesting and exciting. As one helps him open and close his circles, he becomes more and more interested in what one has to say and becomes more tuned in to the world around him.

Whether one-on-one or in a group, whether sharing meanings or using ideas or words in pretend play or conversation, one wants always to be increasing the two-way nature of his communication. When the child is playing out an elaborate fantasy—good guys and bad guys attacking one another, the victors having a wonderful party, where everyone is hugging one another and enjoying a feast of ice cream—one wants to make sure that one is a part of that drama. When the bad guys tromp the good guys, one can circle around, as one of the bad guys, so that the child doesn't ignore the maneuver and makes the good guys act in response. Or, when the child is having his feast, an adult could say he doesn't like ice cream, to prod him to suggest either that one is dumb not to like ice cream or that one can have cake instead. Within the drama, one wants to make sure to open and close circles using ideas.

In terms of logical thinking, this is a child who, when challenged, can easily give up and retreat into his own world. When it is important for him to present his argument to his teacher or to another student in the class about why his way is a better way, he may simply say, "Okay," and go on to daydream about having things his own way. He can develop a wonderful Walter Mitty fantasy where he tells the adult that he has to take a nap, stop drawing, and read instead, or stop playing outside. But he may not discuss any of this fantasy with the adult, just as he did not present his arguments. If the adult asks, "Why do you want it your way?" or "How are you going to do that?" he may feel a little confused. He finds it hard work to answer such questions or to be logical only as part of his interaction with others, and he will be logical only in terms of his own fantasy. The adult should be persistent in using emotional ideals, such as, "Well, why don't you want to go inside? I know you are having a good time outside, but why won't you go inside?" If he says, "Well, I don't know," the response is, "I know you have good reasons," and then very patiently help him articulate his reasons— "Well, maybe you can just tell me one reason." If he won't respond, one might say, "Well, is one reason that you think it is a nice day and children should be outside more on a nice day?" He may say, "Yes, that's right. It's a wonderful day and children should be outside." Even though he has given one of the easier and more obvious answers possible, he has built on someone else's ideas, he is opening and closing logical circles, and he is beginning to get the idea of a "lawyer-to-lawyer" conversation. In time, he will be coming up with imaginative new reasons, such as "being inside is not good for you, because you don't get the sun and the sun is very good for vitamin D and do you want to make me sick?" But no one will hear such imaginative and innovative arguments until the child has been engaged in logical discourse.

Thus, one wants to pull the child who is a little withdrawn or shy out of his inner world. One wants to woo him, help him attend, help him open and close his circles of behaviors, and then to make sure, in terms of using ideas and emotional thinking, that one is always a part of the interaction with him. This will eventually convince him that the world of interaction with others, even though harder, is much more exciting than just marching to his own drummer.

The child who doesn't tune in to the outside world often has a problem with auditory processing or receptive language. He has a hard time figuring out what other people are trying to say to him. As a baby, he may have difficulty decoding or comprehending the rhythm of people's sounds. Whereas many four-month-olds may be able to understand a complicated rhythm, this child may be able to comprehend only a simple, two-cadence rhythm; the more complex vocal rhythms confuse him. Later on, when one gives this child three suggestions: "Please pick up your coat, bring it over here, and then hang it up," he remembers only the first part, "Pick up your coat," and then looks dumbfounded, as if to say, "What do you want me to do next?" The child has a hard time comprehending first in sounds and then in words. He has to work very hard to tune in to other people, because so much of what he is getting from other people involves figuring out their gestures and their words. If this child, who may be creative and bright, has difficulty sequencing other people's communications as they come in to him, he will find it easier to relax and listen only to himself. One needs to convince him that the extra effort he is going to need to put forth is worthwhile.

In summary, with the shy, withdrawn child, the following principles may prove helpful. Respect the slow pace of the child and take one step at a time. Often, bringing the child into a sense of engagement with gestures, so that he has only to point or to lift his finger to indicate a "yes" or a "no," will be a way of getting the relationship going. If this process occurs in a group, such as in an educational setting, the teacher wants to respect the child's slow pace and bring the group to the child. The child, who may also have sensitivities to sound or touch or problems with motor tone or planning, may at first be more comfortable in the corner alone with the teacher or other adult. As the adult begins a series of interactions with gestures and a few words, he can then bring one child to the withdrawn child, and eventually another and another. This interaction may occur over many weeks or even months. The adult serves as a kind of facilitator, but also as a buffer between the child and the world. The adult makes sure the comfort level is always high and the sensory input, in terms of touch or sound, is at a level the child can tolerate. The adult also makes sure the demands for communication are gradual, from the slightest gesture, such as raising a pinky to indicate a "yes" or a "no," to eventual pointing, smiling, and a variety of communicative endeavors.

One can use the security of a small group that one brings to a child's special corner, to help him participate in a bigger group. The child can sit between the two or three friends he has made off in his own corner.

The passive and withdrawn child will probably need extra practice in assertiveness during floor time. The child will need to be encouraged to do more things: to crash the cars or feed the dolls or make the dolls hug, rather than the adult doing too much for the child. Such a child may avoid aggressive themes entirely, even in gesture or in terms of ideas; aggression may never get played out: the wolves never attack the three pigs or the soldiers never attack the enemy. One needs to look for opportunities to move from a pattern where aggression may be inhibited to where it can be played out in gesture and then in ideas. Fearful themes may emerge before aggressive themes or in alternation. One needs to help the child play out these fears of separation or danger. One should not force the child to confront these themes, but should look for natural opportunities, as when the child flirts with a little bit of aggression or a little bit of fear, and then use the occasion as a "window of opportunity" to help the child bring out the theme. There are times when one must pay attention to the need of the withdrawn and passive for increased security. Doing things slowly, step by step, and empathizing with the child's need to feel safe and secure and to have things a certain way, helps the child feel secure in a relationship with the adult. As part of enhancing security, one wants to help the child use his own action and initiative to master his environment. For example, if the child indicates that the adult is sitting too close to him, and he wants the adult to move away, the adult should try to get the child to indicate exactly where he wants the adult, or move himself (the child) to a different position. The child who doesn't like loud noise can learn to lower and raise the volume. Whenever he can be the negotiator of his own security, he is better off.

THE QUICK-TO-ANGER CHILD

Although the quick-to-anger child, particularly as a toddler, is a serious challenge to parents, day care staff, and educators, a wonderful opportunity exists to help this child learn to use his considerable energy in constructive ways.

First of all, one should realize that some children who are quick to anger, even as babies, tend to use their muscles or their motor system to discharge energy. A three- or four-month-old will squawk loudly and move around quite a bit when upset. As seven- and eight-month-olds, they may be well coordinated in the way they crawl, but they may also like to be thrown up in the air and to bang into things. When they get angry, they are likely to bang their hands on the floor. Some bang their heads on the floor, because they have better control over their heads and necks than they do over their arms and legs; and they can make a better sound by thumping their heads on the floor.

This child who likes to use his motor system to communicate may also be blessed with a high level of enthusiasm and energy. He seems to behave as though the world is his oyster, and he's going to take it all in. Naturally, when he gets frustrated, he is not quiet about it; he is not a shrinking violet. He is most unlike the oversensitive child. This child likes to jump into new experiences, to jump into the water first and look later. This child often engages very well, with a lot of enthusiasm and pleasure. He can be very attentive, but often only when he is interested in something. If he is disinterested, he can be inattentive, because the way he clearly makes his needs known is with his motor system.

The challenge for this child, as a toddler, often is in the way he negotiates the second level—two-way communication. Because he gets easily frustrated and angry, he tends to use his motor system to change what he doesn't like. If a toy isn't working, he will want to break it. If his mother and father aren't doing what he wants, he will want to butt them with his head or push them over. If a child has something he wants, he may pinch the child, grab the toy, and even push the child down. Because of his enormous energy level and his desire to do what he wants when he wants, he is less likely to be interested in two-way communication. He will tend to be interested in one-way communication, his way. He is what one may call "The Little Dictator."

If parents and educators can provide extra practice in two-way communication in the toddler phase, there can be an enormous saving of energy and time when this child is older and already in regular school settings. By way of example, the child may be reaching for an electric plug in order to pull it out. The typical parental reaction would be to say, "No!" and quickly pick him up and pull him away from the plug, put him down, only to see him run toward the plug again. Then perhaps the parent might pick him up, hold him while he throws a temper tantrum with squawks and yells; a half-hour later, he finally calms down. The next day, however, the same cycle repeats itself. The parent either becomes very strong or becomes exhausted from these constant fights.

If this child has difficulty with two-way communication and, in particular, with the parent's or educator's side of the two-way communication—not comprehending gestures, especially those meant to limit his assertiveness and aggression—one can take two steps. First, one makes sure one is giving the child a lot of nurturing, that is, the kind of engagement and shared attention appropriate for younger children, as well as for toddlers. Second, make sure that one is trying to open and close circles of communication by giving the child the toy he wants or by playing a game that he finds amusing, for example, pinching your nose while making an interesting sound. The child can learn that two-way communication can make life pleasurable.

The next step is to establish limits to the child's aggression and his doing things that he shouldn't be doing. A parent needs to behave like a policeman directing traffic. When the child starts moving toward the plug, the parent gets down on the floor in front of him and begins to make very clear gestures, indicating "No, No" with head and arms and getting in front of him to block his way. As he tries to get past, the parent blocks his way even more, pointing with head and hands, "No, No." Every time he squawks and tries to get around the parent keeps gesturing "No" again and again. Every time the parent says "No" and he squawks, he's closing a circle and the circle is being closed around limit-setting. Thus, important learning is occurring. The more circles are closed, the more the child is learning how to follow limits in terms of the parent's gestures, not just in terms of physical restraint.

The parent will also have to learn to raise his voice. Voice tone is a very important gestural signal; children know that one means business by the quality of one's voice. They know also by the seriousness of one's facial expression. It is necessary to make one's facial expression very serious and to let one's voice get gradually louder.

One can practice going from one to ten, in terms of loudness of voice and seriousness of facial expression, and also in the intensity of one's gesturing. One can start off at one, then go to two, three, and up to ten, while blocking the child's way to the plug. The same method is useful, whether he wants to grab something on the table he shouldn't, or to do something to another child that he shouldn't, or to touch the forbidden television set. If a parent gets in front of him, gestures, increases the intensity of seriousness, loudness, and animation from one to ten, and he is still trying to overwhelm any opposition, a parent may have to use physical restraint. But this kind of exercise, which combines animated gestures, a sense of authority, that one means business, with physical restraint as needed, will give the child the necessary learning experiences with two-way communication, so he can learn to accept limits. When he gets older and can use ideas, the parent can begin talking about the importance of "No, No" and why he has to follow the parent's advice sometimes. He can play out his frustration and anger in make-believe. Later, when he can use logic, he can present his point of view with great intensity. He may be a great trial lawyer who will stomp and rage in front of the jury, as he stomps and rages at his parent as a four-year-old. But if the parent has done his job well during the toddler stage, the child will learn to accept the parents' authority.

Such an active, assertive, quick-to-anger, quick-to-get-frustrated child can lead many parents or caregivers to let situations get out of hand and lose their tempers. This child's intensity can overwhelm almost anyone and cause him or her to become angry. But a parent is often reluctant to expend the energy necessary to set limits on the child early in the game. Usually, parents try to be the nice guys and don't like to be assertive, or annoyed. So parents like to say in a calm, even-toned way, "Oh, come on, Susie. Don't touch that plug! I said don't. You aren't listening to me. You are going to be punished." Meanwhile the child may just smile and go on her merry way. To raise one's voice a little more in that midrange takes energy and causes discomfort. So parents often try to be nice, nice, nice, until they get so frustrated that they go from zero to ten on the Richter scale, whereupon they frighten the child, because he wasn't ready for their explosive anger. Then they feel guilty after an out-of-control rage and try to make it up to the child by overindulging him. The child experiences an unpredictable, chaotic environment—first nice-nice, then out of control, and then nice-nice again. Instead, a parent needs to move in quickly. As soon as the child starts to challenge the parent, he or she should see the situation as a learning opportunity. One might say to oneself, "Oh, good. He's challenging me again. I can teach him again about limits," and then move in. It is necessary to make a move early in the game before one, as the adult, is out of control.

It is important to realize that the active child may also at times be inattentive, as well as a quick-to-anger child. The most common type of quick-to-anger child is the active child, but sometimes a quick-to-anger child may be similar to the cautious, fearful, shy child mentioned earlier. The child who is oversensitive to experience may also have a short fuse, have tantrums, and be quick to anger, but in a less aggressive way than the very active, quick-to-anger child.

For the oversensitive, quick-to-anger child, one wants to follow the same principles regarding nurturing, improving the gestural level, and setting limits. But armed with the awareness that this child frightens easily, one wants to be much gentler and much more gradual in establishing one's firmness and to provide extra practice in setting limits. Adequate opportunity to develop the nurturing aspect of the relationship is critical.

Once the very active, quick-to-anger child, as well as the sensitive, quick-to-anger child, have gotten to be two to two-and-a-half-years-old, the more one can help them put feelings into words and go from the level of acting out feelings to playing or talking them out. They will be more aware of their feelings and better able to deal with their anger in constructive ways.

Frequently, the very active and aggressive child will also be inattentive. This child may have a hard time processing information, like the withdrawn child mentioned earlier. If he has an auditory processing or mild receptive language problem, he finds tuning into himself easier than tuning into another person. He may need a lot of practice with closing his circles, in terms of behavior and, later on, in terms of ideas and words. On the other hand, this child, because he focuses on his motor system, tends to be a doer; he tends to like to act on and change his environment rather than use ideas or thoughts, even up to the age of four. He appears to be inattentive, even though he is not inattentive. In other words, he tunes a person out, not because he can't comprehend what the person is saying, but because he prefers action to thought. Like the child who has a minor receptive language problem, this child will benefit from extra practice with word over deed, the idea over the act. In pretend play, one can help him describe his feelings or the feelings of the characters in his drama. In problem-solving talks with him, one tries to help him describe his feelings and to give him extra practice with the pleasure of using ideas, so that he can eventually strike a balance between action and idea.

Educators and parents who work with the inattentive and active child often feel capable of doing only one thing at a time. They are so busy setting limits, they forget to give the child extra practice in using ideas instead of actions. For example, a two-and-a-half-year-old girl is active, inattentive, and very charismatic within her group. She loves not only to throw her toys around, but also to get all the children yelling and scream-ing, particularly when the teacher wants everyone to sit down. To the teacher, she is a nuisance, because she tends to disorga-nize the class. Often the teacher will get involved in setting limits with her—punishing her by making her sit down and be quiet or telling her she can't play a game she likes. In fact the teacher is so happy when the child is quiet, that the former won't want to initiate discussion with the latter. The teacher needs to say, "Hey, when you weren't listening to me, what were you thinking and what were you feeling? What are your reactions when I tell you to stop doing something?" Or, alterna-tively, the teacher won't want to begin pretend play with this child to see if she can learn to put the feelings of the dolls into words. This child needs extra practice in verbalizing feelings of frustration and anger, excitement and happiness, because the child likes to channel these feelings into activity rather than into ideas. A teacher, caregiver, or parent has to be working on two fronts at once: to help the child set limits, if the child is quick to anger or overly active; to teach the child to use a more abstract form of expression, ideas and words, to channel behavior.

In summary, the following principles may prove helpful in working with the aggressive child. The aggressive child who doesn't empathize with others may need a lot of extra engagement, a lot of warmth. He needs to be "filled up." Yet he may be fearful of closeness and avoid it. If he is verbal, it is helpful to empathize with his "fear" of "hurt feelings" or another type of worry (e.g., "being left") and continue to woo him gently and on *his* terms. Therefore, the engagement aspect of floor time, which relates to the chemistry of feeling connected to another person, may be very important and should often be worked on first in order to get a good baseline of involvement. As indicated earlier, the aggressive child, two years old and over, may also have a hard time elevating behavior to the level of ideas. He likes to act out or pretend play rather than think out or use ideas to express his various inclinations. The fifteen-month-old who is not ready to use ideas may prefer to act out rather than use gestures. Instead of pointing, grimacing, and motioning in an aggressive way, he may like actually to hit.

The sequence of steps used to deal with aggression takes the child from learning to gesture instead of actually carrying out the act; to using gestures in an anticipatory way or as a warning, to actually using ideas rather than behavior. So the child under two can be taught to use more gestures and learn to modulate his gestures; he can move along a one to ten scale gradually, rather than all at once. This lesson is significantly enhanced if the parent, therapist, or educator who sets limits on the child's behavior also moves gradually on a one to ten scale, rather than at first being nice-nice and then all of a sudden being verbally explosive or using physical restraint.

Therefore, one increases floor time in order to develop a sense of engagement; one then uses engagement to elevate behavior to ideas and words in pretend play. When the child is younger, one tries to move from behavior to gesture, from the reality of behavior to behavior as a gestural signal for anger or caring or closeness. Even the child who is working on using words needs a lot of help to become a better "gesturist"; he needs to learn to use gestures as warnings and as the beginnings of symbols. At the same time as one is working with the child during floor time on improving his gesturing capacities, one needs to use limits, in a very firm way, accompanied by a lot of gesturing.

In other words, there must be clear consequences to behavior. In setting limits, educators and parents need to be aware of the importance of using firm gestures and facial expressions, words, loudness of voice, and of adjusting these elements so that their intensity is gradually increased. In many families with problems of aggression and other conduct, there is a tendency not to use gestures in the early phases of limit-setting and then to go from being overly passive to being explosive or "losing it." Instead, parents need to gradually increase vocal tone, seriousness in facial expressions, assignment of punishments, and finally, physical restraint.

In addition, one should be aware that the aggressive child may need greater physical space and less density of people. Some children who are prone to motor discharge pattern aggression do much better when they have their own space with lots of room to play, so that they are not banging into other children so readily. In one day care center, children who were prone to aggression who had enormous amounts of space in each room did much better than they had done in other, less spacious settings. More space gives a child who is working out his own limits a little extra leeway.

If the aggressive child is also verbal, articulate, and has good problem-solving abilities, it is very important to employ the six-step process described in chapter 15. He gets help in becoming engaged; he experiences empathy for his goals; he is helped to reason out alternative ways to meet these goals without being aggressive; he can collaborate in the creation of a step-by-step process to enable him to curb his aggression and use alternative ways of getting his needs met; and firm limits are set to motivate him. As limits are set, more floor time is used to make sure the relationship with the adult is on solid ground while the limits are implemented. As the child collaborates in this process with the therapist, educator, or parents, he can begin to anticipate situations in which he experiences aggressive feelings, as well as his own escalation—how he goes from a feeling of frustration to annoyance to finally hitting out. Better anticipation will enable him to implement other strategies to meet his needs—to keep another kid away from his toys, to be victorious over someone else in competition, to be liked, or just have physical contact with people.

CAREGIVING PATTERNS IN RELATION TO THE SHY, WITHDRAWN, AND QUICK-TO-ANGER CHILD

A child can draw adults (educators or parents) into certain types of interactions, based on the child's unique differences. There are therefore certain patterns of interaction that, in themselves, can support the child's maladaptive behavior. If the parents and educators are aware of the patterns of these interactions, they can help to change them to give the child more flexibility. The following comments will briefly discuss these patterns for the shy, withdrawn, quick-to-anger child.

For example, parents who intrude upon and overwhelm the shy child (e.g., a father who has a "John Wayne" attitude and believes only in rough-and-tumble play) may constantly so excite and overstimulate such a child that the child feels cautious and frightened. The parent intensifies the shy child's pattern of interaction.

In the case of the child who tends to march to his own drummer and to withdraw, often there are parents who also tend to be self-absorbed and preoccupied or overly cautious and scared of hurting or intruding on the child. Parents who feel sad, depressed, or preoccupied with economic or family stresses, tend to be withdrawn themselves. Whatever the reason, they don't woo their child or pull him or her in enough. Such parental behavior can encourage, or even create, the child's tendency toward a pattern of self-absorption.

Two types of caregiving patterns tend to intensify the aggressive behavior of the child who is very active or quick to anger. When the parents believe in very concrete, black-and-white, law-and-order approaches, and the notions of delay, reasoning, or putting feelings into ideass have no meaning for them, they go head-to-head with the child who is already very intense. The resulting power struggles and conflict may only make the child more aggressive. A cautious child may become so fearful with such intense, concrete parents, that he may become passive. The child who is physically more assertive and likes to use motor activity may take the parent on and become increasingly aggressive. The parent who is constantly overstimulating the child, either because of marital tensions, family problems, or just personality style, may overly increase the child's activity level, and therefore his aggressiveness. Parents who are not providing enough nurturing and soothing experiences leave the child no alternative but to say, "Love by irritation is better than no love at all. So I will irritate the heck out of you." All of these patterns of interaction will contribute to the child's aggression and inattentiveness.

The child who is inattentive often has parents who tend to be fragmented in the way they think and act; in other words, the parents' attention is spread thin by doing many things at once. Such parents don't close their circles, either because they are anxious or easily distracted. Sometimes, due to marital conflicts, each parent has a different agenda for the child and thus fragments the way he or she relates to the child, so that the latter is pulled in many directions at once. The child who is constantly overexcited also can become very anxious. Each of these family patterns can contribute to the tendency of the child to be inattentive.

Clinicians and educators can help to correct these patterns by providing different kinds of interaction, but they have to be aware that they can fall into the same patterns that the parents exhibit and, therefore, only worsen the child's tendencies.

THE INATTENTIVE AND DISTRACTIBLE CHILD

The inattentive and distractible child needs extra practice in his floor time and problem solving, particularly in opening and closing circles of communication. Attention is an aspect of communication, so that the child who is inattentive doesn't open and close many circles. By definition, the more circles of communication that are closed, the more attentive the child is. To close twenty or thirty circles in a row requires a few minutes of consistent attention. The child who withdraws his attention, or goes from wanting something to wanting something else is not opening and closing many circles. Even very young babies can open and close circles by looking or listening and become increasingly attentive. One needs to be very aware during floor time and problem-solving time of the amount of circles being closed, particularly in social interaction. As the child is playing, one can look at his follow-through with toys to see how much he opens and closes circles of communication with the inanimate world.

In order to help a child open and close circles of communication, it is necessary to pay attention to each sensory modality—vision, hearing, touch, smell—that either holds or undermines a child's attention. Loud noises or visually complex designs may distract him; soothing sounds or not too complex vocal input may facilitate his attention. As one identifies the way the child uses sound and sight, one can give the child extra support in the modality in which the child finds himself more easily able to be attentive. Simple, not too loud, repetitive, vocal input may help some children be attentive. One then wants to build and expand on this input by adding greater complexity and range. A certain level of lighting, not too bright or not too dim, may help another child be attentive. Some children may love color or musical rhythms, and those elements may be useful for helping the child maintain his attention. It is important to respect the child's over- or underreactivity and the way he processes information in each sensory modality, so as to help him gradually build units of opening and closing circles of communication using vision, hearing, touch, and his own movement patterns.

Children often find it easier to be attentive when they are active. The fidgety child who needs to walk around to focus should be respected and helped to do anything physically that will help him be more attentive. If he understands his own motor system, he will collaborate if one respects the fact that he cannot necessarily be attentive in the way one would like him to, but he can be attentive in a way that is in keeping with his nature as an individual.

As a child becomes older, smarter, and more able to use ideas, one can empathize with his inattentiveness, and collaborate on ways to foster his attentiveness. Over time, the child will become more flexible and will be able to adjust to routine social situations. If, at first, one meets the child 80 percent of the way to help him be attentive enough to find the world interesting and satisfying, he will find ways to adjust to most environments.

There are a number of specific ways a therapist or a parent may help a distractible, preoccupied, passive, or resistant child to attend. A child who needs to be asked over and over to come to the table or turn off the television and get ready for bed, dawdles and makes therapists and the parents angry; power struggles and temper tantrums ensue.

Parents tend to make a critical error. They often talk on and on and get frustrated, before they even notice whether or not they have the child's attention. One mother reported how embarrassed she was to be yelling at her "spacey type" child; she felt bad about it, because "she couldn't help it." She would say many times, "Come in for dinner," and the child didn't; "Do your homework," and the child didn't; finally she would yell at the child. The therapist asked, "When she doesn't respond, before you yell and get frustrated, do you walk over to her and see if she will look at you, and at least acknowledge what you've asked her to do?" The mother responded with embarrassment, "No, I don't do that." The therapist asked, "Why?" The mother: "That would feel too intrusive to me."

The therapist: "But don't you think your daughter should at least look at you, when you talk to her? The mother: "I know she loves me; it's just she can't always pay attention, because she's so distracted by what she's doing." The therapist: "I would bet that when the principal of her school talks to her, she looks at him!" The mother: "Oh, I know she does; I've seen her do that." The therapist: "Well, it may be harder for her to look at you when she is doing something else, but if the motivation is high enough, she will probably pay attention to you. One of the problems is that you haven't helped her to become motivated to be as attentive to you as she is to the principal." Therapists know that in intimate, loving relationships, it is harder to mobilize respect. People take each other for granted, and when a child is easily distracted, he will be more so in the relationships in which he feels more comfortable.

The mother asked, "You mean I should just go over and say, 'Janie, can you look at me when I talk?' and repeat that until she looks at me?" The therapist: "Yes, and do it like a gentle top sergeant in the military: 'Hey Jane! Whom do you think I'm talking to?' "

The foregoing case illustrates the larger principle that a child who doesn't listen to an adult may have a more primary difficulty. The parent creates an opportunity for failure by speaking to the child without having the child's attention. If the child hasn't opened and closed even one circle of communication, it is unlikely that the parent has his attention. First, one should position oneself in front of the child. Second, one should make sure the child is looking when one speaks; if not, one should stop and say, "Hey, why aren't you looking at me?" One should raise one's voice, until one receives at least a fleeting look. One should shut off the television and eliminate other distractions. As one is talking, if the child begins to tune out, one should stop and say, "What happened?" and find out why the child couldn't keep listening. The ensuing discussion leads to opening and closing many circles of gestures and words, while helping the child stay with the primary task of attending.

If the child decides not to attend, at least it is clearly a volitional, negative, and defiant act, and not an act of inattentiveness.

It is necessary to remember that communication involves four steps: attending, engaging, establishing two-way simple gestural and verbal communication, and then more complex gestural and symbolic communication. The first three processes must be in place before the parent tells the child what he or she wants him to do. A key is never to skip a step and to empathize with the child's tendency to look and listen to everything. The parent must get his attention and make sure circles are closed, before important verbal information is shared.

THE NEGATIVE CHILD AND CONCRETE PARENT

The negative child creates many unique challenges because of his behavior and the response he elicits from his caregiver or therapist. One type of negative child may like to march to his own drummer. The adult may make a running commentary on what the child is doing: "Oh, you are looking out the window," or "You are throwing a ball." Such comments may roll off the child's back like beads of water. The child may seem to take in the comments somewhat indifferently; he perhaps understands some of the words and not others. Only token interaction with the parent takes place. There is only an occasional look or smile or request for assistance for something the child wants to do.

The therapist or caregiver attempts to apply good floor time technique by following the child's lead. However, the child doesn't necessarily amplify or hook into the adult's commentary and say, in so many words, "Thank you for describing what I'm doing. Now let me tell you what I'm going to do next."

It is necessary to realize that at the gestural level of communication, there is only one-way communication and little two-way communication going on. The caregiver tells the child what to do or comments on what the child is doing, instead of creating interactive opportunities. For example, if the caregiver says, "You are looking out the window, and what do you see?" and the child ignores the adult, the adult can take some binoculars, look out the window, and describe what he or she sees. The child is likely to become curious and want to look. Or, if a child is looking in a particular direction, the caregiver can position himself in front of the child and point out something the child perhaps hasn't seen and get him to comment on what the caregiver is pointing out. If the child is bouncing a ball, instead of commenting on what a good ball-bouncer he is, the caregiver can catch the ball, throw it back, or even gently pretend not to throw it back, and thus create an interactive opportunity. Even the verbal child who gets involved in his own pretend play, when he handles and speaks for all the dolls, may not engage in two-way communication at the gestural level and therefore needs opportunities to interact.

Another challenge is when the adult perceives the child does not want to engage in floor time. For example, the child doesn't want to do pretend play or talk or interact with the caregiver; the child wants to play only structured games like Monopoly, or have a book read to him, or play Chutes and Ladders. This behavior often throws the caregiver into a quandary: "What can I do? I'm supposed to follow his lead, but he just wants to sit there and look at the ceiling"; or "He just wants to play Monopoly. How can I follow his lead and do floor time with him, if he won't do spontaneous pretend play with me?" The answer to this dilemma is simpler than it seems, because the dilemma is not what it appears to be. From the parent's point of view, the dilemma is that the child doesn't want to go along with the parent's prescribed activity. Floor time philosophy, however, dictates that whatever the child is saying or doing *is* the activity of floor time. There is no such thing as a child not engaging in floor time. Floor time by definition means simply that the parent is attentive, empathetic, and ready to follow what the child wants to do. For example, a verbal child is sitting like a bump on a log and refuses to get down on the floor with the dolls and begin make-believe play. The parent might empathize, "It looks as if you want to sit there staring at the picture. There must be something interesting about that." If the child ignores the parent, the parent might then sit next to him and try to mimic his behavior, saying "Let's see what it feels like to do what you are doing." The parent might get in front of the child, since he wants to sit and look, and see if he wants to look at his parent, who then might make interesting faces at him. The child may then say, "Get out of here. You're blocking my view." The parent could say, "I didn't know I was blocking your view. What are you looking at?" The child may then point at, but not say, what he is looking at, in which case the parent could say, "Oh, in that direction. You mean where the garden and trees are? I didn't realize that." Meanwhile, parent and child are engaged in a gestural and verbal dialogue. If the child persists in being negative, "I don't want you in front of me, leave me alone," the parent could respond, "Now I understand. You want me to leave you alone. Where should I go?" The child: "Anyplace. Just out of here." The parent: "Like where?" While the slow pace of this dialogue will frustrate the child, who wants the parent to get the message more quickly, the parent is further engaging the child in floor time. After twenty or thirty minutes, regardless of his negativism or indifference, the parent and child have opened and closed many gestural circles and dealt with the child's main issue, "leave me alone." Eventually the reason the child is so negative may emerge. A parent who has too literal a view of floor time insists that the child get down on the floor, engage in pretend play, or make up a story, produces only the illusion of floor time. All of the child's behavior should be considered as potential floor time behavior—silence, staring, negativism, rejection of the parent. If the child says, "I hate you. You are mean to me," the parent should still follow the child's lead rather than becoming defensive and saying, "But I was so nice. Look at all the good things we did today." The parent should suggest that he or she understands that the child must have very good reasons for hating the parent, and that the parent is eager to hear what those reasons are.

Frequently, in an area where he or she has some anxiety, the parent will become more literal or concrete and want to take the child's remarks at face value. The parent who is uneasy with his child's anger, for example, will take the child's "I hate you" as a literal statement, defend himself, or walk out of the room, rather than follow up and elaborate on the statement, as a floor time communication. The parent who is sensitive to negativism may rationalize and say, "Well, if he doesn't want to play with me, and says 'No' to my overtures, I should leave him alone. That's the only way of being respectful."

The point of doing floor time, however, is always to tune in at four levels—to be engaged and attentive, have two-way communication, and then to attempt, with children older than two years, to symbolize feelings, intentions, and behaviors, by putting them into the form of ideas, and to categorize those ideas for purposes of logical communication. One cannot be engaged and have two-way communication if one is out of the room. A parent may protest, "But if he tells me to leave, and I don't leave, I'm not following his lead." No one said that the parent had to do what the child says; the parent should follow the general theme of the child's expression and empathize with it. In other words, if the child, as part of pretend play says, "Now I want you to bang your head against the wall," the parent might only pretend to hit his head. The parent, in other words, makes a distinction between reality and make-believe. Similarly, if the child tells the parent to leave, the parent can empathize with the wish, but not actually do the deed.

The tendency to take children literally interferes with floor time. For example, a particular child was clearly very involved with his mother; he loved to irritate her by criticizing her. She took his criticisms literally and would get upset and argue with him. She could never, for example, wonder out loud why he felt so negative about her or how she disappointed him. She assumed that whatever he was saying to her was accurate; this assumption reinforced her negative self-image as a "bad mother."

Parents need to be aware that what children say and do may be only the tip of the iceberg. When the child sometimes handled aggression impulsively, the mother couldn't see that this behavior was a part of his attitude toward the world that she encouraged by taking his comments literally. The child's annoyance, resentment, feistiness, and dismissal of the parent are all part of his communication, and none of them needs to be taken literally. Instead they should be a basis for exploration of the child's intentions and for helping him abstract his feelings. The goal is to remain engaged and help the child elaborate his negative feelings.

The child who wants only to play structured games, like Monopoly or cards, or to be read to presents a challenge to a parent who is trying to put floor time philosophy into practice. The parent will enter into the game with the child. As the child changes the rules to serve his desire to be the winner, that is, to be the boss or the champion, or to be invulnerable and never lose, the floor time parent should go along. The child exercises his floor time right to give his own meaning to the game. If one plays according to the actual rules, one isn't doing floor time, unless the child has elected to play by those rules. In that case, his drama may cast him as policeman who makes sure no one cheats. The parent should empathize with the child's wish to be either the policeman or to win at any cost by changing the rules. The parent should express pride and pleasure in the child's taking the initiative rather than implying any criticism of his manipulation of the game. Each floor time session may represent an act in the developing drama. Since the child may change both roles and rules, the pattern that emerges may be one of vacillation.

A parent may well ask, "But if I follow his lead during floor time, how will he know with his friends when he shouldn't change the rules? After all, he has to learn to play according to the rules, too." The parent must make it clear to the child the difference between play when he is setting the rules and play according to the "real rules," in order to help the child shift gears appropriately. For example, during floor time, which need not be called "floor time" for the child, when the child changes the rules, the parent may comment, "I see we're going to be playing according to your rules today," and the child will most likely indicate his comprehension. When the child's father, a friend, and the child are playing Monopoly together, and the child seeks to change the rules, the father may point out that with company, they have to play according to the actual rules of the game. The child will benefit from understanding the different contexts. Learning about context is one of childhood's most important lessons.

The parent needs to feel secure about defining different contexts in order to help his child understand that situations, in most instances, determine roles. After all, one can wear a bathing suit at the beach, but not at school. One can use certain kinds of words with friends, but not with teachers. One has to eat a certain way at the dinner table, but one can eat differently in the backyard. The children who do best are usually those who understand and abstract rules from their contexts. Even though there are certain rules that cut across all contexts, such as not hurting other people and being respectful of others, most rules are somewhat context dependent. The principle of consistency needs to be balanced with context-dependent learning.

A floor-time attitude therefore means that whatever the child is doing—a structured game, negativism, rejection, or other activities—is the child's communication; the parent goes along with that communication and lets the child take the lead. It is important not to be too literal—to assume only pretend play takes place on the floor or that floor time is only the child's doing what you want him to do. By definition, floor time is when the child takes the initiative, even though sometimes the initiative will take idiosyncratic forms that include angry and rejecting words or negative or avoidant behavior.

CHILDREN WHO ARE SENSITIVE TO DETAIL AND CHILDREN WHO FOCUS ON THE ABSTRACT PATTERN—"FOREST-TYPE" AND "TREE-TYPE" CHILDREN

Optimally, one can be sensitive to detail and subtlety, and at the same time, understand how all the pieces fit together in a larger pattern. Much of emotional and intellectual life depends on the ability to blend both these skills. But often individuals tend to be stronger in one of these abilities and relatively weak in the other. For example, the "forest-type" person who can abstract and see the big patterns may have difficulty knowing the elements that make up the pattern. Such an individual may try to figure out how he feels based on how he behaves; for example, "Because I hit him, I must be angry." Similarly, a "tree-type" person who perceives details knows that he is angry, sad, happy, or excited, but may have a hard time figuring out the overall pattern that governs his emotions, such as "I get angry when people reject me." The tree person may excel at empathizing with the emotions of each character in a novel but may have difficulty understanding the theme or overall plot. The forest person may have a sense of the novel's plot, but may not be able to figure out the feelings of each character. The tree person may be able to do simple subtraction, addition, and multiplication, but have trouble with advanced math, like calculus, which depends on abstracting special patterns. The forest person may struggle with verbal skills and even mathematics when he is younger, but do better with the more abstract academic tasks when he is older.

Being aware of these different patterns in children helps the adult use both spontaneous floor time and problem-solving discussions to provide a child with practice in the area where he is weak and to help him achieve more balance. For example, a tree-type child may play out a drama of dolls investigating secret passages in a haunted house. The dolls become scared, are captured, escape, find somebody who takes care of them, and are captured again. The drama is filled with rich detail: the child explains that at one moment one character is excited and at another moment, another one is scared. Day after day, such a child plays out getting excited, frightened, overwhelmed, and feeling secure—all within the course of fifteen or twenty minutes. The adult playing this drama out along with the child is excited about moving from detail to detail and nuance to nuance because of the child's sensitivity, subtlety, and wonderful use of language. The adult may forget, or may never even consider, that his child never seems to describe the whole picture or to give an overview of the action: Why are the children investigating the house in the first place? Empathetic comments are necessary to focus the child on the bigger picture. "Let's see now. They were feeling A, and they were feeling B, and they were doing C. How does this all fit together? What are they trying to do?" The child then begins to design (in an architectural sense) a larger structure or plot for his drama. At first, he will go right back into the detail, but after some practice, he may begin to show a knack for seeing the big picture as well.

Similarly, in a problem-oriented discussion, this tree-type child may tell the adult all about school, about what this friend and that friend said, and how this one hurt his feelings and that one made him feel better. The adult may get caught up in the child's excitement or fears without thinking to ask how the child would characterize his entire day. Or if the child is having difficulties with another child who vacillates—he is nice one day and mean the next, excited a third day, frightening a fourth day—one might get lost in the details of each day and never say, "Well, what would you say overall about this other child? How would you size him up?" If the first child says, "Well, he has changing moods, but overall I guess I like him pretty well; I wish he wouldn't change so much," that child is showing perspective and taking in the bigger picture. One will be surprised how often the tree-type child doesn't make general statements, and instead treats each detail as though it were the whole picture. As one verbal child put it, "When I'm mad, I think I will be that way forever." Helping the child who gets lost in detail see the bigger picture can be very reassuring. It helps the child realize that his perceptions and feelings of the moment are part of a large pattern and as such need not dominate his life. The child can gradually feel more integrated rather than fragmented. It is tempting for the therapist to get lost in detail with the child. After all, the therapist might say to himself, isn't it my job to explore his anger or his excitement? But it is also the therapist's goal to explore how different feelings fit together and how the very tendency to feel fragmented or overloaded is in itself a very important feeling and an important pattern.

The child who has difficulty in attending to the details, subtleties, or nuances, or a child who has a hard time discriminating among different sounds and words, has a different kind of challenge. Assume for the moment, that this child is gifted in seeing the forest, the big pattern, and that this ability is supported by an unusually well-developed visual–spatial capacity. Such a child often describes life's patterns in the broadest and most abstract way. "How was your day?" a therapist might ask a child of this sort, and he might think for a second and give what seems like a very sophisticated answer, as one such youngster gave this therapist in response to that question: "My day was typical for a child of my age." When asked about his specific feelings, he said, "What you would expect for a six-year-old." This apparently sophisticated and insightful answer, however, was not matched by an ability to fill in the details. In this instance, when this therapist followed up by wondering what a typical day might be like for a child his age, the boy had a hard time finding the words to describe the details. When asked to talk about feelings in a particular situation, such as when another child was mean to him or when someone was particularly nice to him, he had a hard time identifying a particular behavior or feeling. He continued to speak in vague generalities. Nonetheless, he gave thoughtful answers, and he always seemed to be approximating some important truth. He didn't respond with the same general principle to every question. He looked at life from the broadest and most abstract angle. Some identify their feelings and then abstract what their feelings have in common; he would describe the abstraction first.

It was possible, with patience, to have him gradually fill in the details. When asked what he did at school, or what a youngster his age might do at school, he answered at first with generalities, but was responsive to the question. Then, if the therapist mentioned what children typically do first in the day, such as hanging their coats up or greeting other children, he could chime in and say, "Oh, that's right. I did this or that." Progressing through the day, he could give more specifics. The therapist was helping him put the trees into the forest. Similarly, when he and the therapist talked about feelings, if the therapist mentioned how some children might feel or behave in a certain situation, he would sometimes disagree and say, "No," he would think a child might do or feel something a little different, or that he, in a similar situation, did something different. For every ten words the therapist spoke, he would speak two or three, although he was collaborative and working hard in this endeavor.

Children who see the big patterns do very well when a therapist assists them in filling in the details. It is necessary to progress from the therapist "cuing them up," that is, suggesting possibilities, to finding ways to help them suggest the possibilities themselves. For example, initially a therapist might give examples of how children feel in a specific situation, and eventually ask the child how he thinks different children feel in that situation. If he still couldn't respond in detail, the therapist would have to find a middle road, where he might draw a picture of how some children feel and let the child use the visual cue to stir his auditory–verbal memory. Also, the therapist might remind the child of some friends he has spoken about, who typify certain behaviors and feelings, such as an aggressive friend or a frightened friend, and might wonder out loud if he felt like either of them. In this way, the therapist finds some basis for the child to do a little more of the work. The therapist should gradually let the child do most of the work, so that he can eventually fill in the details on his own.

Therefore, one needs to be aware of distinct "processing styles" that children evince in their approach to floor time and problem solving, in order to help the child take pride in what he does easily, but also to help him practice what he finds difficult. In short, the tree-type children, who appear advanced and precocious in their verbal abilities and are often viewed by their parents and teachers as very bright, may at times need help in constructing the forest. If this help is provided early on, they can develop a conceptual and abstracting ability, which is not demanded of them in the early school years or in their interactions with their parents, because they are so perceptive about details. They are so admired for their verbal ability, that no one challenges them to see the bigger patterns, and the area where they need practice doesn't often get attention.

Similarly, the superabstract, forest-type child may be seen as a child who doesn't use a lot of words or doesn't easily recall details. There is a tendency to assume either that he is a special breed of genius who has his head up in the clouds or to discount him as slow and not gifted. The latter attitude can discourage his future brilliance and creativity; the former attitude fails to give him the kind of balance that will be helpful to him. It is often hard for parents and educators to make the effort required to work patiently with a forest-type child to enable him to identify the trees.

Because the tree-type child often lacks visual–spatial capacity, a particularly valuable exercise is to have him visualize his feelings and experiences. He should be asked to picture a person he's mad at, a person he misses, or how different feelings fit together. The forest-type person who has visual–spatial strength often has a weak auditory–verbal capacity. He should be asked to imagine the sound of someone who is mad or sad or angry. Having him play the sounds in his mind, and even mimic them, can help this child to dramatize the "trees" of an experience.

Occasionally, one finds youngsters who are having trouble in both modalities. They need practice in both abstraction and detail.

THE CLINGING CHILD

The "clinging child," runs after the adult and holds on. The adult usually tries to escape the child; and the more the child senses the escape, the more he clings. Instead, the adult needs to engage the child. The adult should try to set aside a half-hour of floor time at different times during the day in order to engage the child without his asking. Floor time provides an opportunity to initiate gestures indicating warmth and closeness, so the child can be close without holding. With a two-year-old and older child, one tries to use words signifying closeness. One can talk about the dolls hugging or the child's desire to hug. One can also use words for anger and frustration, because sometimes the child clings for those reasons as well. As the adult avoids the escape pattern, proactively engages the child, and uses lots of gestures and ideas to characterize the different feelings involved, he or she should also begin to set limits on the child's intrusiveness. For example, when floor time is over, when one is on the phone, and the child starts clinging, one can be firm on the limits, because he is now being intrusive. One uses lots of gestures and eye contact to stay in touch with him, while one encourages him to play nearby with toys.

"INDIVIDUAL DIFFERENCES" AND FLOOR TIME PROCEDURES

In establishing procedures for floor time and problem solving it is essential to take into consideration individual differences among children. Children manifest significant differences in motor tone and motor planning, word retrieval, and sensory reactivity and processing.

Children who have difficulty with motor planning have a hard time doing rapid, alternating, sequential movements, such as quickly rotating their hands while slapping their thighs and then crossing over. They may have trouble putting together a six-step sequence of routine activities around the house, such as tying their shoes or putting things away in the proper place. Going from thought to action is not automatic but requires a great deal more effort for such children. Most people, for example, when copying rapid, sequential movements from another person, do it almost "on automatic pilot," without thinking. During problem-solving and floor time efforts, one way to take into account children with motor planning delays, which are sometimes associated with differences in motor tone, is to respect the greater effort the child needs to make and to try to provide extra practice.

Once the child becomes verbal, that is, capable of using ideas in a problem-solving mode, it is important to help him understand what he may have noticed only as a terribly frustrating set of activities. For example, a child who appears to be clumsy may have a hard time copying his father's carpentry efforts or imitating complex activities of the educator, therapist, or parent during floor time. The child may be unable to follow along as others move cars in and out of the garage of the playhouse, or play a "Simon Says" game. He may lack the fine motor skills and the sequential movements required to copy or construct complex designs. As the child exhibits his difficulty, the parent, therapist, or educator should empathize with the child's feelings of frustration, but also point out that even though he is gifted with words or thinking up ideas, when he tries to make something out of his ideas, such as by cutting and pasting, drawing, or putting together pieces, implementing the idea is hard for him. The child may say, with a look of amazement, "How did you know?" He may be relieved to know that his problem is no longer just his secret frustration but is now articulated and elevated to an understanding that somehow it is harder for him than he would like, to do things with his hands, legs, or fingers.

Elevating the child's difficulty to the level of conscious thought through problem solving enhances the sense of shared attention to a task and a sense of connectedness. If there is a collaboration through purposeful interactions around a task, there is a shared sense of the challenge. Also, once the problem is identified, the child can verbalize his full range of feelings, from anger and frustration to sadness and disappointment. The child becomes better able to use his strengths to deal with the challenge at hand. For example, if he is a good thinker and planner on the level of ideas but has a hard time implementing his ideas, he can learn to break down a task into small steps, doing one step at a time; for example, he may become able to avoid overloading himself with too much motor activity during a certain period of time, because he realizes how much effort and thought the task will take, and how much it will tire him out. He may use his ideation or verbal ability to keep on with his task by reaffirming for himself what he needs to do, identifying each small piece of the task, and taking one step at a time. In other words, the "turtle" as opposed to the "hare" approach may suit the child with motor planning problems very well.

Such a child may also have slightly low motor tone and may not like to be insecure in space (e.g., he doesn't like to go down slides or on roller coasters). He may need to understand that he likes to take care of his body and be sure of his body and how it is moving, in a very methodical, step-by-step way. Knowing this about himself will help him feel less embarrassed—less like "there is something wrong with me"—when he notices that other children enjoy slides, while he is more cautious. A child can learn to take pride in his more careful and methodical approach.

In addition, sometimes children with motor planning problems that are associated with fine motor delays may make a lot of seemingly "peculiar" movements. They may flap their arms or hold their body in odd ways. When they get excited, they may look very uncoordinated, with arms and legs moving in different directions. Sometimes this kind of unnatural or irregular motor movement is associated with other processing difficulties in the sensory and motor areas. It is easy for professionals to attribute such motor movement to nonspecific neurologic illness or "organicity." However, everyone has some unevenness in maturation; some people show a little more than others do. It is useful to pinpoint the functional aspects of the maturational lag or dysfunction, whether it is in motor planning, auditory processing, visual–spatial processing, or sensory overreactivity. Children who have lags in more than one of these areas may look more "peculiar" in some of their mannerisms. But if, at the same time, the child is an organized thinker, is comfortable with being close to people and being engaged, and has creative problem-solving abilities, the important elements of the child's personality may be well in place, and the seeming peculiarities may be limited to a mild lag in one or another area of motor or sensory processing. It is important not to generalize from what look like some peculiar movements or even some perseveration around motor movements to some vague notion of general organicity. All maturational lags can be thought of as organic in nature, on the one hand, but at the same time can be seen as a continuum in which a large percentage of the population shows some lags in one or another area of development.

Another type of individual difference to take into account manifests itself in children who have difficulty finding the words they want to say—sometimes called word retrieval or word finding problems. A child who is competent on the intake side and has no auditory processing difficulties (that is, no receptive language difficulties) may have a subtle version of an expressive language difficulty, not related to articulation of particular sounds, but rather to a difficulty in finding the word that they want to say. When one asks such a child what happened at school, he may say, "Nothing," or "Same old stuff," or "Can't remember," when in fact, he has a good sense of what went on. He can't find the words to describe it and so he takes the easy way out. If asked to describe a story that the teacher read or later on, in the fourth or fifth grade, to discuss the "theme" of the story that he has read, he may use vague generalities. "The book was good," he may say, or "I liked the book," instead of talking about what the book was actually about. The vagueness may not occur because the child is conceptually weak; some of these children can be quite brilliant. But if a child with this problem cannot easily find the words, he may give up trying. Such a child may have the abstracting ability to produce general answers to questions but never to provide details.

Children with word retrieval problems often need to be cued up by the therapist, educator, or parent in order to find the words to describe their experience. For example, the adult may suggest that it is difficult to remember what happened at school and then say, "Maybe I can help. I know the first thing is free time, and often you like to play with Susie. Remember yesterday you told me she could be mean to you sometimes." "Oh yes," the child may say, "She was mean to me again today. She took my toy away, and I was mad at her." Then the discussion is off and running. One may need to cue the child up for each part of the day, such as, "Well, I know that after your free play, you tend to do circle time. Did the teacher read a story, as she usually does? If so, what was it about?" "I think she did, but I can't remember what it was about." "Well, I know often she reads to you about animals." "Oh yes, she read about a lion today." It is desirable, furthermore, to cue the child up without getting into a power struggle by saying something like this: "Why won't you tell me what you did?"

Therefore, there are two steps that help a child with word retrieval problems. The first is to empathize with the difficulty and frustration of not being able to remember. Helping the child become aware that remembering specifics is hard for him (parallel to the technique used for the child with a motor planning problem) helps him use his problem-solving ability, that is, his ability to use ideas and to reflect on his difficulty. The second is to provide cues to give him reminders of how his day tends to be sequenced. The child can learn to write down for himself the sequence of his day—math, English, free time—and to ask himself certain rhetorical questions that will provide the cues for himself that the parent would have ordinarily provided. It would be hard for a child under eight years to learn to cue himself up, but the older child, the adolescent, and even the adult with such a problem, often learns to do this process automatically.

Another individual difference alluded to earlier occurs in the child with sensitivites in many sensory realms—a child who is overly sensitive to touch or to sound, as well as a child who is undersensitive to such sensations. A child who is overly sensitive is likely to find many experiences overwhelming and will naturally shy away from them. The barrier between the inner self and the world is not well developed, because of the tendency to overreact to sensations. The child who is sensitive to touch, for example, will feel intruded on by a group and want to find a corner where he can be secure against two walls and only have to deal with one person whom he can see. He may overreact to someone just touching him on the back or rubbing up against him. He may not like his hair combed or brushed. During floor time, he may want to face the parent, therapist, or the educator, and always be able to anticipate the next step. Alternatively, the child who is undersensitive to touch may crave contact. He may like to roughhouse. He may go out of his way to bang into or rub up against things. The cautious child, who is easily overwhelmed by sound, won't like loud noises, commotion, or lots of talking. A child who seeks out the stimulation of sound will want the equivalent of a rock-and-roll concert all the time; he may try to create commotion.

One needs to recognize these differences in order to help each child identify how he is unique and special and to incorporate his particular strengths into his growing problem-solving ability. If one approaches the child's differences positively and empathetically, the child can then talk about situations that he enjoys and those that are frustrating for him. The child comes to realize whether or not he enjoys loud noises, or if touch is something he likes to control, and learns to take one step at a time; or, alternatively he may come to realize that he loves to have a lot of contact with people. This dialogue is a valuable part of problem solving that helps the child elevate his physical differences to the world of thought, idea, and judgment, and enables him to reflect on both his joys and his frustrations.

Furthermore, this self-knowledge allows the adult and the child collaboratively to plan strategies to enable the child to achieve better control and modulation. For example, the child who is sensitive to touch can, together with his therapist, educator, or parent, anticipate situations where there are going to be a lot of people and determine how he wants to negotiate those occasions. How will the child be comfortable during circle time? Perhaps he can position himself with his back to the wall. If he is doing to go to a rock concert, he may want to bring earplugs. The child will be more at ease, more willing or anxious to endure a difficult experience and be part of the group, if he knows what to anticipate and that his discomfort stems from a physical difference, rather than from his mind "playing a trick on him." Adults with comparable problems often find it very reassuring to review their history of being overly sensitive to touch or sound—all the times they thought they were "going crazy" at big parties or felt overwhelmed and even suspicious of others' intentions. As they became aware of this trait and could anticipate feeling a certain way, the feeling no longer escalated to the point of feeling "crazy." The adult could say, "Gee, I am getting overloaded. I'd better go to the powder room to relax and regain control of myself. I'd like to get a breath of fresh air or find a quiet corner to regain my equilibrium." A child can do very much the same thing, and it is very reassuring for them to know what to do.

Certain exercises help children who have extra sensitivity to touch reorganize themselves. Squeezing their arms and legs and providing deep pressure or joint compression, such as in a jumping, skipping, or hopping game, or jumping on the bed, may be helpful. Large motor movement as well as firm pressure helps the child overly sensitive to touch to equilibrate. This self-knowledge can give the child control over his body.

Similarly, the child who is undersensitive, who seeks out and craves sensation, may easily lapse into socially inappropriate behavior, such as hitting other children, banging into things, breaking things, roughhousing too much. Understanding his craving may lead the child to figure out appropriate ways of satisfying his need. For example, he can invent a game of bear hugs, so that he and his friends hug each other. He can try to anticipate the activities he'll like during gym class and wait for gym, rather than letting himself go sooner. He can use the corner of the room to play a game that calls for him to rub up against the walls. At home, he can populate his playroom with big punching bag type balloon figures, which he can punch and jump on to give him the needed sensation.

Thus, first of all, it is important to help the child identify his individual differences. Second, it is necessary to help him articulate his feelings about the situations as they occur and to empathize with the child about such feelings.

Third, the child needs guidance to be able to anticipate the variety of situations he confronts in order to handle his needs in a way that will produce self-esteem, to allow him to feel, not different from, but part of the group, that he is coping, and that he is the master, rather than a "victim," of his own body. This process can be accomplished first in the therapeutic or educational setting, then generalized to other settings.

For the younger child who cannot yet use words in a sophisticated enough way to identify and anticipate the situations where problems occur, it is important for the parent, educator, or therapist to collaborate with the child in identifying those kinds of experiences that help the child feel better, as well as to create and structure difficult situations to give the child the time to gain control and confidence.

The child who has motor planning delays can master new motor challenges step by step with a lot of security, reassurance, and support. The child who is sensitive to touch also needs to take slowly, one step at a time, situations that involve physical contact with other people or things. The child who is undersensitive to sensations like sound or touch and who tends to seek out sensation can be helped to find socially appropriate ways of meeting his need. The earlier one identifies individual differences, the more the child can be helped to find activities which enable him to feel a constructive and positive sense of mastery over his body.

CONCLUSION

In this chapter, we considered different types of children and outlined a number of different principles. Common principles apply throughout: to respect the child's individual differences; to work with the child at his level of development; and help him move to high levels to help him to comprehend how he is unique and different and special; to empathize with his special abilities and difficulties; to work with the child collaboratively to find out the best ways for him to meet his own goals in the context of higher organizational capacities. It was seen how floor time and problem-solving time strategies as well as limits can help the child be attentive, engaged, interactive, representational, and logical.

Chapter 17

Parent-Oriented Developmental Therapy

One approach to working with infants and young children is to work predominantly with the parents. Rather than the therapist working only with the child himself, the goal is to help the parents mobilize the four developmental processes which are essential for healthy emotional growth and development: shared attention and engagement; two-way, preverbal communication; representing or symbolizing emotions; and categorizing and connecting experience and emotions. The thesis is that the child's symptoms or difficulties reside in compromises of one or another of these four critical processes. If the parents can reestablish forward momentum in these processes, the child will not only get back on a positive developmental growth track, but will also resolve the particular symptoms.

By way of an example, a four-year-old child who came in for therapy was initially very preoccupied with himself and uninvolved with other people. In addition, he was somewhat compulsive and ritualistic in his behavior, unable to represent any feelings of yearning or dependency, and only occasionally, and barely, able to represent feelings of anger. He came in because he was hitting other children at school. He was perceived as mechanical and aloof by both his teachers and his mother. He was very bright; he was able to do complicated math and language problems above his grade level. During the first year of treatment, two-way communication was established initially through gestures. At the same time, the parents worked on deepening the relationship. After a year, he was able to abstract some of his feelings, particularly anger at other children who frustrated him or who wouldn't play with him. He could assert his will and negotiate what he wanted. It was more difficult for him to represent and communicate feelings of longing and need. When his father was away on a trip the boy would occasionally say that he missed him. On rare occasions, with a flirtatious glance, he would indicate that he wanted to do something special with his mother. He might talk about a particular friend whom he wanted to come over and play. But these expressions were intermittent and often without depth or elaboration. His play still dealt more with themes of competition—being the best and winning, rather than themes of need or longing, although the latter began to show up more frequently. As he became slightly warmer, he grew more flexible and was better liked by his peers and his own parents; his self-esteem improved enormously. His school behavior improved, once a sense of better connectedness and two-way communication at the gestural level were established, even before any of his affects were represented. As he has become better able to represent his angry feelings, he no longer marched out of the room or had tantrums when frustrated. He was gradually becoming more caring and empathetic, as opposed to mechanical and stiff.

To facilitate his progress, his parents had to work through their own anxieties and defensive strategies. His mother described patterns where she used to become depressed and withdraw from him when he would be aloof or mechanical. She worried that he was "disturbed," but wasn't able to reach out or woo him. Instead, she simply interpreted every one of his behaviors as a "sign of disturbance." She could see "no good" in him, because of how he made her feel. As she came to understand the similarity of her feelings toward her son to those of her own mother, who had been aloof and depressed, she was able to reach out and take pride in some of his behaviors. Gradually, she was able to pull him into a deeper relationship. The father was very competitive and controlling and had been the "king" in his own household as a child. He felt if his son "wanted me, he will come after me. I don't run after anyone." As the father became aware of his own fears of rejection, he too was able to woo his son. He found that they had much in common—intellectual pursuits and even a shared arrogance. Soon, there were two "kings" in the family. In the marriage, the couple did the same thing with each other that they did with their son. They felt depressed and withdrawn or competitively aloof and were eventually able to reach out to each other.

After two years of effort on the part of his parents, this child was about halfway to where he should be; progress was likely to continue, because a good foundation had been established. The most critical steps involved broadening and deepening the range of his affect at each of the early presymbolic levels. It is important not to skip over the early steps, particularly when the main problems are found there. In many cases, the problems may be more in the symbolic realm to begin with, if the early steps have been well negotiated.

HELPING PARENTS BALANCE THEIR EMPATHETIC RANGE

The following example will illustrate a challenge in the representational realm. A mother reported to the therapist (the author) that her four-year-old daughter Molly had a history of being subject to tantrums, becoming easily upset, very negative, and resistant. The mother felt so overwhelmed by Molly's behavior, that she tended to either leave the scene of action, whenever Molly would get upset, yell back at her, or punish her for being angry, aggressive, demanding, and unwilling to calm down. Molly could cry literally for hours and then whine.

At first, Molly would hide behind her father's legs and insist that he carry her into the therapist's office. Molly engaged and interacted gesturally; she could be sweet, but ignored the therapist. She impressed the therapist as a very shy, yet warm and playful child, who engaged well with her parents, could get overloaded easily, and be very demanding. She was unable to process complex auditory input, that is, she couldn't answer "why" or "how" questions. She was capable of pretend play, but when she got anxious, she became aggressive, and her play became fragmented and disjointed, and she became preoccupied with people being eaten or hurt. When she got frustrated with her parents she went into a crying fit, and then continued to whine for a considerable period of time. As her parents got angry and impatient with her, she upped the stakes and seemed to become more disorganized—throwing toys, crying, yelling, and screaming. The more angry the parents became or the more they chose to ignore her, the more upset and disorganized her behavior became. In other words, she showed a great range between her capacity for warmth and engagement and a tendency to become easily overloaded, fragmented, and upset.

Her mother worked on her own intolerance of Molly's moods and understood some of her own conflicts about her daughter's behavior. She had done floor time approaches for a month, when she came in and said, "Molly's doing great." The mother reported that she was able to use an insight that she had discussed at an earlier session. She said:

> I finally realized that Molly feels unsure of herself. I couldn't face this fact before, because Molly was always my "success story." She would be the person who would be better than my brother, which I couldn't be. We felt that she was so confident, because she'd been an early talker and had good motor skills. [Molly was a good jumper, runner, and dancer.] I also realized that, even though she was quite verbal in general, she did not find it easy to verbalize feelings, and she tends always to put feelings into behavior.

The mother went on to say, "It's amazing what just being aware that your daughter can feel unsure of herself can do to your approach to her."

By way of an example, she said:

> We were in the middle of drawing, and for no apparent reason, after we had been getting along nicely for fifteen or twenty minutes, and I was thoroughly enjoying the time, out of left field, she started yelling and screaming and breaking the crayons and having a real tantrum—that's typical for her. Normally, I'd be enraged that she'd interfere with our nice play time together. This time, instead of yelling back at her and saying I won't stay in the same room, and leaving her, in which case she would probably have screamed for a good half-hour or more, I counted to ten and thought to myself, there must be something here that she's feeling unsure of herself about. I stayed there and let her cry for a minute or two, and then just talked in a calm voice, asking her to let me know what was so upsetting to her. To my surprise (this has now happened many times), she said, "I messed up what I wanted to do."

The mother then pursued and asked, "Sweetheart, how did you mess up?" Then Molly showed her how she had drawn something that didn't look quite like what she wanted it to look like, how the lines were "messed up." Her mother said, "This time I didn't exit; this time I didn't yell back. I actually felt bad for her. She crept into my lap and cried for a minute or two. I hugged her and then she said, 'I feel okay now.' " They were then able to resume drawing and to enjoy the rest of their time together.

A second example came about when Molly wanted to stay in the kitchen, because her brother was in the kitchen, and she wanted to hear what her brother had to say. Molly and her mother were about to get into a power struggle, because her mother didn't want both children in the kitchen arguing with one another. But instead of yelling or insisting that Molly leave the kitchen immediately, this time her mother accompanied her into the other room, and asked her what was going on, why she was insisting on staying in the kitchen. Molly replied, "I can't explain now; I can't get the words out to say what I want to." The mother was patient and empathized with Molly's inability to find the words, because that seemed to be more frustrating to Molly than what she actually wanted to say. Eventually, Molly said she thought her brother was going to get something to eat that she wasn't going to get, although she didn't use the word *jealous*. The basic issue for her seemed to be the inability to articulate her feeling, when her mother was pressuring her with questions, "Why do you have to be here? I told you to stay in the other room." Her inability to express her reason for wanting to be in the kitchen was what was frustrating her and making her want to cry. As her mother empathized with her about how hard it is sometimes to say what one wants to say, Molly said, "Sometimes I feel my brain needs to be hit." It became clear that the mother's ability to empathize with her daughter's frustration enabled them to discuss the situation and work out a compromise—Molly and her brother each got to be with the mother part of the time.

As her mother was able to engage her daughter with this new approach, Molly was able also to give up her pacifier, begin going to bed at a more reasonable hour, and generally to be less finicky, angry, or belligerent throughout most of the day.

In carrying out floor time, it is important to note that parents often have a perception of a child that makes it hard for them to empathize with a key part of the child's character. In this case, it was the mother's realization that her child did feel vulnerable and unsure of herself at times, in spite of her apparent competence. Being able to see the child's behavior in terms of her uncertainty rather than as a willful act of belligerence was critical in turning around this child's crying and stubborn, angry behavior. But more importantly, the mother's insight allowed her to empathize during floor time, with the full range of the child's emotions. A parent must empathize with all the child's feelings—whether loving feelings or angry feelings, but also vulnerable, sad, helpless feelings. If parents see the child only in one way, there is a lack of empathy for the other part of a child's character. The child feels that one side of his character is cut off; he never has a chance to put that part of his personality into words; instead, that side of his personality often comes out in behavior discharge, such as tantrums. "I feel frustrated or unsure of myself," or "I feel bad about messing up," comes out instead in behavior—angry, belligerent, spoiled behavior. How many adults behave the same way, when they deal with loss, frustration, or vulnerability through belligerence or aggression? Even if the aggression is expressed verbally, it is a behavior-discharge attack use of words, as opposed to a communicative use of words in order to try to share a feeling with someone.

But no parent is able to empathize with the full range of a child's feelings spontaneously or automatically, because all parents view their children through the filter of the parent's own feelings and conflicts. A parent may be predisposed to favor one side of the child, such as competence or helplessness. The resulting empathetic imbalance undermines the child's ability to represent fully their internal world. The therapist's goal is to help the parents increase their empathetic range by helping them understand their own conflicts about one or another set of emotional themes. At times, the therapist's work will be to facilitate the parents' representational access, if he or she tends to be concrete.

The long-term goal is to help the parents understand their own fantasies and behavioral patterns so that they can be more flexible and adaptive. A short-term goal, especially with caregivers who are not self-observing (i.e., symbolic in the way they handle affect), however, is to help the caregiver meet the child's developmental needs in spite of his perceptions or worrisome fantasies. For example, a very self-centered impulsive mother was intrusively overstimulating her infant. We tried to quickly find out what she wanted for her infant. "I want him to want me," she said. "How?" I asked. "To smile, hug, talk, and look at me," she replied. I also wanted to quickly find out what her long-term goals were. "What do you want him to be like as he grows up?" I asked. "Tough and strong; not take shit from anyone," was her reply. This goal was a product of mother feeling she had to be "tough" to deal with abuse by her own father.

With mother's interest in her baby for her own immediate needs ("be hugged") and for her long-term needs ("for him to be tough"), which was an extension of herself, we worked with her on specific types of interactions. She thought "poking" her baby would get him to react and to be tough. We showed her "better" ways to help him react (e.g., talk to him, hand him toys and see if he would hand them back). We also talked about how he would be "strong" if he interacted with her in this new way.

The key point is: New interactive styles must be tied to the caregiver's needs and goals. These needs and goals may change over time and the caregiver may become more self-observing.

GENERAL PRINCIPLES OF PARENT-ORIENTED DEVELOPMENTAL THERAPY

In order to help the parents utilize these processes, the clinician must first conduct an initial evaluation as discussed in the Assessment Section in order to understand how family dynamics and constitutional and maturational factors have contributed to one or another of these processes going awry. The clinician can then initiate a series of sessions to help the parents more fully relate to the child.

Each of the parents should be encouraged to be involved in floor time for a half-hour a day to provide an opportunity to engage warmly and connect, to share attention, and to establish two-way gestural communication with opening and closing of circles, and to follow the child's lead in pretend or other play. As the parents report back each time to the clinician about their successes and failures, he or she will assist or coach them. For example, the father may complain that he daydreams and his mind wanders whenever aggressive themes come up. He may get bored after fifteen minutes and find himself looking at magazines or making the interactions more structured. The mother may complain that she gets anxious that her child will "go out of control," if the dolls are fighting; she may encourage the doctor to come and help the dolls.

The therapist needs to help the parents see where they are having trouble, to empathize with their fears or anxieties, and help them understand how their own history contributes to the way they relate to their child. The father's avoidance of aggression and the mother's tendency to become frightened and make nice-nice, or "call the doctors in," whenever aggression occurs in the floor time, could be explored. At the same time, the therapist has to help the parents understand why it is important for the child to have each experience. The therapist has to explain why the choice is not between aggression and no aggression, but between aggression symbolized and represented, and therefore integrated with the other facets of the child's personality, as opposed to aggression in a prerepresentational form, which is more likely to result in either impulsiveness and behavior discharge, or massive inhibition and passivity. A floor time philosophy should govern daily interactions with the child, even when there is no pretend play or specific floor time activity. A specific floor time dialogue becomes a dialogue about the overall relationship between parent and child.

It is also necessary to explore the effect of an emotion, such as aggression, on the relationship between the parents. Does the father's avoidance and the mother's making nice-nice interfere with their own relationship in any way? Is the mother frustrated with the father's avoidance? Is the father frustrated with her tendency to make nice-nice? How does this process affect the other children in the family?

Therapy focuses on the four stages of development and involves particular themes such as aggression that are hard for the parents to organize at all four levels.

The therapist's goal is not to become fragmented or lost in the family dynamics but to help the parents negotiate shared attention and engagement, two-way communication, representational elaboration or use of emotional ideas, and emotional thinking, through floor time as they apply to the problem affects. The therapist will also need to facilitate problem-solving discussions, and the effective setting of limits, as described in an earlier chapter. When individual differences in the child, like sensitivities to sound or touch or tendencies toward motor discharge, have made it difficult to engage the child, parent consultation sessions can often help get the family to deal with the reality of the child's sensitivities or motor difficulties without distortions or projections. Depending on the degree of family difficulties, short-term work or work over a longer period of time will be needed.

There are many disorganized families that one may wish to discount in order to work with the child alone. It may be easier to see the parents only for support or to give specific advice regarding not overstimulating or being overly punitive with a child. But many therapists give up on the parents too readily. Even in a very dysfunctional family, where one or both parents may have a borderline personality organization or a severe character disorder or where there are serious marital problems, progress is still possible. One may spend the first year simply getting consistent engagement and two-way communication among family members, without much progress symbolizing complicated affects or seeing connections between affects. But even this accomplishment provides a strong foundation, especially if the child does not have the rug pulled out from under him by disengagement or random and chaotic communication patterns. Over time, as a foundation of engagement and simple two-way communication is established, the family's ability to symbolize and categorize complex affects will gradually grow.

To initiate parent-oriented developmental therapy (after the initial evaluation phase when the therapist watches the parents play with the child and observes their interaction patterns), the therapist may have the parents come in and play with the child either on a regular basis or periodically. The therapist then becomes the observing coach, not just a recipient of reports from the parents. For children under two-and-a-half years, it is often preferable to have such active observation and coaching as an important component of most sessions. At times, separate parent sessions will be indicated. For children three years old and older, depending on the parents' ability to report honestly and openly on what happens during floor time and other factors, the topics will decide how often to see parents alone and with their child.

During sessions with parents and children together, the therapist must not take over, for example, to demonstrate a technique, to the extent of demoralizing the parent. The therapist–coach must let the mother and the father take separate turns in the interactive play, and also be available to the chlid without getting caught in the middle of the action. For example, the therapist should, if the child is having the soldiers hit each other and the mother is about to call for "the doctors," wonder out loud, "Mommy, you're bringing in the doctors, although there are no injuries yet. And [looking at the child] he hasn't even asked for help. He is still telling how angry everyone is." The mother may then take the time to watch what is going on and attempt to elaborate on the anger. If the mother again attempts to bring in "doctors" or, alternatively, "the three little pigs" who will distract the child from his fighting drama, the therapist might wonder what it is about the child's theme that frightens the mother. As the child plays, the parent can explore his or her own anxieties on the sidelines with the therapist. The mother can then get back into the drama to see if she can follow the action from the child's perspective.

As coach, listener, and observer of how the parent relates to him, as well as what takes place between parent and child, the therapist operates within his particular framework and asks himself certain rhetorical questions. He wonders how engaged the parents and the child are and how much attention they are sharing. If he doesn't directly observe this interaction, he may ask the parents to talk about what sense of connectedness they felt when playing with the child. Some parents may report feeling distant, aloof, unengaged. Even if the parents aren't so aware of their feelings as they might be, the therapist may see the mechanical style of description as a sign that they are not terribly involved. He may observe the way they engage him and understand that they are not able fully to engage their children, because of how they relate to people in general.

The therapist can directly observe the quality of two-way communication or can get a sense of the interaction between parent and child by asking the parent for examples. If the parent speaks in generalities, the therapist may say, "Can you give me specific illustrations?" He will then get a picture of the way circles are or are not opened and closed and, in the two-year-old and older, which affects are or are not being symbolized.

By observing or listening to the parents of three-year-olds and older, he will also get a sense of how much feelings are being categorized and connected to one another. Is the child saying that the wolves attacked the piglets, because the wolves were mad or because they were hungry, and the piglets had all the food? Or is he saying just that the wolves were mad, with no indication of any reason? Similarly, the therapist will get a sense of the differentiating ability of the parent by the way in which the parent relates to him. Is the parent able to elaborate clearly on the therapist's comments with both detail and a sense of perspective?

In addition, in connection with each developmental level, the therapist will listen for themes of dependency and closeness; pleasure, sexuality, and excitement; assertiveness or overt aggression; self-limit-setting; empathy and caring for others, including altruism; and more mature kinds of love and concern. He will also listen to the counterparts of these themes, such as separation worries, as a part of dependency and closeness; castration anxieties, as part of excitement and sexuality or aggression. He will get a sense of whether a level is reached broadly and flexibly or only in a limited way. For example, the child may be able to organize two-way communication, when the theme of assertiveness or aggression emerges, but when it comes to closeness and dependency, somehow the child seems more chaotic and random. Or dependency may be symbolized in pretend play, but aggression may be acted out behaviorally in hitting or biting, without being symbolized.

The therapist will also observe the stability of the organizational level achieved. Is the child able to represent anger in pretend play only up to a point? Does he act his anger out behaviorally, if he is very angry or if his mother is away for a few hours?

The therapist will find that different themes have different levels of organization. He will get a sense of the particular conflicts or patterns that characterize these themes. Is there aggression and then separation, or is there excitement, sexuality, and then aggression? What is the sequence of themes that is elaborated, either by behaviors at the level of two-way communication or in terms of representations or symbols at the level of emotional ideas? What themes are organized at the highest level of representational differentiation, where there are not only patterns but also connecting links between the elements in the patterns?

The therapist needs to think about the levels of development reached, the themes evidenced at those levels, the breadth as opposed to the restrictiveness of the themes, and the stability of the organizational level. The particular patterns or signatures, that is, the story lines or drama that the parents describe or the child evidences directly, or the parents and the child are negotiating, will emerge. The therapist's role is simply to comment or interact with the child and the parents in such a way as to facilitate the four processes and the broadest range and greatest stability of themes at each level. As parents work on different emotional themes with their child, they too will resolve inner conflicts and grow emotionally. At times marital difficulties will also be partially resolved due to emotional growth in each parent's interactive capacities.

SUMMARY

In summary, a model of developmentally based, parent-oriented therapy has been presented. If the parents can attempt to engage the child at the four levels of development, the therapist can act as a coach to the parents and the family. The child may make progress without being seen alone very often or very intensively by the clinician. Direct parent work alone; parent work and parent–child work, with the clinician observing the interactions; or a combination of parents alone, parent–child together, and some therapist–child work are all sound options. The therapist must have clearly in mind the goal of facilitating the family's and the child's ability to engage in these four processes and then see how his therapeutic strategy will facilitate this goal. In cases when the child's anxiety, negativism, stubbornness, or tendency to withdraw is severe, and a parent's own personality structure is very fragile, it may be essential for the therapist to work directly with the child to enable him to take the lead to work out better interactions with his parents. But most parents are available, if one doesn't get scared off by the marital problems and tendencies to fragmented or seemingly irrational and unpredictable behavior. In most cases, one can work systematically with the parents, as well as with the child.

Many professionals work with multiproblem families where the early goal is to maintain contact with the family, foster a relationship, and stabilize critical parental and family functions such as the physical care, safety, and early nurturing of the infant. The special challenges of working with multiproblem families were considered in some detail in an earlier work entitled *Infants in Multirisk Families* (Greenspan et al., 1987) and is discussed in appendix 4, "Setting Up a Clinical Infant and Child Development Program."

Chapter 18

Developmental Perspectives on Couples and Family Processes: Implications for Therapy

Traditionally, couples, family, and even group therapy in general has rested in part on dynamic and systems understanding of "contents" boundaries, structures, and organizations. For example, in couples therapy there is interest in the mechanism of projective identification. One member of the couple projects certain contents of their own onto their spouse. The spouse unconsciously carries out these projected expectations which may also be unconscious in the mind of the originator. The mechanism of projective identification has also been postulated to operate in families where, for example, an adolescent may be carrying out the unconscious wishes of a parent, much to the parent's chagrin (Greenspan and Mannino, 1974; Shapiro and Zinner, 1975).

Intrapsychic collaborations among the different members of the group, including mechanisms such as pairing and fight–flight, have been postulated (Bion, 1961) to account for the dynamics of groups of eight to ten people. Developmental

557

concepts are well integrated into many of the different approaches to couples, families, and groups (e.g., level of differentiation).

The developmental approach to be discussed below will not offer an alternative to traditional conceptualizations of group process. Rather, it will try to offer a complementary perspective which will explore the application of the model of levels of development postulated in this work to group processes.

The developmental perspective is based on a number of principles. The first principle, well established in many approaches, is that group patterns are an entity in their own right, whether it be a couple, a family, or a small group. Different people are component parts of a larger whole. Participants — family members, group members, or spouses—are the elements in a larger structure.

Consider a family where the male child appears to be "hyper" and is coming for a consultation for a problem with "being destructive." His older sister seems quiet and reserved. She has excellent concentration and is called a "model child." Mother tends to be overprotective and hovers over her children in an infantilizing manner. At other times, however, mother is overstimulating and intrusive. Father is an aloof workaholic who becomes intensely involved in hyperstimulating the family when he is home. He is often away, however, and even when he is home, when not overstimulating his family, he is unavailable, shut away in his study. This is a not atypical family constellation. Each member of the family has a unique character. Even with their unique characteristics, all members of this family had difficulty with one common characteristic—negotiating closeness or dependency. The "hyperactive destructive one" was very uneasy with being too close. In fact, it was at times that he either wanted closeness or closeness was offered to him that he became the most hyper. His older sister had given up on closeness and had withdrawn into a self-contained shell. She only felt close to her books and was too fearful to reach out to be close to people. Mother tried to be close by her overprotectiveness, but was constantly frustrated and feeling "empty" and that "nobody cared." Father had a lifelong difficulty with being close to other people, using a style similar to that of his older daughter—avoidance. He created an artificial sense of security and dependency around his work. Each family member, in their own way, was struggling with closeness; each, however, was marching to a different drummer and had different symptoms or complaints.

Once it became possible to see that they were dealing with a common theme, closeness (even though each one had other themes they were concerned with as well), it was possible to look at a number of parameters of this family's functioning.

One parameter we looked at was the one just stated: What was the theme that they were all concerned about? In this case, it was dependency. Then we asked a number of related questions that follow from our developmental approach to ego functioning.

First, at what developmental level was this family functioning in its common concern? Once we understand that they are interested in something together, we want to know how they are negotiating this issue. Are they negotiating it at a level suggestive of prerepresentational patterns, even preengagement patterns? Where are they as a group in our developmental scheme? Are they engaged? Are they involved in intentional behavioral interactions? Have they made it to the representational level? If so, are they elaborating the different interrelated emotional themes around dependency and closeness or are they representationally constricted? Have they made it to the level of representational differentiation? If so, are they elaborating different themes at a differentiated level?

In this family, they were all engaged to some degree, even the more reserved ones that used aloofness and detachment. They were all purposeful in their behavior, except for the "hyper" one who sometimes regressed to a preintentional chaotic pattern. More often than not even his aggressive behavior was purposeful and targeted. When it came to abstracting affective patterns around dependency and closeness, however, including the anxieties, fears, and coping strategies associated with dependency, the family only had a limited ability to representationally elaborate their concerns (i.e., put feelings into words, complex gestures, rituals, or even playful games). At best, they were marginally at the level of representational elaboration when it came to dealing with dependency. They seemed to be somewhere between an intentional behavioral level and an early representational level. For example, only on rare occasions would mother talk about feeling loving or lonely or gesture father for closeness. More often, she followed her pattern of trying to overprotect and overdo for him. This made him feel suffocated; in turn, he avoided her. This pattern was never discussed but it was played out at the behavioral level.

We also observed that at the level of intentional behavior and representational elaboration, this family was quite constricted. They were not able to negotiate, even at the behavioral level, range of themes. Their ability to negotiate curiosity, excitement, pleasure, and anger and aggression was quite limited. For example, anger would often lead to loss of an attained developmental level. The youngest child would start to behave chaotically and regress to a preintentional level. Mother, when she would get furious, would withdraw, in spite of her overprotective style, regressing to a preengagement level. When angry, father would do the same.

We saw a family that was quite constricted in terms of their representational and prerepresentational range, and which at best, made it up into the late stages of intentional behavior and early stages of representational elaboration. The family members had no capacity for discussing dependency issues in a highly differentiated way, where feelings would be abstracted, verbalized, and examined in terms of their relationships to each other. We have a family who, at best, operated in a constricted way at the level of behavioral and beginning representational elaboration.

The challenge for this family is clear: they need to progress to the point where they can represent more broadly patterns at the level of representational elaboration and then progress to the level of representational differentiation.

As we think about how to help such a family, we should be clear that this family had regressive potential back to preintentional and preengagement levels of ego development. At the same time, we should also be clear that individually each one of the members of this family may have been capable of a higher level of adaptation in terms of their individual psychological functioning. When one talked to father alone (not in the family setting), he would appear to have a capacity for representational elaboration and differentiation as he reflected about himself, his parents, his relationships with siblings, and key relationships at work. At work he was able to be assertive and often compassionate with people who worked for him. He even reflected on his relationship with his own father and mother in a highly elaborative and differentiated way. However, in the family sessions, he operated like a different person, aloof or competitively attacking and overstimulating other family members. Other family members showed similar profiles. Individually, they were capable of a higher level of functioning than they were in the family group.

The family becomes a unique entity. It has its own developmental level which is in part independent from the individual dynamics of each member. There are a number of principles that can be applied to the family group. The group is an entity in its own right: it organizes around a common theme or set of themes. This theme (or set of themes) is organized at a developmental level (engagement, intentionality, representational elaboration, representational differentiation). At the developmental level there is a thematic and affective range that the family is capable of. The range may be constricted or broad and flexible. Each family can be described (or even profiled and diagrammed) in terms of the predominant themes and the developmental level and thematic–affective range.

THERAPEUTIC IMPLICATIONS

The following discussion will focus on how to use these observations of group processes for therapeutic purposes. The therapeutic goal may be stated as follows: to shift the equilibrium of the group to a higher level from the lower level found naturally by the group because of a lack of integrating and differentiating structures within it (be it couples, family, or a larger group). Some social organizations may do this naturally. (Perhaps these are the types of social organizations we should advocate as being therapeutic in their own right.)

But first, let us consider how we do this therapeutically. In the group, be it a couple, family, or other type of group, the role of the therapist is to facilitate the shift upward in both structure and broadening of themes that could be differentiated and integrated at any given structural level. The therapist is constantly trying to get the behavioral and prebehavioral issues onto the representational level by abstracting central affective states. The therapist might comment, "In spite of all the competitive rhetoric in this family, where you criticize one another, you all seem to be struggling with how to be close to one another." Each member may then review his difficulties with closeness in his own history, as well as in the family. Nonetheless, family members might quickly lapse into back-biting critiques of one another.

As the therapist keeps his eye on the difficulty this family has in dealing with dependency, he may continually return to it until the family can abstract a feeling state having to do with dependency. He will point out all the ways in which the family defends against, avoids, or regresses from this issue as a way of helping them see the interrelationships between the main theme and their other behaviors. Over time, they see that what, for them, were seemingly random states of mind are part of a larger pattern, and moreover that each individual's styles are part of this larger pattern. The group is seen as a theme and a series of interrelated ways of dealing with, avoiding, or otherwise defending against this theme.

The overall goal is to switch from the lower level to the higher level. To abstract the feeling states, the couple, family, or group must see which feeling states they are having difficulty with. If, for example, in the family the situation is closeness, the family may nonetheless perceive the difficulty they are having as "we fight too much." Then the therapist's job is to keep abstracting the difficulties with closeness out of each interaction. The family may be involved in behavioral interactions where they attack one another. Around each attack, the therapist sees frustrated dependency longings. At some point after observing this, the therapist may offer a comment such as, "Gee, when mommy attacks daddy or daddy attacks junior, each time it seems to be because the other one wasn't paying enough attention to the first one and wasn't taking care of that person enough. Junior seemed to want mommy to give him a verbal hug, so to speak, and daddy seemed to want something similar from daughter. Each time you folks get angry, there always seems to be some related issue having to do with how can we be close to one another." The family may respond to this initially with anxiety and a further intensification of their behavioral patterns. But over time, they will begin to abstract and represent something about the family's needs. As closeness and dependency are elevated to the representational level, the family can find a higher equilibrium, a way of meeting each other's needs and conceptualizing the family in a different way. The family goes from being a "fighting family" to a family that is struggling to find a way to meet each other's needs. (This is a very different equilibrium and orientation, particularly when this shift is from a behavioral intentional action level.) They may eventually reach a level where feelings are abstracted, experienced, and discussed.

Within a couple's relationship, this pattern sometimes works quickly and dramatically. The couple observes that together they function at a much lower level than either one functions at individually. As they begin exploring how they negotiate dependency, competition, aggression, or other elements, the therapist helps them abstract those feeling states which exist at prerepresentational levels. As they become aware of the way they are behaving toward each other, and as they become aware of those feelings that they can only deal with in a concrete way, they begin learning to abstract those feeling states (whether it has to do with sharing, or competition, or closeness and dependency, or anger, or sexuality, etc.). As they learn to represent these feeling states that had formerly been acted out in intentional or disorganized behavior, or in levels of engagement or in preengagement patterns, they progress up the developmental ladder.

There are many steps that must go on before the traditional therapeutic level of examining meanings is achieved. Many therapists assume the couple, family, or other group is already at this level. Much verbalization goes for naught because the group is really struggling with issues of engagement and purposeful intentional behavioral communication. They are not yet ready to see relationships among affect states, and they continue to be disorganized at their prerepresentational or early representational levels, while the therapist is two levels higher than they are.

In helping the group progress from a lower to a higher level of equilibrium, the therapist's understanding of the group's dynamics is used to help them abstract their feeling states. He also creates a milieu following the general principles that have been discussed earlier. He is engaged and mobilizes each member to be engaged to the entire group. He sets up a structure for intentional, purposeful communication within the group. He communicates a value system that the group organizes around; the essence of this system is that abstracted representational communications will help group members understand earlier patterns of communication and that representational differentiation is to be strived for as a goal. Within this context and with the relationship with the therapist facilitating developmental momentum, over time the group uses the security afforded by constant engagement and purposeful communication, and a focus on abstracting feeling states, as a vehicle for moving into the representational levels. Once there, the therapist helps the group elaborate the representational levels into themes they were incapable of representing earlier and then move into more differentiated patterns.

There is a shifting back and forth between engaging the group in its fantasies and pointing out the limits of realistic thinking.

The group or family or couples' therapist creates a sense of safety and security by focusing on verbalizing rather than acting. He fosters engagement between members, pointing out when one member is isolating himself or disengaging, and helping him reengage (he fosters engagement between the group members just as he fosters it between himself and the group). Similarly, he is always fostering purposeful communication. Disorganized behaviors are always reorganized in the context of group intentions. When a member behaves chaotically, he helps that member communicate what he wants to say more purposefully or helps the group see the unpurposeful communication in a purposeful manner. The person who is lying on the floor comes to see that they are asking for discipline or asking for closeness or trying to be provocative. Lying on the floor now becomes a purposeful behavior for the individual and for the group. The individual side and the group side operate synergistically.

In some respects the group has the opportunity to create an even greater sense of security at the level of engagement and prerepresentational reality testing than individual therapy. The members of the group create multiple connections and engagements. The sense of security can be enormous. Similarly, the ability to negotiate in an organized, purposeful way the group's many nonverbal gestures also provides an enormous sense of security, in part related to the ever-present possibility of chaos.

In the family, the ability for engagement and purposeful communication can often reinstitute a structure that has been dangerously undermined by miscommunications. Sometimes one is putting into place a system that has never been present in the family. To the degree the new family "structure" continues outside the therapy sessions, there is now a new sense of security through engagement and differentiated behavioral communications. The family now has prerepresentational reality testing, the predictability and understanding of each other's gestures, and constant engagement with one another. Earlier, there may have been unpredictable, frightening gestures, overwhelming confusion, withdrawal, and avoidance. We often overlook the importance of establishing the baseline experience of engagement and the interactional logical communication most take for granted.

Similarly, with couples, instituting engagement and the purposeful communication provides a cohesive structure and foundation for that couple. Against this background, it is not surprising that families, couples, and other groups experience relief and can begin engaging in representational elaboration and differentiation.

It must be remembered that people only exist in relative terms in the context of the various groups in which they participate; we exist as part of a nuclear family and an on-going set of relationships, including new families, larger groups in work and play, and various societal structures. One's experiences in the therapeutic group have profound influences not only on that group's level of adaptation, but one's own way of finding equilibrium points in one's natural groups (and vice versa), in a day-to-day life. Group relationships, in part, define one's self just as individual psychodynamics do.

In summary, a family can be described according to its developmental level, its thematic–affective range. Experiences that facilitate individual ego development, when applied to the unique features that characterize families and groups, also facilitate the collective ego development of the family or group as a whole.

Chapter 19

Comments on Selecting the Appropriate Therapeutic Approach

We have talked about specific techniques, such as floor time, working with parents, and working directly with the parent and the child in their interaction patterns. We will now talk about which therapeutic approach is most appropriate for which type of difficulty.

COUNSELING PARENTS IN FLOOR TIME AND PARENT–CHILD INTERACTION

When the child does not require direct work with a therapist, as indicated earlier, a useful technique is to work with the parents in order to improve their ability to interact with the child at home during floor time, and at other times. This approach is ideally suited for a child who is at his appropriate developmental level, but has a constriction in range of emotional themes organized at that stage or in the stability of themes organized. There may or may not be obvious conflicts and/or

567

anxiety. It is suited for parents who are motivated to work with their children and who themselves have mastered the four core developmental processes but may have constrictions in the range of emotional themes they organize.

Floor time becomes a microcosm for the parent–child relationship and for the parents' ability to mobilize and support the child's four levels of development. In short term work, after an initial evaluation, often, it is possible to have the parents come in every other week or monthly for a series of six to eight sessions, during which they get down on the floor to practice their pattern of play while the clinician observes and assists.

As the therapist observes how a parent is or is not able to support a child's particular capacity, he is also focusing on what contributes to the difficulties. One element may be a lack of knowledge, know-how, or cognitive limitation, any of which may be temporary on the part of the parent. More often than not, however, as indicated earlier, the parents' limited knowledge is accompanied by their emotional limitation. In the action-oriented mode of playing with the children, parents can often quickly get in touch with the way their own parents played or did not play with them, or the way their parents did or did not engage them around certain themes or conflicts. Sometimes even just an intellectual understanding can give a parent the perspective they need to engage their children more fully. Sometimes an issue that they have trouble with at home with their spouses, such as closeness or anger, may not be as much of a problem with their child, because the child is less threatening to them and therefore the emotions are not as intense; they can stay at a distance from the problem.

DIRECT THERAPEUTIC WORK WITH CHILDREN

In situations where children are not at the requisite developmental level, often they require a more in-depth and intensive approach, which may require sessions with the child alone or with the parents and the child together, but with the therapist interacting directly with the child and at the same time facilitating the parent–child interaction. In this approach, the therapist calls on his own special floor time skills to relate to the child at the different developmental levels and to help the parent do the same. This will often involve multiple meetings a week. If the parents have significant psychological or psychiatric difficulties or other limitations in their ability to carry out the floor time exercises, direct work by the therapist with the parents in separate sessions may be indicated.

Another type of child with whom this more intensive direct approach is indicated is the child who is at his age-appropriate developmental level, but has very challenging individual differences, such as intense sensory over- or underreactivity, or very poor modulation of impulses and behavior. These extreme patterns may require the therapist's special skills.

Occasionally, if the child is only one developmental level behind, and the family is very competent, the parent–child type of floor time can be used to mobilize forward progress, as well as to broaden the range and themes that the child can accommodate at his developmental level.

COMPREHENSIVE, IN-DEPTH APPROACH

In another type of situation, a comprehensive, intensive, in-depth approach is required for the infant or child. The child and the family may need to meet with a clinician two to four times a week; often auxiliary services, working with language, motor, and/or sensory capacities may be necessary one to two times a week. This comprehensive approach is particularly important for children who have significant lags along multiple lines of development, for example, if language and social and emotional development are delayed, both in terms of developmental level and range and depth. Also, children who are diagnosed as having pervasive developmental disorder with or without autistic features or children with severe conduct or attentional difficulties may require this in-depth, comprehensive approach.

We have seen children who may operate, for example, at a fourteen-month-old level when they are three years old, whose prognosis is oft thought to be dire, in fact respond well to an intensive comprehensive approach. By age four, five, or six, such a child can become warm, supportive, intimate, and capable of relating to peers and adults. The child's specific auditory and/or visual–spatial processing difficulties or motor and sensory problems become available to remediation, because the profound emotional and social difficulties may improve sufficiently so that the earlier ominous social deficit is no longer present.

In this therapist's experience, when children receive only behavior modification therapy or only a focus on so-called splinter skills, such as isolated cognitive skills, rather than a comprehensive therapeutic approach that mobilizes the four levels of development, the results are not nearly as good. Children may learn to inhibit their use of aggression or to follow certain concrete rules, but they don't learn to think emotionally or to be warm and intimate in their relationships. Therefore, a comprehensive, in-depth approach that involves individual work with the child and/or his parents and the therapist, two to four times a week, in addition to speech and language work, occupational therapy, and direct counseling with the parents, is often indicated for these more severe challenges.

Chapter 20

Diagnostic Considerations: Implications for Treatment

The traditional *Diagnostic and Statistical Manual of Mental Disorders* (1987; i.e., DSM-III-R and the emerging DSM-IV) tends to focus on the phenomenology of mental disorders; that is, on clusters of symptoms or patterns of behavior. There has been a deliberate attempt to avoid hypothesizing underlying causes or dynamics, and almost no attempt to take into account developmental patterns.

Mental health professionals are familiar with the traditional diagnostic categories, such as affective disorders and schizophrenia. Childhood categories include attention deficit disorder, anxiety disorder, conduct disorder, pervasive developmental disorder, and others.

However, there is general agreement that in the current diagnostic framework there are very few categories that apply to the first three to four years of life. Attachment disorder of infancy focuses on reactive attachment disorder, such as the baby's reaction to being deprived of a human relationship. Other categories, such as specific developmental disorder, which can relate to a motor or language delay, can also be appropriate for infancy. But there are woefully few symptom-oriented disorders that are geared specifically to infants. Some mental health professionals apply symptom complexes constructed for problems with older children downward toward infancy. For example, anxiety disorders can describe symptoms of excessive fear and anxiety exhibited by infants and young children, as well as by older children. Similarly, mood disorders may also apply to younger children (when they manifest characteristics often seen in depression with older children). Symptoms of distractibility associated with attention deficit disorder are seen in preschoolers and even toddlers. Conduct disorders describe children who have difficulty with social behavior and controlling their impulses. Pervasive developmental disorder and autism are applied to a broad age range and encompass children with severe impairments in social relationships, language, and overall communication.

However, the diagnostic categories applied to older children are inadequate to characterize the difficulties of infants and young children. Furthermore, in addition to symptom-oriented descriptions, therapists require an appropriate developmental approach to diagnosis. It is important to capture the derailment of an entire developmental process, such as failure to attain a specific developmental level, evidenced by the ability to regulate aggression or behavior, to relate to others, or to have self-esteem. In addition, because all learning takes place as part of a relationship, diagnoses must also capture the importance of the parent/caregiver–child relationship (as the process that helps the child develop adaptive capacities).

In order to characterize adequately an infant's or young child's diagnostic patterns, one should look at them from many sides. One needs to discuss the infant's presenting symptoms and behavior (phenomenology), as well as the developmental level or process, and, as indicated, the parent/caregiver–child interactions, family patterns, and other aspects of development. For example, is the symptom just a sign of momentary stress, a sign of adaptation, or a signal that some underlying developmental process, such as relationships, is not being properly negotiated?

Therefore, a multiaxial approach is recommended: (1) a symptom-oriented or phenomenologically oriented diagnosis; (2) a developmentally based diagnosis; (3) a relationship and/or family-based diagnosis; and (4) an "other" category to cover developmental or physical problems (e.g., a motor or language delay or a chronic physical illness). While these multiple diagnoses will not necessarily in themselves always capture the interactive pattern, it would be captured in an accompanying description. Additionally, the interactive pattern would be hinted at in both the family and the infant's pattern. For example, a problem with regulation and shared attention would obviously be a statement not just about the infant's inattentiveness or the parents' inability to engage the infant, but about the way this process is being mediated.

This approach to diagnosis can be applied descriptively to the case studies presented in chapters 2, 3, and 4. The basic model presented in chapter 1 captures the different axes. As indicated earlier, the therapist looks at each developmental level; the child's constitutional and maturational contributions, and the interactive and family contributions, to see how these influence the infant's or child's ability to negotiate each particular developmental level. The symptoms or behaviors that result from this negotiation comprise the symptom-oriented diagnosis. The developmental level and pattern lead to the developmental diagnosis. The family and interactive patterns contribute to the relationship, interactional, or family diagnosis. The "others" category captures other lines of development, such as sensory reactivity and processing; language, motor, physical health, and related systems. One may describe these dimensions formally or in a narrative paragraph, as illustrated in the cases. Next, developmental, family relationship, and symptom-oriented diagnoses will be discussed.

DEVELOPMENTAL DIAGNOSES

The framework for the developmental diagnoses is presented in chapter 1, "The Basic Model" (i.e., the different developmental levels), is illustrated by the cases, and is discussed in the sections on assessment and treatment. If the clinician wishes to formalize the developmental diagnoses, the following format is suggested.

The clinician should make a determination regarding each of the six developmental levels in terms of whether they have been successfully negotiated or not, and whether there is a deficit at any level that has not been successfully negotiated. Sometimes these levels have been successfully negotiated, but are not applied to the full range of emotional themes. For example, a toddler may use two-way gestural communication to negotiate assertiveness and exploration by, for example, pointing at a certain toy and vocalizing for his parent to play with him. The same child may either withdraw or cry in a disorganized way when he wishes for increased closeness and dependency instead of, for example, reaching out to be picked up or coming over and initiating a cuddle. This would indicate a constriction at that level.

Sometimes children are able to negotiate a level with one parent and not the other, with one sibling and not another, or with one substitute caregiver but not another. If it should reasonably be expected that a particular relationship is secure and stable enough to support a certain developmental level, but that level is not evident in that relationship, then there is a constriction at that level as well.

It is useful to indicate which areas or relationships are not incorporated into the developmental level. Consider the following areas of expected emotional range: dependency (closeness, pleasure, assertiveness [exploration], curiosity, anger, empathy [for children over $3\frac{1}{2}$]); stable forms of love, self-limit-setting (for children over 18 months); interest and collaboration with peers (for children over age 2 years); participation in a peer group (for children over age $2\frac{1}{2}$); and the ability to deal with competition and rivalry (for children over 3½ years).

If the child has reached a developmental level, but the slightest stress, such as being tired, having a mild illness (e.g., a cold), or playing with a new peer leads to a loss of that level, then there is an *instability* at that level.

A child may have a defect, constriction, or instability at more than one level. Also, a child may have a defect at one level and a constriction or instability at another. Therefore, the clinician should make a "developmental" judgment based on the following developmental levels.

Developmental Level	Defect	Constriction	Instability
1. Regulation and interest in the world			
2. Attachment			
3. Intentional Communication			
4. Behavioral Organization (complex sense of self)			
5. Representational Elaboration			
6. Representational Differentiation			

INTERACTIVE, RELATIONSHIP, AND FAMILY DIAGNOSES

There are many approaches to looking at interactive, relationship, and family patterns as discussed in chapter 18. For the purposes of focusing the diagnostic process, it is suggested that the clinician use frameworks that provide him or her with the broadest understanding of the interactive and family patterns.

In addition, however, the clinician should attempt to focus his conclusion on how the interactive and family patterns, including the caregivers' special feelings and fantasies, contribute to the processes involved in negotiating each developmental level. For example, an intrusive, anxious caregiver who fantasizes and worries about "hurting" her infant, in a dysfunctional, fragmented way may, nonetheless, be able to support the infant's capacity to form a relationship (attachment). However, she may have difficulty in supporting intentional communication and aspects of self-regulation. A seemingly well-organized caregiver in a rigid, controlled family may, because of a disguised, underlying depression, not be able to foster attachment and the forming of relationships, and only partially be able to support aspects of self-regulation and interest in the world.

Therefore, it is suggested that the interactive and family patterns be summarized in terms of the developmental levels described above. They should also be described narratively in terms of their additional dynamics. Interactive, relationship, and family patterns may be described as influencing a defect, constriction, or instability in the developmental levels, as outlined above.

Simply because an infant experiences a difficulty does not mean the interactive or family dynamics are critical contributors. The infant's constitutional and maturational pattern may exert a determining influence. For example, an infant with a severe motor delay and overreactivity to sound and touch may understandably experience difficulty in mastering intentional communication in the first year of life, even if his caregiver and his family are excellent at supporting two-way intentional communication. Chapter 5 on assessment discusses the specific interactive and family patterns that contribute to an infant's or child's difficulty with one or another developmental stage.

While the approach recommended here is in keeping with the developmental framework which forms a theoretical foundation for this book, there are many colleagues working in the area of relationships and family patterns whose work can also serve as a basis for increased diagnostic perspective, for example, Sameroff and Emde (1989).

In the remainder of this chapter, I will not attempt to discuss further different potential axes. There is, however, a great deal of ongoing interest in diagnosis for infants and young children and their families. For example, a committee of the National Center for Infant Programs (which the author chairs) is working on improved phenomenological or descriptive diagnostic categories and collecting data on types of problems evidenced by infants and young children. Refinements are now being made in the American Psychiatric Association's approach to diagnosis in DSM-III-R; work is in progress on DSM-IV.

SYMPTOM-ORIENTED AND PHENOMENOLOGICALLY BASED DIAGNOSES

This section will suggest an approach to symptom-oriented diagnoses and will comment on related treatment issues as well. Three broad categories will be suggested, under which most symptoms and patterns can be listed. While for each symptom-oriented diagnosis, one must understand the developmental processes that are involved and the contribution of the constitutional–maturational and interactive and family dynamics, the descriptive diagnoses are helpful for administrative and some clinical purposes.

Descriptive symptom-oriented diagnoses may be divided into three general categories, each of which has its specific developmental roots, and preventively oriented psychotherapeutic approaches. These three categories are interactive disorders, regulatory disorders, and multisymptom disorders.

INTERACTIVE DISORDERS

Interactive disorders are characterized by a particular caregiver–child interaction or by the way the child perceives and experiences his emotional world. These disorders lack a significant constitutional or maturational component. Symptoms in this category include anxiety, fears, behavioral control problems, and sleeping and eating difficulties. This category, because it involves symptoms stemming from interactive patterns, would also include situational reactions of a transient nature, such as a mother returning to work or certain responses to trauma where the response does not involve multiple aspects of development.

REGULATORY DISORDERS

Regulatory disorders have a significant and clearly demonstrable maturational or constitutional component (Greenspan, 1989). They also have an interactive component. These disorders involve attentional and behavioral problems, such as irritability, aggression, distractibility, poor frustration tolerance, tantrums, and sleeping and eating difficulties.

MULTISYSTEM DEVELOPMENTAL DISORDERS

A third category of disorders involves multiple aspects of development, including social relationships and language, cognitive, motor, and sensory functioning. The extreme end of the continuum of these disorders is autism. Another type of disorder which involves multiple aspects of development is where an environmental stress leads to a global disruption in multiple areas of functioning. For example, when an infant evidences a failure-to-thrive syndrome, motor, cognitive, language, affective, and physical growth may slow down or cease altogether. Types of neglect or abuse may produce a similar global disruption in functioning. Some of these types of disorders fall into the DSM-III-R category of pervasive developmental disorder.

In summary then, the three types of disorders are (1) interactive; (2) regulatory disorders; and (3) multisystem developmental disorders. Within these groups, one can classify most of the DSM-III-R and planned DSM-IV infant and early child-hood mental health disorders.

It may be useful to look briefly at how the DSM-III-R diagnoses would fit under these three broad categories.

DSM-III-R (1987) disorders that characterize symptoms or behaviors that can be found in infants and young children include the following:

1. Adjustment Disorder
2. Personality Disorders
3. Sexual Disorders
4. Mood Disorders
5. Organic Mental Disorders
6. Developmental Disorders (e.g., retardation)
7. Pervasive Developmental Disorder
   a. Autism
   b. Pervasive Developmental Disorder not otherwise specified
8. Specific Developmental Disorders (including arithmetic, writing, reading, articulation, expressive language, receptive language, coordination)
9. Attention Deficit Hyperactivity Disorder
10. Conduct Disorder
11. Separation Anxiety Disorder
12. Avoidant Disorder of Childhood
13. Overanxious Disorder
14. Eating Disorders
15. Pica
16. Rumination Disorder of Infancy
17. Gender Identity Disorder
18. Tic Disorders
19. Elimination Disorders (encopresis and enuresis)
20. Speech Disorders
21. Elective Mutism
22. Reactive Attachment Disorder of Infancy
23. Stereotyping/Habit Disorder
24. Undifferentiated Attention Deficit Disorder

Under *Interactive Disorders,* the following may be included:

1. Adjustment Disorders
2. Personality Disorders
3. Sexual Disorders
4. Mood Disorders
5. Conduct Disorders
6. Oppositional Defect Disorder
7. Separation Anxiety Disorder
8. Avoidant Disorder
9. Overanxious Disorder
10. Eating Disorders
11. Elimination Disorders (functional)

Under *Regulatory Disorders,* the following may be included:

1. Attention Deficit Hyperactivity Disorder
2. Undifferentiated Attention Deficit Disorder
3. Specific Developmental Disorders
4. Rumination Disorder of Infancy
5. Speech Disorders
6. Stereotyping

Under *Multisystem Developmental Disorders,* the following may be included:

1. Pervasive Developmental Disorder not otherwise specified
2. Autism
3. Reactive Attachment Disorder (of a severe, multisystem, failure-to-thrive type)

Additional disorders that do not fall into these three categories include:

For a detailed discussion of the specific diagnostic categories listed above, consult DSM-III-R (American Psychiatric Association, 1987).

1. Organic Mental Disorders
2. Developmental Disorders (retardation)
3. Pica
4. Tic Disorders

The following chapters will consider each of the three types of broad disorders in terms of general features and treatment implications.

These three categories as indicated include: problems that are part of the infant–caregiver interaction patterns, problems that are part of regulatory difficulties or disorders, and problems that are part of multiproblem or multisystem pervasive developmental difficulties.

As these three broad categories are considered a framework for therapy and prevention will emerge. In the first category, difficulties that are a part of the infant–caregiver interaction pattern, it will be observed that there are only minimal contributions, if any, from constitutional–maturational differences and that there are not significant irregularities, delays, or dysfunctions in core areas of functioning, such as motor, sensory, language, and cognition. In other words, in this category, the primary difficulty is in the interactions between the child and the caregiver. The caregiver's own personality, fantasies, and intentions, the child's own emerging organization of experience, and the way these come together through the interactions, will be the primary focus for understanding the nature of the difficulty and for intervention.

The second category of regulatory disorders focuses on a group of infants and young children where there are significant constitutional and maturational factors. Here sensory over- or underreactivity, sensory processing, or motor tone and motor planning difficulties, along with the child–caregiver interaction, the caregiver's personality and fantasies, and the family dynamics are part of the problem.

One may argue that all infants and children have unique constitutional and maturational variations, including the first group where the focus is the caregiver–infant interaction. To be sure, this statement in a relative sense is true. The distinction is that, for the regulatory disorders, the constitutional and maturational factors are not just present as individual differences, but are a *significant* part of the child's problem. Therefore, in the second group, one wants not just to understand individual differences as part of the nature of the caregiver–infant interaction patterns, one wants to make the constitutional and maturational factors a major focus in their own right (alongside the interaction patterns and the family dynamics). Here, where possible, one will utilize intervention strategies that help the infant strengthen or organize in a more adaptive way constitutional and maturational variations. One will also seek to understand how the infant's constitutional and maturational variations are a stimulus for the parents' particular fantasies and how the infant's constitutional and maturational variations bring out certain maladaptive personality dynamics in the caregivers, parents, or family as a unit.

The third group, the multisystem, pervasive developmental problems, include those groups of infants and young children that in addition to variations in constitutional and maturational patterns, have significant delays or dysfunctions in multiple core areas of functioning, such as language, motor, sensory, and cognition. Here difficulties exist at a number of levels. The child evidences problems in infant–caregiver interaction patterns, parents' perceptions, and family dynamics. There are also regulatory difficulties in terms of significant contributions from constitutional and maturational variations. Furthermore, either these regulatory patterns are so extreme that they are consistent with significant delays in sensory, motor, cognitive, or language patterns, or they are associated with significant dysfunctions and delays in these core areas of functioning. In this third category, therefore, there are three broad areas of concern and focus for intervention—interactive, including family and caregiver variables; the regulatory factors; and the delays and dysfunctions in core areas of functioning.

One may question in this group if the main difficulty isn't only delays and dysfunctions in multiple core areas of functioning in the child. We suggest that there are almost always difficulties in the interactive patterns and caregiver and family dynamics. It is rare, even with the most flexible and adaptive parents, that the infant and young child's developmental challenges, which combine regulatory problems and significant delays and dysfunctions, do not result in difficulties in the caregiver–infant interaction or in the family dynamics. The nature of the challenge the infant or young child presents and the lack of expectable feedback, due to language and visual–spatial–motor processing difficulties, almost always creates a significant stress on the interaction patterns and the family dynamics. Most families and most caregivers seem prepared for certain types of communication patterns with infants and young children. When these, biologically expectable, interaction patterns are not forthcoming, special approaches are often needed. The degree of the family contribution will vary considerably depending on the infant or child or the family's and caregiver's preexisting patterns. With this last group, therefore, interventions must focus simultaneously on the family dynamics, infant–caregiver interaction patterns, the regulatory patterns, and the developmental delays and dysfunctions in core areas, such as motor, language, cognition, and sensory functions. We will now discuss each broad category.

Chapter 21

Interactive Disorders

Interactive disorders occur when anxiety, fear, labile mood, conduct problems, or some other aspect of feeling, thought, or behavior are part of the child's interaction with his caregiver(s) or family, and/or feelings, wishes, and conflicts within the child, or both. Consider the following examples. An eight-month-old may be so fearful, that he does not crawl, interact, or explore; he may cry every time the mother moves a few steps away. He wants to be picked up all the time, and is afraid. A nineteen-month-old toddler may pinch, poke, or bite other children. He hits his mother when she tries to discipline him. A four-year-old avoids his peers and stands off in a corner of the room. If another child behaves assertively, he becomes frightened and freezes. He is fearful of even looking at animals in the zoo. Another four-and-a-half-year-old is aggressive with peers. A three-year-old has nightmares and won't go to her preschool program: see cases 1, (p. 31) 3 (p. 56), 4 (p. 60), 6 (p. 101), 12 (p. 157), 13 (p. 167), 14 (p. 175), and 18 (p. 238), which illustrate interactive difficulties.

In order to understand the interactive patterns associated with these types of symptoms, the first step is to determine which interactive patterns, in terms of the characteristic interactions of each developmental level, have been negotiated successfully and which have not.

By way of an example, consider a withdrawn four-year-old who never engaged or formed relationships well. As a baby, he tended to disengage, particularly when confronted with anger or other intense feelings; the parents never knew quite how to woo him back. Under the pressure of peer competition, he feels angry and withdraws.

On the other hand, another four-year-old child who engaged well, learned the gestural system of communication, learned to represent or symbolize his emotions, tends not to be able to distinguish clearly aggression from warm and loving feelings. This child becomes frightened whenever he feels aggressive; he anticipates rejection, and he rejects first, often becoming aloof and withdrawn. Although the behavior of the two children may look the same, very different sets of reasons and underlying interactive dynamics are involved. When the second child comes into the playroom, he is warm and engaged, he uses interactive gestures, and he plays out themes such as aggression and love, which demonstrates that he can represent experiences. However, in the play, one begins to see that he confuses aggressive and loving themes; as these themes become merged and chaotic, he may withdraw from the play when it reaches a critical point.

The first child, who withdraws because he never engaged, will come into the playroom with a somewhat aloof and cautious manner; he may not warm up at all, or only very slowly; anytime there is some suggestion of emotion or the situation does not feel quite "right," he will withdraw. One senses that the major issue between the adult and the first child is the quality of intimacy and engagement, whereas with the second child, one can feel secure about his engagement and communication and go on to focus on his ability to represent feelings and resolve conflict. A child's behavior in the playroom provides clues to the types of interventions that were difficult to negotiate and the types of interventions that should be a part of the psychotherapeutic process.

The first child had difficulty negotiating the most basic patterns of interaction and relatedness, especially in the context of strong emotion. Both he and his caregivers were unsure of themselves and were unable to woo one another. The therapist will try not to repeat this pattern by waiting for the child to begin talking about his feelings, because the child will experience this as a replay of the interactive pattern he never learned to negotiate. Instead, the therapist will try to empathize with the child's uncertainty about how to be close and explore associated fears.

The second child had difficulty negotiating complex symbolized feelings in the context of an ongoing relationship. The therapist will need to discover what about the child's relationships made it difficult for him to learn that aggressive and loving feelings can be part of the same relationship pattern.

Interactive disorders can be evidenced from early infancy up through childhood (and probably into adulthood as well). The characteristics of these disorders, at each age and developmental phase, will be based on the developmental challenges of the particular phase the infant or child and his caregiver are negotiating. These characteristics and challenges have been described in both the "Clinical Assessment" and "Floor Time" sections (Parts III and IV). One particular type of interactive pattern that has been the subject of a great deal of research relates to attachment patterns (Bowlby, 1969; Ainsworth, Bell, and Stayton, 1974). Clinicians should incorporate this and related research into their clinical thinking, but be cautious about generalizations that take attention away from the unique characteristics of each infant, caregiver, and family. For example, a recent study by Marion Yarrow (personal communication, 1990) suggests that "securely attached infants of depressed mothers had more difficulty as older children than less securely attached counterparts."

THERAPEUTIC APPROACHES TO CHALLENGES STEMMING FROM DIFFICULTIES IN THE CAREGIVER–INFANT INTERACTION PATTERNS

As indicated earlier, there are many different types of fears, anxieties, behavior-control problems, and the like that are part of the difficulties in the infant or child and his interaction patterns with his caregiver. This section will comment briefly on the overall goal of the work with the caregiver and the family, and the infant- or child–caregiver interaction patterns.

The main therapeutic goal is to facilitate the child's progress in two ways: one, toward an age-appropriate developmental level, and two, toward an age-appropriate range of experience and stability of experience at that level. The therapeutic approach is discussed in the various chapters on floor time—how the clinician can work with the infant–caregiver interaction patterns, work directly with the infant to help him or her organize experience, and assist the family in dealing with its own dynamics. For example, if a child is two-and-a-half years old and not yet symbolizing and representing experience, but instead is behaving it out, the goal will be to help that child to symbolize a full range of age-appropriate experiences in a stable manner. An aggressive two-and-a-half-year-old who acts out his angry feelings much as a sixteen-month-old would, by pinching, pushing, or biting, requires assistance in learning how to symbolize his feelings, either through pretend play or verbalization. Although this same child's most prominent symptom is in the area of aggression, he may also have difficulty symbolizing feelings of closeness and dependency; he may cling rather than be able to verbalize or play out such feelings. These limitations suggest that the child doesn't yet have an inner, multisensory picture of this type of feeling. He moves from an inclination directly into behavior rather than through the capacity to represent his feelings in picture, which would allow him to decide which behaviors are appropriate to satisfy or cope with his feeling.

A child who is aloof and disinterested in others needs first to be helped to engage and to feel a part of a relationship. If he hasn't learned two-way gestural communication, this would be the next step. At each of these early steps, one would see also whether he could apply it to the full range of feelings. Can he engage while angry and curious and assertive as well as when he feels needy, or does he become aloof when he explores rather than being able to maintain a sense of connectedness?

The basic goal then is to assist the child to move from his current developmental level into an age-appropriate developmental level with the full range of feelings that he might be capable of in a stable manner. Even when the child is frustrated and annoyed or tired, he should be able to hold on to his highest level of emotional adaptation. Stability will vary enormously. Some will constrict their range when under stress or pressure. In other words, they may be able to represent experience, but they won't be able to represent all types of experience, when deeply frustrated or angry; other children will lose the developmental level entirely. Others will lose it only when the pressures get to be enormous.

To help the child shift to a wide range of emotional themes at an age-appropriate developmental level in a stable manner requires work on a number of fronts—family dynamics, the caregiver's own personality, the infant or child and caregiver interaction patterns, and the infant's or child's own evolving organization of experience. It may be helpful to think about how the child and his or her caregivers and family are negotiating the six critical levels of interventions (described in chapter 10).

The first step, as described, involves fostering attention, focus, and engagement, with regular opportunities for floor time. Before one tackles any problem involving anxiety, fear, behavior control, and the like, it is critical to establish a base line of warm intimacy and engagement. This focus helps the youngster feel secure and cared for and becomes the foundation for all subsequent mastery of the emotional challenge. In some instances this focus in itself will significantly reduce the fears or anxieties that have created a disequilibrium in the family. For example, the child who begins waking up in the middle of the night with nightmares and also becomes more clinging and demanding during the day may so stress his parents and involve them in power struggles on the one hand and overprotectiveness on the other hand, that the parents are trying to indulge the child and, at the same time, escape from him. What gets lost in this dynamic pattern is a warm, intimate relationship, where the child's lead is respected and followed. The first step of engagement and focused concentration through floor time is to reestablish this relationship by helping the parents understand, cope, and find more adaptive ways to handle such feelings.

The second step, which involves problem-solving abilities, involves helping the child learn more cause-and-effect modes of thinking as well as how to anticipate situations, feelings, and alternative behaviors, especially in the problem areas. As indicated earlier, the ability to anticipate can occur at the symbolic level but also through practice at the gestural and behavioral levels. Problem solving challenges the family to be organized, focused, and anticipatory of the child's functioning and is easily compromised under the pressure of a particular symptom. The child who, for example, evidences a great deal of separation anxiety may become so demanding, that his parents not only experience a feeling of rejection, but they also begin to feel so overwhelmed that they deal with every problem concretely—in the here and now. Their goal becomes to "keep him quiet and settled, so we can have a moment to ourselves." Getting back into a problem-solving mode, where the child's challenges are anticipated, their feelings explored, and the behaviors and alternative behaviors discussed, can be exceedingly helpful. Consider, for example, the child who is having a difficult time separating to go to preschool. If the parent's attitude is, "I'd better not bring it up, because then he'll think about it, and he'll throw more of a temper tantrum in the morning," cannot help the child anticipate. On the other hand, in the comfort of his own house, and in the warm security of an intimate relationship with his mother or father, the child might be able to picture what he will feel like at school the next day and how he is likely to behave when he gets that feeling. Together, he and his parents may even be able to design an approach that will ease his sense of anxiety. Perhaps they will negotiate that the first day the mother will be there the whole time, the second day the whole time minus a half hour, the third day the whole time minus an hour, and so forth. Even if these negotiations don't hold up under the pressure of the next day, the ability to anticipate the feeling associated with the situation and the likely behaviors, together with some pattern of potential alternative behaviors, can only prove helpful. However, the parents who have become too concrete, anxious, and overwhelmed to anticipate with their child won't easily be able to move him into his problem-solving mode, unless they are helped with their feelings as well. Often the parents' and family's anger, resentment, and feeling that the child "will never grow up, and will always be a burden on us," needs to be verbalized and explored.

The third step of empathizing with the child's perspective and helping him identify his assumptions can easily be lost in a variety of situations where the parent–infant interaction pattern is the basis for the child's difficulty. Almost by definition, whatever the natural history of the problem has been, once the problem becomes a dominant force in the family life, the ability to empathize by taking the child's perspective to help him see what his basic assumptions are is almost always absent, where there are symptoms of fear, anxiety, or behavior dyscontrol. One or more of the child's emotional themes—dependency longings, or anger, or sense of inner vulnerability or curiosity, or sense of sexual excitement, are not being engaged by certain family members and are often a part of the basis for a particular symptom. A relevant emotional theme may be ignored at different levels within family life. It can be ignored at the level of engagement, two-way behavior communication, representational or symbolic elaboration, and/or representational differentiation. If the theme is not dealt with at any of these levels or several of them at once, its contribution to a particular symptom will play an important role in the maintenance of that symptom and in the potential correction of it. By way of example, an intense, energetic three-year-old obviously enjoyed competition, but his parents denied aggressive, competitive themes and felt that sharing and cooperation were the most important values in life. Whenever the child wanted to compete with his father at the behavioral level, by horsing around and jumping on his father's stomach or wrestling, his father was afraid that this behavior would make his son "too aggressive"; the father had had a hyperactive sibling. The father would quickly discourage his son's "aggressive" behavior and try to get him involved in some kind of more structured activity. The child might come home from preschool and talk to his mother about a child being mean to him; he would be about to say that he had wanted to hit the child back; and before he could get the words out, his mother would say, reflecting only a wish, "just ignore him . . . maybe he is really nice." The mother would negate her son's emotional reaction rather than acknowledge it.

Both parents also disengaged or withdrew somewhat, when their son seemed to be angry with them—perhaps because he resisted a particular bedtime hour or wanted an extra dessert. There existed, therefore, an inability for the family to function adaptively at the levels of engagement, two-way behavioral interaction, the symbolization of feelings, and the differentiated symbolization of feelings, as indicated by the absence of cause-and-effect discussions about school. However, when the situation called for dependency feelings or the child's feelings of curiosity, his parents could engage him at these levels. They had no trouble understanding how much he loved his mother or father, exchanging hugs and kisses, or even hearing about how much he missed them, when they were away at work.

This same child would have frequent nightmares that were filled with aggressive monsters who were burning down his house; he was very worried about his parents' being hurt. When the clinician (this author) first saw this child, heard his history from his parents, and had a chance to observe their interaction, the clinician sensed that the child was quite angry with his parents and was therefore not surprised that the child was constantly having his house burned down. Later on the child was able to verbalize how frustrated and angry he was, especially with regard to having situations at school that he found difficult not only ignored, but reinterpreted to him all the time. Once the clinician could help the family engage, interact, and symbolize with the child the competitive and aggressive aspects of life, as well as the dependent aspects, the child's symptoms receded. Therefore, it is critical to empathize with the child's feelings and, when possible, to tease out underlying assumptions the child may have. The clinician may also try to identify where the parents, due to conflicts of their own or family dynamics, find it difficult to deal with one or another emotional theme that characterizes the child's expected range of experiences.

In step 4, as described earlier, problems in the areas of interaction and feelings must be broken down into many small steps on two fronts at once. The first is the behavioral front, where the child is helped to approach areas that may be causing him some anxiety or fear, such as joining a group in school or separating from his mother and going to school, sleeping through the night, or toilet training. At the same time, one wants also to divide into small steps the child's psychological challenge of being able to symbolize or represent, or even just engage when certain affects or feelings are present. It is sometimes the parents who are reluctant, as in the case described above, but at other times, it is the child who is also reluctant to engage, interact, or symbolize certain feelings. In some instances, the child may have greater difficulty than the parents. Helping the child approach the feelings that tend to be warded off and organize them at an age-appropriate developmental level can be structured in a step-by-step progression. For example, the child who is fearful of his needs and longings may vacillate between excessive clinging and aggression. In addition to helping him control his behavior, he may be helped to play out and verbalize his feelings, especially those of frustration when his needs are not met, in pretend play, as well as in direct conversation. This process will not occur all at once. It may begin with a reference to a doll or even a pet fish or hamster; the doll or animal may play out these feelings as well. Ten steps later he may talk about his frustration in relationship to some other child, but by the twentieth step he may be able to talk about such feelings in relationship to himself.

In interactional, family-based (and other) difficulties, conflicts can be very important. Behind most anxieties, fears, or behavior-control problems is a conflict between the greedy, tyrannical, or aggressive side of the child and his fearful or worried side. The child will always do better with his fears if he feels secure that his greedy or aggressive side cannot get out of control and that he can rely on his parents to assist him by maintaining some structure. This structure should be neither overly punitive nor overly permissive, and it should be created in collaboration with the child, particularly the child who is verbal.

To illustrate why limits are important in interactive and family-based problems, consider the child who is excessively fearful about playing with other children and joining in activities at school; this child may also have nightmares. The child wants to be "with his mother all the time," refuses to go to his preschool program, refuses to let his father even "carry me anywhere," and insists on being able to push and hit his baby sister, whenever he feels like it, because she "scares me when she takes my toys." This is the child clinicians refer to as a "fearful tyrant." The mother's dilemma is that she feels anxiously overprotective but worried that if she's punitive, he'll only get more fearful. "How can I punish him for pushing his sister, when he's already so scared? He'll only have more nightmares." In such a situation, it is critical to establish some structure by setting limits in a few areas at once: first, on the overt action of hitting and pushing his sister; second, on the excessive avoidance of challenging activities like going to preschool, interacting with or playing with his father, or letting his father carry him around; and third, on the excessive demanding that his mother be at his beck and call. If one institutes the first five steps in the process effectively by engagement through floor time, problem-solving discussions, empathizing, and setting up small steps in areas that are challenging (such as going to school), one can introduce additional structure, accompanied by incentives and limits, to motivate the child to move from one step to another. For example, the child should have to deal with sanctions every time he pushes his sister; the argument that punishment only scares him won't hold up, because parents will feel secure that their floor time and their availability is supportive, nourishing, and reassuring enough to enable him to handle the sanction. In problem-solving discussions, there should be anticipation of conflicts, so he is well warned and can consider his feelings and alternative ways of coping with each situation.

In addition, the structure should create incentives for him not to avoid school altogether; he may need to attend at first on a part-time basis and have his mother with him. Each step needs to be negotiated with firmness. In addition, some part of each day should include time with his father, whether the child likes it or not. His father should use floor time strategies and be willing to try to make the experience fun. He should not demand that the child demonstrate some pleasure, but neither should the father leave the room every time his son says, "Get out of here, Daddy." A flirtatious, wooing, and at times playfully provocative parent will help woo the child into a relationship. The mother should become slower to acquiesce in every one of the child's demands. As structure is gradually established in this area, the child should begin to feel more confident that the greedy, tyrannical side of his nature won't get out of control. At the same time, through the floor time and the problem-solving time, he has a chance to explore and put into words his scary feelings.

As indicated earlier as well, every time it is necessary for the structure and limit-setting to be intensified, it is critical to increase the floor time proportionally. Obviously, parents who got into this bind in the first place may not have an easy time reestablishing previously abandoned structure and limits. The parents have their own anxieties, fears, or family dynamics to account for their patterns. The goal is to foster a balance of structure and limits with support for higher-level and more elaborative communication.

The model presented here suggests that certain basic approaches, such as floor time, problem-solving time, and limit setting be applied to six basic goals: to engage and attend; to have problem-solving discussions in which challenges can be anticipated; to empathize and clarify basic assumptions; to create hierarchies in areas of challenges; to set limits; and to balance limits with floor time. The parents' involvement with their child in these ways will reveal family assets and also family or caregiver vulnerabilities or difficulties. As the clinician works with the family on their dynamics, the couple's patterns, the caregiver–child relationship patterns, the child's own way of organizing experience, the ability of the family to negotiate successfully these six types of processes should improve. As a result, the child should not just overcome problems, but also get back on track developmentally. In other words, he should become more and more able to deal with the full range of emotional themes in a stable manner at his age-appropriate level. There are certain tactics or tools to assist the family when it is not able to foster age-appropriate functioning. The tactics include work with the family, couple, infant– or child–caregiver interaction patterns and the child's own organization of experience. Each problem area or set of symptoms becomes not simply a challenge to be met but also a window of opportunity to help the child find a more adaptive way of organizing experience and to get back on track developmentally. In other words, there's always a double goal—to help the child over the symptom of the moment (a particular fear or anxiety or behavior dyscontrol pattern) and at the same time, to use the opportunity to help the child be fully age appropriate in his capacities.

BRIEF CLINICAL ILLUSTRATIONS

Consider the case of an eight-month-old who is very fearful. She avoids assertive behavior; she cries insistently, until her mother picks her up. This infant has no constitutional or maturational problems. As one watches the mother and the child interact, one sees that every time the baby makes a sound, the mother assumes it is a sound of distress, rather than just a sound of "Hey, what a wonderful world this is!" or a sound of assertiveness; the mother moves in right away to find out what's wrong. As a result, the baby never seems to have an opportunity to flex her muscles, to try things out, or to initiate interaction. Talking to the mother reveals that she is a person who feels "empty" inside. She wants to make sure her baby feels "filled up." The father is also overprotective and mother feels distressed when he competes with her.

This baby has some capacity for two-way interaction—she can gesture and signal. However, she is unable to use gestures to deal with assertiveness, aggression, or separation, because the mother intervenes too quickly. One sees the early beginnings of a very passive, fearful character structure.

What therapeutic approach is appropriate here? One wants to encourage the baby to be more assertive, but not at the cost of putting the mother aside. Mother needs to help her baby negotiate the stage of two-way intentional interaction. (The abilities to be calm and attend and to engage well are already in place.)

The goal then is to help the mother read the baby's signals better in order to understand the baby's natural assertiveness. As mother learns to slow down her response a bit and to observe more before she moves in, she can foster not only the baby's dependency needs, but also the baby's need for assertiveness.

Another case involves a two-and-a-half-year-old boy who has nightmares, wakes up, and comes into his mother's bed. He is competent constitutionally and maturationally. When the baby interacts with the mother during play, he vacillates between being very aggressive and very fearful. He has the dolls hitting each other and then becomes overexcited and almost shaky. The father does a lot of roughhousing, because he wants the child to be "tough," but he doesn't help the child represent emotions in his pretend play. Mother is a very cautious person. She is sincere and not overprotective, but when the baby begins playing or talking, the mother seems to be a step behind. The baby will say, "Truck crash." Instead of saying, "Oh, yes, the trucks are crashing. What are they going to do next?" the mother may watch silently for a few seconds, then look perplexed, and then make an indirect comment, such as "Do you want this truck, too?" Her pauses interrupt the rhythm of the interaction.

Many depressed caregivers seem to be a step slow in their interactions. These "empty holes" (as they might be described) in the expected rhythm of communication may create in the child a feeling of grabbing at empty space. I have seen children respond with agitation and increased activity, feelings of uncertainty, distractibility, and dysphoric affects including sadness and emptiness. Both the pattern of early reciprocity and the formation of representational abilities may be affected.

Based on the clues described above, what does one do to help this child get over his nightmares? One sees that the child is not getting support from either parent for symbolizing or representing affect. His mother is cautious and somewhat depressed, and the rhythm of her voice, instead of helping him represent his feelings by confirming them in a representational form, tends to leave the child feeling disconnected. She lacks the ability to cue affects and represent experience with him.

The father pulls in the opposite direction. He pushes the child to, "Go out and be John Wayne," while the mother is saying, "I'm not sure I can offer you all that much security." The father is giving the child support for assertiveness but only in prerepresentational forms. In so doing, he is also overexciting and overwhelming the child.

As a result of these conflicting experiences, the child cannot harness and integrate his emerging ability to symbolize experience and to accommodate his security needs with his assertiveness. Neither parent helps him elevate experiences to representational levels. It is not surprising that he would have scary dreams. The clash of his experiences worries him at night. The fact that he can have nightmares is, in part, a positive sign, because it means that he can at least partially symbolize experiences and use images, although he is not yet able to symbolize them enough to work them through.

The therapeutic approach appropriate for this child calls for sessions for both child and parents. The therapist can help the mother be a little quicker to respond (just the opposite of the previous case), and empathize with her child's feelings. Also the therapist will need to find out more about her depression (which may cause her rhythm to be so slow). The therapist can help the father be more sensitive to the child's dependency needs and help him modulate his approach to his child's assertiveness. Both parents can work to facilitate the child's emerging representational abilities in daily floor time, so that he can fully represent feelings of both dependency and assertiveness.

A group of children who might be described as having impulse control difficulties illustrates the role of preverbal interactive patterns. A number of bright, verbal two- to five-year-olds (with excellent motor and language abilities) had a common problem with either hitting peers or parents and/or unpredictable, provocative behavior, which was quite resistant to routine parental limits. In observing these children over a period of time, I noticed that neither they nor their parents used anticipatory gestural communication, including facial gestures, vocal gestures, affect gestures, motor gestures, and so forth. It occurred to me that perhaps these families, which seemed to evidence a high degree of "poker-faced" individuals, had failed to negotiate an important aspect of gestural communication in the second year of the child's life. During this time, it is likely that gestures serve a number of functions for the child with regard to self-limit-setting. Gestures may help the child identify his own feelings and intentions. Adults in part know their feelings through the feedback from their own facial expressions, clenched fists, or angry voices, and it seems as though affects are, in part, defined by their somatic manifestations. Furthermore, the parents' gestures, such as an angry look, a stern grimace, or a firm finger-pointing may help warn the child of his parents' reaction, before a parental sanction is necessary. Finally, the child's gestures may also help the parents anticipate what the child is about to do, allowing them to intervene in a warning way before the child misbehaves. This system of gestural communication is highly developed in the animal kingdom. Two animals will posture and gesture to one another, seeing who will back down so they can avoid a fight. Similarly this gestural communication appears to play a significant role in the safe handling of interpersonal aggression in humans. It is not surprising that where, for a variety of reasons, psychosocial as well as constitutional, this system has not developed properly, one might see impulsive behavior.

The principal focus of treatment, as suggested above, is to determine what types of interaction patterns contributed to the lack of attainment of a developmental level or breadth of application of a developmental level to the full range of emotional themes.

The various fears, anxieties, moods, and behaviors that are associated with interactive problems between infants, young children, and their families provide a unique opportunity to discover how a particular child and his caregivers and family are negotiating the different developmental levels and the range of emotional themes that can be organized at each of these levels.

Chapter 22

Regulatory Disorders

Regulatory disorders, a new diagnostic construct, involve some of the same behaviors as interactive disorders, including nightmares, withdrawal, aggressiveness, fearfulness, attentional difficulties, and difficulty with groups. But these disorders involve symptoms that are a part of both interactive patterns and *clearly demonstrable constitutional* and *maturational patterns* (see cases 1 [p. 31], 2 [p. 42], 4 [p. 60], 5 [p. 82], 7 [p. 109], 8 [p. 122], 9 [p. 131], 11 [p. 147], 15 [p. 186], 16 [p. 203], 18 [p. 238], 22 [p. 289] for illustrations of regulatory difficulties).

Regulatory disorders[1] are first evident in infancy and early childhood. They are characterized by difficulties the infant has in regulating physiological, sensory, attentional, and motor or affective processes, and organizing a calm, alert, or affectively positive state. The causes of these disorders are unclear. One may observe regulatory difficulties in infants whose prenatal, perinatal, and early developmental functioning (i.e., motor, cognitive, and language) has appeared unremarkable. At the

---

[1]Serena Weider, Ph.D., has collaborated in the clinical definition and description of regulatory disorders.

same time clinically, one may see a large number of infants with regulatory difficulties where there has been maternal substance abuse (Greenspan, 1990; Porges and Greenspan, 1990) and the infant is small for gestational age or of low birth weight. There are suggestions that these infants have difficulties organizing adaptive functions involving feelings, behaviors, and learning. Difficulties can range from mild to severe and may affect one or more areas of development.

For example, poorly organized or modulated responses may show themselves in the following ways:

1. The physiological or state repertoire (e.g., irregular breathing, startles, hiccups, gagging);
2. Gross motor activity (e.g., poor tonus, jerky movements);
3. Fine motor activity (e.g., poorly differentiated or sparse, jerky, or limp movements);
4. Attentional organization (e.g., driven or unable to settle down versus perseverating in a small detail);
5. Affective organization: this would include both the predominant affective tone as well as the range of affect and degree of modulation expressed (e.g., infant can vary from being completely flat to screaming frantically, but be predominantly sober, depressed, or unhappy);
6. Sleep, eating, or elimination patterns (e.g., difficulty with falling or staying asleep or returning to sleep).

Infants and children may clinically present with sleep or feeding difficulties, deficits in their speech and language development, as well as their ability to play alone or with others. Parents may also complain that their children easily lose their temper (e.g., get angry or jealous) and do not adapt well to changes in state or other required transitions. Because sensory, motor, and affective experiences impact upon the infant and young child continuously through routine handling, if such handling is not sensitive to individual differences, irregular conditions in the environment, and/or changes in routine, these infants and children and their caregivers can be strongly affected.

Background

There is a long-standing assumption and growing evidence, including documentation of differences in sensory reactivity and physiologic regulation, that fussy or difficult infants have symptoms that are part of a pattern of constitutional and early maturational variation (Greenspan, 1990; Porges and Greenspan, 1990; Degangi, Pietro, Greenspan, and Porges, 1991). However, it is also recognized that early caregiving patterns can be influenced by and exert considerable influence on how these constitutional and maturational patterns develop and become part of the child's evolving personality (Portales, Porges, and Greenspan, 1990). With regard to the presumed "constitutional" or "biological" base for sensory, motor, and integrative patterns, there has been a tendency toward using general terms such as *overly sensitive* or *reactive* without delineating as specifically as possible the sensory pathway or motor functions involved. As interest in these children increases, it is important to systematize descriptions of the sensory, motor, and integrative patterns that we presume are involved.

Criteria

In order to facilitate this effort, a preliminary classification of regulatory disorders will be suggested below. These disorders will be operationally defined as having a distinct behavioral pattern coupled with difficulty in sensory, sensorimotor, or organizational processing which affects daily adaptation and interactions–relationships. When behavioral and constitutional–maturational elements are not present, other diagnoses may be more appropriate. For example, an infant who is irritable and withdrawn after being abandoned may be evidencing an expectable type of relationship or attachment difficulty. An infant who is irritable and overly reactive to routine interpersonal experiences, in the absence of a clearly identified sensory, sensorimotor, or processing difficulty, may be evidencing an anxiety or mood disorder.

In addition to the behavioral symptoms, therefore, at least one category of sensory, sensorimotor, or processing difficulty must be present to make this diagnosis. These are listed below together with different behavioral categories in the following sections.

1. The child is over- or underreactive to loud or high- or low-pitched noises.
2. The child is over- or underreactive to bright lights or new and striking visual images (e.g., colors, shapes, complex fields).
3. Tactile defensiveness is apparent (e.g., overreactivity to changing clothes, bathing, stroking of arms, legs, or trunk; avoids touching "messy" textures, etc.) and/or underreactive to touch or pain.
4. The child is under- or overreactive to movement in space (e.g., brisk horizontal or vertical movements such as in tossing a child in the air, playing merry-go-round, jumping, etc.).
5. The child is under- or overreactive to odors.
6. The child is under- or overreactive to temperature.
7. Poor motor tone is apparent (gravitational or postural insecurity, oral–motor difficulties—avoids certain textures).
8. The child has less than age-appropriate motor planning skills (e.g., complex motor patterns such as alternating hand banging).
9. The child has less than age-appropriate fine motor skills.
10. The child has less than age-appropriate auditory–verbal discrimination or integration capacity (e.g., an 8-month-old should be able to imitate distinct sounds, a 2-½-year-old follow or repeat requests, or a 3-year-old put together words and actions).

11. Less than age-appropriate visual–spatial discrimination or integration capacity is apparent (e.g., a 2½-year-old should know where to turn to get to a friend's house, an 8-month-old should recognize different facial configurations, a 3-year-old should be able to put together certain spaces, such as a room, with activities).

Regulatory Disorders: Four Types
   Type I: Hypersensitive type

To make this diagnosis, both (1) and (2) in the relevant category must be present.

1. The child is often overly reactive to routine sensory experiences such as light touch, loud noises, or bright lights.
2. The child tends to have at least one of the following:
   a. Tends to be easily upset (e.g., irritable, often crying or unhappy), cannot soothe self, finds it difficult to return to sleep and/or recover from frustration or disappointment.
   b. The child may also be negative and controlling ("the fearful little dictator").
   c. The child can be fearful, cautious, and clinging (e.g., at 4 months, even when sitting in mother's lap, may take more than 15 minutes to "flirt" with a new person, looking serious and worried; or at 8 months, may cry, pull away, and squirm intensely when a new person tries to pick her up even after 15 minutes of gentle wooing).
   d. The child dislikes changes in routine or new experiences, including visiting other people's homes, school, and so on. When frightened of new experiences, he or she clings to mother or father (e.g., wants to be picked up and held). The child will not explore new surroundings even for a few minutes.
   e. The child tends to shy away from new peers even after eighteen months of age.

f. Night wakings tend to be associated with a strong
    desire to be held by mother until sleep again or for
    entire night.
g. In school settings, the child tends to be over-
    whelmed by a large group (circle times tend to be
    difficult) and seeks a one-on-one relationship with
    the teacher.

Type II: Underreactive type

1. The child is often underreactive to and has difficulty
   processing auditory–verbal experiences. In addition, he
   or she may be either over- or underreactive to tactile
   and visual–spatial experiences, as well as having motor
   tone and motor planning difficulties.
2. At least one of the following also applies:
   a. The child tends to be unfocused or inattentive,
       "tuned out."
   b. The child tends to be withdrawn, but responds, to
       some degree, to wooing.
   c. The child will intermittently stare off into space or
       at distant objects.
   d. The child is preoccupied with his own inner sensa-
       tions, or at later ages, with his own thoughts or
       feelings (or private pretend play), and/or is with-
       drawn. For example, at four months of age the
       infant tends to scan his environment but not focus
       in on mother's or father's face and/or voice with
       intentional affect (e.g., focused smiling); at eight
       months of age the infant may play with a block or
       seem to focus on an object for an inordinate
       amount of time, excluding his parents' inviting
       overtures; at two years of age, the child may wander
       about aimlessly; at three-and-a-half years of age, he
       or she may play with building blocks or a special
       doll house, lost in private "thoughts" or fantasy

games. Note that none of these characteristics is so pervasive as to constitute an autistic pattern.

Type III: Active–aggressive type

1. The infant often has a mixed pattern of sensory over- or underreactivity, motor planning difficulties, as well as at times fine motor lags. Also, this child tends toward poor motor modulation and motor discharge patterns, particularly when frustrated, angry, or vulnerable (e.g., crawling or running into things or people, making loud noises or sounds, unable to attend in an age-expected manner). He or she seems to be looking at or listening fleetingly to each sound or sight so that attention and study of any one thing is lacking; is unable to attend in age-expected manner. For example, by four months, an infant should be able to attend for five or more seconds; by eight months, for twenty or more seconds; and by eighteen months, for a few minutes at a time. By nine to twelve months, the infant seems to be looking at or listening fleetingly to each sound or sight so that attention and study of any one thing is lacking.
2. The child also has at least one of the following characteristics:
   a. He tends to be overly active.
   b. He tends to be destructive and/or aggressive. For example, by nine to twelve months, the child may already be pulling other children's hair deliberately; by eighteen months, he may be hurting others with biting and kicking; may break toys and hurt animals.
   c. He tends to find it difficult to inhibit excitement (gets carried away) or shift "states" (e.g., go to sleep).

Type IV: Mixed type

1. The child tends to have mixed features of mild to mod-

erate severity of types I through III, with no one set of characteristics dominating. For example, he or she may be fearful but also aggressive. The child must have at least one each of categories (1) and (2).

2. The child tends to have some mixed features of types I through III, though one or another may predominate, with at least one significant sensory processing difficulty, auditory–verbal, visual–spatial, and/or perceptual–motor, contributing to the behavioral difficulties. When social withdrawal or aimless or idiosyncratic behavior is a significant symptom, it is not so severe as to constitute an autistic disorder because there is either intermittent or ongoing reciprocal social relating or the ability to be socially engaged by a skilled therapist sensitive to both the underlying processing difficulties and their associated emotional patterns.

Clinical Illustrations and Discussion

There are many ways in which regulatory processes influence development. For example, consider a fifteen-month-old who experiments with being independent—walking or crawling away from his mother—as well as maintaining a sense of security. The child begins to abstract, in a preverbal way, a sense of who he is as a person, who the mother is, and who the father is. But, if a child is unable to process sounds across the room, and his mother says, "Hey, that's terrific! You're building a great tower," he looks at her face and is confused. He does not get any reassurance, because he cannot decode the rhythm of her voice. He has to come over and cling to her. Meanwhile, she gets upset with his clinging and, without realizing that he can't decode her sound, she ushers him away. The child who can decode the mother's sounds, plays with his tower, looks over, hears his mother's reassuring sounds, and thinks, "Oh, that's great. You like it. I'll do some more." The child who decodes the rhythm feels as if he's in his mother's lap, because he receives her warmth across space. When one talks to a loved one who is far away, one feels warm on the telephone, because one decodes the affect in the voice. The child who cannot decode sound will therefore have greater difficulty in developing independence.

The child with visual-spacial processing difficulty may have a difficult time maintaining his internal mental representation, especially under the pressure of intense affects. The visual-spacial vulnerability makes it hard to maintain the internal mental image. If for example the representation of a significant caregiver is lost, a child may expectedly experience a sense of loss and even depression or anxiety and fear. An interesting hypothesis regarding depression in children and adults relates to this phenomena. Perhaps the biologic vulnerability for depression is mediated through a visual-spacial vulnerability which in turn creates a vulnerability in the stability of mental representations. The loss of the representation leads to dysphoric affects. The dysphoric affects, in this model, are secondary.

If motor planning is impaired and the child cannot control his body, his difficulty will affect his confidence in dealing with aggression. He tries in play to touch his father's nose, but instead he hits his father in the eye and makes him mad. The child didn't intend to hit his father; his arm didn't work the way he wanted. Thus the child's confidence in his body and his ability to modulate aggression is not going to be optimally established.

For the child who is tactilely hyperreactive, his protection from the outside world is overly fragile. How is that going to affect the way he perceives other people's aggression? How is he going to react when another two-year-old hits him in the back? When mother tries to hold a four-month-old who is sensitive to light touch, if she rubs his skin lightly, he may squirm away, and she may misperceive that he is rejecting her.

We recently studied eight-month-olds (DeGangi and Greenspan, 1988; Doussard-Roosevelt, Walker, Portales, Greenspan, and Porges, 1990; Portales, Porges, and Greenspan, 1990); and were able to further observe how critical the constitutional and maturational factors are to the child's development. In infants with a variety of symptoms, such as eating or sleeping problems and temper tantrums, we were able to demonstrate that a very high percentage had constitutional and maturational differences that were part of the difficulty. The babies were either hypo- or hyperreactive in one or another sensory modality or had sensory processing or motor tone or motor planning difficulties. These differences in turn seemed to contribute to a skewing of the parent–infant interaction pattern, which in turn was affecting personality development. These children were also found to have differences in physiological regulation (DeGangi, DiPietro, Greenspan, and Porges, 1991). These differences persisted and were evident at eighteen months. There were also signs of family distress at eighteen months (Portales, Porges, and Greenspan, 1990). It appeared that the maturational differences were affecting not only the child's personality, but also derailing the family to some extent. A small group of these infants that were followed to age four evidence a greater number of behavioral and learning problems than a comparison group (DeGangi, Porges, Sickel, and Greenspan, submitted). Therefore, children who have constitutional and maturational unevenness tend to be especially challenging. They have a harder time in their interactions with their caregivers. Family functioning tends to be stressed. Eventually there may be more behavioral and learning difficulties.

THERAPEUTIC APPROACHES FOR INFANTS AND YOUNG CHILDREN WITH REGULATORY DISORDERS

Infants and young children with regulatory disorders evidence challenges in their constitutional and maturational variations as well as interactive and family patterns. These variations in turn affect how the children perceive and organize experience. For example, a baby who is excessively needy and demanding, fussy or finicky, intermittently angry, labile in his moods, slow to warm up and adapt to new situations, has an impact on the family, on the nature of interactions between the child and family members, and on the way the child perceives himself and integrates experience. In a sense, all experience is colored in part by the unusual constitutional and maturational variations that infants and young children with regulatory problems evidence. As indicated earlier, these challenges can occur as a result of differences in sensory reactivity, sensory processing, motor tone, and motor planning; these children may evidence patterns of hyper- and hyporeactivity and sensitivity to even routine kinds of day-to-day experience.

In contrast to children whose major difficulties emanate from challenges in the interactional or family patterns, the regulatory disordered infant or young child requires major effort to help him overcome his own constitutional and maturational difficulties with self-regulation; however, the focus on fostering better regulatory capacities cannot and should not occur in isolation from the interactive and family patterns.

Therapeutic approaches for children call for the six steps outlined in chapter 6. Step 1 has to do with using floor time to foster engagement and a sense of connectedness between the infant and caregiver and simultaneously to attempt to focus the child's attention. The floor time tactics described earlier are obviously helpful here. The therapist needs to work simultaneously with the child's constitutional and maturational variations as well as with the child's interactive patterns and feeling tone. The therapist needs to find the pattern that will most likely help the child focus, attend, and engage. It is helpful to incorporate practical suggestions developed by occupational therapists trained in sensory integration work (Ayers, 1964). The therapist needs to be aware of the child's sensory reactivity in terms of touch, sound, sight, smell, and the child's response to movement. The therapist may want to explore the child's reaction to firm pressure, for example, if the child is overly sensitive or reactive to tactile stimuli. For some children, firm pressure, as part of rough-and-tumble type play, can help the child to normalize sensory input and foster better capacities to focus and concentrate. In terms of sights and sounds, the therapist needs to experiment with different intensities in terms of loud-ness, different frequencies, and different rhythms of sounds. The child who is overly reactive to loud noises will do best with soft, soothing sound. The child who is underreactive to sound may need a stronger, more dramatic vocal pattern. Some children will do better with low-pitched sounds, some with high-pitched ones. The child who has a difficulty with processing, that is, abstracting the sequence of sounds, may need simple rhythms, which have only one or two variations of sound, whereas the child who processes sound easily may need the novelty of more complex vocal rhythms, with four or five patterns. Observing how the child looks or doesn't look, or whether he has a knowing sense or a confused sense about him, will inform the clinician about what type of vocal rhythm and sequence is most helpful in fostering attention and a sense of engagement. Similarly, the level of brightness or dimness in the room, the intensity of colors used in play objects, and even the degree of animation the clinician uses in his own facial expressions will need to vary, depending on the child's hypo-or hyperreactivity to different aspects of what he sees. Here, too, the complexity of the visual input (complex design versus simple designs) should vary, depending on the degree of vi-sual–spatial complexity.

In terms of a child's response to his own movement pat-terns, some children focus and attend when moved or involved in slow, rhythmic activities, such as four or five seconds per swing on a swing. Other children will do better when moved rapidly—one second per swing. Others will do best when they have opportunities for both fast and slow rhythms. In addition to the movement rate and rhythm, the position of the child is important. An excessively finicky child may calm down most readily when resting on his stomach, over a parent's knees, with firm pressure on the child's back, while being moved in a very slow rhythm, with the parent's knees creating the movement. Another child may do better in an upright position, resting against the parent's chest, with the child's head crooked into the parent's neck. This more typical, upright position is too activating for some children, and a more horizontal position may be more calming, particularly when the child is experiencing some distress.

Some children attend and focus better when they're involved in large-muscle activity themselves. Some children do best when such an activity is combined with joint-compression activities, where they are getting appropriate receptor feedback. For such children, jumping on a bed or on a trampolinelike device may foster their ability to attend and engage.

Many children who are oversensitive to touch, sound, light, or who are sensitive to their own movement patterns, attend, focus, and engage best when they can be in charge of the interaction patterns. The more in charge they are, the more they can regulate and monitor the sensory input and the motor control they need. As infants grow into toddlers and develop better motor control to take charge of their interactions, fostering their own initiatives often will support their capacities to attend and engage.

Many children with regulatory difficulties also evidence constitutional and maturational difficulties in the areas of motor tone and motor planning. They may have high or low tone or difficulty with planning the motor acts, such as alternating hand movements when drumming on their own legs. As a baby, such a child may have difficulty getting his hand to his mouth. As a toddler, he may knock over things; when he's trying to grab one thing, he knocks over another thing. Practice in coordinating perception and motor acts can be very helpful; it should start with activities a child can master and then work up to more difficult activities. In addition, a child with low motor tone, who tends to tire easily because of it, should be understood to require a great deal of effort to do routine activities that other children do easily; walking, especially upstairs, takes enormous amounts of energy for the child who doesn't have the normal amount of extensor tone. The child is putting a lot of conscious effort into activities that are more automatic for other children. Exercises, such as having the child lie on the floor on his stomach and pretend to be a boat (rocking back and forth, arching his back) or playing the bird game (the child scissors his feet around his father's waist, arches his back, and has his arms flap as his father circles around), encourage extensor tone and help the child with motor coordination, strength, and stamina. Such activities, along with certain types of movement patterns, will help children gradually learn to enjoy activities around the playground, such as going on the swings or the slides. Here, too, it is important to remember to take the child one step at a time, to build fundamental abilities by improving motor tone and motor planning, and then to expose the child to activities which, on the one hand, are routine functions for children, but on the other hand, provide self-support for motor tone and motor planning. Certain kinds of play activities per se support more extensor tone and provide practice in motor planning. For example, simple games of putting objects in certain places or taking them out support motor planning. Games that require the child to change direction rapidly, such as a chase game that doesn't go in a straight line, or putting his body into an extensor pattern, such as the bird game, will improve the child's capacity. These kinds of activities, together with the sensory-normalizing activities and interactions, will foster attention and engagement in both early and later stages of development.

These examples indicate how focusing on constitutional and maturational variations can directly foster this first step of engaging and attending. As described in the first section of the floor time discussion (chapter 10), being able to empathize with the child and follow his lead is critical. The adult must seek to discover the right amount of emotional rhythm and tone that interests the child and helps him feel secure and intimate. There is no substitute here for the parents' natural emotional warmth and flexibility in adjusting to the child's mood and rhythm. The clinician who is naturally empathetic and flexible will find it easier to engage a wide variety of infants and young children, whereas the clinician whose approach is more rigid will find he can work with some infants and young children better than others. As a general rule, for the more cautious, hyperreactive regulatory disordered infants and young children, a very warm and available yet cautious approach on the clinician's part is often most helpful. The approach often needs to contain a very gradual, slow element, together with a flirtatious and playful one. Take the example of a regulatory disordered eight-month-old, who is especially cautious of new experiences and especially fearful. If one approaches the child slowly from afar, with lots of flirtatious glances, one often does better than if one approaches in a more routine way. From across the room, one must look, flirt, and vocalize with the child. The child's probable expectation—that one is going to approach him and try to pick him up—doesn't become realized, as one moves from across the room only an inch at a time, making interesting facial expressions and gestures. The child often relaxes and begins to flirt back at the adult for a second or two from a distance—looking and then hiding his eyes in his mother's chest. As one gets a little closer, one senses when the child starts to become apprehensive and frightened by the changed look in his eyes or by the degree to which he averts his gaze. At this point, one should not move closer but should hold one's position and continue the flirtation. If at this point, one begins talking to the mother and only intermittently flirting with the child, soon many eight-month-olds, even those who are quite cautious and overly sensitive, will begin seeking out the clinician with their eyes and sometimes their motor gestures. Once this begins to happen, an important corner has been turned, and the relationship is moving ahead, and shortly there will be an opportunity for the clinician to engage the child and foster his or her attention more fully.

Often what the clinician learns about the way he can successfully approach a child and enlist his engagement and concentration will be very helpful to the parents. It may be especially helpful to the father, who perhaps still feels rejected by his eight-month-old, and to the mother, who at times feels that she can't get quite that desired look or glow in her baby's eyes, because of the baby's over- or underreactivity.

As indicated, in step 2, once there is a sense of focus and engagement, the child is encouraged toward a problem-solving orientation. This orientation can occur at the gestural and behavioral level, as well as, in the older child, at the symbolic and verbal level. At the gestural and behavioral level, it may involve a simple reality-based, adaptive movement, like rolling a ball to someone or reaching for an object or handing something to someone. For the child with regulatory difficulties, the problem-solving step is oriented toward helping the child anticipate, practice, and master, slowly but surely, those types of behaviors or activities that would be expectedly difficult for the child. This procedure can be applied at both the early behavioral and gestural level with the six- to eighteen-month-old, and with words and thoughts with the preschool or school-age child. For example, the child with tactile sensitivities, who avoids touch and is cautious about any toy, game, new piece of clothing, or even the texture of a new person in his life, can be helped through practice. The parents should gradually introduce him to a new toy with new textures and allow him to play with them in a way that is enjoyable. For example, a typical problem arises when one puts a new shirt on an infant or toddler who is tactilely sensitive and usually cautious about new experiences. Rather than waiting for the in-laws to come over and having the child refuse to let his mother put on the new shirt (a present from the same in-laws), a probatory and anticipatory strategy is preferable. The mother might let the child play with the shirt and enjoy pushing it back and forth between himself and his mother. If the child enjoys this game, he will see, touch, and smell the shirt and begin to get used to its feel. The father might put the shirt over his own head and allow the child to pull it off, so he can see his father's eyes. The child actually touches the shirt before he realizes it is something he might not want to touch. There are many such opportunities to use behaviors and gestures to help the preverbal child anticipate and practice new experiences; the only limitation is the ingenuity of the clinician and caregiver. Children with regulatory difficulties should have extra anticipation and practice in areas where their regulatory system is easily challenged. If they are sensitive to touch or sound or smells or movement patterns, these are the very patterns where practice and anticipation should occur.

For the two-year-old and older, especially for the three- to four-and-a-half-year-old, words and thoughts can be used to anticipate a problem. A problem-solving discussion between the parent and the child could, for example, anticipate what will happen at school the next day. The child is helped to anticipate the feelings he is likely to have and the behaviors he is likely to evidence in response to those feelings. He is asked to picture the feelings and other behaviors that he might try or to review similar past situations, as a way of figuring out what he may expect in the future, in order to reduce the sense of surprise or shock and to feel prepared even for uncomfortable sensations. Many clinicians, parents, and educators carry out this exercise but focus only on the situation and the behaviors. "When you are in circle time, you will tend to sit in a corner by yourself," fails to account for the child's feeling. "When you are in circle time you feel . . . how?" The child who can talk about feeling scared, "Like I can't breathe," or "Like my brain doesn't work," will be at a great advantage over a child who discusses only the situation and the behaviors. The child's ability to understand and verbalize how he feels in a situation will give him a great deal more flexibility to cope with that situation.

How the child will feel when he has to put on a new pair of shoes; how he is likely to behave during circle time or when everyone is drawing and he's expected to draw, too, or when another child pushes him or surprises him from behind; or when another child yells too loudly or won't give that child what he wants or takes something from the child—all of these situations, which are common in the life of any child, will be especially difficult for the child with regulatory difficulties. To the degree that they can be anticipated, in terms of the situation, the feelings, and the likely behavior, the child will have that much more opportunity to prepare and evolve more adaptive coping strategies.

In addition to mental anticipation, with the verbal, thinking child, actual, real practice in anticipation can also be helpful. Trial runs in situations similar to the one where the child is challenged should prove helpful, just as they do for the toddler and infant. For example, a preschooler who is about to experience circle time for the first time and who does poorly in groups, because of the noise and the likelihood of being touched, may benefit by having his parents have him play not just with one child (if he already can do well with only one), but to begin giving him practice playing with two or three children. Practice with a small group will expose him, in the safety of his own house, with his mother present, to situations where he's likely to bump shoulders, deal with aggression, and hear loud noises. Having the children actually sit in a circle and listen to a story may be the culmination of this practice. Then, when the child has to sit in a group of six children at school, without his mother present, he may be more comfortable, because he has already had an actual opportunity to practice and anticipate.

If both practice and discussion are modified to be manageable for the child and gradually increased in level of challenge, they help the child anticipate situations and provide valuable problem-solving assistance.

The third step in working with regulatory disorders is to help the child experience empathy for his difficulty and get a sense (particularly if he's a verbal, thoughtful child) of his basic assumptions about life. For example, the clinician may empathize with the verbal child about how he must feel when he has to sit in a group or hear loud noises. The clinician may also help the parents do this. What the child's experience is like is often not self-evident; using one's self as a reference point may not always work. It may be hard for the clinician or parent or educator to imagine how overwhelmed, disorganized, and fragmented a child with sensory overload may be, when they do not have these kinds of sensitivities themselves. The clinician may think that a child just doesn't want to share the limelight with other children in circle time and therefore begins to behave provocatively, when in fact, the child may feel overwhelmed, fragmented, and "like I'm jumping out of my skin."

Feelings like "my brain doesn't work," or "I'm jumping out of my skin," or "I can't stand it, I've got to get out of here," or "My mind is exploding"; or feeling "like moosh," or "like I'm water, like there's no container," are quite different from an adult's ordinary expectations, as he tries to empathize with a child about his interactions with his peers. The adult has to listen carefully to the child to understand his actual experience and especially his likelihood of sensory overload, which will have its own affective meanings. Each child will develop his own fantasies that elaborate on sensory and affective experience. When voices are too loud, some children may feel that people want to hurt them, and they feel overloaded. Other children may feel that people are trying to manipulate or trick them. Still others may believe that people hate them or want to deprive them of something. It is important to help the verbal child sense that one can understand not just the secondary fantasy that everyone hates him, but also the primary feeling of being overloaded and overwhelmed. The latter feelings are likely to involve emotional and sensory overload in one form or another.

For the preverbal child—the infant and toddler—being empathic is especially difficult, because he can't understand the adult's words, even if the adult characterized his experience accurately. Furthermore, as the child can't use words, the only clue may be a certain feeling tone in his body. Empathy for the preverbal child is expressed in the attitude of the parent, caregiver, clinician, or educator. The impatient, critical looking parent hardly captures the emotional tone of the overwhelmed, frightened twelve-month-old. However, a reassuring, "I-know-it's-scary" look on the parent's part may convey some reassurance to a frightened child. For the younger child, therefore, the parent can convey empathy through facial expressions and gestures, which pick up the child's mood states and convey an expectable understanding of them. There's a difference, for example, in terms of empathetic expectations on the child's part if he is angry and belligerent or frightened and overloaded. Each circumstance requires a different empathetic response. The angry child may benefit from a firm, steady look on a parent's face—a look that says, "You can't do that here, and I'm here to make sure you can't." The frightened child may benefit most from a look of concern for his pain and fear, and a quality of gentleness and tenderness.

In addition to demonstrating empathy, the adult should help the child, especially the verbal child, identify his core assumptions. Examples of core assumptions are: "I shouldn't have any pain," or "I'm entitled to escape anytime I feel uncomfortable." Characterizing these assumptions helps the child understand why he's doing what he's doing. The adult needs to understand that the assumptions serve a role for the child and to show empathy for the child. Even if the child feels like a "fearful dictator" and wants everything done his way, at the same time he is apt to be frightened and not want the adult to compete with him or get angry at him. The goal is to empathize with a verbal child's self-perception. (Fearful dictators may range in age from four months through eighty-four years of age.)

The next step is to figure out a series of small steps to help the child master new experiences. The child with regulatory disorders requires many tiny steps—one toe in the water at a time. Whether there are sleeping or eating problems, difficulty in joining in group time, learning to be more assertive, or to have fewer tantrums, improving focus and concentration, or learning to use words rather than behaviors to characterize distress, parents, educators, and clinicians need to develop a hierarchy of steps, with each step manageable for the child. If the first step is not manageable, it can be broken down into ten smaller steps. The critical challenge for the child with regulatory disorders is to overcome his sense of standing still or even moving backwards and help him get some forward momentum, so that he can feel a sense of mastery over some steps. It doesn't make a difference how small the steps are, so long as he can move forward.

The fifth step in the sequence requires the adult to establish a structure, with both limits and incentives. The small steps will work best when the child possesses a sense of incentive, as well as a sense of finite structure to operate within. Children with regulatory disorders may seem so overwhelmed, helpless, and unhappy most of the time, that clinicians, educators, and parents are reluctant to set limits. Yet limits on some of the child's behavior create a sense of security—that his environment cannot be totally manipulated or intimidated by him. Usually the child breaches some behavioral norm, such as not clearing his place from the table, scratching someone, or throwing his food on the floor. It's important to set broad enough limits and set them in areas where one is relatively certain the child has the capacity to keep within them. For example, the child with too little motor control to prevent his food from falling on the floor is not likely to benefit from limits related to eating more neatly. However, another child with greater planning abilities and control may be able to minimize the amount of food on the floor with some such limits. Similarly, the child who can control his pinching or biting will benefit from limits having to do with hurting other people. While it is generally useful to set limits on children's capacity for or interest in hurting others and/or breaking objects, other limits need to be set in ways appropriate to each child's capacities. Moreover, clinicians, educators, and parents should not attempt to fight battles on four or five fronts at once. It is best to establish limits on only one or two fronts at a time.

In addition to and as complementary to limits, one can provide incentives, which can take the form of stars, checks, goals, or special privileges, or just a sense of warm admiration. Parents should be aware that both external incentives and limits help a child progress toward a goal, particularly when a child has not made a particular goal his own, so that the internal reward of a job well done is not yet well established.

However, limits should not compromise the first four steps of the developmental approach to resolving challenges. For example, a limit that isolates the child and reduces the quality of engagement, or that is so concrete as to undermine a child's problem-solving ability, will not prove helpful in the long run.

On the other hand, useful limits tend to stem from problem-solving discussions, where the child has been able to anticipate from the parent when he will receive limits and what the reasons for the limits will be, and where the parent can express empathy with the child's problem of having dug himself into a hole and having to receive a limit.

Step 6, as indicated earlier, suggests that every time limits or punishments of some sort are used, floor time should be increased in order to balance following a child's lead with engaging him and setting limits. This critical principle is especially hard to establish with regulatory disordered children, because they tend to create a sense of frenzied helplessness with the adults in their environment. The adults find themselves in continuous power struggles with the children and tend to forget that only a small percentage of the time should be spent on limits and whatever time is spent on limits should be balanced by floor time in order to guarantee balance for the child. If the child is defeating the limits, it is necessary to find better and more effective limits, not to use more time focusing on already established limits. One must protect floor time, while at the same time one tries to create better limits.

SLEEPING AND EATING DIFFICULTIES

Typical common regulatory problems often involve sleeping and eating (although controlling aggression and focusing attention are also very common). There are two popular remedies for sleeping problems: let the child cry for ten or twenty minutes, but periodically look in to reassure him and one's self that he's okay. This tough-it-out approach is based on the notion that the child can go back to sleep by himself, but won't until he feels he has to, if he becomes dependent on his parents for this type of self-regulation.

At the opposite extreme is to take the child into the parent's bed to allow him to fall asleep, through the warm and supportive interventions of the parent. This approach assumes that the child will rely on the parent's support and warmth as long as needed and will sleep on his own when he is able.

However, an approach that is consistent with a more general concern with regulation requires the parent to try to identify the source of the sleeping problem. It is not unusual for common day-to-day experiences to unsettle a regulatory disordered child's already fragile equilibrium. Dietary factors, especially when certain types of food are eaten late in the evening; activities that overexcite a child, again, especially late in the evening; even overtiredness can play a role in a child's waking up and not sleeping well. In addition, if a sleeping child is exposed to certain fabrics, odors, or noises to which he is sensitive, this sensitivity can interfere with his sleep. One must also look for certain other causes, such as medical illnesses, side effects of medication, and the like.

Certain types of family behavioral patterns—overstimulation, overprotectiveness, overanxious interaction, or parent conflict and other family strife—may also contribute to sleeping difficulties.

Obviously, identifying and altering specific causes can be the easiest and most important way to help the child not only sleep better but also mobilize his progressive developmental tendencies in a more general way. The factors that interfere with sleeping are also likely to interfere with other aspects of development, which are perhaps too subtle to be noticed initially.

When there is no simple cause or there are multiple causes, which, when addressed, do not result in a child's learning to sleep through the night, the following approach may be helpful. Just as floor time is used to foster a sense of engagement, it may also be used with the verbal child to play out (during the light of day) scary feelings that may occur at night. The child also gets support for his dependency needs with warmth and intimacy in a collaborative way during the day rather than in a demanding way through a power struggle in the middle of the night.

The problem-solving aspects of floor time not only encourage engagement, but also the child's initiative and mobilization of his self-regulatory capacities. Children may become used to their parents taking care of their every need during the day. It is not surprising, therefore, if they wake up at night with the same idea in mind. Development of a child's assertiveness and sense of self-mastery requires interaction with parents that is sensitive to the child's cues in order to support the child's initiative, as discussed in some detail in the floor time chapters (see chapters 10–15). The child's themes that have to do with initiative and aggression, especially anger around unmet dependency needs, need to be facilitated and elaborated, rather than interfered with. During the problem-solving discussions with a verbal child, how he feels in the middle of the night (if he can remember) should be a part of the anticipatory drama. Using animals and dolls in a pretend way to anticipate the nighttime situation will enable the empathetic adult to see how the child plays out the scenario and to figure out the child's assumption, for example, that "Other people should help me when I'm uncomfortable."

The parent, or the parent with a verbal child, should then establish a goal to help the child regulate himself during both the day and the night. This goal should consist of a series of small steps. If the child wakes up six times during the night, the first step might be for the parents to get up only five times, and then four, then three, then two, and then one. A similar approach to daytime activities would allow the child to do some things for himself that he depends on the parents for, whether it's picking himself up after tripping or picking up a toy that falls on the floor.

The forms the actual limits can take depend on the regulatory profile of the child and the parents' personalities. Parents who are very symbiotic in their orientation toward their children almost always have to take a very gradual approach; the tough-it-out approach rarely works. Often it is best for the parent to be able to be in the room with the child, in order to rub his back when he wakes up upset. The parent may progress from picking the child up, to rubbing his back, to soothing the child by voice, to soothing the child with just a presence in the room; or the parent may stay in the child's room and lie down on a cot in view of the child. The parent must eventually extricate himself from the room entirely, but the weaning should be so gradual that the child may only whimper or cry for a few minutes, as the parent leaves. On the other hand, a parent who is more comfortable with letting a child cry may let the child learn that he can calm himself down, by increasing intervals when the child is left alone, starting with five or ten minutes and going up to fifteen or twenty minutes, with the parents only looking in to make sure the child is all right.

A clinician needs to be flexible in order to develop an approach based on the needs of the child and the family. For example, children with severe regulatory disorders tend to cry for hours with the tough-it-out approach and almost always need the more gradual approach. Parents can't behave in ways that are very uncomfortable for them, nor should they be urged to do so. There are many ways a child can learn better self-regulatory skills. The important general principle is that, on the one hand, the child needs practice in self-regulatory skills, in feeling warmly engaged, and in being assertive during the day, and at the same time, the child needs experience at night in being able to regulate his own sleep, especially the ability to fall back asleep after waking up.

Another common example of regulatory problems has to do with eating difficulties, which are susceptible to the same small-step approach described for sleeping problems. In addition to helping the child to engage and feel connected and to experiment with assertiveness, it is important to recognize the regulatory component of the child's eating problem, in terms of his sensitivity to different textures and smells. If he is an overly reactive child orally with relatively extreme tactile sensitivity around the mouth, or if he has low muscle tone or motor planning problems with chewing, eating is a far more difficult, and often more unpleasant, task than for the average person. Therefore one should experiment with different textures and odors and show the child that he can vary them so that he can exercise both maximum control and find ways to enjoy his eating. Eating needs to be enjoyed and should be pleasurable. Going shopping and arranging the menu can often help an older child. Working on textures and odors, along with other regulatory support for constitutional and maturational variables, as mentioned earlier in the section, can help a younger child. Also, the parent or clinician can apply deep tactile pressure on the child's pallet with the thumb; short bursts of pressure will help normalize sensation before the child eats. As with regulatory problems in general, there's no substitute for talking with the verbal child to anticipate the situation, the feeling, and the behavior.

ATTENTIONAL DIFFICULTIES

Attentional problems require the same small-steps approach, with special attention to figuring out which sensory pathways and motor patterns enable a child to be attentive more easily and which require extra practice. Is he more inattentive when hearing words or when seeing spatial designs? How can the two be used together to foster greater attentiveness? Is he tactilely sensitive, does he have motor planning difficulties? Most importantly, opening and closing circles of communication can be helpful—first on a behavioral, gestural level, then on a symbolic level, then at an internal level where the child sustains his attention by asking himself rhetorical questions. The key is for the child to use purposeful activity and purposeful thought and string together these thoughts and activities as a way of sustaining attention. Active problem solving is better than passive listening for the regulatory disordered child.

   It may be useful to consider an example of how a therapist might use a regulatory perspective in his work with a child with attention difficulties. A six-year-old comes in; he is there because the teacher said, "Johnny might be hyperactive and distractible; he is not learning in school, and probably should be on medication, so that he will attend better." The child has a history of "spacing out" a little bit in school and tending to get overwhelmed in groups, but when he has a friend over, he plays nicely; with a parent alone, he does well. But he can get a little "hyper" and distractible in the schoolroom, or if even two or three kids come over to play, or if there's a birthday party.

The child comes in and says, "Hi," and he looks warmly at the therapist. They exchange greetings, and he asks where the toys are. The therapist says, "Well there are some toys over there." "Can I play with them?" "Oh, sure." He goes over to the closet and opens it up. The therapist asks him, "What do you want to play with?" and he takes out three or four trucks and starts rolling and crashing them. The therapist says, "Gee, it's fun to explore." The child picks up a transformer truck and asks, "Do you know how this works?" Then the child starts trying to figure out how the transformer truck works and how the different parts relate to each other. He asks the therapist "Can you help?" "Where do you need help?" the therapist asks. The child might say, "I don't quite know how to change this part." The therapist asks the child if he (the child) could show him (the therapist), and they work on the truck together. As the session progresses and they play out different themes, eventually the therapist asks the child about his family and peers. The child talks easily and says that he has a little sister who really "makes me mad sometimes." "What makes you mad?" "Well, she bugs me. She takes my toys and stuff." Then he describes school and says that he doesn't like it when kids "poke fun at me," or when they call him names. What he likes, he says, is to go out with his father on Sundays and he goes on to describe what they do together.

Later on in the session when the child draws, the therapist notes that the child's fine motor control is behind his general intelligence. As the therapist explores what happens in school, he also notes that the child has a difficult time comprehending complex questions and at times gives up and seems to favor passivity or avoidance or "escape into fantasy."

At the end of such a session, what has the therapist learned? One-on-one, the child evidences many age-appropriate capacities. He is attentive and focused, engaged and related. He uses complex intentional gestures and represents his wishes and feelings in an elaborate and organized manner. There are hints that he has some difficulty with competition and aggression (e.g., "The kids poke fun at me"), but further exploration is required to look at how he deals with specific emotional themes. The therapist talks to the teacher, who confirms that the child "spaces out" in class. The therapist obtains a history from the parents: this is a child who has had some difficulties with auditory processing and fine motor control. He also tends to have tactile sensitivity, and gets quickly overloaded with sensory input; when he does overload, he tends to look distracted and withdraw. He seems, therefore, to have some regulatory components to his difficulties.

His parents are warm and supportive; they are able to use the representational mode around complex feelings, as evidenced, in part, by the child's ability to say when he is feeling "needy" or "angry." The clinical sessions, history, and observation of the family lead the therapist to think that there are many strategies to work with. The therapist decides to help the school to adjust to the child. The medication issue is brought up by the child's teacher and parents, but the therapist suggests that they put it on hold while they see what can be accomplished in a psychotherapeutic and educational program.

In such a case, the therapist may work on several fronts at once. He will organize a program to remediate maturational differences (e.g., have a speech pathologist help with auditory processing difficulties, an occupational therapist help with motor planning, fine motor regulation, and sensory hyperreactivity difficulties). At the same time, he will help the parents through floor time and problem-solving approaches which help the child learn to attend and focus even when anxious. For example, the parents will work on helping the child break down a task into small parts and find ways of linking one part to another, including helping the child use internal cues (e.g., ask himself questions). Most importantly, the parents will learn about their own feelings and counterproductive tendencies, such as overwhelming or withdrawing from, or being too concrete with, their child.

In his session with the child, the therapist will help the child in two ways. He will help him stay organized at both the gestural and representational levels by helping him learn to close circles of communication. He will also help the child identify and label feelings that lead the child to tune out or "avoid" or to lessen his desire to remain focused. Feelings such as anger, humiliation, fear of failure or loss, and fear of success can often trigger regressive patterns. When there are individual differences in ego structure, including processing problems and maladaptive responses to anxiety, both challenges need to be dealt with.

Consider an example of how the therapist might work. The therapist notices that when there is talk about a subject that makes the child uncomfortable, he doesn't close his representational circles. The therapist may say, "Gee, since you were telling me about school, I would like to hear more about what happens." The child says, "Oh, look at this transformer!" The therapist: "It's an interesting transformer, but we were talking about school and your friends." The child: "Oh! Can I play that game over there?" As the child continues to ignore what the therapist says, he evidences his constitutional vulnerability in auditory processing. But he is also deliberately avoiding talking about something that makes him anxious. His problem is a combination of his vulnerability and his way of dealing with anxiety. In a sense he intensifies his vulnerability when anxious. If the therapist then says, "Gee, let me get this right. I want to talk about your friends and school, but you would prefer to ignore that I'm even asking you the question and just play the game." The child might confirm the statement and close the circle, but he might talk about the game some more anyhow. The therapist then focuses on a new theme of how the child has a hard time closing a circle and how a complex statement containing three or four sentences causes him to feel lost.

"When I ask you a question, what happens to your thoughts?" "My mind is empty, I feel lost," the child might say. As the therapist shifts gears and helps the child look at how he "feels lost," together they can begin looking at situations and feelings that lead him to feeling lost, and the maladaptive patterns of avoidance or escape into fantasy that follow the lost feeling. The key is for the therapist to shift from a focus on just the content of the child's play or talk about the process by which the child deals with information.

The therapist should assist the parents in closing circles with the child as well. As parents engage in problem-solving discussions for a fifteen- or twenty-minute period each day and talk about a variety of subjects they will have lots of opportunities to close circles. The parents' goal is to keep the logic of the conversation going. If the child gets off on a tangent, the parent needs to acknowledge that the child would prefer to talk about another subject or feels lost, then try to bring the child back to the original topic. If the child says, "I don't want to talk about that," he has closed the circle; he is getting practice in being logical, and he is not being "spacey."

The therapist helps the parents determine in which emotional areas the child is more likely to display avoidant behavior—when he is talking about rivalry with peers and aggression, or the teacher's disapproval, or being overloaded by all the noise in school? The therapist, along with the parents, explores what happens when the child is in situations where he gets overloaded. What are his characteristic tendencies? For example, they will try to talk to the child about how he feels when people are making noise. He may say, as one child did, "It feels like there are a thousand bees in my head, and I can't hear anything else, and I don't know what I'm doing. It's awful." The therapist may say, "Well, tell me more about what that awful feeling is like," and help him describe the feeling, with as many metaphors as he can. The better the description he is able to give, the more the child learns to understand and anticipate the feeling. He learns to stay with the feeling and not escape from it by withdrawing and "spacing out." The child will be able to look at how he tends to side-step the feeling with direct avoidance or passivity or aggression or by confusing others, once he can describe his core feeling state. The child's ability to identify his tendencies does not mean they are deliberate or that there is not a maturational component to his difficulty. It only means that he can use his ability to represent and observe feelings to become more flexible in his coping. The fact that the therapist is focusing on the child's coping pattern does not mean he isn't following the child's lead. The child's behavior of avoidance or fragmented thinking is a part of his communication.

One tries over time to help children tolerate the dysphoric affect of confusion by realizing that, because they have a mild processing problem, their tendency is to "play ostrich" and tune out what's going on around them. One shows them that they can learn to become more vigilant. If the parents function well, they can help; at the same time, the occupational therapist or speech pathologist can work to strengthen the child's sensorimotor and language systems. The therapist also works with the parents on their characteristic family patterns. The therapist should also consult directly with the teachers, so that they can work with the child in class. Sometimes a school counselor working with children together in a group can be very helpful. The goals and approaches, however, should be coordinated. The teacher can also work on facilitating ego structure without becoming overly intrusive.

Self-Cuing in Children with Attentional Difficulties

A lack of self-cuing is one of the patterns that I have observed clinically with children who evidence attentional difficulties, and especially those who forget their homework, their classroom location, and what they are supposed to do from one minute to the next. Whereas another child, during a transition such as the end of the schoolday, may ask himself, "What is my homework for tonight and which books do I have to take home?" the forgetful, inattentive child simply walks out of school thinking of the green leaves on the trees outside and the friend he wants to talk to on the way home. The books he needs for homework do not enter his thoughts until his angry parent is standing over him yelling. Clinically, I have also noticed that as children learn to ask themselves these rhetorical questions, their seeming inattentiveness can begin changing. In other words, an aspect of the inattentiveness is a lack of a logical infrastructure of thinking where the child uses self-observation, self-reflection, and most importantly self-cuing through rhetorical questions to organize his day, and to maintain his concentration. In this framework, attention and concentration are viewed not as a passive or even natural process or ability. It is viewed as an active process which rests on active thinking. Since many inattentive children can think quite logically and actively, particularly when they are highly motivated, they may be more capable than we think in applying this same active thinking ability to transitions. Applying active thinking to transitions, in terms of self-cuing, would help them stay with a task. In a limited number of clinical cases where this active approach to maintaining attention has been taken, the results have been promising. In such cases, however, in addition to helping the child to think actively, it has been important to also help the child understand his own, at times, latent desire to be forgetful, avoidant, or passive. One child put it beautifully: "When the work gets too hard and too much, I just chuck it over my back by forgetting everything." Family patterns and conflicts over assertiveness and aggression invariably play a role, but the child's tendency, based on constitutional and maturational differences, is not to cue himself with rhetorical questions.

Related to the actual process of attending is a potentially interesting hypothesis. In operant learning theory, different reinforcement schedules maintain behavior under their control at different rates. Some schedules such as a random ratio schedule (behavior is reinforced based on number of responses) maintains behavior at high rates and other schedules maintain behavior at low rates (e.g., a fixed interval schedule with long intervals). Early caregiver responses to the infants attentive behavior may form a pattern which resembles a known schedule.

Such caregiver patterns may therefore be studied as a factor influencing attentive behavior.

It is important not to assume that an attentional disorder is a unitary entity. It is useful to assume that every child has some maturational unevenness, which in each child is quite different. Whether the problem is visual–spatial or auditory processing or motor planning will dictate different approaches to the problem. The psychotherapist has to figure out what the maturational vulnerabilities are and what kind of internal experience they produce. He needs to observe how this is experienced one-on-one, or in a group, and with cognitive and affective challenges. The therapist must determine how the child copes with his experience—by withdrawal, activity, fear, ritualistic behavior, or some other way.

Most educators will be very appreciative if a therapist can pinpoint why the child is so difficult to teach, and how he copes with feeling confused. For example, some children with a visual–spatial processing lag have a hard time picturing experience. This difficulty may explain why they find it hard to do math (math has to be pictured). A child has to be able to picture that $5 \times 3 = 15$. For example, ask a child, "How big is 7, if 1 is this big?" Perhaps he cannot represent the proper proportions, he cannot picture spatial entities. If one tries to teach that child the rules of addition and subtraction, "math facts," by rote, he will never be a good math student. If he learns to picture in his mind different sizes and dimensions and develops a "spatial feel" for numbers, he can learn to enjoy and master math. He may need to go from concrete objects to imagination until he has a sense of spatial proportions. As he tries to master a new way of thinking, he may use all his favorite tactics—withdrawal, avoidance, aggression, and so forth. The therapist's perspective can help a tutor recognize the child's unique patterns of regulatory phenomena and work with him more effectively.

Therefore, in the regulatory disorders, unevenness in maturation is part of the problem along with symptoms associated with attentional difficulties.

FAMILY PATTERNS OF INFANTS AND CHILDREN WITH REGULATORY DIFFICULTIES

In dealing with regulatory disorders, the clinician is likely to see specific types of family dynamics, caregiver fantasies, and interactional patterns between infants and caregivers.

It is not unusual for caregivers or parents to feel frustrated in their efforts to calm their regulatory disordered infant or toddler and to help the child attend to them in order to derive satisfaction from the relationship. At later ages, from around fifteen months on up, parents may also become even more frustrated with their inability to control the child's irritability, temper tantrums, or aggression. Sleeping and eating problems, as indicated, are also frequent. When parents cannot help the child control or regulate his own body, they often feel, in the deepest and most profound sense, like failures—like "bad" parents. In addition, the parents are also likely to be tired, if the child is waking up a great deal at night, or drained, because the child may be in constant motion or having tantrums or being irritable all day long. When the parents' irritability, sense of frustration and failure is coupled with physical exhaustion, the situation may be truly explosive.

Some parents have their own history of regulatory dysfunction. If these parents tend toward aggressive acting out, the clinician needs to be alert for physical abuse as a possible consequence of this interplay of factors. If the parent tends to deal with his or her own patterns of regulatory dysfunction by patterns of withdrawal, depression, or avoidance, one needs to look for various forms of neglect as well.

Where these extremes are not present, one may more typically see parents and caregivers dealing with these circumstances in a number of expectable ways. The parent may be overcontrolling and punitive and may try to insist that the child self-regulate by adhering to certain standards that the parents have set up. When the child fails to respond to the parents' best attempts to establish control and order, coupled with structured punishment and sanctions, certain parents are likely to become more punitive, until they reach a point where they can go no further; they may then seek assistance. By this time, the child's regulatory problems may have gotten so severe that the situation appears to be out of control.

Other parents vacillate between punitive, overcontrolling approaches and states of withdrawal. One day, they feel energized and determined to make their child attend, sleep, eat, or behave; the next day, they've given up and may say, "He'll have to do this on his own, when he wants to." Needless to say, this alternation between unavailability and overcontrolling punitiveness can provide a very unstable milieu for the infant, toddler, or young child. Some parents and caregivers become very fragmented in their own thinking, particularly if they have regulatory dysfunctional tendencies of their own; their behavior tends to match the fragmented behavior of the infant or young child.

Other parents become overtly hostile and rejecting of their children; these parents are very aware of their own fantasies of wanting to escape from their children. Again, their thinking often is conveyed to the child. Some parents, in defending against the impulse to escape, become rigidly and somewhat mechanically nurturing to their children; these parents overprotect, feel overanxious, and therefore do not provide opportunities for the child to learn self-sufficiency. Even parents who lack the underlying desire to escape or reject may focus their frustration by being overprotecting or anxious.

The family dynamics may take on certain characteristic patterns that extend beyond the scope of the individual caregiver or parent. Not infrequently, the mother is exhausted, the father feels unattended to and works harder than usual to stay away from the demanding battle zone of the family; the mother then feels unsupported by the father; the mother and father each feel that the other isn't nourishing enough. There's no sexual intimacy or warmth between them; each one becomes critical of the other. Often many of the angry feelings the parents both feel toward the child get played out between the two adults. In turn, anger stirred up between the two of them may get played out toward the child. Older siblings can become involved in this pattern as well; they may feel ignored on the one hand, and frazzled and caught in the chaos, on the other hand. The siblings may begin to act out more in such a dysfunctional family situation.

When one observes the caregiver–infant interaction patterns, one often sees that those interactions characterize these different emotional themes. The parent may be overly labile, fragmented, and erratic in the way he or she responds to the baby's cues, and the baby, in turn, is even more erratic than he might ordinarily be. The parent may be overly controlled and punitive with the child; the child may become, in response, negative, avoidant, or overtly defiant. Parents who are anxiously overly protective and controlling may stimulate a passive-compliant or avoidant pattern on the part of the infant. Or, as indicated earlier, one may see alternating patterns of control from both the parent and the infant, as seeming indulgence with a child who may play the part of fearful tyrant, may be displaced by parental demands that elicit fearful and tantrumy behavior from the child.

While there are an infinite number of variations one can see in the infant–caregiver–parent or family patterns, it is critical to work with each of them at the same time that one works with the infant's constitutional and maturational contributions. The overall approach usually involves working with the parent and the infant to strengthen the infant's constitutional and maturational coping capacities and to foster age-appropriate, more flexible patterns of relating. The child or infant's assertiveness, self-mastery, and broad emotional range are fostered for each major developmental competency (focus and engagement, two-way communication, using emotional ideas, and categorizing and connecting emotional ideas). As the infant, toddler, or child is helped to negotiate each developmental stage and to incorporate the full range of emotional themes—pleasure, assertiveness, dependency, aggression, and the like—and as his constitutional and maturational capacities for attending and engaging are strengthened, the pressures on the parents and family are lessened. At the same time, through separate but simultaneous meetings with the parents to discuss their feelings—especially their reactions to their infant—and their own personality dynamics in this regard, and to look at and understand the couple's relationship and family dynamics, one often sees gradual improvement. These discussions can be handled sometimes by one clinician working in a setting with the infant, parents, or caregiver; by the caregiver alone; the caregiver and couple; and sometimes the whole family. At other times, two professionals may be involved—one focusing more on the couple or family relationship, and the other one focusing more on the caregiver–infant patterns and the infant's constitutional and maturational capacities. This division of labor depends on the nature of the therapeutic team and the needs of the family.

For infants and young children who evidence significant constitutional and maturational variation as part of their regulatory disorders, it is very helpful to have at least a consultation with an occupational therapist trained in sensory integration work to evaluate the contributions of sensory over- or underreactivity, sensory processing, motor tone, and motor planning problems to the infant's regulatory disorder. At times follow-up sessions with the occupational therapist to help the infant deal with significant difficulties may be appropriate. How much occupational therapy involvement there should be beyond the initial consultation often depends on the clinician's own skill in working with sensory and motor patterns, the degree of challenge the child evidences, and the degree to which the parents themselves are gifted and carrying out the initial suggestions. In a general sense, where a child has a significant developmental delay involving motor tone and motor planning, it is almost always useful to have some follow-up sessions. Where particular sensory reactivity problems are extreme, it is also helpful to have the occupational therapist play a more active role and have follow-up meetings with the parent alongside and with the clinician, who will be focusing on the interactive and family patterns.

Where receptive or expressive language is influenced by the regulatory differences, speech pathologists should also be consulted initially and possibly become part of the follow-up care, again depending on the degree and severity, the family's competencies, and the clinician's own experience in working with the language component of the child's development.

In working with regulatory disorders, therefore, there are a number of principles that may be helpful to the clinician. These govern the way he or she works with the constitutional and maturational variation of the infant or young child, the way he develops and implements a step-by-step program to help the infant or young child engage in the kind of experiences that will foster his or her overall development, and the way in which he works with the caregiver–infant or caregiver–child interaction patterns and the family dynamics.

Chapter 23

Multisystem Developmental Disorders

Multisystem developmental disorders involve problems in social, emotional, and intellectual development, receptive and expressive language development, sensory reactivity and processing, motor tone, and motor planning (see cases 10 [p.139], 16 [p.203], 17 [p.221], 19 [p.252], 20 [p.265], 21 [p.274] for illustrations of these disorders).

Consider pervasive developmental disorder and autism. At present, children (usually between 18 months and 4 years of age) receive a diagnosis of pervasive developmental disorder or communication disorder with autistic features or, if severe enough, autism. Such children evidence a severe disturbance in interpersonal relating, communication, and overall adaptation. Most of the children I have seen with this pattern have significant developmental problems at each of the early stages of ego development. They often, for example, have a severe difficulty with auditory processing and, later, receptive language. They may also have various types of sensory hyperreactivity (e.g., tactile sensitivities) and subtle irregularities in motor tone and

639

planning. These constitutional–maturational patterns are often sufficient to throw off the early negotiation of shared attention, engagement, intentional reciprocal gesturing, and early representational capacities. Even reasonably stable, supportive, and empathetic families often do not have the intuitive skills to help their child successfully negotiate these early challenges. One may hypothesize that a combination of two events not infrequently seems to significantly derail the child's forward momentum between sixteen and twenty-four months. One of these events appears to be the child's own emerging capacities for higher level presymbolic and symbolic functioning. Overloaded with new information about the world (because new information is being processed with a vulnerable and shaky foundation such as poor behavioral causality), he begins regressing in terms of behavioral organization, regulation, interpersonal patterns, and emerging motor control and language. Around this time, for example the toddler is developing a sense of himself in space including a greater sense of potential vulnerability. There may be other cognitive advances that can paradoxically overwhelm certain children. In many cases, careful history taking often reveals environmental stresses around this time, such as the loss of a caregiver, a parent going back to work, preoccupation of a parent with the birth of a sibling, and so forth. For children who already have a tenuous hold on their interpersonal relationships and emerging functional capacities, the combination of these two types of challenges may be overwhelming (although for some even the former challenge alone seems sufficient).

The infant's maladaptive foundation, it is hypothesized, can be functionally described in terms of individual differences and dysfunctions in sensory reactivity, sensory processing (including receptive language), motor tone, and motor planning. Affective and social dysfunctions may be a part of these more basic dysfunctions. The numerous biological differences described in a considerable literature on these children, it is hypothesized, are expressed functionally through differences and dysfunctions in the regulatory, sensory, language and motor systems, as described above.

Furthermore, as the child becomes more challenging he usually succeeds in confusing his parents sufficiently so that they stop offering him developmental support in terms of the four processes outlined earlier (shared attention and engagement, two-way intentional gesturing, representational elaboration, and representational differentiation). Having disengaged, in part because of their confusion and anxiety and in part because of the challenging nature of the child's behavior, a number of parents report growing feelings of alienation, anger, and loss, and unintentionally behave with increasing ambivalence. The child, as he loses his engagement and intentional interactive relatedness to his key caregivers, seems to spin more and more idiosyncratically out of control. For children who are prerepresentational, this may manifest itself by greater motor and behavior randomness and lack of intentionality. For children who have achieved some degree of representational capacity, their use of ideas and words becomes more personalized and fragmented, or it is lost altogether. The lack of an intentional and organizing human relationship mediates this disorganization.

There appear to be many variations and types of multisystem disorders. When extreme in terms of social and affective dysfunction, pervasive developmental disorder (not otherwise classified) or autism is considered. In this discussion there will be a focus on a range of dysfunctions with an emphasis on the moderate to severe end of the continuum.

The biggest challenge to the treatment and prevention of multisystem developmental difficulties is the early detection of massive ego distortion, and opportunities to reestablish an adaptive developmental process. Often, in cases of pervasive developmental disorder, parents may have known something was wrong at thirteen or fourteen months, and they perhaps didn't do anything in the hope that the situation would get better. Perhaps they were told that the child might grow out of the problem. Usually at about twenty months, parents start a developmental assessment, but often waste another four or five months getting workups by speech and occupational therapists and having neurologic and genetic consultations. All the latter may be helpful but they should be done within one week in order to get treatment started. At this age, every month that passes is worth years later on; one should not let six months go by. If the child finally gets a therapist's attention at about two years of age, he has lost important time.

From about twelve months up until two-and-a-half or three, a child is abstracting the rules of social interaction at a very rapid rate. When this does not occur, a child may look as though he has a biologic deficit in social interaction skills when in fact it may be only a lack of learning secondary to processing difficulties. Perhaps the brain structure that is alleged to be biologically deficient in reciprocal social behavior looks deficient only because learning the rules of social interaction would normally occur during the first two years of life. In this context it would be of interest if biological studies of Pervasive Developmental Disorders and autism would compare the children with these severe disorders to children with sensory reactivity language and motor difficulties without affective and social difficulties (in addition to using normally developing children or children with other types of disorders as controls). When a child, because of auditory and/or visual–spatial processing difficulties, makes communication challenging, and the people in his immediate environment do not find a way to engage and interact with him, a critical time in his development may be lost and vital social learning may not occur. Our clinical experience with two- to three-year-olds, however, is that they can still learn gestural communication, adaptive affect expression, and eventually symbolic communication if an intensive program is offered. The earlier such a program can be started, however, the quicker we see progress. When proper treatment is not offered and instead mechanical, stereotyped, or overly structured treatment approaches are offered, the children may look more mechanical and preseverative.

Treatment should have one very simple goal: to get the child back into, or to establish, an intentional pattern of natural, warm communication. Interestingly, many families report, and have videotapes to back it up, that in the first year of life the child was engaged and was beginning reciprocal interactions. Only in the second year of life did the child begin moving away from social interactions, suggesting that for some reason he became move overwhelmed and withdrew as he moved into the second year.

In order to help the initiation of or return to an adaptive pattern of social development, there are a number of important challenges that must be met. These involve helping the child learn to attend, relate, interact, experience a range of feelings, and ultimately think and relate in an organized and logical manner. These challenges involve the caregivers' and therapist's awareness of the steps the child needs to master his core developmental competencies and the selection of a proper educational setting which can offer both special expertise and helpful peer-to-peer feedback. The following sections will discuss the principles of an optimal therapeutic program.

TREATMENT APPROACHES FOR INFANTS AND YOUNG CHILDREN WITH MULTISYSTEM DELAYS AND DISORDERS, INCLUDING PERVASIVE DEVELOPMENTAL DISORDER

The most promising therapeutic approach to children with delays in many areas of functioning, especially those children characterized as having pervasive developmental disorder, is to mobilize the core developmental processes outlined earlier. That is, the child must be encouraged to attend and engage; to communicate intentionally with others (i.e., two-way communication or opening and closing circles of communication); to form abstract representations or symbols as a way of organizing experience, especially affective experience; and to differentiate or make connections between symbolized or represented experiences.

Work with these children is especially challenging because of the difficulty parents, educators, and therapists have in creating experiences that will promote these four developmental processes. The differences and delays in sensory reactivity, sensory processing, motor tone, motor planning, and language make it extremely difficult to find ways to engage, interact, or communicate with these children. For example, the child who won't look at his parent, or who becomes aimless every time his parent tries to gesture at him, or withdraws whenever his parent presses an attempt at communicating, will not easily become engaged or subsequently involved in complex interactive gesturing, let alone interactive verbalizations. The constitutional and maturational patterns of the infant or child are so challenging that parents typically become involved in counterpatterns that not only don't help the child but make his challenge even greater. For example, as the child becomes more withdrawn or more aimless, the parent may instinctively vacillate between overwhelming the child by pressing harder and withdrawing ("I have to give up; nothing works"). Such inconsistency will only detract from the child's ability to master core developmental processes.

Before looking at how one can help this most challenging group of children master the core developmental processes that all children need to master, it may be useful to identify some of the common strategies that are often unhelpful promoting developmental competency in infants and children with multiple and pervasive developmental difficulties.

FRAGMENTED, RIGID APPROACHES

Perhaps one of the most common unhelpful approaches is to lose sight of the developmental progession the child needs, and instead, to zoom in on particular skills in a fragmented or isolated way. This haphazard approach invariably leads to rigid, stereotyped, controlling, or avoidant therapeutic, educational, or parental approaches. For example, a child may be aimless and distracted and seem to be too inattentive to the therapist's or parent's overtures to engage in the simplest kind of interaction. A parent or therapist may be trying, for example, to get the child to put a square block in a square hole. But the child may seem to be looking out the window, staring at the ceiling; the child may bang on the floor or knock over the puzzle. The child may do everything but look at the adult and try to copy what the adult is doing. Frustrated by the child's inattentiveness, the therapist or parent (often the parent copies the therapist) may hold the child's face and insist that the child look at him or her. Next the therapist, and the parent as well, may try to get the child to listen by slowing down and firming up his or her voice. The therapist may talk in a repetitive monotone (much like a computer voice in a tram car at an airport) and say something like, "Look at me. Look at me. Look at me." Perhaps, it is reasoned, this repetitive, simple monotone will provide the child with a very simple and clear stimulus input and will help him organize and carry out the desired behavior. If the therapist has been influenced by behavioral schools of thought, he may add on a reward every time the child does look at him. The therapist might offer verbal praise (also delivered in a computerized monotone), "Good boy. Good boy. Good boy," as well as a piece of candy or other treat.

If a truly objective observer, however, saw an adult sitting next to a child and talking in a computerlike voice—a mechanical monotone, with no emotional variation or spontaneous facial expression, he would not be surprised that the child was taking very little interest: who likes to talk to a machine? If the adult began holding the child's face and insisting that the child look at him, even though the adult was giving the child no incentive to pay attention, it would be obvious that children who tend to be aimless and self-absorbed and adults who tend to be rigid and stereotyped cannot assist one another.

I have a hypothesis that most adults—therapists, educators, and parents—who work with children with pervasive developmental disorders inadvertently begin to copy the child's perseverative and stereotyped patterns. The therapist, parent, and educator tends to be stereotyped and perseverative in a more rigid, focused way, whereas the child tends to vacillate between the rigid, focused, perseverative activities and more aimless, self-absorbed, distractible activities. But there is a remarkable similarity between the behaviors of the adults and those of the child.

Perhaps identification with the child is not surprising. After all, the child is not providing the ordinary feedback most parents, educators, or therapists expect. Even therapists working with very conflicted or anxious children get lots of affective and behavioral feedback. Parents are probably biologically programmed in some way to respond to the feedback they get from their children, and this feedback keeps them going. The smiling baby, the pointing toddler, or the talking preschooler engenders certain feelings in his parents, which, in turn, lead the parents to behave in ways that will further support developmental capacities in this child. The smiling child promotes a smiling parent, and vice versa. The pointing child promotes a pointing parent, and the verbal child promotes an imaginative, vocal parent. When the adult receives only aimless, perseverative, or self-absorbed feedback, he or she is not prepared. The natural response to this confusion may be to become overly rigid and controlling or to withdraw. As a related observation, I have observed children who are developing in a healthy fashion, together (in a one-on-one setting) with an aimless and perseverative child. Often the age-appropriate child may, much as the therapists do, begin intruding and press the child who is not providing feedback as a way of trying to get some response.

The stereotyped, perseverative behavior may be rationalized as "therapeutic." It is important to understand, however, that while the intrusive stereotypical behavior may be a natural, biologic tendency in the face of a child who is not providing the expected feedback, it is most often not therapeutic.

Another example is of a strict behavior-modification approach where the therapist uses systematic reinforcers to support certain behaviors; time-outs and certain abstinence procedures are used to extinguish or discourage certain negative behaviors. The very systemization of the approach and the mechanical quality of the resulting behavioral interactions may be experienced by the child as a rigid, mechanical, and stereotyped interaction with an adult.

One may wonder why children with pervasive developmental disorder look more and more unusual as they become older. It is not atypical for children with autistic spectrum/pervasive developmental disorder patterns to become more stereotyped and more perseverative, as they develop. Even children who develop certain splinter skills and intellectual capacities, such as being able to read or add, may nonetheless become increasingly rigid and stereotyped in their social responses. (The movie *Rain Man* starring Dustin Hoffman provides a good example of a very high-functioning individual with autistic-type patterns.) One needs to consider the hypothesis that the type of interventions that have been organized on behalf of these infants and children in part supports rather than remediates their more mechanical behavior.

Therefore, it may be that, while the pervasively developmentally delayed infant and young child does present special challenges and does not provide the feedback that helps the adults promote certain developmental competencies, at the same time, the adult's tendency to react to the child's challenge in a rigid way only further increases the child's already significant developmental challenge. The key then is to help therapists, educators, and parents develop a pattern of intervention that fosters core competencies of relating and engaging, focusing and concentrating, interacting in flexible and spontaneous ways with two-way communication, and representing (symbolizing) and then differentiating this represented experience. If every time we wish to help a child copy a particular motor behavior or perform a particular academic skill we can, at the same time, work on the child's core developmental competencies in a spontaneous and self-initiating way, we might then be able to see a developmental progression of greater flexibility, warmth, intimacy, and spontaneity, rather than one of increased perseverativeness and rigidity.

PARALLEL COMMENTARY RATHER THAN INTERACTION

In addition, there is a tendency even among the most relationship-oriented therapists to ignore the more delayed child's core needs and employ tactics taken from therapeutic work with less severely delayed children. One such tactic is frequently used in what could be called parallel play with the children. For example, the child may take a block and place it on top of another block, then knock them down and pile them up again, and again. This behavior is manifested by a nonverbal child who is not yet functioning at a symbolic level or even at a level that involves complex interactive gestures. The child is only at the level of reacting to someone else's overture in a simple way. If one gives him a block, he will open his hand and take it, but he won't initiate giving the block back or look at or vocalize at the giver. The therapist who has been trained to work with more neurotic two-, three-, and four-year-olds assumes that he or she can form a relationship with this more delayed child by simply positioning himself next to the child and perhaps copying and/or commenting on what the child is doing. He might say, "Oh, Johnny is putting one block on top of the other. Oh, Johnny is knocking it down now. Now Johnny is building it up again." He may even say, "Oh boy, Johnny is angry at the blocks," or "Now Johnny likes the blocks." Meanwhile, the child may overlook the adult, show no emotion, and not necessarily take in what is being said. A therapist and a child may go on in this kind of a way for weeks, months, and possibly even years, with very little movement or gain. To be sure, the child experiences the therapist's presence, and may or may not enjoy it. And the therapist most likely increases his own daydreaming time between his parallel play and his comments. The therapist may also get annoyed and, from time to time, become more intrusive in his comments. In order for the therapist to remain involved and not give up, he rationalizes that this child needs his presence in this way, because the child is living in his own world and, when the child is ready, the child will accept the therapist.

Some adult therapists have reported sitting in rooms for years, with adult withdrawn schizophrenics, sometimes quietly, and sometimes making occasional comments, until finally the patient seems to open up to the therapist. There is a sense that the potential for relating is there only it is frozen, and that patience, a presence, and occasionally clarifications and interpretations of a verbal nature will help the patient. This approach may be misapplied to adults, and it certainly is misapplied to infants and children who haven't yet developed symbolic and representational capacities or complex two-way communicative gestural capacities. Nevertheless, the therapist will try to support what they are doing with theoretical parallels to what they believe to be similar endeavors.

DEVELOPMENTAL MISMATCH

Another common type of error is to attempt to relate to the child in a way that is developmentally above the child's current level of function. To build a relationship with the child without representation or symbolic capacities or complex, interactive gestural capacity, who is building and knocking down his blocks, the therapist may reason, "Ah ha, the child is building and breaking down. This looks to me like a conflict involving aggression and castration anxiety. Or a conflict involving loss. Or a conflict involving growth and destruction." The therapist may begin to comment to the child that he is destroying his blocks, or destroying his family with the blocks, or building up the blocks and destroying them. The therapist may comment further on the fear of destruction or the fear of growth. As he pursues alleged underlying *conflicts* in the child, the therapist misses the fact that the child is not yet even functioning at a level that enables him to comprehend representational or symbolic type of verbal communications. The therapist rationalizes his behavior by assuming that even though the child has never spoken a word and doesn't even interact gesturally, that the child nonetheless has a preconscious or unconscious capacity to understand everything the adult is saying, and that the child is, in fact, tuning in with words and symbols, even though the child is not letting on that he is doing any such thing. Even if the therapist tries to simply talk to the child about why he is knocking down the blocks, perhaps asking our three-year-old, "Why do you like to do that?" and suggesting simple reasons for the child's actions, the therapist would still be beyond a child who is barely gesturally and not yet verbally interactive.

WORKING ON SPLINTER SKILLS

The tendency to work on "splinter" skills (an isolated, often rote-learned cognitive capacity) is another aspect of working developmentally above a child. The parent understandably wants his cognitively and language delayed child to appear more normal. The therapist would also like some signs of intellectual brilliance from a delayed youngster. Together they may help the child to master certain splinter skills, such as having a child say the days of the week or recognize certain letters or words, or memorize the contents of a book. Some of the rigid, perseverative, and stereotyped approaches described earlier, such as holding the child's face, or using M&Ms as reinforcers to get the child to carry out certain proscribed behaviors in the right circumstances and with the right cues, can enable the child to perform those behaviors. However, a change of place or context or even the verbal sequence used to elicit the behavior will take away the child's ability to recognize the letters or read the book in any but a concrete and perseverative way. Splinter skills may boost the morale of the parent, educator, or clinician, but they rarely help the child very much.

On the other hand, certain mechanical skills may help the child mobilize his core developmental competencies. As long as the method of teaching the child is not overly mechanical, a number of sounds or words that he can use to signal needs or desires, as he might do with complicated hand or facial gesturing, can only be helpful. Later on these same words may be a part of a more complex symbolic capacity. Similarly, teaching certain concepts such as "more" or "less" or "up" or "down" or certain social behaviors such as sitting and concentrating can only be helpful if they are used as part of the child's spontaneous self-initiative. If splinter skills are not integrated into the child's developmental competencies and the method of teaching is overly stereotyped, the child's competencies may actually be undermined.

WORKING BELOW THE CHILD'S DEVELOPMENTAL LEVEL

It is also a common error to approach a child developmentally below his developmental level. To continue with the example of the child at an early gestural level who is knocking down his blocks, one can also assume that this child is very warmly engaged with others, loves to cuddle with his parents and hug, and doesn't mind leaning on a parent while he perseveratively builds or knocks down his blocks. Therapeutic efforts beneath the child would focus only on hugging and cuddling, warmth, and security. The therapist might rationalize his focus on fostering simple engagement in this child, with the notion that the problem is in the attachment and the child needs a more secure and deeper attachment in order to move on in development. Fostering emotional closeness might not have any negative impact on the child, except that mobilizing a developmental competency already attained might be simply practicing something the child is already very well comfortable with. Furthermore, the therapist may interpret the building up and knocking down of blocks as a sign of ambivalence, when it may be nothing of the kind.

There are, therefore, a number of common unhelpful approaches to working with pervasively delayed and disordered infants and young children. These approaches are understandable because the children don't provide the expectable cues that help the parents, educators, and clinicians interact in ways that will promote development. In the absence of these cues, the adults are left to their own devices, and often use therapeutic theories to rationalize what is a maladaptive intuitive response to a challenging situation.

PRINCIPLES OF INTERVENTION

Perhaps the primary goal for children who have significant delays in core areas of functioning, regulatory difficulties, and therefore difficulties in their interaction patterns, including their own family dynamics, is to enable them to form a sense of their own personhood—a sense of themselves as intentional, interactive individuals. One typically observes infants and young children with these kinds of difficulties operating in an aimless, fragmented, often impersonal, idiosyncratic manner. If one tries to imagine what their inner experiences are like, based on how they behave, one would imagine that they are organizing pieces of experience around basic needs and stereotyped interactions with their physical world.

How does one assist these children to organize their experiences, so that they begin to have a more logical, interactive, personal, emotional, and pleasurable relationship to others? In terms of normal development generally, one may hypothesize that the sense of one's self evolves from the infant's or young child's ability to abstract from his interactive experience. The infant or young child has literally a seemingly infinite number of interactions with his caregivers. These interactions, and at times negotiations, create an experiential basis for the infant to extract, that is, to figure out how the world works in general and in particular how that part of the world works that involves the unique set of sensations or feelings that affects his own body and is a part of his intentional, interactive world. This sense of "personhood" doesn't exist initially at a symbolic or representational level. Rather it would seem initially to organize itself around physical sensations, a sense of connection to others (and the affects associated with this sense of connection or engagement). Later the sense of personhood would appear to define itself around a sense of intentionality (two-way communication, involving the use of simple and complex gestures). Next it would define itself in terms of emerging representations or symbols as they became organized and differentiated. As the sense of personhood evolves, earlier and more fundamental levels serve as a foundation for newer levels. The challenge is how to foster this sense of personhood, so critical to an organized, integrated foundation for organizing experience, in a child who has delays and dysfunctions in core areas of functioning.

Interventions with children with such challenges requires one to remember that their sense of their own being derives not simply from their language functioning or their motor functioning or their cognition. Working with each or any of these areas in isolation may only continue a sense of fragmentation. Their sense of themselves derives from how they utilize their bodies as part of intentional engagements and interactions and how they organize the affects these interactions generate. One must always ask how any intervention affects the child's ability to abstract and organize an emotional, sensation-based experience of who he is. Because these children often lack the most basic foundation for interpersonal experiences (e.g., they are often not interactive in the purposeful way that ordinary eight-month-olds are), much of the experience that they might use to abstract a sense of their own personhood is not available to them.

Therefore, for these children, the earliest therapeutic goals must be geared to the first steps in the developmental progression, that is, to foster focus and concentration, engagement with the human world, and two-way intentional communication. These early steps in the developmental sequence, unfortunately, are sometimes ignored (as indicated earlier) in order to pursue splinter skills involving allegedly higher levels of language or cognitive functioning.

FOCUS, ENGAGEMENT, AND TWO-WAY COMMUNICATION

The first principle of treatment of pervasive developmental disorder and multisystem delays in infants and young children is, therefore, to work on the earliest stages in the developmental sequence. It may be easy to state this principle in the abstract, but the practicing clinician may find it hard to implement. The child who is tuning out, seemingly aimless, wandering around the room, banging on the windows, touching the floor, opening and closing doors, seems hardly interested in forming a sense of focused engagement or patterns of two-way communication. It is tempting to begin talking to the child about why he wants to open and close the door, yet such intervention will be too far above the child in terms of developmental feedback to be of any value other than giving him the sense that the clinician is in the room with him.

As one focuses on fostering a sense of focus and a sense of engagement, even before one worries about two-way communication, one is empowered by one's knowledge of how the child responds to different types of sensations and the types of experiences that are likely to influence him. Therefore, one must pay attention to the child's regulatory difficulties and delays and dysfunctions in motor, sensory, language, and cognitive functioning. What are the tools the child potentially brings to his ability to focus and engage? For example, if he's overreactive to sound, talking to him in a normal loud voice may lead him to become more aimless and more withdrawn. If he is overreactive to sights, bright lights and even very animated facial expressions may be overwhelming for him. On the other hand, if he is underreactive to sensations of sound and visual–spatial input, talking in a strong voice and using animated facial expressions in a well-lit room may help him attend. Similarly, in terms of his receptive language skills, if he is already at the point where he can decode a complex rhythm, making interesting sounds in complex patterns may be helpful. On the other hand, if he can only decode very simple, two-sequence rhythms, and perhaps understands a single word here and there, using single words (not as a symbolic communication, but as gestural communication) and using simple patterns of sound may help him engage.

In addition, there may be other experiences that help him attend and overcome his regulatory dysfunctions. One may find that he remains relatively better focused in motion, such as being swung on a swing with someone holding him. And certain rhythms of movement may be more effective than others. For some children, fast movement, rhythms, such as one swing per second, may be ideal. For others, slow rhythms, similar to the breathing rate or one swing every four or five or six seconds, may be ideal. The necessary motion can come from a real swing, or the parent's arms, or the big ball that many occupational therapists use to foster motor development that a child can kind of hang over and gently move. One may also find that different kinds of tactile input foster concentration and focus for some children. Firm pressure on the back or the arms or the legs, applied in a rhythmic manner, may encourage their attention. Certain types of large motor movement may also foster some ability of some children to focus and attend. For example, jumping on the bed, or any trampolinelike motion, may combine both joint compression and large motor experiences to help some children focus.

It is important to realize that each infant and child is different. There is no substitute for the keen eye of the clinician as he observes the impact of various experiences on the child. The clinician attempts to involve the child in certain activities, and to use his understanding of the child's sensorimotor–cognitive–language experiences as a way of mobilizing and helping the child attend and focus. Occupational therapists, trained to work with the infant's way of responding to and processing sensations and integrating them with motor and cognitive and language capacities, are often especially gifted at finding ways to help an infant focus and engage.

In practice, helping the child attend and focus is often best done in spontaneous interaction with the child, when the clinician or caregiver attempts to follow the child's lead. If one observes that a certain quality of voice helps the child to pay attention (or certain rhythms of vocalization, certain activities like jumping or rapid movement, or firm tactile pressure), the clinician may need to create opportunities for these kinds of experiences as part of "spontaneous" interaction patterns in order to convey a sense of spontaneity and self-motivation to the child's ability to concentrate and focus. For example, if a child moves around the room quite a bit, the clinician may move around with the child to take advantage of his movement, interest in and at the same time create some opportunities for joint focus or interaction.

It is especially difficult with children with pervasive developmental disorder to foster warmth, engagement, and a sense of intimacy. Here it is critically important to take advantage of a child's own natural interests; forced intimacy—when the child's head is held or the child is conditioned with certain reinforcements to focus on the adult—may not be associated with the kind of visceral pleasure that occurs in routine development. The goal is to find ways of creating opportunities for that visceral sense of pleasure and intimacy that leads a child to *want* to relate to the human world, not to *have* to relate to the human world.

It requires far more ingenuity to help the child want to relate to others, than to create circumstances under which the child has to relate. For example, in one of the cases described earlier, after weeks and weeks of trying, the father finally found that by turning a wheel in the direction opposite to the way the child was turning it perseveratively led the child to be curious about the father. Whose hand and face was this that was turning the wheel in the opposite direction? As the child looked up at his father with a warm look for the first time in his life, this toddler was gaining a sense of interaction through a mechanical motor activity—one that was actually perseverative in nature, only now the father had joined the perseveration. In other cases where an opening does not present itself easily and a child seems to be actively avoiding human interaction by perseverative activities, it has been necessary to get in the child's way, so to speak. One child, who wanted only to scratch the floor, had to contend with his mother's hand, which always seemed to be on the spot on the floor where he was trying to scratch. As he pulled the hand away, he would look annoyed; annoyance is a type of engagement. His mother did not intrude in an overwhelming way but did make her presence felt. His looks of annoyance and then his pulling her hand away was the basis for their forming a sense of engagement. As his mother varied her intrusion and sometimes made a game out of it, such as beginning to put her hand where his hand was going and then pulling away at the last second, she actually got a grunt of pleasure from her toddler due to the novelty. This response took many, many weeks to elicit, however.

Whether by a glimmer of eye contact, an exchange of facial expressions, focusing together on a ball, or entering into the child's perseverative world—whichever approach one takes—it is important to realize that the days, weeks, and even months that are needed to foster a spontaneous sense of warmth and pleasure and engagement are well worth the time and effort. It is worth the time and effort, because it is a critical step for all subsequent learning. Remember, the child cannot abstract a sense of his own person from an infinite number of experiences with his human world, if he does not have these experiences. (My hunch is that one of the reasons why children with pervasive and multisystem developmental problems evidence patterns of behavior that appear to be increasingly autisticlike is because they are not abstracting from human interactions but from more mechanical, perseverative interactions. If the clinician reinforces splinter skills that do not foster the sense of human intimacy, the child is inadvertently led away from an appropriate developmental progression.) Therefore, the clinician cannot skip the earliest therapeutic steps, since the child's ability to use his natural developmental capacities hinges on mastering some ability to focus and concentrate, to form some warmth and intimacy, and a sense of engagement with people around him.

The third step in the early therapeutic sequence has to do with forming simple and then more complex, gestural communications. When a child has some splinter skills, but nonetheless evidences a pervasive developmental disorder, it is tempting to interact around these emerging splinter skills, such as to say some numbers or letters. One will often see the adult involved in a parallel sort of commentary as he tries to build on the child's cognitive ability by talking to the child, but the child remains tuned out, and there is very little interaction. It is important to remember that, not only focus and attention, not only a sense of engagement, but also a sense of interaction are necessary for the child to begin evolving his own sense of himself as an intentional, interactive being.

Before continuing with the discussion of gestural interaction, it is important to emphasize that these three capacities form the basis of this presymbolic sense of one's own person, and mastering those capacities is what is most difficult for children with multisystem and/or pervasive developmental problems. Once these three presymbolic capacities are put in place, the symbolic capacities not only tend to develop, but they develop as part of a healthy and adaptive personality structure.

To return to the gestural level, a particularly useful guide to fostering a gestural interactive level with children who already have some symbolic splinter skills, is to start an interaction by getting simple, then more complex gestures going and using only symbols as they relate to gestures already operative. As discussed earlier, in opening and closing circles of communication, a particularly important clinical practice is always to build on the gestural before introducing the symbolic. By way of an example, a twenty-eight-month-old boy who had been diagnosed as having pervasive developmental disorder was playing on the floor with his father during an assessment session. The boy was moving a car back and forth, examining how it worked, and then moving it again. His father tried to engage and relate to him by commenting, "That's a nice car. Look how Johnny is moving it. Now it's moving fast. Now it's moving slow." The therapist suggested that he try to be more interactive. Although while he was talking, he was warmly relating, not much was happening between the two of them. The father then did what many caregivers and therapists would do, he continued to talk to his son about the car, asking, "Can you move it here?" and cupped his hands to see if his son would move the car in his direction. He pretended that his hands were a house and said, "Look, move it into my house." Unfortunately, his son just ignored his overtures. He began to look discouraged, as it seemed that he had failed to get some interaction going. As the therapist watched supportively, the father tried different approaches. He made a tunnel with his hands and suggested that his son might want to put his car in the tunnel. He began saying in a more commanding way, "Bring the car here. Give it to me." Finally, in disgust, he took the car out of his son's hands and tried to hide it. His son got angry, threw a mild tantrum, and then didn't want to touch the car anymore; the father became even more discouraged. This behavior reflects common patterns that clinicians and parents evidence: parallel verbal commentary, interactive verbal or symbolic commentary pitched at a higher level than the child is capable of, such as using the hands as a make-believe house. And finally frustration often leads to intrusive and impatient actions.

The therapist then suggested trying first simple gestural interactions that this child was quite capable of, and building more complex gestures and the verbal dialogue on that. The suggestion was to begin by following the child's lead. The child was again examining and moving the car. The therapist said, "Speak, and use any words you want, but make the interaction a very simple gesture-to-gesture one. Use your words only as icing on the cake or an elaboration of the gesture. Try to get something going, using your motor system in interaction with his motor system." As the father looked perplexed, the therapist explained, "You can take out other cars and aim them in his direction, you can play with his car with him. The idea is to get some kind of simple interaction that need be no more complicated than rolling a ball back and forth between the two of you." The father again tried cupping his hands and getting his son to send the car in his direction. The therapist commented in a supportive way that this gesture hadn't worked in the past, either because the son didn't want to respond or didn't understand the complex gestural communication involved or the implied symbolic communication. Then the father tried something much simpler. He put his hand on the car very gently, as his son was exploring it, and pointed to a particular part, as though to say, "What's that?" But in pointing, the father actually moved the car, so the son felt the car moving in his hands and noticed without upset his father's involvement, as it was gentle, slow, and nonintrusive. The son took the car back but looked at where the father had touched with his fingers. This more physical gestural communication seemed to get at least a faint circle closed—the son's interest in the car, the father's pointing to a spot on the car, moving it a little, and the son's looking at that particular spot, even though he took the car back—which, incidently was also a circle-closing response.

After getting this minimal interaction going, as the son was moving the car back and forth, the father got another car and started moving it back and forth next to his son. The father had his car move toward his son's car but did not crash into it. The son initially pulled his car out of the way but then moved his car fast as his father had, toward his father's car. Now three or four circles were closed in a row and a real interaction was going on. Within a few minutes, they were involved in a game where they seemed to be moving their cars toward each other and sometimes even crashing them. Sometimes the father moved the car slowly and sometimes fast. And sometimes the son moved the car slowly, and sometimes he crashed it. So far there was simply a game of gestures, but it was interactive. Now the father again cupped his hands but didn't try to make it into a house; it was a barrier that his son tried to get around.

FROM GESTURES TO SYMBOLS

Even though the father was talking about the cars, at this point the therapist suggested to him, "If you wish, you could now add words in a more interactive and intentional way. You can experiment with different words to see what he can understand." There were simple and complex gestures going on; there was a sense of engagement, a sense of pleasure, some focus and concentration, and it was appropriate to explore symbolic capacities, but only in relationship to the action. At this point, the father started to say, "fast" and "slow." When he moved it fast, he mentioned "fast," and when he moved it slow, he mentioned "slow." After four or five times, once, his son boomed his car into his father's car and said the word *fast*, without pronouncing it quite clearly. The father had a big smile on his face and was amazed that his son could learn a new word and use it appropriately so quickly. The therapist commented that words and symbols can be learned quickly, if they're related to the actual experiences of the child and built on the child's gestures. Words in isolation don't have meaning for the child.

This child had very good fine motor abilities, even though his gross motor skills were clumsy, and all other areas were delayed. At a later point in the session, the father was trying to show off how well his son could draw and identify different shapes. But when he tried to get his son to say, "square," or "circle," his son wouldn't imitate him or say anything. When the father tried to get his son to draw particular shapes by saying, "Draw something," his son would do nothing. The therapist suggested again that they follow the principle of getting the complex gesture going first. The father took a pencil and started scribbling circles, and his son, who had been scribbling on the paper, drew a circle, a remarkably nice one. The father smiled as though to say, "See, I told you so." The child had apparently done this many times at home. As the father scribbled circles, the son seemed interested in copying the father, using his fine motor skills, and his perceptual abilities. They seemed to have a game where the father drew a circle, and the son drew a circle next to it. Once they got this interaction going, I suggested to the father that he might want to introduce words, because the deed was in place, so to speak. The father started to say "circle," as he drew the circle, and much to our surprise, after three or four times, the son started to say "circle," as he drew his circle. The son grinned with satisfaction toward his father, as he said this.

Later on, the son drew a circle on his own, while I was talking to his parents. He looked up at his parents to get their attention to it. The son was now initiating gestural and early symbolic communications.

These few examples with cars and the drawing of the circles illustrate an important principle. The principle is to always build the symbolic on the gestural by trying to relate the two, at least in the early stages of trying to master complex gestural and early symbolic capacities. As one is successful at the gestural communication level with opening and closing circles of communication, and one wants to move into the complex gestural and early symbolic realms, it is very important that these capacities be joined. Parents and clinicians should not focus on symbolic splinter skills, which do not relate to the child's experience. The child organizes his sense of who he is based on an infinite number of interactions with his important caregivers and his surroundings. These interactions get going in a certain sequence of attending, engaging, and then opening and closing circles of communication. Each new level of complexity must build on the former.

FOSTERING REPRESENTATIONAL ELABORATION AND DIFFERENTIATION

As discussed earlier, one works with children to foster their symbolic level of communication by connecting it to the gestural level and then adding on representational or symbolic elaboration. This process is best done by following a child's lead in pretend play or in the functional use of language; for example, by helping him ask for juice or saying he is happy or sad, and so forth. The particular challenge with the pervasive developmental disorder or multisystem delayed child as one moves toward more representational or symbolic elaboration is to also help the child differentiate his experience. In other words, the child needs to learn cause-and-effect communication and to make connections between various representations or ideas.

Those who work with these children are often familiar with the fact that they tend to remain concrete. They don't often learn to use higher-level logic and abstractions. The therapist must foster the children's representational elaborations and differentiations to help them become more logical and abstract. The clinician must overcome hurdles and challenges that the child throws up because of his uneven development. As the child learns to represent experience, he will typically represent it in a highly fragmented and, at times, even emotionally intense or labile way. Sometimes a withdrawn, aimless child becomes so connected to his caregivers, that he is clinging, demanding, and talking all the time, even though a year earlier he was not saying a word. His intense relatedness and continuous "chit-chat," however, tends to operate in short bursts of ideas or fragments of higher level concepts or thoughts. For instance, the child may talk to himself at one moment about cars crashing, but the next moment may say, "Look at the leaves out the window"; then he may say, "Give me my juice," and then he may play out a tea party. Each burst of symbolic or representational activity may only last 30 seconds; there may be no logical bridges from one to the other.

Children without these disorders often develop a less fragmented level of symbolic functioning; even from the beginning there is some logical superstructure supporting the islands of communication. The tendency to fragment is more intense for children with these developmental challenges, however; and there is often a more driven quality to the intensity of their emotionality. This driven quality should be seen as a progression from the withdrawn, aimless state. Even the use of fragmented ideation should be viewed as a real asset, because it suggests symbolic activity is percolating. At the same time, however, the clinician or other adult wants to foster more differentiated, abstract, and logical use of ideas, while respecting the child's self-motivated wish to communicate. He should not interfere with the spontaneity or the personal quality of the child's initiative. It is critical for the clinician or the parent to walk a fine line between empathizing and helping the child elaborate and go with the flow, and helping the child do more than march to his own drummer; that is, be more logical.

SELF-ABSORBED THINKING

Since most children with pervasive and multisystem developmental delays have difficulty with receptive language, that is, auditory processing, and some also have difficulty with visual–spatial processing, it is much easier for them to pay attention to their own ideas rather than the ideas of others. A child with this type of a pattern has to work perhaps 100 times harder to take in the verbal, or at times, visual information from his caregiver or therapist than to comprehend his own thoughts. There is, in fact, an excitement and ease in listening to one's own emerging thoughts, especially because they have been so long in coming. The child, therefore, often uses intense ideation as a way of keeping himself interested and excited and practicing a new skill, but at the same time, he uses it as a substitute for taking in ideation from someone else. At this stage, the child can in a sense remain engaged at the behavioral level and at the level of basic connectedness but fail to be engaged at the symbolic level. A child who is clinging and needy may be speaking and playing according to his own game plan, without using his parents' symbolic or representational feedback. A clinging child may tell a parent about cars racing or a tea party, but as the parent asks questions, "Who is going to sit here?" and "What's happening next?" the child ignores these inquiries as he joyfully marches to his own drummer. If the process continues, a very engaged and related, perhaps even clinging, representationally, or ideationally idiosyncratic child develops. Fantasy and reality are not differentiated, because of the lack of symbolic feedback.

It is important to recognize that the way the child categorizes his experiences at the level of symbols or representations is through feedback. The parent becomes the representative of what is outside the child and the foundation for reality. In other words, if there is a symbolic "me" and a symbolic "you" interacting, this becomes a basis for more differentiated cause-and-effect type symbolic interactions. On the other hand, if there is only a "me" in our interaction, the "me" and "you" don't become differentiated on the symbolic level, even though they may be differentiated at the earlier behavioral and somatic levels and basic ego functions such as separating fantasy from reality do not develop.

The clinician's or parent's ability to enter the child's symbolic world becomes the critical vehicle for fostering differentiation and higher levels of abstract and logical thinking. Just as it is difficult to enter the child's behavioral world, it may be even harder to enter the child's symbolic world. At each symbolic juncture, the child may find it easier to march to his own drummer. For example, when the child ignores the parent's inquiry about who sits where at the tea party, the parent should bring the child back to the comment or question, until the child closes the symbolic circle. The parent needs to do this during floor time and in problem-solving discussions.

During floor time or pretend-oriented play, the parent might about half of the time, gently play dumb (a little like the TV character Columbo), and bring the child back to the point of confusion. For example, when the child has the puppet biting the head of the cat, the parent may say, "Ouch, you hurt me." Then the child looks at the tree outside, the parent may ask, "But, what about the cat? What about his ouch?" If the child then says, "I'll give another ouch," and bites the cat with the puppet, the child has closed the circle of communication. If the parent then says, as the child goes back to the tree, "Don't you want to talk more about the cat?" and if the child says, "No, let's look at the tree," the child has closed yet another circle and also created a logical bridge from one set of ideas to the other. By helping the child create such bridges and by going with the flow, since it is the child's floor time, the child becomes more and more differentiated. But if the parent simply lets the child go on his own and becomes fragmented with the child or becomes too rigid and controlling, differentiation may become compromised.

Negotiating bedtime, talking about food or friends, talking about activities at home, doing floor time and pretend play, or just watching a cartoon on TV, provide opportunities for opening and closing circles of communication at the symbolic level and helping the child connect ideas. All individuals tend to be drawn to what is biologically easier for them. The child will favor his own world over the outside world, not because he isn't interested in others—he may be interested at the level of behavior—but because the communications of the outside world require so much hard work to process.

Because it is easier for the language-delayed child to beat to his own drummer, listen to his own thoughts, rather than the thoughts of others, in attempting to help such a child open and close circles of communication, the adult will often ask the child an endless series of questions; for example, what color the car is, how fast it is going, where it is going. This conversation, even when successful, can take on a contrived sing-song or mechanical quality.

As the child becomes more verbal (and as the adult has been successful in helping the child become more verbal), the adult needs to pay special attention to balancing his interest in the details of the child's verbalizations with his emotional intentions and affects. Consider the example in chapter 13 on page 484, and repeated here.

The child says, "Look at my car!" The adult: "I see it. The child: "It goes fast, zoom!" The adult: "I can see that. It looks exciting that it's going so fast. The child (with a big smile): "Watch, I can make it go like a rocket ship." The adult: "Wow, that's a powerful rocket." The child (beaming with pride): "Here it comes." In this example, the child develops the theme of power with the adult empathizing with the child's affects rather than just the details.

As one can see, the adult, by focusing on affect, gives the child the opportunity to organize his real drama as opposed to stringing out the child's thoughts in a contrived manner; that is, "What color is the car?" and "Where is the car going?" The greater the receptive language problem, the more likely the tendency to get involved in the contrived, sing-song quality and the more the need to pay attention to the affective elements of the child's communications. We have a double agenda, therefore: to open and close symbolic circles and to do it with respect to the child's affective, that is, emotional intentions, not just his words. To do this well, adults not only have to be relaxed when they are with a child, but have to be naturally curious and naturally interactive. The adult cannot fake his own affect without the risk of being contrived. His job is to simplify the words so as not to overwhelm the child's vulnerable receptive language capacities, but at the same time he must be naturally curious and naturally interactive.

Sometimes adults try to talk slowly and clearly so as not to confuse the receptive language-delayed child, which can cause the rhythm and tone to take on a contrived, mechanical quality. But slow, mechanical sounding words are actually harder to understand because they lack the rhythmic variations that support the verbal meanings. It is much harder, for example, to recall numbers that are said slowly and mechanically, in comparison to numbers which are said with rhythm and feeling. In addition, mechanical automatonlike speech will not create an opportunity for the child to respond with speech that has emotional tone to it.

SELF-MOTIVATED OPPORTUNITIES FOR
DIFFERENTIATION

When a child with pervasive developmental disorder is highly motivated and very interested, for example, in trying to negotiate to get a certain kind of food or to go outside, there is often an opportunity to open and close many symbolic circles. The child who is trying to open the door, because he wants to go outside and is angry that he can't, may, in the midst of crying and angry shouting, open and close twenty circles of communication. In fact, during these high states of motivation some children with these types of challenges will be very differentiated in their thinking. It is important not to deliberately frustrate the child, but it is also important to recognize that frustration derived from a difference of opinion is a fine motivator and one that occurs naturally. Stretch the transition times and the periods of negotiation. Often a parent or therapist wants to cut short a power struggle over going outside, for example, or gives indirect feedback ("maybe . . . but why don't you look at your book?") because the child is angry and demanding. It is great for a child to be demanding as long as he is gesturally or verbally opening and closing circles. Stretch out these periods of "motivated" interaction and provide clear and direct feedback ("I want to go out"; "Not now"; "Now"; "Later"; "Not later, now," etc.).

Therefore, perhaps the most important skill for the clinician, parent, and educator to have in order to be able to help the child use his ideas and symbols interactively is the ability to take advantage of the child's own initiative and interests and occasional states of high motivation. Simply playing an interactive game with the child or a turn-taking game around an impersonal cognitive task will not resonate at nearly the same level of emotional depth, as when the child is in a self-motivated state. The goal is not just to teach the child words, but offer him an opportunity to develop a true sense of himself as a person. This sense comes from deeply felt, emotional wishes and needs. Therefore, the ability to connect different ideas or feelings must derive from a deeply felt set of feelings.

It is interesting to speculate here on what factors help children learn to abstract and reason. What separates human reasoning, which is flexible and sensitive to conflict, from rigid computer logic (which we observe all too often in developfully delayed children). It may well be two critical factors. One may be the capacity to learn in relationship to internal viceral (i.e., highly personal affective motivated) states of mind. The other may be the almost infinite number of interactive experiences most children abstract from. Pervasive developmentally delayed children often lack both of these critical learning experiences. And both of these, the internal viceral and the external feedback, provide a type of continuing and constant set of affective and reality based challenges to the child's growing abstracting ability.

WHY AND HOW QUESTIONS

It is easy for the clinician or parent to become frustrated in this effort, because the child with this kind of pattern will not respond easily to "how" or "why" questions, which are in themselves abstractions. In order for the child to be able to answer such abstract questions, he needs to progress through interactive discussions that help him open and close his circles of now symbolic communication. If one asks, "Why did the puppet bite the head of the cat?" the child will look blank, because he doesn't understand what "why" means. The parent or clinician who is not aware of the sequence by which children learn concepts or that children with pervasive and multisystem delays will take a much longer time to master these basic concepts, may give up on interactive communication and let the child march to his own drummer. Alternatively, the parent or clinician may overstructure the dialogue with the child, by asking him to label this or that body part or to say the word that describes what they see in the picture. These tasks are fine for limited periods of time to help children master certain words, but will not help the child develop more differentiated and abstract modes of thinking. In order to foster interactive symbolic dialogue one must take into consideration the sequence by which children with processing problems learn certain abstract concepts. For example, children can handle a "what" question, before a "how" question and a "how" question before a "why" question. But initially, the clinician or parent will have to simplify the question and be aware of the level of abstraction of the question or the comment, until the child can close the circle of communication. For example, "Why do you want to go outside?" Child: "I want to!" "But why?" Child: "Outside now!" "What is outside that you want?" Child: "Bicycle, want ride bicycle." Here, the adult switches from a "why" question to a simpler "what" question to help the child explain why he wants to go outside. One might end the discussion by consolidating the child's gain by saying, "Oh, the reason why you want to go outside is to ride your bicycle." With such discussions, the child will eventually comprehend "why" questions.

The child has to master a lot of differentiated thinking before he can answer a high level "why–because" question with a high level "because" answer. (A low level "because" answer would be, "Because that's the way it is." A high level "because" answer would involve some cause-and-effect thinking: "The child has to sit there because he's big, and this is a big chair.") For the child with pervasive developmental disorder, the ability to respond to such a question would itself be a high achievement. And the achievement would be even more significant when that "because" answer comes in response to a personal question, such as one related to how a child is feeling or why a child wants to do a certain thing.

To facilitate higher level abstractions, clinicians and parents must not fall into the trap of scripting the child's dialogue by asking leading questions, in response to which the child has only to fill in a word or two, or by talking about something for which the child has pat phrases (e.g., the parent says, "And after one comes——; and after two, comes——," etc.). If the child is not surprising you with his comments then you are scripting the conversation too much. If the child is racing his car, don't always cup your hand, sometimes race him; other times create a barrier, still other times, see if you can "blow" his car over. Be more open; do not be too predictable or routine in your gestures or comments. In order to facilitate the child's shift from concrete to abstract modes of thinking, it may be helpful to look at some of the different steps a child must progress through in the journey.

HELPING THE CHILD SHIFT FROM CONCRETE TO ABSTRACT MODES OF THINKING

Children with multisystem developmental delays often find it especially difficult to shift from concrete modes of thinking or using ideas to more abstract ones in part because they do not easily generalize from a specific experience to other similar experiences. In learning that the answer to "Why do you want to go outside?" is "To play," they will not easily figure out the answer to other "why" questions. Understandably, there is a temptation to teach the child answers and repeat the same question, as indicated earlier, by scripting the dialogue. Sometimes this is justified by "I don't want to confuse him with too many new questions." Parents, educators, and therapists frustrated by slow progress may wish to create an illusion of progress through the mastery of some rote-learned statements.

But the same principle that got the child to this level must be continued—the spontaneous, child-initiated opening and closing of symbolic circles. The child can only learn to abstract and generalize through active experience. The slower the going, the more, not less, spontaneous active symbolic interaction the child needs.

The adult needs to be ingenious in setting up opportunities for the child to initiate symbolic interaction and open and close circles of communication. It is often helpful to assist the child in elaborating his communication, going from the general to the specific, always taking advantage of high states of motivation. For example, the child has a man sitting on a car and is rolling the car toward a building. The adult enters the play gesturally, moving another car alongside, and says, "What's going to happen?" The child is silent. Not getting a response to this most general elaboration, the adult moves to the next level, offering alternatives. "Should we go to the garage or the house over here?" Often, with these more concrete alternatives, the child will say, "Garage" or "House" or point to one or the other. If the child remains silent, one may simplify the elaboration even further, still being careful not to tell the child what to do. As the child is moving the car, instead of oversimplifying and saying, "Okay, we are going to the garage," one might say, "Okay, the cars are going into my mouth." The child may find this silly and say, "No, the garage" or may just laugh. In either case, a nice symbolic circle has been closed. If the child ignores you, the challenge is to come up with another set of gestures and ideas that build on his, perhaps using simpler concepts and words.

Sometimes, parents or therapists become discouraged because as the child is learning to use more and more words, he still can't answer simple questions like, "What did you do at school today?" It is easy to lose sight of just how hard a question that is to answer. That question requires the child to have a symbolic sense of himself, not just in the present but in the immediate past. He must also be able to imagine that his symbolized self is in a space (i.e., the school), which is different from his immediate setting. Therefore, to answer this simple question requires the child to be able to represent himself in the context of both time and space. As children are learning to "think," this ability develops slowly, especially for the children with multisystem developmental delays.

It is, therefore, useful to conceptualize the process of learning to use symbols as a gradual one with many steps. These include emotional steps such as (1) using symbols in the here and now for the immediate satisfaction of a need, e.g., "juice," "outside," "car"; (2) for negotiation or communication around a need with the exception of immediate satisfaction, e.g., "Mom, come!" "What that"; (3) for communicating or amplifying on or about an object of interest or an activity in a way that may suggest certain emotions like curiosity or cooperation, e.g., the child points to a flower and says, "Flower" with a look of curiosity and pleasure that he wishes to share; (4) for communicating a variety of emotions that convey flexibility in meeting personal needs and appreciation of the interactive complexity of many feelings, such as pride, pleasure in an activity or accomplishment, curiosity, interest and later empathy in another person, jealousy and/or cooperativeness, etc., e.g., after having been to the circus, a child puts on a silly hat and, with a smile of pride, says, "Me clown," or says simply, "Look!" as he beats his brother in a car race.

While progressing through these, and eventually more advanced, emotional patterns, symbolic communication is also progressing in terms of the bridges being established between ideas. Steps in this process include: (1) the expression of single ideas in the here and now, e.g., "table"; (2) connecting two or more ideas in the here and now, e.g., "drink juice"; (3) connecting two or more ideas in the here and now with various levels of causality, e.g., the child begins answering what, how, and why questions, initially with the simple "what" ones and progressing to the "why" ones (statements such as "I want to go outside because I want to," eventually become "I want to go outside because the sun is out and I like to play in my car when it is nice outside); (4) connecting two or more ideas which require symbolizing self across time and space, e.g., "I want to play house with Sally at school tomorrow because I didn't get to do it today."

These early emotional and causal steps, when mastered, create a foundation for more advanced thinking in both the emotional-social and impersonal realms. The developmentally delayed child, as indicated, will require more, not less, active experience to abstract the principles associated with these steps. The clinician must figure out ways to work around the child's auditory processing difficulties, i.e., find simple words and deal with clearly felt emotions or needs. He must create those experiences in which the child wishes to initiate interaction and that continuously challenge him to use his emerging symbolic capacities in changing situations and contexts.

OVERVIEW OF THE STEPS IN THE RECOVERY FROM MULTISYSTEM AND PERVASIVE DEVELOPMENT DISORDER

As we work with our multisystem and pervasive developmental disorder children, as indicated, it is important to recognize that one can facilitate their moving from one stage to another, only through a certain sequence of steps. Often they begin by being withdrawn, avoidant, and aimless. Next, minimal gestures are used, after the parents, caregivers, and therapists are able to foster enough sense of engagement, concentration, and focus to begin to see simple circles being opened and closed. Initially the circles are opened and closed in a more reactive way, as when the child seems to be reacting to the parent. Slowly but surely the child's initiative takes over, particularly if the parents are careful to follow his lead. Simple gestures and an initial level of engagement and focus give way to more complex gestures—first more reactive, and then more self-initiated and assertive.

The child moves from complex gestures to fragmented symbolic capacities. The capacity will be there one day, then it may not be there for several days; then there may be a word to accompany a gesture or an isolated piece of symbolic play, such as putting a puppet on the hand; and then the capacity may again disappear for a number of days. Because it is a higher level and newer ability, it is not so different from a child who learns to walk by taking a step one day and then giving up for three days. A symbolic or representational capacity requires putting a lot of pieces together, which the child cannot always do easily, particularly the child who is overloaded with sensory input and who has trouble processing and organizing his input and his output. To help a child who is fragmented, it is important not to get fragmented with him. Frequently, as a child mumbles or isn't clear or seems confused, the adult changes the subject to help the child reorganize. But it is far better for the adult to patiently help the child through gesture or words communicate his original intent.

As this piecemeal capacity becomes more routine, we then see a stage that may have never been described before in accounts of the recovery of children with pervasive developmental disorder and multisystem delays—a very intense, driven, hypomanic quality in using representation or ideation. The children become needy and cling almost as though they had discovered the human world is a great place and they don't want to lose it. They can chit-chat endlessly, only the chit-chat has, as indicated earlier, a fragmented quality. Islands of representation emerge rather than organized, complete thoughts. Bridges from one set of communications to another are often not clear.

It is interesting to hypothesize that the reason children get into this intense phase is that they are so excited with their own ideation; they feel they have a new capacity, a new tool to experiment with—ideas. Previously, they did not have ideas the way adults experience them. But for these children to be interactive with their ideas is still difficult, because they do not take in other people's ideas easily due to their auditory and visual–spatial processing problems. Their excitement comes from experimenting with their own ideas and they march more and more to the beat of their own drummers. Thus it is important to make these ideas interactive as a way of fostering logical and more abstract thinking.

After children go through this driven stage, the intensity often evens out, particularly with more differentiation in their thinking. They become more capable of organized thought, as their affect returns to a calmer state; their emotional signaling and gesturing, as well as their use of words, appears to be more and more adaptive.

As children get over their hyperideation phase, where they appear to be excited with their own ability to have ideas, as indicated, they go into a more relaxed, organized phase of thinking. However, during this stage, the thinking is still very much based on the child's imagination, because he still has more difficulty receiving information from others in comparison to ideas generated by his own mind. It is important for caregivers and therapists to help the child open and close symbolic circles, so that he can build on other people's information instead of developing more and more idiosyncratic, obsessional, and ritualistic thinking. In fact, the more the child marches to his own drummer, the more ritualistic and obsessive and idiosyncratic his thoughts may become. In a sense, he is still entertaining himself and keeping himself company with his own thoughts. This process serves many purposes, from relieving anxiety to creating a sense of inner security and comfort. Such thoughts are similar to some of the ritualistic behaviors of a toddler or younger child who does not open and close his behavioral or gestural circles. Now he is not opening or closing his symbolic circles.

However, rather than become concerned about idiosyncratic and ritualistic thought patterns, the clinician should, at least in the first instance, be pleased that such patterns are present insofar as they indicate the degree to which the child has become symbolic. It is only when the youngster remains ritualistic and idiosyncratic in his thinking and does not gradually learn to become more adaptive and reality-based through opening and closing symbolic circles with significant others in his life that the clinician should be concerned. The first reaction, therefore, should be one of pleasure in the child's progress. The second reaction, however, should be one of helping the child shift from idiosyncratic and obsessive thinking to more adaptive and flexible thinking. The tool to helping a child with this is through interactive dialogue around core emotional themes, where the child opens and closes representational or symbolic circles of communication.

As the child attempts to be more logical, we also see the phase where he tends to generalize from one experience to another almost too quickly and he does it in a concrete way. One child, after his father told him that he (Dad) didn't like candy said, "Oh so children like candy and adults don't." This child made such statements repeatedly. It was temporary for his father to explain the illogic of his logic. But instead it was suggested that the best course is to provide feedback that will help his son "time tune" his logic. Frequently, Dad said with a grin, "But Mrs. Green, our neighbor likes candy." Though temporarily confused, this child with active, warm, challenging feedback (and not lectures) slowly learned to think more flexibly.

A few other examples of helping a child think more flexibly may also prove useful. One 4-year-old child was clearly provocative after his therapist's vacation, but "tuned out" at any mention of feelings or vacations and the like. One day, after the child kept the therapist waiting while he played in the waiting room, the therapist said, "You kept me waiting!" The child looked at him. The therapist then said, "I guess I kept you waiting for two weeks." The patient smiled, took the doctor doll and started throwing it and gave the therapist his first warm look since the therapist had returned. This example is mentioned to highlight the importance of simple, direct emotional comments rather than complex interpretations.

Another child who was provocatively and happily ignoring her therapist's going away, finally responded when her therapist said, with a hand gesture, "Soon I go bye-bye (waves his hand)." The child looked scared and sad and eventually played out some relevant themes.

A child became preoccupied with the "ing" at the end of words. Instead of ignoring it or fighting it, his parents and therapist said, "Do you love the 'ing' sound?" Together they found "ing" words and made up "ing" songs. Many symbolic circles were closed around what started out as a perseverative type interest.

A child insisted he was a certain cartoon figure and would tell others they were different people or things. To help him better differentiate, these creative perceptions were used to open and close symbolic and presymbolic circles and were not directly challenged. The child gradually became more differentiated.

One child (as many do) regressed easily going from a verbal symbolic level to a disengaged level. Rather than get upset or intervene, her parents and therapist saw each regression as a communication and a chance to help her learn what it was like to go back up the ladder (i.e., to use gestures and words). Children with large regressive ranges need to learn how to move in both directions.

Children with Pervasive Developmental difficulties attempt to avoid feeling anger and other strong affects. Often rigid behavior and thoughts substitute for the affects. The adults (and children) in the rigid child's world need to become comfortable in responding flexibly (i.e., "throwing curve balls,") and gently violating rigid expectations. One then sees simultaneously increased flexibility and increased direct expression of anger and other affects. Becoming secure with anger seems to be a critical step in the overall process of the child increasing his affective flexibility.

As these children become more organized at the gestural level, the affect system begins on a path that is very unusual for children with pervasive developmental disorder or autistic spectrum problems. The children's affect begins to appear more and more normal. It is typical of children with these challenges to have more idiosyncratic, perseverative, and mechanical-type affects. As one works interactively with these children, however, one observes that they do not go off on an alternate pathway. In fact, while they still have the unique cognitive and processing difficulties, their affect begins getting closer and closer to what we ordinarily expect. A great deal depends on the therapeutic work and the success the parents have with their children, but even where the work is not completely successful, the tendency is more toward expectable kinds of affects than idiosyncratic or unusual types.

It is also important to remember that in working to foster more differentiation in the behavioral, gestural, and symbolic interactions, the child's processing difficulties should not imply a difficulty with central reasoning. In other words, the child may have a difficult time understanding your "why" or your "how" question; he may be able to respond only to sentences with three words in them, rather than sentences with six or ten words; but his difficulty may be more due to the child's processing problems than to a deficiency in his central reasoning or creativity. Watching how the child marches to his own drummer in terms of the complicated spatial relationships he may construct through drawing or with blocks, or fantasy constructions, will give a picture of how creative he is. One might picture an advanced physicist who can speak only a few words of English. Simple words may have to be used to negotiate complex mathematical concepts. The child may be able to comprehend more than his language delay allows him to evidence.

For example, a child may understand "up" and "down," but may not understand the words that express the concept. Using hand gestures to convey "large" or "small" or "more" or "less," combined with simple words, such as "this" or "that," and saying, "This is large and this is small," may get a dialogue going about complex concepts of size and even volume, although the words are quite simple. The key to helping the child become more abstract is the clinicians', educators', and parents' ability to gradually increase the cognitive challenges through interaction. But the adults have to be flexible, trying simple words, combining words with gestures, and taking advantage of the child's self-motivated states, and conceptual potential.

CAREGIVER, PARENT, AND FAMILY PATTERNS

Parents of children with developmental disabilities share a number of patterns that are critical for the therapist to explore. Parents typically feel depressed and therefore withdraw from their children; they deny their sadness and disappointment and become overly perfectionist and controlling; they vacillate between withdrawing, states of depression, and intrusive, over-controlling patterns. In addition, each parent will often have his or her own fantasies and related feelings, such as feelings of guilt: "What did I do to make my child so unresponsive?" Or of anger: "This is unfair. I've worked too hard for this to be true." The anger may be at the child; it may be at the spouse; it may be at the clinicians and service providers.

Sometimes the expectable feelings of disappointment, sadness, or anger are subtle and beneath the surface. For example, one mother, who was a professional educator, appeared to go through all the appropriate moves with her delayed daughter. She tried to read her daughter's signals, tried to be supportive and constructive, but she lacked a certain spirit, a gleam in her eye, and an emotional range in her voice. She seemed preoccupied and mechanical in her approach, although it was well organized, appropriate, and well-thought-out. The clinician commented that she seemed to be working very hard to be a good partner for her child, and went to on say that he imagined she would like to be able to enjoy it more. As he phrased a clarifying comment in a positive and supportive way, as opposed to a critical way, and focused on her wish to enjoy it more and on her skill and awareness of what this child needed, he allowed the mother to open up about her sad and disappointed feelings. She began to cry and to talk about how it feels to have a child who doesn't respond. She said:

> At first, when he wouldn't look at me or smile at me, I would get mad at him and want to shake him. Then I began wondering what I did wrong, and my husband did wrong. I found myself vacillating between trying very hard and then giving up and just feeding him and making sure he was comfortable, before he went to sleep. I couldn't bear the pain of looking into his eyes and not getting a twinkle back. Then I think I began doing what I'm doing now—trying to interact with him, but without any enthusiasm or zest. It's too painful; I can't want too much from him, because I know he can't provide it. I think it's best for me

not to try to get too excited or too happy when he does look at me, because I'll only be disappointed next time.

This is the statement of a mother who was in a chronic moderate state of depression with regard to her preschool child. She'd given up on spontaneous emotional interaction that would include a sense of pleasure, spontaneity, and creativity. She had decided not to withdraw totally and not to overwhelm the child, but instead, without fully thinking through the consequences, she was offering a kind of mechanical, socially appropriate set of overtures.

As we worked with this situation, the mother was encouraged to verbalize more of her sad, depressed, and disappointed feelings. She was able to relate the inner pain she felt with her child to feelings she had had with her own parents when they were not responsive to her. Her own parents could be mechanical and very orderly at times. She related her pain to aspects of her marriage. Her husband was preoccupied with work and didn't have a gleam in his eye for her. She realized that she had been a "good soldier" most of her life, whenever she was disappointed in the emotional glow that others "didn't" offer her. Combining this self-exploration with doing floor time with her child allowed her to do two things at once. She was developing new skills in opening and closing circles of communication and engaging. She focused not just on the mechanics of her motor system or her choice of words, but on the range of her emotion and on the animation in her face. But the combination of working on the mechanics of interaction with self-exploration allowed her to take a chance and experience some joy, especially when her son looked at her with a little grin. As she unfroze her own emotions, just as her son was beginning to experiment with new emotions, a chemistry began to evolve between the two of them. Slowly but surely she unfroze more and more and there was warmth and depth in her emotional gestures. Her son was moving in the same direction.

It is often necessary to establish a process which allows the improved mechanics of interaction to help the child become more engaged, and the supportive self-exploration with the caregiver or parent to help the parent become more excited in a sincere way with the child. The reinvestment of the parent with the child captures some of the hopefulness and expectations present when the baby was born. It can be bolstered by putting new tools in the parents' hands; tools to open and close circles of communication, and experiment with more spontaneous affect. It is a slow and gradual process, but one that is absolutely essential for working with children with this type of disorder.

A process is also needed for parents who are angry and overly punitive, perhaps also as a reaction to their disappointment. Some people who don't feel either sad or mechanical, but are angry and intrusive whenever they do not get what they want, think that by going after something in a more aggressive way, they will get it. One father would yell at his delayed child to smile. He was a very successful businessman, and this approach worked in most areas of life, where he was dealing with adults who were highly competent. The pressure he would put on them led him to believe that, "Everyone needs a little whipping once in a while." He could see, however, that his son's aimlessness and withdrawal only increased as he became more aggressive and intrusive. However, when the father could verbalize some of the pain associated with his disappointment, he was able to relax and be more gentle. Whether the parent's reaction is angry, perfectionistic, overly idealized, or depressed, underneath these patterns is often a struggle with expectable feelings of disappointment that the child doesn't provide the range of cues that most parents not only rely on but secretly wish for when they have a child. All human beings seek some degree of engagement, warmth, and intimacy from other human beings. Parents often expect children to provide this engagement, often in a deep and meaningful way. (It is not uncommon for parents to expect children to make up for the neglect they received during their own childhoods.) Because of these expectations, parental disappointment is not unusual, even when children's development is optimal. The disappointment becomes massive and overwhelming but is often denied or otherwise defended against, whenever the child's development takes an unusual course. Therefore, it is critical for the therapist to deal with parent and family patterns.

Each caregiver's relationship with other family members also will be deeply affected by the reactions to a particular child. For example, a mother who feels deprived by her child may expect more from her husband. A husband who feels deprived may in turn expect more from his wife. An equilibrium that worked earlier in the marriage may no longer suffice, because each one expects more than the other can provide. Each may focus on the character flaws of the other. The husband who is unemotional, and the wife who is overly demanding and emotional may each intensify their particular character trait and lead the other one to feel quite angry. The family dynamics with older children may be affected in turn. With a delayed child, one should assume that there will be strong reactions in each caregiver, in the couple's relationship, and throughout the whole family. One must uncover these patterns, as part of the therapeutic process.

In addition to parents, the clinician should collaborate with other professionals, including occupational therapists, speech pathologists, special educators, and early childhood educators who may work with the infant or young child and his or her family.

SPEECH AND LANGUAGE THERAPY, OCCUPATIONAL THERAPY, EARLY CHILDHOOD AND SPECIAL EDUCATION

Children with pervasive developmental disorders and/or multisystem developmental delays require a team of professionals that can work with the child to promote the core developmental competencies to attend and engage, communicate with gestures simple and complex, and communicate and organize experience with representations or ideas, first in an undifferentiated and then in a differentiated way. The various disciplines each must also pursue their unique approaches to these problems. Occupational therapists, for example, develop strategies that foster fine motor and functional gross motor capacities, and approaches to normalizing sensory dysfunction (hyper- or hyposensitivity, or sensory processing or sensory integration difficulties). Some approaches are controversial, such as using vestibular stimulation as a way of supporting and organizing sensorimotor and attentional capacities. Other approaches are fairly straightforward and uncontroversial, such as practicing certain fine motor patterns or exposing the child to a variety of tactile experiences to normalize tactile reactivity.

Speech pathologists work on the child's comprehension of communication, as well as his ability to communicate. For familiar problems, such as a child who cannot make a certain sound and needs practice in the motor coordination required to make that sound, as well as more complicated situations where children are helped to comprehend the sequence of certain words or sounds, speech pathologists have moved more toward spontaneous and free interaction, as a vehicle for learning communication, and their framework has broadened to include all aspects of communication.

Educators also have a long tradition of figuring out strategies to assist children in learning sensory, motor and conceptual abilities. For example, when a lesson plan is to teach a concept such as "hot or cold" or "more or less than," or certain fine motor capacities, educators may use a series of semistructured tasks.

From the perspective of a developmental approach, however, it is important to combine the traditional approaches that characterize each discipline with certain common developmental principles that focus on the core competencies outlined earlier. The speech pathologist, occupational therapist, and early childhood or special educator, in working with the child, should have as their goal the simultaneous mastery of specific skills and generic core competencies. For example, when an occupational therapist is working on a fine motor pattern and providing the child with extra practice, simultaneously that occupational therapist should be helping the child focus his attention, warmly engage with her, and where possible take the initiative in opening and closing circles of communication. If the task, for example, involves copying designs, it is best to engage the child first, and have the child enjoy the occupational therapist as a person, and then to help the child focus on the activity at hand, perhaps by devising a way that he naturally becomes interested in holding the pencil and making scribbles. If the therapist can entice the child to want to copy his therapist (rather than ordering the child to copy), there has been success at two levels—at fostering the particular fine motor skill and in supporting the core competencies.

Helping the child do something through his own initiative, even if it takes longer, is far better than doing something for or to the child to expedite the learning process. It is not unusual for the physical or occupational therapist to hold the child's hand to show him how to move it; the parents tend to observe and imitate what the therapist does. In fact, the learning process is often not speeded up but circumvented if one does too much for the child, although at times one may have to demonstrate a skill a few times to stimulate the child's self-initiative.

One should also pay attention to the child's self-motivated states and natural desires, so skills can be taught by taking advantage of the child's interest. If one can create incentive in the child by making the activity fun and rewarding, there is a good possibility he will want to practice that skill and use it in a variety of situations. If the rewards or consequences are contrived, such as giving him M&Ms as opposed to natural, social reactions, the child may not be learning how the experience itself can be rewarding. If the feedback the child gets is more mechanical and concrete than spontaneously emotional, the goal of reaching the child's emotional core through natural emotional feedback may be compromised.

Often therapists spend a good portion of the session on more mechanical, "do-as-I-say" type exercises. It is desirable to have at least half a session spent on trying to help the child use a particular skill in spontaneous, self-initiated ways. The session could be divided into two halves: one more traditional and didactically oriented, and interactive in some part; and the second more spontaneous, following the initiative of the child.

Children in a preschool early intervention program may have a half-day program that includes group activities with other children; they also typically spend time with a speech pathologist and an occupational therapist (or a physical therapist).[1] These professionals often consult with the educators in order to integrate principles of speech and language and occupational therapy into the educational routine of the child. It is critical to be aware of the interactions that take place around specific educational tasks, whether it is a paper-and-pencil type of task or listening to a story or a taking-turns kind of activity. The informal interactions are often more important for the child than the structured activity they envelope. Even seemingly informal discussions about what to eat, where to hang up coats, whether to sit here or there, often can and should involve opening and closing many circles of gestural and, if possible, symbolic communication. The more attentive, engaged, and communicative the child is in these interactions, the more moments of learning there are. The gains a child makes are often related to the intuitive ability of his educators, therapists, and caregivers to value the moments of informal interaction with the child and not see them only as mechanical steps leading to something else that's more important. In fact, what is needed is "a process" orientation where interaction processes are seen as the real learning opportunities and concrete exercises and tasks are the vehicles for or occasions for interaction.

It should go without saying that the parents are the true integrators of all that relates to the child, as they are with the child the most hours of the day. They not only need to benefit

---

[1] A physical therapist and occupational therapist may work as a team; the physical therapist may work on the more severe aspects of the motor delay, and the occupational therapist may work on the fine motor and selective functional aspects of gross motor as well as sensory reactivity and sensory processing.

from the insights of all the professionals who work with the child, they need to provide feedback to the professionals about what works and doesn't work at home, as well as the emotional climate there. Team meetings, as well as individual discussions between the relevant parties, need to be organized on a regular basis, as part of the child's treatment.

THE LONG-TERM EDUCATIONAL PLAN FOR CHILDREN WITH PERVASIVE OR MULTISYSTEM DEVELOPMENTAL DISORDERS AND DYSFUNCTIONS

In most communities, children with pervasive developmental disorders and dysfunctions find themselves initially in a part-day, part-week, special education program with occupational and speech therapy added in. As they become older, they become involved in a full-day program, with the same therapeutic elements. The typical program has only a partial mental health component that focuses on the emotional and social capacities of the child, even though these may be the core challenge for that child developing his sense of personhood. The family may meet only periodically with the social worker associated with the special education program or with teachers.

Children tend to be grouped with other children with similar handicaps, so it is common to have a group of eight children with communication problems, such as social isolation, withdrawal, and aimless behavior. Naturally, there will be very little spontaneous interaction between these uncommunicative children; if one child begins spurting ahead in terms of his gestural communication and his ability to open and close circles, he will be unlikely to receive much socially or emotionally relevant feedback from his peers. Because his new ability is somewhat precarious, it will be easy for him to give up his attempted overtures when the feedback is unresponsive. Some children who are participants in an overall program servicing handicapped children may be overly aggressive and disorganized; if the aggressive, overwhelming child is coupled with the passive, frightened, or withdrawn child, there will also be a maladaptive mix in terms of peer-to-peer feedback and interaction. When these poor interaction patterns are coupled with the lack of sufficient mental health input in such settings and the lack of optimal coordination and consultation with parents, the child is not offered an optimal or even adequate intervention program. Most communities need to rethink the way in which they organize education and intervention for children with pervasive and multisystem delays and disorders, as well as for all handicapped children.

Progress may be undermined with a less than optimal program often misleading evaluation using standardized tests inappropriate for infants or children with unusual developmental patterns provides a faulty picture of a child and becomes the basis for a misleading prediction (which unfortunately can become a self-fulfilling prophecy). A cross sectional assessment of a delayed child does not appear to be useful in predicting his course, particularly when there have been interactive difficulties. A far more accurate picture of a child's potential emerges from the slope of his learning curve once a comprehensive intervention program has been in progress for six to twelve months and true interactive learning has begun. Only after a child is pulled back into interactive relationships can one obtain a picture of his learning potential. No infant can learn in complete isolation even when the isolation is due in part to the infants processing difficulties. The child's potential is often quite promising when the rate of learning (once a full program is underway) is near, at, or better than the expected rate of progress month per month for a child of that developmental age (e.g., a two-year-old functioning at an eight month level advance to a twelve month level in three months). If it takes a while to pull the child into relationships, or to get reciprocal interactions going, one should *wait* before judging the rate of learning. In general, one should always focus on how to improve the quality of learning and be cautious especially about negative predictions as they can undermine the learning process.

The following are developmentally derived recommendations for an educational program for infants and young children with pervasive and multiple developmental delays and dysfunctions.

1. The program needs to focus during part of each day on the interaction patterns of the infant or young child and his or her parents. The goal is to assure that these patterns promote the core developmental competencies outlined earlier, that is, to attend, to engage, interact with simple and complex gestures, represent or symbolize experience, and then differentiate this represented or symbolized experience. This work must take into account the child's individual differences, the parents' own personalities, and the family's dynamics. This program can be carried out by educators, speech pathologists, occupational therapists, and mental health professionals. If the parent's own personality dynamics and the core emotional abilities of the child are at issue, a person with a mental health background is especially important.

2. A professional needs to consult with the parents at least once a week to help with family dynamics and interactive patterns at home. Periodic or regular home visits should involve both parents and other family members and caregivers who live with the family, as needed.

3. The child should spend part of each day in a small peer group, where certain conceptual abilities geared to the developmental level of the child are fostered, but where simultaneously, the core developmental competencies are also supported. In this context, early childhood educators or special educators should be well equipped to promote the core competencies as well as offer opportunities to master age-appropriate skills and concepts. A combination of interactive play, semi-structured activities, and selected structured activities is usually appropriate for this goal.

4. The composition of the group that the handicapped child finds himself in should be approximately one or two handicapped children per five nonhandicapped children of a similar age or developmental level. Grouping children with handicaps

together may not be in the interest of any individual child, especially if the handicap involves difficulties in communication or social interaction. In order for children to be able to use peer relationships to learn how to communicate and interact more appropriately, they require peers who can respond in an age-appropriate way to emerging communicative and interactive gestures. Seven withdrawing and uncommunicative children will not be able to assist one another. One or two uncommunicative children with five others who are communicative will find socially and emotionally appropriate feedback, as they make overtures to the more communicative peers, providing the teachers can mobilize peer-to-peer interactions.

5. Teachers should have training and interest in mobilizing peer-to-peer interaction, particularly between the handicapped child and his nonhandicapped counterpart. The best method is not to order the interaction but to create interactive opportunities. For example, a handicapped child may be sitting at a table with three nonhandicapped children. They are trying to make something with glue and paper. In order to facilitate the opening and closing of circles of communication, the teacher might proceed as follows: Jane wants the scissors, which are near Harold who has difficulty in communicating and social interaction. Jane asks the teacher to get the scissors. The teacher says, "They are not near me, they're near Harold. Can you ask him?" Jane, discouraged by prior attempts to ask Harold, looks at the teacher as if to say, "This is going to be hard." The teacher says, "I'll bet you Harold can pass the scissors to you, if you figure out just the right way to ask him." Jane says, "Harold, give me the scissors." Harold doesn't respond. The teacher says, "I think you have to get him to look at you, in order for there to be a chance he'll respond to your request." Jane then focuses her eyes on Harold's and says, "Harold," three times. He slowly looks at her. She then says, "Can you give me the scissors?" but he still doesn't respond. The teacher then suggests that, "If you show him with your hands, as well as with your words, what you want, maybe you'll stand a better chance." As Jane does this, Harold gives her a big smile and

gives her the scissors. Jane has learned an important lesson, and she and Harold have opened and closed a number of circles of communication. The lesson is useful for communication in general—always get the person's attention, and when the person doesn't understand what you are saying in one way, try adding on extra communicative gestures. Jane will certainly benefit from this experience. Harold also benefits enormously, because he gets an opportunity to interact with his peers in a spontaneous way, even though the peer was getting some coaching.

In another situation, Jane and Harold may be sitting on the floor during a free play time; Harold is watching Jane and two of her friends eagerly putting on crowns and pretending to be queens and princesses. The teacher wants to get Harold involved but doesn't want to insist that Jane patronize Harold by saying something to him. Nor does the teacher want to make Harold do something that's not spontaneous and not natural to him, by saying to Harold, "Go put on a crown," or by putting a crown on his head. Instead, the teacher plays the role of instigator–provocateur. As the girls are playing queen and princess, she says, "Who's the king?" And Jane says "Oh, Laura can be the king." And the teacher points out, "No, she's already the princess." Then Jane says, "Well, how about Sally?" The teacher says, "Well, Sally you already have as the other princess, and you're the queen." And then the teacher suggests, "I think, if possible, it might be nice to have a boy be the king, because that's kind of a boy's role." And then Jane finally says, "Well, are you saying that Harold should be the king?" And the teacher says, "That's up to you, but I think he'd be a perfect king, and the question is, can you get him to want to be the king?" With this instigation, the three girls take on as their goal to get Harold to want to be the king. They first ask him if he wants to be the king, but he looks confused. Then they each put the crown on themselves, point to it, and gesture to him, as if to ask if he wants the crown for himself. He smiles and nods and begins interacting in a relatively simple way, in the drama. The principle here is to play off the person who needs to become involved in a peer–peer interaction. Instead of putting pressure on the handicapped child to do something he may not yet be comfortable with or understand, the teacher puts the pressure on the other children to pull him in so that he experiences a more natural social situation.

As Harold begins to enjoy gesturing and interacting, he will get feedback more easily than if he were in a group of children who were as delayed as he is.

In addition to small groups at school, children with developmental challenge require more not less time playing one-on-one at home with peers. Same aged or younger children, who are very interactive, give the delayed child a chance to abstract the principle of social interaction. Four to five play dates per week is not too much. Many children unfortunately do not have this opportunity and feel clumsy and alienated when they are older.

For his long term educational goals the handicapped child needs to be in a small classroom, where the majority of children are progressing adaptively in most areas. In this setting educators can work with the few handicapped children one-on-one around special skill areas, such as speech, concept formation, occupational therapy goals, and others. All members of the group should be considered to be part of the same social milieu.

7. If the child's handicap involves only motor development or a medical illness that does not involve the capacity to communicate, socially interact, or organize thinking, then it is less critical that the child be surrounded by nonhandicapped or non-medically impaired children. For example, children who only have an orthopedic problem or a medical illness may be able to communicate well with each other and give each other good emotional and intellectual feedback. For these children, there are a number of social and emotional issues that are important to consider in terms of constructing the optimal peer group. They too may benefit from being with nonhandicapped children, but their ability to communicate will not depend on it.

It is challenging to develop an educational approach that does not isolate special educational programs from the mainstream. Placing a child in a mainstream environment often means losing professional expertise, such as speech patholo-gists, occupational therapists, and special educators who know how to work with the handicapped child. These professionals are usually at the special school or the special program within the school. The changes suggested here would designate certain settings as integrated settings. The nonhandicapped child, as well as the handicapped child, would both have the advantage of having the special educators, speech pathologists, and early childhood educators available. The nonhandicapped child would not be undermined by the presence of this expertise. Since all children have subtle variations, they would undoubt-edly benefit from participating in an integrated program. They would also gain experience with types of children that they might not ordinarily relate to. Such experience would deepen and broaden their sense of humanity and certainly enhance, rather than compromise, their cognitive, emotional, and social growth. The handicapped child would benefit enormously, be-cause in essence he would have his special needs met in a setting where interactions and communications with peers would be possible. Such a child may not be capable of interacting in an age-appropriate way immediately. He may relate with gestures while others use words. He may withdraw if there is noise or commotion. The educator however will serve as a mediator and inspire the socially outgoing child to pull in the withdrawn child and in so doing help both children learn about real communica-tion. On the other hand, his recovery and his ability to move in this direction would be enhanced and harnessed by access to normative, peer-to-peer interactions.

As children progress to higher grades, the same principle must hold—a few handicapped children must be combined with many nonhandicapped children and be worked with by the educators to make the interactive experiences enriching for both groups. As specific learning disabilities become evident, particularly as the handicapped child becomes more socially interactive and more emotionally secure, these challenges would be worked with as with any child with learning disabili-ties. But even children with profound learning disabilities should not be put into a classroom only with other children with those same learning disabilities, because that too undermines the more normative, peer-to-peer interactions. Sharing art, music, and recess is not the same as being in the same class and is not sufficient.

CONCLUSION

This chapter has outlined some of the therapeutic issues related to children with multisystem developmental delays or pervasive developmental disorders. Central to its recommendations is the concept of helping the child establish an inner sense of his personhood. This sense develops through the child's ability to engage, focus, and concentrate, initiate two-way interaction, use simple and complex gestures, and symbolize and differentiate these symbolic capacities. Facilitating core developmental competencies must be the goal of all therapeutic efforts: interactive play therapy directly with the clinician, work with the parent and caregiver, interactive work with child and caregiver, the educational program, and the speech and occupational therapy program. The educational system must collaborate by making available, as the routine not the exception, normative peer-to-peer interactions to harness the handicapped child's emerging social and emotional capacities.

Appendix 1

Comments on Speech Pathology Evaluation and Intervention

A speech pathologist, and where appropriate an audiologist, should do a thorough evaluation of any child suspected of or evidencing difficulties with receptive or expressive language, or more broadly, with communication. Most speech pathologists say, with good reason, they never see a child too early; most referrals to speech pathologists come when there are already delays in verbal abilities.

Speech pathologists work in two problem areas: receptive language or processing information through sound and visual clues, such as gestures; and expressive language, or being able to make the different sounds and understanding how the sounds come together to make certain words. Work on expressive language involves helping a child who, for example, cannot make the "L" or "M" sound, or learn to move his tongue or his lips in a certain way. The importance of expressive language in communicating feelings, as well as for impersonal cognitive-type communications, is self-evident. The importance of receptive language difficulties is less obvious.

To the degree that one's ability to interpret vocal cues is impaired, there may be an impairment in understanding basic ideas that are communicated emotionally through these channels, such as safety versus danger, acceptance versus rejection, and approval versus disapproval. It is not surprising that children with receptive language problems often have a harder time negotiating basic emotional themes. Whether someone is trying to be friendly or mean is hard to comprehend if the child doesn't understand the meaning of the words or, even earlier in life, the rhythm or tone of vocal gestures. Some learn to compensate naturally with visual cues, but unless the parents are especially empathetic and helpful in creating opportunities for learning, the children will have difficulty.

There may be a sense of inner confusion in a child who cannot comprehend the world of sounds and words. Regressive channels, such as temper tantrums, withdrawal, avoidance, or diffuse aggressive activity, are often used by such a child. Receptive language or receptive communication begins with understanding the simplest gestures (the 4- to 8-month-old), evolves into understanding simple words and complex gestures (8- to 18-month-old), and finally, in the two-year-old and older child, it becomes the typical means used to understand symbols—verbal symbols and eventually the written word.

When the delay starts early, the ability to comprehend one's caregiver will be compromised. It is essential to have children work with a speech pathologist to comprehend gestures, sounds, and, later, words, as well as to learn to communicate.

One should always look for subtle differences in receptive or expressive language as a maturational component of any emotional challenge, such as in the child who is passive and fearful or the counterphobic or aggressive child. The latter may resort to motor discharge when anxious and confused; the anxiety and confusion come about because he doesn't comprehend cues from other people. The creative, bright child who seems lost in fantasy may have functional reasons that explain his difficulty with identifying external reality; he may also have a subtle receptive language problem that makes it easier for him to listen to his own thoughts than to the words of others. One may see receptive language problems in three- to six-year-olds who have some slight delays in reality testing.

Children who are very compulsive and orderly sometimes have subtle receptive language or expressive language problems. The compulsiveness is an attempt to bring order to the sense of internal fragmentation and confusion they feel because of their maturational lag. The compulsiveness can help them adapt in the short run, but if taken to an extreme, it can become maladaptive. Sometimes children who are sad and depressed and seem timid and frightened of aggression may also experience some difficulty abstracting the emotional cues of others and tend to blame themselves for this confusion.

Obviously, there is a combination of factors operating in such cases. One can have any of these patterns without a receptive language problem. For example, children who tend to be sad and depressed may also be gifted in their language abilities. Their sensitive perceptions of the subtleties and nuances may so overload them, that they tend to blame themselves any time someone else is upset.

Therefore, while there may be many reasons for the child's actual behavioral or emotional symptoms, expressive and receptive language problems are a component in many patterns and should be considered and "ruled out," lest one lose the therapeutic leverage that a speech pathologist can offer as part of an overall treatment plan.

We have found that an approach to treatment that is intensive and comprehensive, but sensitive to the child's individual differences, is most helpful. An intensive approach to a condition such as pervasive developmental disorder, includes speech and occupational therapy alongside psychotherapy and family or parent counseling. Even symptoms such as anxiety, depression, avoidance, or passivity; fearfulness, aggressiveness, or impulsivity; or just emotional immaturity may require that occupational and speech therapy be integrated with the overall approach, if there is a motor or language component, or a sensory reactivity or processing component to the symptoms.

If the language, sensory, or motor aspects of a problem are sufficiently mild that the speech pathologist or occupational therapist feels that ongoing occupational therapy or speech intervention is not needed, they will often recommend exercises that parents can do at home, with occasional reevaluations.

Some therapists are concerned about "overloading" or overwhelming a child with too much therapy. A child may already evidence autisticlike patterns of avoidance. He may get speech and occupational therapy two times a week, individual psychotherapy four times a week, and, in addition, family or parent counseling once or twice a week. He may also be in a psychotherapeutic educational setting. Such children are most likely to be undermined by insensitivity on the part of the individual professional or their parents, who may intrude into their lives by moving in on them too quickly, demanding too much of them that they cannot do, or being angry at them. Rigid approaches that demand, for example, that they sit in a time-out box, or types of aversive conditioning to change their behavior, or any approach that compromises empathy and gentle limit-setting tends to have long-term negative consequences, although there may occasionally be a short-term change of behavior. On the other hand, exposing children to three professionals in the same day does not seem to be harmful, so long as they get a break, such as a nap, in between sessions. In fact, the consecutive sessions tend to be very helpful. When the choice is between working with a sensitive, tender, warm, and loving professional and being involved in well-supervised, peer-to-peer activities in a psychoeducational setting or having the child playing perseverative games with himself, sitting and watching television, or accompanying a noninteractive nanny on errands, the former alternatives are far more beneficial.

In summary, well-guided therapeutic efforts balance the child's needs for independence and autonomy and time for himself, as well as for engagement. The therapy supports the child's need for initiative, as a part of a therapeutic relationship or of a normal peer-to-peer relationship, and helps the child mobilize those processes of attending, engaging in two-way communication, and symbolizing of affects that he has, for a variety of reasons, not been able to do on his own or with his family.

A child will not become overloaded with a routine of daily floor times with his parents, two sessions each of speech and occupational therapy, parent counseling once or twice a week, and four individual psychotherapy sessions per week. If the mother is at home, she can do floor time three or four times a day. Such a pattern has helped children with autistic features become more pleasurably engaged in two-way communication within six months. It is critical to respect the child's own rhythm within the context of each session and not overwhelm the child for a half-hour and then give him an hour on his own—two negative experiences and extremes to avoid. Respecting the child's need for a balance of experiences, is the essence of helping children do better.

Appendix 2

Comments on Occupational Therapy Evaluation and Intervention

Many types of disorders require concomitant occupational therapy. Whether the conditions are severe, such as autistic-type patterns or atypical development (pervasive developmental disorder), or the milder types of disorders, occupational therapy is indicated when there is evidence of difficulties or lags in fine motor development; in motor planning skills (the ability to do complex sequential motor acts, such as playing the drum with each hand beating a different rhythm); or when there is difficulty with gross motor coordination, associated with either low or high muscle tone, or asymmetry, or in the capacity for sensorimotor integration. For certain types of motor difficulties a physical therapy evaluation will be indicated. Also, an occupational therapy evaluation and possible treatment should be considered, when there is unevenness in maturation represented through differences in sensory reactivity and sensory processing, in any one or a number of modalities, such as hypersensitivity to touch, sound, light, or movement in space. Hyposensitivity to sensation in any of these modalities also indicates the need for evaluation. Difficulties in integrating experiences across the senses, such as between touch and sound or sound and sight, or in processing information through any modality also suggest the need for an occupational therapy evaluation and possible intervention.

It is important to realize that, particularly in the early years of life, much of the child's intellectual, emotional, and social functioning is mediated through sensory and motor experience. The child decodes affective signals, that is, emotional signals, from his parents through his ability to perceive, which occurs through one or another sensory modality. Therefore, children who are hypersensitive to sensory input may overestimate or misread affective signals.

It is not uncommon to observe multiple fears in children who are overly sensitive to sound or touch, and have difficulties with sensory processing. If a child, for example, confuses auditory input in terms of the sequence of sounds, he will not only confuse a set of instructions but also confuse complex emotional signals conveyed through the person's voice tone and rhythm, as well as his words.

The motor system, both fine and gross, is the main tool a child has for communicating his own intentions and both his intellectual and emotional signals. To the degree that learning occurs through two-way communication, the giving and taking of information, the motor system is critical for the child's intellectual and emotional development. For example, before words become important, the child communicates through his motor gestures (i.e., the ability to put his hands up to ask to be picked up in a clear way is the child's way of communicating dependency). If the child has a motor planning or motor tone problem and hits father in the nose instead of reaching out when the child wants to be picked up, emotional signaling and a sense of cause-and-effect logic are undermined. In addition to the more obvious gestural capacities of the child motor tone and motor planning affects expressive language in terms of control of the tongue, the mouth, and its ability to make sounds.

But perhaps equally important is the sense the child gets of his body doing what he intends it to do. If he sees a ball, his sense of efficacy and self-confidence derives from his ability to initiate action that is in keeping with his wishes; that is, to get the ball. If he can't crawl, or bypasses the ball, or bumps and bangs into things, his confidence in his own body is undermined. Most importantly, the child's confidence in his ability to deal with aggression will be influenced by his confidence in his motor system. If his body seems to be out of control and does not do what he wants it to do, be becomes more fearful that his aggressive feelings can get out of control. Also, he becomes less confident that he can protect himself or escape from danger.

Therefore, the motor system is important for communication—for communicating emotional wishes and needs, for establishing two-way communication, and for dealing with assertiveness and anger, as well as for developing confidence to deal with the aggression and anger of others, as well as their own emotional needs.

In summary, occupational therapy evaluation and possible treatment should be considered in any child where uneven maturation of sensory or motor capacities is contributing to difficulties in overall adaptation. It is critical, however, to make sure the occupational therapy approaches are part of an overall program of fostering better adaptation.

Appendix 3

Clinical Principles of an Integrated Approach to Motor, Language, Cognitive, and Affective Challenges[1]

Due to their motor or language problems, children with motor and/or language delays or disorders often have special emotional difficulties, even in the most optimal family settings. How do we turn such challenges into unique learning opportunities? For example, how do we help the infant with a motor or language disorder to correct the motor and communication difficulty, and at the same time, learn to use his motor and communication system for 'falling in love,' for cause-and-effect emotional signaling, for emotional thinking, and other needs as the baby grows? In light of the importance of integrating the child's physical and emotional needs, a key guiding principle immediately suggests itself.

[1] An appreciation to Georgia DeGangi, Valery DeJon, and Diane Lewis for their discussions of the ideas in this appendix.

PRINCIPLE 1

Each activity aimed at improving motor language or cognitive capacities should also have a central goal of facilitating relevant, age-expected, emotional patterns. For example, in working with an eight-month-old with language lags and abnormal oral–facial tone, an accepted approach would involve the use of manual signs, gestures, and melodic cues to enhance communication development, and the use of facial messages to normalize muscle tone. For instance, one may ask the eight-month-old infant to come, and accompany the verbalization with a gesture, stressing pronunciation of the word *come* to add melodic cues.

In addition, in order to create an opportunity for learning cause-and-effect emotional signaling, one might work toward facilitating motor development by teaching the infant to imitate simple movements of the hands to express him- or herself or tell the parent to come. Similarly, one might help the infant to learn an emotional, relevant, intentional gesture indicating dependency; for example, reaching up to be held. Such patterns often are best learned by responding to the infant's self-motivated, spontaneous activity, whenever possible, rather than using overly structured tasks. After all, intentionality is learned by gaining sensitive responses from a significant other in the immediate surroundings, not by being controlled. To be sure, a complex motor gesture would be shaped through gradual approximation. On the other hand, if each approximation (and eventually the complete pattern) was emotionally age appropriate, relevant, and responded to with a great deal of physical and emotional warmth ("That's great! I love you!" along with a big hug), the infant would learn in his own way to communicate in the emotional world of closeness and dependency. Further, the child would learn that he can communicate his desire for closeness, rather than sensing that closeness is a random entity.

As the example above indicates, there are at least two parts to learning: (a) helping the child organize emotionally and socially relevant patterns and (b) responding to each step in the sequence of the newly learned pattern in a pleasurable manner. Therefore, this point leads us to principle 2.

PRINCIPLE 2

Each emotionally or socially relevant pattern, either in its incipient stages or in its complete form, should receive a timely, phase-specific, pleasurable, emotional response. This guideline includes the caregiver's position (e.g., when possible, in front of infant) and affective disposition (e.g., you can't fake pleasure).

The fact that the caregiver's response should be developmentally phase appropriate is illustrated by the communicatively delayed fifteen-month-old, who manages to say "wuf wuf." Clapping and admiring the infant's accomplishment with communication support (i.e., affective verbal and motor gestures) may at that moment be more phase appropriate than a big hug and cuddle. The infant is learning to balance dependence and independence, and is learning to communicate with word and gesture. Such distal communication modes (i.e., the use of words and gestures) support the infant's emerging ability to be close from across space. Attention should be paid particularly to developing innovative approaches that allow for flexible physical positioning for appropriate, face-to-face, emotional interactions. Parallel with an infant's emerging communication capacities is the toddler's interest in self-control and initiative. This goal thus leads to another principle.

PRINCIPLE 3

Each emotionally relevant interaction should facilitate self-initiative (in generating similar emotional patterns) and the generalization (and abstraction) of these patterns to all areas and contexts of functioning.

For example, in facilitating phase-specific emotional patterns, one should always ask, "Am I doing it *for* the child, or am I creating a learning opportunity where he or she is learning to take initiative?" The nine-month-old who hears a "toot toot" every time he presses his hand near his father's face, understands that he is taking initiative and making things happen. In contrast, the nine-month-old who is only read to without active involvement in the story or who has his arms moved for him, is learning passively to receive information or make movements, but not to practice effective gestures. The application of a new emotional skill to multiple contexts, such as touching Daddy's face to make Daddy say "toot toot," or pulling Mommy's finger to get her to stick out her tongue, facilitates the application of emotional–behavioral and emotional–ideational patterns to multiple contexts.

In addition to learning to take initiative and generalize new coping capacities, the infant and child with developmental disabilities faces another important milestone that must be achieved. This challenge relates to the critical tasks of differentiating an emotional sense of self, which is unique and clearly separated from one's sense of others and nonself. Children with difficulties in motor development or language and communication often have difficulty comprehending and expressing subtle aspects of their sensory–affective experiences (e.g., "I feel angry but my arms do not do what I want them to," or "I feel scared, frustrated." "I know the word but it's stuck." "Does he want to hold me or hurt me?"). Consequently, they find it difficult to separate what's "me" from what's "not me."

Moreover, cognitive lags, where abstracting abilities are limited, may contribute to an inability to order the difficult emotional aspects of one's self into an organized pattern. Similarly, communication difficulties create additional demands to developing a secure sense of self, in terms of body control, assertiveness, and handling aggression (e.g., "If I can't make my mouth do what I want it to, then what can I control, and where does my self-initiative and control end and someone else's begin?").

To facilitate a differentiated sense of self across the full range of human emotions in a child who has difficulties with communication, cognition, general motor planning, or control requires that special experiences be made available.

PRINCIPLE 4

Extra practice for self-differentiation should be provided and supported to accomplish this goal. Two elements are thus necessary: (a) the infant or child needs to experience the full range of human emotions and inclinations, including closeness or dependence, pleasure, assertiveness and curiosity, anger, protest, self-limit-setting, and eventually, empathy, and consistent love. (b) Caregiver responses should be clear and accurate in relation to the child's elaborations, including feedback which provides a sense of being understood and, at the same time, supports further development of self-initiation.

For infants and young children, as described in the Therapeutic Sections, special play times or floor time often afford the context for a variety of interactions. Such floor times, where dolls or animals may implement the emotional theme, may demand a great deal from the caregivers, including understanding their own emotional reactions to the child's dependency or aggression, and consequently extra patience and the realization that the child needs further *extra* repetition, at certain times, and help with moving to the next step.

In some instances, emotional development, as well as motor functioning and communication, may be lagging, and this would be the target of intervention. For example, consider the nine-month-old infant with severe auditory processing delay and motor tone and planning difficulties. Assume that alertness, interest in the world, pleasure in others (a warm attachment), as well as intentional communication is compromised. In such a case, one is working to help the child stabilize head, shoulders, and trunk and, at the same time, offer enough tactile, vestibular, and other sensory input to facilitate increased tone and alertness and interest in the world. Here, the first goal is to find ways to encourage and maintain alertness so that the child eventually can create, without help, those movement patterns and sensory experiences that support increased tone and alertness. At the same time, one is attempting to woo the infant so that he or she finds the human world a lovable place. A game of vigorous dance, nuzzling, and hugging may combine the beneficial effects of movement and touch with the warm, pleasurable emotions of being close. The caregiver will need to be especially alert to slight vocal or motor signals for interaction so that they can be quickly interpreted and responded to in a phase-appropriate manner. A seemingly disorganized tap on the nose during the "nuzzle dance" may provide the opportunity for Daddy to be a "honk honk" car, encouraging similar touches to the baby's nose with novel and entertaining honks. Here, Daddy is simultaneously providing movement, touch, and head, shoulder, and trunk support, as well as wooing (in a loving way) and offering cause-and-effect feedback for emerging motor patterns. In essence, the goal is to integrate the infant's need for increased motor tone and alertness, with sensory interest in the world, a loving attachment, and cause-and-effect emotional signaling.

Lastly, parents and professionals should be aware of potentially adverse interaction patterns (e.g., early resentment, withdrawal, anxious and overexpectation overprotectiveness and inability to let the infant take initiative when he is capable of doing so later in development). In other words, the phase-specific needs of the infant also provide a context for the professional and parent to consider their own attitudes and expectations, in relationship to the infant's emotional growth and requirements.

Appendix 4

Setting Up a Clinical Infant and Child Development Program: Administrative and Programmatic Issues

As the previous discussions suggest, proper diagnosis and preventively oriented interventions and treatments for infants and young children depend on working simultaneously with a number of aspects of the child's development. These aspects include the child's sensory processes, motor, language and emotional development, and interactive capacities with parents and others. It is also necessary to explore the parents' personality dynamics and interactive abilities with their infant, as well as their relationships within the family.

STAFF EXPERTISE

To be able to arrive at an appropriate diagnosis and intervene in all these areas often requires a multidisciplinary group of

711

professionals. Occasionally, one professional will have within his expertise all the necessary skills; however, most professionals will be more expert in one or another area. In most circumstances, it is useful for a program that offers services for infants and young children to have access to three types of professional expertise, either directly or through collaborations.

First, there is a need for a professional skilled at observing the infant's emotional and social development through interaction with parents, as well as through direct interactions and handling by the clinician. The professional may have a background in child psychiatry, pediatrics or behavioral pediatrics, developmental or clinical psychology, social work, early childhood education, nursing, special education, or other disciplines, such as occupational or speech and language therapy.

There is also a need for a person with a strong background in assessing sensory processes and fine and gross motor development. Such experts often come from the field of occupational therapy. However, the occupational therapist must have experience with infants and young children up to three years old in working with both sensory reactivity, processing, and integration, as well as with fine and gross motor development.

Also, it is important to include speech pathologists who have expertise in language functioning, including receptive and expressive language. Occasionally there are individuals in the field of developmental and cognitive psychology who have expertise in assessing language functioning.

To assess the parents' personality functioning and level of psychopathology, as well as the family patterns, one needs a professional with relevant clinical experience. Such a person could come from the fields of child psychiatry, clinical psychology, social work, developmental psychology, pediatrics, or education, if he or she has a good deal of experience in working with parents and families.

In addition to having the various areas of expertise represented, it is critical to have as the clinical leader of the effort a person who is reasonably knowledgeable in all the areas. Certain clinicians have a lot of experience in "putting the pieces together"—the integration of sensory, motor, and language functioning; affective and emotional development; interactive capacities between the infant and parents, the parents and infant, and the parents' personality and family patterns. This clinician must understand how all the elements come together to create either healthy, adaptive development or specific types of problems or difficulties. Such an individual can come from any of a number of disciplines, but in addition to a great deal of clinical experience, he or she should have a background in psychpathology and prevention and treatment of problems in infants and young children, as well as clinical work with parents and adults.

In practice, clinicians from any one of a number of backgrounds can do the on-line work with infants and young children; specialists may be needed only in a back-up capacity. For example, if one is dealing with interactive problems between infants, young children, and their parents, a clinical psychologist, child psychiatrist, behavioral pediatrician, or social worker may assist the family. If there are no primary language problems, or sensory and motor processing problems in most of the children seen, there is less need of occupational or physical therapists or speech pathologists, especially if the clinician can assess these functions in a general way. One caveat is that often a parent may be unaware of a subtle motor, sensory, or language contribution to the child's difficulties. On the other hand, if one offers services for infants and young children with primary motor delays or primary language problems, in addition to emotional and social problems, one may require a large number of speech pathologists or occupational therapists.

REFERRALS

A therapist should establish liaisons with all possible sources of referrals, that is, places where babies and young children are likely to come for health, education, or mental health screening or assessments. There are three groups that one wants to be alert to indications of difficulties in infants and children for appropriate referral for more complete evaluation.

The most important group is the parents themselves, since they intuitively monitor their baby's development every day. However, parents recognize only the more global motor, language, emotional, and social milestones; they are aware of sleeping or eating problems, fussiness, aggression, or tantrums. However, they often don't have a systematic set of criteria to enable them to judge when an evaluation may be appropriate and may come in only when the baby is already far behind. Therefore, it is particularly valuable to talk to parent groups at schools, to reach older children and younger siblings, and to speak at preschool and toddler programs and day care centers. Communication can occur through the media with articles in local newspapers or magazine pieces, or by sending material to parents on various development-oriented mailing lists that provides guidelines for healthy development, as well as for problems or worrisome patterns. Parents need to know when development is proceeding normally, and also to understand when a baby does not evidence a certain expected level of competency or evidences a symptom that may compromise overall competency over time.

In addition to communicating with parents, it is necessary to reach out to pediatricians and other health care providers who work with infants, young children, and families. Communication with pediatricians through the local pediatric society and the professional literature can provide guidelines for monitoring the emotional, sensory, motor, cognitive, and language aspects of well-baby care and lead to appropriate referrals. There is no substitute for ongoing relationships with individual pediatricians and their staffs, including nurses and nurse practitioners, to encourage referrals and follow-up care by the pediatricians.

In addition to pediatricians, mental health colleagues who work with families and with individual adults are a potential source of referrals, particularly if there is family stress, such as depression, that may be contributing to both the parents' and the child's difficulties.

In addition to health professionals, early childhood educators in preschool or day care programs can be important sources of referrals. There are a number of approaches: A therapist may offer free consultative services to such programs, particularly for children who have problems with aggression, inattentiveness, or fear. Taking advantage of speaking and in-service training opportunities, and providing literature to day care and preschool educators will help them identify children in need of evaluation for potential emotional and/or developmental difficulties.

A therapist who is involved with child welfare agencies in the community can provide consultation regarding abused, neglected, and homeless children, including a vast array of problems that most agencies do not handle.

One wants also to be aware that many children who need early and special education services, perhaps because of motor or language delays, will also require mental health services, either in a regular preschool or nursery program or a therapeutic preschool or nursery program, or through various outpatient services.

The therapist should also be aware that insurance plans cover a number of mental health services for infants and young children. Any condition that is diagnosable in an infant, such as attachment disorder of infancy, anxiety disorder, pervasive developmental disorder, or a specific developmental delay in language or motor functioning, may be covered in the same way as is outpatient psychiatric care. Similarly, many elements of an evaluation will be covered as a diagnostic workup under the medical or mental health components of insurance plans. Auxiliary services, like occupational and physical therapy, or language or speech pathology therapy, may or may not be covered, depending upon the individual plans. Some plans will cover these services, if they are part of a psychiatric diagnosis. Others will cover them only if they are part of a medical diagnosis. Other plans will specifically exclude physical or occupational therapy but may include speech pathology or language therapy. One needs to help families examine their insurance plans to discover what coverage they have.

Because infants may have physical and emotional components to their problems, at times a medical and psychiatric diagnosis may be appropriate. For example, a child with a motor and language delay related to perinatal complications may evidence a form of "static encephalopathy," a nonprogressive neurologically based delay. At the same time, this child may evidence an "attachment disorder."

Often, however, a therapist is reluctant to diagnose a baby who may come in with symptoms that are a product of family difficulties. There are diagnoses that can capture and suggest transient reactions, such as an anxiety disorder which can be transient, or a situational reaction of childhood which can also occur in an infant. There are a number of "infant" diagnoses, such as specific developmental delays, attachment disorder, separation anxiety disorder, and pervasive developmental disorder, which may be appropriate for infants and toddlers. Other diagnoses that are ordinarily reserved for older children, like anxiety disorder, conduct disorder, attention deficit disorder, and mood disorder, may be appropriate for young children, or even infants if the criteria are made clear enough and if one can readily see how this is an earlier version of a disorder that is normally seen in older children.

In the future, it is hoped that there will be more appropriate diagnostic categories for infants, young children, and their families that will help facilitate reimbursement for services.

COMPREHENSIVE PREVENTIVE INTERVENTION SERVICES FOR INFANTS AND YOUNG CHILDREN IN MULTIRISK FAMILIES

Severely disturbed multirisk families often have maladaptive patterns which have persisted for generations. These families use the traditional, sometimes fragmented, array of services in the community. A comprehensive approach, combined either directly or through collaborating elements seldom found in a single agency, would include:

1. Services responding to concrete survival needs such as food, housing, and basic medical care;
2. A planned effort to meet the needs of the family and the child for an ongoing, trusting human relationship;
3. At pivotal junctures when the infant's development may be in jeopardy, providing highly technical patterns of care to deal with the infant's and family's individual vulnerabilities and strengths along multiple dimensions; and
4. A special support structure to provide, at one site, partial or full therapeutic day care for the child, innovative outreach to the family, and ongoing training and supervision of program staff.

It is useful to visualize preventive service approaches as a pyramid (Figure A4-1) which includes concrete survival services, an ongoing relationship, and technical approaches. It is also useful to think of service requirements in terms of the stages of a child's development (Table A4-1). The tasks at each stage of development imply that certain components of the service system must be available to assure appropriate support for the function of that stage.

We have outlined here the six steps of a developmental pyramid. At the base of the pyramid is an integrated service system that can provide the services necessary to support the integrity of the family, including supplying missing pieces when necessary, in order to assure basic homeostatic capacities and early capacities for attachment. We have also noted that each step up the pyramid demands very specialized services to help facilitate the special developmental needs of the growing infant, toddler, and young child at that stage. It must be emphasized that, for example, for the eight-month-old child, simply helping

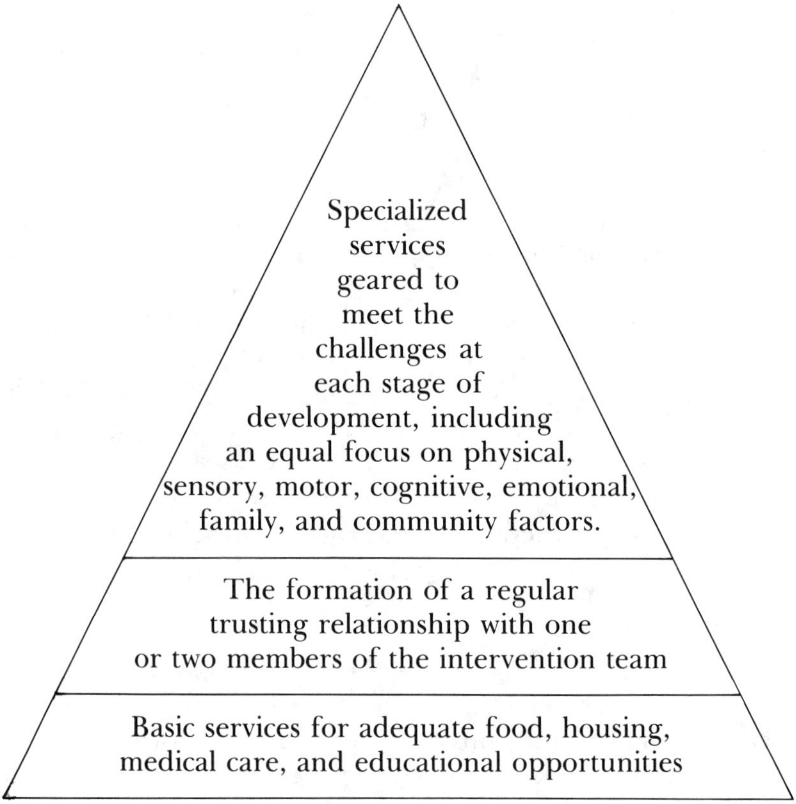

Figure A4-1. Service Pyramid

the family with concrete supports, assuring adequate housing and nutrition, and helping to alleviate crises is often not sufficient to maintain development. The youngster now often needs more differentiated experience. In some families, where financial or other crises are interfering with an otherwise natural capacity to provide the "higher level" experiences, more concrete services may be all that are needed. In most cases, however, this is not so. Where individuals and/or families are chronically fragmented, disorganized, and in recurrent crises, a combination of the concrete services at the base of the pyramid

TABLE A4-1

Schematic Illustration of Levels of Development and Corresponding Service System Requirements and Expected Shifts in the Therapeutic Relationship

Time	Interagency Collaboration	Basic Requirements	Therapeutic Relationship
		Representation, Differentiation, and Consolidation	
24–40 months	Services to permit, as appropriate, more independent functioning and new relationships (e.g. nursery schools).	Facilitation of representational capacity and reality orientation.	Work on capacity to shift between fantasy and reality and integrate wide range of affective and thematic issues.
		Representational Capacity	
17–30 months	Services to permit direct psychotherapeutic work with toddler on as intensive basis as necessary.	Engagement of evolving representational (symbolic) capacities across a wide thematic and affective range.	Work on capacity to use and elaborate fantasy.
		Behavioral Organization, Initiative, and Internalization	
9–18 months	New services to permit direct exploratory work with the toddler now useful. Remedial educational approach should also be available.	Secure availability while admiring and supporting greater behavioral organization initiative and originality.	Further work on self-observing capacity permits integration of affective polarities around dependency and aggression and passivity and assertiveness.

TABLE A4-1 (*continued*)

Time	Interagency Collaboration	Basic Requirements	Therapeutic Relationship
8–10 months	Services incl. educative and psychotherapeutic, and as necessary, auxiliary caretaker to facilitate reading of infant's communications.	*Somatopsychological Differentiation* Reads and responds contingently to range of affective and behavioral cues.	Includes work on capacity for self observation to facilitate empathetic reading of the "other."
2–8 months	Special services to support consistent affective caretaker–infant relationship.	*Attachment* Rich investment in human world; woos and is wooed.	Evolves an attachment that survives negative feelings.
0–2 months	Health, Mental Health, Social Service, Educational, Legal.	*Homeostasis* Protection, care, engagement in world.	Has a pattern that is predictable, regular, comforting.

From: Greenspan, Wieder, Lieberman, Lourie, and Robinson, eds. (1987), *Infants in Multirisk Families*. Madison, CT: International Universities Press, p. 382.

to stabilize the family is only the first step. Then a successive number of specialized services are necessary to support the types of experiences needed to facilitate the child's growth at each stage of his or her development (Table A4-1).

Most often, it has been found that the various levels of experience that need to be supported in the family can be made possible through a program that integrates the existing network of community support services. Such a clinical infant development program serves as a focal point for other community services. While providing, at each level of the pyramid, the specific kinds of technical expertise that will further the youngster's development, the program also provides an integrating focus for the total service system. As suggested, both a center and outreach capacities are necessary to augment more traditional program approaches, because the hardest to reach, most challenging families often require intensive daily care, and, depending on their level in the pyramid, highly specific clinical approaches. It also should be noted that outreach capacities often make it possible to build the slow step-by-step process that forming relationships with the multirisk caregiver requires. Those steps, formulated by Greenspan and Wieder, are summarized in the following table on the dimensions of the therapeutic relationship (Table A4-2).

It is well worth emphasizing that strengthening a family sometimes involves working directly with the youngster. This work, too, undergoes a number of successive stages, helping the youngster, when the parents cannot, to learn to engage the world and regulate: to become involved with people rather than just things; to read human communications; to take pleasure and pride in a growing behavioral organization and initiative; to use an emerging symbolic capacity, and to differentiate this capacity along adaptive lines. These are all tasks that can be enhanced through direct work with the infant and the young child, although it is more advantageous to the child to have the parents in the therapeutic program as well, and have them supporting their child's development. If the parents are not

TABLE A4-2
Dimensions of the Therapeutic Relationship

Regularity and Stability	Steps in the Therapeutic Process Attachment	Process
1. Willingness to meet with an interviewer or therapist to convey concrete concerns.	1. Interest in having concrete needs met.	1. Preliminary communication, including verbal support and information gathering.
2. Willingness to schedule meetings again.	2. Emotional interest in the person of the therapist (e.g., conveys pleasure or anger when they meet).	2. Ability to observe and report single behaviors or action patterns.
3. Meeting according to some predictable pattern.	3. Communicates purposefully in attempts to deal with problems.	3. Focuses on relationships involved in the behavior-action pattern.
4. Meeting regularly with occasional disruptions.	4. Tolerates discomfort or scary emotions.	4. Self-observing function in relationship to feelings.
5. Meeting regularly with no disruptions.	5. Feels "known" or accepted in positive and negative aspects.	5. Self-observing function in relationship to complex and interactive feeling states.
		6. Self-observing function for thematic and affective elaboration.
		7. Makes connections between the key relationships in life including the therapeutic relationship.
		8. Identification of patterns in current, therapeutic, and historical relationships to work through problems and facilitate new growth.
		9. Consolidation of new patterns and levels of satisfaction and preparing to separate from the therapeutic relationship.
		10. Full consolidation of gains in the context of separating and experiencing a full sense of loss and mourning.

From: Greenspan et al., eds. (1987), *Infants in Multirisk Families*. Madison, CT: International Universities Press, pp. 422 and 423.

available during the important stages of the child's early development because of their own psychopathology or other circumstances, direct work with the youngster can help strengthen his adaptive capacities, enabling him often to be a "stronger team member" in the family unit. The child can then help the parents help him. For example, the child who sends his signals in a weak fashion, or who has a parent who does not read his signals at eight months, may, through work with an infant specialist, be taught to strengthen his signals. He can then relate more readily to his depressed mother. As she gets more feedback from her child, she can be drawn out of her depression somewhat, and in turn relate to her infant more. Another example of such direct work involves the child at twenty-two months who has already had a history of difficulties and has a tendency toward negativistic avoidance and fragmented aggressive behavior. Using the existing symbolic modes he may have available, he can explore through play and other symbolic communications the repetitive or maladaptive patterns he may have learned as a way of dealing with stress. Even at a nonverbal level these patterns can be played out symbolically and alternatives presented: In the course of treatment working with a toddler who made her doll "run away" all the time, the therapist took the doll and showed it moving in a more assertive direction toward the parent—reaching out to rather than avoiding the family.

Working with multiproblem families fulfills a critical community need. An infant center is the proper oganizational structure for such an effort. (For a detailed description of our program with multirisk families, see *Infants in Multirisk Families: Case Studies in Preventive Intervention* [Greenspan et al., 1987].)

This appendix has discussed a few of the challenging issues involved in setting up services for infants, young children, and their families. Setting up and implementing such services can be of major benefit to a community.

Appendix 5

An Overview of the Developmental–Structural Approach and the Stages of Ego Development

In an attempt to understand early development, my colleagues and I undertook a clinical descriptive intervention study of multirisk infants and their families as well as normal infants and their families (Greenspan, 1981; Greenspan, Wieder, Lieberman, Nover, Lourie, and Robinson, 1987).

This research, plus intensive clinical work with infants and young children, suggested both the need for and the ingredients of a truly integrated developmental theory reconciling our knowledge of development based on human relationships, cognition, and emerging empirical research on neurophysiological, behavioral, and social development of infants and young children.

In order to meet this challenge, we developed an approach that focuses on the organizational level of personality along multiple dimensions and on mediating processes or "structures" (Greenspan, 1979, 1981, 1989).

There are two assumptions that relate to this approach. One is that the capacity to organize experience is present very early in life and progresses to higher levels as the individual matures. The phase-specific higher levels in this context imply an ability to organize in stable patterns an ever-widening and complex range of experience. For example, it is now well documented that the infant is capable at birth or shortly thereafter of organizing experience in an adaptive fashion. He or she can respond to pleasure and displeasure (Lipsitt, 1966); change behavior as a function of its consequences (Gewirtz, 1965, 1969); and form intimate bonds and make visual discriminations (Klaus and Kennell, 1976; Meltzoff and Moore, 1977). Cycles and rhythms, such as sleep–wake and alertness states, can be organized (Sander, 1962); the infant evidences a variety of affects or affect proclivities (Thomkins, 1963; Ekman, 1972; Izard, 1978), and demonstrates organized social responses in conjunction with increasing neurophysiologic organization (Emde, Gaensbauer, and Harmon, 1976). It is interesting to note that this empirically documented view of the infant is, in a general sense, consistent with Freud's early hypotheses (1900, 1905, 1911) and Hartmann's postulation (1939) of an early undifferentiated organizational matrix. That the organization of experience broadens during the early months of life to reflect increases in the capacity to experience and tolerate a range of stimuli, including responding in social interactions in stable and personal configurations, is also consistent with recent empirical data (Sander, 1962; Escalona, 1968; Brazelton, Koslowski, and Main, 1974; Sroufe, Waters, and Matas, 1974; Stern, 1974a,b; Emde et al., 1976; Murphy and Moriarty, 1976). There are a number of indications that increasingly complex patterns continue to emerge as the infant develops. Between seven and twelve months complex emotional responses such as surprise (Charlesworth, 1969) and affiliation, wariness, and fear (Bowlby, 1969; Ainsworth, Bell, and Stayton, 1974; Sroufe and Waters, 1977), have been observed. Exploration and "refueling" patterns (Mahler, Pine, and Bergman, 1975), and behavior suggesting functional understanding of objects (Werner and

Kaplan, 1963) have been observed in the middle to latter part of the second year of life, along with the eventual emergence of symbolic capacities (Piaget, 1962; Gouin-Decarie, 1965; Bell, 1970).

The interplay between age-appropriate experience and maturation of the central nervous system (CNS) ultimately determines the characteristics of this organizational capacity at each phase. The active and experiencing child uses his maturational capacities to engage the world in ever-changing and more complex ways.

The organizational level of experience may be delineated along a number of parameters, including age or phase appropriateness, range and depth (i.e., animate and inanimate, full range of affects and themes), stability (i.e., response to stress), and personal uniqueness.

In addition to a characteristic organizational level, a second assumption is that for each phase of development there are also certain characteristic types of experience (e.g., interests or wishes, fears, and curiosities) that play themselves out, so to speak, within this organizational structure. Here one looks at the specific drive–affect derivatives, including emotional and behavioral patterns, or later, thoughts, concerns, inclinations, wishes, fears, and so forth. The type of experience is, in a sense, the drama the youngster is experiencing, whereas the organizational level might be viewed metaphorically as the stage upon which this drama is being played out. To carry this metaphor a step further, it is possible to imagine some stages that are large and stable and can therefore support a complex and intense drama. In comparison, other stages may be narrow or small, able only to contain a very restricted drama. Still other stages may have cracks in them and may crumble easily under the pressure of an intense, rich, and varied drama.

According to the developmental–structuralist approach, at each phase of development there are certain characteristics that define the experiential organizational capacity, that is, the stability and contour of the stage. At the same time, there are certain age-expectable dramas, themes characterized by their complexity, richness, depth, and content.

The developmental–structuralist approach is unique in an important respect. In focusing on levels and organizations of experience, it alerts the clinician to look not only for what the infant or toddler is evidencing (e.g., psychopathology) but for what he or she is not evidencing. For example, the eight-month-old who is calm, alert, and enjoyable, but who has no capacity for discrimination or reciprocal social interchanges, may be of vastly more concern than an irritable, negativistic, food-refusing, night-awakening eight-month-old with age-appropriate capacities for differentiation and reciprocal social interchanges. In other words, each stage of development may be characterized according to "expected" organizational characteristics.

In addition to the studies on normal infant emotional development, the developmental–structuralist approach also builds on observations of disturbed development. Interestingly, the study of psychopathology in infancy is a new area, even though the historical foundation for identifying disturbances in the early years of life is very impressive. Constitutional and maturational patterns which influenced the formation of early relationship patterns were already noted in the early 1900s, with descriptions of "babies of nervous inheritance who exhaust their mothers" (Cameron, 1919) and infants with "excessive nerve activity and a functionally immature" nervous system.

Winnicott, who as a pediatrician in the 1930s began describing the environment's role in early relationship problems (1931), was followed in the 1940s by the well-known studies describing the severe developmental disturbances of infants brought up in institutions or in other situations of emotional deprivation (Lowery, 1940; Hunt, 1941; Bakwin, 1942; Spitz, 1945; Bowlby, 1951). Spitz's films resulted in laws in the United States prohibiting care of infants in institutions.

Both the role of individual differences in the infant based on constitutional–maturational and early interactional patterns, and the "nervous" infants described by Rachford in 1905 and Cameron in 1919, again became a focus of inquiry, as evidenced by the observations of Burlingham and Freud (1942); Bergman and Escalona's descriptions of infants with "unusual sensitivities" (1949); Murphy and Moriarty's description of patterns of vulnerability (1976); Thomas, Chess, and Birch's temperament studies (1968); Cravioto and Delicardie's descriptions of the role of infant individual differences in malnutrition (1973); and the impressive emerging empirical literature on infants (Sander, 1962; Lipsitt, 1966; Gewirtz, 1961; Reingold, 1966; Brazelton, Koslowski, and Main, 1974; Stern, 1974a,b; Emde, Gaensbauer, and Harmon, 1976). More integrated approaches to understanding disturbances in infancy have been emphasized in descriptions of selected disorders and clinical case studies (Fraiberg, 1979; Provence, 1983; Greenspan et al., 1987).

So that we could further understand both adaptive and disturbed infant functioning, as indicated, we undertook an in-depth study of normal and disturbed developmental patterns in infancy in order to develop a systematic comprehensive classification of adaptive and maladaptive infant and family patterns (Greenspan, 1979, 1981; Greenspan, Lourie, and Nover, 1979; Greenspan and Lourie, 1981).

The capacities described by the stages are all present in some rudimentary form in very early infancy. The sequence presented suggests not when these capacities begin, but when they become relatively prominent in organizing behavior and furthering development.

The first stage is the achievement of homeostasis, that is, self-regulation and emerging interest in the world through sight, sound, smell, touch, and taste. Once the infant has achieved some capacity for regulation in the context of engaging the world, and central nervous system (CNS) maturation is increasing between two and four months of age, the infant becomes more attuned to social and interpersonal interaction. There is greater ability to respond to the external environment and to form a special relationship with significant primary caregivers.

A second, closely related stage is formation of a human attachment. If an affective and relatively pleasurable attachment (an investment in the human, animate world) is formed, then with growing maturational abilities, the infant develops complex patterns of communication in the context of this primary human relationship. Parallel with development of the infant's relationship to the inanimate world where basic schemes of causality (Piaget, 1962) are being developed, the infant becomes capable of complicated human communications (Charlesworth, 1969; Tennes, Emde, Kisley, and Metcalf, 1972; Brazelton et al., 1974; Stern, 1974a).

When there have been distortions in the attachment process, as occurs when a mother responds in a mechanical, remote manner or projects some of her own dependent feelings onto her infant, the infant may not learn to appreciate causal relationships between people at the level of compassionate and intimate feelings. This situation can occur, even though causality seems to be developing in terms of the inanimate world and the impersonal human world.

Causal relationships are established between the infant and the primary caregiver, as evidenced in the infant's growing ability to discriminate primary caregivers from others. The infant also becomes able to differentiate his or her own actions from their consequences; affectively, somatically, behaviorally, and interpersonally. Usually by eight months of age or earlier, the process of differentiation begins along a number of developmental lines including sensorimotor integration, affects, and relationships.

The third stage is somatopsychologic differentiation, indicating processes occurring at the somatic (sensorimotor) and emerging psychological levels. (In this context, *psychological* refers to higher level mental processes characterized by the capacity to form internal representations or symbols as a way to organize experience.) While schemes of causality are being established in the infant's relationship to the interpersonal world, it is not at all clear whether these schemes exist at an organized representational or symbolic level. Rather, they appear to exist mainly at a somatic level (Greenspan, 1979), even though the precursors of representational capacities are observed. Some are perhaps even prenatally determined (Lourie, 1971).

With appropriate reading of cues and systematic differential responses, the infant's or toddler's behavioral repertoire becomes complicated and communications take on more organized, meaningful configurations. By twelve months of age, the infant is connecting behavioral units into larger organizations as he or she exhibits complex emotional responses such as affiliation, wariness, and fear (Bowlby, 1969; Ainsworth, Bell, and Stayton, 1974; Sroufe and Waters, 1977). As the toddler approaches the second year of life, in the context of the practicing subphase of the development of individuation (Mahler, Pine, and Bergman, 1975), there is an increased capacity for forming original behavioral schemes (Piaget, 1962) and imitative activity and intentionality.

A type of learning through imitation evidenced in earlier development now seems to assume a more dominant role. As imitations take on a more integrated personal form, it appears that the toddler is adopting or internalizing attributes of his or her caregivers.

To describe these new capacities it is useful to consider a fourth stage, that of behavioral organization, initiative, and internalization. As the toddler approaches the end of the second year, internal sensations and unstable images become organized in a mental representational form that can be evoked and is somewhat stable (Gouin-Decarie, 1965; Bell, 1970; Piaget, 1962; Fenson and Ramsay, 1980). While this capacity is fragile between sixteen and twenty-four months, it soon becomes a dominant mode in organizing the child's behavior.

A fifth stage is the formation of mental representations or ideas. The capacity for "object permanence" is relative and goes through a series of stages (Gouin-Decarie, 1965); it refers to the toddler's ability to search for hidden inanimate objects. Representational capacity refers to the ability to organize and evoke internal organized multisensory experiences of the animate object. The capacities to represent animate and inanimate experiences are related and depend both on CNS myelination and appropriate experiences. The process of "internalization" may be thought of as an intermediary process. Internalized experiences eventually become sufficiently organized to be considered representations.

At a representational level, the child again develops capacities for elaboration, integration, and differentiation. Just as causal schemes previously were developed at a somatic and behavioral level, now they are developed at a representational level (Sinclair, 1970; McCune-Nicolich, 1977). Play and intentional interpersonal use of language illustrate these new capacities (Waelder, 1933; Erikson, 1940; Peller, 1954; Kraus and Glucksberg, 1969; Nelson, 1973; Fein, 1975; Lowe, 1975). The child begins to elaborate and eventually differentiate those feelings, thoughts, and events that emanate from within and those that emanate from others. The child begins to differentiate the actions of others from his or her own. This process gradually forms the basis for the differentiation of self representations from the external world, animate and inanimate, and also provides the basis for such crucial personality functions as knowing what is real from unreal, impulse and mood regulation, and the capacity to focus attention and concentrate in order to learn and interact.

The capacity for differentiating internal representations becomes consolidated as object constancy is established (Mahler et al., 1975). In middle childhood, representational capacity becomes reinforced with the child's ability to develop derivative representational systems tied to the original representation and to transform them in accord with adaptive and defensive goals. This permits greater flexibility in dealing with perceptions, feelings, thoughts, and emerging ideals. Substages for these capacities include representational differentiation, the consolidation of representational capacity, and the capacity for forming limited derivative representational systems and multiple derivative representational systems (structural learning [Greenspan, 1979]).

At each of these stages, pathologic as well as adaptive formations are possible. These may be considered as relative compromises in the range, depth, stability, and personal uniqueness of the experiential organization consolidated at each stage. The infant can form adaptive patterns of regulation in the earliest stages of development. Internal states are harmoniously regulated and the infant is free to invest in the animate and inanimate world, thereby setting the basis for rich emotional attachments to primary caregivers. On the other hand, if regulatory processes are not functioning properly and the infant is either hyposensitive or hypersensitive to sensations, he or she may evidence homeostatic difficulties. From relatively minor compromises such as a tendency to withdraw or become hyperexcitable under stress, to a major deviation such as overwhelming avoidance of the animate world, the degrees to which the infant, even in the first months of life, achieves a less than optimal adaptive structural organization can be observed.

Thus, the early attachments can be warm and engaging or shallow, insecure, and limited in their affective tone. There are differences between an infant who reads the signals of the caregivers and responds in a rich, meaningful way to multiple aspects of the communications (with multiple affects and behavioral communications) and one who can respond only within a narrow range of affect (for example, protest) or who cannot respond at all in a contingent or reciprocal manner (for example, the seemingly apathetic, withdrawn, and depressed child who responds only to internal cues). As the toddler becomes behaviorally more organized and complex patterns appear which reflect originality and initiative in the context of the separation and individuation subphase of development, we can observe those toddlers who manifest this full adaptive capacity. They may be compared with others who are stereotyped in their behavioral patterns (reflect no originality or intentionality), who remain fragmented (never connect pieces of behavior into more complicated patterns), or who evidence polarities of affect, showing no capacity to integrate emotions (the chronic negativistic aggressive toddler who cannot show interest, curiosity, or love).

The child who can organize, integrate, and differentiate a rich range of affective and ideational life can be distinguished from one who remains either without representational capacity or undifferentiated (i.e., one who has deficits in reality testing, impulse control, and focused concentration), or who may form and differentiate self and object representations only at the expense of extreme compromises in the range of tolerated experience (e.g., the schizoid child who withdraws from relationships). Similar adaptive or maladaptive structural organizations can be observed in later childhood (the triangular phase), latency, and adolescence.

A more detailed discussion of this framework, including principles of prevention and intervention, is available (Greenspan, 1979, 1981, 1987, 1989). It should also be pointed out that, through videotaped analyses of infant–caregiver interactions (Greenspan and Lieberman, 1980), these patterns evidence temporal stability and can be reliably rated and new raters trained and kept at high levels of reliability (Hofheimer, Strauss, Poisson, and Greenspan, 1981; Hofheimer, Lieberman, Strauss, and Greenspan, 1983; Poisson, Lieberman, and Greenspan, 1981, unpublished). Empirical support for this framework and its related infant–caregiver interaction rating scale (GLOS) is emerging through its application in discriminating clinical disorders and clinical and nonclinical groups (Dougherty, 1991).

This framework has also served as a basis for formulating the stages in early ego development (Greenspan, 1989). (Tables A5-1, A5-2, and A5-3 summarize the developmental structuralist framework, its relationship to the service system, and the stages in early ego development.)

TABLE A5-1
Developmental–Structural Delineation of Stage-Specific Capacities[a]

Stage	Illustrative Adaptive Capacities	Illustrative Maladaptive (Pathologic) Capacities	Adaptive Caregiver	Maladaptive Caregiver
Homeostasis (0–3 months)	Internal regulation (harmony) and balanced interest in the world	Unregulated (e.g., hyperexcitable) or withdrawn (apathetic) behavior	Invested, dedicated, protective, comforting, predictable, engaging, and interesting	Unavailable, chaotic dangerous, abusive; hypo- or hyperstimulating; dull
Attachment (2–7 months)	Rich, deep, multisensory emotional investment in animate world (especially with primary caregivers)	Total lack of or nonaffective, shallow, impersonal involvement (e.g., autistic patterns) in animate world	In love and woos infant to "fall in love"; effective, multimodality, pleasurable involvement	Emotionally distant, aloof, and/or impersonal (highly ambivalent)
Somatopsychological differentiation (3–10 months)	Flexible, wide-ranging, affective, multisystem contingent (reciprocal) interactions (especially with primary caregivers)	Behavior and affects random and/or chaotic or narrow, rigid, and stereotyped	Reads and responds contingently to infant's communications with a range of senses and affects	Ignores or misreads (e.g., projects) infant's communications (e.g., is overly intrusive, preoccupied, or depressed)
Behavioral organization, initiative, and internalization (9–24 months)	Complex, organized, assertive, innovative, integrated behavioral and emotional patterns	Fragmented, stereotyped, and polarized behavior and emotions (e.g., withdrawn, compliant, hyperaggressive, or disorganized behavior)	Admiring of toddler's initiative and autonomy, yet available, tolerant, and firm; follows toddler's lead and helps him organize diverse behavioral and affective elements	Overly intrusive, controlling; fragmented, fearful (especially of toddler's autonomy); abruptly and prematurely "separates"

TABLE A5-1 (*continued*)

Stage	Illustrative Adaptive Capacities	Illustrative Maladaptive (Pathologic) Capacities	Adaptive Caregiver	Maladaptive Caregiver
Representational capacity, differentiation, and consolidation (1½–4 years)	Formation and elaboration of internal representations (imagery); organization and differentiation of imagery pertaining to self and nonself, emergence of cognitive insight; stabilization of mood and gradual emergence of basic personality functions	No representational (symbolic) elaboration; behavior and affect concrete, shallow, and polarized; sense of self and "other" fragmented, undifferentiated, or narrow and rigid; reality testing, impulse regulation, mood stabilization compromised or vulnerable (e.g., borderline psychotic and severe character problems)	Emotionally available to phase-appropriate regressions and dependency needs; reads, responds to, and encourages symbolic elaboration across emotional and behavioral domains (e.g., love, pleasure, assertion) while fostering gradual reality orientation and internalization of limits	Fears or denies phase-appropriate needs; engages child only in concrete (nonsymbolic) modes generally or in certain realms (e.g., around pleasure) and/or misreads or responds noncontingently or unrealistically to emerging communications (i.e., undermines reality orientation); overly permissive or punitive
Capacity for limited extended representational systems and multiple extended representational systems (middle childhood through adolescence)	Enhanced and eventually optimal flexibility to conserve and transform complex and organized representations of experience in the context of expanded relationship patterns and phase-expected developmental tasks	Derivative representational capacities limited or defective, as are latency and adolescent relationships and coping capacities	Supports more complex, phase- and age-appropriate experiential and interpersonal development (i.e., into triangular and posttriangular patterns)	Conflicted over child's age-appropriate propensities (e.g., competitiveness, pleasure orientation, growing competence, assertiveness, and self-sufficiency); becomes aloof or maintains symbiotic tie; withdraws from or overengages in competitive or pleasurable strivings

aThis chart is an illustrative summary and should not imply a level of precision or finality to this conceptualization beyond a relative approximation of important events in early development.
From: Greenspan (1981), Psychopathology and Adaptation in Infancy, Early Childhood: Principles of Clinical Diagnosis and Preventive Intervention. *Clinical Infant Reports*, No. 1. New York: International Universities Press.

TABLE A5-2
Emotional Milestones, Family and Service System Patterns

Stage-Specific Tasks and Capacities	Infant Maldaptive	Family Maladaptive	Service System Maladaptive	Service System Adaptive
Homeostasis (0–3 months) (regulation and interest in the world)	Unregulated (e.g., hyperexcitable) or withdrawn (apathetic) behavior	Unavailable, chaotic dangerous, abusive; hypo- or hyperstimulating; dull	Critical and punitive	Supply support structure and extra nurturing
Attachment (2–7 months) (Falling in love)	Total lack of or nonaffective, shallow, impersonal involvement in animate world	Emotionally distant, aloof, and/or impersonal (highly ambivalent)	Angry and impatient covered by mask of impersonal professionalism	Woo caregiver into a relationship, point out pleasurable aspects of baby
Somatopsychological differentiation (3–10 months) (Purposeful communication)	Behavior and affects random and/or chaotic or narrow, rigid, and stereotyped	Ignores or misreads (e.g., projects) infant's communications (e.g., is overly intrusive, preoccupied, or depressed)	Vacillates between overcontrol and avoidance (of intrusive caregiver) or overprotectiveness (of depressed caregiver)	Combine empathy and limit setting with sensitivity to reading subtle emotional signals, help caregiver read infant's signals
Behavioral organization, initiative, and internalization (9–24 months) (A complex sense of self)	Fragmented, stereotyped and polarized behavior and emotions (e.g., withdrawn, compliant, hyperaggressive, or disorganized behavior)	Overly intrusive, controlling: fragmented, fearful (especially of toddler's autonomy); abruptly and prematurely "separates"	Premature separation from or rejection of family rationalized by notion: "they are okay now"	Support family self-sufficiency, but with admiration and greater rather than less involvement

TABLE A5-2 (continued)

Stage-Specific Tasks and Capacities	Infant Maladaptive	Family Maladaptive	Service System Maladaptive	Service System Adaptive
Representational capacity, differentiation and consolidation ($1\frac{1}{2}$–4 years) (creating ideas and emotional thinking)	No representational (symbolic) elaboration; behavior and affect concrete, shallow, and polarized; sense of self and "other" fragmented, undifferentiated or narrow and rigid; reality testing, impulse regulation, mood stabilization compromised or vulnerable (e.g., borderline psychotic and severe character problems)	Fears or denies phase-appropriate needs; engages child only in concrete (nonsymbolic) modes generally or in certain realms (e.g., around pleasure) and/or misreads or responds noncontingently or unrealistically to emerging communications (i.e., undermines reality orientation); overly permissive or punitive	Infantalizing and concrete with family providing instructions, but no explanations or real sense of partnership	Create atmosphere for working partnership; learn from caregivers and help them conceptualize their own approaches

TABLE A5-3
Stages of Ego Development

Self–Object Relationship	Ego Organization, Differentiation & Integration	Ego Functions
Homeostasis—0–3 months		
Somatic preintentional world self-object	Lack of differentiation between physical world, self, and object worlds	Global reactivity, sensory-affective processing and regulation or sensory hyper- or hyporeactivity and disregulation
Attachment—2–7 months		
Intentional part self-object	Relative lack of differentiation of self and object. Differentiation of physical world and human object world	Part-object seeking, drive-affect elaboration or drive-affect dampening or liability, object withdrawal, rejection, or avoidance
Somatopsychological Differentiation—3–10 months		
Differentiated behavioral part self-object	Differentiation of aspects (part) of self and object in terms of drive-affect patterns and behavior	Part self-object differentiated interactions in initiation of, and reciprocal response to, a range of drive-affect domains (e.g., pleasure, dependency, assertiveness, aggression), means-ends relationship between drive-affect patterns and part-object or self-object patterns
		or
		Undifferentiated self-object interactions, selective drive-affect intensification and inhibition, constrictions of range of intrapsychic experience and regression to stages of withdrawal, avoidance, or rejection (with preference for physical world), object concretization

TABLE A5-3 (*continued*)

Self–Object Relationship	Ego Organization Differentiation & Integration	Ego Functions
Behavioral Organization—Emergence of a Complex Self, 10–18 months		
Functional (conceptual) integrated & differentiated self-object	Integration of drive–affect behavioral patterns into relative "whole" functional self-objects	Organized whole (in a functional behavioral sense), self-object interactions characterized by interactive chains, mobility in space (i.e., distal communication modes), functional (conceptual, abstractions of self-object properties, integration of drive–affect polarities (e.g., shift from splitting to greater integration)
		or
		Self–object fragmentation, self–object proximal urgency, preconceptual concretization, polarization (e.g., negative, aggressive, dependent, or avoidant, self–object pattern, regressive state, including withdrawal, avoidance, rejection, somatic dedifferentiation, object concretization)
Representational Capacity and Elaboration—1½–3 years		
Representational self-object Elaboration 1½–3 yr	Elevation of functional behavioral self–object patterns to multisensory drive–affect invested symbols of intrapersonal and interactive experience (mental representations). Interactive experience (mental representations)	Representational self–objects characterized by mobility in time and space; e.g., creation of object representation in absence of object drive-affect elaboration (themes ranging from dependency and pleasure to assertiveness and aggression now elaborated in symbolic form evidenced in pretend play and functional language), gradual drive affect stability (self–object representations slowly survive intensification of drive–affect dispositions)
		or
		Behavioral concretization (lack of representation), representational constriction (only one or another emotional theme), drive-affect liability, regressive states including withdrawal avoidance, rejection, and behavioral dedifferentiation and object concretization.

TABLE A5-3 (*continued*)

Self–Object Relationship	Ego Organization, Differentiation & Integration	Ego Functions
Representational Differentiation—2–4 years		
Differentiated, integrated representational self–object	Abstractions of self–object representations and drive-affect dispositions into higher level representational organization. Differentiated along dimensions of self-other, time, and space	Representational differentiation characterized by genetic (early somatic and behavioral patterns organized by emerging mental representations) and dynamic integration, (current drive-affect proclivities organized by emerging mental representations) intermicrostructural integration (i.e., affect, impulse, and thought). Basic structure formation (self–object representations abstracted into *stable* patterns performing ongoing ego functions of reality testing, impulse control, mood stabilization, etc.). Self and object identity formation (i.e., a sense of self and object which begins to integrate past, current and changing aspects of fantasy and reality) or Representational fragmentation (either genetic, dynamic, or both). Lack of, or unstable basic structures (e.g., reality testing, impulse control, etc.), defective, polarized or constricted (global or encapsulated) self–object identity formation

Source: Greenspan, S. I. (1981).

Appendix 6

The Sensory and Thematic Affective Contributions to Early Ego Development*

There are two ways of considering how the infant organizes experience; that is, along the interrelated dimensions of sensory and affective–thematic experience. The following section will outline these two dimensions and their clinical implications for a theory of ego development.

HOMEOSTASIS (SELF-REGULATION AND INTEREST IN THE WORLD, 0–3 MONTHS)

During this stage, one may postulate a self–object relationship characterized by a somatic preintentional world self–object. Ego organization, differentiation, and integration are characterized by a lack of differentiation between the physical world, self,

---

*Source: Greenspan (1989).

and object worlds. Ego functions include global reactivity, sensory–affective processing, and regulation, or sensory hyper-, hyporeactivity, and disregulation.

THE SENSORY ORGANIZATION

The infant's first task in the developmental–structuralist sequence is simultaneously to take an interest in the world and regulate himself. In order to compare the ability of certain infants to simultaneously regulate and take an interest in the world with those who cannot, it has been clinically useful to examine each sensory pathway individually as well as the range of sensory modalities available for phase-specific challenges.

Each sensory pathway may be (1) hyperarousable (e.g., the baby who overreacts to normal levels of sound, touch, or brightness); (2) hypoarousable (e.g., the baby who hears and sees but evidences no behavioral or observable affective response to routine sights and sounds—often described as the "floppy" baby with poor muscle tone who is unresponsive and seemingly looks inward); (3) or neither hypo- nor hyperarousable but having a subtle type of early processing disorder (hypo- or hyperarousable babies may also have a processing difficulty). A processing disorder may presumably involve perception, modulation, and processing of the stimulus and/or integration of the stimulus with other sensory experiences (cross-sensory integration), with stored experience (action patterns or representations), or with motor proclivities. Although more immature in form, processing difficulties in infants may not be wholly dissimilar from the types of perceptual–motor or auditory–verbal processing problems we see in older children. In this context, the capacity of babies to habituate to and process the various inanimate sights and sounds may apply to the entire experiential realm of the child, including the affective-laden, interpersonal realm. It is important to note that the differences in sensory reactivity and processing were noted many years ago and continue to be discussed in the occupational therapy literature (Ayers, 1964).

If an individual sensory pathway is not functioning optimally, then the range of sensory experience available to the
infant is limited. This limitation, in part, determines the options
or strategies the infant can employ and the type of sensory
experience that will be organized. Some babies can employ the
full range of sensory capacities. At the stage of homeostasis, for
example, one can observe that such babies look at mother's face
or an interesting object and follow it. When this baby is upset,
the opportunity to look at mother helps the baby become calm
and happy (i.e., a calm smile). Similarly, a soothing voice, a
gentle touch, rhythmic rocking, or a shift in position (offering
vestibular and proprioceptive stimulation) can also help such a
baby to relax, organize, and self-regulate. Also there are babies
who only functionally employ one or two sensory modalities.
We have observed babies who brighten up, alert, and calm to
visual experiences, but who are either relatively unresponsive,
become hyperexcitable, or appear to become "confused" with
auditory stimuli. (A 2-month-old baby may be operationally
defined as confused when instead of looking toward a normal
high-pitched maternal voice and alerting he makes some random motor movements—suggesting that the stimulus has been
taken in—looks past the object repeatedly, and continues his
random movements.) Other babies appear to use vision and
hearing to self-regulate and take an interest in the world but
have a more difficult time with touch and movement. They
often become irritable even with gentle stroking and are calm
only when held horizontally (they become hyperaroused when
held upright). Still other babies calm down only when rocked
to their own heart rate, respiratory rate, or mother's heart rate.
Studies of the role of vestibular and proprioceptive pathways
in psychopathology in infancy are very important areas for
future research.

As babies use a range of sensory pathways, they also integrate experiences across the senses (Lewis and Horowitz, 1977;
Spelke and Owsley, 1979). Yet, there are babies who are able
to use each sensory pathway but have difficulty, for example,
integrating vision and hearing. They can alert to a sound or a

visual cue but are not able to turn and look at a stimulus that offers visual and auditory information at the same time. Instead, they appear confused and may even have active gaze aversion or go into a pattern of extensor rigidity and avoidance.

As higher levels of sensory integration are considered, one may also consider the difference between perception as a general construct and sensory-specific perceptions. In this discussion, the focus will be on individual sensory pathways with the understanding that as sensory and affective information is processed, it can be considered in terms of sensory-specific perceptions and more integrated perceptions.

The sensory pathways are usually observed in the context of sensorimotor patterns. Turning toward the stimulus or brightening and alerting involve motor "outputs." There are babies who have difficulties in the way they integrate their sensory experience with motor output. The most obvious case is a baby with cerebral palsy. At a subtle level, it is possible to observe compromises in such basic abilities as self-consoling or nuzzling in the corner of mother's neck or relaxing to rhythmic rocking. Escalona's classic descriptions (1968) of babies with multiple sensory hypersensitivities therefore require further study in the context of a broader approach to assessing subtle difficulties in each sensory pathway, as well as associated master patterns.

THEMATIC AFFECTIVE ORGANIZATION

At this first stage the affective–thematic organizations can support the phase-specific task which in turn can organize discrete affective–thematic inclinations into more integrated organizations. For example, the baby who wants to calm down is, at the same time, learning the means for obtaining dependency and comfort. The baby who wants to be interested in the world can, with a certain posture or glance, often let his primary caregiver know he is ready for interesting visual, auditory, and tactile sensations.

In the first stages, there are babies who cannot organize their affective–thematic proclivities in terms of the phase-specific tasks. In addition to maladaptive caregiver patterns and infant–caregiver interactions (Greenspan, 1981), babies who are uncomfortable with dependency, either because of specific sensory hypersensitivities or higher-level integrating problems, often evidence a severe compromise on the regulatory part of this equation. Babies with a tendency toward hyper- or hypo-arousal may not be able to organize the affective–thematic domains of joy, pleasure, and exploration. Instead, they may evidence apathy and withdrawal or a total disregard for certain sensory realms while overfocusing on others (e.g., babies who stare at an inanimate object while ignoring the human world).

Excessive irritability, hypersensitivities, tendencies toward withdrawal, apathy, and gaze aversion illustrate some of the dramatic, maladaptive patterns in this first stage of development. If there are maladaptive environmental accommodations, these early patterns may form the basis for later disorders, including avoidance of the human world, and defects in such basic personality functions as perception, integration, regulation, and motility.

ATTACHMENT (2–7 MONTHS)

During this stage, one may postulate a self–object relationship characterized by an intentional part self–object. Ego organization, differentiation, and integration are characterized by a relative lack of differentiation of self and object. There is, however, differentiation of the physical world and human object world. Ego functions include part-object seeking, drive–affect elaboration, or drive–affect dampening or liability, object withdrawal, rejection, or avoidance.

THE SENSORY ORGANIZATION

The second stage involves forming a special emotional interest in the primary caregiver(s). From the perspective of sensory pathways, one can observe babies who are adaptively able to employ all their senses under the orchestration of highly pleasurable affect in relation to the primary caregiver(s). The baby with a beautiful smile, looking at and listening to mother, experiencing her gentle touch and rhythmic movement, and responding to her voice with synchronous mouth and arm and leg movements, is perhaps the most vivid example. Clinically, however, we observe babies who are not able to employ their senses to form an affective relationship with the human world. The most extreme case is where a baby actively avoids sensory and, therefore, affective contact with the human world. Human sounds, touch, and even scents are avoided either with chronic gaze aversion, recoiling, flat affect, or random or nonsynchronous patterns of brightening and alerting. We also observe babies who use one or another sensory pathway in the context of a pleasurable relationship with the human world but cannot orchestrate the full range and depth of sensory experience. The baby who already listens to mother's voice with a smile but averts his gaze and looks pained at the sight of her face is such an example.

THEMATIC AFFECTIVE ORGANIZATION

The task of attachment organizes a number of discrete affective proclivities—comfort, dependency, pleasure, and joy, as well as assertiveness and curiosity—in the context of an intense, affective caregiver–infant relationship. In the adaptive baby, protest and anger are organized along with the expected positive affects as part of his emotional interest in the primary caregiver. A healthy four-month-old can, as part of his repertoire, become negativistic, but then also quickly return to mother's beautiful smiles, loving glances, and comforting.

On the other hand, babies can already have major limitations in certain affect proclivities. Rather than evidencing joy, enthusiasm, or pleasure with their caregivers, they may instead evidence a flat affect. Similarly, rather than evidencing assertive, curious, protesting, or angry behavior in relationship to their primary caregiver, they may only look very compliant and give shallow smiles. In addition to being constricted in their affective range, babies may also evidence a limitation in their organizational stability. An example is a baby who, after hearing a loud noise, cannot return to his earlier interest in the primary caregiver. Where environmental circumstances are unfavorable or for other reasons development continues to be disordered, early attachment difficulties may occur. If these are severe enough, they may form the basis for an ongoing defect in the baby's capacity to form affective human relationships and to form the basic personality structures and functions that depend on the internal organization of human experience.

SOMATOPSYCHOLOGICAL DIFFERENTIATION (PURPOSEFUL COMMUNICATION, 3–10 MONTHS)

During this stage, one may postulate a self–object relationship characterized by a differentiated behavioral part self–object. Ego organization, differentiation, and integration are characterized by a differentiation of aspects (part) of self and object in terms of drive–affect patterns and behavior. Ego functions include part self–object differentiated interactions in initiation of, and reciprocal response in, a range of drive–affect domains (e.g., pleasure, dependency, assertiveness, and aggression), a means–ends relationship between drive–affect patterns, and part self–object patterns. Ego functions may include undifferentiated self–object interactions, selective drive–affect intensification and inhibition, constrictions of range of intrapsychic experience and regression to states of withdrawal, avoidance, or rejection (with preference for the physical world), or object concretization.

SENSORY ORGANIZATION

Building on a solid attachment, the task is now to develop the capacity for cause-and-effect, or means–end type communications. Here, we observe even more profoundly the differential use of the senses. Some babies do not possess the capacity to orchestrate their sensory experiences in an interactive cause-and-effect pattern. A look and a smile on the mother's part do not lead to a consequential look, smile, vocalization, or gross motor movement on baby's part. This baby may perceive the sensory experiences mother is making available but seems unable to organize these experiences, and either looks past mother or evidences random motor patterns. We also observe babies who can operate in a cause-and-effect manner in one sensory pathway but not another. For example, when presented with an object, they may clearly look at the object in a purposeful way and then examine it. However, when presented with an interesting auditory stimulus, instead of responding vocally or reaching toward the person or the object, the infant behaves chaotically with increased motor activity and discharge-type behavior, such as banging and flailing. Similarly, with tactile experience, some babies, instead of touching mother's hand when she is stroking their abdomen begin evidencing random motor responses that appear unrelated to the gentle stimulus. We observe even more profoundly the differential use of the senses as infants are now also learning to "process" information in each sensory mode and between modes in terms of seeing relations between elements in a pattern. For example, some babies learn that a sound leads to a sound or a look to a look. Other infants do not possess the capacity to orchestrate their sensory experiences. The implications for later learning problems of certain sensory pathways not becoming incorporated into a cause-and-effect level of behavioral organization are intriguing to consider (e.g., the differences between children with auditory–verbal abstracting and sequencing problems and those with visual–spatial problems). In organizing cause-and-effect type communications, a compromise in a sensory pathway not only limits the strategies available for tackling this new challenge but may restrict the sensory modalities that become organized at this new development level. Motor differences, such as high or low tone or lags will also obviously influence the infant's ability to signal his wishes. In organizing cause-and-effect type communications, therefore, a compromise in a sensory or motor pathway not only limits the strategies available for tackling this new challenge, but may restrict the sensory and motor modalities that become organized at this new developmental level and, as will be discussed, the associated drive affect patterns as well.

As babies learn to orchestrate their senses in the context of cause-and-effect type interactions, we observe an interesting clinical phenomenon—in relationship to what has been described in the early neurological literature as "proximal" and "distal" modes. At this time, we may begin seeing a shift toward distal rather than proximal modes of communication. Proximal modes of communication may be thought of as direct physical contact, such as holding, rocking, touching, and so forth. Distal modes may be thought of as involving communication that occurs through vision, auditory cuing, and affect signaling. The distal modes can obviously occur across space, whereas the *proximal* modes require, as the word implies, physical closeness. The crawling eight-month-old can remain in emotional communication with his primary caregiver through various reciprocal glances, vocalizations, and affect gestures. Some babies, however, seem to rely on proximal modes for a sense of security. Early limitations in negotiating space will be seen later on to affect the capacity to construct internal representations.

THEMATIC–AFFECTIVE ORGANIZATION

At this stage the full range of affective–thematic proclivities, evident in the attachment phase, become organized in the context of cause-and-effect (means–end) interchanges. The baby joyfully smiles or reaches out in response to a motor movement or affective signal, such as a funny look from the mother, in a reciprocal exchange. Where the caregiver does not respond to the baby's signal, such as returning a smile or a glance, we have observed that the baby's affective–thematic inclinations may not evidence this differentiated organization. Instead they may remain either synchronous, as in the attachment phase, or shift from synchrony to a more random quality, where they appear almost hypomanic, evidencing many affect proclivities in quick succession. The expected range may be present but not subordinated into a cause-and-effect interchange.

There are also many babies who, because of a lack of reciprocal responses from their caregiver, seemingly, evidence affective dampening or flatness and a hint of despondency or sadness. This may occur even after the baby has shown a joyfulness and an adaptive attachment. In some cases at least, it seems as though when not offered the phase specific "experiential nutriments" (the cause-and-effect interactions he is now capable of), but only the earlier forms of relatedness, the baby begins a pattern of withdrawal and affective flattening. It is as though he needs to be met at his own level to maintain his affective–thematic range. Most interesting are the subtle cases where the baby can reciprocate certain affects and themes, such as pleasure and dependency, but not others, such as assertiveness, curiosity, and protest. Depending on the baby's own maturational tendencies and the specificity of the consequences in the caregiving environment, one can imagine how this uneven development occurs. For example, caregivers who are uncomfortable with dependency and closeness may not afford opportunities for purposeful reciprocal interactions in this domain but may, on the other hand, be quite "causal" in less intimate domains of assertion and protest.

The baby's own affective–thematic "sending power," and the degree of differential consequences he is able to elicit, may have important implications for how he differentiates his own internal affective–thematic life (as well as how he organizes these dimensions at the representational or symbolic level later on).

STAGE OF BEHAVIORAL ORGANIZATION, INITIATIVE, AND INTERNALIZATION (9–18 MONTHS); A COMPLEX SENSE OF SELF

During this stage, one may postulate a self–object relationship characterized by a functional (conceptual) integrated and differentiated self–object. Ego organization, differentiation, and integration are characterized by an integration of drive–affect behavioral patterns into relatively "whole" functional self–objects. Ego functions include organized whole self–object interactions (in a functional behavioral sense). These functions are characterized by interactive chains, mobility in space (i.e., distal communication modes), functional (conceptual) abstractions of self–object properties, and integration of drive–affect polarities (e.g., shift from splitting to greater integration). Alternatively, ego functions may be characterized by self–object fragmentation, self–object proximal urgency, preconceptual concretization, or polarization (e.g., negative, aggressive, dependent or avoidant, self–object pattern), and/or regressive states. The latter may include withdrawal, avoidance, rejection, somatic dedifferentiation, and object concretization.

SENSORY ORGANIZATION

This stage involves a baby's ability to sequence together many cause-and-effect units into a chain or an organized behavioral pattern (e.g., the 14-month-old who can take mother's hand, walk her to the refrigerator, bang on the door, and, when the door is opened, point to the desired food). Wish and intention are organized under a complex behavioral pattern. This organized behavioral pattern can be viewed as a task that involves coordinated and orchestrated use of the senses. Here the toddler who is capable of using vision and hearing to perceive various vocal and facial gestures, postural cues, and complex affect signals is able to extract relevant information from his objects and organize this information at new levels of cognitive and affective integration. A toddler who is not able to incorporate certain sensory experiences as part of his early cognitive and affective abstracting abilities (Werner and Kaplan, 1963) may evidence a very early restriction in how his senses process information.

Balanced reliance on proximal and distal modes becomes even more important during this phase of development. The mobile toddler enjoying his freedom in space presumably can feel secure through his distal communication modes. It is interesting in this context to examine traditional notions of separation anxiety and the conflicts that some toddlers have over separation and individuation (Mahler et al., 1975). With the use of the distal modes, the toddler can have his cake and eat it too. If he can bring the caregiving object with him through the use of distal contact with her, he does not have to tolerate a great deal of insecurity. He can "refuel" distally and use proximal contact when necessary. The youngster who has difficulty in using his distal modes to remain in contact with the primary caregiver may need more proximal contact. This difficulty often occurs because of the insecurity generated by an ambivalent primary caregiver, but the limitations of his own sensory organization may also be an important factor.

THEMATIC–AFFECTIVE ORGANIZATION

The piecing together of many smaller cause-and-effect units of experience involves a range of types of experience, such as pleasure, assertiveness, curiosity, and dependency, into an organized chain. For instance, it is not unlikely for a healthy toddler to start with a dependent tone, cuddling and kissing his parents, shift to a pleasurable, giggly interchange with them, and then get off their laps and invite them to engage in an assertive chase game where he runs to a room that is off-limits, such as the living room. When the parents say "no, you can't go in there," protest and negativism may emerge. Under optimal circumstances, the interaction may come to a relative closure with the toddler back in the playroom, sitting on his parent's lap, pleasurably exploring pictures in his favorite book. Here the child has gone full circle, suggesting that he has connected the many affective–thematic areas.

Around eighteen months, as children begin to abstract the meaning of objects, their understanding of the functions of the telephone or a brush may have its counterpart in their experiencing the caregiver as a "functional" being invested with many affective–thematic proclivities. Between twelve and eighteen months, while children are able to integrate many behavioral units, they do not seem to be able to integrate intense emotions. For the moment at least, they lose sight of the fact that this is the same person they love and experience pleasure with. By eighteen to twenty-four months, the sense of split-off fury seems, at least in clinical observations, to be modified at some level by an awareness of love and dependency.

REPRESENTATIONAL CAPACITY (18–30 MONTHS)

During this stage, one may postulate a self–object relationship characterized by a representational self–object. Ego organization, differentiation, and integration are characterized by an elevation of functional behavioral self–object patterns to multisensory drive–affect invested symbols of intrapersonal and interactive experience (mental representations). Ego functions include representational self–objects characterized by mobility in time and space (e.g., creation of object representation in the absence of object); drive–affect elaboration (themes ranging from dependency and pleasure to assertiveness and aggression now elaborated in symbolic form as evidenced in pretend play and functional language). There is gradual stabilizing of drive–affect patterns (self–object representations survive intensification of drive–affect dispositions). Or there is behavioral concretization (lack of representation), representational constriction (only one emotional theme at a time), drive–affect liability, regressive states, including withdrawal, avoidance, rejection, and behavioral dedifferentiation, and object concretization.

SENSORY ORGANIZATION

As a toddler shifts from organizing behavioral patterns to the ability to abstract the functional meaning of objects, and then to the ability to construct mental representations of human and inanimate objects, we observe the establishment of the "representational" capacity. A mental representation is multisensory and it involves the construction of objects from the perspective of *all* the objects' properties (including levels of meaning abstracted from experiences with the object). Therefore, the range of senses and sensorimotor patterns the youngster employs in relationship to his objects is critical, for the object is at once an auditory, visual, tactile, olfactory, vestibular, proprioceptive object, and an object that is involved in various affective and social interchanges. Where the range, depth, and integration of sensory experiences are limited, the very construction of the object will obviously be limited in either its sensory range and depth or affective investment and meaning. Therefore, in such a situation, important limitations in the child's early representational world may result.

THEMATIC–AFFECTIVE ORGANIZATION

As the child learns to construct his own multisensory, affective–thematic image of his experiential world, he organizes affective–thematic patterns at a level of meanings. This new level of organization can be thought of as operating in two ways. The youngster with a representational capacity now has the tool to interpret and label feelings rather than simply act them out. A verbal two-and-a-half-year-old can evidence this interpretive process by saying "me mad," or "me happy." Pretend play is, perhaps, an even more reliable indicator than language of the child's ability to interpret and label. Pretend play is an especially important indicator because many children have language delays. For example, a child soon provides a picture of his representational world as he plays out dramas of dependency (two dolls feeding or hugging each other); of excitement and curiosity (one doll looking under the dress of another); or of assertiveness (searching for monsters).

The representational capacity also provides a higher-level organization with which to integrate affective–thematic domains. Therefore, we observe new experiences as a child develops from two to five years of age. These include empathy, consistent love (object constancy, a love for self and others that is stable over time and survives separations and affect storms such as anger [Mahler et al., 1975]), and later on the ability to experience loss, sadness, and guilt.

Because of the complexities of representational elaboration, the conceptualization of this stage may be aided by subdividing the representational capacity into three levels or subcategories. The first level is the descriptive use of the representational mode (the child labels pictures and describes objects). The second level is the limited interactive use of the representational mode (the child elaborates one or two episodes of thematic–affective interactions, such as statements of "give me candy," "me hungry," or a play scene with two dolls feeding, fighting, or nuzzling). The third level is elaboration of representational, affective–thematic interactions. Often by the age of two-and-a-half or three, the child sequences a number of representational units into a drama—the doll eats, goes to sleep, awakens, goes to school, spanks the teacher, comes home and has a tea party, begins looking under the dress of another doll, becomes overexcited, is comforted by mommy, and then goes back to sleep. Initially, the elements in the complex drama may not be logically connected. Over time, along with representational differentiation, the causal–logical infrastructure of the child's representational world emerges in his pretend play and use of language. Over time, the child's thematic elaboration can be observed to include a range of themes, including dependency, pleasure, assertiveness, curiosity, aggression, self-limit-setting, and eventually empathy and love.

Disorders in this phase include children who remain concrete and never learn to use the representational mode (e.g., only fragments of play or language). Impulsive or withdrawn behavior often accompanies such a limitation. The child's relationship patterns are also usually fragmented.

At a somewhat less severe level, we see children who have developed a representational capacity in both the inanimate and animate spheres but show severe limitations or regressions with even minor stress in certain areas of human experience. For example, they may be able to use symbolic modes only around negativism, dominance, and aggression and consequently look solemn, stubborn, and angry, showing little range of representational elaboration in the pleasurable or intimate domain. When frustrated or angry some children may quickly regress to behavioral modes.

As a feature of the ego's abstracting capacity one must also consider the maturational capacities of the child. If, for example, a child evidences a lag in processing sensory information in either the auditory–verbal, symbolic, or visual–spatial symbolic pathways (e.g., can't sequence, and thereby abstract units of experience), then the ability to abstract large patterns of experience may be compromised. Therefore, organizing early representations will obviously be more challenging to the child with difficulty in perceptual sequencing. Since many children evidence a range of individual differences in sequencing and organizing information, this capacity, as it interacts with interpersonal experiences, must also be considered.

The ego at this stage evidences the adaptive capacity for representational elaboration. It also evidences a range of maladaptive options, including a lack of representation where the physical world can be represented but the drive–affect invested interpersonal world is not represented. This global lack of representational capacity is often associated with interpersonal withdrawal and/or regressive behavioral and somatic discharge patterns. Where there is support for representational elaboration in some areas but not others, or where certain child-initiated themes lead to parental anxiety and/or parental undermining behavior, one observes representational constrictions. One also observes in some instances that these constrictions can be accompanied by intense patterns of behavioral and affective expression. These intense patterns may be in the same or the opposite thematic–affective realm as the representational constriction. One may also observe a lack of representation of delineated self–object thematic patterns (e.g., only dependency with intrusive mother figures) rather than entire areas of emotion (such as dependency with everyone). This limited access to representational elaboration often stems from more circumscribed conflicts in parent–child interaction patterns (e.g., the parent only becomes intrusive or withdraws when the child behaves like the parent's sister) and sets the stage for neurotic conflicts and circumscribed character pathology. Patterns that remain outside of representational life are denied access to unconscious or conscious symbolic processes and are therefore more likely to seed the formation of unconscious neurotic configurations.

How children remain concrete (i.e., do not develop a representational capacity), constrict the representation of certain drive-affect realms, form delineated limited areas of nonrepresented access, and develop compensatory regressive behavioral and affective patterns, reveals the range of functioning available to the ego. The ego organizes current and past experience (behavioral and somatic) in representational configurations. Initially, these are descriptive. They quickly become functional and interactive. The physical, temporal, and spatial properties of experience are the initial organizers. Representational meanings are quickly learned, however. Each representational or interpersonal interaction creates a context for abstracting meanings. To the degree there is a less than optimal interactive experience available (the caregiver is concrete or ignores or distorts certain representational themes), we observe a series of ego operations which include:

1. Concretization of experience (access to representation is never achieved).
2. Behavioral–representational splitting (some areas gain access, but core areas remain at behavioral level).
3. Representational constriction (global dynamically relevant areas remain outside of the representational system).
4. Representational encapsulation—limited dynamically relevant areas remain in more concrete form.
5. Representational exaggeration or lability—domains of experience which are ignored or distorted become exaggerated and/or labile, their opposites become exaggerated and/or labile, or other "displaced" dynamically related thoughts, affects, or behaviors become exaggerated or labile.

REPRESENTATIONAL DIFFERENTIATION (24–48 MONTHS)

During this stage one may postulate a self–object relationship characterized by a differentiated, integrated representational self–object. Ego organization, differentiation, and integration are characterized by an abstraction of self–object representations and drive–affect dispositions into a higher level representational organization, differentiated along dimensions of self–other, time, and space. Ego functions include representational differentiation characterized by:

1. Genetic (early somatic and behavioral patterns organized by emerging mental representations);

2. Dynamic integration, (current drive–affect proclivities organized by emerging mental representations);
3. Intermicrostructural integration (i.e., affect, impulse, and thought);
4. Structure formation (self–object representations abstracted into stable patterns performing ongoing ego functions of reality testing, impulse control, mood stabilization, etc.);
5. Self and object identity formation (i.e., a sense of self and object which begins to integrate past, current, and changing aspects of fantasy and reality); or
6. Representational fragmentation (either genetic, dynamic, or both);
7. Lack of, or unstable, basic structures (e.g., reality testing, impulse control, etc.);
8. Defective, polarized, or constricted (global or encapsulated) self–object identity formation.

THE SENSORY ORGANIZATION

For the child to meet the challenges of organizing and differentiating his internal world according to "self" and "other," "inside" and "outside," dimensions of time and space and affective valence, he is, in part, dependent on the integrity of the sensory organization that underlies his experiential world. Now, even more than earlier, the capacity to process sensory information is critical, including sequencing auditory–verbal and visual–spatial patterns according to physical, temporal, and spatial qualities in the context of abstracting emerging cognitive and affective meanings. The child is now challenged to understand what he hears, sees, touches, and feels, not only in terms of ideas, but in terms of what is me and not-me; what is past, present, and future; what is close and far, and so forth. These learning tasks depend on the ability to sequence and categorize information. Therefore, if anywhere along the pathway of sensory processing there are difficulties, the subsequent ability to organize even impersonal information will likely be compromised. For example, if sounds are confused, words will not be easily understood. If spatial references are confused, spatial configurations will not be easily negotiated. If short-term memory for either verbal or spatial symbols is vulnerable, information will be lost before it can be combined with and compared to other information (to abstract meanings). And if higher level auditory–verbal symbolic or visual–spatial symbolic abstracting capacities are less than age appropriate, the very capacity to categorize experience will be limited. When one considers that the challenge is now to process and organize not only impersonal, cognitive experiences, but highly emotional, interpersonal experiences (which keep moving, so to speak), this challenge to the sensory system is formidable. Furthermore, categories such as "me," "not met," "real," and "make-believe" are high-level constructs. Not surprisingly, learning difficulties often are first evidenced in emotional functioning.

THEMATIC–AFFECTIVE ORGANIZATION

In contrast to earlier views by Freud (1900) and Mahler et al. (1975), our clinical observations suggest that a parallel path of differentiation exists simultaneously with the onset of the representational capacity and its elaboration. The child appears to use his new representational capacity to simultaneously elaborate and differentiate experience. There does not appear to be a period of magical representational thinking followed by one of reality thinking. The child continually differentiates affective–thematic organizations along lines that pertain to self and other, inner–outer, time, space, and so forth. This differentiation is based on the child's capacity to experience the representational consequences of his representational elaborations with the emotionally relevant people in his world, usually parents, family, and friends. The parent who interacts with the child, using emotionally meaningful words and gestures, and engages in pretend in play in a contingent manner (offering, in other words, logical representational feedback) provides the child with consequences that help him differentiate his representational world. In this view, reality testing—the capacity to separate magical from realistic thought—appears to be a gradual process beginning with the onset of the representational capacity proper and stabilizing prior to the child's formal entry into school.

One observes the child's elaborate representational themes along two dimensions. In the horizontal dimension, the child broadens the range of his or her themes to eventually include a range of emotional domains or drive–affect realms, including closeness or dependency, pleasure and excitement, assertiveness, curiosity, aggression, self-limit-setting, the beginnings of empathy and consistent love. For example, not infrequently one observes repetitive pretend play of a feeding or hugging scene suggesting nurturance and dependency. Over time, however, the dramas the child may initiate (with parental interactive support) will expand to include scenes of separation (one doll going off on a trip and leaving the other behind); competition, assertiveness, aggression, injury, death, recovery (the doctor doll trying to fix the wounded soldier), and so forth. At the same time, the logical infrastructure of the child's pretend play and functional use of language becomes more complex and causally connected. The "He Man" doll is hurt by the "bad guys" and therefore "gets them." After the tea party, the little girl doll goes to the "potty" and then decides it is time to begin cooking dinner. In discussions, the three-and-a-half-year-old sounds more and more like a lawyer with "buts" and "becauses"—"I don't like that food because it looks yucky and will make me sick." There is, therefore, both thematic elaboration and differentiation. Even though the themes may be pretend and fantasmagoric, the structure of the drama becomes more and more logical. The rocketship to the land of "He-Man" uses N.A.S.A. rocket fuel.

As indicated, representational differentiation depends not only on a child being representationally engaged in thematic–affective areas but experiencing cause-and-effect feedback at the representational level. Parents have to be able not only to engage but also to interpret experiences correctly. The parents who react to play with a gun as aggression one day, as sexuality another day, and as dependency on a third day, or who keep shifting meanings within the same thematic play session, will confuse the child. This child may not develop meanings with a reality orientation. Parents who confuse their own feelings with the child's feelings, or cannot set limits, may also compromise the formation of a reality orientation.

The primary ego functions now develop from the ego's ability to abstract patterns along dimensions of self and object meanings, affective tendencies, and the dimensions of time, space, and causality. These include reality testing (a representational me separate from a representational other); impulse control (a representational me impacting on, and eliciting consequences from, a representational other); mood stabilization (a representational me and other becomes organized along a dominant mood as affects are abstracted into larger affective patterns); focused attention and a capacity for planning (a representational me causes events to occur in a temporal context); and a more integrated body self–object representation (the parts of me and object are abstracted in spatial contexts).

During this stage, ambivalence can be dealt with in a new way and an integrated representational self can be organized, or one may observe a lack of integration. Different self–object representational units may exist, depending on interpersonal factors or maturational factors, at various degrees of differentiation. The sexual self–object, assertive self–object, dependent self–object, and so on, may each achieve its own relative degree of differentiation. As indicated earlier, sensory processing difficulties may undermine differentiation in auditory–verbal or visual–spatial modes. Or a lack of representational feedback or distorted or illogical feedback in certain realms of experience will tend to leave those areas of representational life relatively undifferentiated.

As is well known, anxiety and conflict now tend to play a new role, but perhaps earlier than previously thought. With growing representational capacity anxiety can be interpreted via the emerging representational system. Conflicts between self–object representations can occur in terms of an "internal debate" at the level of ideas (e.g., the good me and you versus the angry evil me and you). Conflicts between self–object representations and external expectations can also occur (the "greedy" me and the "strict" limiting other). Therefore, while anxiety and internal conflict have been thought to be dominant only in the late oedipal and postoedipal phases (because of the necessity of internalized prohibitions, i.e., superego formation), our clinical observations of young children suggest that representational differentiation alone may be a sufficient condition.

What operations are now available to the ego to deal with anxiety and conflict? The ego now has new approaches in addition to the primitive mechanisms described earlier.

Observations of both normal and disturbed young children suggest that the approaches available to the ego at this stage, include:

1. Global lack of differentiation (reality and the object ties that provide reality feedback are too disruptive or "scary").
2. Selective dedifferentiation (blurring of boundaries and changing meanings, as with "my anger won't make mother leave because we are the same person").
3. Thought–drive–affect dedifferentiations ("I can think anything, but I won't have feelings so I won't be scared").
4. Thought–behavior (impulse) dedifferentiation ("If I do it, it's not me. Only when I think and plan it is it me").
5. Selective constrictions of drive–affect–thematic realms (areas such as anger or sexual curiosity are avoided and may remain relatively undifferentiated, often due to being associated with disorganizing interactive experience such as withdrawal, overstimulation, etc.).
6. Affect, behavioral, or thought intensification ("If I exaggerate it or its opposite, it can't scare me").

7. Differentiated representational distortions (changing meanings along lines of drive–affect dispositions—"I am supergirl, the strongest." But basic reality testing is maintained—e.g., "It is only pretend").

8. Encapsulated distortions (dynamically based conflict driven, highly selective shifts of meanings; e.g., "I am the cause of mother's anger").

9. Transforming differentiational linkages. This is an early form of rationalization. As the child's capacity to connect representational units is forming, he or she can elaborate. ("I like mommy because she is home all the time and am mad at daddy because he travels a lot.") These logical links can undergo subtle shifts to change meanings for defensive purposes. ("I like daddy to travel a lot because he brings me presents. I am mad at mommy," etc.)

10. Compromises in representational integration and representational identity. The integration of somatic, behavioral (and representational self–object organizations) and associated drive–affect proclivities are not fully maintained, as evidenced by the irritable-looking three-year-old who "feels fine" or the hitting three-year-old who "loves everyone."

Appendix 7

Selected Assessment Instruments

- *DeGangi-Greenspan Test of Sensory Functions in Infants* (TSFI) (Western Psychological Services, Los Angeles, CA). Measures sensory processing and reactivity in infants, focusing on evaluation of responses to tactile deep-pressure, visual–tactile integration, adaptive motor skills, ocular motor control, and reactivity to vestibular stimulation.
- *DeGangi-Berk Test of Sensory Integration* (TSI) (Western Psychological Services, Los Angeles, CA). Measures overall sensory integration in three- to five-year-old children with delays in sensory, motor, and perceptual skills.
- *Touch Inventory for Preschoolers* (TIP) (*American Journal of Occupational Therapy*, 1986, Vol. 40, pp. 414–419). Measures tactile defensiveness in preschoolers.
- *Fagan Test of Infant Intelligence* (Infantest Corp., Cleveland, OH). Measures the infant's differential fixation to one of two visual targets, one novel, the other familiar.
- *Greenspan-Lieberman Observation Scale* (GLOS) (Reginald S. Lourie Center for Infants and Young Children [Susan Poisson, contact], Rockville, MD, 1980). Designed to provide a

system for coding videotapes of free play interactions between caregiver and infant or child. There is an infant version and a preschool version.

•*Family APGAR* (*Journal of Family Practice*, 1982, Vol. 15, pp. 303–311). Screens for family dysfunction.

•*Parenting Stress Index* (University of Virginia, Charlottesville, VA). Standardized assessment measuring child characteristics and dimensions of parent stress.

•*McMaster Family Assessment Device* (*Journal of Marital and Family Therapy*, 1983, Vol. 9, pp. 171–180). Self-report assessment of family functioning.

•*Infant/Child Characteristics Questionnaire* (ICQ) (Bates) (Indiana University, Bloomington, IN). Measures child temperament.

•*The Revised Dimensions of Temperament Survey* (DOTS-R) (*Journal of Adolescent Research*). Items related to various temperamental characteristics.

•*Sequenced Inventory of Communication Development* (SICD) (University of Washington Press, Seattle, WA). Measures receptive and expressive language in children, four months to four years of age, or for persons who are developmentally delayed.

•*Receptive Expressive Emergent Language Scale* (REEL) (University Park Press, Baltimore, MD). Assesses prelinguistic skills in infants between one month and three years of age.

•*Communication and Symbolic Behavior Scales* (CSBS) (Special Press, Inc., San Antonio, TX). Assesses communicative, social, affective, and symbolic abilities of children between nine months and two years of age.

•*Test for Auditory Comprehension of Language* (TACL) (Teaching Resources Corp., Hingham, MA). Measures receptive language in children between three years and six years of age, and requires no verbal responses.

•*Peabody Picture Vocabulary Test, Revised Edition* (PPVT-R) (American Guidance Services, Circle Pines, MN). Measures receptive vocabulary between two-and-a-half and forty years of age.

•*Bayley Scales of Infant Development* (Psychological Corp., New York, NY). The Mental Development Index (MDI) measures cognitive and perceptual abilities.

●*Bayley Scales of Infant Development, Infant Behavior Record* (IBR) (Psychological Corporation, New York, NY). Descriptive rating scales of behavior characteristics of children up to thirty months of age.

●*McCarthy Scales of Children's Abilities* (Psychological Corp., New York, NY). Test of general cognition and motor abilities for children from two-and-a-half to eight-and-a-half years of age.

●*Vineland Adaptive Behavior Scales* (American Guidance Services, Circle Pines, MN). A revision of the Vineland Social Maturity Scale by Edgar A. Doll. The scales are available in three versions: Interview Editions, Survey Form; Interview Edition, Expanded Form; and Classroom Edition. Assesses adaptive behavior of both nonhandicapped and handicapped individuals from birth to adulthood.

●*Child Behavior Checklist* (University of Vermont, Burlington, VT). Measures children's competencies and problems, as reported by their parents or parent–surrogates.

●*Brazelton Neonatal Behavioral Assessment Scale* (J. P. Lippincott Co., 1973). Assesses infant's ability to process stimuli and organize adaptive responses.

●*Peabody Developmental Motor Scales* (PDMS) (Teaching Resources Corp., Hingham, MA, 1983). Assesses gross motor and fine motor skills.

●*Behavior Rating Instrument for Autistic and Other Atypical Children* (C. H. Stoelting Co., 1976). Evaluates low-functioning and atypical children.

●*Cattell Infant Intelligence Scale* (The Psychological Corporation, New York, NY, 1960). Downward extension of Stanford-Binet (Form L-M). Tests at levels one month apart from one to twelve months, two-month intervals from twelve to twenty-four months; three-month intervals from twenty-four to thirty months.

●*Denver Developmental Screening Test* (DDST). Screens four developmental areas: personal–social, fine motor-adaptive, language and gross motor.

●*Gesell Development Schedules* (Nigel Cox, 1940). Assesses five areas: adaptive, fine motor, gross motor, personal–social, and language.

●*Uzgirus Hunt Ordinal Scales of Infant Psychological Development* (University of Illinois, 1975). Constructed following Piagetian sequences: visual pursuit to object permanence; instrumental action; vocal and gestural imitation; operational causality; object relations in space; and development object relations schema.

●*Stanford-Binet (L-M)* (Riverside Publishing, 1972). Assesses verbal, quantitative, and abstract/visual reasoning, and short-term memory.

●*Stanford-Binet* (4th ed.) (Riverside Publishing, 1985). Same as above.

References

Ainsworth, M., Bell, S. M., & Stayton, D. (1974), Infant–mother attachment and social development: Socialization as a product of reciprocal responsiveness to signals. In: *The Integration of the Child into a Social World*, ed. M. Richards. Cambridge, UK: Cambridge University Press, pp. 99–135.

American Psychiatric Association (1987), *Diagnostic and Statistical Manual of Mental Disorders*, 3rd ed. rev. (DSM-III-R). Washington, DC: American Psychiatric Press.

Ayers, A. J. (1964), Tactile functions: Their relation to hyperactive and perceptual motor behavior. *Amer. J. Occupat. Ther.*, 18:6–11.

Bakwin, H. (1942), Loneliness in infants. *Amer. J. Dis. Child.*, 63:30–42.

Bates, E., Benigni, L., Bretherton, I., Camaioni, L., & Volterra, V. (1979), *The Emergence of Symbols: Cognition and Communication in Infancy*. New York: Academic Press.

Behar, D., Rapoport, J. L., & Adams, A. J. (1984), Sugar challenge testing with children considered behaviorally "sugar reactive." *Nutrit. & Behav.*, 1:277–288.

Bell, S. (1970), The development of the concept of object as related to infant–mother attachment. *Child Develop.*, 41:219–311.

Bergman, P., & Escalona, S. (1949), Unusual sensitivities in very young children. *The Psychoanalytic Study of the Child*, 3&4:333–352. New York: International Universities Press.

Bion, W. (1961), *Experiences in Groups*. London: Tavistock.

Bloom, L. (1973), *One Word at a Time: The Use of Single Word Utterances Before Syntax*. The Hague: Mouton.

Bolton, R. (1984), The hypoglycemia–aggression hypothesis: Debate vs. research. *Curr. Anthropol.*, 25:1–53.

Bowlby, J. (1951), *Maternal Care and Mental Health*. World Health Organization (WHO) Monogr. Series No. 2. Geneva.

———— (1969), *Attachment and Loss*, Vol. 1. New York: Basic Books.

———— (1979), *Attachment and Loss*, Vol. 3. New York: Basic Books.

Brazelton, T., Koslowski, B., & Main, N. (1974), The origins of reciprocity: The early mother–infant interaction. In: *The Effect of the Infant on Its Caregiver*, ed. M. Lewis & L. Rosenblum. New York: John Wiley, pp. 49–76.

———— Cramer, B. (1990), *The Earliest Relationship: Parents, Infants, and the Drama of Early Attachment*. Reading, MA: Addison-Wesley Publishing Co. (A MerLoyd Lawrence Book).

Brown, R. (1975), *A First Language: The Early Stages*. Cambridge, MA: Harvard University Press.

Burlingham, D., & Freud, A. (1942), *Young Children in Wartime*. London: Allen & Unwin.

Cameron, H. S. (1919), *The Nervous Child*. London: Oxford Medical Publications.

Charlesworth, W. R. (1969), The role of surprise in cognitive development. In: *Studies in Cognitive Development: Essays in Honor of Jean Piaget*, ed. E. Elkind & J. H. Flavell. London: Oxford University Press, pp. 257–314.

Connors, C. K., & Blouin, A. G. (1982–1983), Nutritional effects on behavior of children. *J. Psychiat. Res.*, 17:193–202.

―――― Caldwell, J., & Caldwell, L. (in press), Experimental studies of sugar and aspartame on autonomic, cortical and behavioral responses of children. In: *Diet and Behavior: An Interface Among Psychology, Medicine and Nutrition,* ed. B. Spring, J. Chiodo, & J. Elias. Lubbock, TX: Texas Technical University Press.

Cravioto, J., & Delicardie, E. (1973), Environmental correlates of severe clinical malnutrition and language development survivors from kwashiorkor or marasmus. In: *Nutrition, the Nervous System and Behavior.* Washington, DC: PAHO Scientific Publication No. 251.

DeGangi, G., DiPietro, J. A., Greenspan, S. I., & Porges, S. W. (1991), Psychophysiological characteristics of the regulatory disordered infant. *Infant Behav. Develop.,* 14:37–50.

―――― Greenspan, S. I. (1988), The development of sensory functioning in infants. *J. Phys. & Occupat. Ther. in Pediat.,* 8/3.

―――― ―――― (1989a), The assessment of sensory functioning in infants, *J. Phys. & Occupat. Ther. in Pediat.,* 9:21–33.

―――― ―――― (1989b), *Test of Sensory Functions in Infants.* Los Angeles: Western Psychology Services.

―――― Porges, S. W., Sickel, R., & Greenspan, S. I. (submitted), Longitudinal outcomes of regulatory disordered infants.

Dougherty, S. C. (1991), *An Investigation of Depression in Infancy and Early Childhood from a Transactional, Developmental Structuralist Perspective.* Doctoral dissertation. Saybrook Institute, San Francisco, CA.

Doussard-Roosevelt, J. A., Walker, P. S., Portales, A. L., Greenspan, S. I., & Porges, S. W. (1990), Vagal tone and the fussy infant: Atypical vagal reactivity in the difficult infant. *Infant Behav. & Develop.,* 13:352 (abstract).

Egger, J., Carter, C. M., Wilson, J., Turner, M. W., & Soothill, J. F. (1983), Is migraine food allergy? *Lancet,* 2:865–869.

―――― ―――― Graham, P. J., Gumby, D., & Soothill, J. F. (1985), Controlled trial of oligo antigenic treatment in the hyperkinetic syndrome. *Lancet,* 1:540–544.

Ekman, P. (1972), Universals and cultural differences in facial expressions of emotion. In: *Nebraska Symposium on Motivation*. Lincoln: University of Nebraska Press.

Emde, R. N., Gaensbauer, T. J., & Harmon, R. J. (1976), Emotional Expression in Infancy: A Biobehavioral Study. *Psychological Issues*, Monogr. No. 37. New York: International Universities Press.

Erikson, E. H. (1940), Studies in Interpretation of Play: I. Clinical Observation of Child Disruption in Young Children. *Genetic Psychology*, Monogr. 22.

—— (1943), Clinical studies in childhood play. In: *Child Behavior and Development*, ed. R. C. Barker. New York: McGraw-Hill, pp. 411–428.

Escalona, S. (1968), *The Roots of Individuality*. Chicago: Aldine.

Fein, G. (1975), A transformational analysis of pretending. *Develop. Psychol.*, 11:291–296.

Fenson, L., Kagan, J., Kearsley, R., & Zelazo, P. (1976), The developmental progression of manipulative play in the first two years. *Child Develop.*, 47:232–236.

—— Ramsay, D. (1980), Decentration and integration of play in the second year of life. *Child Develop.*, 51:171–178.

Ferguson, H. B., Stoddart, C., & Simeon, J. G. (1986), Double blind challenge studies of behavioral and cognitive effects of sucrose-aspartame ingestion in normal children. *Nutr. Rev.*, 44(Suppl.):144–150.

Flavell, J. H. (1963), *The Developmental Psychology of Jean Piaget*. Princeton, NJ: Van Nostrand.

—— Botkin, P., Fry, C., Wright, J., & Jarvis, P. (1968), *The Development of Role-Taking and Communication Skills in Children*. New York: John Wiley.

Fraiberg, S. (1979), Treatment modalities in an infant mental health program. Presentation at the training institute on "Clinical Approaches to Infants and Their Families" sponsored by the National Center for Clinical Infant Programs, Washington, DC.

—— (1980), *Clinical Studies in Infant Mental Health: The First Year of Life*. New York: Basic Books.

Freud, S. (1900), The Interpretation of Dreams. *Standard Edition*, 4 & 5. London: Hogarth Press, 1953.

———— (1905), Three essays on the theory of sexuality. *Standard Edition*, 7:135–242. London: Hogarth Press, 1953.

———— (1911), Formulations on the two principles of mental functioning. *Standard Edition*, 12:218–226. London: Hogarth Press, 1953.

Gewirtz, J. L. (1961), A learning analysis of the effects of normal stimulation, privation and deprivation on the acquisition of social motivation and attachment. In: *Determinants of Infant Behavior*, Vol. 1, ed. B. M. Foss. London: Methuen, pp. 28–35.

———— (1965), The course of infant smiling in four child rearing environments in Israel. In: *Determinants of Infant Behavior*, Vol. 1, ed. B. M. Foss. London: Methuen, pp. 205–260.

———— (1969), Levels of conceptual analysis in environment–infant interaction research. *Merrill-Palmer Quart.*, 15:9–47.

Gouin-Decarie, T. (1965), *Intelligence and Affectivity in Early Childhood: An Experimental Study of Jean Piaget's Object Concept and Object Relations*. New York: International Universities Press.

Greenspan, N. T. (1991), Infants, toddlers, and indoor air pollution. *Zero to Three* (Bulletin of the National Center for Clinical Infant Programs), Vol. XI, No. 5, pp. 14–21.

Greenspan, S. I. (1975), A Consideration of Some Learning Variables in the Context of Psychoanalytic Theory. *Psychological Issues*, Monogr. 33. New York: International Universities Press.

———— (1979), Intelligence and Adaptation: An Integration of Psychoanalytic and Piagetian Developmental Psychology. *Psychological Issues*, Monogr. 47/68. New York: International Universities Press.

———— (1981), *Psychopathology and Adaptation in Infancy and Early Childhood: Principles of Clinical Diagnosis and Preventive Intervention*. New York: International Universities Press.

———— (1989), *The Development of the Ego*. Madison, CT: International Universities Press.

———— (1990), Regulatory disorders: Clinical perspectives. Presented at the National Institute on Drug Abuse RAUS Review Meeting on Methodological Issues in Controlled Studies on Effects of Prenatal Exposure to Drugs of Abuse, June 8–9, Richmond, VA; to appear in NIDA monograph, December, 1991.

———— Greenspan, N. T. (1985), *First Feelings: Milestones in the Emotional Development of Your Baby and Child from Birth to Age 4.* New York: Viking.

———— ———— (1989), *The Essential Partnership.* New York: Viking.

———— Lieberman, A. F. (1980), Infants, mothers, and their interaction: A quantitative clinical approach to developmental assessment. In: *The Course of Life: Psychoanalytic Contributions Toward Understanding Personality Development,* Vol. 1, ed. S. I. Greenspan & G. H. Pollock. DHHS Publication No. [ADM] 89–786. Washington, DC: U.S. Government Printing Office.

———— ———— (1989a), Infants, mothers, and their interaction: A quantitative clinical approach to developmental assessment. In: *The Course of Life, Vol. I: Infancy,* ed. S. I. Greenspan and G. H. Pollock. Madison, CT: International Universities Press, pp. 503–560.

———— ———— (1989b), A quantitative approach to the clinical assessment of representational elaboration and differentiation in children two to four. In: *The Course of Life, Vol. II: Early Childhood,* ed. S. I. Greenspan and G. H. Pollock. Madison, CT: International Universities Press, pp. 387–442.

———— ———— Nover, R., Lourie, R., & Robinson, M., eds. (1987), Infants in Multirisk Families: Case Studies in Preventive Intervention. *Clinical Infant Reports,* No. 3. Madison, CT: International Universities Press.

———— Lourie, R. S. (1981), Developmental structuralist approach to the classification of adaptive and pathologic personality organization: Application to infancy and early childhood. *Amer. J. Psychiat.,* 138:725–736.

————— ————— & Nover, R. (1979), A developmental approach to the clasification of psychopathology in infancy and early childhood. In: *The Basic Handbook of Child Psychiatry*, Vol. 2, ed. J. Noshpitz. New York: Basic Books, pp. 157–164.

————— Mannino, F. V. (1974), A model for brief intervention with couples based on projective identification. *Amer. J. Psychiat.*, 13:1103–1106.

Gross, M. D. (1984), Effect of sucrose on hyperkinetic children. *Pediatrics*, 74:876–878.

Hartmann, H. (1939), *Ego Psychology and the Problem of Adaptation*. New York: International Universities Press.

Hofheimer, J. A., Lieberman, A. F., Strauss, M. E., & Greenspan, S. I. (1983), Short-term temporal stability of mother–infant interactions in the first year of life. Presented at the 93rd Meeting of the American Psychological Association, Los Angeles, CA.

————— Poisson, S., Strauss, M., Eyler, F., & Greenspan, S. I. (1983), Perinatal and behavioral characteristics of neonates born to multi-risk families. *J. Develop. & Behav. Pediat.*, 4, 3:163–170.

————— Strauss, M. E., Poisson, S. S., & Greenspan, S. I. (1981), The reliability, validity and generalizability of assessments of transactions between infants and their caregivers: A multi-center design. Working Paper, Clinical Infant Development Program, National Institute of Mental Health.

Hunt, J. M. (1941), Infants in an orphanage. *J. Abnorm. & Soc. Psychol.*, 36:338.

Izard, C. (1978), On the development of emotions and emotion–cognition relationships in infancy. In: *The Development of Affect*, ed. M. Lewis & L. Rosenblum. New York: Plenum Press.

Klaus, M., & Kennell, J. (1976), *Maternal–Infant Bonding: The Impact of Early Separation or Loss on Family Development*. St. Louis, MO: C. V. Mosby.

Kraus, R., & Glucksberg, S. (1969), The development of communication: Competence as a function of age. *Child Develop.*, 40:255–266.

Kruesi, M. J. P., Linnoila, M., & Rapoport, J. L. (1985), Carbohydrate craving, conduct disorder, and low 5-HIAA. *Psychiat. Res.*, 16:83–86.

Lewis, M., & Horowitz, L. (1977), Intermodal personal schema in infancy: Perception within a common auditory–visual space. Paper presented at the meeting of the Eastern Psychological Association, April.

Lipsitt, L. (1966), Learning processes of newborns. *Merrill-Palmer Quart.*, 12:45–71.

Lourie, R. S. (1971), The first three years of life: An overview of a new frontier for psychiatry. *Amer. J. Psychiat.*, 127:1457–1463.

Lowe, M. (1975), Trends in the development of representational play: An observational study. *J. Child Psychol. & Psychiat.*, 16:33–47.

Lowery, L. G. (1940), Personality disorders and early institutional care. *Amer. J. Orthopsychiat.*, 10:546–555.

Mahler, M. S., Pine, F., & Bergman, A. (1975), *The Psychological Birth of the Human Infant.* New York: Basic Books.

Mattes, J. A., & Gettelman, R. (1978), An intensive crossover study of the effects of artificial food colorings in a hyperactive child. *Amer. J. Psychiat.*, 135:987–988.

McCune-Nicolich, L. (1977), Beyond sensorimotor intelligence: Measurement of symbolic sensitivity through analysis of pretend play. *Merrill-Palmer Quart.*, 23:89–99.

Meltzoff, A., & Moore, K. (1977), Imitation of facial and manual gestures by human neonates. *Science*, 198:75–78.

Milich, R., & Pelham, W. E. (1986), Effects of sugar ingestion on the classroom and playgroup behavior of attention deficit disorder boys. *J. Consult. & Clin. Psychol.*, 54:714–718.

Monro, J., Carini, C., & Brostoff, J. (1986), Migraine is food–allergic disease. *Lancet*, 2:719–721.

Murphy, L. (1974), *The Individual Child.* DHEW Publication No. (OCD) 74-1032. Washington, DC: U.S. Government Printing Office.

——— Moriarty, A. (1976), *Vulnerability, Coping and Growth.* New Haven, CT: Yale University Press.

Nelson, K. (1973), Structure and strategy in learning to talk. *Monographs of the Society for Research in Child Development*, 38 (1–2, Serial No. 149).

Nemiah, J. C. (1977), *Alexithymia: Theories and Models.* Proceedings of the Eleventh European Conference on Psychosomatic Research. Basel, Switzerland: Karger.

Parens, H. (in press), Development of aggression. In: *The Course of Life*, Vol. 2, ed. S. Greenspan & G. Pollock. Madison, CT: International Universities Press.

Pearson, D. J., & Rix, K. J. B. (1983), Food allergy: How much in the mind? *Lancet*, 1:1259–1261.

Peller, L. (1954), Libidinal phases, ego development, and play. *The Psychoanalytic Study of the Child*, 9:178–198. New York: International Universities Press.

Piaget, J. (1952), *The Origins of Intelligence in Children.* New York: International Universities Press.

———— (1954), *The Constriction of Reality in the Child.* New York: Basic Books.

———— (1962), The stages of the intellectual development of the child. In: *Childhood Psychopathology*, ed. S. Harrison & J. McDermott. New York: International Universities Press, pp. 157–166.

———— (1968), *Structuralism.* New York: Basic Books, 1970.

Poisson, S., Hofheimer, J., Strauss, M., & Greenspan, S. I. (unpublished), Inter-observer agreement and reliability assessments of the GLOS measures of caregiver infant interaction. Rockville, MD: The Reginald Lourie Center for Infants and Children.

———— Lieberman, A., & Greenspan, S. I. (unpublished), *Training Manual for the Greenspan-Lieberman Observation System (GLOS).* Rockville, MD: The Reginald Lourie Center for Infants and Children.

Porges, S. W., & Greenspan, S. I. (1990), Regulatory disordered infants: A common theme. Presented at the National Institute on Drug Abuse RAUS Review Meeting on Methodological Issues in Controlled Studies on Effects of Prenatal

Exposure to Drugs of Abuse, June 8–9, Richmond, VA; to appear in NIDA monograph, December, 1991.

Portales, A. W., Porges, S. W., & Greenspan, S. I. (1990), Parenthood and the difficult child. *Infant Behav. & Develop.*, 13:573 (abstract).

Prinz, R. J., Roberts, W., & Huntaranj, E. (1980), Dietary correlates of hyperactive behavior in children. *J. Clin. & Consult. Psychol.*, 40:760–769.

Provence, S. (1983), *Infants and Parents: Clinical Case Reports*, No. 2. New York: International Universities Press.

—— Naylor, A. (1983), *Working with Disadvantaged Parents and Their Children: Scientific and Practical Issues*. New Haven, CT: Yale University Press.

Rachford, B. K. (1905), *Neurotic Disorders of Childhood*. New York: E. B. Treat & Co.

Rheingold, H. (1966), The development of social behavior in the human infant. *Monogr. Soc. Res. Child Dev.*, 31:1–28.

Rix, K. J. B., Ditchfield, J., Freed, D. L. J., Goldberg, D. P., & Hillier, V. F. (1985), Food antibodies in acute psychoses. *Psychol. Med.*, 15:347–354.

Sameroff, A., & Emde, R. (1989), *Relationship Disturbances in Infancy*. New York: Basic Books.

Sander, L. (1962), Issues in early mother–child interaction. *J. Amer. Acad. Child Psychiat.*, 1:141–166.

Shapiro, R., & Zinner, J. (1975), Family organization and adolescent development. In: *Task and Organization*, ed. E. Miller. New York: John Wiley.

Sinclair, H. (1970), The transition from sensorimotor to symbolic activity. *Interchange*, 1:119–126.

Spelke, E., & Owsley, C. (1979), Intermodal exploration and knowledge in infancy. *Infant Behav. & Develop.*, 2:13–27.

Spitz, R. A. (1945), Hospitalism: An inquiry into the genesis of psychiatric conditions in early childhood. *The Psychoanalytic Study of the Child*, 1:53–74. New York: New York University Press.

Spring, B., Miller, O., Wurtman, J., Digman, L., & Cozolino, L. (1982–1983), Effects of protein and carbohydrate meals on mood and performance: Interactions with sex and age. *J. Psychiat. Res.*, 17:155–167.

Sroufe, L. A., & Waters, E. (1977), Attachment as an organizational construct. *Child Develop.*, 48:1184–1199.

—— —— Matas, L. (1974), Contextual determinants of infant affective response. In: *The Origins of Fear*, ed. M. Lewis & L. Rosenblum. New York: John Wiley, pp. 49–72.

Stern, D. (1974a), Mother and infant at play: The dyadic interaction involving facial, vocal and gaze behaviors. In: *The Effect of the Infant on Its Caregiver*, ed. M. Lewis & L. Rosenblum. New York: John Wiley.

—— (1974b), The goal and structure of mother–infant play. *J. Amer. Acad. Child Psychiat.*, 13:402–421.

—— (1985), *The Interpersonal World of the Infant: A View from Psychoanalysis and Developmental Psychology*. New York: Basic Books.

Tennes, K., Emde, R., Kisley, A., & Metcalf, D. (1972), The stimulus barrier in early infancy: An exploration of some formulations of John Benjamin. In: *Psychoanalysis and Contemporary Science*, Vol. 1, ed. R. Hold & E. Peterfreund. New York: Macmillan, pp. 206–234.

Thomas, A., Chess, S., & Birch, H. (1968), *Temperament and Behavior Disorders in Children*. New York: New York University Press.

Thomkins, S. (1963), *Affect, Imagery, Consciousness*, Vol. 1. New York: Springer.

Virkkunen, M. (1983), Insulin secretion during the glucose tolerance test in antisocial personality. *Brit. J. Psychiat.*, 142:598–604.

—— (1984), Reactive hypoglycemic tendency among arsonists. *Acta Psychiat. Scand.*, 69:445–452.

—— Huttunen, M. D. (1982), Evidence for abnormal glucose tolerance test among violent offenders. *Neuropsychobiol.*, 8:30–34.

Waelder, R. (1933), The psychoanalytic theory of play. *Psychoanal. Quart.*, 2:208–224.

Werner, H., & Kaplan, B. (1963), *Symbol Formation*. New York: John Wiley.

Winnicott, D. W. (1931), *Clinical Notes on Disorders of Childhood*. London: Heinemann.

Wolff, P. (1963), Developmental and motivational concepts in Piaget's sensorimotor theory of intelligence. *J. Amer. Acad. Child Psychiat.*, 2:225–243.

Wolraich, M., Milich, R., & Stumbo, P. (1985), Effects of sucrose ingestion on the behavior of hyperactive boys. *J. Pediat.*, 106:675–682.

Name Index

Adams, A. J., 376
Ainsworth, M., 23, 587, 726, 731
Ayers, A. J., 611, 744

Bakwin, H., 728
Behar, D., 376
Bell, S. M., 23, 587, 726, 727, 731
Bergman, A., 726, 731, 732, 754, 757, 762
Bergman, P., 729
Bion, W., 557
Birch, H., 729
Bolton, R., 375
Bowlby, J., 587, 726, 728, 731
Brazelton, T., 5, 726, 729, 730
Burlingham, D., 729

Caldwell, J., 376
Caldwell, L., 376
Cameron, H. S., 728, 729
Carter, C. M., 376
Charlesworth, W. R., 726, 730
Chess, S., 729
Connors, C. K., 376
Cramer, B., 5
Cravioto, J., 729

DeGangi, G., 14, 15, 317, 603, 609, 610, 705n

DeJon, V., 705n
Delicardie, E., 729
DiPietro, J. A., 603, 610
Dougherty, S. C., 385–386, 734
Doussard-Roosevelt, J. A., 609

Egger, J., 376
Ekman, P., 726
Emde, R. N., 577, 726, 729, 730
Erikson, E. H., 732
Escalona, S., 726, 729, 746
Eyler, F., 385–386

Fein, G., 732
Fenson, L., 731
Ferguson, H. B., 376
Fraiberg, S., 5, 729
Freud, A., 729
Freud, S., 726, 762

Gaensbauer, T. J., 726, 729
Gewirtz, J. L., 726, 729
Glucksberg, S., 732
Gouin-Decarie, T., 727, 731
Graham, P. J., 376
Greenspan, N. T., 379
Greenspan, S. I., 5, 6, 14, 15, 16, 317, 385–386, 435, 556, 557, 602, 603, 609, 610, 719–720t, 721,

Subject Index

disorder, 658–661
during floor time, 453–562
fostering of, 434–435
functional emotional assessment
of, 395–397
gestural, 72
history of, 328–332
in parent-infant relationship,
19–20
in three-year-old, 11–12
Communication and Symbolic Behavior Scales (CSBS), 768
Complex interaction, eliciting ability
for, 422–423
Comprehensive, in-depth therapeutic approach, 569–570
Comprehensive preventive intervention services, for infants and
children in multirisk families,
716–723
Compulsiveness, receptive language
difficulties and, 697
Concentration, 342
Concreteness, 165–166, 758
and aggressive behavior, 519
in children with multisystem developmental disorder, 663
and organization of experience,
759–760
in parent, and negative child,
523–528
vs. symbolization, 20–21
undermining of use of ideas by,
465–468
Concrete reinforcers, dependence
on, 435
Concrete thinking
helping child shift from, to abstract
thinking, 671–674
during representational capacity
phase, 756
Conflict
in interactive problems, 594
resolution of, 432
between self-object representa-

tions, 765
Connectedness
building of, 482–483
helping child develop sense of, 589
Constitutional/maturational capacities, 3
individual difference in, 438,
728–729
strengthening of, 147–157
relative effect of, on developmental
level, 4
Constitutional/maturational patterns,
13–15
assessment of, 388
effect of, on family and interactions, 610–611
importance of, in development,
609–610
problems with, in regulatory disorders, 603
variations in
sensory integration work for, 637
working with, in children with
regulatory disorders,
611–615
Constitutional vulnerability, in premature infant, 122–131
Contributing factors, evaluation of,
313
Coping capacities
development of, 119–121
learning to generalize, 708
range and flexibility of, 387
Couples
developmental perspectives on,
557–566
engagement and intentional communication in, 566
functioning of, at low developmental level, 563–564
projective identification in, 557
reaching higher developmental
level in, 462–466
sense of safety and security in, 565
Crying spells, case study of, in five-